PUBLIC PAPERS OF THE PRESIDENTS

OF THE UNITED STATES

PUBLIC PAPERS OF THE PRESIDENTS

OF THE UNITED STATES

Herbert Hoover

*Containing the Public Messages, Speeches, and
Statements of the President*

JANUARY 1 TO DECEMBER 31, 1931

1931

UNITED STATES GOVERNMENT PRINTING OFFICE

WASHINGTON : 1976

PUBLISHED BY THE
OFFICE OF THE FEDERAL REGISTER
NATIONAL ARCHIVES AND RECORDS SERVICE
GENERAL SERVICES ADMINISTRATION

For sale by the Superintendent of Documents, U.S. Government Printing Office
Washington, D.C. 20402 - Price $14   Stock Number 022–003–00920–5

PREFACE

IN THIS VOLUME are gathered most of the public messages and statements of the President of the United States that were released by the White House during 1931. Similar volumes covering 1929 and 1930 are available. The final volume of the Hoover administration, covering January 1, 1932—March 4, 1933, is under preparation.

Annual volumes for the years 1945 through 1974, containing the papers of Presidents Truman, Eisenhower, Kennedy, Johnson, Nixon, and Ford, are also available.

The series was begun in 1957 in response to a recommendation of the National Historical Publications Commission. Until then there had been no systematic publication of Presidential papers. An extensive compilation of the messages and papers of the Presidents, covering the period 1789 to 1897, was assembled by James D. Richardson and published under Congressional authority between 1896 and 1899. Since then various private compilations have been issued but there was no uniform publication comparable to the *Congressional Record* or the *United States Supreme Court Reports*. Many Presidential papers could be found only in mimeographed White House releases or as reported in the press. The National Historical Publications Commission therefore recommended the establishment of an official series in which Presidential writings and utterances of a public nature could be made promptly available.

The Commission's recommendation was incorporated in regulations of the Administrative Committee of the Federal Register issued under section 6 of the Federal Register Act (44 U.S.C. 1506). The Committee's regulations, establishing the series and providing for the coverage of prior years, are reprinted as Appendix F.

CONTENT AND ARRANGEMENT

The text of this book is based on historical materials held in the Herbert Hoover Presidential Library at West Branch, Iowa. In a few instances, when the Library had no official copy of a statement known to have been made public, the text has been supplied from news accounts or other contemporary sources.

President Hoover's news conferences are published for the first time in full text in this series since, at the time they were held, direct quotation of the President's replies frequently was not authorized. Transcripts by White House stenographers were used in this publication. The news conferences have been numbered in sequence on the basis of existing transcripts.

For some addresses by the President, varying texts are in the files, and newspaper clippings point to additional departures from his official text. Because of the scarcity of sound recordings of the speeches, it has not been possible in every instance to verify and print "as delivered" transcripts. Accordingly, the editors have used, when available, official texts printed by the Government Printing Office. When no such official printing was found, they have selected the "best available" version from those in the Library's holdings. When stenographic records were kept of textual changes during the delivery of a public address, the "as delivered" version is used. For researchers interested in possible changes between the prepared text, and the version actually delivered, President Hoover's file of public statements, containing a large number of reading copies with changes in his handwriting, is available for examination at the Herbert Hoover Presidential Library.

An addition to this volume is the inclusion of a diary account of the President's involvement in negotiating the moratorium on intergovernmental debts. This diary account appears in Supplement I. Another addition is the inclusion of statements made by the President during an interview with correspondent Frazier Hunt. Excerpts from this interview appear in Supplement II.

Certain Presidential materials issued during the period covered by this volume have not been printed as items but are listed in Appendix A. Routine messages to Congress, not included as items, are listed in Appendix B. Proclamations and Executive orders appear in full in a companion publication, *Proclamations and Executive Orders, Herbert Hoover, 1929–1933,* published in 1974, and are therefore merely listed in Appendix C.

The President is required by statute to transmit numerous reports to the Congress. Those transmitted during the period covered by this volume are listed in Appendix D.

A selected list of the President's calendar of activities for 1931 appears in Appendix E.

Preface

The items published in this volume are presented in chronological order, rather than being grouped in classes. Most needs for a classified arrangement are met by the subject index.

The dates shown at the end of item headings are White House release dates. In instances where the date of the document differs from the release date, that fact is shown in brackets immediately following the heading. Textnotes, footnotes, and cross references have been supplied where needed for purposes of clarity.

Remarks or addresses were delivered in Washington, D.C., unless otherwise indicated. Similarly, statements, messages, and letters were issued from the White House in Washington unless otherwise indicated.

Dr. Ellis W. Hawley, professor of American history at the University of Iowa, served as consultant in the preparation of the volume. Materials to be considered for inclusion were compiled by Dwight M. Miller, senior archivist of the Herbert Hoover Presidential Library, who also assisted in their selection and annotation. Thomas T. Thalken, Director of the Library, provided his support for completion of the volume.

The planning and publication of the series is under the direction of Fred J. Emery, Director, and Ernest J. Galdi, Deputy Director, of the Office of the Federal Register. Editors of the present volume were Faye Q. Rosser, Michael J. Sullivan, and Carol L. Minor.

Design of the volume was developed by the Government Printing Office's Division of Typography and Design. Rudie Diamond of that Division provided continuing consultation.

Preface

The frontispiece is from an oil painting by Douglas Chandor which was commissioned by Time magazine. Completed in 1931, the original work remained the property of the artist and his heirs until it was acquired in 1968 by the National Portrait Gallery where it is now a part of their collections.

JAMES B. RHOADS
Archivist of the United States

JACK M. ECKERD
Administrator of General Services
October 1976

CONTENTS

LIST OF ITEMS

List of Items

List of Items

List of Items

68-611 O - 76 - 2

List of Items

List of Items

List of Items

List of Items

List of Items

List of Items

List of Items

List of Items

List of Items

List of Items

List of Items

List of Items

XXXIII

List of Items

List of Items

List of Items

List of Items

List of Items

List of Items

List of Items

List of Items

List of Items

President . . . . Herbert Hoover

Vice President. . . . . Charles Curtis

THE CABINET

Secretary of State. . . . . Henry L. Stimson

Secretary of the Treasury. . . . . Andrew W. Mellon

Secretary of War. . . . . Patrick J. Hurley

Secretary of the Navy. . . . . Charles F. Adams

Attorney General. . . . . William D. Mitchell

Postmaster General. . . . . Walter F. Brown

Secretary of the Interior. . . . . Ray Lyman Wilbur

Secretary of Agriculture. . . . . Arthur M. Hyde

Secretary of Commerce. . . . . Robert P. Lamont

Secretary of Labor. . . . . William N. Doak

Herbert Hoover

1931

1

The President's News Conference of
January 2, 1931

GEORGE E. AKERSON

THE PRESIDENT. The only news item I have at the moment is that Mr. Akerson is leaving the White House service. Someone has offered him two or nearly three times the pay the Government can afford, and he has responsibilities to his family that I cannot deny. I do greatly regret to lose an old friend out of my personal service.

RAILROADS

I would like to talk to you for a moment about the railway situation—but not for publication or for any use. It will be disclosed as I go on. It might be interpreted as being rather pessimistic in a time of sensitive public mind, but I would like for you to know something about the background that lies behind this whole position, largely for your own instruction—wholly for your own instruction—so that you may know what sort of a problem we are confronted with.

The situation of the railways—not in the immediate sense of the depression, because we will come out of that in due time, but in the longer sense—is one of the, if not the greatest, economic problems that we have confronting us. The competition of the buses and the trucks, the automobiles, of the waterways, and especially of the pipelines and of electric power, have—all of them—contributed to steadily undermine the railway traffics. Probably the most menacing one of those is the pipelines. We are now engaged in building gas pipelines from Texas and Oklahoma into Chicago and Minneapolis and Washington, D.C., and the net result is a constant diminution of coal traffics, which particularly affects cooperating roads. The electrical power gets the coal traffics. The gasoline pipes that are now being laid throughout the Midwest in

1

particular are taking a tremendous area of traffic away from the railroads. So that we have to look forward to a period of either reorganization or of continued distress in what amounts to our largest single industry, and the one on which probably public recovery depends more than any other one industry.

The lines open to the railways to meet the situation lie either in reducing their operating expenses through the elimination of duplications and the building up of sounder methods of transportation through electrification, through more economical operating terminals and other devices which require very large expenditures, or alternatively, wage reductions. If they are to get back the traffics which they have been losing, they must get them back by being able to meet that competition. It means lower rates, and lower rates cannot be made except by broad economies in methods, or alternatively, by wage reductions. If they do not get their traffic back they cannot reemploy their men, and the stress of those pressures which have become particularly acute in the last few years, more especially in the last year by the extension of pipelines, give no little anxiety for the recovery of that industry. When you come to the practical results of recovery, the difficulties of recovery will not lie in the rich and strong roads so much as in the weak sisters around about.

So that I am greatly impressed with the fact, and I know that every other thinking person, who has given the matter long study, is anxious that we do not enter into a period here of railroad distress that will prolong our whole national depression. A good deal of our Government business is built not only on the operation of the railroads but upon the expenditure of $1,500 million of improvements and betterments. And with these forces working against the traffics, the financial consideration becomes more difficult all the time, and the consolidation—the unification—of the roads tends to build up their financial stability and their ability to secure resources with which to carry out the fundamental engineering improvements that they must make if they are to meet the situation. More especially, in the eastern territory here, there was domination of railways which are impregnable in their situation by virtue of their connections between the large centers of production and distribution, but other groups have not the entry into these points which gives them anything like equality nor stability of competition. So that a group of railroads in such a fashion as to give each one of four groups the connection between each one of the producing and distributing centers would bring about a stronger competition and better fundamental public service.

Now the details of the plan that has been evolved will probably be subject to criticism. Probably five or six thousand miles of weak railroads involved in the plan, which none of the stronger railways want to take, and those which have taken them may be subjected to criticism from one point of view or another. In any event, I have no doubt that when the details of the plan are known they will be subject to criticism, as any plan will be. The plan follows the five-system plan of the Interstate Commerce Commission except upon the division of weak roads among the strong roads. The difficulty with the plan was the fact that the five-system was an aggregation of the weak roads, and they have to be distributed around amongst some of the stronger brothers.

So far as this office is concerned, I have taken no part in the formulation of the details of the plan. I could not tell you at this minute the details. It is a matter the railways have to work out for themselves with the Interstate Commerce Commission, who has the full obligation and the courage and independence to take care of it and make any such readjustments in it as they think necessary, or deny it altogether, or do what they like with it. But in any event, the purpose is not only to give a little more courage to the American people but a little more confidence. The purpose at this time is that this country is not as yet entirely devoid of enterprise and ability to reconstitute itself for larger exertions, and also that the whole Nation looks forward for a term of years ahead. It is no new notion, as you know. It is no invention of mine. Congress itself had laid down the lines 10 years ago on which it was then thought and is still thought, I think, by most people is the necessary and ultimate development.

And that is all that I have today.

3

George E. Akerson

Q. Will you permit us to go back for a minute to our friend Akerson, and ask whether you care to make any announcement as to his successor?

THE PRESIDENT. I haven't anybody in mind whatever. I have got to look around and find somebody.

Q. Mr. President, when is it to take effect?

THE PRESIDENT. There is no special date. Sometime in the middle of the month, whenever I can find a successor, and he can be spared.

NOTE: President Hoover's one hundred and sixty-fifth news conference was held in the White House at 4 p.m. on Friday, January 2, 1931.

On the same day, the White House issued a text of the President's statement about the resignation of George E. Akerson as Secretary to the President (see Item 2).

For the consolidation plan involving the eastern railroads, see 1930 volume, Items 428 and 429.

2

Statement About the Resignation of George E. Akerson as Secretary to the President. *January 2, 1931*

THE PRESIDENT said:

"The only news item I have at the moment is that Mr. Akerson is leaving the White House service. Someone has offered him two or three times the pay the Government can afford, and he has responsibilities to his family that I cannot deny. I do greatly regret to lose an old friend out of my personal service."

NOTE: Mr. Akerson, Secretary to the President since March 4, 1929, resigned to become a member of the executive staff of the Paramount Publix Corporation.

3

Message of Sympathy on the Death of Hugh Campbell Wallace.
January 2, 1931

My dear Mrs. Wallace:

I was deeply grieved to learn yesterday of the death of your husband. Both Mrs. Hoover and I wish you to know of our sincere sympathy in your great loss.

Yours faithfully,
HERBERT HOOVER

[Mrs. Hugh Wallace, 1800 Massachusetts Avenue, Washington, D.C.]

NOTE: Mr. Wallace, United States Ambassador to France from 1919 to 1921, died on January 1, 1931, at his home in Washington, D.C.

4

Message to President Gaston Doumergue of France on the Death of Marshal Joseph Joffre.
January 3, 1931

I AM DISTRESSED by the news of the death of Marshal Joffre who is so affectionately remembered by the American people. Both in their name and personally I wish to express to Your Excellency the deep sorrow which is felt in this country at the passing of this great patriot.

HERBERT HOOVER

[His Excellency Monsieur Gaston Doumergue, President of the French Republic, Paris, France]

NOTE: Joseph Joffre served as commander in chief of the French Army from August 5, 1913, to December 13, 1916, when he became Marshal of the French Army and technical adviser to the French Government regarding World War I.

5

Message to the Congress Transmitting the Final Report of the Yellowstone National Park Boundary Commission. *January 5, 1931*

To the Congress of the United States:

I am transmitting herewith for the consideration of Congress the final report of the Yellowstone National Park Boundary Commission on an inspection of areas involved in the proposed adjustment of the southeast, south, and southwest boundaries of the Yellowstone National Park, made pursuant to Public Resolution No. 94, Seventieth Congress, approved February 28, 1929.

HERBERT HOOVER

The White House,
    January 5, 1931.

NOTE: The message and accompanying report are printed as House Document 710 (71st Cong., 3d sess.).

For appointments to the Commission, see 1929 volume, Item 31.

6

Letter to the Speaker of the House Transmitting a Supplemental Estimate of Appropriation for the Relief of Farmers in Drought Stricken Areas. *January 5, 1931*

Sir:

I have the honor to transmit herewith for the consideration of Congress a supplemental estimate of appropriation for the Department of Agriculture, amounting to $45,000,000, for the fiscal year 1931, to remain available until June 30, 1932, for the purpose of making advances or loans to farmers, as contemplated by the joint resolution entitled "Joint resolution for the relief of farmers in the drought and/or storm stricken areas of the United States," approved December 20, 1930.

The details of this supplemental estimate of appropriation, the necessity therefor, and the reason for its transmission at this time are set forth in the letter of the Director of the Bureau of the Budget transmitted herewith, with whose comments and observations thereon, I concur.

Respectfully,

HERBERT HOOVER

The White House,
    January 5, 1931.

[The Speaker of the House of Representatives]

NOTE: The letter and accompanying papers are printed as House Document 706 (71st Cong., 3d sess.).

The President referred to Senate Joint Resolution 211, which is Public Resolution, No. 112 (46 Stat. 1032).

7

The President's News Conference of *January 6, 1931*

THE PRESIDENT. There won't be anything to take Miss Shankey. You need not wait.

[At this point, Anne Shankey, the President's stenographer, left the office. The exchange of remarks, as set forth below, follows the text of a contemporary news account.]

Q. Can we be of any assistance to you in selecting a new secretary?

THE PRESIDENT. Yes, I would like to have your united opinion on the matter. [*Laughter*]

NOTE: President Hoover's one hundred and sixty-sixth news conference was held in the White House at 12 noon on Tuesday, January 6, 1931.

8

Telephone Remarks to the National Automobile Chamber of Commerce.
January 6, 1931

I AM GLAD to extend this greeting to the automobile industry of the United States as represented at your banquet in New York City tonight.

I am informed that if I were speaking to every person whose livelihood is directly or indirectly dependent upon the industry, I should be speaking to 1 person in every 10 of the people of our country. Therefore, the prosperity of the industry is in the anxious thoughts of the Nation, and everybody wishes you well in your plans to expand the manufacture and use of your product.

The despondency of some people over the future is not borne out by the statistical evidence or prospects in respect to the automobile industry. I am informed by the Department of Commerce that despite the depression you have manufactured and sold during this year, 1930, over 3,500,000 new automobiles. You have also disposed of the large inventories of a year ago. Hundreds of miles of new roads are being constructed every day in the world and these increasing miles must be equipped with more automobiles. I am informed also that the consumption of gasoline during the last year shows an increase of 5 percent over even the highly optimistic year of 1929. This certainly means that we have been cheerful in the use of our automobiles. I do not assume they are being used for transportation to the poorhouse. While I am aware that many people are using the old automobile a little longer, it is obvious that they are still using it and that it is being worn out. Altogether the future for the industry does not warrant any despondency.

No one needs to recall the utility and importance of the automobile in our national life. I have often wondered, however, if part of its popularity was not due to the exhilarating sense of power that we all inhale through the mastery over time and space we gain from it. It brings a sense of freedom that makes our spirits rise even though it sometimes

8

invites for some people the depressing ministrations of a motorcycle policeman.

I wish you success in your meeting and in the organization plans which you put forward for the new year. Every automobile and truck which you make and sell adds to employment in a hundred different trades. Yours is indeed a great and vital industry, the success of which is important to every one of us. I sincerely wish you a prosperous new year.

NOTE: The President spoke at approximately 9:40 p.m. via telephone to the annual dinner gathering in the Hotel Commodore in New York City. The dinner was held in conjunction with the 31st Annual Automobile Show.

9

Letter to the Speaker of the House Transmitting a Supplemental Estimate of Appropriation for the Bureau of Immigration. *January 9, 1931*

Sir:

I have the honor to transmit herewith for the consideration of Congress an estimate of appropriation for the Department of Labor for salaries and expenses, Bureau of Immigration, for the fiscal year 1932, amounting to $500,000, which is supplemental to the estimate of $9,617,740 contained in the Budget for the fiscal year 1932.

The details of this estimate, the necessity therefor, and the reason for its submission at this time are set forth in the letter of the Director of the Bureau of the Budget, transmitted herewith, with whose comments and observations thereon I concur.

Respectfully,

HERBERT HOOVER

The White House,
    January 9, 1931.

[The Speaker of the House of Representatives]

NOTE: The letter and accompanying papers are printed as House Document 715 (71st Cong., 3d sess.).

10

Message to the Congress Transmitting
Report of the American Samoan Commission.
January 9, 1931

To the Congress of the United States:

I transmit herewith for the information of the Congress the official report of the American Samoan Commission, appointed in pursuance of the joint resolution of Congress, approved February 20, 1929, being Public Resolution No. 89 of the Seventieth Congress, and of the joint resolution of Congress approved May 22, 1929, being Public Resolution No. 3 of the Seventy-first Congress, together with an appendix containing a copy of a bill.

HERBERT HOOVER

The White House,
    January 9, 1931.

NOTE: The message and accompanying report are printed as Senate Document 249 (71st Cong., 3d sess.).

The Commission was established to devise a civil government for American Samoa.

11

Message to the Congress Requesting an Appropriation for the
International Water Commission, United States and Mexico.
January 9, 1931

To the Congress of the United States:

I commend to the favorable consideration of the Congress the inclosed report from the Secretary of State to the end that legislation may be enacted to authorize an appropriation of $287,000 to defray the expenses of the American section of the International Water Commission, United States and Mexico, in continuing its study, in cooperation with representatives of Mexico, of a plan for the equitable use of the waters of the lower Rio Grande, the lower Colorado, and Tia Juana Rivers, for submission to the Congress, pursuant to the provisions of the act of May 13, 1924, entitled "An act providing for a study regarding the equitable use of the waters of the Rio Grande below Fort Quitman, Tex., in cooperation with the United States of Mexico," as amended by the act of March 3, 1927.

HERBERT HOOVER

The White House,
    January 9, 1931.

NOTE: The message and accompanying report are printed as Senate Document 250 (71st Cong., 3d sess.).

12

Message to the Senate Refusing to Return
Senate Resolutions of Advice and Consent
for Appointments to the Federal Power Commission.
January 10, 1931

To the Senate of the United States:

I am in receipt of the Resolution of the Senate dated January 5, 1931, "That the President of the United States be respectfully requested to return to the Senate the resolution advising and consenting to the appointment of George Otis Smith to be a member of the Federal Power Commission, which was agreed to on Saturday, December 20, 1930".

I have similar resolutions in respect to the appointment of Messrs. Claude L. Draper and Colonel Marcel Garsaud.

On December 20, 1930, I received the usual attested resolution of the Senate, signed by the Secretary of the Senate as follows: "Resolved, that the Senate advise and consent to the appointment of the following-named person to the office named agreeably to his nomination:

FEDERAL POWER COMMISSION
George Otis Smith, to be a member of the
Federal Power Commission".

I received similar resolutions in respect to Colonel Garsaud and Mr. Draper.

I am advised that these appointments were constitutionally made, with the consent of the Senate formally communicated to me and that the return of the documents by me and reconsideration by the Senate would be ineffective to disturb the appointees in their offices. I cannot admit the power in the Senate to encroach upon the Executive functions by removal of a duly appointed executive officer under the guise of reconsideration of his nomination.

I regret that I must refuse to accede to the requests.

HERBERT HOOVER

The White House,
    January 10, 1931.

NOTE: The Senate resolution was adopted following a decision by the three commissioners to dismiss Solicitor Charles A. Russell and Chief Accountant William V. King.

On the same day as the President's message, the Senate voted to restore the nominations to the calendar, claiming that the relevant Senate rule allowed a confirmation to be reconsidered in either of the two executive sessions following it, and that since the recess had prevented these from being held the confirmation was incomplete. On January 23, 1931, the Senate voted to recommit the names to the Senate Commerce Committee and to consider court action.

For documents relating to appointments to the Federal Power Commission, see 1930 volume, Items 182, 195, 218, 236, and 240.

13

Statement About Refusal To Resubmit Federal Power Commission Appointments to the Senate.
January 10, 1931

THE PRESIDENT said:

"I have today notified the Senate that I will not accede to their resolution requesting the return to the Senate of the resolutions advising and consenting to the appointment of Mr. George Otis Smith, Col. Marcel Garsaud and Mr. Claude L. Draper, members of the Federal Power Commission.

"I am advised by the Attorney General that these appointments were constitutionally made, are not subject to recall, and that the request cannot be complied with by me. In any event, the objective of the Senate constitutes an attempt to dictate to an administrative agency upon the appointment of subordinates and an attempted invasion of the authority of the Executive. These, as President, I am bound to resist.

"I cannot, however, allow a false issue to be placed before the country. There is no issue for or against power companies.

"It will be recalled that on my recommendation the Federal Power Commission was reorganized from the old basis of three Cabinet members giving a small part of their time, to a full commission of five members, in order that adequate protection could be given to public interest in the water resources of the country, and that I further recommended that the Commission should be given authority to regulate all interstate power rates. The law establishing the new Commission [1] became effective last June although legislation giving it authority to regulate rates has not yet been enacted.

"The resolutions of the Senate may have the attractive political merit of giving rise to a legend that those who voted for it are "enemies of the power interests," and, inferentially, those who voted against it are "friends of the power interests." And it may contain a hope of symbol-

---

[1] Public, No. 412, 46 Stat. 797, June 23, 1930.

izing me as the defender of power interests if I refuse to sacrifice three outstanding public servants, or to allow the Senate to dictate to an administrative board the appointment of its subordinates, and if I refuse to allow fundamental encroachment by the Senate upon the constitutional independence of the Executive. Upon these things the people will pass unerring judgement.

"Much of the debate indicates plainly that those who favored this resolution are intent upon removing Messrs. Smith, Draper, and Garsaud, not because they are unqualified but to insist upon the Senate's own selection of certain subordinates. Irrespective of the unique fitness of these Commissioners for their positions and before they have given a single decision in respect to any power company, they are to be removed unless they are willing to accept employees not of their choosing. It is not only the right but it is also the duty of the Commission under the law to appoint its own employees. It must assume the responsibility for the conduct of its office. The fitness of its subordinates for the fulfillment of their respective duties must be determined by the Commissioners and no honorable man could accept such responsibilities upon any other terms. If the appointments of these Commissioners are withdrawn, it is obvious that their successors must accept the Senate's views of these subordinates.

"The resolution raises the question of the independence of the executive arm of the Government in respect of the appointment and removal of executive officials. Many Presidents have had to meet this particular encroachment upon the Executive power in some form. Every one of them has repelled it, and every President has handed on this authority unimpaired. It reaches to the very fundamentals of independence and vigor of the Executive, whose power comes from the people alone and the maintenance of which is vital to the protection of public interest and the integrity of the Constitution.

"The President is responsible to the people to see that honest and capable officials are employed by or appointed to the various administrative agencies of the Government. I do not appoint nor recommend any subordinate of the Power Commission. Under the law the Commission appoints those officers untrammeled. If the Power Commission shall

14

fail to employ honest and capable officials, it is within my power to remove such officials as well as the members of the Commission. I have not and shall not hesitate to exert that authority. The House of Representatives has the right to impeach any public official and if the Power Commission shall be derelict in the performance of its duties, the orderly and constitutional manner of procedure by the legislative branch would be by impeachment, and not through an attempt by the Senate to remove them under the guise of reconsidering their nominations, or any attempt to force administrative agencies to a particular action.

"In July last, I nominated to the Senate Colonel Garsaud and Messrs. Draper and Williamson as members of the new Commission. Their character and fitness for its duties were inquired into by a committee of the Senate and favorably reported. Owing to the press of business in the last session, these nominations were not considered at that time. Their names remained before the country for 4 months, and in December I renominated them to the Senate together with Mr. George Otis Smith and Mr. Frank R. McNinch. The qualifications of all five members were again searchingly investigated by the committee, the nominations were favorably reported to the Senate and they were confirmed on December 19 and 20 after full consideration and debate.

"Mr. George Otis Smith has been in public service, as a member and head of the Geological Survey for 30 years through Democratic as well as Republican administrations. He has distinguished himself as an independent devoted public official with a larger knowledge of waterpower resources of the United States than any other man. He was chosen as Chairman of the Commission. Colonel Garsaud is an eminent engineer and had a distinguished service as colonel in the Army during the World War. Mr. Draper served for 10 years as chairman of the Public Utilities Commission of his State with the universal approval of the citizens of that State. Not a single member is in the remotest way connected with power interests.

"Upon confirmation, official notice was forwarded to me by the Secretary of the Senate in accordance with the precedents of many years. I thereupon issued the commissions and the appointees were duly sworn into office.

15

"Messrs. Smith, Draper, and Garsaud, the only members who were then in Washington, met and assumed the responsibility of office, and I understand, notified all employees of the old Commission that under the new law their employment was automatically terminated. Arrangements were made with the Civil Service Commission to temporarily continue the clerical employees and further action was deferred upon the secretary, a solicitor, and an accountant, and others, until a meeting of the full Commission, including Messrs. Williamson and McNinch, which was held early in January. At that time all employees, including the three men whose dismissal has been the subject of controversy, were informed they could apply for reappointment and their qualifications would be examined. I am informed that the solicitor and accountant have applied for reappointment but no action has been taken by the Commission upon their applications. The Chairman of the Commission has, however, expressed disapproval especially of the former secretary and the solicitor because of long continued bickerings and controversies among employees of the old Commission.

"I regret that the Government should be absorbed upon such questions as the action of the Power Commission in employment or nonemployment of two subordinate officials at a time when the condition of the country requires every constructive energy."

14

Statement on the Death of Nathan Straus.
January 11, 1931

THE DEATH of Mr. Nathan Straus removes from our national life a venerable figure who will be sadly missed. A Jewish leader whose vision transcended all limits of race or creed, a philanthropist whose benefactions, especially in behalf of children, were of permanent value.

NOTE: Mr. Straus was a prominent philanthropist and leader of the Zionist movement, especially active in such causes as child health, poor relief, and aid to Palestine.

15

Letter to the Chairman of the American National Red Cross on the Drought Relief Campaign.
January 12, 1931

[Released January 12, 1931. Dated January 10, 1931]

My dear Mr. Chairman:

In accordance with our conferences during the past week I am glad, as President of the American Red Cross, to approve an appeal for public assistance to the association in the relief work it has undertaken in the rural sections.

Last fall the Red Cross undertook the burden of personal relief throughout the drought states. At that time you set aside $5,000,000 of the Association's funds and established a vigorous and active organization throughout the drought area. In our discussions then it was considered that further funds might be required and it was contemplated that at an appropriate time an appeal should be made to the generosity of the American people to assist the Red Cross in its burden. It was felt then that it would not be possible to measure the volume of requirements until we had reached the early stages of winter and that, in any event, it was desirable that the Red Cross postpone any appeal until such time as the Community Chests and committees on Unemployment Relief in the larger cities should have further advanced the raising of their funds.

The problem as now developed, requires more than the available funds and is not wholly one of food, clothing, and other personal care among farmers who have suffered from the drought. There is also difficulty in the smaller rural and industrial towns as a double reaction from the drought and depression. I understand that these towns are unable to organize to effectively meet their problems as are the municipalities.

The arrangement made by Secretary Hyde and yourself by which a representative of local Red Cross Chapters will sit upon the local committees created by the Department of Agriculture for administration of the crop relief will assure that every one truly deserving will be looked after with care and without waste.

I am confident you will command the never failing generous instincts of our people toward those who are less fortunate.

I remain,

Yours truly,

HERBERT HOOVER

[Hon. John Barton Payne, Chairman, American Red Cross, Washington, D.C.]

NOTE: The local committees to which the President referred were those established as part of the drought relief organization in August 1930. See 1930 volume, Item 265.

On January 5, 1931, the Senate adopted an amendment to the drought relief bill, adding $15 million for food loans. The next day Chairman Payne testified before the Senate Appropriations Committee that the American National Red Cross could handle the need for food relief. On January 10, Chairman Payne recommended a special Red Cross drive to the President. The Congress, on January 14, passed the Drought Relief Act (46 Stat. 1039) appropriating $45 million for feed, seed, and production loans but nothing for food loans.

16

The President's News Conference of *January 13, 1931*

RED CROSS DROUGHT RELIEF CAMPAIGN

THE PRESIDENT. I am issuing this morning a proclamation on behalf of the Red Cross stating that there must be a very material increase in the resources of the American Red Cross to enable it to bear the burden which it has undertaken in the drought area and smaller communities over 21 States during this winter. Within the last 10 days the Red Cross has had to increase the rate of expenditures to an amount greater than during the entire preceding 4 months.

The American Red Cross is the Nation's sole agency for relief in such a crisis. It is meeting the demand, and must continue to do so during the remainder of the winter.

The disaster reserve of the Red Cross which was pledged to this emergency last August is not sufficient to meet the increased demands. It is imperative in the view of the experienced directors of the Red Cross that a minimum of at least $10 million be contributed to carry the relief program to completion.

The familiarity of this situation, due to months of press reports of its progress, should not blind us to the fact that it is a real emergency, nor dull our active sympathies toward our fellow countrymen who are in actual want and in many cases will lack the bare necessities of life unless they are provided for.

As President of the United States and as President of the American Red Cross, I, therefore, appeal to our people to contribute promptly and most generously in order that the suffering of thousands of our fellow countrymen may be prevented. I am doing so with supreme confidence that in the face of this great humanitarian need your response will be immediate.

Just one word beyond the proclamation. The problem in the broad way and in certain rural areas is also a problem of the general depression, but it is not alone the farmers but its reactive effect upon villages and especially villages with small industries, from the depression and the drought which calls upon the Red Cross for services entirely beyond any form of agricultural relief. We have now organized the Red Cross in cooperation with the Department of Agriculture so that there will be a complete interlocking of their committee setup throughout the entire region, and thus there can be no failure at care for everybody who is in need. The amount indicated is necessary. It has been placed at a minimum of $10 million, which with the disaster relief appears at the present moment to be sufficient to adequately care for the problem, but it certainly does require this minimum amount. And I am in hopes that out of common interest you will spread our proclamation.

Thank you very much.

NOTE: President Hoover's one hundred and sixty-seventh news conference was held in the White House at 12 noon on Tuesday, January 13, 1931.

On the same day, the White House issued a text of the President's message to the Nation urging support for the drought relief campaign of the American National Red Cross (see Item 17).

19

17

Message to the Nation Urging Support
for the Drought Relief Campaign
of the American National Red Cross.
January 13, 1931

To My Fellow Countrymen:

There must be a very material increase in the resources of the American Red Cross to enable it to bear the burden which it has undertaken in the drought area and smaller communities over twenty-one states during this winter. Within the last ten days the Red Cross has had to increase the rate of expenditures to an amount greater than during the entire preceding four months.

The American Red Cross is the nation's sole agency for relief in such a crisis; it is meeting the demand and must continue to do so during the remainder of the winter.

The disaster reserve of the Red Cross which was pledged to this emergency last August is not sufficient to meet the increased demands. It is imperative in the view of the experienced directors of the Red Cross that a minimum of at least ten million dollars be contributed to carry the relief program to completion.

The familiarity of this situation, due to months of press reports of its progress, should not blind us to the fact that it is an acute emergency, nor dull our active sympathies toward our fellow-countrymen who are in actual want and in many cases will lack the bare necessities of life unless they are provided for.

As President of the United States and as President of the American Red Cross, I, therefore, appeal to our people to contribute promptly and most generously in order that the suffering of thousands of our fellow-countrymen may be prevented. I am doing so with supreme confidence that in the face of this great humanitarian need your response will be immediate.

HERBERT HOOVER

18

Message to Felix M. Warburg on His 60th Birthday.
January 13, 1931

I AM PLEASED to remember that tomorrow is your sixtieth birthday and to congratulate you most cordially upon this milestone in your useful career of public service in so many constructive philanthropies not only of distinguished value to the Jewish people but also of outstanding benefit to all especially the children.

HERBERT HOOVER

[Felix M. Warburg, 1109 Fifth Avenue, New York City]

NOTE: Mr. Warburg, member of the banking firm of Kuhn, Loeb and Company, was active in numerous philanthropic activities and chairman of the Federation for the Support of Jewish Philanthropic Societies.

19

Message to Viscount Willingdon, Governor General of Canada, on His Departure From Office.
January 14, 1931

[Released January 14, 1931. Dated January 13, 1931]

ON YOUR departure from Ottawa Mrs. Hoover joins me in sending to you and Lady Willingdon best wishes for a pleasant journey and for continued success in India. The relations of Canada and the United States have been happy indeed during your distinguished term as Governor General and we shall always have the most pleasant recollections of your visit to Washington.

HERBERT HOOVER

[His Excellency Viscount Willingdon, Governor General of Canada, Government House, Ottawa]

NOTE: Freeman Freeman-Thomas, Viscount of Willingdon, served as Governor General of Canada from 1926 to 1931. He left Canada to become Viceroy and Governor General of India.

20

Message to the Association of Community Chests and Councils About the Red Cross Drought Relief Campaign.
January 15, 1931

I WISH to express my gratification at the action of the Community Chest Association in giving such whole-hearted support to the appeal of the Red Cross in this emergency. It exemplifies the response which the country will unquestionably give.

HERBERT HOOVER

[J. Herbert Case, President, Association of Community Chests and Councils, 33 Liberty Street, New York City]

NOTE: The message was in response to a telegram from J. Herbert Case. The telegram, dated January 14, 1931, and released with the President's message, follows:

My dear Mr. President:

I desire to advise you as President of the American Red Cross, that we are today sending the following telegram to all community chests throughout the United States: "The Officers of the Association of Community Chests and Councils urge your local Community Chest organization to give vigorous and whole-hearted support to the National Red Cross Drive intended to meet a great national emergency. The opportunity has now come to our organizations which have rendered such great service in meeting local needs to demonstrate that they are able and willing to make a like contribution of service to the needs of the nation."

Faithfully yours,

J. HERBERT CASE, *President,*
Association of Community Chests and Councils

[The President, White House, Washington, D.C.]

21

Letter to the Speaker of the House
Transmitting a Supplemental Estimate
of Appropriation for the District of Columbia.
January 15, 1931

Sir:

I have the honor to transmit herewith for the consideration of Congress a supplemental estimate of appropriation for the District of Columbia for the fiscal year 1932, to be immediately available, in the sum of $1,500,000 for beginning the construction of the first unit of the municipal center.

The details of this estimate, the necessity therefor, and the reason for its submission at this time are set forth in the letter of the Director of the Bureau of the Budget transmitted herewith, with whose comments and observations thereon I concur.

Respectfully,
HERBERT HOOVER

The White House,
    January 15, 1931.

[The Speaker of the House of Representatives]

NOTE: The letter and accompanying papers are printed as House Document 720 (71st Cong., 3d sess.).

22

Letter to Governor Harry G. Leslie
About the Indiana Conference
on Child Health and Protection.
January 16, 1931

[Released January 16, 1931.   Dated January 14, 1931]

My dear Governor Leslie:

I will be obliged if you will express my cordial greetings to the Indiana Conference on Child Health and Protection and my regret that a previous engagement prevents me from speaking to them directly by telephone. There is an especial reason for wishing to speak to this first of many State and regional groups who will carry forward the work of the White House Conference. The conclusions of that Conference, so far as they propose immediately practical measures in behalf of childhood, depend for their application chiefly upon the States and the local communities. The Federal Government can help with information and research, and toward the creation of administrative agencies and the funds to assist in support of them, but they rest primarily with States and counties, cooperating often with private agencies and dealing with the problem at close range and in the light of local conditions. The work in behalf of children is so intimately a part of the life of the people that its control and direction need to be kept very close to them. I look forward with high anticipation to the success of your Conference.

Yours faithfully,

HERBERT HOOVER

[Honorable Harry G. Leslie, State House, Indianapolis, Indiana]

NOTE: The letter was read to the conference, meeting in Indianapolis, Ind. The group was the first State organization to follow up the work of the White House Conference on Child Health and Protection. See 1930 volume, Item 376.

23

Remarks on Presenting a Special Congressional Medal to Lincoln Ellsworth.
January 16, 1931

ON BEHALF OF the Congress of the United States it gives me great pleasure to hand you this gold medal for your conspicuous courage, sagacity, and perseverance on your polar flight of 1925, and transpolar flight of 1926. Please accept my congratulations, and the congratulations of the American people.

In reading of your explorations, I learn of the noble assistance rendered you at all times by your sister, Mrs. Bernon S. Prentice. I regret that she has not lived to see you receive this medal. Her life was a fine example of the fortitude of our American women.

NOTE: The President spoke in a presentation ceremony on the South Lawn of the White House at 12:30 p.m. During the ceremony the President received an American flag that had been carried in the *Norge*.

Mr. Ellsworth was co-leader with Roald Amundsen and Umberto Nobile in the flight of the dirigible *Norge* over the North Pole in 1926. The 1925 polar flight of Ellsworth and Amundsen ended when bad weather grounded their plane.

24

Message to a Luncheon Honoring George E. Akerson.
January 16, 1931

[Released January 16, 1931.   Dated January 13, 1931]

My dear Mr. Zukor:

I congratulate you cordially upon acquiring the services of my long time friend and co-laborer, George Akerson, whose ability, personality and loyalty I hold in the highest esteem. He is equally to be congratulated upon the opportunity of such a profitable and congenial association with yourself in your increasingly important field of activity.

Yours faithfully,

HERBERT HOOVER

[Mr. Adolph Zukor, President, Paramount Publix Corporation, Paramount Building, New York City]

NOTE: The message was read at a luncheon at which Mr. Akerson was introduced to the executives of the motion picture industry. Adolph Zukor hosted the luncheon at the Ritz-Carlton Hotel in New York City.

25

Message to the Congress Recommending an Appropriation for the International Geological Congress.
January 17, 1931

To the Congress of the United States:

I commend to the favorable consideration of the Congress the inclosed report from the Secretary of State to the end that legislation may be enacted to authorize an appropriation of $110,000 for the expenses of the sixteenth session of the International Geological Congress to be held in the United States in 1932.

HERBERT HOOVER

The White House,
  January 17, 1931.

NOTE: Secretary of State Henry L. Stimson's report, dated January 17, 1931, follows:
The President:

The geological groups in the United States have extended an invitation to the International Geological Congress to hold its sixteenth session in the United States in June 1932.

International Geological Congresses have been held throughout the civilized countries of the world since 1878 at three or four year intervals, except during the period of the Great War. The United States has been host to but one of these congresses, the fifth, held in Washington, D.C., in 1891. Sweden was host to the

Congress in 1910, Canada was host in 1913, and the Union of South Africa was the host to the Congress held in 1929.

One of the best ways to bring about the advance of scientific knowledge in a given field, including the better understanding of the discoveries, their relations and values in that field, is through congresses and organizations of this character, in which scientists are brought together for deliberation and discussion.

These congresses are attended by the leading educators in research and applied geology, and the leading practicing geologists and geological engineers of the civilized countries. The technical sessions are devoted to the discussion of topics of world-wide interest in geology, and the excursions are devoted to direct examinations of the most significant geologic features that are displayed in the host country. Each of the recent congresses has adopted, as a major topic for discussion, one or more of the most important of the world's mineral resources, and, as a consequence, the proceedings of that congress contain an authoritative résumé of the existing information on those resources; these proceedings thus become compendia of information on the selected topics for years to come. The eleventh congress, held in Sweden in 1910, issued a volume on the Iron Ore Resources of the World; the twelfth congress, held in Canada in 1913, issued a volume on the Coal Resources of the World; and the fifteenth congress, held last year in South Africa, will issue a volume on the Gold Resources of the World. The major topic adopted for the sixteenth congress in 1932 is the Petroleum Resources of the World, and in conformity with the practice of other governments it is proposed that this Congress issue a technical report of the congress and a scientific volume on the Petroleum Resources of the World. The information, when compiled, should be of great value.

At the request of the Secretary of the Interior, I therefore have the honor to recommend that the Congress be asked to enact legislation authorizing an appropriation of $110,000 for the expenses of the sixteenth session of the International Geological Congress to be held in the United States in 1932.

Respectfully,
Henry L. Stimson

26

White House Statement on the Formation of a Committee of Leading Citizens To Aid the Red Cross Drought Relief Campaign.
January 18, 1931

AT THE REQUEST of Honorable John Barton Payne, the Chairman of the Red Cross, the President has invited a committee of leading citizens to sponsor and aid the National Red Cross and its local chapters in the drive for funds in aid of the drought sufferers.

The President's request read as follows:

I am appointing a nation-wide committee to sponsor the American Red Cross effort to raise ten millions of dollars for the relief of the sufferers in the drought-stricken areas. Mr. [Calvin] Coolidge has consented to act as Honorary Chairman. Knowing your public spirit I am most desirous that you should be a member of this committee.

We are faced with a national emergency. Those in need in our larger cities are being and will be provided for through the generosity and self-reliance of the citizens of those communities. The people however in the drought-stricken areas in twenty-one states are not in a position adequately to help themselves and must look to their fellow citizens for temporary assistance.

The American way of meeting such a relief problem has been through voluntary effort and for many years this effort has been centered in the American Red Cross, created by the people themselves to act in just such emergencies. It has met its responsibilities magnificently in times of war and of peace.

It is essential that we should maintain the sound American tradition and spirit of voluntary aid in such emergency and should not undermine that spirit which has made our Red Cross the outstanding guardian of our people in time of disaster.

HERBERT HOOVER

NOTE: On the same day, the White House issued a list of leading citizens who had accepted the President's invitation to join the nationwide committee.

27

Message to the Congress Transmitting
Report of the National Commission
on Law Observance and Enforcement.
January 20, 1931

To the Congress:

The first deficiency appropriation act of March 4, 1929, carried an appropriation for a thorough investigation into the enforcement of the prohibition laws, together with the enforcement of other laws.

In pursuance of this provision I appointed a commission consisting of former Attorney General George W. Wickersham, chairman, former Secretary of War Newton D. Baker, Federal Judges William S. Kenyon, Paul J. McCormick, and William I. Grubb, former Chief Justice Kenneth Mackintosh of Supreme Court of Washington, Dean Roscoe Pound of Harvard Law School, President Ada L. Comstock of Radcliffe College, Henry W. Anderson of Virginia, Monte M. Lemann of New Orleans, and Frank J. Loesch of Chicago.

The commission thus comprises an able group of distinguished citizens of character and independence of thought, representative of different sections of the country. For 18 months they have exhaustively and painstakingly gathered and examined the facts as to enforcement, the benefits, and the abuses under the prohibition laws, both before and since the passage of the eighteenth amendment. I am transmitting their report immediately. Reports upon the enforcement of other criminal laws will follow.

The commission considers that the conditions of enforcement of the prohibition laws in the country as a whole are unsatisfactory but it reports that the Federal participation in enforcement has shown continued improvement since and as a consequence of the act of Congress of 1927 placing prohibition officers under civil service, and the act of 1930 transferring prohibition enforcement from the Treasury to the Department of Justice, and it outlines further possible improvement. It calls attention to the urgency of obedience to law by our citizens and to the imperative necessity for greater assumption and performance by State and local governments of their share of responsibilities under the "concurrent enforcement" provision of the Constitution if enforcement is to be successful. It recommends that further and more effective efforts be made to enforce the laws. It makes recommendations as to Federal administrative methods and certain secondary legislation for further increase of personnel, new classification of offenses, relief of the courts, and amendments to the national prohibition act clarifying the law and eliminating irritations which arise under it. Some of these recommendations have been enacted by the Congress or are already in course of legislation. I commend those suggestions to the attention of the Congress at an appropriate time.

The commission, by a large majority, does not favor the repeal of the eighteenth amendment as a method of cure for the inherent abuses of the liquor traffic. I am in accord with this view. I am in unity with the spirit of the report in seeking constructive steps to advance the national ideal of eradication of the social and economic and political evils of this traffic, to preserve the gains which have been made, and to eliminate the abuses which exist, at the same time facing with an open mind the difficulties which have arisen under this experiment. I do, however, see serious objection to, and therefore must not be understood as recommending, the commission's proposed revision of the eighteenth amendment which is suggested by them for possible consideration at some future time if the continued effort at enforcement should not prove successful. My own duty and that of all executive officials is clear—to enforce the law with all the means at our disposal without equivocation or reservation.

The report is the result of a thorough and comprehensive study of the situation by a representative and authoritative group. It clearly recognizes the gains which have been made and is resolute that those gains shall be preserved. There are necessarily differences in views among its members. It is a temperate and judicial presentation. It should stimulate the clarification of public mind and the advancement of public thought.

HERBERT HOOVER

The White House,
    January 20, 1931.

NOTE: The report, entitled "A Report of the National Commission on Law Observance and Enforcement Relative to the Facts as to the Enforcement, the Benefits, and the Abuses Under the Prohibition Laws, Both Before and Since the Adoption of the Eighteenth Amendment to the Constitution," is printed in House Document 722 (71st Cong., 3d sess., Government Printing Office: 1931).

On Monday, January 19, 1931, the White House issued an advance text of the Commission's summary and conclusions, which emphasized opposition to repeal of the eighteenth amendment. The full text of the report, made available on Tuesday, January 20, reflected a badly divided Commission, with two Commissioners advocating outright repeal, five favoring revisions to allow some sales, and four favoring a further trial of prohibition.

28

Message to the Congress Recommending an Appropriation for Participation in the Conference on the Limitation of the Manufacture of Narcotic Drugs.
January 21, 1931

To the Congress of the United States:

I commend to the favorable consideration of the Congress the inclosed report from the Secretary of State to the end that legislation may be enacted to authorize the appropriation of $35,000, for the expenses of participation by the United States in the Conference on the Limitation of the Manufacture of Narcotic Drugs to be held at Geneva, Switzerland, on May 27, 1931.

HERBERT HOOVER

The White House,
    January 21, 1931.

NOTE: The message and accompanying papers are printed as Senate Document 256 (71st Cong., 3d sess.).

29

Radio Address on the Drought Relief Campaign of the American National Red Cross.
January 22, 1931

Judge Payne, ladies and gentlemen:

It is a real obligation that I should join in this appeal. The American Red Cross is a great voluntary organization, created by the people themselves, on whom the Nation places reliance in time of need and times of disaster. For some months it has been providing for those of our fellow citizens who have suffered from the devastating effects of the long-extended drought. The area affected is roughly limited to the States bordering upon the Potomac, the Ohio, and the Mississippi Rivers, with limited acute areas in some Southwestern and Northwestern States. The people in this area lost a large part of their crops, and many thousands are even short of food supplies.

The Red Cross now appeals for $10 million of additional funds in order that that essential task may be adequately performed. There is no question but that funds are needed. It is unthinkable that any of our people should be allowed to suffer from hunger or want. The heart of the Nation will not permit it. It is to the heart of the Nation that I am appealing tonight. I urge all of my fellow countrymen to contribute promptly and in accordance with their means. It is a call to citizenship and to generosity in time of trial, but it is a call for protection to our greatest American institution of charity and above all a call on behalf of those in need.

I want to take this occasion to thank the thousands of devoted members of the Red Cross throughout the land who in the drought-stricken areas are devoting their time and effort to the relief of suffering and in the other parts of the country to providing the means of doing so. In the face of calamity let us unite in a common effort to drive suffering and want from our country. There can be no higher duty. To the call of that duty the Nation will respond.

NOTE: The President spoke over the National Broadcasting Company radio network from the White House.

John Barton Payne was Chairman of the American National Red Cross.

As printed above, the text follows the President's reading copy of the address. On the same day, the White House issued an advance text of the address.

30

Message to the One Hundred Year Club of New York.
January 22, 1931

[Released January 22, 1931.   Dated January 21, 1931]

I WILL be obliged if you will express my cordial greetings to those present at the third annual dinner of the One Hundred Year Club of New York. The existence of such a society, representing so many industrial and professional organizations still flourishing after one hundred years of unbroken activity is in itself a demonstration of the inherent stability of American life with its endless opportunities for profitable enterprise through all temporary vicissitudes. I send you my confident good wishes for continued success.

HERBERT HOOVER

[Charles C. Paulding, President, The One Hundred Year Club of New York, New York City]

NOTE: The message was read at the club's third annual dinner, held in the Savoy Plaza Hotel in New York City. The organization comprised New York City firms a century or more old.

31

The President's News Conference of
January 23, 1931

BENEDICT CROWELL

THE PRESIDENT. I have today forwarded to the Senate the nomination of Mr. Benedict Crowell, of Cleveland, as a brigadier general of the

Reserve Corps of the Army. As you know, Mr. Crowell has long been a member of the Reserve Corps, and he did very distinguished service during the war as Assistant Secretary of War and subsequently as the Director of Munitions. And this promotion in itself is not so material as it affords an opportunity to indicate the feeling of his Army associates and his friends in the War Department and my own feeling toward what we have always considered was an inadvertent but very grave injustice.

FEDERAL POWER COMMISSIONERS

I have some inquiries here for the Attorney General's opinion on the three Power Commissioners. The Attorney General will release that opinion for you this afternoon if you want it.

Otherwise, I have nothing on this occasion.

NOTE: President Hoover's one hundred and sixty-eighth news conference was held in the White House at 4 p.m. on Friday, January 23, 1931.

On the same day, the White House issued a text of the President's statement on the nomination of Benedict Crowell as brigadier general of the Army Reserve Corps (see Item 32).

In his remarks the President referred to the Attorney General's opinion on the Federal Power Commission appointments; that opinion, dated January 10, 1931, follows:

Sir:

You have asked my opinion on the legal aspects of the resolutions of the Senate, passed January 9, 1931, requesting you to return to the Senate the certified copies of the resolutions of the Senate expressing its consent to the appointment of George Otis Smith, Marcel Garsaud, and Claude L. Draper as members of the Federal Power Commission.

These men were nominated for these positions, and their nominations were considered by the Senate, which passed resolutions consenting to their appointment. Formal notification of this action was transmitted to you by the Secretary of the Senate, and in reliance thereon you made the appointments. The question is now presented whether, if you comply with the Senate's request and the Senate goes through the form of withdrawing its consent to the appointments, such action would have any legal effect or operate to remove or oust the appointees.

The nomination of Mr. Draper was confirmed on December 19, 1930, by the passage of a resolution in the following form:

"Resolved, That the Senate advise and consent to the appointment of the following-named persons to the offices named agreeable to their respective nominations: Federal Power Commission. . . . Claude L. Draper, of Wyoming, to be a member for the term expiring June 22, 1931."

The nominations of Mr. Smith and Mr. Garsaud were confirmed by the passage of a similar resolution on December 20, 1930. In the cases of Smith and Draper, after the votes were taken the presiding officer caused to be entered in the Record without objection a statement that—

"The Senate advises and consents to the nomination, and the President will be notified." (Cong. Rec., Dec. 19, 1930, p. 1101; Cong. Rec., Dec. 20, 1930, p. 1266.)

The Executive Journal of the Senate for December 19, 1930, in recording the passage of the resolution on confirming the nomination of Draper, contains the following:

"Ordered, that the foregoing resolution of confirmation be forwarded to the President of the United States."

There is a similar entry and order in the Executive Journal of December 20, 1930, relating to the Smith appointment. In the case of Garsaud the Congressional Record does not disclose a statement by the presiding officer that the President would be notified, but the Executive Journal of the Senate for December 20, 1930, contains, in addition to the resolution consenting to the appointment of Garsaud, the following:

"Ordered, that the foregoing resolution of confirmation be forwarded to the President of the United States."

On December 20, 1930, the Senate recessed until January 5, 1931. On December 20, 1930, the Secretary of the Senate duly notified you of the confirmation of the nomination of Draper, and on December 22, 1930, the Secretary of the Senate duly notified you of the confirmations of Smith and Garsaud. In each case the notice was in the regular form, delivered by messenger, and consisted of a copy of the resolution of the Senate certified by the Secretary of the Senate. On December 22, 1930, in reliance upon these formal notifications that the Senate consented to the appointments, you appointed Smith, Garsaud, and Draper, who, on December 22, 1930, took the oath of office and entered upon the discharge of their duties. The appointments were effected by signing and delivering commissions to the appointees. On January 5, 1931, which was within two days of actual executive session of the Senate following the confirmation, motions to reconsider the nominations, accompanied by motions to request the return of the notifications, were made in the Senate and, having been passed on the 9th of January, are now before you.

The action of the Senate in such matters is governed by Rule XXXVIII of the Standing Rules of the Senate, of which paragraphs 3 and 4 are as follows:

"3. When a nomination is confirmed or rejected, any Senator voting in the majority may move for a reconsideration on the same day on which the vote

35

was taken, or on either of the next two days of actual Executive session of the Senate; but if a notification of the confirmation or rejection of a nomination shall have been sent to the President before the expiration of the time within which a motion to reconsider may be made, the motion to reconsider shall be accompanied by a motion to request the President to return such notification to the Senate. Any motion to reconsider the vote on a nomination may be laid on the table without prejudice to the nomination, and shall be a final disposition of such motion.

"4. Nominations confirmed or rejected by the Senate shall not be returned by the Secretary to the President until the expiration of the time limited for making a motion to reconsider the same, or while a motion to reconsider is pending, unless otherwise ordered by the Senate."

It is provided in Article II of the Constitution that the President

"shall nominate, and by and with the Advice and Consent of the Senate, shall appoint Ambassadors, other public Ministers and Consuls, Judges of the Supreme Court, and all other Officers of the United States, whose Appointments are not herein otherwise provided for, and which shall be established by Law; . . ."

This clause contemplates three steps. There is, first, the nomination, which is a mere proposal. Next comes action by the Senate consenting or refusing to consent to the appointment. Finally, if the Senate consents to the appointment there follows the executive act of appointment. It has long been recognized that the nomination and the appointment are different acts, and that the appointment is not effected by the Senate's so-called confirmation of the nomination. After the Senate has consented to the appointment, the nominee is not entitled to the office until the consent is followed by the executive appointment. After a nomination is sent to the Senate and has received the approval of that body, the President may, having changed his mind, decline to make the appointment. See *Marbury* v. *Madison,* 1 Cranch 137; 12 Op. Atty. Gen. 32, 42; 12 Op. Atty. Gen. 304, 306; 3 Willoughby on The Constitution, 2d Ed. (1929), Sec. 987.

As the Executive Act of appointment follows the Senate's consent, the necessity for and the important function of a formal notification to the President, expressing the Senate's consent, become at once apparent.

Upon the foregoing facts the ultimate question in this case is whether the appointments were made with the consent of the Senate. If the appointments were made without that consent they were ineffective and invalid, but if made with the Senate's consent the function of the Senate in respect of the appointments is ended.

The formal notifications of confirmation sent you by the Secretary of the Senate were sent by authority of the Senate before the expiration of the time allowed for reconsideration by paragraph 3 of Rule XXXVIII. While these orders for notification to the President did not explicitly state that the notifications should be sent forthwith, there seems to be no substantial dispute about the fact that the orders were so intended and that orders in that form for immediate notification of the President are in accordance with the traditional practice of the Senate, and that the Secretary of the Senate was justified in treating these orders as authority for immediate notification.

The contention has been made that although the Senate intended to and did convey to the President a formal notice of consent to the appointments, unconditional in form, there was an implied qualification that the Senate might reconsider and withdraw the consent and therefore the President should have withheld action until the expiration of the period allowed by Senate rules for reconsideration.

While the Senate rules are not very explicit, a reasonable and fair interpretation, with a view to reconciling all their provisions and in the light of established legislative and executive practice, leads only to the conclusion that the Senate intended to and did constitutionally consent to your making the appointments when you did. Reasonably construed there is nothing about the rules which renders them obnoxious to any constitutional provision. One provision of these rules is that when a nomination is confirmed, a motion for reconsideration may be made within either of the next two days of actual executive session. This must be read in connection with paragraph 4, which provides that nominations confirmed or rejected shall not be returned by the Secretary to the President until the expiration of the time limited for making a motion to reconsider or while such a motion is pending "unless otherwise ordered by the Senate". That rule was intended to protect and preserve the power of the Senate to reconsider. It carries the inference that if notification of confirmation be transmitted to the President, the Senate loses the power of reconsideration if the President should act on the notification by making an appointment before a request for return of the notification is delivered to him.

The rules also plainly recognize that before the time for reconsideration has expired or even while a motion for reconsideration is pending, the Senate may order an immediate notification of its consent to the appointment to be transmitted to the President. If the Senate makes no order directing immediate notification to be sent to the President, the notification would be withheld until the expiration of the time allowed for reconsideration; but where the Senate orders a notification to be sent forthwith and without waiting for the expiration of the reconsideration period, some purpose must be attributed to that action. Why order immediate notification to be sent to the President unless he is expected to act upon it? The only conceivable purpose in expediting the notice is to make it possible for the President to expedite the appointment. If ordering the notification of confirmation to be sent to the President in advance of the expiration of the time allowed by the rules for reconsideration is not intended as a formal announcement and expression of the Senate's consent to an immediate appointment, the advanced notification would have no purpose whatever. The rules provide in such a case for no second notification, and if the first one be not effective so that the President may rely on it, he never will receive a notification of final consent, to the appointment. The President would never be able to rely on any notification and would be obliged to inform himself as best he might as to whether the Senate had finally consented to the appointment.

It has been suggested that even though a notification of the confirmation has been sent by the Senate to the President in advance of the expiration of the period allowed for reconsideration, it is subject to recall at the pleasure of the Senate without regard to what the President has done in reliance on it, and that this is implied in the provision in paragraph 3 of Rule XXXVIII to the effect that where a motion for reconsideration is made it shall be accompanied by a motion to request the President to return the notification. The fallacy of that argument rests in the assumption that paragraph 3 contemplates that the notification is under all circumstances subject to recall during the reconsideration period. This rule assumes that a request for a return of the notification may be effective if it reaches the President before he has made the appointment. In that case he would, no doubt, comply with the request. It also assumes that where nominations have been rejected and the President consequently makes no appointments, there is no difficulty about recalling the notification. It is consistent, however, with the idea that the request for return of the notification will be too late if it fails to reach the President before the appointment is made. Senate practice lends weight to these conclusions.

The position that the Senate did consent that these appointments be immediately made, subject to revocation on reconsideration by the Senate is wholly untenable. That would allow the Senate to encroach upon executive functions by removing an officer within a limited time after his appointment because of dissatisfaction with his official acts. Any rule that provided for such a course would be void. The consent required by the Constitution is a consent absolute and irrevocable when acted on by the Executive. With such a condition attached it would be a case, not of a void condition, but of an invalid appointment. Either these appointments are valid because made with the unqualified consent of the Senate or they are void. There is no middle ground.

Ordinarily the Senate is the judge of its own rules, but where it makes a retroactive interpretation applicable to past transactions which involve action of the executive branch of the Government, the question becomes a legal one and open to judicial inquiry. I cannot escape the conclusion that, fairly construed, the rules of the Senate contemplate that where it orders notification of the Senate's consent to an appointment to be forthwith transmitted to the President without waiting for the expiration of the period for reconsideration, that action is intended as a deliberate expression to the President of the Senate's unqualified consent to the immediate appointment, and that it amounts to a decision by the Senate, not under suspension of its rules but in accordance with them, to place reconsideration beyond its power if the President should act and make the appointment before a request of the Senate for a return of the papers reaches him.

I am of the opinion, therefore, that what transpired in this case amounted to an expression by the Senate of its consent to these appointments and that the appointments were constitutionally made and became effective; and that the return of the papers to the Senate would serve no lawful purpose because no action which the Senate could now take would disturb or operate to revoke the appointments.

Respectfully,

WILLIAM D. MITCHELL
Attorney General

[The President, The White House]

On February 4, 1931, the Senate voted to confirm Messrs. Garsaud and Draper but not to confirm Mr. Smith. In a subsequent court case the Supreme Court upheld the President's position that confirmation could not be reconsidered and rescinded.

32

Statement on the Nomination of Benedict Crowell as Brigadier General of the Army Reserve Corps. *January 23, 1931*

I HAVE today forwarded to the Senate the nomination of Mr. Benedict Crowell of Cleveland as Brigadier General in the Reserve Corps of the Army.

Mr. Crowell has long been a member of the Reserve Corps and gave most distinguished service to the country in important capacities during the war. This promotion in itself is not so material as the opportunity it affords to indicate the feeling of his many associates and friends in the War Department and my own feeling over what we have always considered was an inadvertent but yet a grave injustice.

HERBERT HOOVER

The White House,
    January 23, 1931.

NOTE: Benedict Crowell served as Assistant Secretary of War during the Wilson administration. In December 1922, he was indicted on charges of defrauding the Government under wartime contracts. The indictment was thrown out on January 30, 1925, in a judgment vindicating Crowell and six other defendants.

33

Message on the 21st Anniversary of the Boy Scouts of America. *January 23, 1931*

[Released January 23, 1931.   Dated November 26, 1930]

BOYHOOD is the period of development. By the time he comes of age a boy has acquired, in body, brains, and character, the tools he must use in life. His work and play, his love of camping and knowledge of nature, his courage, his sportsmanship, his desire to serve his fellow men, have become a part of him, of what he will always be.

Scouting, too, has come of age. Through twenty-one years it has summoned Youth to the great adventure of lofty living. As the twenty-first year marks Youth's formal passage to legal maturity, so the coming of the twenty-first year of the Boy Scout movement in America marks its entry into an era of maturer service. I hope it may continue through years of increasing usefulness to release that deep love of humanity, that eagerness to make life fuller and sturdier, that is the very core of democracy itself.

HERBERT HOOVER

[Myron Stearns, Boy's Life, 2 Park Ave., New York City]

NOTE: The headquarters of the Boy Scouts of America released the message in conjunction with the announcement of a week-long celebration to begin on February 8, 1931, the 21st anniversary of the founding of the organization.

34

Message of Sympathy on the Death of Walter S. Dickey.
January 23, 1931

I HAVE been shocked and grieved to learn of the death of your father. His energetic and valuable service to his community, his State and his Country will be greatly missed. He was my good friend. Please accept the deep sympathy of Mrs. Hoover and myself.

HERBERT HOOVER

[Mr. Lawrence Dickey, Journal-Post, Kansas City, Missouri]

NOTE: Mr. Dickey, owner of the W. S. Dickey Clay Manufacturing Co., and the Kansas City Journal-Post, died on January 22, 1931, at his home in Kansas City, Mo.

35

Message to the Congress About the Claim of George J. Salem Against the Government of Egypt.
January 26, 1931

To the Congress of the United States:

I inclose herewith a report which the Secretary of State has addressed to me in regard to the claim of George J. Salem against the Government of Egypt. This claim grows out of the improper exercise of jurisdiction over Mr. Salem by the native courts of Egypt respecting a charge of forgery of deeds and out of the retention by the Egyptian authorities of Mr. Salem's deeds for a period of over four years. These actions caused him to lose opportunity for the advantageous sales of his land and entailed the expenses necessary in defending himself in the native courts of Egypt and also in the mixed tribunals of Egypt. In the latter tribunals he sought a remedy for the injury above recited, but he received a further injury through what is considered by this Government to be a denial of justice.

It will be noted that the Egyptian Government in a note addressed to the American minister at Cairo, dated March 20, 1930, agreed to the arbitration of the claim.

I recommend that an appropriation in the amount suggested by the Secretary of State be authorized in order that the expenses which it will be necessary to incur on the part of the Government of the United States in the prosecution of the claim to final settlement may be met.

HERBERT HOOVER

The White House,
    January 26, 1931.

NOTE: The message and accompanying report are printed as Senate Document 261 (71st Cong., 3d sess.).

36

Message to the Congress Recommending Payment of Claims of Certain Chinese Citizens Against the Navy Department.
January 26, 1931

To the Congress of the United States:

I transmit herewith a report of the Secretary of State requesting the submission to the Congress of claims against the Navy Department in the total amount of $4,657.20 United States currency in behalf of Yao Ah-Ken and Chiang Ah-erh (Tsiange Ah Erh) for personal injuries received; the family of Ts'ao Jung-k'uan (Dzao Yong Kwer) for damages sustained due to his death; and in behalf of the Shanghai Electric Construction Co. (Ltd.) for property losses sustained by it as the result of a collision between United States Marine Corps truck No. 1130 and tram car B 168, owned by the company, in Shanghai, China, on November 29, 1929. The total amount requested to be appropriated will be allotted as follows: To Yao Ah-Ken and Chiang Ah-erh (Tsiange Ah Erh), $1,500 each; to the family of Ts'ao Jung-k'uan (Dzao Yong

Kwer), $1,500; and to the Shanghai Electric Construction Co. (Ltd.), $157.20.

I recommend that, as an act of grace and without reference to the question of the legal liability of the United States in the premises, an appropriation in the total amount of $4,657.20 United States currency be authorized to effect settlement of these claims, in accordance with the recommendations of the Secretary of the Navy and the Secretary of State.

HERBERT HOOVER

The White House,
    January 26, 1931.

NOTE: The message and accompanying papers are printed as Senate Document 262 (71st Cong., 3d sess.).

37

The President's News Conference of *January 27, 1931*

NIAGARA FALLS

THE PRESIDENT. I have an inquiry here about Niagara Falls. Some years ago we appointed a joint control board on Niagara Falls with the Canadian Government. And in view of the press inquiries this morning that I had from this neighborhood, I have asked the War and State Departments to suggest that that board should have another meeting and see what revision they might need to make in their previous proposals, or alternatively, how imminently necessary it is for the Senate to proceed with the treaty which was formulated to cover the question of the failure of the scenery at Niagara.[1]

---

[1] The press inquiries, to which the President referred, related to a recent massive rock slide at Niagara Falls.

On February 18, 1931, the Senate Foreign Relations Committee voted to reject the treaty that had been presented to the Senate by President Calvin Coolidge. The chief objections were to the portions of the treaty calling for agreements with private power companies.

For the message transmitting the final report of the Special International Niagara Board, see 1930 volume, Item 109.

GENERAL DISARMAMENT CONFERENCE

The matter I would like to talk to you about today is absolutely as background and not for publication at all, but I want for you to understand the problem which is coming along a little later—nothing for quotation or even for publication about it, but simply to have you forearmed.

It is with relation to the World Disarmament Conference in February 1932. As you know, there has been a great deal of preparation and work done in the last 6 years, in which this Government has participated during the preliminary conference leading up to this final conference which is to be held, as I have said, in 1932.

We have regarded that matter as one of a good deal of importance, both as to the promotion of peace and especially the reduction of economic burdens in Europe. The progress made with naval limitation in the meantime is such that naval questions are not likely to be a matter of any great importance at that Conference. It is likely it will be almost wholly confined to land armaments. We have already demobilized our Army down to the point where it is not a threat against nations. As a matter of fact, it is in numbers less than the number of policemen on our streets. So that we are not primarily concerned. Our interest is purely one in promotion of a general cause and, therefore, one of friendly interest in promoting the negotiations. The economic importance of it is somewhat indicated, in direct importance to us by the fact that there are about 3 million men in standing armies outside of Russia, not including their reserves in it, and there is a large budget of $1,500 million for their support. All of which has an interest to us in the promotion of economic progress.

But we have felt that with the experiences of the [London] Naval Conference we are progressing, and assurance of success in conferences of this kind requires a large amount of preliminary negotiation between the governments which are primarily concerned. Those negotiations, of course, we are hopeful will go forward but are not negotiations in which we have any direct interest at all, and which we could not be a party to otherwise than perhaps just friendly suggestions.

Furthermore, we do not believe that in the situation where we are so indirectly concerned that we should undertake the leadership of such a conference; that that responsibility must rest on those nations which are primarily concerned, and who must, if the Conference is to be a success, make the sacrifices and arrangements that lead to limitation and reduction of arms.

I want you to have just that much when the problem arises, which is likely to be at any time. It is an attitude of entire friendliness and desire on our part to wish to help in anyway we can. It is not our major problem, and the success of such a conference must come from the nations which are concerned.

Otherwise than that I have nothing.

Q. Will our interest in air armaments, Mr. President, be taken up at the Conference?

THE PRESIDENT. I hadn't given that any particular thought, so I cannot give you any competent answer to it. The development of air transportation has not reached a point where it can get across the Atlantic, so it is not very direct. Our air armament, I might mention, is on a parity with any other nation in the world right now.

Q. Mr. President, in connection with not using this in anyway, Secretary Stimson talked about this at his conference yesterday—that we did have a vital interest in the question. I was just wondering if we could not more or less use this as background.

THE PRESIDENT. I would a little rather you would not give publication at all now. You can have this in mind when the subject will come up in the next few weeks, and you will know what our attitude is.

NOTE: President Hoover's one hundred and sixty-ninth news conference was held in the White House at 12 noon on Tuesday, January 27, 1931.

38

Message on the 50th Anniversary of the International Christian Endeavor Society.
January 28, 1931

THE CELEBRATION of the fiftieth anniversary of Christian Endeavor is indeed an occasion for world wide gratification to all who have witnessed its steadfast service of high ideals of life and character. I join its multitudes of friends in best wishes for continued success and growth.

HERBERT HOOVER

[Daniel A. Poling, President, International Interdenominational Christian Endeavor Society, 41 Mount Vernon Street, Boston, Mass.]

NOTE: The message was released in Washington, D.C., in conjunction with publicity on the organization's Golden Jubilee Conference, which was held from July 11 to July 16, 1931.

39

The President's News Conference of
January 30, 1931

PRIME MINISTER RICHARD B. BENNETT

THE PRESIDENT. I have been very glad to welcome here today the Canadian Premier on his informal visit to Washington. We have no formal matters under discussion. We are mutually interested in the common welfare of both nations, and we will have, no doubt, some informal conversations on problems of the future, and that sort of conversations always leads to better working understandings. I consider it a very great compliment that Mr. Bennett has found it possible to come to Washington in such a fashion.

VIRGIN ISLANDS

The only other matter of interest that I have today is that we have undertaken to reorganize the Government of the Virgin Islands. The

Navy Department has asked to be relieved of the administration, and I am assigning it to the Department of the Interior.

I am proposing to forward to Congress the name of Dr. Paul M. Pearson, of Pennsylvania, for Governor. Other civilian officials will be appointed in replacement of naval officers.

Congress recently made some appropriations for reorganization and developmental work in the islands, and the new organization is intended to make that more effective.

The Director of the Budget and the Director of the Bureau of Efficiency have worked out a plan for the new administration which will be carried into action by the Department of the Interior.

QUESTIONS

Q. Mr. President, is that effective today—immediately?

THE PRESIDENT. Yes, I will send the name of the new Governor up to Congress, and as soon as he is confirmed or otherwise we will make the changes.

Q. Mr. President, you spoke of Mr. Bennett having set a fashion in coming down here.

THE PRESIDENT. I didn't say "set a fashion." I said "in such a fashion."

NOTE: President Hoover's one hundred and seventieth news conference was held in the White House at 4 p.m. on Friday, January 30, 1931.

On the same day, the White House issued texts of the President's statements on the visit of Canadian Prime Minister Richard B. Bennett (see Item 40) and the reorganization of the Government of the Virgin Islands (see Item 41).

40

Statement on the Visit of Canadian Prime Minister Richard B. Bennett.
January 30, 1931

THE PRESIDENT said:

"I have been very glad to welcome today the Canadian Premier upon his informal visit to Washington. We have no formal matters under discussion. We are mutually interested in the common welfare of our peoples. Informal conversations on problems of the future always lead to better understanding. I consider it a great compliment that Mr. Bennett has found it possible to come to Washington."

NOTE: The Canadian Prime Minister arrived in Washington, D.C., on January 30, 1931, dined with the President that evening, and spent the next 2 days in informal conferences. The chief item of discussion was the projected St. Lawrence Seaway.

41

Statement on the Reorganization of the Government of the Virgin Islands. *January 30, 1931*

THE PRESIDENT said:

"We have undertaken to reorganize the Government of the Virgin Islands. The Navy Department has asked to be relieved of the administration, and I am assigning it to the Department of the Interior.

"I am proposing to forward to Congress the name of Dr. Paul M. Pearson, of Pennsylvania, for Governor. Other civilian officials will be appointed in replacement of naval officers.

"Congress recently made special appropriations for reorganization and developmental work in the islands, and the new organization is intended to make these provisions more effective.

"Mr. Herbert Brown of the Bureau of Efficiency and Colonel [J. Clawson] Roop, Director of the Budget, have drafted plans for the new administration which are being carried into action."

42

Message to a Testimonial Dinner Honoring Dr. James Ewing. *January 31, 1931*

[Released January 31, 1931. Dated January 29, 1931]

Gentlemen:

I thank you warmly for your kind invitation to attend the testimonial dinner in honor of Dr. James Ewing on January 31st, and deeply regret that my duties here do not permit me to be present. I should like to share in person in paying honor to such a useful and distinguished citizen, whose work as scientific researcher, teacher, and author has done so much to forward the attack upon the problem of cancer in particular and of disease in general. Such a career is a service and an inspiration to humanity, and deserves the tribute of public praise.

Yours faithfully,

HERBERT HOOVER

[The Medical Board of the Memorial Hospital, New York, N.Y.]

NOTE: The message was read at a testimonial dinner, held at the Hotel Pierre in New York City. Dr. Ewing, of Cornell University, was one of the Nation's leading cancer researchers.

43

The President's News Conference of *February 3, 1931*

PUBLIC VS. PRIVATE FINANCING OF RELIEF EFFORTS

THE PRESIDENT. I have rather a long statement today, which we will give to you mimeographed, so that you won't have to take notes on it.

Certain Senators have issued a public statement to the effect that unless the President and the House of Representatives agree to the appropriations from the Federal Treasury for charitable purposes, they will force an extra session of Congress. I don't want to add acrimony to a discussion, but would rather state the case as I see it in its fundamentals.

This is not an issue as to whether the people are going hungry or cold in the United States. It is solely a question of the best method by which hunger and cold can be prevented. It is a question as to whether the American people on the one hand will maintain the spirit of charity and of mutual self-help through voluntary giving and the responsibility of local government as distinguished on the other hand from appropriations out of the Federal Treasury for such purposes. My own conviction is strongly that if we break down this sense of responsibility, of individual generosity to individual, and mutual self-help in the country in times of national difficulty and if we start appropriations of this character we have not only impaired something infinitely valuable in the life of the American people but have struck at the roots of self-government. Once this has happened it is not the cost of a few score millions, but we are faced with the abyss of reliance in future upon Government charity in some form or other. The money involved is indeed the least of the costs to American ideals and American institutions.

President Cleveland, in 1887, confronted with a similar issue stated in part:

"A prevalent tendency to disregard the limited mission of this power and duty should, I think, be steadfastly resisted, to the end that the lesson should be constantly enforced that though the people support the Government, the Government should not support the people.

"The friendliness and charity of our countrymen can always be relied upon to relieve their fellow citizens in misfortune. This has been repeatedly and quite lately demonstrated. Federal aid in such cases encourages the expectation of paternal care on the part of the Government and weakens the sturdiness of our national character, while it prevents the indulgence among our people of that kindly sentiment and conduct which strengthens the bonds of a common brotherhood."

And there is a practical problem in all this. The help being daily extended by neighbors, by local and national agencies, by municipalities, by industry, and a great multitude of organizations throughout the country today is many times any appropriation yet proposed. The opening of the doors of the Federal Treasury is likely to stifle this giving and thus destroy far more resources than the proposed charity from the Federal Government.

The basis of successful relief in national distress is to mobilize and organize the infinite number of agencies of self-help in the community. That has been the American way of relieving distress among our own people and the country is successfully meeting its problem in the American way today.

We have two entirely separate and distinct situations in the country— the first is the drought area; the second is the unemployment in our large industrial centers—for both of which these appropriations attempt to make charitable contributions.

Immediately upon the appearance of the drought last August, I convoked a meeting of the Governors, the Red Cross and the railways, the bankers and other agencies in the country and laid the foundations of organization and the resources to stimulate every degree of self-help to meet the situation which it was then obvious would develop. The result of this action was to attack the drought problem in a number of directions. The Red Cross established committees in every drought county, comprising the leading citizens of those counties, with instructions to them that they were to prevent starvation among their neighbors, and, if the problem went beyond local resources, the Red Cross would support them.

The organization has stretched throughout the area of suffering. The people are being cared for today through the hands and with sympathetic understanding and upon the responsibility of their neighbors who are being supported in turn by the fine spirit of mutual assistance of the American people. The Red Cross officials, whose long devoted service and experience is unchallenged, inform me this morning that, except for the minor incidents of any emergency organization, no one is going hungry and no one need go hungry or cold.

To reinforce this work, at the opening of Congress I recommended large appropriations for loans to rehabilitate agriculture from the drought and provision of further large sums for public works and construction in the drought territory which would give employment in

51

further relief to the whole situation. These Federal activities provide for an expenditure of upward of $100 million in this area and it is in progress today.

The Red Cross has always met the situations which it has undertaken. After careful survey and after actual experience of several months with their part of the problem, they have announced firmly that they can command the resources with which to meet any call for human relief in prevention of hunger and suffering in drought areas and that they accept this responsibility. They have refused to accept Federal appropriations as not being consonant either with the need or the character of their organization. The Government departments have given and are giving them every assistance. We possibly need to strengthen the Public Health Service in matters of sanitation and to strengthen the credit facilities of that area through the method approved by the Government departments to divert some existing appropriations to strengthen agricultural credit corporations.

In the matter of unemployment outside of the drought areas important economic measures of mutual self-help have been developed, such as those to maintain wages, to distribute employment equitably, to increase construction work by industry, to increase Federal construction work from a rate of about $275 million a year prior to the depression to a rate now of over $750 million a year, to expand State and municipal construction—all upon a scale never before provided or even attempted in any depression. But beyond this to assure that there shall be no suffering, in every town and county voluntary agencies in relief of distress have been strengthened and created and generous funds have been placed at their disposal. They are carrying on their work efficiently and sympathetically.

But after and coincidently with voluntary relief, our American system requires that municipal, county, and State governments shall use their own resources and credit before seeking such assistance from the Federal Treasury.

I have indeed spent much of my life in fighting hardship and starvation both abroad and in the Southern States. I do not feel that I should be charged with lack of human sympathy for those who suffer, but I recall that in all the organizations with which I have been connected over these many years, the foundation has been to summon the maximum of self-help. I am proud to have sought the help of Congress in the past for nations who were so disorganized by war and anarchy that self-help was impossible. But even these appropriations were but a tithe of that which was coincidently mobilized from the public charity of the United States and foreign countries. There is no such paralysis in the United States and I am confident that our people have the resources, the initiative, the courage, the stamina and kindliness of spirit to meet this situation in the way they have met their problems over generations.

I will accredit to those who advocate Federal charity a natural anxiety for the people of their States. I am willing to pledge myself that if the time should ever come that the voluntary agencies of the country, together with the local and State governments, are unable to find resources with which to prevent hunger and suffering in my country, I will ask the aid of every resource of the Federal Government because I would no more see starvation amongst our countrymen than would any Senator or Congressman. I have the faith in the American people that such a day will not come.

The American people are doing their job today. They should be given a chance to show whether they wish to preserve the principles of individual and local responsibility and mutual self-help before they embark on what I believe is a disastrous system. I feel sure they will succeed if given the opportunity.

The whole business situation would be greatly strengthened by the prompt completion of the necessary legislation of this session of Congress and thereby the unemployment problem would be lessened, the drought area indirectly benefited and the resources of self-help in the country strengthened.

NOTE: President Hoover's one hundred and seventy-first news conference was held in the White House at 12 noon on Tuesday, February 3, 1931.

On the same day, the White House issued a text of the President's statement on public vs. private financing of relief efforts (see Item 44).

44

Statement on Public vs. Private
Financing of Relief Efforts.
February 3, 1931

THE PRESIDENT said:

Certain Senators have issued a public statement to the effect that unless the President and the House of Representatives agree to appropriations from the Federal Treasury for charitable purposes they will force an extra session of Congress. I do not wish to add acrimony to a discussion, but would rather state this case as I see its fundamentals.

This is not an issue as to whether people shall go hungry or cold in the United States. It is solely a question of the best method by which hunger and cold shall be prevented. It is a question as to whether the American people on one hand will maintain the spirit of charity and mutual self-help through voluntary giving and the responsibility of local government as distinguished on the other hand from appropriations out of the Federal Treasury for such purposes. My own conviction is strongly that if we break down this sense of responsibility of individual generosity to individual and mutual self-help in the country in times of national difficulty and if we start appropriations of this character we have not only impaired something infinitely valuable in the life of the American people but have struck at the roots of self-government. Once this has happened it is not the cost of a few score millions, but we are faced with the abyss of reliance in future upon Government charity in some form or other. The money involved is indeed the least of the costs to American ideals and American institutions.

President Cleveland, in 1887, confronted with a similar issue stated in part:

"A prevalent tendency to disregard the limited mission of this power and duty should, I think, be steadfastly resisted, to the end that the lesson should be constantly enforced that though the people support the Government, the Government should not support the people.

"The friendliness and charity of our countrymen can always be relied upon to relieve their fellow citizens in misfortune. This has been repeatedly and quite lately demonstrated. Federal aid in such cases encourages the expectation of paternal care on the part of the Government and weakens the sturdiness of our national character, while it prevents the indulgence among our people of that kindly sentiment and conduct which strengthens the bonds of a common brotherhood."

And there is a practical problem in all this. The help being daily extended by neighbors, by local and national agencies, by municipalities, by industry and a great multitude of organizations throughout the country today is many times any appropriation yet proposed. The opening of the doors of the Federal Treasury is likely to stifle this giving and thus destroy far more resources than the proposed charity from the Federal Government.

The basis of successful relief in national distress is to mobilize and organize the infinite number of agencies of self-help in the community. That has been the American way of relieving distress among our own people and the country is successfully meeting its problem in the American way today.

We have two entirely separate and distinct situations in the country— the first is the drought area; the second is the unemployment in our large industrial centers—for both of which these appropriations attempt to make charitable contributions.

Immediately upon the appearance of the drought last August, I convoked a meeting of the Governors, the Red Cross and the railways, the bankers and other agencies in the country and laid the foundations of organization and the resources to stimulate every degree of self-help to meet the situation which it was then obvious would develop. The result of this action was to attack the drought problem in a number of directions. The Red Cross established committees in every drought county, comprising the leading citizens of those counties, with instructions to them that they were to prevent starvation among their neighbors and, if the problem went beyond local resources, the Red Cross would support them.

The organization has stretched throughout the area of suffering, the people are being cared for today through the hands and with sympathetic understanding and upon the responsibility of their neighbors who are being supported, in turn, by the fine spirit of mutual assistance of the American people. The Red Cross officials, whose long, devoted service and experience is unchallenged, inform me this morning that, except for the minor incidents of any emergency organization, no one is going hungry and no one need go hungry or cold.

To reinforce this work at the opening of Congress I recommended large appropriations for loans to rehabilitate agriculture from the drought and provision of further large sums for public works and construction in the drought territory which would give employment in further relief to the whole situation. These Federal activities provide for an expenditure of upward of $100 million in this area and it is in progress today.

The Red Cross has always met the situations which it has undertaken. After careful survey and after actual experience of several months with their part of the problem they have announced firmly that they can command the resources with which to meet any call for human relief in prevention of hunger and suffering in drought areas and that they accept this responsibility. They have refused to accept Federal appropriations as not being consonant either with the need or the character of their organization. The Government departments have given and are giving them every assistance. We possibly need to strengthen the Public Health Service in matters of sanitation and to strengthen the credit facilities of that area through the method approved by the Government departments to divert some existing appropriations to strengthen agricultural credit corporations.

In the matter of unemployment outside of the drought areas important economic measures of mutual self-help have been developed such as those to maintain wages, to distribute employment equitably, to increase construction work by industry, to increase Federal construction work from a rate of about $275 million a year prior to the depression to a rate now of over $750 million a year, to expand State and municipal construction—all upon a scale never before provided or even attempted in any depression. But beyond this to assure that there shall be no suffering, in every town and county voluntary agencies in relief of distress have been strengthened and created and generous funds have been placed at their disposal. They are carrying on their work efficiently and sympathetically.

But after and coincidently with voluntary relief, our American system requires that municipal, county, and State governments shall use their own resources and credit before seeking such assistance from the Federal Treasury.

I have indeed spent much of my life in fighting hardship and starvation both abroad and in the Southern States. I do not feel that I should be charged with lack of human sympathy for those who suffer, but I recall that in all the organizations with which I have been connected over these many years, the foundation has been to summon the maximum of self-help. I am proud to have sought the help of Congress in the past for nations who were so disorganized by war and anarchy that self-help was impossible. But even these appropriations were but a tithe of that which was coincidently mobilized from the public charity of the United States and foreign countries. There is no such paralysis in the United States, and I am confident that our people have the resources, the initiative, the courage, the stamina and kindliness of spirit to meet this situation in the way they have met their problems over generations.

I will accredit to those who advocate Federal charity a natural anxiety for the people of their States. I am willing to pledge myself that, if the time should ever come that the voluntary agencies of the country together with the local and State governments are unable to find resources with which to prevent hunger and suffering in my country, I will ask the aid of every resource of the Federal Government because I would no more see starvation amongst our countrymen than would any Senator or Congressman. I have the faith in the American people that such a day will not come.

The American people are doing their job today. They should be given a chance to show whether they wish to preserve the principles of individual and local responsibility and mutual self-help before they embark on what I believe is a disastrous system. I feel sure they will succeed if given the opportunity.

The whole business situation would be greatly strengthened by the prompt completion of the necessary legislation of this session of Congress and thereby the unemployment problem would be lessened, the drought area indirectly benefited, and the resources of self-help in the country strengthened.

NOTE: On January 17, 1931, the Senate adopted the Robinson amendment to the Interior Department appropriation bill which added $25 million to provide the American National Red Cross with a relief fund. The Red Cross declared that it would refuse the money, and the House of Representatives voted to reject the Senate amendment. In a letter to the President, Chairman John Barton Payne spelled out the position of the Red Cross.

The White House released a text of Chairman Payne's letter, dated February 3, as follows:

Dear Mr. President:

Answering your inquiry as to whether the drouth sufferers are being provided for, I beg to state:

Relief is being given to drouth sufferers throughout the drouth area by our local Chapters and Branches. These are manned by the most public-spirited and helpful people in the different counties and states; the neighbors and friends of the drouth-stricken who know many of them personally, are sympathetic with them, determine their needs and give them an order on the local country store for their requirements. We know of no better method of helping them.

We invite suggestions. A few have come to us from Senators and Members of the House. Every suggestion from whatever source is welcomed and is given prompt attention.

From the beginning we have not withheld support from a single drouth sufferer for want of funds. Sufficient funds for current needs have always been on hand and relief where necessary has been given. In addition to ordinary feeding, we are providing a hot lunch at noon for the school children in Arkansas and some other places where it seemed to be necessary.

Our campaign for Ten Million Dollars is proceeding with reasonable satisfaction. Subscriptions to date exceed Five Million. We are confident of our ability to raise sufficient funds to continue adequately to meet the needs. When this task, assumed by the American Red Cross, is completed the public will be satisfied, as has always been the case with the work of the Red Cross.

Respectfully yours,
JOHN BARTON PAYNE,
Chairman

45

The President's News Conference of
February 5, 1931

DROUGHT RELIEF LEGISLATION

THE PRESIDENT. I haven't anything today for publication or quotation. There is some background on the latest discussion going on about the relief bill [1] that may be of interest to you, but strictly background material.

The leaders of the House and Senate are working on a suggestion that I made last Tuesday in respect to the strengthening of the agricultural credit corporations in the drought area. Some of you will recollect that last September when we had meetings of the Governors and of the bankers from the drought States, the project was put forward then of establishing agricultural credit corporations, or more of them—there are a good many now in existence—with view to meet the heart of the difficulty for those who have ample security but where there is an inability to finance due to the failure of local banks and other difficulties in the drought territory. So that the leaders on both sides are endeavoring to develop that question as reaching to the heart of the problem. That is where people have security but where there is inadequate finance, the Secretary of Agriculture may help out in the building up of those credit corporations. That is not in the nature of compromise, because it all implies the abandonment of all charitable appropriations of all kinds and cutting out one of the primary difficulties which has arisen in the drought territory, and that is the lack of credit for people who have security but who are unable under the present circumstances to finance themselves. That, in addition to the work of the Red Cross and the other agencies, the $45 million bill,[2] should meet every corner of the problem.

APPROPRIATIONS FOR PUBLIC WORKS

There is one thing in the present appropriation bills that we must not overlook—one reason for expedition. Under the setup which I

---

[1] Robinson amendment to the Interior Department appropriation bill (H.R. 14675).

[2] As enacted, H.J. Res. 447, approved January 15, 1931, is Public Resolution, No. 114 (46 Stat. 1039).

arranged with the Budget this year, all of the construction programs in the Government carried the provision that the appropriations are immediately available. That was part of the whole employment setup, so that an expeditious passing of the appropriation bills all along the line in the construction work, which I think appears in at least five departments, will materially expedite our work in giving employment on public works of one kind of [or] another. So that if the leaders up there find a solution of the broad problem to get the bills immediately available, it will help us out on the unemployment side considerably.

That is all I have.

Q. Mr. President, what is the total of that construction fund again— the approximate total?

THE PRESIDENT. Well, that is a little difficult to get at offhand. Construction funds embrace three different approaches. First, in the present budget sums which we are now expending. Second, are the emergency construction bills which have already passed and the authority is in the budget for 1932, in which we made the whole appropriation of the construction work immediately available. Now, if you combine all of those into the calendar year 1932 as to what the total, direct and indirect, construction expenditures will amount to—somewhere from $750 million to $775 million. As I have said before, that compares with the rate of about $275 million before the depression.

I made a statement for you just before Christmas[3] giving out an itemized statement of what those construction activities were likely to be. The appropriation bills—the deficiency bills—carry some further items. I don't know how much that would aggregate—about $25 million to $30 million.

DROUGHT RELIEF LEGISLATION

Q. Mr. President, if you will permit me to return to that relief bill, will the amount of it figure in the settlement?

THE PRESIDENT. There is a discussion from $25 million to $15 million. It is not the amount we are worrying about—it is the question of important principle concerned.

---

[3] See 1930 volume, Item 423.

Q. Mr. President, in the matter of security, would that mean this year's crops could be adequate security?

THE PRESIDENT. That is a complex question. In the $45 million the loans are secured on this next year's crop. It does not follow that the loans made by the agricultural credit corporations are dependent entirely on the crop. They may be for other purposes than that. The agricultural credit corporations happened to be an avenue of financing of wider dimensions, and that is one object of opening up that avenue of crop loans on a wider and more substantial basis.

NOTE: President Hoover's one hundred seventy-second news conference was held in the White House at 4 p.m. on Thursday, February 5, 1931.

46

Letter to Senator Thomas D. Schall
About the Appointment of a District Judge for Minnesota.
February 6, 1931

[Released February 6, 1931.   Dated February 3, 1931]

My dear Senator Schall:

I have your letter of recent date in which you again urge the appointment of Mr. Ernest Michel as a United States Judge for the District of Minnesota, and I have borne in mind your long continued and earnest representations as to this appointment. I regret that I cannot do so. The Department of Justice, after careful investigation, as early as last June indicated its disapproval of Mr. Michel for this position. The Attorney General has given you his reasons therefor.

You appreciate, I am sure, my own responsibility in making appointments to the federal judiciary. The Constitution provides that the President shall first nominate and then, with the advice and consent of the Senate, make the appointment. The initiative of making the nomination is clearly with the President. It is apparent, therefore, that I have an independent obligation, as President, to nominate men for the federal judiciary who are not subject to any question as to their fitness.

I keenly realize the difficulties of your own personal situation. As you say, Mr. Michel is strongly supported by various political groups in Minnesota. I recognize the fact that he is a partner of an important supporter in your recent campaign. I am aware also of the implications which have been made of reprisals against this administration if I fail to agree to this appointment. My conception of my responsibilities does not, however, permit of my placing the appointment of judges on this basis.

No question of corporate influence or personal popularity does or should enter into this question. In the making of a nomination to fill the existing vacancy, I shall be glad to receive any suggestions which you may care to submit and suggest that you present to me eight or ten names of men whom you think would make fit appointees for United States District Judge in Minnesota—men whom you are sure will be dominated by no one—and from such a list I shall hope to find someone with fitness for that position.

Yours faithfully,
HERBERT HOOVER

[Honorable Thomas D. Schall, United States Senate, Washington, D.C.]

NOTE: The President referred to Attorney General William D. Mitchell's letter of January 28, 1931. A copy of this letter is available for examination at the Herbert Hoover Presidential Library.

47

Message to the France-America Society.
February 6, 1931

[Released February 6, 1931.   Dated February 5, 1931]

My dear Mr. Guthrie:

The celebration of the anniversary of the signing of the treaties with France at Paris on February 6, 1778 is a valuable manifestation of an historic friendship and helps keep alive the feelings of international understanding and good will which are so essential as the firm foundations of world peace. I send to you and the France-America Society my cordial greetings and good wishes.

Yours faithfully,
HERBERT HOOVER

[Mr. William D. Guthrie, President, France-America Society, 270 Madison Avenue, New York City]

NOTE: The message was read at a luncheon in New York City commemorating the Franco-American Alliance of 1778.

48

Message to the Real Estate Board of New York.
February 7, 1931

I WILL BE obliged if you will express my cordial greetings to those gathered at the thirty-fifth annual banquet of the Real Estate Board of New York and my best wishes for an inspiring meeting.

HERBERT HOOVER

[Peter Grimm, President, The Real Estate Board of New York, Inc., Hotel Commodore, New York City]

NOTE: The message was read at the annual dinner of the Real Estate Board of New York, held in the Commodore Hotel in New York City.

49

Veto of a Bill for the Relief of Homer N. Horine.
February 7, 1931

To the House of Representatives:

I am returning herewith without my approval H.R. 1036, entitled "An act for the relief of Homer N. Horine."

This enactment would bring Homer N. Horine within the provisions of the pension laws conferring benefits upon honorably discharged members of the military forces who served 90 days or more during the War with Spain. I am advised by the Secretary of War that no record has been found of the enrollment, muster-in, or service in Company G, Fourth Regiment Kentucky Volunteer Infantry, during the war with Spain, of any man named Homer N. Horine. The Veterans' Administration has no information as to whether Mr. Horine was or was not in the military service of the United States during the war with Spain except a statement from him in connection with a claim for pension based upon a short period of service in 1916 as a member of the First Regiment Kentucky National Guard, when that organization was called for border defense, to the effect that he had had no military service prior to 1916. He is now receiving a pension of $17 per month under a special bill enacted by the Congress after he failed to show a disability of service origin during his service in 1916.

It does not, therefore, appear that he was engaged in the service upon which this legislation is based.

HERBERT HOOVER

The White House,
    February 7, 1931.

NOTE: The House of Representatives sustained the President's veto on the same day.

50

Message to the Senate Minority Leader on Drought Relief Legislation.
February 9, 1931

My dear Mr. Senator:

As to our conversation this morning, I am glad to confirm at once that the proposed additional drought relief measure was suggested for the purpose of real aid to the weakened credit situation in the drought area and that in the administration of it the Secretary of Agriculture assures me he has no other intention and that he will interpret it fairly and sympathetically.

Yours faithfully,
HERBERT HOOVER

[The Honorable Joseph T. Robinson, United States Senate, Washington, D.C.]

NOTE: The proposed measure, a substitute for the previously rejected Robinson amendment to the Interior Department appropriation bill, would provide $20 million for loans to agricultural credit corporations and drought rehabilitation. It became law on February 14, 1931, as Public, No. 666 (46 Stat. 1115). Passage came after Secretary of Agriculture Arthur M. Hyde declared that there could be no ban against spending some of the rehabilitation loan proceeds for foods.

51

Message to the Annual Dinner of the Society of the Genesee Honoring George Eastman.
February 9, 1931

I AM indeed sorry that I cannot be present at the dinner given in your honor by the Society of the Genesee in New York this evening but I warmly share in spirit in this tribute to your outstanding service to country and humanity as great industrialist, philanthropist and patron of education, music and public health.

HERBERT HOOVER

[Mr. George Eastman, in care of Thomas J. Watson, 270 Broadway, New York City]

NOTE: The message was read at the 32d annual dinner of the society, held in the Hotel Commodore in New York City. Mr. Eastman was chairman of the board of Eastman Kodak Co.

52

Message to the Congress Recommending an Appropriation for the National Council of Intellectual Cooperation.
February 9, 1931

To the Congress of the United States:

I commend to the favorable consideration of the Congress the inclosed report from the Secretary of State, to the end that legislation may be enacted authorizing an annual appropriation of $21,000 for the maintenance of headquarters for the National Council of Intellectual Cooperation for the United States.

HERBERT HOOVER

The White House,
February 9, 1931.

NOTE: The message and accompanying report are printed as House Document 746 (71st Cong., 3d sess.).

The Inter-American Congress of Rectors, Deans, and Educators, meeting in Havana in 1930, adopted a measure calling for the establishment of a National Council of Intellectual Cooperation in each of the member republics. The functions of the councils were to collect and disseminate information regarding institutions of learning and research, encourage cultural exchange programs, and organize cooperative research projects.

53

Letter to the Speaker of the House Transmitting a Supplemental Estimate of Appropriation for the Bureau of Immigration.
February 9, 1931

Sir:

I have the honor to transmit herewith for the consideration of Congress an estimate of appropriation for the Department of Labor for salaries and expenses, Bureau of Immigration, for the fiscal year 1932, amounting to $500,000, which is supplemental to the estimate of $10,117,740 contained in the Budget for the fiscal year 1932 as increased by the supplemental estimate of $500,000 transmitted to Congress on January 9, 1931.

The details of this estimate, the necessity therefor, and the reason for its transmission at this time are set forth in the letter of the Director of the Bureau of the Budget, transmitted herewith, with whose comments and observations thereon I concur.

Respectfully,

HERBERT HOOVER

The White House,
    February 9, 1931.

[The Speaker of the House of Representatives]

NOTE: The letter and accompanying papers are printed as House Document 745 (71st Cong., 3d sess.).

54

The President's News Conference of *February 10, 1931*

EMPLOYMENT STABILIZATION ACT OF 1931

THE PRESIDENT. I have just signed the Wagner bill for advance planning of construction and Federal works with a good deal of pleasure. Senator Wagner and Congressman Graham have worked out a very admirable measure, in which they adopted the constructive suggestions of the various Government departments. The act sets up, in tangible form, the organization which we have in fact carried on for the last 14 months in planning Federal or public works. It is not a cure for depression, but it is a better organization of relief for future depressions.

I feel that I should take this occasion to make known two men who have had a very large part in the development of these ideas, Edward Hunt of the Department of Commerce, and Otto Mallery, of Harrisburg, who first proposed this sort of setup for advance planning of public works against depression in the unemployment conference in 1921. And they were members of two subsequent committees that were appointed to investigate it, and as a result it was placed before Congress at various times, but it takes a depression in order to bring home the utility of such proposals. They are not welcome in times of prosperity.

But in any event, it has accomplished a very useful piece of organization, and I place the organization of the act in the Department of Commerce. The bill provides that the President is to assign its administration to some department.

And that is all that I have today.

NOTE: President Hoover's one hundred and seventy-third news conference was held in the White House at 12 noon on Tuesday, February 10, 1931.

On the same day, the White House issued a text of the President's statement on the Employment Stabilization Act of 1931 (see Item 55).

The Employment Stabilization Act of 1931 (Public, No. 616, 46 Stat. 1084) established the Federal Employment Stabilization Board.

55

Statement on the Employment Stabilization Act of 1931. *February 10, 1931*

THE PRESIDENT said:

"I have today had great pleasure in approving the act providing for advance planning of construction and Federal public works in preparation for future unemployment relief. Senator Wagner and Representative Graham have worked out an admirable measure in which they adopted the constructive suggestions of the various Government departments.

"The act gives wider authority and specific organization for the methods which have been pursued by the administration during the past 14 months in respect to the planning and acceleration of Federal construction work for purposes of relief to unemployment in times of depression. It is not a cure for business depression but will afford better organization for relief in future depressions.

"I feel it is just that I should take this occasion to make known two men who have had a large part in development of these ideas and their ultimate consummation—Mr. Edward Eyre Hunt of the Department of Commerce, and Mr. Otto Mallery, of Harrisburg, Pa. Proposals of such an organization for advanced planning were first advocated at the unemployment conference in 1921 by these men. The subject was exhaustively investigated by committees in which these two gentlemen participated in 1923 and 1928. The principles of this act were suggested to Congress at various times during the past 5 years, but it was not until we experienced this depression that their usefulness was recognized. I shall place the organization set up under the act, under the Secretary of Commerce."

NOTE: The Employment Stabilization Act of 1931 (Public, No. 616, 46 Stat. 1084) established the Federal Employment Stabilization Board.

56

Message to the Congress Requesting an Appropriation for Participation in the Second Polar Year Program.
February 10, 1931

To the Congress of the United States:

I commend to the favorable consideration of the Congress the inclosed report from the Secretary of State, to the end that legislation may be enacted authorizing an appropriation of $30,000 for participation by the United States Government in the second polar year program, August 1, 1932–August 31, 1933.

HERBERT HOOVER

The White House,
     February 10, 1931.

NOTE: The message and accompanying report are printed as Senate Document 270 (71st Cong., 3d sess.).

On December 10, 1931, the President resubmitted this message to the Congress which was printed as Senate Document 16 (72d Cong., 1st sess.).

57

Message to the Senate Transmitting the International Load Lines Convention.
February 11, 1931

To the Senate:

With a view to receiving the advice and consent of the Senate to ratification of the international load-line convention and its accompanying final protocol, I transmit herewith a certified copy of those instruments, signed on July 5, 1930, by the respective plenipotentiaries of the United States of America and of 29 other governments participating in the international load-line conference which met at London on May 20, 1930, for the purpose of formulating international rules and regulations to determine the load lines of merchant vessels engaged in international trade.

The convention and protocol are accompanied by the final act of the conference signed at the same time, which I transmit for the information of the Senate. This act embraces a declaration by the delegates of the United States of America and certain recommendations of the conference. The declaration made by the delegates of the United States is designed as a safeguard against any possible misconstruction of the position of the United States that its participation in a multilateral convention with the regime now functioning in Russia known as the Union of Soviet Socialist Republics, does not operate as a recognition of that regime by the Government of the United States.

I also transmit an accompanying report on the convention submitted by the Secretary of State.

HERBERT HOOVER

NOTE: The report referred to is entitled "International Conference on Load Lines" (85 pp. plus illustrations) and is published as State Department Publication No. 125 and as Senate Executive Report I (71st Cong., 3d sess.).

58

Radio Address on Lincoln's Birthday.
February 12, 1931

BY THE MAGIC of the radio I am able to address several hundred public gatherings called this evening throughout our country in celebration of the birth of Abraham Lincoln.

It is appropriate that I should speak from this room in the White House where Lincoln strived and accomplished his great service to our country.

His invisible presence dominates these halls, ever recalling that infinite patience and that indomitable will which fought and won the fight for those firmer foundations and greater strength to government by the people. From these windows he looked out upon that great granite shaft which was then in construction to mark the country's eternal tribute to the courage and uncompromising strength of the founder of this Union of States.

Here are the very chairs in which he meditated upon his problems. Above the mantelpiece hangs his portrait with his Cabinet, and upon this fireplace is written:

"In this room Abraham Lincoln signed the Emancipation Proclamation of January 1, 1863, whereby 4,000,000 slaves were given their freedom and slavery forever prohibited in these United States."

It was here that he toiled by day and by night that the Union created by the fathers might be preserved and that slavery might be ended.

Most of the business of this room in Lincoln's time was concerned with the conduct of war against destructive forces. From here he could oft hear the sound of approaching cannon, and yet the thought that he should desert his place, this city and this house, never entered into his considerations. Lincoln was a builder in an epoch of destruction. It was his assignment by Providence to restore the national edifice, so badly shattered in its social and economic structure that it had wellnigh failed. His undying idealism and inflexible resolve builded a new temple of the national soul in which our succeeding generations have since dwelt secure and free and of a richer life.

71

And if Lincoln could today resurvey the scene of his country he would find a union more solidly knit and more resolute in its common purpose than ever in its history. He would find the States of the South recovered from the wounds of war, inspired by the splendid leadership of a new generation to a brilliant renaissance of industry and culture.

He would indeed find the consummation of that great moving appeal of his inaugural in which he said: "The mystic chords of memory stretching from every battlefield and patriot grave to every living heart and hearthstone all over this broad land will yet swell the chorus of the Union when again touched, as surely they will be, by the better angels of our nature." It was indeed a great prophecy.

If Lincoln were living, he would find that this race of liberated slaves, starting a new life without a shred but the clothes in which they stood, without education, without organization, has today by its own endeavors progressed to an amazingly high level of self-reliance and well-being. To Lincoln it would have been incredible that within a lifetime the millions of children of these slaves would be graduating from the public schools and colleges; that the race could have builded itself homes and accumulated itself a wealth in lands and savings; that it should have carried on with success every calling and profession in our country.

While the dramatic period of Lincoln's life was engrossed with these tremendous problems, yet he was a man of many interests. He was a believer in party government. He realized, as we also must realize, that fundamentally our whole self-government is conceived and born of majority rule, and to enable the majority to express itself we must have party organization. Lincoln led in founding the Republican Party and he gloried in his party. His tradition has dominated it to this day. It was and is a party of responsibility; it was and is a party of the Constitution.

While many of the issues of that time are dead and gone, some of our present problems were equally vivid in his day. You will find Lincoln addressing the country in strong and urgent support of the protective tariff with vivid declamation against the party opposing that policy. You will find him advocating Federal Government aid in internal development of waterways, rivers and harbors, and transportation. You will find him pounding at the public mind against nullification and for adherence to constitutional processes of government. No stronger statement has ever been made than that of Lincoln upon obedience to law as the very foundation of our Republic.

In Lincoln's day the dominant problem in our form of government turned upon the issue of States rights. Though less pregnant with disaster, the dominant problem today in our form of government turns in large degree upon the issue of the relationship of Federal, State, and local government responsibilities. We are faced with unceasing agitation that the Federal Government shall assume new financial burdens, that it shall undertake increased burdens in regulation of abuses and in the prosecution of crime.

It is true that since Lincoln's time many forces have swept across State borders and have become more potent than the State or local community can deal with alone either financially or by jurisdiction. Our concept of Federal, State, and local responsibilities is possible of no unchangeable definitions and it must shift with the moving forces in the Nation, but the time has come when we must have more national consideration and decision of the part which each shall assume in these responsibilities.

The Federal Government has assumed many new responsibilities since Lincoln's time, and will probably assume more in the future when the States and local communities cannot alone cure abuse or bear the entire cost of national programs, but there is an essential principle that should be maintained in these matters. I am convinced that where Federal action is essential then in most cases it should limit its responsibilities to supplement the States and local communities, and that it should not assume the major role or the entire responsibility, in replacement of the States or local government. To do otherwise threatens the whole foundations of local government, which is the very basis of self-government.

The moment responsibilities of any community, particularly in economic and social questions, are shifted from any part of the Nation to Washington, then that community has subjected itself to a remote bureaucracy with its minimum of understanding and of sympathy. It has lost a large part of its voice and its control of its own destiny. Under

Federal control the varied conditions of life in our country are forced into standard molds, with all their limitations upon life, either of the individual or the community. Where people divest themselves of local government responsibilities they at once lay the foundation for the destruction of their liberties.

And buried in this problem lies something even deeper. The whole of our governmental machinery was devised for the purpose that through ordered liberty we give incentive and equality of opportunity to every individual to rise to that highest achievement of which he is capable. At once when government is centralized there arises a limitation upon the liberty of the individual and a restriction of individual opportunity. The true growth of the Nation is the growth of character in its citizens. The spread of government destroys initiative and thus destroys character. Character is made in the community as well as in the individual by assuming responsibilities, not by escape from them. Carried to its logical extreme, all this shouldering of individual and community responsibility upon the Government can lead but to the superstate where every man becomes the servant of the State and real liberty is lost. Such was not the government that Lincoln sought to build.

There is an entirely different avenue by which we may both resist this drift to centralized government and at the same time meet a multitude of problems. That is to strengthen in the Nation a sense and an organization of self-help and cooperation to solve as many problems as possible outside of government. We are today passing through a critical test in such a problem arising from the economic depression.

Due to lack of caution in business and to the impact of forces from an outside world, one-half of which is involved in social and political revolution, the march of our prosperity has been retarded. We are projected into temporary unemployment, losses, and hardships. In a nation rich in resources, many people were faced with hunger and cold through no fault of their own. Our national resources are not only material supplies and material wealth but a spiritual and moral wealth in kindliness, in compassion, in a sense of obligation of neighbor to neighbor and a realization of responsibility by industry, by business, and the community for its social security and its social welfare.

74

The evidence of our ability to solve great problems outside of Government action and the degree of moral strength with which we emerge from this period will be determined by whether the individuals and the local communities continue to meet their responsibilities.

Throughout this depression I have insisted upon organization of these forces through industry, through local government and through charity, that they should meet this crisis by their own initiative, by the assumption of their own responsibilities. The Federal Government has sought to do its part by example in the expansion of employment, by affording credit to drought sufferers for rehabilitation, and by cooperation with the community, and thus to avoid the opiates of government charity and the stifling of our national spirit of mutual self-help.

We can take courage and pride in the effective work of thousands of voluntary organizations for provision of employment, for relief of distress, that have sprung up over the entire Nation. Industry and business have recognized a social obligation to their employees as never before. The State and local governments are being helpful. The people are themselves succeeding in this task. Never before in a great depression has there been so systematic a protection against distress. Never before has there been so little social disorder. Never before has there been such an outpouring of the spirit of self-sacrifice and of service.

The ever-growing complexity of modern life, with its train of ever-more perplexing and difficult problems, is a challenge to our individual characters and to our devotion to our ideals. The resourcefulness of America when challenged has never failed. Success is not gained by leaning upon government to solve all the problems before us. That way leads to enervation of will and destruction of character. Victory over this depression and over our other difficulties will be won by the resolution of our people to fight their own battles in their own communities, by stimulating their ingenuity to solve their own problems, by taking new courage to be masters of their own destiny in the struggle of life. This is not the easy way, but it is the American way. And it was Lincoln's way.

The ultimate goal of the American social ideal is equality of opportunity and individual initiative. These are not born of bureaucracy. This ideal is the expression of the spirit of our people. This ideal obtained at the birth of the Republic. It was the ideal of Lincoln. It is the ideal upon which the Nation has risen to unparalleled greatness.

We are going through a period when character and courage are on trial, and where the very faith that is within us is under test. Our people are meeting this test. And they are doing more than the immediate task of the day. They are maintaining the ideals of our American system. By their devotion to these ideals we shall come out of these times stronger in character, in courage, and in faith.

NOTE: The President spoke at 10 p.m. from his office in the White House. The National Broadcasting Company and the Columbia Broadcasting System carried the address.

59

Foreword to the Writings of George Washington. *February 15, 1931*

[Released February 15, 1931.   Dated November 19, 1930]

THE PEOPLE of the United States are justly proud of their literary men and women. They likewise are proud of their outstanding statesmen. Literary power and statesmanship were combined in George Washington, the greatest political leader of his time and also the greatest intellectual and moral force of the Revolutionary period. Everybody knows Washington as a quiet member of the Virginia Assembly, of the two Continental Congresses, and of the Constitutional Convention. Few people realize that he was also the most voluminous American writer of his period, and that his principles of government have had more influence on the development of the American commonwealth than those of any other man.

Unfortunately, Washington for many years was interpreted to his countrymen chiefly through warped biographies written upon a great deal of legendary assumption. Until very recently no readable biography of George Washington in reasonable compass made him stand for what he was—the most potent human and intellectual force in a firmament of American intellect. Nowadays good biographies of Washington are available, written from the sources. Many of them are devoted to a particular phase of his activity—the military side, the political side, the personal side. Hence when the United States George Washington Bicentennial Commission began its work it did not attempt to inspire new biographies. It selected as its most important literary duty the making Washington better known, by spreading abroad his own thoughts and plans and hopes and inspirations in the exact form in which he framed them.

Thus one of the first decisions of the Commission was to provide an edition of Washington's writings as complete as possible, in a form which would make it available for the present generation and forever hereafter. Of the two previous editions of Washington's Writings the first, a hundred years ago, was the twelve-volume edition, edited by Jared Sparks, a pioneer in collecting and publishing historical documents. Proper canons in historial editing were not yet developed, and it hurt the feelings of Sparks if the great man misspelled or seemed to him ungrammatical. Therefore the Sparks edition can not be relied upon to tell us what Washington actually did say. The edition of Worthington C. Ford, forty years ago, was scholarly and carefully edited, but materials were then lacking for a complete edition, the production was limited by commercial considerations, and it is now out of print.

The Commission has set out to publish a definitive edition of all the written and printed words of George Washington in the form in which they left his hands, including several volumes of General Orders, almost the whole of which up to now had remained in manuscript only. Most of his original writings of every kind are fortunately preserved in the Library of Congress. Other libraries and private owners of manuscripts have permitted photostats to be made for inclusion in the great publication. When this series is completed, therefore, almost the whole of his reported thoughts will be within the reach of readers, investigators, and writers.

The George Washington Commission takes great satisfaction in rendering this public service; for as the publication of the new series progresses it will become more and more clear that the reputation of George Washington as a soldier, statesman, and man is enhanced by the record of everything that he is known to have committed to pen and paper.

One deviation has been made from the plan of including all of Washington's writings in this edition. The Diary has been recently published by a skillful editor, enlivened by interesting notes. It has therefore been left out of the new set. On the other hand, the General Orders, which are of great significance for the history of the Revolution, are now for the first time made available in print, and will be distributed in the order of their dates.

What is the message from Washington revealed by this complete and scholarly edition? First of all it includes Washington's own graphic records of his experiences on the frontier while it was still in the possession of the Indians. Throughout the series will be found letters and documents showing that he was the American of his time who had the liveliest sense of the absolute necessity of occupying the West and making it a part of an American commonwealth.

The materials on his activity as a man of affairs, which are here brought into relief, bring home to the reader the picture of Washington as a landowner, land developer, and land cultivator. A much neglected side of his character is Washington as an engineer. His countrymen have not realized how modern he was in his engineering operations—as reclaimer of the Dismal Swamp; as advisor and engineer of the Potomac and James River Canal; as the first advocate of a combined highway and waterway from the Atlantic Coast to the Ohio River; as a bank director; as an investor; as one of the earliest Americans to recognize the possibilities of power transportation by water; and the first to suggest that air navigation might be very useful to the people of the United States.

What Washington says for himself will also be the foundation of our appreciation of his great abilities and immense services as the leader of the Continental Army. He was a thoroughly modern soldier, intensely interested in drill and tactics and plans of campaign, but equally unwearied in recruiting and supply and officering and in maintaining the morale of his troops. All the efforts to show that Washington had no military genius will fade away under the searchlight of this publication of his military material, much of it for the first time.

If nothing had been written by others about Washington's leadership in forming a new nation, his papers and correspondence while President would forever establish him as a great constructive statesman. His private virtues are set forth from the earliest boy's letters down to the last entry that he made in his diary. Washington with his wife's children and grandchildren stands out as clearly as Washington at Yorktown.

The United States George Washington Bicentennial Commission is undertaking to throw light upon the character of Washington in many ways. None will be more enduring than this collection of his own words and thoughts. The addresses, the pageants, the public meetings, and the memorials of every kind which the Commission will encourage and support, will call public attention to the most striking of the events in his life. But a hundred years after 1932, Washington will still be appealing to the sense, the interest, the public spirit, and the patriotism of that later age, by the great thoughts of his mind, by his great hopes for his country, and by the simple, straightforward, elevated, manly, and patriotic spirit of which these WRITINGS will be the imperishable record.

HERBERT HOOVER
President of the United States
Chairman of the George Washington
Bicentennial Commission.

Washington, D.C.,
   November 19, 1930.

NOTE: Congress established the George Washington Bicentennial Commission in December 1924 (S.J. Res. 85, 43 Stat. 671) and, in February 1930, authorized the preparation of a definitive edition of Washington's writings. The Commission asked the President to write the foreword, which was made public in conjunction with Washington's birthday celebrations in 1931.

John C. Fitzpatrick edited the series entitled, "The Writings of George Washington from Original Manuscript Sources, 1745–1799," which was published in 39 volumes between 1931 and 1944.

60

Letter to the Speaker of the House Transmitting
a Supplemental Estimate of Appropriation
for the Bureau of Labor Statistics.
February 16, 1931

Sir:

I have the honor to transmit herewith for the consideration of Congress a supplemental estimate of appropriation for the Department of Labor for salaries and expenses, Bureau of Labor Statistics, for the fiscal year 1932, amounting to $200,000, of which $50,000 is to be immediately available.

The details of this estimate the necessity therefor, and the reason for its transmission at this time are set forth in the letter of the Director of the Bureau of the Budget transmitted herewith, with whose comments and observations thereon I concur.

Respectfully,
HERBERT HOOVER

The White House,
     February 16, 1931.

[The Speaker of the House of Representatives]

NOTE: The letter and accompanying papers are printed as House Document 769 (71st Cong., 3d sess.).

The appropriation was requested to implement the recommendations of the President's Advisory Committee on Employment Statistics. See 1930 volume, Items 244 and 247.

61

Letter to the Speaker of the House Transmitting
a Supplemental Estimate of Appropriation
for the United States Employment Service.
February 16, 1931

Sir:

I have the honor to transmit herewith for the consideration of Congress a supplemental estimate of appropriation for the Department of Labor, Employment Service, for the fiscal year 1932, to be immediately available, amounting to $500,000.

The details of this estimate, the necessity therefor and the reason for its transmission at this time, are set forth in the letter of the Director of the Bureau of the Budget, transmitted herewith, with whose comments and observations thereon I concur.

Respectfully,

HERBERT   HOOVER

The White House,
      February 16, 1931.

[The Speaker of the House of Representatives]

NOTE: The letter and accompanying papers are printed as House Document 770 (71st Cong., 3d sess.).

62

The President's News Conference of
February 17, 1931

44-HOUR WORKWEEK FOR POST OFFICE EMPLOYEES

THE PRESIDENT. I have some questions here which I do not propose to reply to at the moment. But I have signed the 44-hour bill for the Post Office employees. I shall, some time before the end of the session, be sending a suggestion to Congress that they should appoint some sort of a body or authorize the committees of Congress to make an investigation into methods by which the postal revenues can be increased.

The Post Office deficit outside of the services being given to merchant marine and aviation and the free franking privileges now shows close to $100 million, and that deficit is largely due to the necessities to increase the pay of postal employees and the reduction of hours of service, et cetera. And it seemed to me to be only just to the country that there should be some increase in postal revenues to meet these increased expenses imposed upon the Post Office.

Other than that I haven't anything.

Q. Mr. President, will you make any suggestions in that communication?

THE PRESIDENT. No, it is essentially a matter for Congress to find a revenue to meet these difficulties.

Q. Mr. President, can you say just what part of this deficit this increased revenue will cover?

THE PRESIDENT. I can't say. It is just cumulative. . . .

Otherwise than that I haven't anything this morning.

NOTE: President Hoover's one hundred and seventy-fourth news conference was held in the White House at 12 noon on Tuesday, February 17, 1931.

The President referred to H.R. 6603, a bill to lower the workweek for Post Office employees from 48 to 44 hours. As enacted, H.R. 6603 is Public, No. 672 (46 Stat. 1164). The projected message on postal revenue increases was never sent to the Congress.

63

Letter to the Chairman of the Senate Finance Committee About the Emergency Adjusted Compensation Bill.
February 18, 1931

My dear Senator Smoot:

I have given thought to your request that I should express to you and to the Senate Finance Committee my views upon the bill passed by the

House of Representatives, increasing the loans to World War veterans upon the so-called bonus certificates. In view of the short time remaining in this session for its consideration I shall comply with your request.

The proposal is to authorize loans upon these certificates up to 50% of their face value. And to avoid confusion it must be understood that the "face value" is the sum payable at the end of the 20 year period (1945) being based on the additional compensation to veterans of about $1,300,000,000 granted about six years ago, plus 25% for deferment, plus 4% compound interest for the 20 year period. As the "face value" is about $3,423,000,000, loans at 50% thus create a potential liability for the government of about $1,712,000,000, and, less the loans made under the original Act, the total cash which might be required to be raised by the Treasury is about $1,280,000,000 if all should apply. The Administrator of Veterans Affairs informs me by the attached letter that he estimates that if present conditions continue, then 75% of the veterans may be expected to claim the loans, or a sum of approximately $1,000,000,000 will need to be raised by the Treasury.

I will not undertake to enumerate all of the grounds for objection to this proposal. There are a number of most serious objections, some of which are matters of method and some of which are matters of fundamental principle affecting the future of our country and the service men themselves.

I have supported, and the nation should maintain, the important principle that when men have been called into jeopardy of their very lives in protection of the nation, then the nation as a whole incurs a special obligation beyond that to any other groups of its citizens. These obligations cannot be wholly met with dollars and cents. But good faith and gratitude require that protection be given to them when in ill health, distress and in need. Over 700,000 World War Veterans or their dependents are today receiving monthly allowances for these reasons. The country should not be called upon, however, either directly or indirectly, to support or make loans to those who can by their own efforts support themselves.

By far the largest part of the huge sum proposed in this bill is to be available to those who are not in distress.

The acute depression and unemployment create a situation of unusual economic sensitiveness, much more easily disturbed at this time than in normal times by the consequences of this legislation, and such action may quite well result in a prolongation of this period of unemployment and suffering in which veterans will themselves suffer with others.

By our expansion of public construction for assistance to unemployment and other relief measures, we have imposed upon ourselves a deficit in this fiscal year of upwards of $500,000,000 which must be obtained by issue of securities to the investing public. This bill may possibly require the securing of a further billion of money likewise from the public. Beyond this, the Government is faced with a billion dollars of early maturities of outstanding debts which must be refunded aside from constant renewals of a very large amount of temporary Treasury obligations. The additional burdens of this project cannot but have damaging effect at a time when all effort should be for the rehabilitation of employment through resumption of commerce and industry.

There seems to be a misunderstanding in the proposal that the government securities already lodged with the Treasury to the amount of over $700,000,000 as reserve against these certificates constitute available cash to meet this potential liability. The cash required by the veterans can only be secured by the sale of these securities to the public.

The legislation is defective in that this $700,000,000 of government securities is wholly inadequate to meet either a potential liability of $1,280,000,000 or approximately $1,000,000,000 estimated as possible by the Administrator of Veterans' Affairs, and provision would need to be made at once for this deficiency.

The one appealing argument for this legislation is for veterans in distress. The welfare of the veterans as a class is inseparable from that of the country. Placing a strain on the savings needed for rehabilitation of employment by a measure which calls upon the government for a vast sum beyond the call of distress, and so adversely affecting our general situation, will in my view not only nullify the benefits to the veteran but inflict injury to the country as a whole.

Yours faithfully,

HERBERT HOOVER

84

[Honorable Reed Smoot, Chairman, Senate Finance Committee, United States Senate, Washington, D.C.]

NOTE: In his letter to Senator Smoot, the President referred to a letter from the Administrator of Veterans' Affairs, dated February 17, 1931, which follows:

My dear Mr. President:

You have requested that I advise you as to the estimated number of veterans who would be eligible for loans, and the amount which would be borrowed on adjusted service certificates in the event H.R. 17054 becomes a law.

When I appeared before the Committee on Ways and Means, House of Representatives, February 12, 1931, in connection with this measure, I made the following statement in reply to Congressman Ramseyer:

"* * * Based on your experience and knowledge of the ex-service men, are you prepared to make any estimate as to the increased borrowers that a bill like this would probably bring about?

"General Hines. Well, it depends a great deal, Congressman, on whether the present employment conditions are going to continue. If there is a period still of another year where unemployment is not going to improve, it would be my judgment that there would be an increase of at least 25 per cent in the men who would borrow."

In accordance with the above, it is my estimate that 2,550,000 veterans will avail themselves of the full loan value under the proposed measure, and that the total amount of such loans will be $1,283,625,000. From the amount there should be subtracted the $325,000,000 which has previously been borrowed, making a total additional amount which will be borrowed of $958,625,000 or approximately $1,000,000,000.

Respectfully,

FRANK T. HINES,
Administrator

[The Honorable, The President of the United States]

64

Message to a Dinner Honoring Disabled Veterans.
February 18, 1931

I WILL BE obliged if you will express my cordial greetings to the Grand Street Boys' Post Number ten twenty-five of the American Legion and to their guests the Disabled Veterans of the World War of the metropolitan area of New York at the dinner this evening. The disabled veterans by their service to our country have earned its undying gratitude and I gladly share in the honors you are paying them.

HERBERT . HOOVER

[Dr. Abraham Jablons, Grand Street Boys' Post No. 1025, 106 West 55th Street, New York City]

NOTE: The message was read at a dinner given by the Grand Street Boys' Association for some 400 wounded and disabled veterans of World War I. The dinner was an annual affair, begun in 1930.

65

Veto of Indian Claims Legislation.
February 18, 1931

To the Senate:

I return herewith without my approval the bill S. 3165, entitled "An act conferring jurisdiction upon the Court of Claims to hear, consider, and report upon a claim of the Choctaw and Chickasaw Indian Nations or Tribes for fair and just compensation for the remainder of the Leased District lands."

This act undertakes, by indirection, to revive the claims of the Choctaw and Chickasaw Nations for compensation for parts of the so-called "Leased District."

The "Leased Districts" lands of these Indians comprised approximately 7,000,000 acres, lying between the ninety-eighth and one-hundredth degrees of west longitude in the State of Oklahoma. By treaty of June 22, 1855, the United States paid the Choctaws $600,000 and the Chickasaws $200,000 for the lease of this land to the United States in perpetuity, as well as for the cession to the United States of their land west of the one-hundredth degree of west longitude. By treaty of April 28, 1866, involving an additional payment of $300,000 the Choctaws and Chickasaws ceded the Leased District land to the United States, thereby parting with all rights of any kind in that land.

In 1891 Congress appropriated $2,991,450 to pay the Choctaws and Chickasaws for approximately 2,293,000 acres of the Leased District land granted by Congress to the Cheyennes and the Arapahoes. In signing the general appropriation bill containing this item President Harrison protested at paying for land that already belonged to the Federal Government, saying in a message to Congress that he would have disapproved the bill because of this item were it not for the disastrous consequences that would result from the defeat of the entire appropriation bill. In December, 1892, Congress passed a resolution containing the following provisions:

Provided, however, That neither the passage of the original act of appropriation to pay the Choctaw tribes of Indians for their interest in the lands of the Cheyenne and Arapahoe Reservation, dated March 3, 1891, nor of this resolution shall be held in any way to commit the Government to the payment of any further sum to the Choctaw and Chickasaw Indians for any alleged interest in the remainder of the lands situated in what is commonly known and called the "Leased District."

In 1899 the Court of Claims decided that the title to the remaining acreage of Leased District land was in the United States in trust for the Choctaw and Chickasaw Indians. However, the United States Supreme Court, in its decision of December 10, 1890, reversed the Court of Claims, and held that the treaty of 1866 vested in the United States complete title to the Leased District land.

The present claim of the Choctaw and Chickasaw Indians is for 5,224,346 acres at $1.25 per acre.

The bill does not send this claim to the Court of Claims for adjudication and settlement, as is normally the case with respect to Indian claims. That would, indeed, be futile, since the Supreme Court has ruled that neither it nor the Court of Claims has jurisdiction to decide that the United States shall pay for lands that it already owns. The result of the bill would seem to be, through a report to Congress from the Court of Claims, to create a lawful aspect to a claim which has no present legal standing.

This case raises a very wide issue of whether we are to undertake revision of treaties entered into in the acquiring of Indian lands during the past 150 years. The values of such lands have obviously increased, and the undertakings entered into at the time the agreements were made may naturally look small in after years. But the increased values have been the result of the efforts of our citizens in building this Nation.

This case would I feel, create a dangerous precedent which could conceivably involve the Government in very large liabilities.

If it is the thought of Congress that justice requires the revision of Indian treaties in the light of subsequent events, then the whole of these treaties should be considered together not by incidental creation of precedents.

It is the purpose of the United States Government to do justice by the Indians and assist them to citizenship and participation in the benefits of our civilization. And in the case of these tribes the Government has during the past 18 years expended a total of approximately $3,500,000 out of the taxpayers' money and they will in a few years exceed the totals of these claims.

HERBERT HOOVER

The White House,
    February 18, 1931.

NOTE: The Senate referred the veto message to the Committee on Indian Affairs, on February 20, 1931, and no further action was taken.

66

Message to the Trust Company Division
of the American Bankers Association.
February 19, 1931

[Released February 19, 1931.   Dated February 4, 1931]

My dear Mr. Stephenson:

I will be obliged if you will express my cordial greetings to those present at the 20th annual banquet of the Trust Companies of the United States on Thursday evening, February 19th. The Trust Companies have been an influence of high value in the economic life of the nation, by conserving accumulated resources, stabilizing investments and providing continuity of conservative policy in business. Their remarkable increase in numbers and influence has on the whole been an important service in the life of the nation.

Yours faithfully,

HERBERT HOOVER

[Mr. Gilbert T. Stephenson, President, Trust Company Division, The American Bankers Association, Wilmington, Delaware]

NOTE: The message was read at the organization's 20th annual banquet, held in the Commodore Hotel in New York City.

67

The President's News Conference of *February 20, 1931*

EMERGENCY ADJUSTED COMPENSATION BILL

THE PRESIDENT. I will be ready to act on the bonus bill about the middle of next week.

PUBLIC WORKS AND EMPLOYMENT

I have just had a survey made of the various departments as to the progress of the construction program, and I find that whereas we had approximately 150,000 men directly and indirectly employed in construction activities of one kind or another prior to the depression, with the contracts now let we should have a full force of 450,000 within the next 30 days. That is both direct and indirect employment. It is a little bit less than that now, but we take it on the basis of fulfilling the complement of contracts let.

There is one phase of the present appropriation bills that are before Congress that is of a good deal of importance. In all of this year's supply bills, that is for the fiscal year 1932, there is with a very few exceptions a provision making all of the construction appropriations immediately available. And of the total appropriations amounting to over $700 million in the 1932 budget, over $500 million would be immediately available—not that it would all be spent at once, but it would enable us to still further expedite our program if we can have those bills completed.

RESIGNATION OF WALTER E. HOPE

I have with regret accepted the resignation of Mr. Walter Hope as Assistant Secretary of the Treasury. He has been here for a matter of about 18 months in charge of the Bureau of Internal Revenue and the Bureau of Engraving, et cetera. He has found it is necessary to return to New York to practice law and becomes one of the principal partners in one of the leading firms. It is always a loss to lose men of such character and distinction from the Government service. I am in hopes we can get him back sometime.

That is all I have today.

NOTE: The President's one hundred and seventy-fifth news conference was held in the White House at 4 p.m. on Tuesday, February 20, 1931.

On the same day, the White House issued a text of the President's statement about the resignation of Walter E. Hope as Assistant Secretary of the Treasury (see Item 68).

68

Statement About the Resignation of Walter E. Hope as Assistant Secretary of the Treasury.
February 20, 1931

THE PRESIDENT said:

"It is with extreme regret that I have to announce the resignation of Walter Ewing Hope as Assistant Secretary of the Treasury, to become effective March 1, 1931. Mr. Hope was appointed on November 21, 1929. He is a lawyer and prior to his appointment was a member of the firm of Masten and Nichols, New York City. He now finds it necessary to return to the practice of law.

"As Assistant Secretary of the Treasury, Mr. Hope has been in charge of the Bureau of Internal Revenue, the Bureau of Engraving and Printing, the Office of the Comptroller of the Currency, the Bureau of the

Mint, the Secret Service, and other services. He has devoted especial attention to the elimination of delays and the speeding up of work in the Bureau of Internal Revenue and establishing better relations between the Bureau and the taxpaying public.

"Mr. Hope is a life trustee of Princeton University, and a member of its administrative committee, a trustee of Presbyterian Hospital in New York, and president of the Institute for the Crippled and Disabled.

"During the war he served with the United States Fuel Administration and also served under appointment of President Wilson as chairman of a special commission upon fuel conditions in England, France, Italy, and other allied countries, reporting to the Paris Peace Conference."

69

Message to the World Conference on Narcotic Education.
February 20, 1931

I DEEPLY sympathize with the steadfast campaign of American organizations working to bring about international agreements for limiting the manufacture of narcotic drugs and to energize the police power of the several states of this Union to destroy illicit traffic in narcotics.

HERBERT HOOVER

[President of the 4th Conference of Committees of the Affiliated Narcotic Organizations, McAlpin Hotel, New York City]

NOTE: The message was made public at the conference, meeting in the McAlpin Hotel in New York City.

70

Letters to Senator Thomas D. Schall
About the Appointment of a District Judge for Minnesota.
February 20, 1931

[Released February 20, 1931.   Dated February 10, 1931]

My dear Mr. Senator:

It is extremely desirable that a new District Judge for the State of Minnesota should be appointed and confirmed at the present session of Congress. I would be glad if you could accept the suggestion in my letter of February 3rd that you give me a list of the names of men who may be investigated as to fitness for this appointment.

It would be a misfortune if Minnesota should not have the advantage of the establishment of this Court during the present session of Congress.

Yours faithfully,

HERBERT HOOVER

[The Honorable Thomas D. Schall, United States Senate]

[Released February 20, 1931.   Dated February 18, 1931]

My dear Mr. Senator:

The need for an additional United States Judge in Minnesota is pressing.

On February 3rd, and again on the 10th I wrote you asking that you suggest the names of men you would consider fit for this place but you have not done so.

Among those who seem to have substantial support from citizens of Minnesota are:

CHARLES LORING, of Crookston, Associate Justice, Supreme Court of Minnesota

JULIUS E. HAYCROFT, of Fairmont, Judge of District Court, 17th District

FRED W. SENN, of Waseca, Judge of District Court, 5th District

GUNNAR H. NORDBYE, of Minneapolis, Judge of District Court, Hennepin County

NORMAN E. PETERSON, of Albert Lea, Judge of District Court, 10th District

ALFRED L. THWING, of Grand Rapids, Judge of District Court, 15th District

CARLTON P. MCNALLY, Judge of District Court of Ramsey County

EDWIN J. KENNY, of Duluth, Judge of District Court, 11th District.

If you have any information as to the qualifications of any of these men for the position of Federal Judge, I should be pleased to have it.

Yours faithfully,

HERBERT HOOVER

[The Honorable Thomas D. Schall, United States Senate]

[Released February 20, 1931.   Dated February 19, 1931]

My dear Mr. Senator:

I have your letter of February 18 acknowledging mine of that date and presenting the names of various men from Minnesota for the District Judgeship. You do not, however, give me your views as to the men whose names I submitted to you in my letter.

I consider it desirable in the interest of the people of Minnesota that the man appointed shall not only have had judicial experience, but shall be entirely free from any private connections which might be challenged.

None of the men you have suggested have been proposed by the citizens of Minnesota and the Department of Justice is lacking in information regarding them. It would require a considerable period of time to investigate these men as to fitness and connections, and since it is necessary, if we make the appointment at this session, that the name should be sent up not later than tomorrow, I would be glad indeed if you would express to me your views on the men whose names I submitted to you yesterday.

Yours faithfully,

HERBERT HOOVER

[The Honorable Thomas D. Schall, United States Senate]

NOTE: In his letter of February 18, 1931, Senator Schall suggested the following 10 lawyers for the judgeship: Frank Ellsworth, M. M. Joyce, Mark Wooley, Thomas McMeekin, Frank Murphy, John Roeser, John P. Devaney, Thomas Mangan, George Smith, and Charles H. March.

On February 20, the White House issued biographical data and a list of endorsers for Gunnar H. Nordbye in connection with his appointment as United States District Judge for the District of Minnesota. The President signed a recess commission for Mr. Nordbye on March 30.

71

Message to the Senate Transmitting a Report on United States Relations With Nicaragua.
February 21, 1931

To the Senate of the United States:

In response to Senate Resolution 386 of January 5, 1931, I transmit herewith a report by the Secretary of State inclosing a memorandum and copies of documents referred to therein.

HERBERT HOOVER

NOTE: The Secretary of State's report is printed in Senate Document 288 (71st Cong., 3d sess.).

In 1931, the United States had approximately 1,500 marines stationed in Nicaragua. The Senate passed Resolution 386 following an incident in which insurgents, loyal to Augusto Cesar Sandino, killed eight American marines.

Secretary of State Stimson's letter accompanying the report follows:

The President:

The undersigned, the Secretary of State, to whom was referred Senate Resolution 386, of January 5, 1931, reading as follows:

"Resolved, that the Secretary of State be, and he is hereby requested to transmit to the Senate all communications, documents, reports, and agreements, since 1924, or copies thereof, relating to the landing or maintenance of United States marines in Nicaragua; and all notes, communications, or agreements, or copies thereof, passing between the Governments of the United States and Nicaragua, concerning elections to be held in Nicaragua, the formation and training of the constabulary or native police of Nicaragua; the duties to be performed by said constabulary and by United States marines; the mode of compensating said constabulary and the amount thereof"—

has the honor to inform the President that there are attached hereto, with a view to their transmission to the Senate should the President's judgment approve thereof, copies of all notes, communications, or agreements passing between the Governments of the United States and Nicaragua concerning the elections in Nicaragua, the formation and training of the constabulary or native police in Nicaragua, the duties to be performed by said constabulary and by United States marines, and the mode of compensating said constabulary and the amount thereof.

There is also attached hereto a statement regarding the landing or maintenance of United States marines in Nicaragua since the present administration took office, together with copies of all communications, documents, reports, or agreements relating to the landing or maintenance of such United States marines in Nicaragua since the present administration took office.

The Secretary of State has the honor to inform the President after thorough consideration of the matter and an examination of the papers that he has reached the conclusion that it would not be compatible with the interests of the United States to furnish the papers relating to the landing or maintenance of United States marines in Nicaragua prior to the present administration. He will, however, be glad to go before the Foreign Relations Committee of the Senate in executive session with copies of all these documents should that be the desire of the Senate or of the Foreign Relations Committee.

HENRY L. STIMSON

72

Veto of Legislation To Confer Certain Benefits on Civilian Employees of the Quartermaster Corps.
February 23, 1931

To the House of Representatives:

I am returning without approval House bill 6997 entitled,

"An Act to confer to certain persons who served in the Quartermaster Corps or under the jurisdiction of the Quartermaster General during the war with Spain, the Philippine insurrection, or the China relief expedition the benefits of hospitalization and the privileges of the Soldiers' Homes."

This bill proposes to open the doors of the hospitals and homes under the jurisdiction of the Veterans' Administration, which have been constructed from funds authorized by the Congress for the care and treatment of disabled ex-members of the military and naval forces of the United States, to a group of civilians employed by the Quartermaster Corps during the war with Spain, the Philippine insurrection and the China relief expedition. It is thus a departure from the policy of the Government with respect to the extension of such privileges.

It would commit the Government to a policy which, if once embarked upon, could not justifiably be restricted to this selected group of civilians who served during the three periods of hostility mentioned. In every war, the Government is obliged to avail itself of the assistance of many who are not a part of the enlisted, enrolled or commissioned personnel of the Army and Navy, but who perform their duties under contracts providing, we must assume, for their proper compensation, inasmuch as they are entirely voluntary and terminable at the will of the employee. Their services under such contracts, no matter how effective or valiant, have never been regarded as giving them the same claim upon the bounty of the Government as those who entered the military or naval service and were subject to military law and to the rigors and hazards of war, until the restoration of peace or disability or death released them. The Committee on Pensions, House of Representatives, was probably impressed by this thought when they amended the bill originally to eliminate the provision for a pension for this group.

I do not think we may lose sight of the fact that during the World War, there were thousands of civilians engaged in occupations necessary to the carrying on of the combat forces, who might argue as consistently as this group that they are entitled to consideration and hospitalization at the hands of the Federal Government. We quickly recall the arduous service performed by the many civilians who served with the troops overseas during the World War, to say nothing of those who served in cantonments and ports of embarkation and debarkation in the United States. Some were in the employ of the Government and others were not but they worked in a common cause and it would be hard to draw the line between them.

I am advised by the Administrator of Veterans' Affairs that it has not been possible to estimate the number who would become eligible for admission to hospitals and homes should this bill be approved but that the Secretary of the Interior has furnished figures indicating that there were approximately 14,000 who had such service as would bring them within the provisions of this bill, approximately 7,000 of whom are now living.

From the legislative history, I note that no consideration was given to this bill by the Committee on World War Veterans' Legislation, House of Representatives, the Committee on Finance of the Senate, or the Committee on Military Affairs of either House. These committees, under the rules, handle all legislation providing for the construction of additional hospital and domiciliary facilities for beneficiaries under the laws administered by the Veterans' Administration. They now have before them for action several bills which propose to authorize millions of dollars for additional construction for ex-service men who are already within the purview of the provisions of law relating to hospital and domiciliary care, but for whom facilities are not available. I am informed that there are now on the waiting list 2,440 veterans who are in immediate need of hospitalization and 7,417 who are in need of treatment but whose necessities may be characterized as less urgent. Certainly this bill should not be approved before the number of persons who might be eligible under it has been considered in relation to the present hospital construction program.

For these reasons, I do not feel that I can approve this legislation.

HERBERT HOOVER

The White House,
     February 23, 1931.

NOTE: The House of Representatives referred the veto message to the Committee on Pensions on February 23, 1931.

73

Veto of a Bill for the Relief of Joseph Marko.
February 23, 1931

To the House of Representatives:

I am returning without approval House Bill No. 3368, entitled "An Act for the relief of Joseph Marko".

This bill proposes to provide that Joseph Marko who was honorably discharged as a private, Battery E, Three hundred and tenth Field Artillery, on the 6th day of December, 1918, on account of being a neutral alien nondeclarant of Russia, shall, upon application within six months after the passage of this Act, be entitled to all the rights, privileges, and benefits of the World War Adjusted Compensation Act, notwithstanding his discharge on account of alienage.

From the report of the Secretary of War to the Committee on Military Affairs, House of Representatives, at the time this bill was pending before it, I note that Mr. Marko was honorably discharged from the service on December 6, 1918, pursuant to the telegram dated November 14, 1918, from the War Department directing that "neutral alien nondeclarants will be discharged upon their own request. For the purpose of these instructions Russia will be considered neutral."

I further note that there were thousands of men who were discharged under like conditions and that there is no special or peculiar merit in Mr. Marko's case which would single him out for relief that is not extended to all others in the same class. As long as Congress deems it wise to exclude from the benefits of the World War Adjusted Compensation Act all persons who, at any time during the war period or thereafter, were discharged from the military or naval forces on account of alienage, I do not feel that it would be just or proper for me to approve a bill selecting a particular individual for exception from that general provision.

HERBERT HOOVER

The White House,
    February 23, 1931.

NOTE: The House of Representatives referred the veto message to the Committee on Military Affairs on February 23, 1931, and no further action was taken.

74

The President's News Conference of *February 24, 1931*

THE PRESIDENT. I always feel like apologizing when you all come here and I haven't anything to tell you, but that is the case today. I have nothing that I can properly comment on at the present moment, so I have nothing for you this morning.

NOTE: President Hoover's one hundred and seventy-sixth news conference was held in the White House at 12 noon on Tuesday, February 24, 1931.

75

Veto of Indian Claims Legislation. *February 24, 1931*

To the House of Representatives:

I return herewith without my approval H.R. 13584—An Act to amend an Act approved May 14, 1926 (44 Stat. 555), entitled "An Act authorizing the Chippewa Indians of Minnesota to submit claims to the Court of Claims".

The Act of May 14, 1926, authorized the Chippewa Indians of Minnesota to submit to the United States Court of Claims for adjudication any legal and equitable claims which they may have against the United States arising under or growing out of the Act of January 14, 1889, or any subsequent act of Congress, in relation to the affairs of these Indians.

This bill would amend that act of May 14, 1926, by adding to Section 1 the following language:

"In any such suit or suits the plaintiff, the Chippewa Indians of Minnesota, shall be considered as including and representing all those entitled to share in either the interest or in the final distribu-

99

tion of the permanent fund provided for by section 7 of the act of January 14, 1889 (25 Stat. L. 642), and the agreements entered into thereunder. That nothing herein shall be construed to affect the powers of the Secretary of the Interior to determine the roll of the Chippewa Indians of Minnesota for the purpose of making the final distribution of the permanent Chippewa fund. This act shall apply to any and all suit or suits brought under said act of May 14, 1926, whether now pending or hereafter commenced."

A number of suits have been filed by these Indians and are now pending in the Court of Claims.

The Act of January 14, 1889 was entitled "An Act for the relief and civilization of the Chippewa Indians in the State of Minnesota." These Indians were tribal Indians under the guardianship of the United States living upon their reservations as tribal lands comprising approximately 4,700,000 acres. Pursuant to that Act of 1889, these tribal lands, except portions thereof needed for allotments to these Indians, were ceded to the United States to be sold and the net proceeds thereof to be held in the United States Treasury for fifty years, to bear interest at the rate of 5% to be expended for the benefit of the Indians. Three-fourths of the interest was to be paid annually to the Indians in equal shares per capita and one-fourth to be devoted to the establishment and maintenance of free schools for these Indians, and the Act further provided that at the expiration of said fifty years the said permanent fund shall be divided and paid to all of said Chippewa Indians and their issue then living, in cash, in equal shares.

Many of these Indians since 1889 have severed all of their tribal relations and are scattered in various sections of the country but the Chippewa tribe still exists in the White Earth and Red Lake Reservations under the guardianship of the United States which is continuing to maintain free schools for their civilization.

Quite a number of these Indians who had severed their tribal relations continued to receive their distributive share of the interest fund until 1927 when the Solicitor of the Interior Department held that the fund established from the sale of these lands was a tribal fund administered by the United States for the benefit of the tribe which had not been dissolved but was recognized by Congress and that, therefore, the right to share in the interest annuities depended upon existing tribal membership. Accordingly, such Indians who had severed their tribal relations were stricken from the roll by the Secretary of the Interior and no longer entitled to participation in the interest annuities.

Several of these Indians in the case of *Wilbur* vs *the United States* petitioned for a writ of mandamus commanding the Secretary of the Interior to restore them to the rolls of the Chippewa Indians and to pay to each of them their per capita share of these interest annuities and of all future distributions of interest and principal from the fund created under the act of 1889. The Supreme Court of the United States denied this writ of mandamus holding that the Secretary of the Interior had administrative jurisdiction to make such a decision which was not contrary to the provisions of the Act of 1889, whose purpose was to accomplish a gradual rather than an immediate transition from the tribal relation and independent wardship to full emancipation and individual responsibility. The Supreme Court also said in this case which was decided in April 1930 that the time fixed for the final distribution of the fund is as yet so remote that no one is now in a position to ask special relief or direction respecting that distribution.

It thus appears that it is unnecessary to amend the Act of May 14, 1926, to bring in as parties plaintiff those Indians who have severed their tribal relations as their claim for a distributive share of this interest fund has been adjudicated by the decision of the Supreme Court in the above case *Wilbur* vs *the United States* known as the Kadrie case.

Neither is it necessary to amend the Act of May 14, 1926, for the purpose of compelling restoration by the United States to the interest fund of amounts that may have been heretofore erroneously distributed to Indians who had severed their tribal relations. Obviously the plaintiffs in such an action would be only those who had not severed their tribal relations and were still entitled to their distributive share of this interest fund.

The Supreme Court of the United States has said that the Secretary of the Interior had administrative jurisdiction to determine the rights of these Indians to that interest fund and that his decision was not contrary to the provisions of the Act of 1889. I am not in favor of legislation designed to have the courts again review that decision and assume such administrative jurisdiction.

HERBERT HOOVER

The White House,
    February 24, 1931.

NOTE: The House of Representatives referred the veto message to the Committee on Indian Affairs on February 24, 1931, and no further action was taken.

76

Message to State Head Constantine Pasts on Estonia's Independence Day.
February 24, 1931

ON THIS Independence Day of the Estonian Republic, I extend to you and your fellow countrymen most cordial felicitations.

HERBERT HOOVER

[His Excellency Constantine Pasts, Head of State, Tallin, Estonia]

77

Message Honoring Haym Salomon.
February 24, 1931

[Released February 24, 1931.   Dated February 21, 1931]

THE NOBLE and distinterested public services of Haym Salomon deserve the undying gratitude of all Americans. The aid of his financial genius and his wealth was of critical importance in the Revolutionary struggle which created us a Nation. It is indeed fitting that these services should be commemorated with an enduring monument that will remind us ever of his patriotism and self-sacrifice.

HERBERT HOOVER

[Mr. Z. Tygel, Executive Director, Haym Salomon Monument Committee, 32 Union Square, New York City]

NOTE: The message was read at a meeting of the Haym Salomon Monument Committee, held at the Hotel Delmonico in New York City, Haym Salomon, a Polish Jew, migrated to the American colonies in 1772 and later helped to finance the American Revolution.

78

Veto of the Emergency Adjusted Compensation Bill. *February 26, 1931*

To the House of Representatives:

I return herewith, without my approval, H.R. 17054, "An Act to increase the loan basis of adjusted service certificates."

In order that it may be clearly understood, I may review that the adjusted compensation act (bonus bill) passed on May 19, 1924, awarded to 3,498,000 veterans approximately $1,365,000,000 further compensation for war service. To this sum was added 25 per cent, said to be consideration for deferring the payment until about 1945, the whole bearing 4 per cent compound interest. Immediate payment to dependents upon death was included, thus creating an endowment insurance policy represented by a certificate to each veteran showing the sum payable at the end of the period—the "face value." The total "face value" of the outstanding certificates to-day after paying the sums due of less than $50 and payments in full to dependents is $3,426,000,000 held by 3,397,000 veterans or an average of about $1,000 each.

The burden upon the country was to be an amount each year sufficient as a yearly premium to provide for the payment of the "face value" of these certificates in about 1945, and to date has involved an appropriation averaging $112,000,000 per annum. The accumulation of these appropriations is represented by Government obligations deposited in a reserve fund, which fund now amounts to about $750,000,000. A loan basis to certificate holders was established equal to 90 per cent of the reserve value of the certificates, such loans now in the sixth year being authorized to 22½ per cent of the "face value."

When the bonus act was passed it was upon the explicit understanding of the Congress that the matter was closed and the Government would not be called upon to make subsequent enlargements. It is now proposed to enlarge the loan rate to 50 per cent of the "face value," at a low rate of interest, thus imposing a potential cash outlay upon the Government of about $1,700,000,000, if all veterans apply for loans, less about $330,000,000 already loaned. According to the Administrator of Veterans' Affairs the probable number who will avail themselves of the privilege under this bill will require approximately $1,000,000,000. There not being a penny in the Treasury to meet such a demand, the Government must borrow this sum through the sale of the reserve fund securities together with further issues or we must need impose further taxation.

The sole appeal made for the reopening of the bonus act is the claim that funds from the National Treasury should be provided to veterans in distress as the result of the drought and business depression. There are veterans unemployed and in need to-day in common with many others of our people. These, like the others, are being provided the basic necessities of life by the devoted committees in those parts of the country affected by the depression or drought. The governments and many employers are giving preference to veterans in employment. Their welfare is and should be a matter of concern to our people. Inquiry indicates that such care is being given throughout the country, and it also indicates that the number of veterans in need of such relief is a minor percentage of the whole.

The utility of this legislation as relief to those in distress is far less than has been disclosed. The popular assumption has been that as the certificates average $1,000 then each veteran can obtain $500 by way of a loan. But this is only an average, and more than one-half will receive less than this amount. In fact over 800,000 men will be able to borrow less than $200, and of these over 200,000 will be able to borrow only an average of $75. Furthermore, there are 100,000 veterans whose certificates have been issued recently who under the proposed law will have no loan privilege until their certificates are two years old. It is therefore urgent in any event that local committees continue relief to veterans, but this legislation would lead such local committees and employers to assume that these veterans have been provided for by the Federal Treasury, and thereby threatens them with greater hardships than before.

The breach of fundamental principle in this proposal is the requirement of the Federal Government to provide an enormous sum of money to a vast majority who are able to care for themselves and who are caring for themselves.

Among those who would receive the proposed benefits are included 387,000 veterans and 400,000 dependents, who are already receiving some degree of allowance or support from the Federal Government. But in addition to these, it provides equal benefits for scores of thousands of others who are in the income-tax paying class, and for scores of thousands who are holding secure positions in the Federal, State, and local governments and in every profession and industry. I know that most of these men do not seek these privileges, they have no desire to be presented to the American people as benefiting by a burden put upon the whole people, and I have many manifestations from veterans on whom the times are bearing hardly that they do not want to be represented to our people as a group substituting special privilege for the idealism and patriotism they have rejoiced in offering to their country through their service.

It is suggested as a reason for making these provisions applicable to all veterans, that we should not make public distinction between veterans in need and the others who comprise the vast majority lest we characterize those deserving help as a pauper class. On the contrary, veterans in need are and should be a preferred class, that a grateful country would be proud to honor with its support. Adoption of the principle of aid to the rich or to those able to support themselves in itself sets up a group of special privilege among our citizens.

The principle that the Nation should give generous care to those veterans who are ill, disabled, in need or in distress, even though these disabilities do not arise from the war, has been fully accepted by the Nation. Pensions or allowances have been provided for the dependents of those who lost their lives in the war; allowances have been provided to those who suffered disabilities from the war; additional allowances were passed at the last session of Congress to all the veterans whose earning power at any time may be permanently impaired by injury or illness; free hospitalization is available not only to those suffering from the results of war but to large numbers of temporarily ill. Together with war-risk insurance and the adjusted compensation, these services now total an annual expenditure of approximately $600,000,000 and under existing laws will increase to $800,000,000 per annum in a very few years for World War veterans alone. A total of five thousand millions of dollars has been expended upon such services since the war.

Our country has thus shown its sense of obligation and generosity, and its readiness at all times to aid those of its veterans in need. I have the utmost confidence that our service men would be amongst the first to oppose a policy of Government assistance to veterans who have property and means to support themselves, for service men are as devoted to the welfare of our country in peace as in war and as clearly foresee the future dangers of embarking on such a policy. It could but create resentments which would ultimately react against those who should be given care.

It is argued that the distribution of the hundreds of millions of dollars proposed by this bill would stimulate business generally. We can not further the restoration of prosperity by borrowing from some of our people, pledging the credit of all of the people, to loan to some of our people who are not in need of the money. If the exercise of these rights were limited to expenditure upon necessities only, there would be no stimulation to business. The theory of stimulation is based upon the anticipation of wasteful expenditure. It can be of no assistance in the return of real prosperity. If this argument of proponents is correct, we should make Government loans to the whole people.

It is represented that this measure merely provides loans against a future obligation and that, therefore, it will cost the American people nothing. That is an incomplete statement. A cost at once arises to the people when instead of proceeding by annual appropriation the Government is forced to secure a huge sum by borrowing or otherwise, especially in the circumstances of to-day when we are compelled in the midst of depression to make other large borrowings to cover deficits and refunding operations. An increased rate of interest which the Government must pay upon all long-term issues is inevitable. It imposes an additional burden of interest on the people which will extend through the whole term of such loans. Some cost arises to the people through the tendency to increase the interest rates which every State and municipality must pay in their borrowing for public works and improvements, as well as the rate which industry and business must pay. There is a cost to some one through the retardation of the speed of recovery of employment when Government borrowings divert the savings of the people from their use by constructive industry and commerce. It imposes a great charge upon the individual who loses such increased employment or continues unemployed. To the veteran this is a double loss when he has consumed the value of his certificate and has also lost the opportunity for greater earnings. There is a greater cost than all this: It is a step toward Government aid to those who can help themselves. These direct or indirect burdens fall upon the people as a whole.

The need of our people to-day is a decrease in the burden of taxes and unemployment, yet they (who include the veterans) are being steadily forced toward higher tax levels and lessened employment by such acts as this. We must not forget the millions of hard-working families in our country who are striving to pay the debts which they have incurred in acquiring homes and farms in endeavor to build protection for their future. They, in the last analysis, must bear the burden of increasing Government aid and taxes. It is not the rich who suffer. When we take employment and taxes from our people it is the poor who suffer.

There is a very serious phase of this matter for the wives and children of veterans and to the future security of veterans themselves. Each of these certificates is an endowment insurance policy. Any moneys advanced against them, together with its interest, will be automatically deducted from the value of the certificates in case of death or upon maturity. No one will deny that under the pressures or allurements of the moment, many will borrow against these certificates for other than absolutely necessary purposes. The loss to many families means the destruction of the one safeguard at their most critical time. It can not be contended that the interests of the families of our country are conserved by either cashing or borrowing upon their life-insurance policies.

I have no desire to present monetary aspects of the question except so far as they affect the human aspects. Surely it is a human aspect to transfer to the backs of those who toil, including veterans, a burden of those who by position and property can care for themselves. It is a human aspect to incur the danger of continued or increased unemployment. It is a human aspect to deprive women and children of protection by reckless use of an endowment policy. Our country is rich enough to do any justice. No country is rich enough to do an injustice.

The patriotism of our people is not a material thing. It is a spiritual thing. We can not pay for it with Government aid. We can honor those in need by our aid. And it is a fundamental aspect of freedom among us that no step should be taken which burdens the Nation with a privileged class who can care for themselves.

I regard the bill under consideration as unwise from the standpoint of the veterans themselves, and unwise from the standpoint of the welfare of all the people. The future of our World War veterans is inseparably bound up with the future of the whole people. The greatest service that we can render both veterans and the public generally is to administer the affairs of our Government with a view to the well-being and happiness of all of the Nation.

The matter under consideration is of grave importance in itself; but of much graver importance is the whole tendency to open the Federal Treasury to a thousand purposes, many admirable in their intentions but in which the proponents fail or do not care to see that with such beginnings many of them insidiously consume more and more of the savings and the labor of our people. In aggregate they threaten burdens beyond the ability of our country normally to bear; and, of far higher importance, each of them breaks the barriers of self-reliance and self-support in our people.

HERBERT HOOVER

THE WHITE HOUSE,
    February 26, 1931.

NOTE: Congress enacted H.R. 17054 over the President's veto on February 27, 1931, as Public, No. 743 (46 Stat. 1429).

79

The President's News Conference of
February 27, 1931

EMERGENCY ADJUSTED COMPENSATION ACT, 1931

THE PRESIDENT. Although I have been a good deal opposed to the passage of the bonus legislation in its provisions for loans from the Treasury to people who do not need the money, now that the law is passed we propose to facilitate this work in every possible way.

The physical task of making loans to 3½ million people, or any percentage of them, is enormous. It will require a very intensive organization, and would require a good deal of time—probably months to get through with all of the cases—so that I have this afternoon requested General Hines to give complete priority to applications from veterans who are in need. And I have asked him to set up some machinery for the certification of these cases from the veterans' organizations and the local unemployment relief committees over the country that are dealing with the veterans at the present time. The survey which General Hines made of the larger industrial cities shows that, in his opinion, there are about 6 percent of the total number of veterans in the industrial areas that are being taken care of by the local unemployment and other relief organizations. This bill will relieve some of the burden now carried by those committees, but as the amount possible for a great many veterans to draw is so very small, it is very urgent that those committees continue their work.

I also want to compliment the veterans' service organizations for their cooperation in undertaking a campaign amongst all the veterans urging them not to take advantage of the loan provisions except in absolute necessity. I understand from General Hines that they are going to put on that campaign at once and vigorously. I understand they are placing it on the ground of assistance to the Federal Government in minimizing the amount of money which the Treasury will need to borrow and on the basis that loans made on the bonus certificates exhaust the protection to veterans' families under the endowment insurance features of the plan.

Taking General Hines' survey of the number of veterans being assisted by the local committees as a basis, it would appear that if all the loans were confined to need, the drain on the Treasury might be limited to 10 percent of the potential liability created by the law.

And further than that I have nothing to say today.

MUSCLE SHOALS

I might for your own information be able to give you something on Muscle Shoals tomorrow or Monday.

NOTE: President Hoover's one hundred and seventy-seventh news conference was held in the White House at 4 p.m. on Friday, February 27, 1931.

On the same day, the White House issued a text of the President's statement on the Emergency Adjusted Compensation Act, 1931 (see Item 80).

Frank T. Hines was Administrator of Veterans' Affairs.

80

Statement on the Emergency
Adjusted Compensation Act, 1931.
February 27, 1931

THE PRESIDENT said:

"Although I have been greatly opposed to the passage of the bonus legislation in its provisions for loans from the Treasury to people not in need, now that it is a law we propose to facilitate the working of it in every way possible.

"Inasmuch as the physical task of making loans to 3,500,000 veterans, or even half that number, who might apply, will require many months, even with the most intensive organization, I have requested General Hines to give complete priority to applications from veterans who are in need, and have asked him to set up some machinery for the certification of these cases, especially giving regard to the certification of the veterans' service organizations and the various relief organizations dealing with unemployment. The recent survey of the larger cities shows, in the opinion of the Administrator of Veterans' Affairs, that about 6 percent of the total number of veterans in industrial centers, are now receiving support from the local unemployment and other relief committees. This bill will relieve some of the burden now being carried by these committees, but as the amount possible for many veterans to borrow under the bill is so small, it is urgently necessary that the local committees shall continue their service to many veterans.

"I wish to compliment the veterans' service organizations for their cooperation in undertaking a campaign amongst all veterans, urging them not to take advantage of the loan provisions except in cases of absolute necessity. I understand they are placing it on the ground of assistance to the Federal Government in minimizing the amount of money we shall be called upon to borrow and upon the fact that loans upon the bonus certificates exhaust the protection to veterans' families under the endowment insurance features of the certificates.

"Taking General Hines' survey of the number of veterans being assisted by local committees as a basis, it would appear that if all loans were confined to need, the drain on the Treasury may be limited to 10 percent of the potential liability created by the law."

NOTE: On the same day, the White House issued the text of a letter, dated February 26, 1931, from Frank T. Hines, Administrator of Veterans' Affairs. The letter with inclosed reports follows:

My dear Mr. President:

I am inclosing herewith as complete information as it has been possible to secure as to the number of veterans and veterans' families who are receiving relief through organized charity.

These returns represent the reports from eighteen cities whose veteran population is estimated as approximating 898,469. While, in my opinion, the figures on relief extended are indexes only including, as they doubtless do, some duplication, and on the other hand in some instances probably not including all cases to whom relief is being extended, it is interesting to note that from these figures the percent of veteran population represented who is actually in receipt of relief approximates 8, as some 72,310 cases are represented by the attached reports. If we apply this percent to the 3,400,000 holders of bonus certificates there would result a figure of approximately 272,000, which is at least indicative of the number of veterans at this time so in need as to seek relief from organized charity.

I might add it is my personal opinion, however, that these figures on the average are higher than probably the actual facts warrant when we take into account possible duplications and also minor forms of relief which may be comprehended. I would say that a better average figure might be 6%. Further, I have checked back on certain reports originally received, and modified figures have been used.

Very sincerely yours,
FRANK T. HINES
Administrator

[Honorable Herbert Hoover, The President of the United States]

VETERAN POPULATION AND RELIEF REPORTED
EXTENDED TO IT BY THE AMERICAN RED CROSS AND OTHER
CHARITIES FOR THE PAST NINETY DAYS FOR CITIES SPECIFIED

City	Total population	Estimated military population	Number of veterans, or veterans' families to whom relief reported afforded	Note
Boston.........	781,188	45,000	2,936	Includes relief rendered by Red Cross to disabled veterans only and excludes relief rendered by Family Welfare Society, Catholic Charitable Bureau, St. Vincent de Paul Society and Industrial Aid Society, data for which organizations do not distinguish between veterans and others.
Buffalo.........	573,076	[1] 20,058	6,004	Value of relief $150,908 include relief extended by Red Cross, American Legion, Disabled American Veterans, Veterans of Foreign Wars, City Public Welfare Department, extent of duplication and period covered not shown.
Philadelphia....	1,950,961	101,932	4,803	Includes 3,953 families of veterans, average number in family, five. Does not include relief extended by individual posts of veterans' organizations.
New York.....	6,930,446	258,733	[1] 20,000	Some 1,200 charitable organizations in New York City, most of which do not differentiate between veterans and others. While it is estimated 20,000 are actually in receipt of relief at this time, it is further estimated that an additional 20,000 have requested relief. American Legion has estimated 50,000 have applied for relief in New York City.
Cincinnati......	451,160	22,820	735	Does not include returns from associated charities to be submitted later.
Birmingham....	259,678	[2] 9,089	1,025	Does not include relief afforded by churches, Salvation Army, community kitchen as veterans not distinguished from others.

See footnotes at end of table.

VETERAN POPULATION AND RELIEF REPORTED
EXTENDED TO IT BY THE AMERICAN RED CROSS AND OTHER
CHARITIES FOR THE PAST NINETY DAYS FOR CITIES SPECIFIED—Continued

City	Total population	Estimated military population	Number of veterans, or veterans' families to whom relief reported afforded	Note
New Orleans...	458,762	17,500	493	Excludes relief afforded by church and small welfare organizations.
Chicago........	3,376,438	[3] 130,000	[2] 10,900	Relief afforded does not include that furnished by relief agencies suburban villages in Cook County. General estimate is that 10 percent of veteran population being furnished relief. Does not include aid extended by individual legion posts.
Indianapolis....	364,161	[1] 12,746	1,061	Includes estimates from 21 Red Cross and 6 associated charity agencies.
Detroit.........	1,568,662	60,000	1,500	Report based upon Director, Service Men's Bureau and does not include those of veterans reported receiving clothes as well as meals and lodging from Mayor's Welfare Committee.
Milwaukee.....	578,249	[1] 20,239	4,150	Cash allowances $77,000 in addition to other allowances.
St. Louis.......	821,960	55,000	1,721	Does not include number veterans seeking employment and for whom employment obtained, former being 3,500; later 1,027.
San Antonio....	231,542	7,000	1,085	Includes applications for relief to Red Cross and associated charities and applies to residents and transients.
Kansas City (Missouri).	399,746	30,000	2,600	
Minneapolis....	464,356	23,000	6,492	Cost of relief $60,093.
Denver.........	287,861	13,552	672	Relief afforded by Red Cross and Community Chest agencies.
Seattle.........	365,583	16,000	1,813	
Los Angeles....	1,238,048	56,000	4,320	

[1] Estimated.
[2] City of Chicago alone.
[3] Cook county.

81

Message to President Rafael Leonidas Trujillo on the Dominican Republic's Independence Day.
February 27, 1931

ON THIS anniversary of the Independence of the Dominican Republic, I extend to Your Excellency and your fellow countrymen sincere felicitations.

HERBERT HOOVER

[His Excellency General Rafael Leonidas Trujillo, President of the Dominican Republic, Santo Domingo]

82

Statement on Muscle Shoals Legislation.
February 28, 1931

THE FOLLOWING statement was issued by the President today:

I have received a multitude of telegrams from Governors and citizens in the Southern States urging approval of Senator Norris' Muscle Shoals project, and requesting that I express my views upon it. Some of them express dissatisfaction with its principles but consider it expedient to approve it. I have also many telegrams from citizens of the Southern States and other parts of the country protesting against the principles of the bill.

It is obvious from the debate, the press, and these many communications that Muscle Shoals legislation is no longer a question of disposing of a war activity to the advantage of the people primarily concerned. It has by this legislation been transformed into a political symbol and is expected to be a political issue. To be against Senator Norris' bill appears to be cause for denunciation as being in league with the power companies. It appears also to be emerging as the test of views upon Government operation and distribution of power and Government manufacture of commodities. In other words, its adaptation to the use of the people

115

of the Tennessee Valley and to farmers generally is now enmeshed in an endeavor to create a national political issue.

One side issue of this political phase is the use which has been made of Muscle Shoals to sidetrack effective action on the Federal regulation of interstate power in cooperating with the States. Before and since taking office I have proposed this as a measure of essential protection to the 75 million consumers and several million investors in power securities in all walks of life, who use and own the 35 million horsepower of the country. This public necessity has been held aside for 18 months and time of Congress given to 1 percent of the power and the interests of 1 percent of the people of the United States which is the proportion of the Muscle Shoals problem to the whole.

The bill calls for expenditure of $90 or $100 million from the Federal Treasury to expand a powerplant which has been a byproduct of other major purposes of navigation and national defense, into a large undertaking by the Government, the major purpose of which is to be the generation and distribution of power and the manufacture of fertilizers.

In acting on the bill I have to consider whether it is desirable to adopt a change in Federal policies from regulation of utilities to their ownership and operation; whether the lease provision in respect to the fertilizer plant is genuinely workable; whether the method proposed in this bill will produce cheaper fertilizers for the farmers; whether the project is required for national defense; whether the proposals in this bill are, in reality, in the interest of the people of the Tennessee Valley; and in general to consider the commonplace unromantic facts which test the merits and demerits of this proposition as a business.

This happens to be an engineering project and so far as its business merits and demerits are concerned is subject to the cold examination of engineering facts. I am having these facts exhaustively determined by the different departments of the Government and will then be able to state my views upon the problem.

NOTE: The White House issued the statement following a meeting between the President, Secretary of War Patrick J. Hurley, Representative B. Carroll Reece of Tennessee, and Senator J. Thomas Heflin of Alabama.

83

Message to the Baith Israel Anshei Emes Congregation on the 75th Anniversary of Its Founding.
March 1, 1931

[Released March 1, 1931.   Dated February 28, 1931]

I WILL BE obliged if you will express to the congregation Baith Israel Anshei Emes my cordial congratulations upon the celebration of the seventy-fifth anniversary of its founding and my best wishes for long continuance of its high service to the spiritual life of the community.

HERBERT HOOVER

[Harry G. Anderson, Chairman, Program Committee, Baith Israel Anshei Emes, 32 Court Street, Brooklyn, N.Y.]

NOTE: The message was read at exercises at the synagogue in Brooklyn, N.Y.

84

Message of Sympathy on the Death of Representative Henry Allen Cooper of Wisconsin.
March 2, 1931

My dear Mrs. Cooper:

I send you my deepest sympathy in your bereavement and I do pray that you may find consolation in the memory of his long and useful career. Congressman Cooper's courage and high ideals rendered him a truly valuable servant of our country.

Yours faithfully,

HERBERT HOOVER

[Mrs. Henry Allen Cooper, The Washington, Washington, D.C.]

NOTE: Representative Cooper served in the Congress from 1893 to 1919 and from 1921 to his death on March 1, 1931.

85

Message on the Inauguration of President Gabriel Terra of Uruguay.
March 2, 1931

[Released March 2, 1931.   Dated March 1, 1931]

ON THIS DAY of good auspices in the destiny of Uruguay, permit me to offer Your Excellency, with my most cordial congratulations, my heartiest good wishes for your happiness in the high office to which you have been led by the confidence and esteem of your fellow countrymen.

HERBERT HOOVER

[His Excellency Gabriel Terra, President of The Oriental Republic of Uruguay, Montevideo, Uruguay]

86

Proclamation 1939, Revoking Embargo on Exportation of Arms and Munitions of War to Brazil.
March 2, 1931

By the President of the United States of America a Proclamation:

WHEREAS, by Proclamation No. 1923, issued on October 22, 1930, under a joint resolution of Congress entitled "Joint resolution to prohibit the exportation of arms or munitions of war from the United States to certain countries, and for other purposes," approved January 31, 1922 (42 Stat. 361), it was declared that there existed in Brazil such conditions of domestic violence as were or might be promoted by the use of arms or munitions of war procured from the United States; and

WHEREAS, by the joint resolution above mentioned, it thereupon became unlawful to export arms or munitions of war from the United States to Brazil except under such limitations and exceptions as were prescribed in the said proclamation;

Now, THEREFORE, I, HERBERT HOOVER, President of the United States of America, do hereby find, as has been formally represented to this

Government by the Government of Brazil, that the conditions on which the proclamation of October 22, 1930, was based no longer obtain, and I do hereby declare and proclaim that the said proclamation of October 22, 1930, is accordingly hereby revoked.

IN WITNESS WHEREOF, I have hereunto set my hand and caused the seal of the United States to be affixed.

DONE at the City of Washington this 2d day of March, in the year of our Lord nineteen hundred and thirty-one, and of the Independence of the United States of America the one hundred and fifty-fifth.

[SEAL]

HERBERT HOOVER

By the President:
   HENRY L STIMSON
      Secretary of State.

NOTE: See also 1930 volume, Item 337.

87

Letter to the Speaker of the House Transmitting a Supplemental Estimate of Appropriation for Participation in the Conference on the Limitation of the Manufacture of Narcotic Drugs.
March 3, 1931

Sir:

I have the honor to transmit herewith for the consideration of Congress a supplemental estimate of appropriation for the Department of State for the fiscal year 1931, to remain available until June 30, 1932, amounting to $35,000, for the expenses of participation by the Government of the United States in the Conference on the Limitation of the Manufacture of Narcotic Drugs to be held at Geneva, Switzerland, on May 27, 1931.

The details of this estimate, the necessity therefor, and the reason for its transmission at this time are set forth in the letter of the Director of the Bureau of the Budget transmitted herewith, with whose comments and observations thereon I concur.

Respectfully,

HERBERT HOOVER

The White House,
    March 3, 1931.

[The Speaker of the House of Representatives]

NOTE: The letter and accompanying papers are printed as House Document 797 (71st Cong., 3d sess.).

88

Veto of the Muscle Shoals Resolution.
March 3, 1931

To the Senate:

I return herewith, without my approval, Senate Joint Resolution 49, "To provide for the national defense by the creation of a corporation for the operation of the Government properties at and near Muscle Shoals in the State of Alabama; to authorize the letting of the Muscle Shoals properties under certain conditions; and for other purposes."

This bill proposes the transformation of the war plant at Muscle Shoals, together with important expansions, into a permanently operated Government institution for the production and distribution of power and the manufacture of fertilizers.

Disregarding for the moment the question of whether the Federal Government should or can manage a power and fertilizer manufacturing business, we should examine this proposal from the point of view of the probabilities of success as a business, even if efficiently managed. Such an analysis involves a consideration of the capital invested, the available commercial power, the operating costs, the revenue to be expected, and the profit and loss involved from this set-up. The figures and estimates given herein are furnished by the War Department upon the authority of the Chief of Engineers.

VALUE OF THE OLD PLANT AND FURTHER CAPITAL OUTLAY REQUIRED

The following properties and proposed extensions are embraced in the proposed project:

(a) Wilson Dam and its hydroelectric equipment valued at $37,000,-000 being the original cost of $47,000,000 less $10,000,000 applicable to navigation.

(b) The steam power plant at Muscle Shoals valued at $5,000,000 being a reduction from depreciation of $7,000,000 from the original cost of $12,000,000.

(c) Proposed further additions to the electrical plant at Muscle Shoals costing $9,000,000.

(d) Proposed construction of Cove Creek Dam with hydroelectric plant with transmission line to Wilson Dam $41,000,000 of which $5,000,000 may be attributed to flood control and improvement of navigation or, say, $37,000,000.

(e) Proposed construction of transmission lines for wholesale distribution of power within the transmission area—$40,000,000.

(f) Nitrate plants, quarries, etc., at Muscle Shoals which originally cost $68,555,000 but upon which no valuation is placed at present.

The total valuation of the old property to be taken over for the power portion of the project is therefore $42,000,000 after the above deductions from original cost. The new expenditures from the Treasury applicable to the power business are estimated at $90,000,000, less $5,000,000 which might be attributable to flood control, or a total of $127,000,000 of capital in the electrical project. This sum would be further increased by accumulated interest charge during construction. As shown later on several millions further would be required for modernizing the nitrate plants. The total requirement of new money from the Federal Treasury for the project is probably $100,000,000 even if no further extensions were undertaken.

AMOUNT OF POWER AVAILABLE FROM THIS PROJECT

Assuming the additional power given by the construction of the Cove Creek Dam and the use of steam power for five months in the dry season each year, and taking the average load factor from experience in that region, about 1,300,000,000 kilowatt-hours of continuous power could be produced annually. Considered as a general power business a portion of this must be held in reserve to protect consumers, leaving a net of about 1,000,000,000 kilowatt-hours annually of salable power. This amount would be somewhat increased if a large proportion of 24-hour load were applied to fertilizer manufacture.

The secondary power for a period of less than seven months in the year is not regarded as of any present commercial value.

OPERATING COSTS

The following is the estimated annual overhead and operating cost of the electrical end of the project including the steam plant necessary to convert 7-month secondary power into primary power as stated above:

Interest at 4 per cent per annum on capital of $127,000,000	$5,080,000
Amortization	1,890,000
Operating and maintenance cost of hydroelectric plant	775,000
Operating and maintenance cost of steam plant	850,000
Operation and maintenance cost of transmission lines	550,000
Total	$9,145,000

The estimated cost of production and distribution is, therefore, about 9.1 mills per kilowatt-hour. If only part of the transmission lines were constructed it would decrease capital and operating charges but would not comply with the requirement of equitable distribution through the transmission area.

ESTIMATED GROSS INCOME

The purpose of the bill is to provide production and wholesale distribution of surplus power and to give preference to States, municipalities, and cooperative organizations. It further provides that the policy of the Government must be to distribute the surplus power equitably amongst States, counties, and municipalities within transmission distance of Muscle Shoals and provides for the construction of transmission lines to effect this purpose. Such a transmission system for wholesale purposes only is estimated to cost $40,000,000. If it is proposed to sell power at retail to householders, then there would need be a great increase in the estimates of capital outlay and operation costs for such distribution.

The average gross income of the power companies in that territory, including retail as well as wholesale power, is about 12 mills per kilowatt-hour. This includes retail residential power averaging something over 50 mills per kilowatt-hour. Miscellaneous industrial power realizes about 10 mills per kilowatt-hour. The power sold wholesale to other companies and those engaged in municipal distribution averages about 7.2 mills per kilowatt-hour.

It is impossible to compute Muscle Shoals income under this project upon a basis which includes retail power sales, as this is a project for wholesale distribution only. It is impossible to compute it upon the basis of miscellaneous industrial rates as sales for industrial purposes from Muscle Shoals would presumably be mainly for manufacture of fertilizers and it would not be possible to average 10 mills per kilowatt-hour. A rate of not over 2 mills would be a large charge for such power. While the load factor would be improved by large use for this purpose, the net result, however, would be to diminish the gross income below the above rates from municipal and miscellaneous industrial services.

Assuming that the whole 1,000,000,000 kilowatt-hours should be sold to municipalities or other power distributors, it would on the basis of the realizations of the private companies of 7.2 mills yield a gross annual income to this project of about $7,200,000, or a loss upon this basis of nearly $2,000,000 annually. This territory is now supplied with power and to obtain such an income it would be necessary to take the customers of the present power companies. To secure these customers it would be necessary to undercut the rates now made by them. It is difficult to estimate the extent to which it would be necessary to go in such rate cutting in order to secure the business. In any event it would of course diminish estimated income and increase the losses.

It is obvious that any estimate of income contains a large element of conjecture as the proportions of industrial and municipal load can not be foretold. But any estimate of the income of the project as set up by this legislation will show a loss.

FERTILIZER MANUFACTURE

The plants at Muscle Shoals were originally built for a production of nitrates for use in war explosives. I am advised by the War Department that the very large development in the United States by private enterprise in the manufacture of synthetic nitrogen now affords an ample supply covering any possible requirements of war. It is therefore unnecessary to maintain this plant for any such purposes.

This bill provides that the President for a period of 12 months may negotiate a lease of the nitrate plants for fertilizer manufacture under detailed limitations, but in failure to make such a lease the bill makes it mandatory upon the Government to manufacture nitrogen fertilizers at Muscle Shoals by the employment of existing facilities or by modernizing existing plants or by any other process. I may state at once that the limitations put upon lessees in the bill are such that this provision is of no genuine importance. Inquiries have been made of the most responsible and experienced concerns that might possibly undertake such lease and they have replied that under the conditions set out in the bill it is entirely impractical for them to make any bid. The leasing provision is therefore of no utility; it may at once be dismissed. In consequence the project we have to consider under this bill is the manufacture of fertilizers by the Federal Government.

The Department of Agriculture reports that these plants are now more or less obsolete and that with power at even 2 mills per kilowatt-hour, with proper charges included, could not produce the products for which they are constructed as cheaply as these products are now being sold in the wholesale markets. Therefore, it would be necessary to modernize the equipment at an unknown cost in millions. There is no evidence as to the costs of nitrogen fertilizers by the newer equipment, and there is therefore no basis upon which to estimate the results to the Government from entering upon such a competitive business. It can, however, be stated with assurance that no chemical industry with its constantly changing technology and equipment, its intricate problems of sales and distribution, can be successfully conducted by the Government.

PROPOSED ADMINISTRATION

The first essential of all business is competent management. Although the bill provides for the management by three directors, the Congress must from the nature of our institutions be the real board of directors and with all the disadvantages to a technical business that arise from a multitude of other duties, changing personnel, changing policies, and regional interests. These three directors are to have political qualifications, as it is stipulated that not more than two shall be of one political party. They are to receive $50 per diem, but are limited to $7,500 each for the first year and $5,000 annually thereafter. The act provides that:

> "All members of the board shall be persons that profess a belief in the feasibility and wisdom, having in view the national defense and the encouragement of interstate commerce, of producing fixed nitrogen under this act of such kinds and at such prices as to induce the reasonable expectation that the farmers will buy said products, and that by reason thereof the corporation may be a self-sustaining and continuing success."

In other words, they are to say that they believe in Government manufacture of fertilizers, and that it can be made a success on this set-up. We are thus supposed to appoint business administrators on the basis of their beliefs rather than their experience and competency. These directors are manifestly to have a political complexion and apparently the entire working force is likewise to have such a basis of selection, as the usual provision for the merit service required by law in most other Federal activities is omitted. Three men able to conduct a one hundred and fifty million dollar business can not be found to meet these specifications.

GENERAL CONSIDERATIONS

I am firmly opposed to the Government entering into any business the major purpose of which is competition with our citizens. There are national emergencies which require that the Government should temporarily enter the field of business, but they must be emergency actions and in matters where the cost of the project is secondary to much higher considerations. There are many localities where the Federal Government is justified in the construction of great dams and reservoirs, where navigation, flood control, reclamation or stream regulation are of dominant importance, and where they are beyond the capacity or purpose of private or local government capital to construct. In these cases power is often a by-product and should be disposed of by contract or lease. But for the Federal Government deliberately to go out to build up and expand such an occasion to the major purpose of a power and manufacturing business is to break down the initiative and enterprise of the American people; it is destruction of equality of opportunity amongst our people; it is the negation of the ideals upon which our civilization has been based.

This bill raises one of the important issues confronting our people. That is squarely the issue of Federal Government ownership and operation of power and manufacturing business not as a minor by-product but as a major purpose. Involved in this question is the agitation against the conduct of the power industry. The power problem is not to be solved by the Federal Government going into the power business, nor is it to be solved by the project in this bill. The remedy for abuses in the conduct of that industry lies in regulation and not by the Federal Government entering upon the business itself. I have recommended to the Congress on various occasions that action should be taken to establish Federal regulation of interstate power in cooperation with State authorities. This bill would launch the Federal Government upon a policy of ownership and operation of power utilities upon a basis of competition instead of by the proper Government function of regulation for the protection of all the people. I hesitate to contemplate the future of our institutions, of our Government, and of our country if the preoccupation of its officials is to be no longer the promotion of justice and equal opportunity but is to be devoted to barter in the markets. That is not liberalism, it is degeneration.

126

This proposal can be effectively opposed upon other and perhaps narrower grounds. The establishment of a Federal-operated power business and fertilizer factory in the Tennessee Valley means Federal control from Washington with all the vicissitudes of national politics and the tyrannies of remote bureaucracy imposed upon the people of that valley without voice by them in their own resources, the overriding of State and local government, the undermining of State and local responsibility. The very history of this project over the past 10 years should be a complete demonstration of the ineptness of the Federal Government to administer such enterprise and of the penalties which the local community suffers under it.

This bill distinctly proposes to enter the field of powers reserved to the States. It would deprive the adjacent States of the right to control rates for this power and would deprive them of taxes on property within their borders and would invade and weaken the authority of local government.

Aside from the wider issues involved the immediate effect of this legislation would be that no other development of power could take place on the Tennessee River with the Government in that field. That river contains two or three millions of potential horsepower, but the threat of the subjection of that area to a competition which under this bill carries no responsibility to earn interest on the investment or taxes will either destroy the possibility of private development of the great resources of the river or alternately impose the extension of this development upon the Federal Government. It would appear that this latter is the course desired by many proponents of this bill. There are many other objections which can be raised to this bill, of lesser importance but in themselves a warranty for its disapproval.

It must be understood that these criticisms are directed to the project as set up in this bill; they are not directed to the possibilities of a project denuded of uneconomic and unsound provisions nor is it a reflection upon the value of these resources.

I sympathize greatly with the desire of the people of Tennessee and Alabama to see this great asset turned to practical use. It can be so turned and to their benefit. I am loath to leave a subject of this character without a suggestion for solution. Congress has been thwarted for 10 years in finding solution, by rivalry of private interests and by the determination of certain groups to commit the Federal Government to Government ownership and operation of power.

The real development of the resources and the industries of the Tennessee Valley can only be accomplished by the people in that valley themselves. Muscle Shoals can only be administered by the people upon the ground, responsible to their own communities, directing them solely for the benefit of their communities and not for purposes of pursuit of social theories or national politics. Any other course deprives them of liberty.

I would therefore suggest that the States of Alabama and Tennessee who are the ones primarily concerned should set up a commission of their own representatives together with a representative from the national farm organizations and the Corps of Army Engineers; that there be vested in that commission full authority to lease the plants at Muscle Shoals in the interest of the local community and agriculture generally. It could lease the nitrate plants to the advantage of agriculture. The power plant is to-day earning a margin over operating expenses. Such a commission could increase this margin without further capital outlay and should be required to use all such margins for the benefit of agriculture.

The Federal Government should, as in the case of Boulder Canyon, construct Cove Creek Dam as a regulatory measure for the flood protection of the Tennessee Valley and the development of its water resources, but on the same bases as those imposed at Boulder Canyon—that is, that construction should be undertaken at such time as the proposed commission is able to secure contracts for use of the increased water supply to power users or the lease of the power produced as a by-product from such a dam on terms that will return to the Government interest upon its outlay with amortization. On this basis the Federal Government will have cooperated to place the question into the hands of the people primarily concerned. They can lease as their wisdom dictates and for the industries that they deem best in their own interest. It would get a war relic out of politics and into the realm of service.

HERBERT HOOVER

The White House,
     March 3, 1931.

NOTE: The Senate sustained the President's veto on March 3, 1931.

89

Statement on the Franco-Italian Naval Agreement.
March 4, 1931

THE FRANCO-ITALIAN naval settlement marks the completion of the work which began 2 years ago in naval reduction and the ending of competition in naval construction among the five leading naval powers. Throughout the long-continued process toward the completion of this plan, the cause of disarmament has been fortunate in the devotion and application of the men charged with the conduct of foreign affairs. In the last phase of the negotiations, Mr. Henderson, Mr. Briand, and Mr. Grandi have given it the full measure of their statesmanship and the successful result is a matter for congratulation in the whole world. I am happy also to acknowledge the impetus given the settlement by the suggestions of Ambassador Gibson conveyed in Paris and Rome last November. I feel that the responsible heads of governments and the peoples of the world owe a debt of gratitude to the infinite patience and ability of all who have collaborated so effectively toward the settlement and that they realize the fortunate augury which the solution of this problem by direct conversations between the interested parties contains for the progress in the removal of the obstacles on the path of a general and reasonable limitation of all armaments.

NOTE: The statement referred to Arthur Henderson, British Foreign Minister; Aristide Briand, French Foreign Minister; Dino Grandi, Italian Foreign Minister; and Hugh S. Gibson, United States Ambassador to Belgium.

Efforts to implement the agreement failed when the French interpreted its provisions as allowing them to begin a large bloc of replacements in 1934. The British and Italians refused to accept this interpretation.

90

Message to a Dinner Honoring Albert Einstein.
March 4, 1931

I AM GLAD of this opportunity to express my admiration of your distinguished service to mankind through your scientific speculations and researches, and my hope that your visit to the United States has been as satisfying to you as it has been gratifying to the American people.

HERBERT HOOVER

[Professor Albert Einstein, Hotel Astor, New York City]

NOTE: The message was read at a dinner sponsored by the American Palestine Campaign, held in the Hotel Astor in New York City. Professor Einstein, world-renowned physicist and exponent of the theory of relativity, was completing an 11-week visit to the United States.

91

Message About Limitation of Oil Imports.
March 5, 1931

SECRETARY of Commerce Lamont is in negotiation with the larger oil companies in respect to imports in the interest of both the producers and consumers.

HERBERT HOOVER

NOTE: The message was in response to telegrams from Governors William H. Murray of Oklahoma, Ross D. Sterling of Texas, Harry H. Woodring of Kansas, and Arthur Seligman of New Mexico, who were urging a national conference to limit the imports of oil.

92

The President's News Conference of
March 6, 1931

FEDERAL FARM BOARD

THE PRESIDENT. I have to announce to you something that I think you all know, and that is Mr. [Alexander] Legge's resignation. And I know that I reflect the view of the agricultural community when I express intense regret that his private affairs have made it necessary for him to leave the Board. He has been urged I think by every farm organization in the United States to continue as Chairman of the Farm Board, and I have urged him with all the pressures that I could bring to bear, but he feels obligations elsewhere.

I have appointed Mr. James C. Stone as the Chairman of the Board, and Mr. [Charles C.] Teague has been elected Vice Chairman. We, therefore, have a vacancy on the Board which will require some 2 or 3 weeks to fill.

RICHARD N. ELLIOTT

I have given an interim appointment to Congressman Elliott as Assistant Comptroller General.

And that is all the news I have got today.

ALEXANDER LEGGE

Q. Mr. President, does that resignation take effect immediately?
THE PRESIDENT. Yes.

NOTE: President Hoover's one hundred and seventy-eighth news conference was held in the White House at 4 p.m. on Friday, March 6, 1931.

Richard N. Elliott served as Representative from Indiana from 1917 until his appointment as Assistant Comptroller General.

68-611 O - 76 - 12

93

Message to Emperor Haile Selassie of Ethiopia
on the Birth of His Son.
March 7, 1931

[Released March 7, 1931.   Dated March 5, 1931]

I HAVE received Your Majesty's telegram informing me of the birth
of a son.

I participate sincerely in the satisfaction which this happy event has
afforded Your Imperial Majesty and the Royal Family and I hope that
the life of the young Prince may be a long and illustrious one.

HERBERT HOOVER

[His Imperial Majesty Haile Selassie I, Emperor of Ethiopia, Addis Ababa]

94

Statement on the Disapproval of a Bill To Provide for the
Establishment of a National Employment System.
March 8, 1931

[Released March 8, 1931.   Dated March 7, 1931]

THE PRESIDENT stated today:

I have given earnest study to the so-called Wagner bill for improvement of public employment agencies, in an effort to find a method
to make it of use in the present employment situation. I find upon study,
however, that if I would prevent a serious blow to labor during this
crisis, I should not approve the bill. I have repeatedly urged a proper
extension of public employment agencies, but this bill, unfortunately,
abolishes the whole of the present well-developed Federal Empoyment
Service, and proposes after certain requirements are complied with, to
set up an entirely new plan by subsidies to the States from the Federal
Treasury. And even were there no other objections to the plan, it cannot be made effective for many months or even years. It is not only

changing horses while crossing a stream but the other horse would not arrive for many months. This situation alone required that legislation be deferred, as it will not help in emergency but will do great damage.

"The fundamental questions involved also require more consideration. This bill proposes, as I have said, to destroy the Federal Employment Service in the Department of Labor, which has developed out of many years of experience, and to substitute for it 48 practically independent agencies, each under State control, the Federal Government paying for them as to 50 percent, and based not upon economic need of the particular State but upon mathematical ratio to population. On the other hand, the existing Federal Employment Service is today finding places of employment for men and women at the rate of 1,300,000 per annum. It cooperates and coordinates with the service already established by some 30 States. It applies its energies to interstate movements, and, being a mobile service, it concentrates upon the areas in need. Beyond this, however, the present Federal Service has special divisions devoted to the planting and harvest movement in agriculture and a special organization for veterans. There is no provision for the continuation of these two very important special services under the new plan, and the interstate quality of the Federal Service is destroyed. In any event, the bill required effective action by the legislatures and Governors of the various States at a minimum time requiring so long a period for its establishment as to be of no purpose in this emergency. And there is, therefore, ample time to consider the whole of the questions involved. There is no financial loss to labor in allowing this bill to lapse. While the bill provides for $1,500,000 expenditure over the next 15 or 16 months, one-half of it would be absorbed in relieving one-half the present expenditure of the States without any additional service on their part. On the other hand, the present Federal Service has available over the next 15 or 16 months nearly $1 million for the conduct of its agencies, which are being rapidly expanded through the emergency appropriations.

"I am asking the Secretary of Labor to cooperate with the various interested organizations to draft a plan for presentation to the next session of Congress which will avoid the difficulties presented by this bill.

"A more ample statement indicating the difficulties of the bill is given in the reports to me by the Secretary of Labor and the Attorney General, which are attached."

NOTE: Congress adjourned on March 3, 1931, making the President's action technically a pocket veto.

In his statement the President referred to a letter from the Attorney General, dated March 6, 1931, and a letter from the Secretary of Labor, dated March 7, 1931, which follow:

Dear Mr. President:

I have examined the provisions of S. 3060, the Act to provide for the establishment of a national employment system for cooperation with the States in the promotion of such system and for other purposes, which has not yet received your approval.

This examination made in conjunction with the Secretary of Labor has been for the purpose of ascertaining what the effect of this Act would be during the next year upon the efforts of the Department of Labor to relieve unemployment. The Labor Department now has an employment bureau which is rendering excellent service. Section One of this Act expressly provides:

"The Employment Service now existing in the Department of Labor is hereby abolished."

If this bill becomes a law, the present employment bureau would thus be immediately abolished and steps would then have to be taken under this Act to construct an entirely new employment service along new lines. It is obvious that months must elapse before substantial progress could be made in setting up the new service. The state authorities would have to be consulted, the action of state legislatures awaited, and when some progress had been made in setting up new agencies to aid the unemployed, the restrictive provisions of this Act such as that for apportionment of funds, would deprive the system of flexibility and hamper efficient action in the present emergency.

Without attempting here to analyze in detail all the complicated provisions of this Act, it is obvious that by its terms it would have the effect at this time when labor is in greatest need of assistance, of destroying the employment service now being maintained in the Department of Labor and making it impossible for months to come to replace it with a working organization.

Respectfully yours,
WILLIAM D. MITCHELL
Attorney General

[The President, The White House]

My dear Mr. President:

I have to submit to you my recommendation that you should not sign Senate Bill 3060, the so-called Wagner Bill.

As you can imagine, I have all my life most urgently advocated the maintenance and development of national employment services. This bill seeks to destroy the present Federal Employment Service by substituting Federal subsidies to the forty-eight States for conduct of separate agenices based upon population, not upon need. It destroys the interstate phase of service to labor movement, submits labor to the idiosyncracies of state politics and gains nothing to the worker. Of the utmost immediate importance, its first provision is the abolition of the Federal Employment Service, which Service has been built up over years and out of great experience.

In the midst of our emergency we are to be compelled to abandon this vital help to labor and the new system, founded upon an old plan of State subsidies, could not be subsituted for many months and even years. It would destroy the interstate character of the Federal service, which is vital to employment and which is essentially a Federal function, and would set up these forty-eight independent employment services with no practical method of effective control.

In amplification I may say:

(1) The idea in this bill is not new. It has been proposed and rejected at different times over many years. Hearings were held on the subject in the Sixty-sixth Congress by Joint Committee of both houses, and this plan was completely abandoned. Notwithstanding statements to the contrary, the principles on which the present bill are based are directly contrary to the recommendations of the Employment Conference of 1921 of which you were Chairman. Its details likewise antagonize the conclusions of the Senate Committee on Education and Labor of February, 1929. This bill was passed by the Senate in May, 1930. The House took no action upon it until recently. Upon my accepting this office, you requested that I should take up the matter and endeavor to find a practical basis for strengthening of the Federal Employment Service, and you authorized an increase in appropriations therefor. After persistent negotiation I was unable to secure such amendment to this bill as would make it practicable, and a substitute measure was prepared by the Department of Labor and submitted to the Judiciary Committee of the House, and was approved last month. This substitute was predicated upon a decade of experience of the Department, and proposed to strengthen our present flexible interstate system, which stimulates cooperation with the States, permits freedom of action to meet local and regional need. In the proposal which I made we especially undertook to serve in the so-called technological unemployment. We have an emergency appropriation of $500,000 for our present Service, which would be lost if this bill becomes a law.

135

(2) As I have said, by the first paragraph of the pending measure the present Employment Service is abolished. Therefore, should this bill become a law the government, now in the midst of a serious emergency in unemployment, is faced with the destruction of all the practical machinery it has set up in the past decade and which is now functioning and the Labor Department is compelled to abandon duties of the utmost importance to labor of the United States. It would take months and even years to work out the cumbersome plans proposed by this measure, with all of its detail of submission to the respective States for rejection or adoption. I will not go into the complicated details by which the system was proposed to be worked out, but even if workable it involves enormous delay when agencies tested by experience are of the utmost value. The present Federal Service in the past twelve months, in cooperation with State agencies, has placed over 1,300,000 persons in employment. In addition to its general functions, it contains two special functions, that is, nation-wide service to agriculture and nation-wide service to veterans. Both of these special services are totally abolished by the bill and no provision is made for their continuation. During the past year 700,000 farm laborers have been found employment, largely in inter-state movement, and many scores of thousands of veterans have been placed in profitable work. I wish to emphasize that both of these special services will end under this bill. I cannot approve a measure which proposes to scrap these agencies.

(3) The present Federal Employment Service is founded upon the idea of coordination with State and local employment agencies and especially for purposes of aid in which may be termed interstate placements. The President's Conference on Unemployment and the report made by the Senate Committee on Education and Labor on February 25, 1929, emphasized this important interstate function. This primary Federal function is destroyed under this bill. This bill, as I have said, seeks to set up by substitute forty-eight separate organizations in the United States, based not upon need but upon population, with no definite authority of control by the Federal government and no function of interstate movement of labor. Railway and other interstate public services have always presented especial difficulties to State employment agencies. It is well known that some of the railroads and labor organizations have been forced to maintain their own bureaus because of the interstate problems involved. No interstate service would be possible under the set-up proposed in this bill.

(4) The pending measure is so framed that there can be no definite certainty whether it would ever come into complete operation. With the present Service abolished, if by the end of June, 1933, some of the States were unable or unwilling to appropriate funds or to cooperate as this measure requires, then there would be no service in those States or no interstate movement to and from those States.

(5) There are a great many other objections to this bill. The whole question of Federal subsidy to State governments is subject to the great question as in some States it would be used to set up agencies, given over largely to politics. In others the Federal appropriations would be used merely to relieve the State of one-half its present expenditure, with no increase in services. There is no provision to guarantee the character of State employees who would be partly paid by Federal funds. There can be no basis in our form of government for the Federal Government to force State legislative policies, such as this bill might imply. The measure provides for the establishment of forty-nine advisory councils, which means the widest variety of opinion and the maintenance of permanent friction, dispute and interference with administration. It would be difficult to devise a better plan to defeat the unification of employment policy.

The measure lacks that practical flexibility essential for a function of this character. Unemployment is not a factor of population as this bill purports. It is a factor of industry and the economic situation of the times and the variation of the economic ebb and flow. To unite successfully men with jobs, effort must be timed to actual employment conditions. This bill simply sets up forty-eight separate establishments with no respect to the problems of the times.

In conclusion:

I cannot in the interest of the working people of the United States give my approval to a proposal which, while abolishing the tested machinery of a decade of service, leaves the government at a critical moment without any practical instrumentality to carry forward its necessary services. The existing Employment Service is fortunately in possession of funds with which to carry forward the work in which it has been efficiently engaged and which assure that the interest of the wage-earners will be protected.

Nor can I conclude without again emphasizing that this is not in essence emergency legislation. On the contrary, if it would be made workable at all, it would require a long period for coordination and establishment. Far from assuring the cooperation of the States in the development of a public employment system, as the title of this measure suggests, it destroys all existing cooperation and makes the future development of any substitute system dependent upon acceptance or rejection of the provisions of the bill by forty-eight separate States. I cannot, therefore, give my approval to a proposal which, while ostensibly in the interest of labor, would, practically, and directly operate to the immediate injury of the wage-earner.

As it serves no emergency purpose and in fact destroys our emergency action, it is in the interest of labor that carefully and constructively formulated legislation should be undertaken rather than to approve this measure. Furthermore, there is nothing in the present set-up of the United States Employment Service which would prohibit any of the States appropriating any money they may see fit in carrying forward employment work within the States and in cooperation with the Federal Government.

Faithfully yours,
W. N. DOAK

[The President, The White House]

95

Message to Justice Oliver Wendell Holmes On His 90th Birthday.
March 8, 1931

[Released March 8, 1931.   Dated March 7, 1931]

My dear Mr. Justice:

I most cordially congratulate you upon your ninetieth birthday anniversary, but yet more do I congratulate our country upon the continuance of your splendid services, and hope that you may long live in health and strength to carry them forward.

Yours faithfully,
HERBERT HOOVER

[Hon. Oliver Wendell Holmes, 1720 Eye Street, N.W., Washington, D.C.]

NOTE: The message was made public in conjunction with ceremonies in Washington, D.C., honoring Associate Justice Holmes. The ceremonies were broadcast over the Columbia Broadcasting System radio network.

96

Message Endorsing Plans for a Memorial to Nathan Straus.
March 9, 1931

[Released March 9, 1931.   Dated March 3, 1931]

My dear Mr. Janssen:

I always had the highest admiration for the late Nathan Straus and when plans for a suitable memorial to his memory reach the stage where all are agreed as to what it shall be, I shall be glad to help further that project.

I appreciate warmly your pleasant personal references.

Yours faithfully,

HERBERT HOOVER

[Mr. August Janssen, Broadway, 52nd and 53rd Streets, New York City]

NOTE: The message was read at a meeting of the Broadway Association, held in the Hotel Astor in New York City.

97

Statement on the Death of Joseph P. Cotton, Under Secretary of State.
March 10, 1931

THE PRESIDENT said:

"Mr. Cotton's passing is a great loss to the Government and to our country. He was my friend for over 20 years. He has given much of his life to public service and has never refused a demand of the public interest. His abilities, his character, his devotion to the highest of purposes made him a great citizen."

NOTE: Mr. Cotton, a prominent corporate lawyer, served as Under Secretary of State from 1929 until his death.

98

Message on the III Olympic Winter Games.
March 11, 1931

[Released March 11, 1931.   Dated February 4, 1931]

Dear Dr. Dewey:

I am interested to learn of the III Olympic Winter Games to be held at Lake Placid in 1932. The friendly rivalry of the athletes of the nations not only develops sportsmanship but also contributes to the advance of international good-will and fellowship.

Yours faithfully,

HERBERT HOOVER

[Dr. Godfrey Dewey, President, III Olympic Winter Games Committee, Lake Placid, New York]

NOTE: The message was read at a luncheon meeting of the Olympic Winter Games Committee, held at the India House in New York City. The meeting was held to launch a fundraising campaign to raise $250,000 for the games through private subscriptions.

99

The President's News Conference of *March 12, 1931*

OIL IMPORTS AND PRODUCTION

THE PRESIDENT. I haven't anything of startling interest. I have been trying to get together a little statement as to the situation in the oil industry, and I will have it ready and give it to you mimeographed in the course of half an hour or so. It bears on the question of proration being brought about by the Oil Conservation Board in the different States under their State authorities, and the effort being made by the Board on the proration of imports.

I have had several hundred telegrams from different parts of the country, and this is in the nature of a statement as to what the present situation is all around.

Otherwise than that I haven't anything today.

NOTE: President Hoover's one hundred and seventy-ninth news conference was held in the White House at 4 p.m. on Thursday, March 12, 1931.

The White House issued a text of the President's statement on oil imports and production (see Item 100).

100

Statement on Oil Imports and Production.
March 13, 1931

I HAVE RECEIVED several hundred telegrams from the West and Southwest either inquiring or making suggestions as to the situation in the oil industry.

In order to make the matter clear I may state:

"In order to prevent enormous waste of gas and oil and to prevent the ruin of the independent oil producers, the Federal Oil Conservation Board brought about over a year ago, under the leadership of Secretary Wilbur, an almost entire restriction of production from the newly discovered, great oil pool at Kettleman Hills, California, a large part of which is the property of the Federal Government. The State authorities of Oklahoma have brought about similar restraint upon an enormous new pool discovered at Oklahoma City. Coincident with these efforts, the State commissions working with other producers of California, Oklahoma, and Texas, brought about proration agreements amongst themselves. A third great pool has been recently developed in eastern Texas, upon which no proration has yet been brought about, but I am advised that the Governor is making an effort to bring it about. The question of prorating of imports has been under agitation as also having a bearing upon the problem.

"We import approximately 105 million barrels of petroleum and its products per annum and export about 156 million barrels, the imports coming largely from certain South American and Mexican oil pools.

"The consumption of the United States is approximately 900 million barrels per annum, the imports thus representing something over 11 percent and the exports about 16 percent of the total.

"On the 29th of January the Oil Conservation Board recommended to Congress that authority be given to the Federal Trade Commission to effect proration of imports, it being the Board's hope that a proration of production in the foreign pools exporting to the United States could [be] brought about as well as a proration of imports into the United

States. No action was taken by Congress upon this recommendation nor upon other plans proposed by the independent oil producers.

"On March 5, therefore, the Board, with my approval, requested that importers should each voluntarily prorate their production from foreign pools and their imports into the United States, in order to give mid-continent and California fields an opportunity to further readjust their position. The Board considers that in the present situation a substantial reduction in imports can be brought about without distributing the price of oil to the consumer, the Atlantic Seaboard can be supplied from domestic storage. These negotiations are making favorable progress. But such action would have little effect, however, unless the east Texas pool shall be prorated on the same basis as other new pools. It it believed that if these two results could be brought about, the industry will soon readjust itself."

NOTE: A voluntary import limitation program went into effect on April 1. 1931.

101

Statement on the Appointment of John R. Alpine to the United States Employment Service.
March 13, 1931

IN COOPERATION with Secretary Doak, I have appointed Mr. John R. Alpine of New York as Special Assistant to the Secretary of Labor in charge of the United States Employment Service activities to include the application at once of the emergency appropriation of $500,000 [1] made, at my suggestion, at the end of the last session of Congress over and above the usual $380,000 per annum.

Mr. Alpine comes to the service with a long, successful record in the organized labor movement and large experience in employment management. He was international president of the United States Association of Plumbers and Steamfitters; vice president of the American Federation of Labor; was acting president of the Federation in 1918 during

---

[1] Second Deficiency Act (Public, No. 869, 46 Stat. 1552).

the absence of President Gompers in Europe. Since 1921, he has been an official of the Grinnell Company with special relationship to employment questions. He served on the United States Cantonment Construction Adjustment Commission during the late war, and was a delegate in the Labor Section of the Paris Peace Conference in 1918. He has had long experience in employment problems and will take up his new duties at once.

It is proposed by Secretary Doak and Mr. Alpine to add at once several divisions to the Federal Employment Service. These divisions will cover mining, building, metal trades, transportation, needle trades, textiles, office and mercantile, seamen and longshoremen.

In addition to the extension of the Federal Employment Service in these directions, which are interstate in character, and which will be set up in cooperation with the existing public agencies, it is proposed that an extensive study of the whole question of free public employment agencies shall be made both in the United States and abroad. Special examination will be made of the system needed for placement to meet the so-called technological unemployment—the whole with view to devising a sound basis for the extension of employment services.

102

White House Statement on the President's Caribbean Tour.
March 14, 1931

TO SECURE a short rest and to settle certain administrative problems regarding American possessions in [the] Caribbean, President Hoover will go to Porto Rico and probably to the Virgin Islands next week on the reconditioned battleship *Arizona* which is undertaking its 10-day test run at sea. Announcement of the voyage was made by the White House late today.

This will be the first vacation of the President since assuming office, with the exception of a 7-day fishing trip to Florida something more than a year ago. The trial run of the *Arizona* has been scheduled to the

Caribbean to start on March 17. The journey will give the President an opportunity to confer with Governor [Theodore] Roosevelt at Porto Rico.

On the return voyage the President will stop off at the Virgin Islands, the jurisdiction of which has been recently transferred by the President's order from the Navy to the Department of the Interior. The *Arizona* will sail from Norfolk. The exact date of departure will be announced later. The President will travel from Washington to Norfolk by train and will be away from Washington about 10 days.

103

White House Statement on the Appointment of Delegates
to the Conference on the Limitation of the
Manufacture of Narcotic Drugs.
March 14, 1931

THE PRESIDENT HAS appointed the following as delegates on the part of the United States to the Conference on the Limitation of the Manufacture of Narcotic Drugs to be held at Geneva, May 27, 1931.

> MR. JOHN K. CALDWELL, Foreign Service officer of Class I, representative of the Secretary of State on Federal Narcotics Control Board for 5 years; representative of the United States at the last four annual sessions of the League of Nations Opium Advisory Committee; representative of the United States at the Preliminary Conference on the Limitation of the Manufacture of Narcotic Drugs held in London in October, 1930
>
> MR. HARRY J. ANSLINGER, Commissioner of Narcotics
>
> DR. W. L. TREADWAY, Chief of Bureau of Mental Hygiene, Public Health Service (in charge of the "Narcotic Farms" created by the Porter Bill)
>
> THE HONORABLE SANBORN YOUNG of California, chairman, California State Narcotic Commission, 1925–1931

Participation by this Government was authorized by Public Resolution 130, approved March 3, 1931 [46 Stat. 1516].

In view of his familiarity with this subject through attendance as the representative of this Government at the sessions of the League of Nations Opium Advisory Committee and at the Preliminary Conference on the Limitation of the Manufacture of Narcotic Drugs, held in London, Mr. Caldwell will be named Chairman of the delegation.

NOTE: The Conference met from May 27 to July 31, 1931, and produced a convention limiting the manufacture of specified drugs and controlling their movement through licenses.

104

The President's News Conference of
March 17, 1931

THE PRESIDENT. I haven't anything for you this morning at all, I am sorry to say. I have just said that part of you, at least, will have a chance to get seasick for the next 3 days to see whether you can find any news out of that. Otherwise than the fact that we are going, I haven't got anything to give you.

NOTE: President Hoover's one hundred and eightieth news conference was held in the White House at 12 noon on Tuesday, March 17, 1931.

The President referred to his forthcoming tour to Porto Rico and the Virgin Islands.

105

Message to the Kips Bay Boys' Club.
March 18, 1931

[Released March 18, 1931.   Dated March 16, 1931]

I CORDIALLY congratulate the Kips Bay Boys' Club upon the formal opening of their new building and warmly hope that the boys may find much happiness in enjoyment of its greater opportunities for their benefit and pleasure.

HERBERT HOOVER

[Chester Aldrich, Kips Bay Boys' Club, 340 East 54th Street, New York City]

NOTE: The message was read at the dedication of the new Kips Bay Boys' Club Building.

106

The President's News Conference of *March 20, 1931*

SAMUEL H. THOMPSON

THE PRESIDENT. There is nothing new aside from the appointment of Sam Thompson as a member of the Federal Farm Board. This is the most excitement Washington has had. I have no news further than this. Nothing that you could term new. You can ask verbal questions this time, if you wish.

QUESTIONS

Q. How about the telephone call from your son?

THE PRESIDENT. It has not worked today. He was trying to get it through on the set he made.

Q. Are you going to do any fishing off the boat?

THE PRESIDENT. I would like to, but I don't believe I can go fishing. It seems very inapropos to catch small fish with a large boat.

Q. Is there any chance of staying longer in the Virgin Islands, or carrying the trip any further?

THE PRESIDENT. No, I do not think so. I want to stick close to American soil.

Q. What will be your program in Porto Rico?

THE PRESIDENT. I have not given a great deal of attention to this, I shall probably give a 10 or 15 minute speech at some point.

Q. Have you considered giving a speech?

THE PRESIDENT. This is going to be merely a response of greetings. There will be no expression of policy. I want to see something of the government and visualize the sentiment of the people.

Q. Is Governor [Theodore] Roosevelt to meet you?

THE PRESIDENT. Yes, at Ponce. He will meet us at Ponce.

Q. What is the program at the Virgin Islands?

THE PRESIDENT. I haven't any at all. You could shake hands with the whole population of the Virgin Islands in 4 hours. These are days to sleep and I do not think that anyone expects you to send many news dispatches.

Q. Do you expect to renew your exercises?

THE PRESIDENT. It all depends how everyone feels. There are no rules about this voyage. If there is anyone who feels like it I shall have preparations made for it. I think 3 days sleep would do us all good. I am taking it all out mostly in sleep.

NOTE: President Hoover's one hundred and eighty-first news conference was held on board U.S.S. *Arizona*, en route from Norfolk, Va., to Ponce, P.R., at 2 p.m. on Friday, March 20, 1931.

107

Message to the American Jewish Joint Distribution Committee. *March 21, 1931*

[Released March 21, 1931.   Dated March 16, 1931]

My dear Mr. Strauss:

I have been much interested to learn that you and your associates are continuing the work of the Joint Distribution Committee. I am able to review in memory the period of more than twelve years of its constructive endeavors, many of them in concert with organizations over which I presided.

I trust that the forthcoming national conference of the Joint Distribution Committee will result in continuation of the hearty cooperation and support which have made possible the success that has hitherto accompanied its benevolent activities.

Yours faithfully,

HERBERT HOOVER

[Mr. Lewis Strauss, 52 William Street, New York City]

68-611 O - 76 - 13

NOTE: The message was read at the opening session of a conference of the committee, held in the Hotel Pennsylvania in New York City. The American Jewish Joint Distribution Committee, founded in 1914, was the major Jewish welfare agency engaged in overseas reconstruction activities.

108

Remarks at Ponce, Porto Rico.
March 23, 1931

Fellow citizens:

I deeply appreciate your welcome and I am extremely glad of the opportunity to visit you and learn more about your problems. I am glad to visit the only part of the United States visited by Columbus. We regard it as the oldest part of the United States.

It is also a great satisfaction to confer with your able Governor, whose distinguished father was the first to promote the welfare of this island. I have been greatly impressed by the courage with which you have faced your difficulties. I only wish I could stay longer and enlarge the acquaintance of my fellow citizens here.

NOTE: The President spoke at approximately 8 a. m. from a balcony at Ponce City Hall in response to welcoming remarks of Mayor Emilio Fagot and Governor Theodore Roosevelt. Following the welcoming ceremony, the President went by motorcade to San Juan.

As printed above, this item follows the text set forth in a contemporary news account.

109

Address to the Porto Rican Legislature.
March 24, 1931

Gentlemen of the legislature, my fellow American citizens:

I am grateful for the courtesy and generosity of the reception which I have received in Porto Rico. It is indeed a great pleasure for me to be here and to have this opportunity of meeting you personally.

Ever since I became President of the United States I have wished to visit this part of the Union and to have an opportunity of that fuller acquaintance with your problems which comes of personal contact. The time at my disposal is unfortunately too limited to visit many of your communities and inspect all of their various activities and institutions. I wish it were possible for me to do so. I should also like to see more of the beauties and resources of the island of which you are so justly proud.

I want you to realize that it is not lack of interest or of good will on my part that prevents more extended visit and the making of larger acquaintance, but simply the limitations of other responsibilities.

Though I come for the first time to Porto Rico, my contact with the island and my opinion of her people do not date merely from the time when I assumed the position of President. More than a decade ago, as Food Administrator during the troublous times of the war, I came to know Porto Ricans, to become acquainted with their abilities, and, above all, to realize their splendid devotion to our country in time of national danger.

Our Nation is proud of the progress made by the people of Porto Rico. Endowed with liberty, freedom, with self-government and individual opportunity through incorporation under the American flag, the island by the efforts of its citizens and the cooperation of the whole United States has in a single generation emerged from stagnation to a high place in the march of progress.

Porto Rico is, indeed, a magnificent example of what a capable and intelligent people may accomplish under free institutions. You have, indeed, shown courage and initiative under these impulses of freedom and liberty. In proof of this progress I need but recall a few evidences. You have in this single generation since joining in our citizenship increased more than 60 percent in population, increased over 500 percent in material wealth and over 800 percent in attendance upon public schools. You have decreased illiteracy by almost 50 percent and the death rate has been diminished by more than 60 percent.

I know of no finer achievement than that of the people of this island who from their gaining wealth have builded up from a few public schools with but 25,000 scholars at the time of the occupation to a great system of several thousand schools, colleges, and universities, which today gives instruction to over 200,000 scholars.

You are temporarily suffering not alone from the aftermath of the devastating hurricane of 1928, when a tenth of all the property of the island and a much larger percentage of the tools of livelihood were destroyed, but you are involved with us all in the worldwide business depression. Discouraging as these disasters may be for the moment, we know that they are but passing events in our history; that with the courage of your people and under the benevolent institutions which have been builded here, their effects will be overcome and the Nation and this island will resume their march in prosperity and progress.

In Washington we are sensible of these many serious difficulties with which you are struggling at the moment. We also realize not only these difficulties with which you are confronted, but we realize also your possibilities for future progress. This administration has given proof of the continued solicitude of our citizens on the mainland for your welfare by the measures recommended to the Congress and authorized by it. It has been the policy of the Federal Government to contribute even more liberally to the development of Porto Rico in this period of her upgrowth toward freedom and liberty than has been given to our States.

Not only has the island enjoyed the invaluable privileges of full inclusion in our economic system but all of the Federal revenues from the island have been assigned to the island treasury, and now a large measure of the Federal welfare services in public works, public roads, education, agriculture, and in public health, are being extended to the island without costs to its people.

The suffering of the people of the island from the great hurricane found a generous response not only from the contribution of your fellow citizens in the United States but by large measures of relief from the Federal Treasury. The American people have been glad to cooperate in this upbuilding and in the reconstruction from present difficulties, and they take great pride in the progress you have made.

Basically what we are all striving for in our economic life is to provide, for all of our citizens on this island as well as the mainland, the opportunity to gain for themselves and their families by their own effort a fair and adequate livelihood. We have confidence in the advancement of your part of our Nation through economic development, through the education, and through the ordered liberty, which have created the great sister commonwealths upon the mainland.

We wish to see every Porto Rican with the same opportunities in life to which we believe every American citizen is entitled. Economic advancement is not necessarily the foundation of moral and spiritual advancement, but it can be made so if we so conduct our institutions that prosperity shall be diffused among all our citizens. If we use its surplus to advance the cultural, the moral, and spiritual welfare of our people, then economic advancement serves not alone these purposes, but becomes the bulwark of liberty and freedom itself.

I have been particularly impressed with the splendid efforts that you are making in the education and in health and care of children. They are the responsibility of every man and woman of the community, for in them as a whole lies the future. If each generation of youth enter upon the responsibilities of life and of the Nation better equipped in body and mind and in character than their parents the Nation will advance. If we fail in that no amount of legislation, no amount of wealth, no amount of culture or scientific discovery will assure progress.

I would be remiss if I should not on this occasion refer to the distinguished and devoted services to the people of Porto Rico of your Governor, Theodore Roosevelt, Jr. Not only has he devoted himself with success to the problems of reconstruction and development in every proper direction, but he has realized, as we all must realize, the peculiar and grave problems presented by the increase in your population more rapidly than adequate livelihood can be gained from the older and established industries. His efforts to secure new industrial development and to expand your markets are of the first importance to the people of the island. He has proven himself the true friend of the Porto Rican people.

I should wish to convey to you a word of encouragement for the future. The achievements of your past should be your assurance. You have shown splendid ability at cooperation, building new institutions of government, and in disaster, magnificent courage. That courage and that spirit of cooperation will bring to you the blessings of prosperity. You are endeavoring, as all our people are endeavoring, to build a system where men may have an opportunity of livelihood, where insecurity is no longer a spectre in the home of those who have the will to work, and where upon the soil of this prosperity you shall find richer fruits of culture and wider opportunities of mind and spirit. Those possibilities are before the people of Porto Rico. Your fellow citizens upon the mainland will cooperate with you to those ends.

NOTE: The President spoke at 8 a.m. from the steps of the capitol at San Juan.

Following his address, the President visited Morro Castle and then returned to the U.S.S. *Arizona* for departure to the Virgin Islands.

A reading copy of this item with holograph changes by the President is available for examination at the Herbert Hoover Presidential Library.

110

Inscription in the Book of Records of the Colonial Council of the Virgin Islands. *March 25, 1931*

I HAVE RECEIVED the Resolutions in deep appreciation and with a vivid hope of the welfare of the Islands under cooperation with the United States.

HERBERT HOOVER

NOTE: Following a reception in the Administration Building on St. Thomas Island, the President wrote the above inscription in acknowledgment of the resolutions, printed below, presented by the Colonial Council of the Virgin Islands.

RESOLUTION

From: The Colonial Council for St. Thomas and St. John, Virgin Islands of the United States.
To: The President of the United States of America.

WHEREAS His Excellency, Herbert Clark Hoover, thirty-first President of the United States of America, has signally honored the Virgin Islands by visiting these shores;

WHEREAS our illustrious guest is the first President of the United States to set foot on our soil;

WHEREAS this visit is due to the President's desire to personally see this beautiful little national possession in which he has evinced such deep interest;

WHEREAS his recent order creating civilian government for the Virgin Islands manifests such interest in a special manner;

WHEREAS we desire to record our inexpressible pleasure at His Excellency's presence in our midst, and for other reasons aforesaid;

Resolved further, that the Colonial Council, while affirming its loyalty to the the Citizens of the Municipality, tender this testimonial of its profound gratification at the President's visit, and hearty acknowledgement of his solicitude for their welfare;

Resolved further, that the Colonial Council, while affirming its loyalty to the Nation's Chief Magistrate, desires that a similar expression of appreciation, through him, be conveyed to the Congress and people of the United States.

Most respectfully submitted.

Signed, sealed and delivered at Saint Thomas, Virgin Islands, March 24th, 1931.

LEROY NOLTE,
Chairman.

BENITO SMITH, *Secretary*	ABRAM E. SMITH
J. E. KUNTZ	JOSEPH REYNOLDS
V. A. MILLER	G. A. MOOREHEAD
SVEND A. MYLNER	C. CORNEIRO
LIONEL ROBERTS	ALBERT MADURO
KNUD KNUD-HANSEN	CHRISTIAN PETERSEN
THEODORE BOSCHULTE	CARL E. FRANCIS

111

The President's News Conference of *March 26, 1931*

PORTO RICO

THE PRESIDENT. The people of Porto Rico have made magnificent progress in self-government and the establishment of democratic institutions. The government is ably conducted by Porto Rican-born citizens and there are today only three or four important officials upon the island who were not born there. I am advised from every quarter in the island that there would not be a popular vote of 5 percent in favor of independence.

The people are making progress from the effects of hurricane, drought, and the business depression, all of which were imposed upon a century-old poverty. They are showing great courage and initiative in this rehabilitation. They will this season, in large degree, have recovered their crops.

The devastating effect of the hurricane is still represented in the thousands of one-room shacks housing whole families. The most constructive contribution of the Federal Government is to continue and expand the present policies of aid to and cooperation with their institutions in education, health, better adaptation of agriculture, expansion of industry and markets.

The Virgin Islands

The Virgin Islands may have some military value sometime—opinion upon this question is much divided. In any event when we paid $25 million for them we acquired an effective poorhouse comprising 90 percent of the population.

The people cannot be self-supporting either in living or government without the discovery of new methods and resources.

The purpose of the transfer of the administration from the naval to a civil department is to see if we can develop some form of industry or agriculture which will relieve us of the present costs and liabilities in support of the population or the local government from the Federal Treasury or from private charity.

Viewed from every point except remote naval contingencies it was unfortunate that we ever acquired these islands. Nevertheless, having assumed the responsibility, we must do our best to assist the inhabitants.

Questions

Q. Will the present policy towards Porto Rico be continued?

THE PRESIDENT. Yes. Porto Rico, I think, stands as a great credit to the American people. It has a population of nearly 900,000; under self-government it would probably have a living standard nearly as high as any people in the Western Hemisphere. There are 760 police in the island. That includes all forms of peace officers. They are showing a great ability in building up a substantial state, they are making fine progress and are sending many men abroad. Many graduates in many South American countries and many in the United States from Porto Rican institutions. In other words some groups in Porto Rico are capable of a great deal of development.

Q. Will anything be done about the suggestion of using Porto Ricans in our diplomatic service?

THE PRESIDENT. The Porto Ricans have an ambition to enter our diplomatic service. I was a great deal struck with the many capable men there, especially the judges, and the chief justice. He is a man of very considerable parts. We could use them to advantage. We should give them an opportunity in our diplomatic service.

Q. Is there any line of industry to be developed in Porto Rico?

THE PRESIDENT. The work of Governor Roosevelt has uncovered many lines of development. The next step is to build up more industries. They have taken up very systematically all kinds of production which might be increased. They have developed a large market. I was very much encouraged by a very large order received from one of the mail order houses in the United States. They have established agencies in New York City. That is one line of attack. They need someone to look after their interests outside. We need a transformation in the Department of Agriculture to have a number of tropical plants developed in Porto Rico which look very promising. These may help out in the Virgin Islands as well. The sugar business in the Virgin Islands is practically gone. They do not produce one-third as much an acre of what is produced in other parts of the West Indies, and probably has no hope at all. The harbor of St. Thomas is not likely to be built up like it was before the war. Steamers are now going to other ports where they can take on oil. I do not see much hope for the restoration of the business of their harbor. It must follow some other direction. Intensive [omission] appears as a means of possible livelihood.

Q. Is there any suggestion that we might give up the Virgin Islands?

THE PRESIDENT. I don't think so. We have reduced expenses by doing away with the Governor at St. Johns. We thought it was not necessary to maintain more than two posts where the total collected taxes amounted to only $700 a year.

Q. How about the idea of transferring Porto Rico to the Interior Department?

THE PRESIDENT. I have not given any great thought to that question.

Q. Do the same arguments in general apply to Porto Rico as to the Virgin Islands?

THE PRESIDENT. No, because Porto Rico, with the assistance of the Government, is able to carry on. The Interior Department has to be a daily nurse to the Virgin Islands. We have not given any serious thought to this transfer. So far as the actual Federal relationship is concerned we have more relationship through military departments than we do through any other one agency. We have barracks made up of Porto Rican recruits with American officers. It was not until this last winter that we extended any of the Federal services to Porto Rico. The island has been a success from a commercial view. We have a large trade with Porto Rico. The trade comes to us, of course. I think our exports are $60 or $70 million a year.

Q. Is there any question of American competition?

THE PRESIDENT. The Department of Agriculture has been looking for tropical plants to supplement our agricultural products. That would not be a very serious competition.

Q. Is there likely to be an increase in Federal aid?

THE PRESIDENT. Yes. I suppose we will spend $5 or $600,000 here in that direction.

Q. Has the Governor been doing anything to start new industries?

THE PRESIDENT. Yes. He has been very successful. They have been extending their markets and have been making some shipments to England of bananas, with success. They are stimulating the banana trade. All together the situation is satisfactory and full of hope.

Q. Is there any possibility of growing rubber in Porto Rico?

156

THE PRESIDENT. I have no idea. I could not tell you. They would have grown it before this. They have some success in Haiti. American companies have gone there and worked 15 or 18,000 acres.

NOTE: President Hoover's one hundred and eighty-second news conference was held on board the U.S.S. *Arizona* about 225 miles north of Porto Rico at 4 p.m. on Thursday, March 26, 1931.

On the same day, the White House issued a text of the President's statement on Porto Rico and the Virgin Islands (see Item 112), which was telegraphed from the *Arizona*.

112

Statement on Porto Rico and the Virgin Islands. *March 26, 1931*

THE PEOPLE OF Porto Rico have made magnificent progress in self-government and the establishment of democratic institutions. The government is ably conducted by Porto Rican-born citizens and there are today only three or four important officials upon the island who were not born there. I am advised from every quarter in the island that there would not be a popular vote of 5 percent in favor of independence.

The people are making progress from the effects of hurricane, drought, and the business depression, all of which were imposed upon a century-old poverty. They are showing great courage and initiative in this rehabilitation. They will this season in large degree have recovered their crops.

The devastating effect of the hurricane is still represented in the thousands of one-room shacks housing whole families. The most constructive contribution of the Federal Government is to continue and expand the present policies of aid to and cooperation with their institutions in education, health, better adaptation of agriculture, and expansion of industry and markets.

The Virgin Islands may have some military value sometime. Opinion upon this question is much divided. In any event, when we paid $25 million for them, we acquired an effective poorhouse, comprising 90 percent of the population.

The people cannot be self-supporting either in living or government without the discovery of new methods and resources.

The purpose of the transfer of the administration from the naval to a civil department is to see if we can develop some form of industry or agriculture which will relieve us of the present costs and liabilities in support of the population or the local government from the Federal Treasury or from private charity.

Viewed from every point except remote naval contingencies, it was unfortunate that we ever acquired these islands. Nevertheless, having assumed the responsibility, we must do our best to assist the inhabitants.

113

White House Statement on Government Policies To Reduce Immigration.
March 26, 1931

PRESIDENT HOOVER, to protect American workingmen from further competition for positions by new alien immigration during the existing conditions of employment, initiated action last September looking to a material reduction in the number of aliens entering this country. At his request, the Department of State examined the operation of the immigration law and reported that the only important provision of the law useful in the circumstances is that one requiring the exclusion of those who are liable to become public charges. Since then consular officials, charged with the duty of issuing visas to intending immigrants, have carefully examined each applicant. A tabulation completed today shows that during the first 5 months ending February 28, 1931, of the administration of the "likely to become a public charge" provision approximately 96,883 aliens did not receive visas who normally would have immigrated into this country.

Reports from American consuls assigned to 21 countries whose annual quotas total 148,466 of the total quota of 153,714 indicate that only 10,277 visas were issued during the 5-month period against a possible 74,233 allowable under law, or an under-issue of 86 percent.

Incomplete reports from the remaining 46 countries with annual quotas totalling 5,248 indicate an issue of 270 visas, a reduction of 90 percent.

Canada and Mexico furnished 70 and 19 percent, respectively, of the 61,504 nonquota visas reported issued during the fiscal year ended June 30, 1930, remaining 11 percent having been issued to natives of Central and South America.

During the 5-month period involved only 3,876 visas were issued to natives of Canada and 884 visas to natives of Mexico, as compared to 15,997 and 19,336 visas, respectively, in the corresponding 5 months of the last completed normal fiscal year, thus representing decreases of 76 and 95 percent.

NOTE: For the inauguration of the new immigration policy, see 1930 volume, Item 288.

Tables released with the statement follow:

TABLE I.—IMMIGRATION QUOTA VISA STATISTICS

OCTOBER 1930, TO FEBRUARY 1931, INCLUSIVE, COUNTRIES WITH QUOTAS OF 300 OR MORE

Country	Half of annual quota [1]	Relatives of American citizens	Farmers	Relatives of aliens	Nonpreference	Total quota visas reported issued	Percent issued [2]	Percent under-issued [2]	Percent nonpreference issued [3]	Percent nonpreference under-issued [3]
	1	2	3	4	5	6	7	8	9	10
Austria......	706	17	14	27	32	90	13	87	05	95
Belgium......	652	9	17	21	57	104	16	84	09	91
Czechoslo-vakia......	1,437	113	23	273	6	415	29	71	01	99
Denmark.....	591	11	24	36	70	141	24	76	13	87
Finland......	284	12	63	47	1	123	43	57	01	99
France.......	1,543	14	19	52	221	306	20	80	15	85
Germany.....	12,979	95	51	482	784	1,412	11	89	06	94

See footnotes at end of table.

159

TABLE I.—IMMIGRATION QUOTA VISA STATISTICS—Continued

Country	Half of annual quota [1]	Preference			Nonpreference	Total quota visas reported issued	Percent issued [2]	Percent under-issued [2]	Percent nonpreference issued [3]	Percent nonpreference under-issued [3]
		Relatives of American citizens	Farmers	Relatives of aliens						
	1	2	3	4	5	6	7	8	9	10
Great Britain and Northern Ireland.....	32, 860	39	4	573	1, 819	2, 435	07	93	06	94
Greece.......	154	74	....	59	2	135	88	12	09	91
Hungary.....	434	133	17	62	14	226	52	48	06	94
Irish Free State.......	8, 927	11	....	27	283	321	04	96	03	97
Italy........	2, 901	1, 097	2	508	70	1, 677	58	42	05	95
Lithuania....	193	60	11	49	....	120	62	38	00	100
Netherlands..	1, 576	14	32	41	354	441	28	72	24	76
Norway......	1, 189	24	43	68	164	299	25	75	16	84
Poland.......	3, 262	407	27	194	....	628	19	81	00	100
Portugal.....	220	25	....	146	....	171	78	22	00	100
Russia.......	1, 392	135	16	81	376	608	44	56	32	68
Sweden......	1, 657	14	30	41	193	278	17	83	12	88
Switzerland ..	853	14	17	30	79	140	16	84	10	90
Yugoslavia...	423	70	46	33	58	207	49	51	21	79
Total..	74, 233	2, 388	456	2, 850	4, 583	10, 277	14	86	07	93

[1] Only 10 percent of quotas which are 300 or over may be issued each month.

[2] Percent of possible issue actually issued or under-issued.

[3] The figures given under column 9 represent the percentage of nonpreference visas issued as compared to the 5 months possible issue after reduction of the preference cases listed under columns 2, 3, and 4. The figures under column 10 represent the corresponding under-issue of visas.

NOTE.—The above figures represent visas actually reported as issued under each quota. In some instances reports on other visas for which quota numbers have been allotted to distant consulates are received by the quota control officers too late for inclusion in reports to the Department of State. The figures given for visas issued are therefore in some cases provisional in character and are slightly less than the total obtained at a later date.

160

TABLE II.—IMMIGRATION QUOTA VISA STATISTICS

OCTOBER 1930, TO FEBRUARY 1931, INCLUSIVE, COUNTRIES WITH QUOTAS OF LESS THAN 300
TOTALING 5,248 ANNUALLY [1]

Month	Average monthly issue	Actual issue	Numerical decrease
October.....................................	524	101	423
November....................................	525	41	484
December....................................	525	34	491
January.....................................	525	55	470
February....................................	525	39	486
Total.................................	2,624	270	2,354

[1] Includes 46 countries, most of which have quotas of 100 annually.

TABLE III.—NONQUOTA IMMIGRATION VISA STATISTICS REGARDING NATIVES OF CANADA

OCTOBER 1930, TO FEBRUARY 1931, INCLUSIVE, WITH COMPARISON OF SAME PERIOD LAST FISCAL YEAR

	5 months ended Feb. 28, 1931	5 months ended Feb. 28, 1930	Numerical decrease
October.....................................	1,608	6,117	4,509
November	808	3,770	2,962
December....................................	603	2,109	1,506
January.....................................	483	2,115	1,632
February....................................	374	1,886	1,512
Total.................................	3,876	15,997	12,121

161

TABLE IV.—NONQUOTA IMMIGRATION VISA STATISTICS REGARDING NATIVES OF MEXICO

OCTOBER 1930, TO FEBRUARY 1931, INCLUSIVE, WITH COMPARISON OF SAME PERIOD LAST FISCAL YEAR BEFORE THE PRESENT ADMINISTRATIVE MEASURES WERE PLACED IN OPERATION

	5 months ended Feb. 28, 1931	5 months ended Feb. 28, 1930	Numerical decrease
October	236	4,030	3,794
November	189	3,963	3,774
December	217	3,743	3,526
January	157	3,425	3,268
February	85	4,175	4,090
Total	884	19,336	18,452

114

Message to King Fuad I of Egypt on His Birthday.
March 28, 1931

[Released March 28, 1931.   Dated March 26, 1931]

I SEND TO Your Majesty my sincere felicitations on the occasion of your birthday. May the ties of friendship and good understanding existing between Egypt and the United States continue to increase and prosper.

HERBERT HOOVER

[His Majesty Fuad I, King of Egypt, Cairo]

115

Message Endorsing Military Training Camps.
March 28, 1931

[Released March 28, 1931.   Dated April 19, 1930]

My dear Mr. James:

The Citizens' Military Training Camps have through ten years proved themselves important agencies of physical and moral health in the individual and of civic welfare in the Nation. The willingness of young men to devote a month to this training program for better citizenship is proof of good-will in the generation on which will presently devolve the maintenance of our social and political institutions.

I commend the Citizens' Camps to all fathers and mothers and to young men of suitable age in the hope and belief that the camps will show themselves as useful in the future as they have been in the past.

Yours faithfully,

HERBERT HOOVER

[Mr. George F. James, National Executive Secretary, Military Training Camps Association, 705 Tower Building, 6 North Michigan Avenue, Chicago, Illinois]

NOTE: The letter was made public by Maj. Gen. Hanson E. Ely. The Military Training Camps program, which provided summer camps for civilians to receive military instruction, was established by the War Department in 1921.

116

The President's News Conference of
March 31, 1931

FEDERAL TAXES AND SPENDING

THE PRESIDENT. I have canvassed the financial situation in the Government exhaustively with our different departments, and I can state that there will be no increases in taxes if the next Congress imposes no increases on the budget or the expenditure proposals which the administration will present. But for Congress to do this the people must cooperate to effectively discourage and postpone the consideration of demands of sectional and group interest.

WILLIAM R. CASTLE, JR.

I have to announce that Mr. Castle will be the new Under Sectary of State.

ADMINISTRATIVE ASSISTANT TO THE PRESIDENT

Mr. [French] Strother will by the first of June have completed the 2 years for which he agreed to come to the White House, and he will be returning to his work, much to our regret. In the meantime, Mr. Joslin will carry on, at least for sometime to come—carry on Mr. Strother's work as well as his own.

EARTHQUAKE IN MANAGUA, NICARAGUA

The flash has just come in that Managua, the capital of Nicaragua, has been destroyed by an earthquake and is now burning up. I have directed the Red Cross to take the matter in hand at once, and the Army and Navy will cooperate with them.

Further than that I have no news.

NOTE: President Hoover's one hundred and eighty-third news conference was held in the White House at 12 noon on Tuesday, March 31, 1931.

On the same day, the White House issued a text of the President's statement on Federal taxes and expenditures (see Item 117).

Theodore G. Joslin was Secretary to the President.

Managua, Nicaragua was struck by an earthquake at 10:02 a.m. on March 31, 1931. An estimated 1,000 people were killed, and 25,000 were left homeless. On April 3, relief and rehabilitation operations were organized under a Central Relief Committee, composed of Americans and Nicaraguans, headed by Matthew E. Hanna, American Minister to Nicaragua.

164

117

Statement on Federal Taxes and Expenditures.
March 31, 1931

THE PRESIDENT said:

"There will be no increases in taxes if the next Congress imposes no increases upon the budget or other expenditure proposals which the administration will present. But for Congress to do this the people must cooperate to effectively discourage and postpone consideration of the demands of sectional and group interests."

118

Message of Sympathy to President José María Moncada
About the Earthquake in Nicaragua.
April 1, 1931

[Released April 1, 1931.   Dated March 31, 1931]

I AM appalled at the catastrophe which has overwhelmed Managua and in my own name and that of the American Government and people I extend heartfelt sympathy to Your Excellency and the people of Nicaragua.

HERBERT HOOVER

[His Excellency General José María Moncada, President of Nicaragua, Managua, Nicaragua]

119

Message of Sympathy on the Death of Knute Rockne.
April 1, 1931

I KNOW that every American grieves with you. Mr. Rockne so contributed to a cleanness and high purpose and sportsmanship in athletics that his passing is a national loss.

HERBERT HOOVER

NOTE: The message was sent to Mrs. Knute Rockne, South Bend, Ind.

Knute Rockne, football coach at the University of Notre Dame since 1914, died in a plane crash near Cottonwood Falls, Kans., on March 31, 1931.

120

The President's News Conference of
April 3, 1931

RUMORS OF CABINET RESIGNATIONS

THE PRESIDENT. I haven't anything of any great importance today. Just for background and to quiet some of the recent rumors for you, I can tell you that Messrs. [Ray Lyman] Wilbur, [William D.] Mitchell, and [Arthur M.] Hyde are not going to resign from the Cabinet. That is not for quotation but just so that you will know. And in case that hardy perennial about Mr. [Andrew W.] Mellon turns up, you can be satisfied that that won't happen either.

Q. That comes on Thursday.

THE PRESIDENT. Yes. The Wilbur one seems to be happening every Friday now.

But otherwise I haven't anything at all today. If you can think up some device by which we can stir public interest you might let me know.

NOTE: President Hoover's one hundred and eighty-fourth news conference was held in the White House at 4 p.m. on Friday, April 3, 1931.

121

The President's News Conference of
April 7, 1931

THE PRESIDENT. I haven't anything myself today, but Secretary Hyde has just been through the whole of the major drought area and he can tell you direct—and much more useful to you than if I told you indirectly—what is going on. So I am going to leave the job in his hands.

INSPECTION OF DROUGHT AREA BY SECRETARY OF AGRICULTURE

SECRETARY HYDE. Gentlemen, for your information, all of our drought area is covered by the Memphis, St. Louis, and Washington offices. I went out and covered St. Louis and Memphis, and then made a rather extended trip out in the field—into Arkansas.

These drought relief loans have undoubtedly reached the spot. All through Tennessee and the northern part of Mississippi and Louisiana, and in Arkansas you can see new garden fences. The ground is prepared and they have the seed and the means for making a new crop. They are going at it on a better basis than they have been before because one of the requirements of our loans has been that they should put in a garden for the purpose of maintaining the farm family, and that requirement, I am delighted to find, has been followed out so far as I could observe in every case. Those gardens are beginning to come through the ground. Of course, the crops are not yet visible. Planting has not gone very far but the preparation has.

Now, the extent of this thing may be interesting to you. Up until this morning we had made 186,632 separate loans, for an aggregate amount of $27,472,000. That is an average of $153 a family.

In talking to men by the side of the road and driving in to farmhouses and talking to local committees that are interested in the distribution of these loans, I find that there is a very much more hopeful attitude all through the country, not only out on the farms but in the towns. I didn't find a single criticism. One old fellow by the side of the road did have a criticism to the effect that the Red Cross had not fed too little but that they fed too much. So I take it they have done a splendid job all through that part of the country. I talked with the head of the Red Cross, with the Extension [Service] directors, and with bankers, and without any exception they were loud in their praise of these seed loans and the Red Cross operations.

If there are any questions I will be glad to answer.

A very important feature of that is the fact that they have had some very fine rains out there—not the torrential rain that washes everything out, but nice slow drizzling rain that soaks down into the ground.

QUESTIONS

Q. How about the livestock?

SECRETARY HYDE. Livestock—they just don't have very much—a pair of mules and perhaps in some rare instances a cow, but that is one of the criticisms of their agriculture out there.

Q. Do you loan money to buy a cow?

SECRETARY HYDE. No, we can loan money to feed one and are doing that, but if they don't have one they are out of luck.

THE PRESIDENT. There has been no loss of livestock in that territory?

SECRETARY HYDE. No.

Q. Are those loans made on collateral?

SECRETARY HYDE. The only collateral with them is the crop to be made.

Q. No difficulty about any of the needy persons putting up collateral?

SECRETARY HYDE. No; we have been very lenient in scanning all loans of $100 or less, and have indulged in rather hopeful optimism about the crop they are going to have.

Q. Was there any human suffering that you heard about?

SECRETARY HYDE. They didn't tell me of a bit. There undoubtedly was some until the Red Cross got in operation. There undoubtedly would have been a great deal except for the operation of the Red Cross, but from every quarter I receive the information that that need had been met in a splendid way.

Q. Does this $27 million about clean up the situation?

SECRETARY HYDE. I tried to find out something about that but the committees were absolutely undecided. One committee reported 95 percent through, another said 75 percent, and another said 40 percent— and I don't know what to say. My guess would be that we have made more than half of the loans that will need to be made.

Q. You have $45 million for that purpose?

SECRETARY HYDE. $55 million, that includes the agricultural.

THE PRESIDENT. You have $65 million altogether.

SECRETARY HYDE. Yes. We have $10 million set aside for the agricultural credit; $45 million for seed; and $10 million for feed and fertilizer.

168

Q. Mr. Secretary, can you tell me anything about the permanence of those agricultural credit operations?

SECRETARY HYDE. We are trying very determinedly to have them settled on a basis of permanence. We are finding the committees in the various States working along that same basis. We require a little bit of contribution of local credit in order to guarantee a continuing local interest and the type of management that will make them successful. We are working very closely with the State committees and the intermediate credit banks that cover these areas.

Q. Do you calculate that the agricultural credit corporations will be a permanent understructure to the intermediate credit banks?

SECRETARY HYDE. I hope so—yes.

Q. You don't need any further legislation to do that?

SECRETARY HYDE. No. That is the whole purpose of that act. And we hope to do it on a basis that will be permanent.

Mr. Joslin suggests that the question might arise as to whether or not these rains had broken the drought and offered a prospect for a good crop this year. I think we can answer very positively—they have broken the drought and if normal precipitation is figured through the season we could say they would have a very fine crop down there. That to some extent depends upon what happens hereafter, but there is nothing pessimistic in the present outlook.

NOTE: President Hoover's one hundred and eighty-fifth news conference was held in the White House at 12 noon on Tuesday, April 7, 1931.

Secretary of Agriculture Arthur M. Hyde left Washington on March 30 for a 4-day inspection tour of conditions in the drought areas.

Theodore G. Joslin was Secretary to the President.

122

Letter to the Chairman of the United States Tariff Commission
on Duties on Cherries and Tomatoes.
April 7, 1931

[Released April 7, 1931.   Dated April 1, 1931]

My dear Mr. Chairman:

I am returning without approval, the reports of the Commission on
tomatoes, prepared or preserved in any manner, and on cherries, sul-
phured or in brine. No criticism of the work of the Commission, either
direct or indirect, is implied but this investigation was of necessity based
upon conditions maintaining before the emergency created by the
drought and in some cases upon data over a period of so short experience
as make it desirable that the Commission be afforded more time.

I should like it therefore if the Commission would undertake to review the facts upon the basis of the forthcoming crops and make another
report.

Yours faithfully,

HERBERT HOOVER

[Hon. Henry P. Fletcher, Chairman, U.S. Tariff Commission, Washington, D.C.]

123

Message to the Salvation Army
in Philadelphia, Pennsylvania.
April 7, 1931

[Released April 7, 1931.   Dated April 6, 1931]

My dear Brigadier Harvey:

The people of Philadelphia have done a splendid work in providing
local relief of local distress in these difficult times. The Committee for
Unemployment Relief under the Chairmanship of Mr. Horatio G.
Lloyd has accomplished a great humanitarian task. The independent

cooperation of the Salvation Army in this work has been invaluable. I am deeply interested in your efforts to finance the continuance of these labors through the private generosity of the people of Philadelphia, and I shall hope that you may meet with the most generous response.

Yours faithfully,

HERBERT HOOVER

[Brigadier James A. Harvey, The Salvation Army, 701 North Broad Street, Philadelphia, Pa.]

NOTE: The message was made public in conjunction with the opening of a fundraising campaign by the Salvation Army in Philadelphia.

124

Message Endorsing the Children's Charter.
April 7, 1931

CHILDREN ARE our most precious possession. The Children's Charter was written by 3,500 experienced men and women, after many months of study. It condenses into few words the fullest knowledge and the best plans for making every child healthier, safer, wiser, better and happier. These plans must be constantly translated into action. Fathers and mothers, doctors and teachers, the churches and the lay organizations, the officers of government in the states and counties and towns, all have one common obligation—to advance these plans of better life for the children. I urge upon you an even larger interest in it.

HERBERT HOOVER

NOTE: The message was printed in a brochure of the Children's Charter, distributed by the White House Conference on Child Health and Protection. A text of the Charter follows:

THE CHILDREN'S CHARTER

PRESIDENT HOOVER'S WHITE HOUSE CONFERENCE ON CHILD HEALTH AND PROTECTION RECOGNIZING THE RIGHTS OF THE CHILD AS THE FIRST RIGHTS OF CITIZENSHIP PLEDGES ITSELF TO THESE AIMS FOR THE CHILDREN OF AMERICA

FOR every child spiritual and moral training to help him to stand firm under the pressure of life

II For every child understanding and the guarding of his personality as his most precious right

III For every child a home and that love and security which a home provides; and for that child who must receive foster care, the nearest substitute for his own home

IV For every child full preparation for his birth, his mother receiving prenatal, natal, and postnatal care; and the establishment of such protective measures as will make child-bearing safer

V For every child health protection from birth through adolescence, including: periodical health examinations and, where needed, care of specialists and hospital treatment; regular dental examination and care of the teeth; protective and preventive measures against communicable diseases; the insuring of pure food, pure milk, and pure water

VI For every child from birth through adolescence, promotion of health, including health instruction and a health program, wholesome physical and mental recreation, with teachers and leaders adequately trained

VII For every child a dwelling place safe, sanitary, and wholesome, with reasonable provisions for privacy, free from conditions which tend to thwart his development; and a home environment harmonious and enriching

VIII For every child a school which is safe from hazards, sanitary, properly equipped, lighted, and ventilated. For younger children nursery schools and kindergartens to supplement home care

IX For every child a community which recognizes and plans for his needs, protects him against physical dangers, moral hazards, and disease; provides him with safe and wholesome places for play and recreation; and makes provision for his cultural and social needs

X For every child an education which, through the discovery and development of his individual abilities, prepares him for life; and through training and vocational guidance prepares him for a living which will yield him the maximum of satisfaction

XI For every child such teaching and training as will prepare him for successful parenthood, homemaking, and the rights of citizenship; and, for parents, supplementary training to fit them to deal wisely with the problems of parenthood

XII For every child education for safety and protection against accidents to which modern conditions subject him—those to which he is directly exposed and those which, through loss or maiming of his parents, affect him indirectly

XIII For every child who is blind, deaf, crippled, or otherwise physically handicapped, and for the child who is mentally handicapped, such measures as will early discover and diagnose his handicap, provide care and treatment, and so

172

train him that he may become an asset to society rather than a liability. Expenses of these services should be borne publicly where they cannot be privately met

XIV For every child who is in conflict with society the right to be dealt with intelligently as society's charge, not society's outcast; with the home, the school, the church, the court and the institution when needed, shaped to return him whenever possible to the normal stream of life

XV For every child the right to grow up in a family with an adequate standard of living and the security of a stable income as the surest safeguard against social handicaps

XVI For every child protection against labor that stunts growth, either physical or mental, that limits education, that deprives children of the right of comradeship, of play, and of joy

XVII For every rural child as satisfactory schooling and health services as for the city child, and an extension to rural families of social, recreational, and cultural facilities

XVIII To supplement the home and the school in the training of youth, and to return to them those interests of which modern life tends to cheat children, every stimulation and encouragement should be given to the extension and development of the voluntary youth organizations

XIX To make everywhere available these minimum protections of the health and welfare of children, there should be a district, county, or community organization for health, education, and welfare, with full-time officials, coordinating with a state-wide program which will be responsive to a nation-wide service of general information, statistics, and scientific research. This should include:

(*a*) Trained, full-time public health officials, with public health nurses, sanitary inspection, and laboratory workers

(*b*) Available hospital beds

(*c*) Full-time public welfare service for the relief, aid, and guidance of children in special need due to poverty, misfortune, or behavior difficulties, and for the protection of children from abuse, neglect, exploitation, or moral hazard

For EVERY child these rights, regardless of race, or color, or situation, wherever he may live under the protection of the American flag

125

Message to Albert, King of the Belgians, on His Birthday.
April 9, 1931

[Released April 9, 1931.   Dated April 8, 1931]

IT GIVES me much pleasure on this anniversary of Your Majesty's birth to send to you hearty congratulations and best wishes for a long and prosperous reign.

HERBERT HOOVER

[His Majesty Albert, King of the Belgians, Brussels]

126

Message to a Dinner Honoring James H. Kimball.
April 9, 1931

[Released April 9, 1931.   Dated April 8, 1931]

I WILL BE obliged if you will express my cordial greetings to those present at the dinner in honor of Dr. James H. Kimball tomorrow evening, and to Dr. Kimball himself my warm appreciation of his signal services in promoting the success of aviation in general and transatlantic flights in particular through his scientific skill and judgment so characteristic of the entire weather forecasting service of our country.

HERBERT HOOVER

[Mr. Lewis Yancey, Transatlantic Fliers Committee, Hotel Roosevelt, New York City]

NOTE: The message was read at a dinner held in the Hotel Roosevelt in New York City. James H. Kimball, associate meteorologist at the Weather Bureau in New York City, had prepared North Atlantic maps for transatlantic flying and was consulting meteorologist for many pilots and explorers.

127

Message to a Dinner of the American Institute.
April 9, 1931

I WILL BE obliged if you will express my cordial greetings to those present at the dinner of the American Institute on Thursday evening. It is distinctly worthwhile to remind the public not only that many great industrial enterprises are based upon the technical and mechanical requirements of the Army and Navy but also that many inventions and new processes of the greatest value to mankind are the outgrowth of researches undertaken in behalf of these national establishments.

HERBERT HOOVER

[A. Cressy Morrison, President, The American Institute, Fisk Building, Broadway at 57th Street, New York City]

NOTE: The message was read at a dinner held in the Hotel Astor in New York City.

128

Statement on the Death of Nicholas Longworth, Speaker of the House of Representatives.
April 9, 1931

MR. LONGWORTH served his fellow countrymen in State and Nation for over 33 years—nearly the whole of his adult life. In his service he contributed greatly to the welfare of the American people. His happy character, his sterling honesty, his courage in public questions, endeared him and held the respect not alone of his myriad of friends but of the country at large. His passing is a loss to the Nation.

NOTE: Nicholas Longworth served in the House of Representatives from 1903–1913 and from 1915 until his death, and was Speaker of the House from 1925.

129

Message of Sympathy
on the Death of Nicholas Longworth,
Speaker of the House of Representatives.
April 9, 1931

My dear Mrs. Longworth:

I am profoundly grieved to learn of the passing of your husband, and wish you to know how deeply Mrs. Hoover and I sympathize with you in your bereavement. He was endeared to the whole people by his charm and graciousness, and his distinguished public services entitled him to the honors which he bore so modestly and yet so worthily. He will be mourned by the Nation and long held in their affectionate and grateful memory.

> Yours faithfully,
> HERBERT HOOVER

[Mrs. Nicholas Longworth, care of James F. Curtis, Aiken, South Carolina]

130

Executive Order 5595,
Death of Nicholas Longworth,
Speaker of the House of Representatives.
April 9, 1931

THE HONORABLE NICHOLAS LONGWORTH

AS A MARK of respect to the memory of the Honorable Nicholas Longworth, late Speaker and Member of the House of Representatives of the United States, it is hereby ordered that the flags on the White House and public buildings in the District of Columbia and the State of

Ohio be placed at half mast today and on the day of the funeral service at Cincinnati, Ohio, Saturday, April 11, 1931.

HERBERT HOOVER

The White House,
    April 9, 1931.

131

Message to the Aeronautical Chamber of Commerce of America.
April 11, 1931

[Released April 11, 1931. Dated April 10, 1931]

PLEASE CONVEY to the members of the Aeronautical Chamber of Commerce my hope that the conferences and exposition which open today will contribute to the substantial development of the aircraft industry. As I indicated to the delegation representing your body on March fifth, it is my great desire to see commercial aviation established on the right basis. This can best come through air transport and after air transport through business and private flying.

HERBERT HOOVER

[Charles L. Lawrance, President, Aeronautical Chamber of Commerce of America, Inc., Book-Cadillac Hotel, Detroit, Michigan]

NOTE: The message was read at a luncheon opening the National Air Show for 1931. The exposition was held at Detroit's Municipal Airport.

132

Message on the 42d Anniversary
of the Slovak Amerike.
April 12, 1931

[Released April 12, 1931. Dated February 26, 1931]

THE SLOVAK people in the United States have brought to this new land of their choice many valuable qualities of mind and character that have enriched our national life. Their loyalty to American institutions and ideals is an earnest of continued service of country.

HERBERT HOOVER

NOTE: The message was read at a dinner, held in the Commodore Hotel in New York City, commemorating the founding of the Slovak Amerike, a Slovakian newspaper published in New York City. The message was sent to C. L. Orbach, president of the newspaper.

133

Address to the Annual Convention of the
American National Red Cross.
April 13, 1931

I AM PARTICULARLY glad to welcome this annual convention of the American Red Cross. During this past year this great mutual institution of the whole people has been put again to severe tests, not only as to its practical ability to meet national disaster but a test involving its whole moral and spiritual purpose. You have, under most difficult handicaps, again demonstrated that it can meet and relieve human suffering in any national disaster.

The drought presented a new type of problem for the Red Cross—the problem of famine in over 2 millions of people. Your leaders, alive to the possibility of suffering which would be the inescapable result during the winter, began as early as last August to mobilize the Red Cross to meet the inevitable burden. It was that far-sighted action and that early action which enabled the saving of this multitude of people from infinite suffering. Unfortunately, men less familiar with the resources and the ability and the courage of the American people in mutual action under their own Red Cross, men no doubt genuinely concerned over the growing seriousness of the situation, were skeptical of your abilities and the forces which give it strength, and were insistent that the Red Cross should abandon its voluntary character, should abandon its independence and its foundations in service which are part of the spiritual life of our country, and become in effect a Government bureau through Federal appropriations as the source of its funds. They did not realize that the Red Cross represents a vital and precious force in our people— their ability and strength in voluntary action and their sense of service and of moral responsibility. For the Red Cross springs from the people; it is of the people—it is a part of their spiritual expression. It was a momentous decision which confronted you, to refuse the easy course that was proposed, and it has been due to you, officers and members of the Red Cross in every city and hamlet of the United States, to your courage, your resolution, and devotion, that it has been possible even in a time of extreme economic difficulty to prove your strength and ability to meet national emergencies, by finding from your members the financial resources on the one hand and the ability and the sense of service for distribution on the other. If your officers had yielded on this occasion the Red Cross would have been rendered impotent in the face of every future national emergency, for it would have been inevitable to turn to the Government and the taxpayer; it would have meant the destruction of the spirit of the Red Cross and it would have been the destruction of something even greater than voluntary service—it would have injured the spiritual responses of the American people. It would have been a step on the pathway of Government doles.

In problems of this kind we are dealing with the intangibles of life and ideals. We are dealing also with the highest thing in our civilization, that is, the sense of personal responsibility of neighbor for neighbor, the spirit of charity and benevolence in the individual, the holding alight the lamp of voluntary action in American life. A voluntary deed

179

by a man impressed with the sense of responsibility and brotherhood of man is infinitely more precious to our national ideals and national spirit than a thousandfold poured from the Treasury of the Government under the compulsion of law. Your organization is indeed the highest form of self-government, that is, for our people to organize themselves without the force of law.

The spiritual question is not solely a problem of giving and raising funds; it is equally a question of their distribution—for here again is mobilized the sense of voluntary service. There is within it the solicitude and care given to the individual in distress based upon his need and not upon his claim of right or influence. The very spirit that makes the Red Cross possible assures it a probity and devotion in service which no government can ever attain.

In all this there is the imponderable of spiritual ideal and spiritual growth. It is indeed the spiritual in the individual and in the Nation which looks out with keen interest on the well-being of others, forgetful of ourselves, beyond our own preoccupation with our own selfish interests and gives us a sense of belonging to the great company of mankind, sharing in the great plan of the universe and the definite order which pervades it. To impose this burden upon someone else by the arm of the law does not awaken the spirit of our people. A great spiritual value comes to those who give from the thankful heart who give because of their sensibility to suffering. It is this spiritual value, which is exemplified in the Red Cross, that is of transcendent value to our Nation. It is because of the courage and maintenance of this spirit and this value that I wish on this occasion to pay tribute to each and every man of you and to your board of governors, and more especially to your Chairman. You have not alone served our country in distress but you have contributed to preserve a great ideal in our people. You have proved yourselves not only a practical instrument of mercy and relief but you have renewed and invigorated the spiritual life of the Nation.

You are inscribing another bright chapter in the history of the American Red Cross; and you are inserting a chapter of spiritual growth of our country.

180

NOTE: The President spoke at 10:30 a.m. to the opening meeting of the annual convention of the American National Red Cross, assembled in Constitution Hall, Washington, D.C.

134

Radio Remarks to the National Recreation Association. *April 13, 1931*

I AM GLAD to welcome the directors of the National Recreation Association at the White House on this occasion. The Association was organized at the White House 25 years ago, and it is a most fitting place for your 25th anniversary meeting.

I have followed the work of the Association for many years. It has taken a most significant and a magnificent part in the whole recreational development of the country. Its work today is of increasing importance because of the growing congestion of cities on one hand, and the increasing leisure of our people on the other. The whole recreational movement is one not only vital to public health but it is vital to public welfare. The growing congestion of the cities presents constantly new problems of physical and moral and mental training of children on one hand, and the growing leisure by shortened hours of labor presents increasing problems in provision of opportunity for proper use of increasing leisure for adults. Many less problems in government arise which concern people while they are at work than while they are at leisure. They do not often go to jail for activities when they are on their jobs. Most of our problems arise when the people are off the job. Every progress in constructive recreation for leisure time not only improves health but also morals.

The Federal Government during the period of the Association's activities and to a considerable degree due to the efforts of the Association, has developed in itself a great number of recreational activities. I assume that the growth of social aspects of government will increase the interest of the government in recreational questions, and we need the assistance of the Association in directing these policies. If there is anything that we can do to cooperate with the Association in any direction you will find a most hearty welcome to the views of the Association in every section of the Government.

I wish to express to you the most profound admiration that I hold for the work of the Association and to extend to you my best wishes for its further development.

NOTE: The President spoke in the Cabinet Room of the White House. The event commemorated a meeting of the founders of the Association in the White House on April 12, 1906, at the invitation of President Theodore Roosevelt.

135

Address to the Pan American Union.
April 14, 1931

Gentlemen of the Governing Board:

I am glad to be your guest at this special session of the Governing Board of the Pan American Union which you are holding in honor of Pan American Day. I recently issued a proclamation,[1] calling upon our people to give this day due observance, and this proclamation has received general approval throughout the country. Exercises are being held at this time in public schools and universities and by civic organizations in every section of the Union. Pan American Day will become an outward symbol of the constantly strengthening unity of purpose and unity of ideals of the Republics of this hemisphere.

In the latter part of 1928, I had the privilege of visiting 11 of the countries of Latin America.[2] This visit made a deep and lasting impression upon me. It was inspiring to observe, at first hand, not only the progress that Latin America is making along social, economic, and cultural lines, but also the important part which the countries you represent are destined to play in world affairs. It was clear, too, that the nations of America have everything to gain by keeping in close touch with one another

[1] See 1930 volume, Item 169.
[2] See 1929 volume, Supplement IV.

and by developing that spirit of mutual confidence which has its roots in a reciprocal understanding of national aims and aspirations.

Although each of the Republics of this hemisphere possesses problems peculiar to itself, there are certain basic questions relating to democratic progress and social betterment common to us all and in the solution of which we can be most helpful to one another. This spirit of mutual helpfulness is the cornerstone of true Pan Americanism. The Pan American Union not only symbolizes this spirit, but gives to it concrete expression in many practical and constructive ways.

It is of the greatest importance that the people of the United States become better acquainted with the history, the traditions, the culture, and the ideals of the other Republics of America. To an increasing extent, courses on the languages, literature, and history of the nations of Latin America are being offered in the educational institutions of the United States. A similar realization of the importance of becoming better acquainted with the history and development of the United States exists in the countries of Latin America. Increasing numbers of students from the countries to the south are being enrolled in the colleges and universities of the United States. I cannot emphasize too strongly this important aspect of inter-American relations. These cultural currents not only contribute to better international understanding, but also emphasize the essential unity of interest of the American Republics.

Through the Pan American Society and its branches established in different sections of the country, the importance and significance of the culture of the Latin American nations are being brought home to our people. We owe much to the unselfish men who have devoted so much time and energy to this work. The activities of the Pan American Society admirably supplement the important work that is being done by the Pan American Union.

A peculiarly heavy responsibility rests upon the nations of the Western Hemisphere; a responsibility which, at the same time, is a high privilege. Richly endowed by nature, we enjoy the great advantage of inhabiting a hemisphere free from the jealousies and antagonisms which have proved such obstacles to progress and prosperity in other sections of the world. We have developed an international system based on the principle of equality, combined with a full recognition of the obligations as well as the rights of states.

The American Republics are today rapidly approaching the time when every major difference existing between them will be settled by the orderly processes of conciliation and arbitration. In this respect, the Western Hemisphere has placed an enviable record before the nations of the world. From the earliest period of their history, the governments of the Republics of this hemisphere have been earnest advocates of the peaceful settlement of international disputes. They have demonstrated their willingness and even eagerness to adopt and apply mediation, conciliation, and arbitration. The common purpose to eliminate war and the determination to achieve peace and security represent a major contribution of the Americas to modern civilization.

The full significance of this achievement is not always realized, for it carries with it heavy obligations to posterity. Future progress along these lines can only be assured through constant vigilance and by an unswerving determination to make the union of the American Republics, as now expressed in the Pan American Union, an example to the world. We are not attempting in any way to develop a superstate, or to interfere with the freedom of action of any of the states, members of the Union, but rather to develop an atmosphere of good will—a spirit of cooperation and mutual understanding—in which any difference that may arise, no matter how important, will find a ready solution.

I cordially congratulate you, gentlemen of the Governing Board, on your happy initiative in establishing Pan American Day and, at the same time, I send a message of fraternal greeting, in the name of the people of the United States, to all the inhabitants of our sister Republics.

NOTE: The President spoke at 12:30 p.m. in the Pan American Building.

136

Radio Address on the 50th Anniversary of the Founding of Tuskegee Institute.
April 14, 1931

I CONSIDER IT a great privilege to take even a small part in this celebration of the 50th anniversary of Tuskegee Institute. Established half a century ago by Booker T. Washington through initial aid from the State of Alabama, it has grown into a great national educational institution devoted to the development of the Negro race and maintaining at all times a leadership in its advancement.

It is now over 60 years since the Negro was released from slavery and given the status of a citizen in our country whose wealth and general prosperity his labor has helped create. The progress of the race within this period has surpassed the most sanguine hopes of the most ardent advocates. No group of people in history ever started from a more complete economic and cultural destitution. The 50th anniversary of the founding of Tuskegee marks at the same time almost the semicentennial of Negro progress. Within that period the race has multiplied its wealth more than 130 times, has reduced its illiteracy from 95 percent to 20 percent, and reduced its death rate by one-half. It has risen to the ownership of more than 750,000 homes, has accumulated property to the value of billions, has developed a far-reaching internal network of social, religious, and economic organizations for the continued advancement of its people, has produced leadership in all walks of life that for faith, courage, devotion, and patriotic loyalty ranks with all the other groups in our country.

The greatest single factor in the progress of the Negro race has been the schools, private and public, established and conducted by high-minded, self-sacrificing men and women of both races and all sections of our country, maintained by the States and by private philanthropy, covering the whole field of education from primary school through to college and university. These public and private schools, particularly under the leadership of Tuskegee and other universities and colleges, have been the most effective agents in solving the problems created by the admission to citizenship of 4 million ex-slaves without preparation for their new responsibilities. That such a revolution in the social order did not produce a more serious upheaval in our national existence has been due to the constructive influence exerted by these educational institutions whose maintenance of further development is both a public and a private duty.

The Nation owes a debt of gratitude to the wisdom and constructive vision of Booker T. Washington, the founder of Tuskegee. His conception of education based fundamentally upon vocational and moral training has been worthily continued by his able successor, Dr. R. R. Moton, who likewise deserves the gratitude of the Nation for his many contributions to the solution of one of our most difficult national problems. His ability and sanity and modesty have been powerful forces in progress and good will.

We have still many problems to solve in this matter and no section of our country is without its responsibility or without room for progress and improvement. I am convinced that there are within the Negro race, as the result of these institutions, of which Tuskegee stands in the first rank, a body of men whose leadership and unselfishness can be depended upon to accomplish advancement and adjustment.

A notable example of the proper spirit of approach in sane handling of these problems is that developed in our Southern States by the Interracial Commission. This movement developed in the area where problems of interracial adjustment are presented on a large scale, has been represented in its leadership and direction by the best element of both races working in effective cooperation for the good of each and rendering valuable service to the whole country. Tuskegee Institute has greatly contributed to this movement. There can be no solution either in the communities or government that is not based upon sympathetic understanding and absolute justice.

Tuskegee has thus made a notable contribution not only to the day-to-day training of the members of its race for their part in the life of the Nation, but its leaders have made a higher contribution to the

186

adjustment of interracial problems which must awaken the gratitude of the Nation.

NOTE: The President spoke at 5:50 p.m. from the White House. The address was carried over the National Broadcasting Company and Columbia Broadcasting System radio networks.

Dr. Robert R. Moton was president of Tuskegee Institute.

A reading copy of this item with holograph changes by the President is available for examination at the Herbert Hoover Presidential Library.

137

Message to the New Jersey Conference on Child Health and Protection. *April 16, 1931*

[Released April 16, 1931. Dated April 13, 1931]

My dear Governor Larson:

I am deeply gratified that the State of New Jersey is undertaking at this time to crystalize and make applicable to New Jersey the recommendations of the recent White House Conference on Child Health and Protection and am especially gratified that you are lending your personal encouragement and appreciation to this work. I will be obliged if you will make known to the meeting on Thursday my warm appreciation of this great cooperative effort in behalf of childhood.

Yours faithfully,

HERBERT HOOVER

[Honorable Morgan Larson, Governor of New Jersey, care of New Jersey Conference of Social Work, 42 Bleecker Street, Newark, N.J.]

NOTE: The message was read by Governor Larson at a dinner welcoming delegates to the conference, held in Brunswick, N.J.

138

The President's News Conference of
April 17, 1931

NICARAGUAN BANDIT ACTIVITY

THE PRESIDENT. I have no statement for quotation today. I thought perhaps it might be helpful if I reviewed and gave you a little background
about this Nicaraguan situation. You will recollect that Sandino [1] has
been operating his group of bandits up in the north central part of
Nicaragua in the mountains on the borders of Honduras, and the
Marines and the National Guard have policed the country in such a
fashion that he has given no great disturbance for the last 3 or 4 years.
He has recently—in the last week or two—sent out three and possibly
four small bands of organized assassins coming down the rivers in
canoes to the west coast. That is in the territory that has hitherto been
entirely undisturbed by bandits. They have directed their activities towards isolated Nicaraguan and American plantations and have acted in
a fashion that would do discredit to an Iroquois Indian—with
free murder and assassination of isolated Americans and isolated
Nicaraguans.

You will recollect that the Nicaraguan Government undertook the
building up of a constabulary under American marine officers. That
constabulary has been built up to the point where it was able to take over
the responsibility for maintaining order, and we, therefore, were in a
position to withdraw the great bulk of our Marines. That constabulary
is much better adapted to hunting bandits and assassins than the normal
marines because they are better habituated to the bush and the kind of
fighting that that implies, so that we were in position to make very
large withdrawals in accordance with our previous undertakings and
agreements.

You have also to bear in mind that the whole of these forces of [the]
Guardia, except for perhaps 100 of the guards, that is, the constabulary, and the Marines are all concentrated on the west coast; that it is

---

[1] Augusto Cesar Sandino was the leader of a rebel group in Nicaragua.

200 miles across Nicaragua without a road; that to move forces from the west coast sections over into the sections near Bluefield on the east coast would be a matter literally of weeks; and they could not move any adequate army of equipment across. So that the Navy has done the very sensible thing of putting new forces into the east coast. And that in no way changes the fact that we have a surplus on the west coast, and there is no reason why we should not remove some of those marines and put whatever is necessary of forces along the east coast in order to protect the Americans in that quarter. Furthermore, the Navy is assisting the Nicaraguan Government to transport [the] Guardia across by airplanes to strengthen up their local force. These, as I say, are much better adapted to hunting bandits or assassins of this character, and they are taking over the job of working further inland and the American Marines will take care of the situation that arises along the coast.

There are some things that one could say about Mr. Sandino. Many of you have realized that he has been set up in some of our Latin American countries as a great patriot. He heads no political cause. He was a member of Mr. Moncada's [2] own army and part of Moncada's forces at the time of the revolution with which we had to deal 6 years ago. Moncada and his forces in an election held under American auspices—and a fair election—won out. In other words, Mr. Sandino's own party and his own political party, if he ever had one, is now in government of Nicaragua under Moncada. So that he is just a plain bandit. He has all the qualities and character of a city gangster in the United States. He is no patriot or he would not at the moment when Nicaragua is involved in a great calamity start more disturbances and embarrassments to his own country. That, however, is only a comment of a Nicaraguan citizen.

So far as Americans are concerned, they will be protected in the accessible places along the coast, and those who happen to be inland, of whom there are very few, are coming out to the coast. And the Guardia will get busy to see if they can get hold of Mr. Sandino. It does not look as if 100 men who are involved in it could do so much

---

[2] José María Moncada was President of Nicaragua.

but 100 men running loose in inaccessible country can make a lot of uncertainty and create a lot of harm and embarrassment to all citizens.

That is the actual situation. There is some confusion in the minds of the public over the fact of our withdrawal of marines from the west coast. But it would have no more relationship than if they were somewhere in the United States, 2,000 miles apart, because there is no communication between the two places. Such forces as we need to put on the east coast we can handle from Panama and Guantanamo in a third of the time—probably a tenth of the time—that we could handle them from the west coast. I do not myself anticipate that it is going to require any great force to take care of 100 or 150 assassins and gangsters, and that, therefore, it is not a national disturbance of the first order.

NOTE: President Hoover's one hundred and eighty-sixth news conference was held in the White House at 4 p.m. on Friday, April 17, 1931.

On April 11, 1931, rebels loyal to Augusto Cesar Sandino attacked Logtown, and on April 15, looted the coastal town of Cape Gracias a Dios. In this new outbreak of fighting, an American missionary and eight American employees of the Standard Fruit and Steamship Company were killed. By April 17, American gunboats arrived at ports on Nicaragua's east coast.

139

Message to the Annual Conventions of the Press Associations.
April 17, 1931

[Released April 17, 1931.   Dated April 15, 1931]

I HOPE the members of the press associations meeting in the next few days, the American Society of Newspaper Editors, the Associated Press, and the American Newspaper Publishers Association, may find renewed inspiration in their high service of country in these gatherings.

HERBERT HOOVER

NOTE: The message was printed in Editor and Publisher. The conventions of the press associations were being held in New York City during the week of April 21–24, 1931.

140

The President's News Conference of
April 21, 1931

THE PRESIDENT. I have two questions—one on Honduras and the other on Nicaragua.

HONDURAS

On Honduras we have no news other than what you have already in the press this morning.

NICARAGUAN BANDIT ACTIVITY

On Nicaragua our advices are that the Nicaraguan Government has now placed in the field a total of something over 1,300 men in the newly organized National Guard in a drive to clean up [Augusto Cesar] Sandino and his fellow bandits. Our representatives also advise that this force is several times the size of Mr. Sandino's group. His raids on important points have been frustrated by the disposition which has been made of the guard and the protection of our citizens on the coast has been doubly sure by the presence of naval vessels.

Sandino placed himself and his band outside the civilized pale by the coldblooded murder of eight or nine American citizens and many Nicaraguans at isolated places in the interior. The Nicaraguan Government has shown itself fully cognizant of its responsibilities. It is moving vigorously in spite of the difficulties created by the earthquake. It may require some time to accomplish their purpose due to the mountainous and jungle character of the territory in which Sandino operates, but I am perfectly confident that Sandino will be brought to justice.

Otherwise than that I have no news.

NOTE: President Hoover's one hundred and eighty-seventh news conference was held in the White House at 12 noon on Tuesday, April 21, 1931.

The President referred to a revolt in Honduras, which had begun on April 18, under the leadership of Gen. Gregoria Ferrera.

On the same day, the White House issued a text of the President's statement on the disturbance in Nicaragua (see Item 141).

141

Statement on Nicaraguan Bandit Activity.
April 21, 1931

THE PRESIDENT said:

"Our advices are that the Nicaraguan Government has now placed in the field a total of over 1,300 men of the newly created National Guard in a drive to clean up [Augusto Cesar] Sandino and his fellow bandits. Our representatives advise that this force is several times that of Sandino and his bands. His raids upon important points have been frustrated by the dispositions of the guard and protection of our citizens on the coast is made doubly sure by the presence of our naval vessels.

"Sandino has placed himself and his band outside the civilized pale by the coldblooded murder of eight or nine American civilians and many Nicaraguans at isolated places in the interior.

"The Nicaraguan Government has shown itself fully cognizant of its responsibilities. It is moving vigorously despite the difficulties created by the earthquake. While it may require some time to accomplish their purpose due to the mountainous and jungle character of the country, I am confident Sandino will be brought to justice."

142

Remarks on the Presentation of the Collier Trophy to Harold F. Pitcairn.
April 22, 1931

Mr. Pitcairn and gentlemen:

The invention of the autogiro by Mr. Juan de la Cierva is one of the outstanding improvements in heavier-than-air craft. Its ability to arise and descend with safety almost vertically makes it a practical and decided step forward. Six years ago you, Mr. Pitcairn, recognized its value and later brought it to the United States where you and your associates have continually developed the device. By widespread demonstrations you have inspired public confidence to the point where the National Aeronautic Association felt justified in awarding it the Collier Trophy "for the greatest achievement in aviation in America, the value of which has been demonstrated by actual use during the preceding year." On behalf of the National Aeronautic Association, it gives me great pleasure to present to you and your associates the Collier Trophy for your development and demonstration of the practicability of the autogiro in the United States. This trophy is emblematic of the highest award in American aeronautics.

I congratulate you.

NOTE: The President spoke at 12 noon at a presentation ceremony on the White House grounds.

Harold F. Pitcairn was president of the Autogiro Company of America. During the ceremonies, James G. Ray, a company pilot, demonstrated the autogiro in a vertical descent and take-off.

143

Exchange of Messages With President Wilhelm Miklas on the Inauguration of Radiotelegraphic Service Between Austria and the United States.
April 22, 1931

THE LINKING of the various countries of the world by rapid communications is a means for the enhancing of closer friendly relations, and the importance of which our peoples realize more and more as advances are made. It therefore gives me great pleasure to be able to inaugurate with you this new direct radio telegraph service between Austria and the United States.

HERBERT HOOVER

NOTE: President Miklas' message follows:

On the occasion of the opening of direct radiotelegraphic communication between the two countries, I have the honor to send you my best greetings, and to express the wish that this new channel of communication may contribute to extend and deepen relations between the United States of America and Austria.

MIKLAS

144

Message to the Second Pan American Conference of Directors of Health.
April 22, 1931

Mr. President and Gentlemen of the Conference:

It has been most gratifying to me to be able to receive and welcome you individually on the occasion of your Second Quinquennial meeting in the capital of this Republic.

I now take the opportunity of expressing to you collectively my sympathetic interest in your present important deliberations which are for the purpose of protecting the health and promoting the well-being of all the people of all the American Republics. Indeed, if I may judge from your program, your recommendations with regard to yellow fever and aerial transportation will have profound effect throughout the world.

It is pleasant to recall that, during the last thirty years, through advances made in the science of medicine and through the cooperation of the health authorities of all the American Republics, as manifested in your Pan American Sanitary Conferences, in the activities of the Pan American Sanitary Bureau and in your conferences of Directors of Health, the ravages of the major quarantinable diseases, such as yellow fever, plague, cholera, smallpox and typhus fever, diseases which formerly often decimated whole cities have nearly ceased. These pestilences are now almost entirely robbed of their power for harm. This being the case, you are able to turn your attention to the combating of other diseases and other unhealthful conditions which still interfere with the happiness and comfort of our people.

I note with satisfaction in your program the provision for the interchange of ideas with regard to the securing of safe water supplies, safe milk, the prevention of blindness, the welfare of the child, the study of nutrition and of many other interesting and important topics.

I wish to bid you God-speed in your humanitarian work.

Yours faithfully,
HERBERT HOOVER

NOTE: The message was sent to Surgeon General Hugh S. Cumming, who was president of the Second Pan American Conference of Directors of Health. The Conference was held at the Pan American Building in Washington.

145

Message Endorsing the Annual "Buddy Poppy" Sale.
April 23, 1931

[Released April 23, 1931.   Dated April 15, 1931]

My dear Commander:

I warmly commend the annual "Buddy Poppy" Campaign which is conducted under the auspices of the Veterans of Foreign Wars of the United States as a means of general civilian contribution in the relief work for disabled and needy veterans and their dependents. It not only gives employment to disabled veterans, but also it aids in the maintenance of a National Home for Widows and Orphans of deceased veterans in Eaton Rapids, Michigan.

Yours faithfully,
HERBERT HOOVER

[Commander-In-Chief, Veterans of Foreign Wars of the United States, Washington, D.C.]

NOTE: The message was released in conjunction with ceremonies at the White House when Hazel Viola Markinson, 7-year-old daughter of a deceased veteran, presented a "buddy poppy" to the President.

68-611 O - 76 - 16

146

Message to Emperor Hirohito on the Visit of Prince Takamatsu of Japan. *April 23, 1931*

[Released April 23, 1931.   Dated April 21, 1931]

I THANK Your Majesty for your telegram and assure you that it has been a sincere pleasure to have as our guests your distinguished brother and his Princess Consort. The cordial friendship evinced by our imperial guests have completely won our hearts and their visit will remain a most pleasant memory.

HERBERT HOOVER

[His Majesty Hirohito, Emperor of Japan, Tokyo]

NOTE: Prince Takamatsu and his Princess Consort were on an around-the-world honeymoon. They arrived in New York on April 10, 1931, and sailed from San Francisco on May 28.

147

The President's News Conference of *April 24, 1931*

THE BUDGET

THE PRESIDENT. At the Cabinet meeting this morning, its session was devoted to the consideration of expenditure for the next fiscal year. They had before them the compilations of the budget on a functional basis as has been customary for the last 2 years, and I thought perhaps you might want to see it.

If you will look at it you will see that the expenditures for the present fiscal year are about $4,435 million as compared with $4,994 [$3,994] million for the last fiscal year and $4,119 million for the next fiscal year, that is the appropriations for the next fiscal year. And in all of these tables the Post Office is included only as to the deficit—not as to the working expenditure or working basis.

The budget for the whole of these years, of course, is greatly increased by the increased expenditures on construction work, in relief of unemployment and relief to agriculture, and by the increase in expenditures on veterans, and as against that there have been some reductions of expenditures in other directions.

The heading of "Public Buildings and Public Works," this item 31, which amounts to $434 million for this present fiscal year and $458 million for the next fiscal year includes the highways, but it does not include the construction expenditures of the Army and Navy or military structures. It does not include the merchant marine loans to the Shipping Board or construction for aviation and park improvements and other minor items. Those are distributed by the budget over other items.

A total of all construction work including these items are now progressing, as you know, at the rate of about $725 million a year or somewhere about $500 million a year in excess of the rate under predepression conditions.

The expenditure shown as aids to agriculture is item no. 26. The total for this year of $341 million includes farm relief and Farm Board expenditures, together with the other expenditures of the Department of Agriculture, but does not include the highways, which is under "Public Works."

The expenditures on veterans' relief, which appear in items 11 and 12 show an increase for this fiscal year of about $190 million, but that includes $112 million of normal payment on the bonus fund, which was advanced by Congress from the next fiscal year budget for the present fiscal year. The statement does not cover the loans made on the bonus. They are represented there in the budget as $112 million a year of regular payments into that account. The loans on the certificates necessarily affect Treasury business, and for your information, General Hines informs me that the new loans made under the recent law, together with those already outstanding under the old law, now amount to $912 million. And in addition to this, the applications in hand which they have not yet reached amount to about $140 million more, making a total expenditure already in sight on loans to veterans on the bonus certificates of something about $1,050 million. Of course, the applications are still coming in. That latter figure corroborates the estimates we made at the time the act was passed.

I have no doubt you might find something in here that may be of interest to you. I cannot add much more to it.

QUESTIONS

Q. Mr. President, is there anything in there—I am trying to figure out on what the deficit was based. Did you get the deficit by taking $4,119 million from $4,435 million?

THE PRESIDENT. No, this is wholly expenditures. There are no receipts. We are not able to make any calculation on receipts or revenues. This relates solely to the expenditures.

Q. Mr. President, the June 30, 1931, expenditures are represented as estimates. Aren't they amounts already appropriated?

THE PRESIDENT. These budget matters of appropriation or expenditure do not always run accurately with appropriations. Of course, we are always striving to get below the appropriations where we can do it without injuring the major purpose of the appropriations themselves. The estimate for June 1931 would be as at the middle of this month, so there are 2½ months to run, and therefore, they are given as estimates rather than the actual fact.

Q. Mr. President, there is considerable of a cut there as between the figures for 1931 and 1932. Could you indicate where the economies come in?

THE PRESIDENT. Well, you can run down between '31 and '32—public debt charges are much the same—about $8 million increase. The War Department expenditure shows a decrease of $12 million. The Navy Department shows an increase of about $25 million. The veterans' services show a decrease of $203 million. A good part of that is due to the shift, however, of $112 million from next year into this year. Then there is a decrease of about $10 million in the estimated postal deficit. There is a decrease in agricultural aids from $341 million to $160 million showing thereby a saving there of about $180 million.

Q. Mr. President, that saving on agriculture—is that doing away with State assistance?

THE PRESIDENT. No, it has to do with the appropriations for farm relief. I think the appropriations were $200 million or thereabouts in the present fiscal year and $100 million for next year, and the drought relief is in this year's budget and not in next year's.

Q. Mr. President, on the items of veterans' relief. You said that the loans would amount to $1,050 million ultimately. How is that $112 million in that accounted for? How do we account for that?

THE PRESIDENT. Those are loans. They have to be arranged by corresponding loans from the Treasury.

Q. Will it appear, Mr. President, in the figure in the debt?

THE PRESIDENT. It will be in the figure in the debt.

Q. Mr. President, am I right in believing that General Hines estimated that $1 billion would be the total required?

THE PRESIDENT. His estimate was that the total would be a minimum of $1 billion.

Q. That includes past loans?

THE PRESIDENT. Yes, it is $1,050 million.

Q. Isn't there $700 million in the Treasury to meet that?

THE PRESIDENT. Yes, the previous annual payments for the bonus will aggregate about $750 million as I recollect—something about that figure. When it is paid out of cash it has to be borrowed from somewhere.

Q. Mr. President, is there any comparison between this 1932 expenditure and the amount appropriated by Congress for this purpose?

THE PRESIDENT. These are based upon appropriations.

Q. These are actual appropriations?

THE PRESIDENT. Yes.

Q. Mr. President, what big general lesson would you draw from these figures?

THE PRESIDENT. Nothing but public information.

Q. These figures indicate that the fiscal year 1932 will be less than that for June 1931?

THE PRESIDENT. Yes, and with the constant striving to reduce expenditures wherever we can, we are going into the necessary aid to unemployment, agriculture, et cetera—we may get it even less than this.

Q. You do not estimate any unusual expenditure to narrow that gap?

THE PRESIDENT. No, unless we get it from Congress.

NOTE: President Hoover's one hundred and eighty-eighth news conference was held in the White House at 4 p.m. on Friday, April 24, 1931.

On the same day, the White House issued a text of the President's statement on the Federal budget (see Item 148).

Frank T. Hines was Administrator of Veterans' Affairs.

A copy of the question and answer portion of the news conference, as revised by the President, is available for examination at the Herbert Hoover Presidential Library.

148

Statement on the Federal Budget.
April 24, 1931

THE PRESIDENT said:

"The Cabinet session this morning was devoted to consideration of Government expenditure for the next fiscal year. The members of the Cabinet had before them the compilation of the budget on a functional basis, as has been customary during the past 2 years.

"Copies of the budget will be handed to you. You will note that the expenditures for the present fiscal year will be about $4,435 million as compared with $3,994 million in the last fiscal year and as compared with the appropriations of $4,119 million for the next fiscal year. These totals include only Post Office deficits, not the whole working expenditure of the Post Office Department.

"The budgets for all 3 years are greatly influenced by the increased expenditures for construction work in aid of unemployment, for relief to agriculture, and for increased services to veterans, but it will be seen that these increased expenditures are somewhat offset by reductions in other directions.

"The heading of public buildings and public works, amounting to $434 million for this fiscal year and estimated at more than $457 million for next year, includes highways but does not include construction expenditures of the Army and Navy for military purposes, or the Veterans' Bureau, or merchant marine through loans from the Shipping Board, or for aviation and park improvements and sundry other minor construction items. The total of all construction work including these items is now progressing at the rate of over $725 million per annum, being about $500 million per annum in excess of the rate of expenditure for construction previous to the depression.

"The expenditure shown as aids to agriculture of a total for this year of $341 million includes drought relief and Farm Board expenditures, together with other expenditures of the Department of Agriculture, but does not include highway construction.

"The expenditure on veterans' relief shows an increase of about $190 million for the present fiscal year but includes $112 million of the normal payment into the bonus fund for the next fiscal year which was advanced by Congress to the present fiscal year.

"This statement of the budget does not include loans upon the bonus except so far as they are represented in the annual payment into the bonus fund, of about $112 million. But loans on the bonus certificates necessarily affect the Treasury finance. General [Frank T.] Hines, Administrator of Veterans' Affairs, informs me that the new loans made under the recent law together with those already outstanding under previous law, amount to about $912 million. In addition to these amounts applications are at hand amounting to about $140 million more, making a total of expenditure already in sight of about $1,050 million."

NOTE: The following tables of expenditures classified on a functional basis were issued with the statement.

EXPENDITURES CLASSIFIED ON A FUNCTIONAL BASIS, FISCAL YEARS 1932, 1931, 1930

	Estimated expenditures		Actual expenditures
	June 30, 1932 (estimated)	June 30, 1931 (estimated)	June 30, 1930 (actual)
GROUP I			
Public debt:			
1. Principal....................	$467, 584, 900	$442, 985, 912	$553, 883, 603. 25
2. Interest.....................	593, 400, 000	610, 000, 000	659, 347, 613. 07
	1, 060, 984, 900	1, 052, 985, 912	1, 213, 231, 216. 32
National defense:			
Army			
3. General....................	302, 118, 800	304, 140, 800	299, 240, 712. 69
4. Buildings and other structures..	24, 274, 000	26, 949, 000	10, 718, 467. 76
5. Vessels.....................	200, 000	200, 000	....
6. Aircraft and accessories.......	16, 100, 000	22, 901, 000	16, 765, 474. 62
Total, Army...........	342, 692, 800	354, 190, 800	326, 724, 655. 07
Navy			
7. General....................	295, 834, 272	284, 781, 640	299, 994, 223. 19
8. Buildings and other structures.	16, 500, 000	13, 500, 000	2, 425, 000. 00
9. Vessels (ship construction and major alterations).........	70, 000, 000	50, 000, 000	58, 050, 214. 67
10. Aircraft and accessories.......	16, 200, 000	14, 900, 000	14, 431, 859. 00
Total, Navy...........	398, 534, 272	363, 181, 640	374, 901, 296. 86
Total, National Defense..	741, 227, 072	717, 372, 440	701, 625, 951. 93

EXPENDITURES CLASSIFIED ON A FUNCTIONAL BASIS, FISCAL YEARS 1932, 1931, 1930—Continued

	Estimated expenditures		Actual expenditures June 30, 1930 (actual)
	June 30, 1932 (estimated)	June 30, 1931 (estimated)	
GROUP I—Continued			
Veterans of former wars:			
11. General.....................	725, 371, 000	¹ 935, 337, 000	745, 436, 827. 72
12. Buildings and other structures..	20, 167, 000	12, 950, 000	9, 947, 923. 00
Total, veterans.............	745, 538, 000	948, 287, 000	755, 384, 750. 72
Total, group I.............	2, 547, 749, 972	2, 718, 645, 352	2, 670, 241, 918. 97
GROUP II			
13. Legislative....................	11, 601, 000	12, 053, 816	11, 778, 503. 24
14. Executive.....................	468, 700	419, 700	416, 784. 22
15. Judicial, Law Enforcement, and Regulatory Commissions.........	106, 701, 481	96, 892, 650	85, 849, 548. 62
16. Fiscal Administration and Control of Currency and Banking.........	76, 546, 210	75, 454, 900	73, 455, 304. 12
17. Foreign Relations................	17, 308, 100	15, 005, 300	13, 946, 612. 28
18. Administration of Territories and Dependencies...................	4, 875, 100	4, 687, 900	6, 310, 372. 82
19. Service Agencies to the Departments and Independent Establishments.	42, 290, 173	39, 900, 367	35, 764, 255. 97
20. Civil Pensions and Allowances......	20, 900, 000	20, 950, 000	20, 500, 000. 00
21. Balance of postal deficiency after deducting losses due to contract air mail routes, foreign air mail routes, and to transportation of foreign mail in American vessels..	98, 283, 000	108, 978, 000	63, 496, 272. 50
Total, group II...............	378, 973, 764	374, 342, 633	311, 517, 653. 77
GROUP III			
22. Public Health...................	22, 424, 900	20, 493, 700	18, 501, 366. 37
23. Education.....................	16, 424, 310	14, 692, 075	14, 329, 545. 11
24. Indian Affairs..................	25, 728, 800	28, 880, 700	19, 491, 273. 12
25. Conservation of National Resources.	54, 362, 850	52, 111, 500	44, 105, 654. 50
26. Aids to Agriculture...............	160, 872, 025	341, 645, 134	208, 935, 759. 08
27. Aids to Labor...................	7, 798, 820	7, 089, 100	7, 176, 137. 28

See footnote at end of table.

203

EXPENDITURES CLASSIFIED ON A FUNCTIONAL BASIS, FISCAL YEARS 1932, 1931, 1930—Continued

	Estimated expenditures		Actual expenditures
	June 30, 1932 (estimated)	June 30, 1931 (estimated)	June 30, 1930 (actual)
GROUP III—Continued			
28. Aids to Aviation, including losses on contract air mail routes and foreign air mail routes..........	29, 288, 667	28, 577, 733	21, 925, 434. 83
29. Aids to Industry and Trade.........	16, 812, 910	16, 388, 251	15, 678, 701. 51
30. Aids to Merchant Marine, including losses on transportation of foreign mail in American vessels.........	134, 978, 950	96, 791, 234	78, 779, 570. 73
31. Public buildings and public works, exclusive of construction included in other items..................	457, 931, 700	434, 622, 200	272, 011, 188. 09
32. Bureau of the Census..............	8, 750, 000	16, 000, 000	14, 648, 226. 82
Total, group III..............	935, 373, 933	1, 057, 291, 627	715, 582, 958. 44
GROUP IV			
33. Refunds.........................	116, 951, 500	105, 480, 000	152, 118, 461. 30
34. Settlement of War Claims Act, 1928.	....	37, 000, 000	....
35. Trust Funds.....................	90, 960, 200	91, 007, 500	93, 885, 740. 63
36. District of Columbia..............	48, 040, 000	50, 419, 500	45, 596, 319. 80
37. Miscellaneous....................	1, 181, 280	843, 120	5, 209, 434. 18
Total, group IV.................	257, 132, 980	284, 750, 120	296, 809, 955. 91
Total, exclusive of Postal Service payable from postal revenues...	4, 119, 230, 649	4, 435, 029, 732	3, 994, 152, 487. 09

[1] Includes bonus payment $112,000,000 advanced from 1932 to 1931.

149

Message to the Committee on Negro Housing
of the White House Conference on
Home Building and Home Ownership.
April 24, 1931

PROMPTED by a fine spirit of public service, you have assembled here today to consider what program may be devised to improve conditions of housing for our colored citizens. This committee is one of many special committees, each of which is charged with some important phase of the broad problem of homebuilding and homeownership. Since the health and welfare of all citizens, and particularly of children, are vitally affected by conditions of housing and homelife, your committee has unselfishly undertaken to give careful consideration to urgent questions which affect directly the welfare of more than 10 million persons.

Your studies will lead you into the consideration of problems of the design, construction, and financing of houses, of conditions of ownership and tenancy, of remodeling, equipping, and furnishing of homes in city and country. Thoughtful consideration is needed in order to determine what can be accomplished by the Negroes themselves in the improvement of conditions of housing and homelife and of what can be done by public authorities or other agencies to aid them in bringing housing conditions to higher standards of sanitation, convenience, and wholesomeness. Wherever conditions are found to be below a reasonable standard the problem is one of determining what next steps can best be taken in improving the conditions and how information and service can be mobilized to prevent future recurrence of conditions of housing that may impair health or character.

Many of you will doubtless be asked to help in the work of other committees, but I feel that a judicious consideration of the special problems assigned to this committee may lead to a service of unusual value to your country. Self-help is a primary principle of progress, but self-help involves wise stimulation and thoughtful leadership. It is my hope that you, who are among the acknowledged leaders of your race, may find in the work of this committee an opportunity to carry the study of this subject farther than it has been carried before, and that your recommendations may help to coordinate and direct the forces which will lead to a more rapid solution of the important problems of housing with which you are concerned.

NOTE: The message was read to the committee, which was one of approximately 30 study groups preparing reports for the forthcoming White House Conference on Home Building and Home Ownership, at its initial organization meeting.

For the establishment of the White House Conference on Home Building and Home Ownership, see 1930 volume, Item 250.

150

Executive Order 5610, Amendment of the Civil Service Rules Relating to Veterans' Preference.
April 24, 1931

THE CIVIL-SERVICE rules are hereby amended as indicated below.

Rule VI, paragraph 1, is amended to read as follows by eliminating the sentence "Applicants for entrance examination who, because of disability, are entitled either to a pension by authorization of the Bureau of Pensions or to compensation or training by the Veterans' Bureau, and widows of honorably discharged soldiers, sailors, and marines, and wives of injured soldiers, sailors, and marines who themselves are not qualified, but whose wives are qualified for appointment, shall have ten points added to their earned ratings," and substituting therefor the sentence "Applicants for entrance examination who are honorably discharged and who establish by official records the present existence of a service-connected disability, and widows of honorably discharged soldiers, sailors, and marines, and wives of honorably discharged soldiers, sailors, and marines who because of service-connected disability are themselves not qualified but whose wives are qualified for appointment, shall have ten points added to their earned ratings; and this shall also apply to retired officers and enlisted men who establish through official sources the present existence of a service-connected disability in the same manner as is required of others who are granted disability preference":

Examination papers shall be rated on a scale of 100, and the subjects therein shall be given such relative weights as the commission may prescribe. Honorably discharged soldiers, sailors, and marines shall have five points added to their earned ratings in examinations for entrance to the classified service. Applicants for entrance examination who are honorably discharged and who establish by official records the present existence of a service-connected disability, and widows of honorably discharged soldiers, sailors, and marines, and wives of honorably discharged soldiers, sailors, and marines who because of service-connected disability are themselves not qualified but whose wives are qualified for appointment, shall have ten points added to their earned ratings; and this shall also apply to retired officers and enlisted men who establish through official sources the present existence of a service-connected disability in the same manner as is required of others who are granted disability preference. In examinations where experience is an element of qualifications, time spent in the military or naval service of the United States during the World War or the war with Spain shall be credited in an applicant's ratings where the applicant's actual employment in a similar vocation to that for which he applies was temporarily interrupted by such military or naval service but was resumed after his discharge. Competitors shall be duly notified of their ratings.

Rule VI, paragraph 2, is amended to read as follows by eliminating the clause "but the names of disabled veterans, their wives, and the widows of honorably discharged soldiers, sailors, and marines shall be placed above all others," and substituting therefor the clause "but the names of persons entitled to disability preference as defined in paragraph 1 of this rule shall be placed above all others":

All competitors rated at 70 or more shall be eligible for appointment, and their names shall be placed on the proper register according to their ratings; but the names of persons entitled to disability preference as defined in paragraph 1 of this rule shall be placed above all others.

The foregoing amendments to Civil-Service Rule VI will apply to future examinations conducted by the Civil Service Commission.

Rule VII, paragraph 1(*b*), is amended to read as follows by eliminating the sentence "An appointing officer who passes over a veteran eligible and selects a nonveteran with the same or lower rating shall place in the records of the department his reasons for so doing," and substituting therefor the sentence "An appointing officer who passes over a veteran eligible and selects a nonveteran with the same or lower rating shall file with the Civil Service Commission the reasons for so doing, which reasons will become a part of the veteran's record but will not be made available to the veteran or to anyone else except in the discretion of the appointing officer":

The nominating or appointing officer shall make selections for the first vacancy from not more than the highest three names certified, or on the register, with sole reference to merit and fitness, unless objection shall be made and sustained by the commission, to one or more of the persons certified, for any of the reasons stated in Rule V, section 4. For the second vacancy he shall make selection from not more than the highest three remaining, who have not been within his reach for three separate vacancies, or against whom objection has not been made and sustained in the manner indicated. The third and any additional vacancies shall be filled in like manner. More than one selection may be made from the three names next in order for appointment, or from two names if the register contains only two, subject to the requirements of section 2 of this rule as to the apportionment. An appointing officer who passes over a veteran eligible and selects a nonveteran with the same or lower rating shall file with the Civil Service Commission the reasons for so doing, which reasons will become a part of the veteran's record but will not be made available to the veteran or to anyone else except in the discretion of the appointing officer. Any eligible who has been within reach for three separate vacancies in his turn may be subsequently selected, subject to the approval of the commission from the certificate on which his name last appeared, if the condition of the register has not so changed as to place him in other respects beyond reach of certification.

The Civil Service Commission is authorized to hold quarterly examinations for positions for which there are existing registers of eligibles, such examinations to be open only to the men and women entitled to disability preference as herein provided, the names of the resulting eligibles to be entered at the head of the existing registers in the order of ratings attained in competition with the disability-preference eligibles, if any, whose names may already appear at the head of such registers.

HERBERT HOOVER

The White House,
   April 24, 1931.

NOTE: This Executive order resulted from recommendations in the "Report of the President's Advisory Committee on Veteran Preference," dated April 21, 1931. On the same day, the White House issued a text of the report, which follows:

The President:

We have the honor to report to you in the matter of veteran preference affecting the Executive civil service of the United States. Recommendations will appear at the end of this report.

You will recall that at the time you decided to appoint this Advisory Committee on Veteran Preference two groups of organized citizens were making representations to you as to the granting of veteran preference in connection with Federal employment.

Veterans organizations were claiming that veterans were not securing the proper consideration by appointing officers in the filling of positions in the Executive civil service; and especial point was made that disabled veterans should receive a greater proportion of appointments.

The other group found representation in the National Civil Service Reform League, a committee of which made report in general adverse to veteran preference. This organization later sent a letter to your committee under date of December 22, 1930, in which it stated as its view that the two serious objections to the Executive order of March 2, 1929, are:

   1. The preference is not restricted to those veterans who were disabled in the actual performance of military or naval service in the war, and whose disability actually still exists; and

   2. The order does not require that the veterans secure at least a normal passing mark of 70 percent before they may be eligible for any preference or other special dispensation.

The Reform League believed that the Act of July 3, 1930, whereby World War veterans are given disability allowance for disabilities which are not of service origin would so greatly increase the number of veterans entitled to disability preference in connection with civil service examinations as seriously to affect the efficiency of the Government service.

The study which your Committee has given to veteran preference has been directed and controlled not only by the fact that there is a statute requiring the granting of veteran preference, but also by the desire to ascertain the facts.

With this object in view the Committee addressed communications to the National Civil Service Reform League and to each of the recognized service organizations asking that they present to the Committee by January 1, 1931, briefs outlining their views and recommendations with respect to the Executive order of March 2, 1929, and its operation. The representatives of all these organizations and of two or three organizations which asked for hearings, were given opportunity for oral presentation of their views. Detailed statistical information was also secured.

The organizations or individuals who filed briefs with your Committee are The American Legion, through the Chairman of its National Committee on Veterans Preference; The Disabled American Veterans of the World War, through its National Commander and the Chairman of its National Legislative Committee; The United Spanish War Veterans, through its Commander in Chief, and a special committee; the National Civil Service Reform League, through its Secretary; the Retired Men's News of Arcadia, California; the Ex-Service Men's League of the Washington, D.C. Navy Yard, through its counsel; Engineer Clerks in whose behalf Mr. Truman J. Mead of Chicago, Illinois, addressed a letter to the Committee; Captain Harlan Wood, Past Department Commander, District of Columbia American Legion; Bureau of Engraving and Printing Post No. 23, The American Legion, Washington, D.C.; Veterans of Foreign Wars, through its Commander in Chief, Baltimore, Maryland, and its District of Columbia representative; and a committee of civilian employees of the Naval Gun Factory, Washington, D.C.

At hearings conducted by your Committee appeared Mr. Madison L. Hill representing the Ex-Service Men's League, District of Columbia; Captain Harlan Wood representing the District of Columbia Department of the American Legion; Mr. Paul J. McGahan representing the national organization of The American Legion; Captain Edwin S. Bettelheim representing the Veterans of Foreign Wars; Commander in Chief Matthias, Ex-Senator Rice W. Means, and Past Department Commander James G. Yaden, representing the United Spanish War Veterans; Captain Thomas Kirby representing the Disabled American Veterans of the World War; and Mr. Harry W. Marsh, Member of the Executive Committee, and Mr. H. Eliot Kaplan, Secretary, representing the National Civil Service Reform League.

President Coolidge, in creating the Advisory Committee whose report brought about the Executive order of March 2, 1929, stated that, "Its main purpose will be to ascertain ways and means for making Government positions available for the disabled veterans." The disabled veteran was again the object of solicitude on the part of the persons who wrote to and appeared before your Committee.

One statistical study showed that as a consequence of the Executive order of March 2, 1929, the number of disabled veterans appointed for the fiscal year 1930 reached a total of 1,996, as compared with the average number of 1,227 appointments each year for the six years ending with June 30, 1929.

It was found that of the 1,996 disabled veterans appointed last fiscal year, 447 attained earned ratings of less than 70 per cent in the examinations which resulted in their appointments, their entrance on the eligible registers being due to the fact that because of their disability they received a bonus of 10 points in their examination ratings. Your Committee believing that the information would be valuable in arriving at recommendations to be made to you, secured from the Civil Service Commission the names of these 447 disabled veterans, the examinations taken, the ratings therein, and the positions and departments and offices to which appointed; and asked their respective appointing officers for comment as to the efficiency and work performance of these disabled veterans.

The replies received covered 352 of the 447 disabled veterans, no reports being received concerning 25, and 70 others having been separated from the service or not reported on in sufficient detail to be statistically noted. The reports of appointing officers showed that in 51 cases the disability was a handicap in the performance of work, and in 288 cases not a handicap, and the effect of the disability was not stated in 13 cases. The appointing officers reported that the work of 177 of these employees compared favorably with that of employees who had earned 85 per cent or higher in the entrance examination; the work of 146 of these disabled veterans did not compare favorably with such employees; and in 29 cases no comparison was made. The reports of appointing officers showed that the work of 242 of these disabled veterans who had earned less than 70 per cent in the entrance examination compared favorably with the work of employees who had earned between 70 per cent and 85 per cent in such examinations; that in 90 cases the comparison was unfavorable; and that in 20 cases the comparison was not shown.

It is true that in proportion to the number of veterans who compete in examinations the operation of the preference statute as made effective by Executive orders results in a higher comparative percentage of appointments going to veterans and disabled veterans. This is shown by statistics compiled over a period of years. The last fiscal year is illustrative of previous years. During that year the *disabled veterans* furnished *3* per cent of the *competitors, 3.6* per cent of the *eligibles,* and received *5.3* per cent of the *appointments.* The *nondisabled veterans* furnished *17.6* per cent of *competitors, 18.9* per cent of the *eligibles,* and received *18.8* per cent of the *appointments. Nonveteran competitors* comprised *79.4* per cent of the total, provided *77.5* per cent of the *eligibles,* and received *75.9* per cent of the *appoint-*

ments. It will thus be seen that the bonus of 5 and 10 points materially assisted the veterans and disabled veterans in attaining eligibility, and that the additional preference accorded disabled veterans of placing their names at the head of eligible registers added greatly to the proportion of appointments they received in comparison with their percentage of eligibles on the registers.

Your Committee recognizes, of course, that under the preference statutes of Congress this larger proportion of appointments to veterans is warranted.

The Committee gave especial consideration to the classes of positions in the examinations for which veterans have competed and received appointment. The total number of veterans who received appointment in the Executive civil service last fiscal year was 9,269. Of this number 8,100 were appointed to positions where the maximum salary they could receive on appointment was $1,800 a year, and many of them received much less than $1,800. There were 883 veterans appointed as unskilled laborers. More than 2,500 entered the Postal Service; 1,755 received mechanic appointments in the Navy Yard Service; 337 in the Engineer Department at Large; more than 500 in the Prohibition Enforcement Service; 635 in the Immigration and Customs Services; and 488 were appointed as guards. Only 73 veterans were appointed in the group of positions with a salary range from $3,200 to $4,000 a year; 25 in the salary range from $4,000 to $5,200 a year; 1 was appointed as principal agronomist at $5,600, and 1 was appointed as assistant technical director at $8,000.

This showing as established from the official records of the Civil Service Commission, in the view of your Committee, does not seem to support any claim that veteran preference as at present administered *seriously* affects the efficiency of the Government service.

In expressing the view that the disabled veteran should receive special consideration, the representatives of veterans organizations who wrote to, or appeared before, your Committee seemed to believe that this special consideration beyond that accorded the nondisabled veteran should be based on a showing that the disability existed at the time of applying for civil service examniation, and also that it should have service connection. In other words, the veteran who at the time of filing application was not suffering from a disability or if suffering from a disability it was not of service origin, should receive only the preference accorded veterans generally by operation of the preference statute of July 11, 1919. Your Committee finds itself in accord with this view.

A further study by your Committee was founded on the complaint that appointing officers generally were not observing the preference statute, and were attempting to avoid appointments of veterans, and especially disabled veterans, as far as possible. As this is a serious charge your Committee gave it unusual consideration. In a general memorandum which accompanies this report appear two tables showing by actual figures and percentages the number of eligibles certified, appointed, passed over, declined or failed to reply, and on unused certificates or not reached for selection, divided into three groups, namely, disabled veteran eligibles, non-disabled veteran eligibles, and nonveteran eligibles. The complaint filed with your Committee was that, especially as concerns the disabled veteran eligibles, a too high proportion of those certified were passed over by appointing officers in their making selections for appointment from the certificates issued by the Civil Service Commission. The tables referred to show that 32 per cent of the disabled veterans whose names were certified were appointed, 39 per cent of the nondisabled veterans certified were appointed, and 36 per cent of the nonveteran eligibles certified were appointed.

Your Advisory Committee does not believe that this supports any claim that appointing officers deliberately attempt to avoid appointing disabled veterans or nondisabled veterans. Your Committee was so desirous of securing the facts in this particular study that it asked for specific instances where the claim was made that the appointing officer had improperly passed over the disabled veteran in filling the vacancy. For your information only one illustration among those considered is cited. The claim was made that a disabled veteran was passed over on a certificate issued for filling a position of occupational therapy aide. The vacancy was in a neuro-psychiatric hospital where his disability—deafness—was a complete bar to appointment, whereas for a similar position in a general hospital he could have been appointed. The vacancy, however, was in a mental disease hospital, and so his case appears in the statistical table as one where the disabled veteran was passed over and not selected. Similar facts were found to exist in other cases considered by your Committee.

RECOMMENDATIONS

Your Committee recommends the following changes in the present practice with respect to according preference to veterans under the Act of July 11, 1919.

1. That with respect to honorably discharged soldiers, sailors, or marines, their widows, or the wives of seriously disabled veterans, 10-point preference be granted only where it is officially established by the records of the War Dpeartment, the Navy Department, the Coast Guard, or the Veterans' Administration that there is an existing service-connected disability; and that the veterans found eligible hereunder have their names placed at the head of the eligible register. For all other classes of veterans 5-point preference will continue to be applied, the names of eligibles with their augmented ratings to be placed on the registers in the order of such ratings.

The essential change in this recommendation is the requirement that the disability for which the 10-point disability preference may be granted must exist at the time of application and must have service connection. The present practice is to grant 10-point, or disability, preference to "applicants for entrance examination who because of disability are entitled either to a pension by authorization of the Bureau of Pensions, or to compensation or training by the Veterans' Bureau, and widows of honorably discharged soldiers, sailors, and marines, and wives of injured soldiers, sailors, and marines, who themselves are not qualified, but whose wives are qualified to hold such positions."

It will be observed that under present practice the special disability preference of 10 points and of having the names placed at the head of eligible registers need not be founded on establishments of existing or service-connected disability.

2. That this same recommendation be applied to cover officers and enlisted men retired for service-connected disability which exists at the time of filing application for examination, and also to those officers and enlisted men retired not for disability but for age or length of service, who establish through official sources the present existence of service-connected disability in the same manner as is required of others who are granted disability preference.

The principal change from present practice in this recommendation is the latter clause permitting the granting of disability preference to officers and enlisted men retired not for disability but for age or length of service, who establish through official sources the present existence of service-connected disability in the same manner as other veterans who are granted disability preference.

3. That any changes herein recommended be applied to future examinations conducted by the Civil Service Commission.

4. That whenever an appointing officer passes over a veteran eligible and selects a nonveteran eligible with the same or lower rating, the reasons for such action shall be filed with the Civil Service Commission to become a part of the veteran's record, but that no copy of these reasons shall be furnished to the veteran concerned or to anyone else except in the discretion of the appointing officer.

Your Committee asks that special consideration be given to this recommendation; it was arrived at with hesitation and only after most careful study. The basis for the recommendation is that as the law requires that preference in appointment shall be given to veterans, no veteran eligible whose name is certified should be passed over in selection for appointment except for sound reasons; and that if these reasons are reduced to writing to be filed with the Commission, their adequacy as a basis for rejecting the veteran will receive due consideration before they are sent to the Commission for its records. Since an essential part of this recommendation is that the reasons are not to be made available to the veteran or to anyone else except upon approval of the appointing officer, no foundation is afforded for any charge that this filing of the reasons with the Commission would be an unwarranted invasion of the appointing power.

5. That the Civil Service Commission be authorized to hold quarterly examinations for positions for which there are existing registers of eligibles, such examinations to be open only to the men and women entitled to 10-point disability preference, as provided for in Recommendations Nos. 1 and 2 above, the names of the resulting eligibles to be entered at the head of the existing registers in the order of ratings attained in competition with the disability preference eligibles, if any, whose names may already appear at the head of such registers.

This recommendation will increase to some extent the work of the Civil Service Commission in preparing series of examination questions for the more difficult examinations, and will also increase the volume of rating work; but its approval will make possible the elimination by the Commission of its present practice of reopening competitive examinations to veterans under certain conditions. Approval of this recommendation would also give recognition to the principle that there is a social obligation on the Government to assist as far as possible with employment those veterans who were disabled in its service, and who, because the Commission holds examinations not more frequently than once in one, two, or three years, are afforded no special opportunity after the regular examination date to establish their qualifications for consideration for Federal employment.

If the foregoing recommendations meet with your approval, the attached draft of Executive order is submitted for signature.

Your Committee studied the following preference, among others, now accorded veterans, and does not recommend any change:

1. Release from the requirement that the apportionment of appointments in the departmental service at Washington, D.C., among the States and Territories be observed.

2. Waiver of age limits.

3. Retention preferences under certain conditions.

4. Unlimited reinstatement preference for war veterans who have served in the classified civil service.

In the accompanying memorandum are given statistical information and general information as to the history of veteran preference.

We have the honor to be,

Very respectfully,

THOMAS E. CAMPBELL, *Chairman, Civil Service Commission*

FRANK T. HINES, *Veterans' Administration*

ROYAL C. JOHNSON, *Chairman, House of Representatives Committee on Veterans' Legislation*

SETH W. RICHARDSON, *Assistant Attorney General*

JOHN THOMAS TAYLOR, *Vice Chairman, Legislative Committee, The American Legion*

151

Statement on Better Homes Week.
April 25, 1931

I CORDIALLY commend to all the people the observance of Better Homes Week beginning April 26. The Better Homes movement has for several years played a highly important part in encouraging a more beautiful home architecture, improved decoration of house interiors, more practical kitchen arrangements, better planning of gardens, and in every way an enhancement of the comfort and attractiveness of home-life. Everything that can be done to encourage homeownership and to make homelife pleasanter is a distinct contribution not only to social well-being but to the highest spiritual values of life. The Better Homes movement has done distinguished service in this field and deserves the warmest support of all our people.

NOTE: Better Homes Week was sponsored by Better Homes in America, a voluntary public service corporation that President Hoover had helped organize while Secretary of Commerce. The activities of the Better Homes Week consisted of an annual campaign of exhibits and educational projects aimed at improving housing and household management.

216

152

Message on National Boys' Week.
April 25, 1931

THE CELEBRATION of National Boys Week is a yearly reminder of the priceless qualities of youth, when faith is highest and ambition strongest, with their constant inspiration and encouragement to the fathers and sons. Interest in boys and comradeship with them is a privilege to their elders and a guiding service to the boys. I commend the observance of National Boys Week to all our people.

HERBERT HOOVER

NOTE: The message was sent to Louis B. Mayer, Culver City, Calif., and made public in conjunction with the beginning of National Boys' Week sponsored by the Rotary International.

153

Message to a Dinner Honoring Henry Morgenthau.
April 25, 1931

[Released April 25, 1931.   Dated April 8, 1931]

My dear Mr. Levine:

I am glad to learn of the honor that you and your associates of the Bronx House Committee are paying to the Honorable Henry Morgenthau on the occasion of his seventy-fifth birthday, and I will be obliged if you will express to Mr. Morgenthau my hearty congratulations upon his anniversary and my warm appreciation of his many services in behalf of humanity and of high ideals.

Yours faithfully,
HERBERT HOOVER

[Mr. Joseph M. Levine, 30 East 42nd Street, New York City]

NOTE: The message was made public at a dinner honoring Henry Morgenthau, former United States Ambassador to Turkey. The dinner was held in the Bronx House in New York City, a social settlement founded by Mr. Morgenthau in 1911.

154

Message on the 33d Anniversary
of the Battle of Manila Bay.
April 26, 1931

[Released April 26, 1931.   Dated April 24, 1931]

I WILL BE obliged if you will express to your comrades, the survivors
of Admiral Dewey's squadron, my warm appreciation of their historic
service to country.

HERBERT HOOVER

[Harry A. Neithercott, care of James J. Burke, 4339 Brown Street, Philadelphia, Pa.]

NOTE: The message was released in conjunction with a celebration in Philadelphia
of the 33d anniversary of the Battle of Manila Bay, Philippines.

155

Address to the Gridiron Club.
April 27, 1931

Members and guests of the Gridiron Club:

I know that I have your full authority to express the gratitude of every
guest to the Gridiron Club for its hospitality and its always unique entertainment—an occasion without counterpart in the world. These occasions are a contribution to public life. They illuminate dark places with
satire and dismal places with wit. Their streams of humor refresh the
political soul and their streams of ridicule quench the fires of ambition.
I would not say that the Gridiron Club is the gyroscope of the ship of
state; nor that it pours oil upon troubled waters; but it does serve to
keep humility in the crew.

I rise with this humility in the knowledge that the accumulated and
highly distilled wisdom of the Gridiron Club has already indelibly
written conclusions in your minds upon all public questions and public

218

men. Much could be said in refutation by some of the folks who have been referred to, but they will all take solace in the knowledge that the magic spell of wit and the illusions of hyperbole will fade before the responsibilities of your daily chore. But it is good to live a few hours in the land of illusions whether they be illusions of fairies, illusions of wit, or illusions of wisdom, and we are all grateful to the club for such an occasion.

The Gridiron Club has a reputation deservedly of being original. Yet sometimes it repeats. It became quite exercised at a dinner earlier in my administration over the appointment of committees and commissions to investigate facts as a useful preliminary to the determination of policies in the Government. Two of your skits tonight reveal that the club is still concerned.

I have noted from time to time that some of our opponents in Congress also show concern to the extent of heavy combatant oratorical anxiety at this sort of action. Although I lay no claim to authorship of the idea of securing facts before action, it is comforting to observe that this terrible and destructive practice has infected the Congress. The national legislative body has created no less than 13 commissions during its last session. Furthermore, there is even greater encouragement in the fact that the recent Progressive Conference[1] adopted this pernicious practice and as the ultimate and only conclusion of its deliberations appointed four commissions, all of their own faith, and thereby assuring to a nicety the recommendations they will present during the autumn for the edification of the next Congress, and to make news for the members of the Gridiron Club.

It is faintly possible that this new crop of commissions in and out of Congress may be intended to have political purpose in the next election. Indeed, this is the period of comparative calm when old campaign issues are trustfully taken out of the political stable, rubbed down, reshod, and

---

[1] The Progressive Conference convened at the Carleton Hotel on March 11 and 12, 1931, with the purpose of offering solutions to social and economic problems of the moment. The President referred to committees formed during the conference to investigate problems concerning agriculture, public utilities, unemployment and industrial stabilization, and tariff changes.

given a trial heat; or new campaign issues are being earnestly sought for in every nook and corner.

I am reminded of a great and burning issue by the pleasure of listening to the song of "The Bells of Saint Mary's" this evening. That issue is the abuses which have arisen in the land from bells. Indeed it is the only issue which I can learn of that hasn't some exponent. It arises from a malevolent force in the land which invades liberty, stimulates grief, terror, and hate; it is more all-embracing, ever-present, nationwide and more terrible than the power trust. That issue is the abuses which have arisen in the land from bells. It is true that bells were one time devoted to poetic and religious purposes, but people no longer listen with delight to the call of the church bell to Sunday worship. No one longer writes poems upon bells. The sweet sound of the old-fashioned cowbell has been undermined by the barbed wire fence. And this change in the purpose of bells is a serious matter. They have degenerated into an instrument of terror and an attack upon freedom.

There is an untouched issue in this perversion of bells. However inconsequential this issue may appear at first blush, with deeper thought I believe it will appeal to you as an issue worthy of great effort. The whole bell evil has been increasing over a great number of years. The telephone company alone prides itself on having installed over 10 million bells since the Great War. There is no noise in the world so fills one's heart with alarm and foreboding as the telephone bell. This is especially true of officeholders, for good tidings always arrive by mail. But even the press suffers. For its imperious commands you must get out of bed at night. It endangers public health and it engenders agnosticism. It interrupts free speech. Moreover, our manufacturers have installed mass production in those bells attached to clocks for the evil purpose of an early morning alarm. To interrupt a man's sleep and jerk him from the realm of real bliss into the cold realities of another day is a greater invasion of human liberty than any yet wrought by the 18th amendment. Wherever one turns there are new and clamorous bells. In the middle of your meals you are summoned to the front door by their strident clang. They even interfere with free burglary. Bells have been attached lately to the "stop" and "go" signs, compelling us to adjust our pleasure rambles amongst historic scenes to the offensive command of rings on every street corner and crossroad. They have been extended to induce the terror in fire engines and ambulances. There are probably 30 million more strident bells clamoring in the Nation than before the war.

I commend the cure of this abuse to the Gridiron Club. It is an issue of more human importance than a vast number of the reforms now agitating Washington. It offers to your body an opportunity to convert your purely critical party into one of constructive action. It offers opportunity for a courageous stand upon States rights, States responsibilities, unemployment, public health, and the trusts.

No meeting of this club could assemble at this period without some reference to the hard times which surround us. From these references tonight you have witnessed both the joys, if there are any, and sorrows of business depression. It is a subject of necessity uppermost in the minds of all, not only in the daily manifestations of hardship but in its portent for the future. Although these strains in our economic structure exhibit its weaknesses, they invigorate and stimulate new thought for correction of the faults in the system. They also give birth to panaceas and fantasies which bring us sleepless anxieties.

Business depressions are not new to the United States or the world, but I am in hopes that the history of this particular depression will be written, at least so far as the United States is concerned, in different terms from that of its predecessors. It is possible, indeed, that this chapter of history, instead of being written wholly in terms of darkness and despair, may yet be recorded as the turning point in great social and economic progress.

This depression has now, in the view of our leading economists, proceeded to as great a depth in its fundamental forces of diminished production and distribution as any in a century, in fact, has its only parallels in the world depression which followed about a decade after the Napoleonic Wars and that which followed 10 years after the Civil War. And like those depressions it has its roots in the destruction of war and the dislocation of social and political institutions which flow from them down to today.

I have recently read accounts by a careful historian of the depression of 1873. Three major characteristics stand out in that period—the general bankruptcy, the widespread social disorder, and the actual physical suffering of the people. Strikes, lockouts, and riots dominated the times; police forces were increased, the militia called out, and Federal troops mobilized. These were but surface indications of the violence and hatred which the period developed. That depression was accompanied by monetary panics, bank failures, receiverships for nearly half the railway systems, and unparalleled foreclosures on homes and farms. It was estimated at the time that half the industrial population was without income. Actual starvation occurred in practically every city.

In contrast, we can say with satisfaction of this period of nearly 20 months of continuous economic degeneration that we have had fewer strikes and lockouts than in normal times; that we have had no mob violence worth noting to trouble the police or the militia; we have not summoned a single Federal soldier to arms. The first duty of the Government—that is, to secure social tranquillity and to maintain confidence in our institutions—has been performed. That has been accomplished by the good will and cooperation in the community and not by either force or legislation.

At the approach of the present depression I and my colleagues realized that while no action of the Government could stem the gigantic forces which had accumulated to dominate production and distribution of commodities in our country, more especially as the larger portion of the forces swept upon us from abroad, yet it was our duty to constantly encourage the organization of the community to mitigate the destruction of the storm with the utmost minimum of legislative action. The unparalleled growth of cooperative sense in the American people over the last half century has proved its strength. This mobilized voluntary action has preserved the social system free from hate and ill will, and has held the economic machinery in such order that it can quickly resume upon amelioration of these destructive forces. With only local and unnecessary exceptions there has been no starvation.

I can give you an encouraging thought on the depression, although I make no prophecies. It is either a coincidence or a profound action of economic forces that while every major depression has started at a different period of the year, yet our statisticians inform me that every major recovery has begun in the summer. It may possibly be due to the assurance of the crops at that time. Of the crops we have today great encouragement.

If, by the grace of God, we have passed the worst of this storm, the future months will be easy. If we shall be called upon to endure more of this period, we must gird ourselves for even greater effort, for today we are writing the introduction to the future history of civilization in America. The question is whether that history shall be written in terms of individual responsibility, and the capacity of the Nation for voluntary cooperative action, or whether it shall be written in terms of futile attempt to cure poverty by the enactment of law, instead of the maintained and protected initiative of our people. This is a period when the ideals and hopes which have made America the envy of the world are being tested. So far our people have responded with courage and steadfastness. If we can maintain this courage and resolution we shall have written this new chapter in national life in terms to which our whole idealism has aspired. May God grant to us the spirit and strength to carry through to the end.

NOTE: The President spoke at a dinner meeting held in the Willard Hotel.

The Gridiron Club is an organization of Washington newspapermen, who met semiannually for a dinner and satirical review of current political events.

Gridiron Club addresses are traditionally off-the-record, but the above text was later made public.

156

Message on the 100th Anniversary of the Founding of New York University.
April 28, 1931

[Released April 28, 1931.   Dated April 27, 1931]

I CORDIALLY congratulate you and the other authorities of New York University on the celebration tomorrow of the Centenary of this historic institution of learning with its long and honorable record of service to community and nation. I regret that I may not be present to take part personally in the expressions of pride and appreciation of its distinguished achievements which I know will flow in from every quarter of the world.

Herbert Hoover

[Dr. Elmer E. Brown, Chancellor, New York University, 100 Washington Square East, New York City]

NOTE: The message was made public in conjunction with exercises commemorating the anniversary.

157

Message Supporting Fundraising Activities of the American Jewish Joint Distribution Committee. *April 29, 1931*

[Released April 29, 1931. Dated April 22, 1931]

My dear Mr. Ottinger:

I extend to you my best wishes for the success of your effort to raise $1,000,000 in New York City for the aid of suffering Jewry in Eastern and Central Europe.

The work of the Joint Distribution Committee is well known to me and I consider it a remarkable piece of human engineering.

A people who have for a period of over fifteen years provided funds for the rehabilitation of their unfortunate co-religionists in foreign lands, will, I feel sure, continue to work in this noble purpose and will contribute again so that the program affording opportunities of self-help and relief for these people on the other side may be carried on.

Yours faithfully,

Herbert Hoover

[Mr. Albert Ottinger, 415 Lexington Avenue, New York, N.Y.]

NOTE: The message was read at a dinner of the executive council of the committee, held in the Hotel Biltmore in New York City.

158

Message of Sympathy on the Death of Mrs. Elizabeth Mills Reid.
April 29, 1931

IT WAS A great shock to both Mrs. Hoover and me to learn this morning of the passing of your mother. She has been so true and loyal a friend and has contributed so much to national welfare in a thousand directions that her death becomes both a personal and a national loss. We wish you and Mrs. Reid to know that you have our deepest sympathy.

HERBERT HOOVER

NOTE: The message was sent to Mrs. Reid's son, Ogden Reid, publisher of the New York Herald Tribune. Mrs. Reid, widow of former Ambassador Whitelaw Reid, had been active in welfare and philanthropic endeavors.

159

Message to a Luncheon Honoring William C. Creamer.
April 30, 1931

[Released April 30, 1931.   Dated April 24, 1931]

My dear Mr. Creamer:

I cordially congratulate you upon the completion of seventy consecutive years in the employ of Arnold, Constable & Company, and I am deeply interested to learn of your recollections of Mrs. Abraham Lincoln, President Roosevelt and others. I wish you many more years of health and happiness.

Yours faithfully,
HERBERT HOOVER

[Mr. William C. Creamer, Arnold, Constable & Company, Fifth Avenue at 40th Street, New York City]

NOTE: The message was read at a luncheon honoring Mr. Creamer.

160

Message to the Convention of the American Trade Association Executives. *April 30, 1931*

[Released April 30, 1931.   Dated April 29, 1931]

IN 1927 as Secretary of Commerce, I wrote the foreword to a bulletin on "Trade Association Activities" in which I said: "While our industry and commerce must be based upon incentive to the individual, yet the national interest requires a certain degree of cooperation between individuals in order that we may reduce and eliminate industrial waste, lay the foundation for constant decrease in production and distribution costs, and thereby obtain the fundamental increase in wages and standards of living.

"Trade Associations, like many other good things, may be abused, but the investigation of the Department of Commerce shows that such abuses have become rare exceptions. Within the last few years trade associations have rapidly developed into legitimate and constructive fields of the utmost public interest and have marked a fundamental step in the gradual evolution of our whole economic life."

No facts have come to my attention which would cause me to change the opinions expressed at that time, rather every development of industry renders trade associations more essential to sound development of our economic system.

HERBERT HOOVER

[Mr. Leslie C. Smith, Convention of American Trade Association Executives, Atlantic City, New Jersey]

NOTE: The message was read at a dinner of the association in the Ambassador Hotel in Atlantic City, N.J. The dinner was held in conjunction with the annual convention of the Chamber of Commerce of the United States.

161

Message to the Girl's Service League of America.
May 1931

[Released May 1931.   Dated April 29, 1931]

My dear Mrs. Hadden:

I appreciate very warmly what you and the members of the Girl's Service League of America have done in cooperation with the President's Emergency Committee for Employment. This work has been of the greatest social value besides its obvious humanitarian aspects. I will be obliged if you will convey to your associates my cordial thanks.

Yours faithfully,

HERBERT HOOVER

[Mrs. Alexander M. Hadden, President, Girl's Service League of America, 138 East Nineteenth Street, New York, N.Y.]

NOTE: The message was published in a pamphlet entitled "A Service for Girls," issued by the league in May 1931. The league's employment exchange in New York established an emergency program to provide relief and placement services for unemployed young women.

Similar messages were sent to other organizations cooperating in the emergency employment relief program.

162

The President's News Conference of
May 1, 1931

INTERNATIONAL CHAMBER OF COMMERCE

THE PRESIDENT. I haven't anything of news character today at all. There are some matters in the background of the meeting of the International Chamber of Commerce that may be of interest to you, but I have no statement to make either direct or indirect—simply for your own information.

There are a great many distinguished men coming to that confer-

227

ence, and it is likely to be a very illuminating session on the whole question of the business depression and international relations that have grown out of it—international economic relations. We are hoping to give them a very warm welcome. The American businessmen are making large preparations for their reception, and we are all in hopes that they will develop valuable discussions—and I believe they will.

That body has accomplished a great deal in matters that are sometimes regarded as of secondary importance in international economic relations, but they have served to promote a great many things that have a great value—problems of double taxation, handling of international air transport, commercial arbitration in its international phases, reduction of red tape in handling of international trade through customs regulations, and scores of problems of that kind. They have made a very profound accomplishment. They will no doubt discuss—and I have a question or two here that raises it in my own mind—problems of international finance. They have on their programs the question of silver and international loans. And I wanted you to know for your own information that there is no change in the policy of the American Government in respect to our international debt. That subject may be up for discussion. I don't know how far they will get with it. Some of the papers that have been submitted do enter upon that subject.

Further than that I don't see any news openings for you for the end of this week.

QUESTIONS

Q. Mr. President, are you going to let us have these remarks of yours?

THE PRESIDENT. No, I am giving you this as background only.

Q. I thought it might help a little in the foreground.

THE PRESIDENT. No.

Q. Mr. President, could you give us any guidance as to the American attitude on proposals to restore international prosperity by currency control, such as spoken of in the British press a good deal—through the central banks?

THE PRESIDENT. Our policy in that matter is not changed at all. You know the attitude we have taken about it. We are glad to cooperate, but we have no governmental connection with it.

Q. Mr. President, when will your speech be available?

THE PRESIDENT. I don't know. I have tried to get a minute to do it. I have dictated three or four pages, and that is as far as I have got. It is very short. It will be confined to words of welcome and two or three serious subjects. But it will not be a document that will require any great telegraphic space.

NOTE: President Hoover's one hundred and eighty-ninth news conference was held in the White House at 4 p.m. on Friday, May 1, 1931.

The Sixth General Congress of the International Chamber of Commerce met from May 4 to May 9, in Washington, D.C.

163

Message on the Completion of the Empire State Building.
May 1, 1931

[Released May 1, 1931.   Dated April 29, 1931]

I MOST CORDIALLY congratulate you and your associates upon the completion of the Empire State Building and the opening of its doors to the service of the public. This achievement justifies pride of accomplishment in everyone who has had any part in its conception and construction and it must long remain one of the outstanding glories of a great city.

HERBERT HOOVER

NOTE: The message was read at ceremonies opening the Empire State Building in New York City. During the ceremonies, the President turned on the lights in the building by touching a golden telegraph key in the White House.

The message was sent to Alfred E. Smith, former Governor of New York and president of the Empire State Corporation.

164

Message of Sympathy on the Death
of Edwin Anderson Alderman.
May 1, 1931

[Released May 1, 1931.   Dated April 30, 1931]

I AM DISTRESSED to learn of the sudden death of your distinguished husband. Mrs. Hoover joins with me in expressing heartfelt sympathy.

HERBERT HOOVER

[Mrs. E. A. Alderman, University of Virginia, Charlottesville, Va.]

NOTE: Dr. Alderman, president of the University of Virginia and the author of books on Southern history and culture, died on April 29, 1931, while en route to a speaking engagement at the University of Illinois.

165

Message on the Award of the M. Carey Thomas Prize
to Jane Addams.
May 2, 1931

[Released May 2, 1931.   Dated April 22, 1931]

My dear Miss Park:

I am glad to learn that the M. Carey Thomas Prize is to be awarded to Miss Jane Addams at Bryn Mawr College on May 2nd.

Miss Addams' distinguished achievements and her eminence in American life deserve every possible recognition, in addition to that which she already possesses in nationwide admiration and affection.

Yours faithfully,

HERBERT HOOVER

NOTE: The message was read at ceremonies held in Goodheart Hall at Bryn Mawr College. Contributions by the alumnae association made the prize possible. The prize was awarded to recognize American women of eminent achievement.

Marion Edwards Park was president of Bryn Mawr College.

230

166

Message Commemorating the Birthday of Ulysses S. Grant.
May 3, 1931

[Released May 3, 1931.   Dated April 29, 1931]

My dear Major Harmon:

I am glad to learn of the exercises to be held by the Veterans of Foreign Wars of New York City honoring the memory of General Ulysses S. Grant on Sunday next. Beyond his fame as a great military leader, his memory will forever be cherished by the whole country for his chivalrous consideration in victory and for his nobility of spirit in desiring the immediate healing of the spiritual wounds of war.

Yours faithfully,

HERBERT HOOVER

[Major Leonard J. Harmon, 898 West End Avenue, New York City]

NOTE: The message was read at exercises commemorating the 109th anniversary of Grant's birth. The New York County Council of the Veterans of Foreign Wars sponsored the exercises, which were held at Grant's Tomb in New York City.

167

Message to the American Jewish Congress.
May 3, 1931

[Released May 3, 1931.   Dated May 1, 1931]

I WILL be obliged if you will express my cordial greetings to those present at the Sixteenth Anniversary Dinner of the American Jewish Congress and my appreciation of the many valuable contributions made to our National life by our citizens of the Jewish race.

HERBERT HOOVER

[Bernard G. Richards, Executive Director, American Jewish Congress, 33 West 42nd Street, New York City]

NOTE: The message was read at the 16th annual dinner of the Congress, which was held in the Hotel Roosevelt in New York City.

168

Address to the International Chamber of Commerce.
May 4, 1931

Members of the International Chamber of Commerce:

I bid you welcome to the United States. You have come from many lands and at a time of grave responsibilities at home to participate in discussions that will contribute to world advancement. The consideration and the full and frank discussion of worldwide economic problems and of the economic relations between nations by men who have had to deal with the results of economic forces can be most helpful to world understanding and world cooperation in their solution.

It is needless for me to emphasize the high degree of economic interdependence of the world—we require no more emphatic demonstration than the present worldwide depression. Although the United States enjoys a singular economic independence—greater than any other country perhaps—yet we have been gravely affected by world forces.

The present depression is comparable in its extreme depth and its extent only to those which have followed about the same distance after the former great wars in modern history. This depression is no doubt contributed to by many very important, immediate, economic causes to which each of you will give different weight, but I believe you will all agree with me that the destruction of life and property, the great tax burdens, and the social and political instability which resulted from the Great War have had large responsibility in its origins. Over three-quarters of the commercially important population of the world has been in a state of social and political upheaval at sometime even during the past 3 years. Although some secondary part of this political instability may have been the result of immediate economic causes, we cannot ignore the malign inheritances from the Great War. These political and social disturbances necessarily undermine that confidence upon which economic life, both domestic and international, must thrive.

This is not an occasion for me to review the action and interaction of such a multitude of forces, but I do wish to give emphasis to one of these war inheritances in which international cooperation can effect a major accomplishment in reduction of the tax burdens of the world, removing a primary cause of unrest and the establishment of greater confidence for the long future. That is the limitation and reduction of armaments. The world expenditure on all arms is now nearly five billions of dollars yearly, an increase of about 70 percent over that previous to the Great War. We stand today with near 5½ million men actively under arms and 20 million more in reserves. These vast forces, greatly exceeding those of even the prewar period, still are to be demobilized, even though 12 years have passed since the Armistice was signed, and because of fear and of inability of nations to cooperate in mutual reductions. Yet we are all signatories to the Kellogg-Briand Pact, by which we have renounced war as an instrument of national policy and have agreed to settle all controversies by pacific means. Surely with this understanding, the self-defense of nations could be assured with proportionately far less military forces than we have. This vast armament continues not only a burden upon the economic recuperation of the world, but, of even more consequence, the constant threats and fears which arise from it are a serious contribution to all forms of instability, whether they be social, political, or economic.

Endeavor as we must in support of every proposal of international economic cooperation that is just to our respective peoples, yet we must recognize that the reduction of this gigantic waste, this competition in military establishments is in the ultimate of an importance transcendent over nearly every other form of economic effort.

International confidence cannot be builded upon fear. It must be builded upon good will. The whole history of the world is filled with chapter after chapter of the failure to secure peace through either competitive arms or through intimidation.

I am not unaware of the difficulties of this question. No one would suggest that either national defense should be abandoned nor that so great a task as reasonable limitation and reduction of arms can be accomplished over night.

We have made considerable progress in the limitation and reduction of naval arms. We have laid the foundations for still further progress in the future. Those agreements have contributed greatly to the reduction of the burden of taxes and to the reestablishment of confidence and good will amongst the nations who have been signatory to them. Within a short time the principal nations of the world will meet to discuss the broad question of reduction in land armaments. The very calling of this conference is in itself not only proof of need but it is an emphatic evidence of progress in the world demand for relief—for economic relief and for peace. Of all proposals for the economic rehabilitation of the world, I know of none which compares in necessity or immediate importance with the successful results of that conference. The United States has a less direct interest in land armament reduction than any of the large nations because our forces have been already demobilized and reduced more than most others. We have, however, a vast indirect interest in greater assurance of peace, order and the increased economic prosperity of other nations. It is within the power of the businessmen of the world to insist that this problem shall be met with sincerity, with courage, and with constructive action. It is within the power of statesmen to give to the world a great assurance for the future and a great moral victory for humanity.

I wish to thank you for your coming here. I wish to you a successful conference. I have confidence that it will be fruitful of progress.

Thank you.

NOTE: The President spoke at 10:45 a.m. to the opening meeting of the 6th General Congress, meeting in Constitution Hall. The Congress met from May 4 to May 9, 1931, with delegates from 35 countries in attendance.

The above text is a transcript taken from a sound recording of the address. An advance text of the address was released on the same day.

169

Message to President Ignacy Moscicki
on Polish National Day.
May 4, 1931

[Released May 4, 1931.   Dated May 3, 1931]

IT GIVES ME much pleasure to extend to Your Excellency on this auspicious occasion the sincere good wishes of my Government in which I personally join most heartily.

HERBERT HOOVER

[His Excellency Ignacy Moscicki, President of the Republic of Poland, Warsaw]

NOTE: Polish National Day celebrated Polish independence under the Third of May Constitution of 1791.

170

Message to Dedication Ceremonies
for a Monument of Admiral Comte de Grasse
at the Trocadero Palace in Paris, France.
May 4, 1931

THE SCROLL of French history is so long, and inscribed with so many illustrious names, that a Frenchman might be permitted a moment of uncertainty in establishing the place of the Comte de Grasse. For an American, however, no such uncertainty can exist. The circumstances of 1781 in which Admiral de Grasse anchored his flagship, the *Ville de Paris,* at the gate of Chesapeake Bay, were too momentous for us to forget. The energy and independence of his character, moreover, are preserved for us in the letters of General Washington. "The resolutions that you have taken in our circumstances," wrote the Commander in Chief of the Continental Army, soon after the arrival from the West Indies of the French fleet, "prove that a great mind knows how to make personal sacrifices to secure an important general good." And when that important general good had been secured, Washington was the first to acknowledge how large a share of the honor pertained to de Grasse. He wrote on the eve of the Admiral's departure: "The triumphant manner in which Your Excellency had maintained the mastery of the American seas, and the glory of the French flag, lead both nations to look to you as the arbiter of the war."

In that lofty place the Admiral remains. The name of de Grasse, and of his famous ship, are woven into the web of American history. I, therefore, consider it an honor, on an occasion so interesting to my fellow countrymen and to myself, to participate in this act of homage to the memory of a great man who belongs alike to France and to the United States.

NOTE: Ambassador Walter E. Edge read the President's message at unveiling ceremonies, held on Monday, May 4, 1931. A. Kingsley Macomber, of Morristown, N.J., commissioned the monument, and Paul Landowsky, a Polish sculptor, designed it.

In 1781, Admiral Comte de Grasse commanded the French fleet which blocked the British retreat from Yorktown and facilitated the American victory.

171

Message to an American Legion Banquet Honoring German and Austrian Veterans of the World War. *May 4, 1931*

I AM GLAD to learn that the American Legion is taking the initiative in wiping out the animosities of the War by so gallant an action in good will as the Dinner you are giving this evening for the men who served in the German armed forces and who are now prospective citizens of our own Republic.

HERBERT HOOVER

[The Commander, Lexington Post, American Legion, Banquet Hall, Hotel Astor, New York City]

NOTE: The message was read at a dinner honoring 150 German and Austrian war veterans who were becoming citizens of the United States. Lexington Post 108

236

of the American Legion, in cooperation with the Steuben Society, arranged the banquet.

172

Message of Sympathy
on the Death of George F. Baker.
May 4, 1931

[Released May 4, 1931.   Dated May 3, 1931]

I GREATLY regret to learn of the death of your father. His long and successful career, his many public services and his great benefactions marked him as one of our most eminent citizens. Mrs. Hoover and I join in extending to you our deep sympathy.

HERBERT HOOVER

[George F. Baker, Jr., New York City]

NOTE: Mr. Baker, chairman of the board of the First National Bank of New York and director of numerous corporations, died at his home in New York City on May 2, 1931.

173

The President's News Conference of
May 5, 1931

APPOINTMENTS

THE PRESIDENT. This is a day of appointments. I have appointed Mr. Wayland W. Magee of Bennington, Nebraska as the farmer member of the Federal Reserve Board. Mr. Magee has been an active farmer over many years, and was educated in the public schools of Nebraska and Universities of Nebraska and Iowa. He has been the president of various farm organizations and is endorsed by a wide variety of important folks.

I have appointed Mr. F. D. Letts, former Congressman, to the District

Court in the District of Columbia and am promoting Judge Soper, of the District Court of Baltimore, to the circuit bench in this district.

WAR DEPARTMENT ECONOMY CONFERENCE

I have a question on whether we are going to the Rapidan Camp this week. I am calling a meeting of the Secretary of War and the Chief of Staff, the Quartermaster General, the Chief of Engineers, and the two Assistant Secretaries of War at the Rapidan on next Saturday. We shall leave here sometime during the day Saturday and return in time for dinner Sunday night. We are taking advantage of that occasion and the opportunity to discuss various matters in connection with the War Department over the weekend.

Otherwise I have nothing this morning.

Q. Mr. President, can you give us anything more specific as to what you will discuss?

THE PRESIDENT. No. We will discuss the whole of the work of the Department—to a large extent public works.

NOTE: President Hoover's one hundred and ninetieth news conference was held in the White House at 12 noon on Tuesday, May 5, 1931.

F. Dickinson Letts was appointed Associate Justice of the Supreme Court of the District of Columbia.

On the same day, the White House issued biographical data and lists of endorsers for Mr. Magee and Mr. Letts. On May 7, 1931, the White House also issued biographical data and a list of endorsers for Morris A. Soper, in connection with his appointment as a judge in the Fourth Judicial Circuit of the Circuit Court of Appeals of the United States.

174

Letter Accepting the Resignation of Wendell P. Stafford as Associate Justice of the Supreme Court of the District of Columbia.
May 5, 1931

[Released May 5, 1931.   Dated May 4, 1931]

My dear Mr. Justice:

It was with great regret that I received your letter of resignation today. I deeply appreciate your kind personal note of friendship.

I must, of course, accept your resignation. At the same time I would like to express to you the appreciation I have, and that I know the public has for the long and devoted service given to the country, and for the high ideals of the Federal Bench which you have so consistently maintained.

In the release from your responsibilities of office, I wish for you every happiness.

Yours faithfully,

HERBERT HOOVER

[The Honorable Wendell P. Stafford, Justice of the Supreme Court, Washington, D.C.]

NOTE: Justice Stafford's letter of resignation and an accompanying letter, both dated May 4, 1931, and released with the President's letter, read as follows:

Dear Mr. President:

Enclosed herewith is my formal resignation. But I feel that I cannot let it go to you without a warmer and more human word.

I pray earnestly for your welfare and success, not only because they mean the welfare and success of the whole country, but also because, with great admiration, I am,

Faithfully and devotedly yours

WENDELL P. STAFFORD

[The President, The White House]

Sir:

Having attained the age of seventy years, and having held under commissions and continuously since the 9th day of June, 1904, the office of Associate Justice of the Supreme Court of the District of Columbia, and electing to avail myself of the rights conferred upon me by the statutes in such case made and provided, to-wit, Section 260 of the Judicial Code as amended March 1, 1929; U.S. Code Title 28, Section 375, I hereby resign said office.

Respectfully,
WENDELL P. STAFFORD

175

Message to King Prajadhipok of Siam About His Visit to Washington, D.C.
May 6, 1931

[Released May 6, 1931. Dated May 5, 1931]

I HAVE received Your Majesty's message and am most gratified that you found your visit to Washington a pleasant one. It was a privilege and a pleasure to welcome Your Majesty and Her Majesty The Queen to Washington as our guests. In my own name, and on behalf of my fellow officials, I extend to Your Majesties our sincere best wishes and the assurance that your visit has forged more strongly the bonds of traditional friendship uniting Siam and the United States.

HERBERT HOOVER

[His Majesty Prajadhipok, King of Siam, Purchase, New York]

NOTE: King Pradjadhipok was in the United States for optical surgery. The President hosted a state dinner for the King and Queen on April 29, 1931.

176

Message to President Gaston Doumergue
of France on the Opening of the International
Exposition of Colonial and Overseas Countries.
May 6, 1931

[Released May 6, 1931. Dated May 5, 1931]

IT AFFORDS ME special pleasure on the occasion of the opening of
the International Colonial and Overseas Exposition to extend to Your
Excellency my cordial greetings and to assure you of the best wishes
of the United States for the success of the Exposition. From a historic
as well as from a modern point of view the exhibits will have great
educational value. France is to be congratulated on the enterprise and
vision which have assembled in Paris so much of interest from such
distant parts of the world.

HERBERT HOOVER

[His Excellency Gaston Doumergue, President of the French Republic, Paris]

177

The President's News Conference of
May 8, 1931

PUBLIC BUILDING PROJECTS

THE PRESIDENT. I have two or three inquiries from the press and some
from associations as to the progress of the building program of the
Treasury. We haven't had time to get the detail of it, but we will, sometime next week, be able to give you a list of all the buildings which have
been authorized and what their status is on the road to construction.

The summary of the situation is that there are buildings which have
been completed in the last 18 months or are under contract, 119 million;
sites have been secured, plans have been made, specifications have been
gotten out, and contracts will be let within the next 90 days for 58 mil-

lion further. In the subsequent 90 days a still further 60 million will be let on contract, and in the further 90 days again 40 millions more. That is, within the next 6 months we will have completed or in actual construction under contract 277 million. It covers a total of about 395 different buildings. We will, however, in order that every community may know exactly where it stands, give you a list of all the buildings and exactly where we have got to as to securing the sites, plans, contracts, and everything.

DISTRICT COURT OF MARYLAND

The other item I have today is that Mr. Calvin Chesnut of Baltimore has been selected for the District Court to succeed Judge [Morris A.] Soper.

Further than that I haven't anything today.

NOTE: President Hoover's one hundred and ninety-first news conference was held in the White House at 4 p.m. on Friday, May 8, 1931.

On the same day, the White House issued biographical data and a list of endorsers for Mr. Chesnut in connection with his appointment as a United States Judge of the District Court of Maryland.

178

Message on the Celebration of Parents' Day in Central Park.
May 9, 1931

[Released May 9, 1931.   Dated April 29, 1931]

THE LOVE and respect of parents and children are the root of a very large part of all the happiness in the world.

[Uncle Robert, Uncle Robert Foundation, 333 West End Avenue, New York City]

NOTE: The message was sent to Uncle Robert, a popular children's radio entertainer and sponsor of a number of civic and charitable activities. Uncle Robert read the message during Parents' Day ceremonies held on the Central Park Mall on May 10, 1931.

179

Messages of Sympathy on the Death of Walter A. Strong.
May 10, 1931

I AM DEEPLY shocked to learn of the passing of Mr. Strong. He was so fine an American, so staunch in every righteous course that his loss is a loss to all our people. Mrs. Hoover joins me in expression of our greatest sympathy and our prayers that strength may come to you.

HERBERT HOOVER

[Mrs. Walter A. Strong, care of Mr. Charles H. Dennis, The Chicago Daily News, Chicago, Ill.]

MR. WALTER STRONG was an outstanding publisher of a great journal. Courageous, independent, wise, staunch in every course that led to betterment of the city and the nation. His passing is a national loss. It is a deep personal loss to his myriad of friends.

HERBERT HOOVER

[The Chicago Daily News, Chicago, Ill.]

NOTE: Mr. Strong was publisher of the Chicago Daily News.

180

Message to King Carol II on Rumania's Independence Day.
May 12, 1931

[Released May 12, 1931. Dated May 11, 1931]

I TAKE PLEASURE in extending to Your Majesty and the Rumanian people felicitations on this auspicious anniversary of Rumanian independence.

HERBERT HOOVER

68-611 O - 76 -19

NOTE: As printed above, this item follows the text set forth in a contemporary news account.

181

The President's News Conference of
May 12, 1931

SURGEON GENERAL

THE PRESIDENT. I have appointed Mr. Robert U. Patterson to the rank of major general, to be head of the Medical Corps in succession to General [Merritte Weber] Ireland, Surgeon General of the Army. Major Patterson's career is set out in great detail here for your use.

ARMY POSTS

About a month ago I asked the General Staff to make a renewed study of the whole question of Army posts from the point of view of gaining the maximum efficiency through the concentration of the Army, and the secondary purpose of economy in the War Department. The Staff has insisted for great numbers of years that the Army must be more largely concentrated if it is to be the most effective body, and it becomes even more necessary now in view of the very large mechanization of the Army and the number of subsidiary mechanical services, such as aviation, and so on.

We have actually abandoned 13 posts during the past 2 years. They will probably report 20 or 30 more posts that should be abandoned if we are to have the most effective Army and if we are to accomplish some very considerable economies.

Now, I have appointed a committee [1] representing the Army, the Department of Justice, the Department of Agriculture, and the Vet-

---

[1] The committee, to study future disposition of abandoned posts, consisted of: Brig. Gen. Robert E. Callan, War Department General Staff; Sanford Bates, Department of Justice; A. F. Woods, Department of Agriculture; and Louis H. Tripp, Veterans' Administration. By September 1931, it had inspected 53 posts scheduled for abandonment and recommended the transfer of 9 of them to other departments.

erans' Bureau to study these proposed abandonments and see which of them could be used by other departments of the Government with view to economies in those departments in saving construction and location in the necessary expansions in their work. And there are some of these posts that might be of very great value to the States for institutional purposes—educational or otherwise. It would relieve the feeling of deprivation of the local communities if these posts could be substituted for public purposes. So that we are endeavoring to work out the program in such a fashion as to create as little hardship as possible.

DROUGHT LOANS

One other item—I have a report from the Secretary of Agriculture this morning showing that out of the $67 millions appropriated for drought loans in one form or another, $47 million has been loaned to 380,000 different persons, and that probably consummates the total program.

Of the $10 million allocated to assist agricultural credit corporations, only $471,000 has been called for.

Of the $45 million appropriated for seed and fertilizer purposes, 39 million has been loaned.

Of the 10 millions allocated for agricultural rehabilitation, about $5,140,000 has been loaned.

And of the 2 millions which was reappropriated from a former fund applicable to the Southeastern States, about 1½ million have been loaned.

In a few minutes we will give you a mimeographed statement of not only all those points but the States to which this money has been loaned, in detail.

And I think that is the whole of my budget this morning.

PUBLIC BUILDING PROJECTS

We have partially mimeographed the statement as to public buildings which I promised you. We had expected to have it for this conference, but it will probably be 2 o'clock before the mimeographers will have it done. You will then get in detail the location of every building in the United States which has been authorized by Congress, and what stage of advancement it is now in, so that you will have some material for every State and town in the country.

As I said, you will have that at 2 or 3 o'clock, this afternoon. That is presumed to be for Wednesday morning papers.

NOTE: President Hoover's one hundred and ninety-second news conference was held in the White House at 12 noon on Tuesday, May 12, 1931.

For the White House statement on public building projects, see Item 184.

On the same day, the White House issued the following information relating to drought loans:

AID TO AGRICULTURAL CREDIT CORPORATIONS

($10,000,000 Allocated from the Appropriations)

State	Number of individual loans	Number of corporations benefited	Amount loaned
Alabama	39	2	$38,254.17
Arkansas	64	3	65,500.00
Georgia	143	1	21,466.49
Illinois	3	1	12,000.00
Louisiana	16	1	21,000.00
Mississippi	10	1	8,500.00
Missouri	29	2	42,500.00
Montana	5	1	15,000.00
North Dakota	3	1	20,840.00
Oregon	5	1	22,500.00
South Carolina	20	1	2,930.00
Tennessee	7	3	67,500.00
Texas	19	5	75,300.00
Washington	10	1	58,000.00
Total	373	24	471,290.66

SEED AND FERTILIZER LOANS

($45,000,000 Appropriated)

State	Number of loans	Amount approved
Alabama...	14, 039	$2, 194, 875
Arkansas..	51, 453	7, 621, 471
Delaware..	13	3, 195
Florida..	1, 259	158, 695
Georgia...	12, 738	1, 915, 846
Illinois..	2, 042	263, 115
Indiana..	5, 572	762, 835
Kansas..	1, 076	138, 441
Kentucky..	24, 726	2, 175, 031
Louisiana..	15, 319	2, 518, 081
Maryland..	480	101, 914
Michigan..	917	135, 854
Minnesota.......................................	187	26, 780
Mississippi......................................	21, 635	3, 729, 767
Missouri...	14, 837	1, 971, 188
Montana...	7, 697	1, 998, 205
New Mexico.....................................	2, 188	310, 768
North Carolina..................................	12, 212	1, 805, 876
North Dakota....................................	8, 231	1, 587, 640
Ohio..	1, 300	200, 590
Oklahoma.......................................	14, 569	1, 382, 548
Oregon..	4	3, 225
Pennsylvania....................................	33	7, 595
South Carolina..................................	519	86, 984
South Dakota....................................	1, 798	397, 805
Tennessee.......................................	16, 552	1, 889, 583
Texas...	20, 090	2, 536, 932
Virginia...	15, 715	2, 101, 686
Washington......................................	725	428, 185
West Virginia....................................	5, 107	493, 337
Wyoming..	344	68, 755
Total......................................	273, 377	39, 016, 802

AGRICULTURAL REHABILITATION LOANS

($10,000,000 appropriated)

State	Number of loans	Amount approved
Alabama	3, 367	$176, 536
Arkansas	25, 528	1, 552, 290
Georgia	175	8, 383
Illinois	86	4, 054
Indiana	367	24, 088
Kansas	17	780
Kentucky	7, 631	318, 960
Louisiana	9, 867	675, 083
Maryland	2	150
Mississippi	9, 569	728, 571
Missouri	2, 908	254, 746
Montana	79	8, 255
New Mexico	144	8, 899
North Carolina	2, 302	103, 938
Ohio	9	411
Oklahoma	3, 761	207, 784
Tennessee	7, 212	440, 532
Texas	8, 749	477, 216
Virginia	2, 728	138, 076
Washington	12	1, 850
West Virginia	263	9, 890
Total	84, 766	5, 140, 492

REAPPROPRIATIONS OF FORMER SEED LOAN BALANCES IN SOUTHEASTERN STATES OF $2,000,000

State	Number of loans	Amount approved
Alabama	1, 259	$220, 612
Florida	356	39, 940
Georgia	3, 291	426, 945
North Carolina	788	121, 997
South Carolina	5, 621	686, 417
Total	11, 315	1, 495, 911

248

SUMMARY

(All Loans, by States)

State	Number of loans	Amount approved
Alabama.	18, 665	$2, 592, 023
Arkansas.	76, 981	9, 173, 761
Delaware.	13	3, 195
Florida.	1, 615	198, 635
Georgia.	16, 204	2, 351, 174
Illinois.	2, 128	267, 169
Indiana.	5, 939	786, 923
Kansas.	1, 093	139, 221
Kentucky.	32, 357	2, 493, 991
Louisiana.	25, 186	3, 193, 164
Maryland.	482	102, 064
Michigan.	917	135, 854
Minnesota.	187	26, 780
Mississippi.	31, 204	4, 458, 338
Missouri.	17, 745	2, 225, 934
Montana.	7, 776	2, 006, 460
New Mexico.	2, 332	319, 667
North Carolina.	15, 302	2, 031, 811
North Dakota.	8, 231	1, 587, 640
Ohio.	1, 309	201, 001
Oklahoma.	18, 330	1, 590, 332
Oregon.	4	3, 225
Pennsylvania.	33	7, 595
South Carolina.	6, 140	773, 401
South Dakota.	1, 798	397, 805
Tennessee.	23, 764	2, 330, 115
Texas.	28, 839	3, 014, 148
Virginia.	18, 443	2, 239, 762
Washington.	737	430, 035
West Virginia.	5, 370	503, 227
Wyoming.	344	68, 755
Total.	369, 468	45, 653, 205

In addition to approved loans included in the foregoing statement, it is estimated that at least ten thousand applications which are being held in our various offices for additional information will be approved within the next few weeks. This will represent an additional expenditure of approximately $1,500,000. Thus out of a total of $67,000,000 appropriations about $47,500,000 will be required.

182

Message to the Dental Society of the State of New York.
May 12, 1931

I AM DEEPLY interested to learn of the wish of the Dental Society of the State of New York to cooperate in furthering the ideals set forth by the White House Conference on Child Health and Protection by emphasis upon the dental care of children and especially the preschool child. I will be obliged if you will express to the Society my deep appreciation of their cooperation in this great work in behalf of our most precious National asset.

HERBERT HOOVER

[Alfred Walker, President, Dental Society of the State of New York, Hotel Pennsylvania, New York City]

NOTE: The message was read at the society's 63d annual meeting, which was held in the Pennsylvania Hotel in New York City.

183

Message to Bishop William T. Manning on His 65th Birthday.
May 13, 1931

I MOST CORDIALLY congratulate you upon the triple celebration of this day in your life when your sixty-fifth birthday coincides with the fortieth anniversary of your ministry and the tenth of your bishopric and I send you best wishes for every blessing in the years to come.

HERBERT HOOVER

[Right Reverend William T. Manning, Bishop's House, Cathedral Heights, New York City]

NOTE: William T. Manning was Bishop of the New York Episcopate of the Protestant Episcopal Church. The message was made public in conjunction with a festival service held in the Cathedral of St. John the Divine.

184

White House Statement on Public Building Projects.
May 13, 1931

THE CONSTRUCTION of public buildings involves several sequent stages of progress:

(1)—Legislation:
    Examination of projects;
    Preparation of estimates.
(2)—Determination of site:
    Advertisement;
    Examination of sites offered;
    Selection.
(3)—Acquirement of site;
    Negotiation or condemnation.
(4)—Preparation of plans.
(5)—Advertisement for construction bids.
(6)—Letting of contract.
(7)—Construction.
(8)—Completion.

During the past 2 years, 51 projects have been completed, total limits of cost for land and building $23,516,876.00. (See Statement No. 1).

At the present time, sites have been acquired, contracts let either in whole or in part and construction in progress for 150 projects, total limits of cost for land and building $120,213,900.00. (See Statement No. 2).

Plans have been completed for 56 projects, total limits of cost for land and building $20,097,000. Specifications are now being prepared for approximately one-half of this number, and the remaining projects are on the market for construction bids. (See Statement No. 3).

Sites have been acquired for 190 building projects and plans for same are partially completed, total limits of cost for land and building $192,173,723.22. (See Statement No. 4).

Sites for 115 projects have been determined and have recently been acquired or are in course of negotiation or condemnation, total limits of cost for land and building $50,622,941.00. (See Statement No. 5).

Some 196 projects have been specifically authorized by Congress and the sites are in the process of selection. (See Statement No. 6).

NOTE: Statements 1–6 issued with the White House statement are not printed but are available for examination at the Herbert Hoover Presidential Library.

185

Message to the Army Chief of Staff on the Completion of the Survey by the Interoceanic Canal Board.
May 14, 1931

My dear General MacArthur:

I am much gratified with the conduct of the survey of the route for an Interoceanic canal across the Republic of Nicaragua which the Army Engineer Battalion is bringing to a successful conclusion. For a year and a half the officers and enlisted men of the Battalion have toiled in the tropical jungle in the accomplishment of this task. Their work has been done, not for financial reward, but in that willing and faithful performance of duty which is the tradition of the Army, in peace and in war. I should be pleased to have you convey to these troops my appreciation of their devoted service.

HERBERT HOOVER

[The Chief of Staff, War Department]

NOTE: On December 10, 1931, the President transmitted the report of the Interoceanic Canal Board to the Congress. The report is printed in House Document 139 (72d Cong., 3d sess.).

For the appointment of the Interoceanic Canal Board, see 1929 volume, Item 125.

186

Message to President José P. Guggiari
on Paraguay's Independence Day.
May 14, 1931

I EXTEND my hearty congratulations to Your Excellency and your
fellow countrymen on this anniversary of Paraguayan independence.

HERBERT HOOVER

[His Excellency José P. Guggiari, President of Paraguay, Asunción]

187

Message to Hall of Fame Ceremonies
at New York University.
May 14, 1931

[Released May 14, 1931.   Dated May 12, 1931]

My dear Dr. Johnson:

I am deeply interested to learn of the unveiling of busts in the Hall of
Fame in recognition of the enduring quality of the works of President
Monroe, Maury the scientist, Whistler the artist and Whitman the poet.
Naturally my first interest is in my great predecessor, whose enuncia-
tion of the Monroe Doctrine was conceived in the friendliest spirit toward the struggling republics of Latin America and which has formed
the firm foundation upon which has steadily grown an ever-increasing
mutual respect and good will between our own country and these advancing nations to the south of us. It has been one of the great satisfactions of my tenure of the Presidency that it has given opportunity for this
Administration in many ways to show its deep sympathy with and interest in the well being of our sister republics.

Yours faithfully,

HERBERT HOOVER

[Honorable Robert Underwood Johnson, Director, Hall of Fame, New York University, 26 East 55th Street, New York City]

253

NOTE: The message was read at ceremonies unveiling the bronze busts of James Monroe, Matthew Fontaine Maury, James Whistler, and Walt Whitman.

188

Message on the Death of David Belasco.
May 15, 1931

FROM HIS BOYHOOD in San Francisco David Belasco brought to his national career an adventurous quality of imagination and a freedom from precedent that helped him to pioneer those new paths in the world of the theatre which were so distinctly his contribution to the art of the theatre. His vivid personality will be deeply missed by the whole country.

HERBERT HOOVER

[A. J. McCosker, Director WOR, 1440 Broadway, New York City]

NOTE: The message was made public in conjunction with radio memorial services for David Belasco, owner and manager of New York's Belasco Theatre and a prominent figure in the theatrical world. He died on May 14, 1931.

189

The President's News Conference of
May 15, 1931

ASSISTANT SECRETARY OF STATE

THE PRESIDENT. I have appointed Mr. Harvey H. Bundy, of Boston, as Assistant Secretary of State, to the vacancy created by the promotion of Under Secretary [William R.] Castle. We will give you a small statement about Mr. Bundy's antecedents to help fill up the columns if they need it.

IMMIGRATION

I have secured from the Acting Secretary of Labor a statement as to the movement of immigration during the last 3 months that I thought might be of some interest to you. You will recollect that last autumn

I gave the direction that all immigrants who might in our present un-employment situation become public charges should be refused visas. That direction, of course, did not apply to the preferred classes. The result has been that the average of the first 3 months, that is, the 3 months of a year ago, were 12,605 per month. That has now been reversed to a net departure of 3,551 per month during the average of the last 3 months. So that the effect on unemployment is considerable. That would make a difference of somewhere in the neighborhood of 150,000—more than that—175,000 people in the United States looking for employment—with its operation over a year. However, the figures are here in detail and may be of some interest to you.

NATIONAL FORESTS

Something over a year and a half ago I suggested to the Secretary of Agriculture that the Bureau of Forests would contribute both to national conservation and at the same time to the commercial situation in the wood industries, if they would make no more important leases or if they would slacken down on leasing the national forests. I have given a renewed direction to the Secretary narrowing it even further than that which we had previously put into force so as to practically cease the use of the national forests except where leases are already extant, and except in the case of Alaska for pulpwood and small transactions not over $500. The latter in order to protect the farmers. I don't think it will have any gigantic effect on the timber industry, but at least it shows good will.

Otherwise than that I have nothing.

NOTE: President Hoover's one hundred and ninety-third news conference was held in the White House at 4 p.m. on Friday, May 15, 1931.

On the same day, the White House issued biographical data on Mr. Bundy and a text of the report to the President, dated May 14, on immigration by the Acting Secretary of Labor, which follows:

My dear Mr. President:

In response to your request for information as to the effect upon our unemploy-ment situation of your order restricting immigrants who might become public charges, and for information upon the removal from the country of those found to be unlawfully in the United States, I beg to submit the following figures and facts.

During the last three months of which our statistics are complete the number of arrivals has been a total of 10,815 or 3,605 per month, as compared with a total of 56,619, or 18,873 per month, for the similar period a year ago.

The departures, including deportations, for the last three months have been a total of 21,468, or 7,156 per month, as compared with a total of 16,438, or 5,479 per month, for the similar period a year ago.

The actual figures over the twelve month period ending with March, 1931, were as follows:

Month	Immigrant aliens admitted	Emigrant aliens departed and deported
April 1930..	22,261	6,620
May 1930...	19,414	6,089
June 1930...	14,944	6,095
July 1930..	13,323	7,047
August 1930.......................................	14,816	7,300
September 1930....................................	17,792	7,702
October 1930......................................	13,942	8,021
November 1930....................................	9,209	7,178
December 1930....................................	6,439	7,691
January 1931......................................	4,091	6,921
February 1931.....................................	3,147	6,985
March 1931.......................................	3,577	7,562
Total..	142,955	85,211

It will be noted that the net arrivals were 12,605 per month in the first three months of the period, which has been reversed to a net departure of 3,551 per month during the past three months. The effect upon the unemployment situation is of large importance.

The term "Immigrant aliens" includes aliens whose permanent residence has been outside the United States and who have come here for permanent residence.

The term "Emigrant aliens" designated those whose permanent residence was in the United States and who have now departed for permanent residence abroad.

The number of unlawfully resident aliens deported and those who voluntarily departed when their attention was called to their infraction of the Immigration Laws during the twelve months ending with March, 1931, were as follows:

April 1930	2,673
May 1930	2,369
June 1930	1,775
July 1930	2,229
August 1930	2,055
September 1930	2,602
October 1930	2,669
November 1930	2,227
December 1930	2,241
January 1931	2,524
February 1931	2,265
March 1931	2,869
Total	28,498

The term "Aliens Deported" means those aliens illegitimately in the country who have been expelled under warrant proceedings.

Faithfully yours,

ROBE CARL WHITE

Acting Secretary

[The President, The White House]

190

Message to the Secretary of Agriculture Requesting Restriction of Leases of the National Forests for Wood Production. *May 15, 1931*

[Released May 15, 1931.   Dated May 14, 1931]

My dear Mr. Secretary:

In view of the manifest over-production of wood products, it seems to me it would be of assistance both to the commercial situation and to the real conservation of our forests, if the Department of Agriculture would still further temporarily restrict the leasing of the national forests for wood production. I believe it would be desirable now to more positively define the limitation of all leases by the Bureau of Forests except

257

for pulp purposes in Alaska, to occasions when a sum of not more than $500 is involved and to cases where some cutting privileges must be given to actually maintain sawmills that are in operation, and this only where the mills cannot obtain raw material elsewhere.

The only reason I am moved to make these exceptions is that we should not deprive farmers and small industries of wood supply and should not create local unemployment by inconsiderate action.

Yours faithfully,

HERBERT HOOVER

[The Honorable, The Secretary of Agriculture, Washington, D.C.]

NOTE: The new policy of greater curtailment of leases and timber sales was implemented by Department of Agriculture administrative order on May 20, 1931.

191

Message to the Southern Baptist Convention.
May 16, 1931

PLEASE ACCEPT for yourself and express to the Convention my deep appreciation of your heartening and encouraging message. I am grateful for your prayers.

HERBERT HOOVER

[Dr. William J. McGlothlin, Southern Baptist Convention, Birmingham, Alabama]

NOTE: The message was made public in conjunction with the closing session of the convention which was held in Birmingham, Ala. The convention adopted a resolution commending the President for his efforts in regard to law observance and enforcement and urged approval by the Senate of the protocol of the International Court of Justice.

192

Message of Sympathy
on the Death of David Belasco.
May 16, 1931

[Released May 16, 1931.   Dated May 15, 1931]

My dear Mrs. Gest:

I am at one with the whole Nation in mourning the loss of your
father, David Belasco, whose genius brought so much of pleasure to so
many thousands. You have my deepest sympathy.

Yours faithfully,

HERBERT HOOVER

[Mrs. Morris Gest, 71 East 52nd Street, New York City]

NOTE: Mr. Belasco, owner and manager of New York's Belasco Theatre and a
prominent figure in the theatrical world, died on May 14, 1931.

193

Message on the Opening of the Trans-Lux
Movie Theatre in New York City.
May 18, 1931

[Released May 18, 1931.   Dated May 15, 1931]

I EXTEND congratulations on the opening tonight of your New York
theatre. The showing of news pictures throughout the country cannot
but be educational and instructive. The bringing of world events into
the lives of great numbers of our people will serve to promote better
understanding and closer world relations.

HERBERT HOOVER

[Cortland Smith, President, Trans-Lux Movies Corporation, 247 Park Avenue,
New York City]

NOTE: The message was made public in conjunction with ceremonies opening the
theatre. The Trans-Lux Theatres specialized in showing newsreels and short
features.

259

194

Message to President Gerardo Machado y Morales
on Cuba's Independence Day.
May 20, 1931

IN THE NAME of the people of the United States, and in my own,
I desire to extend to Your Excellency and to the people of Cuba on this
memorable anniversary, most cordial greetings and best wishes.

HERBERT HOOVER

[His Excellency General Gerardo Machado y Morales, President of Cuba, Habana]

195

Address to the American National Red Cross.
May 21, 1931

THE RED CROSS is one of the most beautiful flowers of the American
spirit and the American democracy. It represents our people in their
most generous, unselfish, and spontaneously warmhearted character.
And it represents them in the most effective exercise of their powers of
organization and self-government. Supported wholly by the voluntary
gifts of the people, it is managed by the voluntary service of high-
minded private citizens. And yet it occupies a unique position in the
public mind as a truly national institution, a living organism of the
people, vitalized by their affection, fed by their gladly given money, and
firmly rooted in their trust. Through the loftiest of all spiritual qualities—charity—it has become the guardian of the people from suffering
in times of disaster. It has commanded the recognition of governments,
its charters are conferred by special act, its position in international
activities is guaranteed by treaty. By its very purpose it compels the
respect for its own flag and its own passports.

The 50 years of the life of the Red Cross, which the American people
celebrate today, have been years of evolution of an impulse and an idea
and a method to produce this greatest institution in alleviation of human

suffering that we have ever known. Its beginnings were small, and it grew because it expressed the humanity and the generosity and the practical helpfulness natural to our people. And, like so many of the benign social agencies that bless our democracy, it sprang from the mind and the heart of a woman. Clara Barton was in her own person and her own life all that the Red Cross has since become. She in turn gained much of her inspiration from another great woman—Florence Nightingale. The magnificent structure of today grew up around Miss Barton's passionate pity for the sick and the distressed and her practical genius and energy in their relief. She was the ministering angel of the battlefields and hospitals of the Civil War. When peace returned she still lived like a soldier, with her field tent and equipment always packed and ready to respond instantly to the call of duty. The Johnstown flood found her ready, and within an hour after it was reported she was on her way to the stricken city. She responded to a thousand such calls, but her service on the battlefield and her service at Johnstown especially captured the public imagination, and it is these two things that have largely directed the development of the character of the American Red Cross. It has evolved into an agency for the nursing of the wounded in war and for the relief of the victims of disaster in time of peace.

Clara Barton did not look to government for support for her work. Governments are always too slow, frequently too shortsighted, to meet the sudden, sharp demands of critical emergencies in human suffering. She depended upon the instant response of the individual human heart to finance the instant need. This gave her the flexibility and freedom of private initiative in her work. The Red Cross has grown in this tradition. Hundreds of times it has appealed to the American people for funds to meet an immediate situation, and invariably the American people have immediately responded. It has raised millions in a week when millions were needed. No finer illustration has ever been given of the tremendous practical power of pure and unselfish emotion than these outbursts of American generosity to finance relief of suffering caused by conflagration, flood, earthquake, and drought. No finer illustration has ever been given of the tremendous practical capacity of an organized free citizenry than the skill and efficiency with which the Red Cross has administered this relief. This combination of the warm heart and the cool head in action is a perpetual source of just pride to the American people, for it represents them at their best.

A woman founded the Red Cross and a woman has enlarged its usefulness. Miss Mabel Boardman enjoys a deserved national honor for her tireless and effective work in the enlargement of its powers. The men of America, too, have had their indispensable part in its growth. Judge John Barton Payne has earned equal honor for his long years of devoted leadership across a score of disasters and for his steadfastness in holding the organization to its national ideal as a nongovernmental agency for the free expression of the private generosity and humanity of the people. His wisdom and courage and zeal are beyond praise.

But the greater glory of the Red Cross belongs to the people themselves. It is a living embodiment of their heart and soul. It has lived and grown because it is a natural outgrowth of their spiritual impulse. Its sap is drawn from the soil of their spirit, its leaves are colored with their thought, and its flowers are fragrant of their sweetest emotion. It is as truly theirs as the flag or the public school. They wished it, and they willed it into being. It grows with their growth. They support it as spontaneously as they support the church or the lodge. They control it as simply and as naturally as they control the operations of the district school. They will thus support it and control it so long as it continues what it is: the natural repository of their generosity, the effective practical instrument of their eager wish to relieve human suffering. It will remain, as it has been and is, a chief glory and pride of the American democracy.

NOTE: The President spoke at a dinner held in the Willard Hotel, in Washington, D.C. The ceremonies were part of a nationwide celebration of the organization's 50th anniversary and were linked by radio with hundreds of local observances.

196

The President's News Conference of
May 22, 1931

RAILWAY EMERGENCY BOARD

THE PRESIDENT. Two or three people have been told about the report of the emergency board which I appointed [Proc. 1949] on the Louisiana and Arkansas Railway dispute. That was a dispute involving 125 men. The board was appointed. It has made its report and the managers of the railway, I understand, are coming to Washington to discuss the matter with the railway mediation board,[1] and I have agreed not to publish the report until they have had an opportunity to see whether they can settle their disturbance. The object of those processes is to bring about arbitration and if that can be brought about I am only too glad to see it settled up.

SPECIAL SESSION OF CONGRESS

I have memorials from several associations, chiefly of religious character, and others, and there have also been some statements made in the press in respect to an extra session of Congress. I want to say that I do not propose to call an extra session of Congress. I know of nothing that would so disturb the healing processes now undoubtedly going on in the economic situation. We cannot legislate ourselves out of a world economic depression. We can and we will work ourselves out. A poll of the Members of Congress would show that a very large majority of them are in entire agreement with me on that subject.

And that is all I have got for today.

NOTE: President Hoover's one hundred and ninety-fourth news conference was held in the White House at 4 p.m. on Friday, May 22, 1931.

On the same day, the White House issued a text of the President's statement about a special session of Congress (see Item 197).

The railroad emergency board report, filed July 9, 1931, concluded that the wage cuts of February 9, 1931, had been unjustified, that they ran counter to the admin-

---

[1] United States Mediation Board.

istration's policy of wage maintenance and that earlier pay schedules should be restored.

197

Statement About a Special Session of Congress.
May 22, 1931

THE PRESIDENT said:

"I do not propose to call an extra session of Congress. I know of nothing that would so disturb the healing processes now undoubtedly going on in the economic situation. We cannot legislate ourselves out of a world of economic depression; we can and will work ourselves out. A poll of the Members of Congress would show that a large majority agree with me in opposing an extra session."

198

Radio Remarks Introducing Dr. Robert A. Millikan
to the National Advisory Council on Radio in Education.
May 22, 1931

DR. MILLIKAN'S address tonight on "Radio's Past and Future" is the first of a series arranged by the National Advisory Council on Radio in Education, of which society he is the president. It is the purpose of the association to provide the radio audience with addresses from the leading authorities upon significant developments in the fields of science, arts, and the professions. It is distinctly a public service that the leaders in thought in our country have banded themselves together to give to the radio audience this opportunity of knowing from those who can speak with authority the progress that we are making in the fundamentals of civilization.

Dr. Millikan is one of America's foremost scientists. He ranks among the world's greatest physicists. He is the director of one of the most successful of our great physics research laboratories. He has given to

America great contributions in the whole field of education and science. Dr. Millikan is more than a physicist. He is one of America's leaders in philosophic thought.

Dr. Millikan will now speak to you from Los Angeles, California.

NOTE: The President spoke at 9 p.m. from the White House.

Dr. Millikan, of the California Institute of Technology, spoke via radio to the first annual assembly of the council meeting at the New School for Social Research in New York City.

199

Radio Remarks on the Dedication of the Cornell University War Memorial.
May 23, 1931

FOURTEEN YEARS AGO this morning a group of American boys carried an American flag into the fighting on the Aisne front, and thereby made a splendid gesture symbolical of the might of the new world mustering for the decisive issue.

This unit was composed of undergraduates of Cornell University and was under the leadership of Capt. Edward Tinkham, a Cornell student in the class of 1916. It was a vanguard of a mighty army of American youth that flowed across the Atlantic in the months that followed. In this army were 9,000 other Cornellians who followed Tinkham's unit in the Nation's service.

Two hundred and sixty-four of them did not return. I am happy today to take part in the dedication of a permanent memorial to those men of Cornell University who lost their lives in the World War. Significant in itself, this memorial takes on a broader aspect. While we pay tribute specifically to the service of the 264 Cornell men whose names are carved in this beautiful shrine, the occasion recalls the great part in our war effort played by the men of all our universities and colleges.

The towers and cloister in which the memory of Cornell's heroic dead is enshrined—distinctive, beautiful, and useful though they are—are not mere buildings. They are symbols, fitting and lasting symbols, of the ideals for which the men of Cornell, of all our universities and colleges, of our whole country, fought and died. They commemorate the contribution of youth to the cause of America, a free gift of devoted young lives to an ideal they deemed worth cherishing and defending.

These young men of the Tinkham unit were typical American boys. Their experiences and their reactions typify the response of American youth everywhere in the hour of crisis. Volunteers sprang up right and left. Young men eagerly offered to risk their future—their lives—because they wanted to do their man's share in a crisis of the world. Without one atom of selfishness, they sought to carry out their ideal of manhood. It involved hardships, danger, even death, but they were unafraid. With heads erect, with vibrant tread, they left their training camps. Alive with purpose, alive with honor, alive with faith, their only anxiety was how quickly they could get over there. They had no illusions about what was ahead of them. Life to them had been sweet, joyous, and care free. Tomorrow it might be ended. Yet they never faltered and gave up all for a cause which they believed to be right. There was no searching for hidden motives or for ulterior purposes. They accepted whatever came with a smile, and they did not ask questions. They had no hatred in their hearts, but they went about their job with a full resolve to play the man's part in a terrible business.

Their patriotism never wavered but rather their devotion grew and found its way back to the quiet campuses which they had left in the full flush of their youthful enthusiasm.

To them and to all those from Cornell who followed them we dedicate this memorial. In speaking for the Cornell dead I am drawing the attention of this Nation to all of its university war dead, indeed, to all our youth who went over, never to come back.

In this memorial, as in all our other memorials, we do not seek to glorify war or to perpetuate hatreds. We are commemorating not war, but the courage and the devotion and the sacrifice of those who gave their lives for their fellows and for their country. We raise these because we are able to remember the ideals which possessed us at the time. We do not condemn our own action or belittle the high motives and ideals

266

which based our efforts when we acknowledge that the war was a catastrophe.

Here in the scenes which they loved you have built a loving monument to their memory. We cannot add to their glory, but we and our descendants will be the better for remembering them.

NOTE: The President spoke at 12:40 p.m. over a nationwide radio and telephone hookup from his summer camp on the Rapidan River.

200

White House Statement on the Economy Conference With Post Office Department Officials.
May 23, 1931

THE CONFERENCE this afternoon was devoted to consideration of methods of reducing expenditures below appropriations. The result of the drive last year to reduce expenditures was reviewed, as were plans for reducing expenditures during the next year. The discussion covered the activities of each branch of the Post Office Department. It was preliminary to a second conference held tonight.

At the afternoon conference the difficulty presented itself of reducing expenditures and at the same time not discharging any employees. The heads of the various departments of the Post Office Department reported that representative employees in many sections of the country have indicated they would be glad to make their contribution to reducing expenses by deferring increases in salary. They feel that they are performing a real and patriotic service in so doing.

Post Office Department officials said there would be no reduction in pay in any particular; neither is it proposed to reduce the number of employees except through death and natural separation from the service.

It is expected that the conference tonight will develop figures, in which event they will be made public tomorrow.

NOTE: The White House issued the statement following a conference at Rapidan Camp between the President, Postmaster General Walter F. Brown, and Assistant

Postmasters General Arch Coleman, Warren I. Glover, Frederic A. Tilton, and John W. Philp.

As printed above, this item follows the text set forth in a contemporary news account.

201

White House Statement on Economy in the Post Office Department.
May 24, 1931

A COMPREHENSIVE program to increase efficiency in the Post Office Department and to effect economies was formulated at conferences in which President Hoover, Postmaster General Brown and Assistant Postmasters General Coleman, Glover, Tilton and Philp participated over the weekend. A review of the drive for economy which the President instituted last summer revealed a saving for this year of about $38 million out of the appropriation of $843 million made for the year that ends June 30. Minute study was made of the obligations confronting the Department for the next fiscal year.

The appropriation for next year is approximately $841,500,000. Officials reported that enactment by Congress of the law reducing the working week in all branches of the service from 48 to 44 hours would of itself obligate the Government to an additional expenditure of about $13 million, making the total of approximately $854,500,000.

They advised the President, however, that studies already made indicate preliminary reductions for next year of $28 million, or a total of $826,500,000. Thus it is probable there will be a net saving of $15 million under the original appropriation, the additional cost of the shorter workweek to the contrary notwithstanding.

Further examination of possible economies was outlined at the conference with the results to be considered later. The total will be enhanced beginning next year when the building program will begin to offset the great rental charges. In effecting the savings there will be no decrease in personnel excepting only as develops through natural changes incident to death and resignations. It was emphasized that the economies are no wise at the expense of dismissals from the service or through reductions in salaries, President Hoover insisting that there be no economies that would enhance the present unemployment situation.

The Post Office economies would exceed the sums indicated but for the decreased volume of postal business incident to the depression. Because of the business conditions, postal receipts this year probably will be some $58 million below the original estimates. It is noteworthy however, that the receipts for the last month show an increase for the first time since the depression started.

A significant fact developed by the conference is that the postal savings deposits are the largest in history today, totaling $310 million. This is an increase since last July of $175 million, indicating the tremendous increase in savings by the public. The Post Office officials advise the President that the indefensible practice of payment to political organizations for Post Office appointments in some Southern States has been absolutely stamped out as a result of his appointment 2 years ago of committees of leading citizens to pass upon all candidates for such appointments. He was gratified to know that his efforts to end the practice have been successful.

NOTE: As printed above, this item follows the text set forth in a contemporary news account.

202

Message on the Dedication of a World War Shrine in Hoboken, New Jersey.
May 24, 1931

[Released May 24, 1931.　Dated May 14, 1931]

My dear Dr. Armstrong:

I am deeply interested to learn of the dedication at St. Paul's Church, Hoboken, on Sunday May 24th, of a World War Shrine commemorating Hoboken as the Port of Embarkation and Debarkation and the place where so many of our soldier dead lay under the flag upon their return from service abroad. It is indeed fitting that such a Shrine should be adorned with memorials of their supreme sacrifice, and that our country-men should resort there for remembrance.

Yours faithfully,

HERBERT HOOVER

[Rev. Frank C. Armstrong, Chairman, World War Shrine, St. Paul's Church, Hoboken, N. J.]

NOTE: The message was read at ceremonies dedicating the shrine in St. Paul's Protestant Episcopal Church.

203

Message to President José Francisco Uriburu on Argentina's Independence Day.
May 25, 1931

PLEASE ACCEPT my sincere congratulations on this occasion of the anniversary of the Independence of our great sister Republic of Argentina.

HERBERT HOOVER

[His Excellency José Francisco Uriburu, President of Argentina, Buenos Aires]

204

Address to the Union League of Philadelphia, Pennsylvania.
May 29, 1931

Mr. President, members of the Union League Club:

I am deeply honored by your courteous hospitality. When your committee came to me and made the invitation extended to every President of the United States, that I should come to your club, as your guest, I said that in these times of extra and heavy burdens, that I should defer that date in order that I might be prepared, under easier circumstances perhaps, to discuss public questions as my predecessors have done—as they have felt honored to do before this body.

They, however, extended to me a delicate consideration that brooked no refusal—the suggestion that the club would like to extend its hand of encouragement by a reception, with no request for a public address. In these times, when a large number of segments of our population are seeking relief, that was indeed the greatest and most considerate relief ever extended to the President of the United States.

Your generous reception has gone beyond even the frontiers of hospitality. You have presented to Mrs. Hoover and myself a portrait by a skillful artist. It is difficult for me to express, with my natural—I hope natural—modesty, that it gives one pleasure to see oneself presented in a better fashion than the normal snap photograph, and perhaps a justifiable admiration that it may serve as an antidote to some of the current portraits under which I suffer. Yet, I would not criticize that phase of the gift, otherwise it would seem something like the old term about the "gift horse."

I have felt all evening that this club represents more than a comradeship. It is the sanctuary of a great tradition—the tradition of the preservation of our Union, and the preservation of the tradition of loyalty to our Government in the greatest of our trials. That service of the club—protection of the Union—finds its expression in every portion of this building, and all these years the club has stood steadfast for the patriotic solution of the recurring difficulties which have met the Republic. It has pierced the fallacy of many specialized causes; it has favored great measures of progress; it has stood unfailingly in times of public stress with confidence in the ultimate growth and security that distinguishes all thinking men.

After 2 years of fever and tumult in Washington, I assure you this is a gratifying occasion. In these quiet halls, there is a restfulness and a feeling of security—an inspiration of faith in one's country. I shall remember this occasion always with appreciation, not alone for the fine and encouraging words of your President—and even public officials need encouragement—but for the opportunity you have given me to meet many old friends, and, I hope, to make new ones; and to come in contact with that spirit of the living men who have to carry the responsibilities of our community, and of our Nation as a whole. On Mrs. Hoover's and my own behalf I do thank you.

NOTE: The President spoke at a dinner meeting of the league. The address, as printed above, was recorded by court stenographers employed by the Union League. On the same day, the White House issued an advance text of the address.

Preceding the President's address, George S. Patterson, president of the Union League, presented the President with a life-size portrait painted by Philides Costa.

205

Memorial Day Address at Valley Forge, Pennsylvania.
May 30, 1931

WE ARE upon the eve of the celebration of the 200th anniversary of the birth of George Washington. It is, therefore, appropriate that our observance of Memorial Day should this year be at this place, so intimately associated with the moral grandeur of the Father of our Country.

This national shrine needs no description; the events enacted here require no recounting to the American people. The very name, Valley Forge, swells within us a pride of nationality. These peaceful fields hold a glory peculiarly their own. The sufferings of Washington's army in that dreadful winter of privation have made this place famous among all men.

It was not the glory of battle for which these fields are remembered. No great battle was fought here. It was not the pomp of victory, for no martial triumph was won here. It was not the scene where peace was signed by which independence of a great nation was won. It was not the tombs of courageous men who, facing the enemy, gave the supreme sacrifice for their country to which we bow in reverence. A thousand other fields mark the courage, the glory, the valor, the skill, the martial triumph of our race. Yet the instinct and the judgment of our people after the abrasion of the years has appraised this place as a foremost shrine in the War of Independence and in our Nation. It is a shrine to the things of the spirit and of the soul.

It was the transcendent fortitude and steadfastness of these men who in adversity and in suffering through the darkest hour of our history held faithful to an ideal. Here men endured that a nation might live.

George Washington and his men at any moment could have accepted the counsels of an easy path to an easy end of their privations. They could have surrendered their ideals to the widespread spirit of despair and discouragement. They could have abandoned their claims to freedom. They could have deserted their hopes and forsaken their faith. Instead, they chose the harder way of steadfast fortitude and for many of death.

Here Washington and his little band of hungry and almost naked patriots kept alive the spark of liberty in the lowest hours of the Revolution. They met the crisis with steadfast fortitude; they conserved their strength; they husbanded their resources; they seized the opportunity, which, with the turn and the tide of war, led on to victory. It was a triumph of character and idealism and high intelligence over the counsels of despair, of prudence, and material comfort. This was one of those moral victories that are the glory of the race. Without such victories the life of man would descend to a sheer materialism for "where there is no vision the people perish." Lacking these high inspirations mankind could claim no distinction higher than the beasts of the field, that sing no songs, dream no dreams, inspire no hope, and grasp no faith.

It is this high spirit that we commemorate when we pay our yearly tribute of reverence to those who in all wars have stood steadfast and those who have died in the service of our country. Our citizens in every war have flocked to arms at the call of country. They have responded willingly, because in every emergency they have had up before them an ideal of liberty and the freedom of their country. Some wars in history have been instigated by old and cynical men for cruel or selfish reasons. Some wars have been fought for power and possessions. The ends of some wars could have been more nobly won and more wisely won by patience and negotiation. But war for liberty has

273

endowed the race not alone with the most precious possessions of freedom but has inspired every succeeding generation with that idealism which is the outpouring of man's spiritual nature.

An ideal is an unselfish aspiration. Its purpose is the general welfare not only of this but of future generations. It is a thing of the spirit. It is a generous and humane desire that all men may share equally in a common good. Our ideals are the cement which binds human society. They provide the mainspring of progress. Idealism was forged into the souls of the American people by the fires of the Revolution. It is this quality of spirit which has made possible the success of our great democratic experiment. It has tempered our acquisitiveness, has strengthened our sense of civic responsibility, and has made service to fellow man a part of our national character.

This peculiar significance of Valley Forge in our American annals should strike us all with especial force in this particular moment of our national life. The American people are going through another Valley Forge at this time. To each and every one of us it is an hour of unusual stress and trial. You have each one your special cause of anxiety. So, too, have I. The whole Nation is beset with difficulties incident to a worldwide depression. These temporary reverses in the march of progress have been in part the penalty of excesses of greed, of failure of crops, and the malign inheritances of the Great War and a storm of other world forces beyond our control. Their far-reaching effects have fallen heavily upon many who were in no wise concerned with their causes. Many have lost the savings of a lifetime, many are unemployed, all know the misgivings of doubt and grave concern for the future.

No one who reviews the past and realizes the vast strength of our people can doubt that this, like a score of similar experiences in our history, is a passing trial. From it will come a greater knowledge of the weaknesses of our system, and from this knowledge must come the courage and wisdom to improve and strengthen us for the future. Numerous are the temptations under the distress of the day to turn aside from our true national purposes and from wise national policies and fundamental ideals of the men who builded our Republic. Never was the lure of the rosy path to every panacea and of easy ways to imagined security more tempting.

For the energies of private initiative, of independence, and a high degree of individual freedom of our American system we are offered an alluring substitute in the specious claim that everybody collectively owes each of us individually a living rather than an opportunity to earn a living, and the equally specious claim that hired representatives of a hundred million people can do better than the people themselves, in thinking and planning their daily life.

The Revolution, of which Valley Forge was the darkest but perhaps the most glorious moment, was fought not alone for national independence but to retain our freedom to continue unhampered the most promising social experiment in all human history. Our American ideals had already been in process of development for a century when the War for Independence began. Our Government was an experiment in securing to a people the maximum of individual freedom. Amazing success has proved it is no longer an experiment. Under it has grown a social and economic system new in the world and distinctly our own. Human initiative has been inspired, human energies released, local cooperation has solidly knit together communities into self-governing democracies, and the human spirit has blossomed in an atmosphere of a new independence and self-respect. It brought America to a greatness unparalleled in the history of the world.

We must ever continue that fight. Amid the scene of vastly growing complexity of our economic life we must preserve the independence of the individual from the deadening restraints of government, yet by the strong arm of government equally protect his individual freedom, assure his fair chance, his equality of opportunity from the encroachments of special privileges and greed or domination by any group or class.

We are still fighting this war of independence. We must not be misled by the claim that the source of all wisdom is in the Government. We know that the source of wisdom is in the people; that the people can win anew the victory. But that wisdom is not innate. Rather is it born out of experience, and most of all out of precisely

275

such experience as is brought to us by the darkest moments—the Valley Forges—of our individual and national careers. It is in the meeting of such moments that are born new insights, new sympathies, new powers, new skills. That is precisely why the wisdom of the few instead of the many fails to build an enduring government or an enduring people. Such battles as we are in the midst of today can not be won by any single stroke, by any one strategy sprung from the mind of any single genius. The necessary multitude of individuals and group adjustments to new conditions is altogether too vast and too complex for that. Rather must we pin our faith upon the inventiveness, the resourcefulness, the initiative of every one of us. That cannot fail us if only we keep the faith in ourselves and our future, and in the constant growth of our intelligence and ability to cooperate with one another.

Sirens still sing the song of the easy way for the moment of difficulty, but the common sense of the common man, the inherited tradition of an independent and self-reliant race, the historical memory of Americans who glory in Valley Forge even as they glory in Yorktown—all these tell us the truth for which our ancestors fought and suffered, the truth which echoes upward from this soil of blood and tears, that the way to the Nation's greatness is the path of self-reliance, independence, and steadfastness in times of trial and stress.

Valley Forge met such a challenge to steadfastness in times and terms of war. Our test is to meet this challenge in times and terms of peace. It is the same challenge. It is the same test of steadfastness of will, of clarity of thought, of resolution of character, of fixity of purpose, of loyalty to ideals and of unshaken conviction that they will prevail. We are enduring sufferings and we are assailed by temptations. We, too, are writing a new chapter in American history. If we weaken, as Washington did not, we shall be writing the introduction to the decline of American character and the fall of American institutions. If we are firm and farsighted, as were Washington and his men, we shall be writing the introduction to a yet more glorious epoch in our Nation's progress. We have seen many precious fruits of the sturdy pioneering virtues that have made our country first free and then strong and now proudly in the forefront of the world. If, by the grace of God, we stand steadfast in our great traditions through this time of stress, we shall insure that we and our sons and daughters shall see these fruits increased many fold.

Valley Forge has come indeed to be a symbol in American life. It is more than the name for a place, more than the scene of a military episode, more than just a critical event in history. Freedom was won here by fortitude not by the flash of the sword. Valley Forge is our American synonym for the trial of human character through privation and suffering, and it is the symbol of the triumph of the American soul. If those few thousand men endured that long winter of privation and suffering, humiliated by the despair of their countrymen, and deprived of support save their own indomitable will, yet held their countrymen to the faith, and by that holding held fast the freedom of America, what right have we to be of little faith? God grant that we may prove worthy of George Washington and his men of Valley Forge.

NOTE: The President spoke at 10:45 a.m. to an estimated 20,000 people assembled at Valley Forge Park. The National Broadcasting Company and the Columbia Broadcasting System carried the address to the Nation.

206

Message to the Children's Hour.
May 30, 1931

[Released May 30, 1931.   Dated May 28, 1931]

My dear Mr. Warner:

I am interested to know of your weekly broadcast of a children's hour, and particularly of your program for Memorial Day.

The White House Conference on Child Health and Protection recognizes the rights of the child as the first rights of citizenship. The Children's Charter, which it promulgated, sets forth the aspirations and objectives of those who are seeking the protection and the rounded development of the children of America.

I enclose a copy of the Children's Charter, which states succinctly the rights of children, regardless of race or color or situation, wherever they may live under the protection of the American flag.

Yours faithfully,

HERBERT HOOVER

[Mr. Henry Edward Warner, c/o The Baltimore Sun, Baltimore, Md.]

NOTE: The letter and the Children's Charter were read as the opening feature of the Children's Hour, a program originating from WCAO radio in Baltimore, Md.

207

Message on the 75th Anniversary of Berea College.
May 30, 1931

[Released May 30, 1931.   Dated May 21, 1931]

My dear Dr. Hutchins:

I thank you cordially on my own behalf and that of Mrs. Hoover for your kind invitation that we attend the exercises in celebration of the seventy-fifth anniversary of Berea College. It would give us great pleasure if it were possible for us to be present, but other engagements will not permit.

I will be obliged, however, if you will express my cordial greetings to those gathered for this happy occasion and my profound appreciation of the tremendous service which Berea College, both by its own work and by its example, has done in widening the service of education and in development of the character of the previous youth of our country. The service of the College has been memorable and I speak the heart of the Nation in wishing for it many years of ever increasing usefulness.

Yours faithfully,

HERBERT HOOVER

[Dr. William J. Hutchins, Berea College, Berea, Kentucky]

NOTE: The message was made public in conjunction with ceremonies celebrating the founding of the college.

208

Message to the General Assembly
of the Presbyterian Church.
May 30, 1931

[Released May 30, 1931.   Dated May 29, 1931]

I SHALL appreciate it if you will express my cordial greetings to the General Assembly of the Presbyterian Church, now in session in your city. The constant advancement of the spiritual welfare of our country is its primary necessity, and your efforts are a very substantial contribution to that objective.

HERBERT HOOVER

[Rev. Hugh T. Kerr, D.D., Retiring Moderator, General Assembly of the Presbyterian Church, c/o Shadyside Presbyterian Church, Pittsburgh, Pa.]

NOTE: The message was read at a session of the General Assembly meeting in Pittsburgh, Pa.

209

Exchange of Messages With Albert,
King of the Belgians, on Memorial Day.
May 30, 1931

To His Majesty The King of the Belgians:
   I am deeply moved by Your Majesty's tribute to the memory of those of my countrymen who gave their lives in the great cause and whose bodies rest in Belgian soil. All Americans with one accord thank Your Majesty and the Belgian people for this evidence of affection and for the Belgian flowers which tomorrow will lie on American graves.

HERBERT HOOVER

NOTE: The President's message was in response to a message from the King, dated May 29, 1931, which follows:
   The memory of the heroism of the American troops who fought by our side for the liberation of our land is forever graven on the hearts of the Belgian people.

It is with deep emotion and gratitude that, on the thirtieth of May, my fellow-countrymen will again strew flowers upon the graves of the sons of the great Republic who sleep in Belgian soil.

United in our sentiment of gratitude, we address to the friendly American Nation our cordial wishes for its prosperity.

ALBERT

210

Letter Accepting the Resignation of Charles C. Teague as a Member of the Federal Farm Board.
June 1, 1931

[Released June 1, 1931.   Dated May 25, 1931]

My dear Mr. Teague:

I beg to acknowledge your letter of May 22nd on completion of your term with the Federal Farm Board. I greatly regret that your personal situation is such that you cannot continue on the Board for the present.

I wish to take this occasion to express my appreciation, and the appreciation which I know the whole agricultural industry holds, for the great service you have rendered and the devotion you have shown in the difficult times of the past two years.

Yours faithfully,

HERBERT HOOVER

[Mr. C. C. Teague, Federal Farm Board, Washington, D.C.]

NOTE: Mr. Teague's letter of resignation, dated May 22, 1931, and released with the President's letter, follows:

Dear Mr. President:

When I accepted appointment on the Federal Farm Board it was with the understanding that it was to be for a year, or during the organization and policy formation period of the Board. At your request I have continued as a Member of the Board and you have been good enough to accept my resignation, effective on June 1 of this year, in order that I may return to my personal affairs and the affairs of organizations which I have handled for many years and which would not permit of my continuing longer on the Board.

In retiring from the Federal Farm Board permit me to say that it has been a privilege to participate for the past nearly two years in the administration of the Agricultural Marketing Act. It was indeed fortunate, during the present serious economic condition through which the country has been passing, that the farmers of the country have had this important legislation, with adequate finances and administered by a group of men of your selection, who have had such a deep and sympathetic attitude toward the problems of agriculture. In the time that I have been on the Board I have never observed any action influenced by section or politics. The Board has always sought for the most helpful solution of any of the problems that have been presented. They have brought to these problems broad business experience and a thorough knowledge of agriculture and cooperative marketing.

It has, of course, been impossible to be helpful under these most difficult and trying conditions without at times taking some chances of loss to the revolving fund. Had it been administered as a banking trust or fund it would have been of little help to agriculture under existing conditions. I am frank to say that when I accepted your request to become a Member of the Board I had some misgivings as to the possibility of too much importance being attached to the revolving fund and the loan provisions of the Act, as I had the very definite conviction that the greatest benefits would come from Federal sanction and assistance in the developing of a cooperative marketing system for agriculture.

There are two distinct methods of stabilization of markets. Probably the one that has been emphasized most in the publicity relating to Farm Board action has been the stabilization operations on wheat and cotton, which were entirely emergency operations undertaken to meet emergency conditions and which I believe are entirely justified and which will have resulted in benefits to agriculture and business generally far outweighing any cost to the Treasury. However, in my judgment the greatest benefit will come through another type of stabilization of markets, which will come through the long-time project of developing a system of cooperative control of agricultural products, which will effect a better control of production and a better control of distribution and thus have an important influence in the stabilization of markets.

Of course no one could foresee the conditions brought about by the world-wide depression and its effect upon all business, including agriculture. Had it not been for the revolving fund a large number of the cooperatives that have performed a very definite and valuable service to the farmers of this country, would have perished through the inability to finance themselves and to adjust their business practices to the changed conditions brought about by unprecedented declines in values; so, I say without hesitation that many of these cooperatives owe their continuing existence to the assistance given them by the Board. As these facts become better known and understood by agricultural producers and the public, I believe they will recognize the importance of rallying to the support of the Board and of the Agricultural Marketing Act. I am firmly convinced that during the last two years more progress has been made in cooperative marketing than has been made in any previous ten year period in our history. This perhaps can not be demonstated by an inventory of the increased membership of cooperatives but in appraising this gain there should be taken into consideration the great advance that has been made in the support of educational institutions, national farm membership organizations and by broad gauge business men and the public generally.

I am retiring from the Board in no spirit of discouragement but with the definite feeling that the time I have spent on the Board and such contribution as I have been able to make have been distinctly worth while. Permit me at this time to extend to you assurance of my continued respect and regard.

Respectfully,

CHARLES C. TEAGUE
Vice Chairman

[The President, The White House]

211

The President's News Conference of *June 2, 1931*

ARMY AIR CORPS MANEUVERS

THE PRESIDENT. I have sent a letter to the Secretary of War congratulating the Department for the success in the conduct of the maneuvers. That is the largest maneuver of airplanes ever executed and done without any serious mishap—a very remarkable performance.

AGRICULTURE DEPARTMENT ECONOMY CONFERENCES

The conferences in the Department—with the Secretary and the heads of the divisions of the Department of Agriculture—bring out the fact that the appropriations available for expenditure by the Department during the fiscal year ending this month, together with the unexpended balances carried forward from last year—out of those they have saved

$11 million during the year, scattered over the various divisions of the Department. They will carry forward a good many balances from this year over the 1st of July, a great many of which are obligated in contracts let, but disregarding the carryover, which is merely a financial transaction, the cuts for next year, that is the fiscal year beginning the 1st of July, is estimated at about $20 million.

APPOINTMENTS

There are two appointments. We have appointed Roy St. Lewis, of Oklahoma, Assistant Attorney General to fill the place made vacant by the resignation of George Farnum. I will give you a note on his experience. And as soon as Mr. St. Lewis is sworn in we will appoint Mr. Herbert Hyde, who is now assistant to Mr. St. Lewis, as United States Attorney for the Western District of Oklahoma.

AGRICULTURE DEPARTMENT

In the matter of the Department of Agriculture statement I think you had better quote that as from the White House. It is not a matter that I care to announce personally.

AMBASSADOR CHARLES G. DAWES

Q. Do you care to say anything about your conference with Ambassador Dawes?

THE PRESIDENT. I have had no serious conferences with him yet. I had breakfast with him.

NOTE: President Hoover's one hundred and ninety-fifth news conference was held in the White House at 12 noon on Tuesday, June 2, 1931.

On the same day, the White House issued a text of the letter to the Secretary of War about Army Air Corps maneuvers (see Item 212), and the text of a White House statement on the expenditures of the Department of Agriculture (see Item 213).

212

Letter to the Secretary of War About Army Air Corps Maneuvers.
June 2, 1931

My dear Mr. Secretary:

I wish to congratulate you and the Air Corps on the remarkable success achieved in the maneuvers just terminated.

To have mobilized, from all parts of the country, a force of 672 airplanes and maneuvered it from the middle west to, and along, the eastern seaboard from Maine to Virginia without any serious mishap, is very convincing evidence of the efficiency of the Army's air forces.

I am especially gratified to know that all three components of the Army of the United States—Regular Army, National Guard, and Organized Reserve—participated so creditably in this instruction.

You and your subordinates in the War Department by the successful organization and execution of these exercises have reflected great credit upon our military establishment.

Faithfully yours,

HERBERT HOOVER

[Colonel Patrick J. Hurley, Secretary of War]

213

White House Statement on the Expenditures of the Department of Agriculture.
June 2, 1931

SECRETARY HYDE and the chiefs of the Department of Agriculture report that out of the appropriations available for expenditure by the Department during the fiscal year ending this month, together with unexpended balances carried forward from last year, they have during the year saved about $11 million by economies throughout the various divisions. Considerable unexpended balances will be carried forward into the next fiscal year beginning July 1 to cover obligations and contracts entered into.

Of the appropriations for this next year and these balances, it is expected that about $20 million will be saved during the next year.

214

White House Statement on Federal Expenditures.
June 2, 1931

IN REPLY to inquiries from the press the following information in round numbers has been furnished by the Director of the Budget as to the economies made during the past year and the probable fiscal situation upon July 1.

Present indications are that the financial transactions of the Government for the fiscal year ending June 30, 1931, will show an increase of about $500 million in the national debt. The deficit is from about $900 million to $950 million, of which about $440 million will be due to the statutory redemption of the debt.

The deficit is principally due to a falling off in receipts of the Treasury, from taxes and other sources caused by the depression which will apparently be about $840 million below the fiscal year ended June 30, 1930. Added to this is the additional burden of about $50 million fall in postal receipts.

There have also been large increases in expenditures for construction work and agricultural relief and for veterans' services amounting to about $540 million above that of the last fiscal year.

These figures alone—a reduction of $890 million in receipts and an increase of nearly $540 million in expenditures in the above items—would indicate that the Government would be over $1,430 million worse off this year than last.

However, deferments and reductions in expenditures in other parts of the Government largely due to the economy drive last summer amount to about $180 million. During the fiscal year ended last June the debt was reduced by $305 million in excess of statutory amount while this

year it is held to the legal requirements. These two sums make a difference in the situation of about $485 million and result in a final deficit of
about $900 million or $950 million.

As stated, of this deficit of $900 million or $950 million, about $440
million will be expended in the statutory redemption of the public debt
so that the net increase in the debt for the fiscal year will probably be
about $500 million.

The Administrator of Veterans' Affairs reports that the loans so far
made upon bonus certificates now total $1,098,947,000 to 1,971,966 in-
dividuals of which $284,481,000 has been furnished from insurance and
other funds, about $60 million from the banks, and $754,466,000 from sale
of Treasury obligations.

215

Telegram to Senator Reed Smoot
About an International Conference on Silver.
June 3, 1931

[Released June 3, 1931. Dated June 2, 1931]

I AM NOW ABLE to inform you that informal discussions among
nations some of whose participation is vitally necessary develop the fact
that they do not consider this a proper time to call an international
conference on silver and would oppose holding such a conference now.

HERBERT HOOVER

[The Honorable Reed Smoot, Salt Lake City, Utah]

NOTE: The silver industry and Congressmen from silver-producing States
inaugurated a movement for a silver stabilization agreement. In February 1931,
the Senate passed the Pittman resolution (S. Res. 442) urging the President to
undertake international negotiations, and the State Department subsequently
sounded out the British and the Japanese.

216

Message to King George V of Great Britain Offering Birthday Greetings.
June 3, 1931

MAY I TAKE this occasion of the sixty-sixth anniversary of Your Majesty's birth to reiterate the cordial good wishes of the American people and to add my sincere personal congratulations.

HERBERT HOOVER

[His Majesty George V, King of Great Britain, London, England]

217

Message to Prince Takamatsu of Japan on His Departure From United States Territory.
June 3, 1931

[Released June 3, 1931.   Dated June 2, 1931]

YOUR GRACIOUS message of appreciation and farewell has been duly received and I have taken the liberty of giving it to the press for publication to the American people.

Mrs. Hoover cordially joins me in renewed good wishes for the continued welfare of Your Imperial Highness and Princess Takamatsu.

HERBERT HOOVER

[His Imperial Highness Prince Takamatsu, Passenger Steamship Ohiohibu Maru]

NOTE: The message was in response to Prince Takamatsu's message upon his departure from Honolulu, Hawaii, the last American territory visited on his round-the-world trip.

218

The President's News Conference of
June 5, 1931

GOVERNMENT EMPLOYMENT STATISTICS

THE PRESIDENT. I have this morning the occasional return that I secure from the departments as to the number of employees in the Government service and the number of people employed on construction work and furnishing the supplies for such work. I thought perhaps it might interest you. The Government employees include, of course, the military services. They have not varied at the different periods more than 1,000. The construction employees, since January 1930, however—that is a year and 5 months ago—have increased from 235,000 to 655,000 at the present moment, and based on the contracts which have been made and the calculation as to the number of people employed under them, they will increase to 805,000 by the first of September. However, we will give you that table.

INTERNATIONAL SILVER CONFERENCE

I have had some questions on the silver situation, and I am able to talk to you about it simply as background. As was stated the other day, the informal discussions amongst a good many governments developed the fact that they would feel opposed to the holding of such a conference at the present time. I notice that Senator Smoot has suggested that under the agency of the International Chamber of Commerce, which was one of the international bodies that passed strong resolutions recommending such a conference, that there might be held an informal conference of experts and people interested. It is my own impression that that might be of some advantage—that they might be able to develop a program which at least would be worth consideration by the governments. The problem in silver is the fact that whereas production has not materially increased, the demonetization of silver in certain localities and the exigencies of certain other governments have led to the sale of considerable amounts of silver on the top of production. And there are three or four phases that have been suggested by the different people interested in the problem that no doubt such a conference would develop further and might exhaust their possibilities—such things as a coordination in production and cessation of government sales and the increase of minor coinage, increase of consumption in the arts, and other things which might very rightly be developed. And it certainly would do no harm if there was an informal conference, much as there was over wheat or many other conferences that are constantly going on over the world. It tends to educate the public mind and may develop something of practical importance.

APPOINTMENT

Other than the appointment of Collector of Customs at Los Angeles, California, I have no other news today.

AUTOGIRO

Q. Mr. President, can you tell us if Mr. Adams is to fly down to the camp in an autogiro. That rumor has been going around.

THE PRESIDENT. I hadn't heard the rumor at all. I doubt whether he could alight at the camp.

NOTE: President Hoover's one hundred and ninety-sixth news conference was held in the White House at 4 p.m. on Friday, June 5, 1931.

Howard W. Seager was appointed Collector of Customs at Los Angeles, Calif., on June 4, 1931.

The press question referred to Secretary of the Navy Charles F. Adams and the President's camp on the Rapidan River, where Secretary Adams and other naval officials attended the Navy Department economy conference. The Secretary did fly to the camp in an autogiro, landing in a nearby field.

Following the news conference, the White House released a table providing Government employment statistics, which follows:

FEDERAL GOVERNMENT

	January 1930	October 1930	June 1931	Estimated September 1931
Regular employees except construction workers..............................	902, 000	899, 000	901, 000	901, 000
Persons employed upon construction work and furnishing supplies therefor........	235, 000	420, 000	655, 000	805, 000
Total............................	1, 137, 000	1, 319, 000	1, 556, 000	1, 706, 000

219

White House Statement on the Economy Conference With Navy Department Officials.
June 6, 1931

EVERY DIVISION of the Navy was gone over with great care at the conference this afternoon to ascertain the economies that could be made in the Navy without sacrificing efficiency.

The President was advised that the economies during the past year have amounted to $10 million, the result largely of the fleet operating program established by Admiral Pratt.

Navy officials said preliminary estimates of economies for the next year would run from $10 to $15 million. Exhaustive studies are in progress in all different operations of the Navy with a view to increasing savings wherever possible without injury to needed employment and efficiency in training.

It was determined, in view of a report by the Navy that Guam no longer has any military value, that all activities there would be reduced to the minimum basis required for the civil government of the island.

NOTE: The White House issued the statement following a conference at the President's camp on the Rapidan River. Secretary of the Navy Charles F. Adams,

Assistant Secretaries David S. Ingalls and Ernest Lee Jahncke, Chief of Naval Operations Adm. William V. Pratt, Commandant of the Marine Corps Maj. Gen. Ben Fuller, and other naval officials attended the meeting.

The statement, as printed above, follows the text of a contemporary news account, which printed the release in full.

220

Message on the 150th Anniversary of the Phillips Exeter Academy. *June 6, 1931*

[Released June 6, 1931.   Dated June 1, 1931]

Dear Mr. Lamont:

One cannot contemplate the history of the Phillips Exeter Academy, which substantially parallels the existence of the American Republic, without recognizing in the celebration of the one hundred and fiftieth anniversary of the Academy an event of national interest and significance.

The record and ideals of this pioneer school are a major contribution to education in the United States. From the institution has flowed for a century and a half a stream enriching the public service and the culture of our country. The school has achieved in practice the high ideals of education envisaged by its founders and their successors. I wish, therefore, to extend my most cordial congratulations and good wishes on the occasion of the memorable milestone attained on June sixth.

Faithfully yours,
HERBERT HOOVER

[Mr. Thomas W. Lamont, 23 Wall Stree, New York City]

NOTE: The message was read at exercises commemorating the anniversary of the academy in Exeter, N.H.

Thomas W. Lamont, a prominent banker who graduated from the academy in 1888, presided over the afternoon program.

221

Message to President Pascual Ortiz Rubio of Mexico on the Death of Emilio Cortes Rubio.
June 8, 1931

I HAVE just learned with deep regret of the report that two Mexican students, one of them a relative of Your Excellency, were killed this morning at Ardmore, Oklahoma. I have ordered a minute investigation of the circumstances of this profoundly regrettable incident.

HERBERT HOOVER

NOTE: On June 7, 1931, Emilio Cortes Rubio, cousin of Mexican President Ortiz Rubio, and his companion Manuel Garcia Gomez were shot and killed by deputy sheriffs in Ardmore, Okla. Murder charges were filed but at the trial, the responsible police officer was acquitted.

222

Message of Sympathy on the Death of Franklin Henry Giddings.
June 13, 1931

[Released June 13, 1931.   Dated June 12, 1931]

I AM SADDENED to learn of the death of your husband Dr. Franklin Henry Giddings and extend my deep sympathy to you. Dr. Giddings' career as an educator and author was an unusually fruitful one, and his thinking has made a permanent and significant contribution to the science of sociology.

HERBERT HOOVER

[Mrs. Franklin Henry Giddings, Scarsdale, New York]

NOTE: Dr. Giddings, a pioneer sociologist and professor emeritus of sociology and history at Columbia University, died in Scarsdale, N.Y., on June 11, 1931.

223

Remarks at Charleston, West Virginia.
June 15, 1931

Mr. Governor, my dear fellow citizens:

It is most kind of you to come to the station to greet Mrs. Hoover and me this morning. It is again a gracious proof of the hospitality of the people of West Virginia. I have greatly enjoyed the journey over the State this morning. The scenery, the homes of West Virginia are always inspiring.

I have also had the pleasure this morning of following the Kanawha, a project in which I have been much interested for many years but have not before seen. This important Federal project is now nearing the stage of completion. I believe it will greatly aid the progress of the State.

But I am not here to address you upon serious subjects. I have to deliver a serious speech tonight. I do wish to express to you the gratitude of Mrs. Hoover and myself for the kindliness and cordiality of your welcome.

NOTE: The President spoke to an estimated 2,500 people gathered around the rear platform of the Presidential train, which was en route to Indianapolis, Ind. In his remarks, the President referred to Governor William G. Conley.

224

Remarks at Huntington, West Virginia.
June 15, 1931

Governor Conley and fellow citizens:

It is most kind of you to give to Mrs. Hoover and me this courteous and beautiful welcome. It is a greeting so warm and so generous that it is difficult to find terms in which to respond. We do deeply appreciate it. I have greatly enjoyed this journey through West Virginia. The Nation shares with the State its pride in its beautiful scenery, its homes, and its industries.

I have the opportunity for renewed contact with your Governor and with your most able and devoted Senator. Huntington may well be proud of their citizens who take so large a part in National Government. It has been a pleasure to again meet with your Mr. Hallanan and Mrs. Yost, who represent you upon the Republican National Committee.

All one can say in response to greetings of so warm and cordial a character is wholly inadequate. I wish I could adequately thank you on behalf of both Mrs. Hoover and myself.

NOTE: The President spoke to an estimated 5,000 people gathered around the rear platform of the Presidential train, which was en route to Indianapolis, Ind. In his remarks, the President referred to Governor William G. Conley, Senator Henry D. Hatfield, Republican national committeewoman Lenna L. Yost, and Republican national committeeman Walter S. Hallanan.

225

Remarks at Greensburg, Indiana.
June 15, 1931

MRS. HOOVER and I want to express our appreciation for this beautiful greeting. It is a fine welcome to the State of Indiana. It is encouraging to be a President, to receive such a greeting and such a welcome as this.

Thank you.

NOTE: The President spoke to a group gathered around the rear platform of the Presidential train, which was en route to Indianapolis, Ind. The American Legion had organized a welcoming demonstration.

226

Address to the Indiana Republican Editorial Association at Indianapolis.
June 15, 1931

My dear fellow citizens:

It is difficult for me to find adequate expression for my appreciation of the reception given to me today by the people of Indiana. You have provided a marvelous occasion this evening, one in which I know you gentlemen join with me in gratitude to your committee. Never before have I known of 5,000 people sitting down to dinner—of Indiana food at least—so beautifully served, so capably managed, and with the assistance of the girls of a modern university.

It is a genuine pleasure to meet the Republican editors of the State of Indiana and their guests.

The editor in an American community has a most serious responsibility today. It is upon him, in a large measure, that the responsibility rests of molding and interpreting public opinion in his community. It is upon him also that we lean for leadership in every civic movement— political, economic, and social. And, above all, it is in you, the editors, that we must rest the first defense of American idealism. I can say in all fairness that our editors fulfill these responsibilities in a fashion which entitles them to the gratitude of the country.

You of this special association have a great responsibility as the representatives of the party to which we all belong. Many look upon the science of politics with suspicion. While ours is a government of, by, and for the people, it always has and it always must find its expression through organized political parties. Organization is essential to enable the people to express their will for the proper functioning of government in a democracy.

Without organized political parties, striving to serve the best interests of the American people, we would descend into political anarchy and be torn into political factions representing selfish, sectional, and group minorities. The purpose of party organization must be to promote the national welfare. Nothing is more certain than that good government is good politics.

I am glad to have this opportunity to meet with many old friends—Indiana's representatives in Washington—and to express to you, the editors of the State, the appreciation which we hold in Washington for the service which they have given the National Government. Your Senators, your Congressmen, and the many Indiana men who occupy places of high responsibility in Washington are an important part of our Federal system.

Your senior Senator—Senator Watson—has the high distinction of being the majority leader of the Senate. It is a great honor. You of Indiana all know the strength and quality of your junior Senator—Senator Robinson.

Your Congressmen have by ability and long service risen to leadership in the House of Representatives. We might be without any money in the Federal Treasury if it were not for the chairman of the Appropriations Committee,[1] who comes from your State. Mr. Vestal, Mr. Purnell, and your other Republican Representatives are all men who contribute to the unbiased and unselfish government of our country. I have a personal obligation to your able Governor [2] because of his many acts of cooperation with the Federal Government which have eased these many months.

I shall not take your time with encomiums. It it sufficient to say that Indiana always has and always will take a large and distinguished part in the government of our Republic.

The business depression is the dominant subject before the country and the world today. Its blight stretches from all quarters of the globe to every business place and every cottage door in our land. I propose to discuss it and the policies of the Government in respect to it.

Depressions are not new experiences, though none has hitherto been so widespread. We have passed through no less than 15 major depressions in the last century. We have learned something as the result of each of these experiences. From this one we shall gain stiffening and eco-

---

[1] Representative William R. Wood.
[2] Governor Harry G. Leslie.

nomic discipline, a greater knowledge upon which we must build a better safeguarded system. We have come out of each previous depression into a period of prosperity greater than ever before. We shall do so this time.

As we look beyond the horizons of our own troubles and consider the events in other lands, we know that the main causes of the extreme violence and the long continuance of this depression came not from within but from outside the United States. Had our wild speculation; our stock promotion with its infinite losses and hardship to innocent people; our loose and extravagant business methods; and our unprecedented drought, been our only disasters we would have recovered months ago.

A large part of the forces which have swept our shores from abroad are the malign inheritances in Europe of the Great War—its huge taxes, its mounting armament, its political and social instability, its disruption of economc life by the new boundaries. Without the war we would have no such depression. Upon these war origins are superimposed the over-rapid expansion of production and collapse in price of many foreign raw materials. The demonetization of silver in certain countries and a score of more remote causes have all contributed to dislocation. Some particular calamity has happened to nearly every country in the world, and the difficulties of each have intensified the unemployment and financial difficulties of all the others. As either the cause or the effect, we have witnessed armed revolutions within the past 2 years in a score of nations, not to mention disturbed political life in many others. Political instability has affected three-fourths of the population of the world.

I do not at all minimize the economic interdependence of the world, but despite this the potential and redeeming strength of the United States in the face of this situation is that we are economically more self-contained than any other great nation. This degree of independence gives assurance that with the passing of the temporary dislocations and shocks we can and will make a large measure of recovery irrespective of the rest of the world. We did so with even worse foreign conditions in 1921.

We can roughly indicate this high degree of self-containment. Our average annual production of movable goods before the depression was about $50 billion. We exported yearly about 5 billions, or 10 percent. The world disruption has temporarily reduced our exports to about 3½ billions. In other words, the shrinkage of foreign trade by 1½ billions amounts to only 2 or 3 percent of our total productivity. Yet as a result of all the adverse forces our production has been reduced by, roughly, 10 or 12 billions. This sharp contrast between a national shrinkage of, say, $12 billion and a loss of $1,500 million from export trade is an indication of the disarrangement of our own internal production and consumption entirely apart from that resulting from decreased sales abroad. Some of this enlarged dislocation is also due to the foreign effects upon prices of commodities and securities. Moreover, the repeated shocks from political disturbance and revolution in foreign countries stimulate fear and hesitation among our businessmen. These fears and apprehensions are unnecessarily increased by that minority of people who would make political capital out of the depression through magnifying our unemployment and losses. Other small groups in the business world make their contribution to distress by raids on our markets with purpose to profit from depreciation of securities and commodities. Both groups are within the law; they are equally condemned by our public and business opinion; they are by no means helpful to the Nation.

Fear and apprehension, whether their origins are domestic or foreign, are very real, tangible, economic forces. Fear of loss of a job or uncertainty as to the future has caused millions of our people unnecessarily to reduce their purchases of goods, thereby decreasing our production and employment. These uncertainties lead our bankers and businessmen to extreme caution, and in consequence a mania for liquidation has reduced our stocks of goods and our credits far below any necessity. All these apprehensions and actions check enterprise and lessen our national activities. We are suffering today more from frozen confidence than we are from frozen securities.

With no desire to minimize the realities of suffering or the stern task of recovery, we must appraise the other side of this picture. If we proceed with sanity, we must not look only at the empty hole in the middle of the doughnut.

We must bear in mind at all times our marvelous resources in land, mines, mills, manpower, brainpower, and courage. Over 95 percent of our families have either an income or a breadwinner employed. Our people are working harder and are resolutely engaged, individually and collectively, in overhauling and improving their methods and services. That is the fundamental method of repair to the wreckage from our boom of 2 years ago; it is the remedy to the impacts from abroad. It takes time, but it is going on. Although fear has resulted in unnecessary reduction in spending, yet these very reductions are piling up savings in our savings banks until today they are the largest in our history. Surplus money does not remain idle for long. Ultimately it is the most insistent promoter of enterprise and of optimism. Consumption of retail goods in many lines is proceeding at a higher rate than last year. The harvest prospects indicate recovery from the drought and increased employment in handling the crop. Revolutions in many countries have spent themselves, and stability is on the ascendancy. The underlying forces of recovery are asserting themselves.

For the first time in history the Federal Government has taken an extensive and positive part in mitigating the effects of depression and expediting recovery. I have conceived that if we would preserve our democracy this leadership must take the part not of attempted dictatorship but of organizing cooperation in the constructive forces of the community and of stimulating every element of initiative and self-reliance in the country. There is no sudden stroke of either governmental or private action which can dissolve these world difficulties; patient, constructive action in a multitude of directions is the strategy of success. This battle is upon a thousand fronts.

I shall not detain you by long exposition of these very extensive activities of our Government for they are already well known. We have assured the country from panic and its hurricane of bankruptcy by coordinated action between the Treasury, the Federal Reserve System, the banks, the Farm Loan and Farm Board system. We have steadily urged the maintenance of wages and salaries, preserving American

299

standards of living, not alone for its contribution to consumption of goods but with the far greater purpose of maintaining social good will through avoiding industrial conflict with its suffering and social disorder.

We are maintaining organized cooperation with industry systematically to distribute the available work so as to give income to as many families as possible.

We have reversed the traditional policy in depressions of reducing expenditures upon construction work. We are maintaining a steady expansion of ultimately needed construction work in cooperation with the States, municipalities, and industries. Over two billions of dollars is being expended, and today a million men are being given direct and indirect employment through these enlarged activities. We have sustained the people in 21 States who faced dire disaster from the drought. We are giving aid and support to the farmers in marketing their crops, by which they have realized hundreds of millions more in prices than the farmers of any other country. Through the tariff we are saving our farmers and workmen from being overwhelmed with goods from foreign countries where, even since our tariff was revised, wages and prices have been reduced to much lower levels than before. We are holding down taxation by exclusion of every possible governmental expenditure not absolutely essential or needed in increase of employment or assistance to the farmers. We are rigidly excluding immigration until our own people are employed. The departures and deportations today actually exceed arrivals. We are maintaining and will maintain systematic voluntary organization in the community in aid of employment and care for distress. There are a score of other directions in which cooperation is organized and stimulation given. We propose to go forward with these major activities and policies. We will not be diverted from them.

By these and other measures which we shall develop as the occasion shall require, we shall keep this ship steady in the storm. We will prevent any unnecessary distress in the United States, and by the activities and courage of the American people we will recover from the depression.

300

I would be remiss if I did not pay tribute to the business, industrial, labor, and agricultural leaders for their remarkable spirit of cooperation. Their action is magnificent proof of the fundamental progress of American institutions, of our growth in social and economic understanding, of our sense of responsibility, and of human brotherhood.

Leaders of industry have cooperated in an extraordinary degree to maintain employment and sustain our standards of living. There have been exceptions, but they represent a small percent of the whole. Labor has cooperated in prevention of conflict in giving greater effort and consequently in reducing unit costs. We have had freedom from strikes, lockouts, and disorder unequaled even in prosperous times. We have made permanent gains in national solidarity.

Our people can take justifiable pride that their united efforts have greatly reduced unemployment which would have otherwise been our fate; it is heavy but proportionally it is less than one-half that of other industrial countries. Great as have been our difficulties no man can contrast them with our experiences in previous great depressions or with the condition of other important industrial countries without a glow of pride in our American system and a confidence in its future.

While we are fostering the slow but positive processes of the healing of our economic wounds, our citizens are necessarily filled with anxiety, and in their anxiety there is the natural demand for more and more drastic action by the Federal Government. Many of their suggestions are sound and helpful. Every suggestion which comes within the proper authority and province of the Executive is given most earnest consideration. We are, of course, confronted with scores of theoretical panaceas which, however well intended, would inevitably delay recovery. Some timid people, black with despair, have lost faith in our American system. They demand abrupt and positive change. Others have seized upon the opportunities of discontent to agitate for the adoption of economic patent medicines from foreign lands. Others have indomitable confidence that by some legerdemain we can legislate ourselves out of a worldwide depression. Such views are as accurate as the belief we can exorcise a Caribbean hurricane by statutory law.

For instance, nothing can be gained in recovery of employment by detouring capital away from industry and commerce into the Treasury of the United States, either by taxes or loans, on the assumption that the Government can create more employment by use of these funds than can industry and commerce itself. While I am a strong advocate of expansion of useful public works in hard times, and we have trebled our Federal expenditure in aid to unemployment, yet there are limitations upon the application of this principle. Not only must we refrain from robbing industry and commerce of its capital, and thereby increasing unemployment, but such works require long engineering and legal interludes before they produce actual employment. Above all, schemes of public works which have no reproductive value would result in sheer waste. The remedy to economic depression is not waste but the creation and distribution of wealth.

It has been urged that the Federal Government should abandon its system of employment agencies and should appropriate large sums to subsidize their establishment in other hands. I have refused to accept such schemes, as they would in many places endow political organizations with the gigantic patronage of workmen's jobs. That would bring about the most vicious tyranny ever set up in the United States. We have instead expanded our Federal Government agencies which are on non-political basis. They are of far greater service to labor.

We have had one proposal after another which amounts to a dole from the Federal Treasury. The largest is that of unemployment insurance. I have long advocated such insurance as an additional measure of safety against rainy days, but only through private enterprise or through cooperation of industry and labor itself. The moment the Government enters into this field it invariably degenerates into the dole. For nothing can withstand the political pressures which carry governments over this dangerous border. The net results of governmental doles are to lower wages toward the bare subsistence level and to endow the slacker. It imposes the injustice of huge burdens upon farmers and other callings which receive no benefits. I am proud that so representative an organization as the American Federation of Labor has refused to approve such schemes.

There have been some complaints from foreign countries over the revision of our tariff and it is proposed that we can expedite recovery by another revision. Nothing would more prolong the depression than a session of Congress devoted to this purpose. There are no doubt inequities and inequalities in some of our tariff rates; that is inherent in any congressional revision. But we have for the first time effective machinery in motion through a Tariff Commission with authority for any necessary rectification. And that machinery is functioning.

An analysis indicates that the large majority of these foreign complaints are directed against added protection we have given to agriculture. I believe that some of these countries do not realize the profound hardship which they themselves—with no malevolent purpose—have imposed on the American farmer. Improved machinery, the development of refrigeration, and cheapening of sea transportation have created for them great resources from their virgin lands and cheaper labor. As a result these countries have taken profitable export markets from the American farmer. There have been complaints from older nations who import a portion of their food products and export another portion. Yet these nations look upon their own agriculture as a way of life and as vital to their national security, and have long since adopted protective tariffs against the special farm products of the United States. We do not reproach them, for we, too, look upon a healthy agriculture as indispensable to the Nation. The growth of our industrial population will ultimately absorb the production of our farmers, but our agriculture was attuned to the export business and is of necessity passing a prolonged crisis in its shift to a domestic basis. Our tariff had proved so low that our farmers were being crowded even from the domestic market in many products which by use as diversification they can substitute to take up the slack in export business. From that condition we have given him protection, and we stand upon it.

In this connection I noted with interest that the International Chamber of Commerce in its recent meeting in Washington in effect recommended to the world the adoption of this method of the American tariff, although it was not referred to by name. Our visitors found the American tariff act unique in the field of tariff legislation, as it defines

303

the principle of our tariff by law. That is the difference in cost of production at home and abroad. They found in our new Tariff Commission the creation of a tribunal open to every interested party empowered and ready to deal with any variations from this principle. They found a tariff without discriminations among nations. They recommended universal adoption of similar principles. Indeed, such a course would greatly modify tariffs in general. It would promote the commerce of the world by removing discriminations, preferences, and uncertainties.

But it is not my purpose upon this occasion to discuss the relations of our many economic problems to the problems of other nations. I am not unmindful of our responsibilities or our vital interest in their welfare. The very first service to them must be to place our own house in order; to restore our own domestic prosperity. It is from increases in our reservoir of economic strength that has and must come our contribution to the development and recovery of the world. From our prosperity comes our demand for their goods and raw materials. A prosperous United States is the beginning of a prosperous world.

With industry as well as agriculture we are concerned not merely in the immediate problems of the depression. From the experience of this depression will come not only a greatly sobered and more efficient economic system than we possessed 2 years ago but a greater knowledge of its weaknesses as well as a greater intelligence in correcting them. When the time comes that we can look at this depression objectively it will be our duty searchingly to examine every phase of it.

We can already observe some directions to which endeavor must be pointed. For instance, it is obvious that the Federal Reserve System was inadequate to prevent a large diversion of capital and bank deposits from commercial and industrial business into wasteful speculation and stock promotion. It is obvious our banking system must be organized to give greater protection to depositors against failures. It is equally obvious that we must determine whether the facilities of our security and commodity exchanges are not being used to create illegitimate speculation and intensify depressions. It is obvious that our taxes upon capital gains viciously promote the booms and just as viciously intensify depressions. In order to avoid taxes, real estate and stocks are withheld from the market in times of rising prices, and for the same reason large quantities are dumped on the market in times of depression. The experiences of this depression indeed demand that the Nation carefully and deliberately reconsider the whole national and local problem of the incidence of taxation. The undue proportion of taxes which falls upon farmers, homeowners, and all real-property holders as compared to other forms of wealth and income demands real relief. There are far wider questions of our social and economic life which this experience will illuminate. We shall know much more of the method of still further advance toward stability, security, and wider diffusion of the benefits of our economic system.

We have many citizens insisting that we produce an advance "plan" for the future development of the United States. They demand that we produce it right now. I presume the "plan" idea is an infection from the slogan of the "5-year plan" through which Russia is struggling to redeem herself from the 10 years of starvation and misery. I am able to propose an American plan to you. We plan to take care of 20 million increase in population in the next 20 years. We plan to build for them 4 million new and better homes, thousands of new and still more beautiful city buildings, thousands of factories; to increase the capacity of our railways; to add thousands of miles of highways and waterways; to install 25 million electrical horsepower; to grow 20 percent more farm products. We plan to provide new parks, schools, colleges, and churches for this 20 million people. We plan more leisure for men and women and better opportunities for its enjoyment. We not only plan to provide for all the new generation, but we shall, by scientific research and invention, lift the standard of living and security of life to the whole people. We plan to secure a greater diffusion of wealth, a decrease in poverty, and a great reduction in crime. And this plan will be carried out if we just keep on giving the American people a chance. Its impulsive force is in the character and spirit of our people. They have already done a better job for 120 million people than any other nation in all history.

Some groups believe this plan can only be carried out by a fundamental, a revolutionary change of method. Other groups believe that any system must be the outgrowth of the character of our race, a natural outgrowth of our traditions; that we have established certain ideals over 150 years upon which we must build rather than destroy.

If we analyze the ideas which have been put forward for handling our great national plan, they fall into two groups. The first is whether we shall go on with our American system which holds that the major purpose of a state is to protect the people and to give them equality of opportunity, that the basis of all happiness is in development of the individual, that the sum of progress can only be gaged by the progress of the individual, that we should steadily build up cooperation among the people themselves to these ends. The other idea is that we shall directly or indirectly regiment the population into a bureaucracy to serve the state, that we should use force instead of cooperation in plans and thereby direct every man as to what he may or may not do.

These ideas present themselves in practical questions which we have to meet. Shall we abandon the philosophy and creed of our people for 150 years by turning to a creed foreign to our people? Shall we establish a dole from the Federal Treasury? Shall we undertake Federal ownership and operation of public utilities instead of the rigorous regulation of them to prevent imposition? Shall we protect our people from the lower standards of living of foreign countries? Shall the Government, except in temporary national emergencies, enter upon business processes in competition with its citizens? Shall we regiment our people by an extension of the arm of bureaucracy into a multitude of affairs?

The future welfare of our country, so dear to you and to me for ourselves and our children, depends upon the answer given.

Our immediate and paramount task as a people is to rout the forces of economic disruption and pessimism that have swept upon us. The exacting duty of government in these times is by use of its agencies and its influence to strengthen our economic institutions; by inspiring cooperation in the community to sustain good will and to keep our country free of disorder and conflict; by cooperation with the people to assure that the deserving shall not suffer; and by the conduct of government to strengthen the foundations of a better and stronger national life. These have been the objectives of my administration in dealing with this, the greatest crisis the world has ever known. I shall adhere to them.

If, as many believe, we have passed the worst of this storm, future months will not be difficult. If we shall be called upon to endure more of this period, we must gird ourselves to steadfast effort, to fail at no point where humanity calls or American ideals are in jeopardy.

Our transcendent momentary need is a much larger degree of confidence among our business agencies and that they shall extend this confidence in more than words. If our people will go forth with the confidence and enterprise which our country justifies, many of the mists of this depression will fade away.

In conclusion, whatever the immediate difficulties may be, we know they are transitory in our lives and in the life of the Nation. We should have full faith and confidence in those mighty resources, those intellectual and spiritual forces, which have impelled this Nation to a success never before known in the history of the world. Far from being impaired, these forces were never stronger than at this moment. Under the guidance of Divine Providence they will return to us a greater and more wholesome prosperity than we have ever known.

NOTE: The President spoke at 8:30 p.m. to an audience of approximately 5,000 people assembled in Manufacturers Hall on the Indianapolis Fair Grounds, following a dinner given in his honor by the Indiana Republican Editorial Association. The National Broadcasting Company and the Columbia Broadcasting System radio networks carried the address.

A reading copy of this item with holograph changes by the President is available for examination at the Herbert Hoover Presidential Library.

227

Message to the Annual Convention of the Advertising Federation of America.
June 15, 1931

[Released June 15, 1931. Dated May 11, 1931]

Gentlemen:

It seems to me most appropriate that at your annual convention you propose to clarify the function of advertising as an economic force, so

307

that its benefits may be better understood not only by those who employ it, but by the public to which in the aggregate it renders its greatest service.

Advertising has played an important part in raising our standard of living, in stimulating invention and in maintaining competition. By promoting production and distribution, it has brought within the reach of the many comforts and conveniences previously enjoyed by the few.

The theme of your convention is especially timely, because of the part sound, constructive advertising is bound to play in accelerating the return of normal business activity.

Yours faithfully,

HERBERT HOOVER

[Advertising Federation of America, 420 Lexington Avenue, New York City]

NOTE: Gilbert T. Hodges, president of the federation, read the message at the organization's annual convention held in the Hotel Pennsylvania in New York City.

228

Address at the Dedication of the Harding Memorial at Marion, Ohio.
June 16, 1931

I DEEM it a privilege to join here in the dedication of the tomb of Warren G. Harding, 29th President of the United States. This beautiful monument, erected by the voluntary subscriptions of the people, symbolizes their respect for his memory. It has been their response with tender remembrance to a kindly and gentle spirit. As future years come and go each of them will be marked by gatherings here of his friends and the people of a grateful democracy, for democracy has ever paid respect and tribute to those who have given her service.

Warren G. Harding came from the people. Born just at the close of the Civil War, it became his responsibility to lead the Republic in a period of reconstruction from another great war in which our democracy had again demonstrated its unalterable resolve to withstand encroachment upon its independence and to deserve the respect of the world. We cannot too often emphasize the difficulties to accomplishment which Warren Harding met in his task.

Great as are the problems of the conflict, the burdens of statesmanship are equally difficult in the rehabilitation of social and economic life after the dislocation of war. Above all, the burden is heavy in composing the hates and prejudices which smoulder and threaten long after the formal documents of peace are signed.

As the aftermath of war our national finances were disorganized, taxes were overwhelming, agriculture and business were prostrate, and unemployment widespread. Our country was torn with injustices to those racial groups of our own citizens descended from the enemy nations. Violent bitterness had arisen over the Treaty of Versailles.

These evil spirits aroused by war, augmented by inestimable losses, deep animosities, the dislocations of industry, the vast unemployment in a world still armed and arming confronted Warren G. Harding. He brought to the Office of President a long experience in public affairs together with the character and spirit of which the Republic was then in need. His was a mind and character fitted for a task where the one transcendent need was the healing quality of gentleness and friendliness. He was inspired by a devoted wife, who gave unstintingly of her strength to aid him. Mrs. Harding rests here beside him in death as she labored beside him in life. It was Mr. Harding's mission to compose the prejudices and conflicts at home, to lessen the threats of renewed wars through the world. He succeeded in those tasks. When in 2 years he died, new peace treaties had been made in terms which won the support of our people; tranquility had been restored at home; employment had been renewed and a long period of prosperity had begun.

And he succeeded further. The Washington Arms Conference for the reduction and limitation of battleships identified his administration with the first step in history toward the disarmament of the world. That step was accompanied by the momentous treaties which restored good will among the nations bordering upon the Pacific Ocean and gave to all the world inestimable blessings of peace and security.

The new and changing problems of later years have not obscured the many other constructive acts of his administration. The reorganization and reduction of the public debt, the reduction in taxation, the creation of the budget system, the better organization of industry and employment, new services to agriculture, the establishment of a permanent system of care for disabled veterans and their dependents—are but some of the enlightened measures which he inspired and advanced.

But this is neither the time nor place for me in historic retrospect to catalogue his many services to our country. They will be recorded and gratefully remembered by his countrymen.

Our thoughts today turn to the man himself. My first meeting with Warren Harding ever lingers in my memory. It was during the war and in a time of the greatest strain and anxiety. Late one evening the then Senator Harding, whom I had never met, came to my office. When he was announced, there flashed into my mind the thought that here was some complaint or a request for some appointment. Instead the Senator said simply: "I have not come to get anything. I just want you to know that if you wish the help of a friend, telephone me what you want. I am there to serve and to help." That statement, I came to learn, was typical of him. I refer to it now because it reveals the nature of the man.

I was one of those who accompanied the late President on his fateful trip across the continent and to Alaska. He had wished to learn from the people their needs and to translate to them his own aspirations. Those who were his companions on that journey realized full well that he had overstrained even his robust strength in the gigantic task which confronted him during the previous 2 years. And we came also to know that here was a man whose soul was being seared by a great disillusionment. We saw him gradually weaken not only from physical exhaustion but from mental anxiety. Warren Harding had a dim realization that he had been betrayed by a few of the men whom he had trusted, by men whom he had believed were his devoted friends. It was later proved in the courts of the land that these men had betrayed not alone the friendship and trust of their staunch and loyal friend but they had betrayed their country. That was the tragedy of the life of Warren Harding.

310

There are disloyalties and there are crimes which shock our sensibilities, which may bring suffering upon those who are touched by their immediate results. But there is no disloyalty and no crime in all the category of human weaknesses which compares with the failure of probity in the conduct of public trust. Monetary loss or even the shock to moral sensibilities is perhaps a passing thing, but the breaking down of the faith of a people in the honesty of their Government and in the integrity of their institutions, the lowering of respect for the standards of honor which prevail in high places, are crimes for which punishment can never atone.

But these acts never touched the character of Warren Harding. He gave his life in worthy accomplishment for his country. He was a man of delicate sense of honor, of sympathetic heart, of transcendent gentleness of soul—who reached out for friendship, who gave of it loyally and generously in his every thought and deed. He was a man of passionate patriotism. He was a man of deep religious feeling. He was devoted to his fellow men. No revelation of his character can equal that of his own words just before his death. They were a part of his last public statement. I quote:

"We need less of sectarianism, less of denominationalism, less of fanatical zeal and its exactions, and more of the Christ spirit, more of the Christ practice, and a new and abiding consecration and reverence for God. I am a confirmed optimist as to the growth of the spirit of brotherhood. . . . We do rise to heights at times when we look for the good rather than the evil in others, and gave consideration to the views of all. The inherent love of fellowship is banding men together, and when envy and suspicion are vanquished, fraternity records a triumph and brotherhood brings new blessings to men and to peoples. . . . Christ was the Prince of Peace, and we who seek to render His name glorious must move in the ways of peace and brotherhood and loving service."

He gave his life in that spirit, and in that spirit we pay tribute to his memory.

NOTE: The President spoke at 2 p.m. As printed above, the text follows the address as actually delivered by the President. On the same day, the White House issued an advance text of the address.

229

Remarks at Columbus, Ohio.
June 16, 1931

THIS STOP has been one of unusual welcome and enthusiasm. There is not time for me to shake hands with each of you, for it is about time for your dinner.

Mrs. Hoover and I want to express our appreciation for this welcome—for this is an unusual welcome—so I will shake hands collectively with all of you.

NOTE: On arriving in Columbus, the President was greeted by some 20,000 persons. For 40 minutes he reviewed a Grand Army of the Republic parade with Governor George White. Afterward President and Mrs. Hoover received several hundred persons in the rotunda of the State House. The President, unable to greet all those waiting in line, spoke to them from the steps of the State House.

As printed above, this item follows the text set forth in a contemporary news account.

230

Message to King Gustaf V of Sweden on His Birthday.
June 16, 1931

[Released June 16, 1931.   Dated June 15, 1931]

IT GIVES ME much pleasure on this anniversary of Your Majesty's birth to send you sincere felicitations and best wishes for a long and prosperous reign.

HERBERT HOOVER

[His Majesty Gustaf V, King of Sweden, Stockholm, Sweden]

231

Message to the Christian Family Crusade.
June 16, 1931

[Released June 16, 1931.   Dated June 11, 1931]

My dear Mr. Holderby:

The importance of the family as the unit for spiritual and social progress, and the spiritual values of family life, cannot be overestimated. Anything which strengthens the family and gives a deeper significance to family life is salutary, not only for the family but for the nation. This was recognized in the deliberations of the recent White House Conference on Child Health and Protection.

You have no doubt noted that one of the first rights of the child as set forth in the Children's Charter adopted by the Conference was "for every child spiritual and moral training to help him to stand firm under the pressure of life." This Charter also emphasizes the importance of training for parents, "to fit them to deal wisely with the problems of parenthood."

Yours faithfully,

HERBERT HOOVER

[Rev. William Matthew Holderby, General Director, Christian Family Crusade, 218 S. Wabash Ave., Chicago, Ill.]

NOTE: The message was released in Chicago in conjunction with publicity given the Christian Family Crusade, a nonsectarian religious organization.

232

Address to a Joint Session
of the Illinois State Legislature in Springfield.
June 17, 1931

I WISH to thank you for your courteous and most generous greeting. It is a great honor to meet with the joint session of the Illinois Legislature.

It is a fitting thing that the celebration of this day should be participated in officially by the assembly of the State of Illinois, in which Mr. Lincoln took so distinguished a part, and by the President of the United States, in whose office Mr. Lincoln became the savior of our Republic. In the presence of this assembly one thought expressed by Mr. Lincoln recurs to my mind in the relation of the State legislatures to the whole function and scheme of our Government. It is indeed a much larger part than the immediate problems of the States with which they deal, for the legislatures today, as in Mr. Lincoln's time, are the laboratories in which new ideas are developed and in which they are tried out.

A study of national legislation and national action will show that an overwhelming proportion of the ideas which have been developed nationally have first been born in the State legislatures as the result of the problems which have developed within the States. They have been given trial; they have been hammered out on the anvil of local experience. It is true that not all of the ideas come through this successfully. But even the negative values of the trial, especially in some parts of the Union, are of themselves of inestimable value to the Nation as a whole. And the ideas which develop with success become of vital importance to our people at large. Ours must be a country of constant change and progress because of one fact alone amongst many others, and that is that the constant discoveries in science and their product in new invention shift our basis of human relationships and our mode of life in such a fashion as to require a constant remodeling and the remoulding of the machinery of the government. That does not imply that the eternal principles of justice and right and ordered liberty, upon which the Republic was founded, are subject to change, for they are not. But our machinery of government must shift in order to enable us to enforce these principles against the shift of economic and social forces due to constant discovery and invention. And in these great processes our State legislatures occupy a position of dominant importance to the Nation as a whole.

I wish again to thank you for the cordiality of your reception.

NOTE: The President spoke at 11 a.m. to the Illinois State Legislature and an audience of approximately 6,000, assembled in the State arsenal in Springfield.

314

A reading copy of this item with holograph changes by the President is available for examination at the Herbert Hoover Presidential Library.

233

Address at Lincoln's Tomb in Springfield, Illinois.
June 17, 1931

Governor Emmerson, my dear fellow citizens:

The people of Illinois are the trustees of the Nation for the care of the remains of one of our greatest Americans. In the discharge of this trusteeship this memorial was erected some 57 years ago. The people of the State have taken a just pride in the restoration and its beautification. When it was dedicated, another great citizen of Illinois, the 18th President of the United States—Ulysses S. Grant—made the address on that occasion. It is proper that a President of the United States should take part in its rededication at this time.

Over 2 million people, I am informed, have registered their names at this shrine since its erection, and thus this, the tomb of Lincoln, has become a shrine to all Americans.

The instinct of our people with the passing of time sifts out those men and those events and those places which become the marks on the national road of progress. The stone and the marble of all of our great national shrines are more than physical reminders of the mighty past of our country and the great deeds of America. They are symbols of things of the spirit. Through the men and deeds they commemorate they renew our national ideals and our aspirations. It is a refreshment of the national soul to assemble in these places and to direct the thoughts of our people to these occasions and to recall the men and their deeds which builded the Republic. It is an awakening of pride in the glories of the past and an inspiration to faith in the future. These are the springs which replenish that most sacred stream of human emotions— patriotism.

Nothing that we may say here can add to the knowledge or devotion of our people to the memory of Abraham Lincoln. Nothing we may do can add to his stature in history. All that words can convey has long since been uttered by his grateful countrymen.

This is an occasion of sentiment rather than an occasion of words, for we cannot by expression in words convey those great things of the spirit which inspire a nation.

We gather here today that we of our generation may again pay tribute to the man who not only saved the Union and gave freedom to a race but who recreated the ideals and inspirations of American life.

A nation in its whole lifetime flowers with but a few whose names remain upon the roll of the world in after generations. Lincoln after all these years still grows, not only in the hearts of his countrymen but in the hearts of the peoples of the world.

It is not new, yet it is eternally true, to state that Lincoln made a universal appeal to the minds and hearts of men. His every aspiration was for the unity and welfare of his country. He became a triumphant force in achieving that ideal, because he saw the problems of his time not only from the standpoint of the statesman but of the average citizen whose outlook he understood and whose trials and hopes he shared.

No man gazes upon the tomb of Lincoln without reflection upon his transcendent qualities of patience, fortitude, and steadfastness. The very greatness which history and popular imagination have stamped upon him sometimes obscures somewhat the real man back of the symbol which he has become. It is not amiss to reflect that he was a man before becoming a symbol. To appreciate the real meaning of his life we need to contemplate him as the product of the people themselves, as the farm boy, the fence builder, the soldier, the country lawyer, the political candidate, the legislator, and the President, as well as the symbol of union and of human rights.

Time sifts out the essentials of men's character and deeds, and in Lincoln's character there stands out his patience, his indomitable will, his sense of humanity of a breadth which comes to but few men. Of his deeds those things which remain in the memory of every schoolchild in America are the preservation of the Union, the emancipation of the

316

slaves, the infusion of the new conception of popular government. Those are the transcendent services for which he is enshrined by his countrymen. In these accomplishments Lincoln not alone saved the Union, emancipated a race, and restored the Government to the people, but made the United States a power so potent in the world as to turn the tide of human affairs.

It is fitting that we should rededicate his hallowed resting place, that we should thus recall to every American mind and heart the contribution which Lincoln made to the greatness of our Nation. But it was Lincoln himself whose insight and splendid expression illuminated the true purpose of our assembly at national shrines. It was he who at Gettysburg called upon the people not so much to mourn the dead as to honor them by a rededication of themselves to the service of their country. He said in that memorable address: "It is for us the living rather to be dedicated here . . . to the great task remaining before us." That should be our purpose and resolve today.

The six decades which have passed since Lincoln's death have written on the scroll of history changes bewildering in their variety, momentous in their consequences. They have broadened and enriched life beyond the imaginations of Lincoln's contemporaries. The years have not only yielded rich treasures, material and spiritual, but they have brought challenges to readjustment, both by government and individuals, to a changing world. Our country has become powerful among nations. It is charged with infinitely new responsibilities both at home and abroad.

What a poet has called the endless adventure, the government of men, discloses new and changing human needs from generation to generation. As we scan our history even since his day, who can doubt Lincoln's own words that our national heritage is "worth the keeping." And it was Lincoln who stated and restated in impressive terms that its keeping rests upon obedience and enforcement of law. There can be no man in our country who, either by his position or his influence, stands above the law. That the Republic cannot admit and still live. For ours is a government of laws and a society of ordered liberty safeguarded only by law.

The eternal principles of truth, justice, and right, never more clearly stated than by Lincoln, remain the solvent for the problems and perplexities of every age and of our day. It is to those who, like Lincoln, have made these principles serve the needs of mankind that the world pays its homage. At his shrine we light the torch of our rededication to the service and ideals of the Nation which he loved and served with the last full measure of devotion.

NOTE: The President spoke at 2:30 p.m. to a large audience assembled for the rededication ceremonies of the tomb. Before speaking, the President placed a wreath on the new sarcophagus marking Lincoln's burial spot.

In his opening remarks, the President referred to Louis L. Emmerson, Governor of Illinois.

A reading copy of this item with holograph changes by the President is available for examination at the Herbert Hoover Presidential Library.

234

Remarks at Danville, Illinois.
June 17, 1931

I DEEPLY appreciate this greeting. You have shown a cordiality and a welcome that sounds like Illinois itself. No one could pass through Danville without memories of a great citizen whom Danville contributed to the United States for a period of nearly 40 years, in the shape not of Mr. Cannon but of Uncle Joe. He was indeed a rugged American citizen, and he represented the character of our people in the Middle West.

I greatly appreciate your coming down. It is a greeting with a warmth of welcome that is an encouragement to anyone in public life, and it is not alone an opportunity to greet myself and Mrs. Hoover, but your own able Senator. You ought to know more of your Senator and the work which he is accomplishing in Washington.

There is very little that one can say on these occasions. We have been today engaged in celebrating a matter that is of deep interest to our whole country. I have no doubt that you have taken part in it in spirit at least over the radio, because Mr. Lincoln came originally from this part of Illinois. Part of his life was spent in your town. He practiced law in this region, and Mr. Lincoln was a part and parcel of this section of the community.

I do thank you for your greeting.

NOTE: The President spoke from the rear platform of the Presidential train, which was en route to Washington, D.C. Senator Otis F. Glenn introduced the President to the reception committee.

In his remarks, the President referred to former Representative Joseph G. Cannon.

235

Remarks at Decatur, Illinois.
June 17, 1931

I AM DEEPLY grateful for the cordial reception and the generous welcome which you have extended to Mrs. Hoover and myself.

We have today taken part in a remarkable gathering in Springfield to do honor to the name of Abraham Lincoln. Never before has so great a group of people gathered together in his memory. I have no doubt that many of you have participated in those ceremonies in spirit and in thought.

The days we are now passing through are times of stress and times that require the unremitting service of the men whom you have elected to high office. You can have no appreciation of the encouragement that you give to me by your presence here at the station to greet me and by the cordiality of your welcome. It is indeed a welcome and an encouragement which I have received from every point which we have touched in the State of Illinois. I wish to thank you for it.

NOTE: The President spoke to a reception committee from the rear platform of the Presidential train, which was en route to Washington, D.C.

236

Statement About Conferences on the Economic Situation in Germany.
June 19, 1931

THE PRESIDENT said:

"Since my return from the Central West yesterday I have conferred with those leaders of both political parties who are present in Washington with respect to certain steps which we might take to assist in economic recovery both here and abroad.

"These conversations have been particularly directed to strengthening the situation in Germany. No definite plans or conclusions have yet been arrived at but the response which I have met from the leaders of both parties is most gratifying.

"Any statement of any plan or method is wholly speculative and is not warranted by the facts."

NOTE: Since June 5, 1931, the administration had been considering a possible one-year moratorium on intergovernmental debts and reparations.

For the President's Diary of Developments of the Moratorium, see Supplement I.

237

Statement on the Death of Ralph Harmon Booth, United States Minister to Denmark.
June 20, 1931

THE DEATH of Ralph Harmon Booth, U.S. Minister to Denmark, which occurred today, deprives the public service of an able and devoted man. Appointed to the post in January 1930, after a distinguished career in American journalism, he had already rendered valuable diplomatic service. His death is a loss to the country.

NOTE: Mr. Booth headed Booth Newspapers, Inc., a chain of Michigan dailies, before he was appointed United States Minister to Denmark. He died in Salzburg, Austria, where he was undergoing treatment for a heart ailment.

238

The President's News Conference of
June 20, 1931

THE MORATORIUM

THE PRESIDENT. We have a statement here which we will give you mimeographed in a moment.

The American Government proposes the postponement during 1 year of all payments on intergovernmental debts, reparations, and relief debts, both principal and interest—of course, not including the obligations of governments held by private parties. Subject to confirmation by Congress, the American Government will postpone all payments upon the debts of foreign governments to the American Government payable during the fiscal year beginning July 1, conditional on a like postponement for 1 year of all payments on intergovernmental debts owing the important creditor powers.

This course of action has been approved by the following Senators: Henry F. Ashurst, Hiram Bingham, William E. Borah, James F. Byrnes, Arthur Capper, Simeon D. Fess, Duncan U. Fletcher, Carter Glass, William J. Harris, Pat Harrison, Cordell Hull, William H. King, Dwight W. Morrow, George H. Moses, David A. Reed, Claude A. Swanson, Arthur Vandenberg, Robert F. Wagner, David I. Walsh, Thomas J. Walsh, James E. Watson; and by the following Representatives: Isaac Bacharach, Joseph W. Byrns, Carl R. Chindblom, Frank Crowther, James W. Collier, Charles R. Crisp, Thomas H. Cullen, George P. Darrow, Harry A. Estep, Willis C. Hawley, Carl E. Mapes, J. C. McLaughlin, Earl C. Michener, C. William Ramseyer, Bertrand H. Snell, John Q. Tilson, Allen T. Treadway, and Will R. Wood. It has been approved by Ambassador Charles G. Dawes and by Mr. Owen D. Young.

The purpose of this action is to give the forthcoming year to the economic recovery of the world and to help free the recuperative forces already in motion in the United States from retarding influences from abroad.

The worldwide depression has affected the countries of Europe more severely than our own. Some of these countries are feeling to a serious extent the drain of this depression on national economy. The fabric of intergovernmental debts, supportable in normal times, weighs heavily in the midst of this depression.

From a variety of causes arising out of the depression such as the fall in the price of foreign commodities and the lack of confidence in economic and political stability abroad there is an abnormal movement of gold into the United States which is lowering the credit stability of many foreign countries. These and the other difficulties abroad diminish buying power for our exports and in a measure are the cause of our continued unemployment and continued lower prices to our farmers.

I might say to some of you that this is a release for tomorrow morning's papers—not for today.

Wise and timely action should contribute to relieve the pressure of these adverse forces in foreign countries and should assist in the reestablishment of confidence, thus forwarding political peace and economic stability in the world.

Authority of the President to deal with this problem is limited as this action must be supported by the Congress. It has been assured the cordial support of leading Members of both parties in the Senate and the House. The essence of this proposition is to give time to permit debtor governments to recover their national prosperity. I am suggesting to the American people that they be wise creditors in their own interest and be good neighbors.

I wish to take this occasion also to frankly state my views upon our relations to German reparations and the debts owed to us by the Allied Governments of Europe. Our Government has not been a party to, or exerted any voice in determination of reparation obligations. We purposely did not participate in either general reparations or the division of colonies or property. The repayment of debts due to us from the Allies for the advance for war and reconstruction were settled upon a basis not contingent upon German reparations or related thereto. Therefore, reparations is necessarily wholly a European problem with which we have no relation.

I do not approve in any remote sense of the cancellation of the debts to us. World confidence would not be enhanced by such action. None of our debtor nations has ever suggested it. But as the basis of the settlement of these debts was the capacity under normal conditions of the debtor to pay, we should be consistent with our own policies and principles if we take into account the abnormal situation now existing in the world. I am sure the American people have no desire to attempt to extract any sum beyond the capacity of any debtor to pay, and it is our view that broad vision requires that our Government should recognize the situation as it exists.

This course of action is entirely consistent with the policy which we have hitherto pursued. We are not involved in the discussion of strictly European problems, of which the payment of German reparations is one. It represents our willingness to make a contribution to the early restoration of world prosperity in which our own people have so deep an interest.

I wish further to add that while this action has no bearing on the conference for limitation of land armaments to be held next February, inasmuch as the burden of competitive armaments has contributed to bring about this depression, we trust that by this evidence of our desire to assist we shall have contributed to the good will which is so necessary in the solution of this major question.

There is some background, and it is not for quotation. I thought you would be interested in the governments that benefit by this proposal so far as the postponement of our debt is concerned; that is: France, Great Britain, Italy, Austria, Belgium, Czechoslovakia, Estonia, Finland, Greece, Hungary, Latvia, Lithuania, Poland, Rumania, and Yugoslavia. Those are the governments with whom we have made settlements and funded the debt.

Now, I want you to understand clearly that this proposal is subject to acceptance by all of the creditor governments. It is not a proposal singly to each one or separately. It is a proposal for action all the way around.

I had expected to have a little more time both in our relations abroad and at home, and would have been able to have assembled an even larger list of support, as in no case where we have been able to have personal contact in explanation of the situation have we received other-

323

wise than the most cordial support. There is a great deal of difficulty in explaining subjects as complex as this over the telephone. I have discussed the matter over the telephone with Senator Robinson and Senator Couzens, and I am assured that there will be no opposition from them. I have no doubt that many other Members of the House and Senate would have been glad to have added their names if we had the time to have reached them with an adequate statement of what the situation is.

This is naturally a national problem. It is not a political question or partisan in any sense. It bears on the whole foreign relations of the United States, which are not in their conduct of a political character.

This arrangement so far as we are concerned does not require an extra session of Congress. By the support evidenced here I should think it would be ample to indicate the support that Congress will give to the proposal.

I think that is all that I can give you.

Q. Mr. President, with that support will this go forward without waiting for the regular session in December? Or does the law require definite action by Congress?

THE PRESIDENT. The law will require action by Congress, but with this support I assume that Congress will act favorably.

Q. Mr. President, is no action necessary between now and when Congress meets?

THE PRESIDENT. No, no payments due until the 15th of December.

Q. Mr. President, do we understand that your proposal has been laid before foreign governments interested?

THE PRESIDENT. They are aware of it. You can put it that way. It has not been formally made.

Q. In view of the fact, Mr. President, that this is contingent upon acceptance by European nations, they will be formally notified, will they not, sir?

THE PRESIDENT. Oh, no doubt.

NOTE: President Hoover's one hundred and ninety-seventh news conference was held in the White House at 6:15 p.m. on Saturday, June 20, 1931. Following the news conference, the White House issued a text of the President's statement announcing the proposal for the moratorium on intergovernmental debts (see Item 239), which was embargoed for release on June 21.

239

Statement Announcing the Proposal
of the Moratorium on Intergovernmental Debts.
June 21, 1931

THE PRESIDENT made the following statement:

The American Government proposes the postponement during 1 year of all payments on intergovernmental debts, reparations, and relief debts, both principal and interest, of course, not including obligations of governments held by private parties. Subject to confirmation by Congress, the American Government will postpone all payments upon the debts of foreign governments to the American Government payable during the fiscal year beginning July 1 next, conditional on a like postponement for 1 year of all payments on intergovernmental debts owing the important creditor powers.

This course of action has been approved by the following Senators: Henry F. Ashurst, Hiram Bingham, William E. Borah, James F. Byrnes, Arthur Capper, Simeon D. Fess, Duncan U. Fletcher, Carter Glass, William J. Harris, Pat Harrison, Cordell Hull, William H. King, Dwight W. Morrow, George H. Moses, David A. Reed, Claude A. Swanson, Arthur Vandenberg, Robert F. Wagner, David I. Walsh, Thomas J. Walsh, James E. Watson; and by the following Representatives: Isaac Bacharach, Joseph W. Byrns, Carl R. Chindblom, Frank Crowther, James W. Collier, Charles R. Crisp, Thomas H. Cullen, George P. Darrow, Harry A. Estep, Willis C. Hawley, Carl E. Mapes, J. C. McLaughlin, Earl C. Michener, C. William Ramseyer, Bertrand H. Snell, John Q. Tilson, Allen T. Treadway, and Will R. Wood. It has been approved by Ambassador Charles G. Dawes and by Mr. Owen D. Young.

The purpose of this action is to give the forthcoming year to the economic recovery of the world and to help free the recuperative forces already in motion in the United States from retarding influences from abroad.

The worldwide depression has affected the countries of Europe more severely than our own. Some of these countries are feeling to a serious extent the drain of this depression on national economy. The fabric of intergovernmental debts, supportable in normal times, weighs heavily in the midst of this depression.

From a variety of causes arising out of the depression such as the fall in the price of foreign commodities and the lack of confidence in economic and political stability abroad there is an abnormal movement of gold into the United States which is lowering the credit stability of many foreign countries. These and the other difficulties abroad diminish buying power for our exports and in a measure are the cause of our continued unemployment and continued lower prices to our farmers.

Wise and timely action should contribute to relieve the pressure of these adverse forces in foreign countries and should assist in the reestablishment of confidence, thus forwarding political peace and economic stability in the world.

Authority of the President to deal with this problem is limited as this action must be supported by the Congress. It has been assured the cordial support of leading Members of both parties in the Senate and the House. The essence of this proposition is to give time to permit debtor governments to recover their national prosperity. I am suggesting to the American people that they be wise creditors in their own interest and be good neighbors.

I wish to take this occasion also to frankly state my views upon our relations to German reparations and the debts owed to us by the Allied Governments of Europe. Our Government has not been a party to, or exerted any voice in determination of reparation obligations. We purposely did not participate in either general reparations or the division of colonies or property. The repayment of debts due to us from the Allies for the advance for war and reconstruction were settled upon a basis not contingent upon German reparations or related thereto. Therefore, reparations is necessarily wholly a European problem with which we have no relation.

I do not approve in any remote sense of the cancellation of the debts to us. World confidence would not be enhanced by such action. None of our debtor nations have ever suggested it. But as the basis of the settlement of these debts was the capacity under normal conditions of the debtor to pay, we should be consistent with our own policies and principles if we take into account the abnormal situation now existing in the world. I am sure the American people have no desire to attempt to extract any sum beyond the capacity of any debtor to pay and it is our view that broad vision requires that our Government should recognize the situation as it exists.

This course of action is entirely consistent with the policy which we have hitherto pursued. We are not involved in the discussion of strictly European problems, of which the payment of German reparations is one. It represents our willingness to make a contribution to the early restoration of world prosperity in which our own people have so deep an interest.

I wish further to add that while this action has no bearing on the conference for limitation of land armaments to be held next February, inasmuch as the burden of competitive armaments has contributed to bring about this depression, we trust that by this evidence of our desire to assist we shall have contributed to the good will which is so necessary in the solution of this major question.

NOTE: The White House issued the President's statement following the news conference on June 20, 1931, and embargoed its release until June 21.

240

Telegram to Members of the Congress
About the Moratorium on Intergovernmental Debts.
June 23, 1931

YOU NO DOUBT have seen my statement in Sunday's press of the proposals of the American Government in respect to postponement for one year of all intergovernmental debts.

Inasmuch as the proposal is of course contingent upon action by Congress and as the matter is one of national interest having no partisan character in that light I consulted before action the Senators and Representatives of both parties present in Washington and as many as possible who were accessible in the country.

This list of generous support from members was shown in the public statement referred to above. I regret that difficulties of communication rendered it impossible to contact with all members of the Senate and House.

I do not wish to press any member for reply as to his views if he prefers not to give them at this time yet if you are favorable to the proposal in the first paragraph of the statement above mentioned it would undoubtedly be helpful to the general situation if you could inform me thereof.

HERBERT HOOVER

NOTE: The telegram was sent to 33 Members of Congress on June 22, 1931, and 30 others on June 23.

241

Message to the American Olympic Committee.
June 23, 1931

[Released June 23, 1931.   Dated April 15, 1931]

My dear Mr. Brundage:

When the young men and women from the nations of the world assemble at the opening of the Games of the Tenth Olympiad in Los Angeles in August of 1932 it will be expected by all Americans that their teams will be represented with full strength and be of the best in character and ability to perform that we have to offer.

To gather together, train, coach and present for competition five hundred of the youth of our land needs both organization and money. It is especially gratifying to note that now as always America's participation is to be financed by voluntary gifts, thus being an expression of good will and cooperation on the part of our generous and sport-loving general public.

Yours faithfully,

HERBERT HOOVER

[Avery Brundage, Esq., President, American Olympic Committee, 110 South Dearborn Street, Chicago, Illinois]

NOTE: The message was printed in the June 1931 issue of the Olympic News.

242

Letter Accepting the Resignation of Samuel R. McKelvie as a Member of the Federal Farm Board. *June 24, 1931*

[Released June 24, 1931. Dated June 20, 1931]

My dear Mr. McKelvie:

On my return to Washington I find your letter of June 15th conveying your resignation from the Farm Board. You already know how much I regret that personal affairs compel you to leave the Board and how anxious I was for you to continue.

You have contributed a real public service to American agriculture during your term on the Board which I know will be recognized by the farmers of the country.

Yours faithfully,

HERBERT HOOVER

[The Honorable Samuel R. McKelvie, Federal Farm Board, Washington, D.C.]

NOTE: Mr. McKelvie served on the Federal Farm Board from 1929 to 1931. His letter of resignation, dated June 15, 1931, and released with the President's letter, follows:

My dear Mr. President:

I retire from the Federal Farm Board with mixed feelings of regret and happiness: The work of the Board is of such far reaching importance and so interesting that I wish I might feel privileged to continue on. Yet, I prefer private life and these are times when if one has a business he may be pardoned for wanting to give it his attention. I will be happy to be back home.

The undertakings of the Federal Farm Board have been twofold, first, to assist farmers in establishing an enduring marketing system owned and controlled by them; second, the application of emergency measures that would prevent precipitate declines in farm commodity prices due to world-wide economic conditions. In both respects substantial progress has been made.

In the development of cooperative marketing more has been accomplished since the Federal Farm Board was established than could have been achieved in ten years without the assistance of such an agency of Government. Largely the funds and energies of the Board have been expended to that end. Cooperatives that were purely local or regional in character have been welded into national sales agencies on a commodity basis, thus giving the farmer the volume of business, bargaining power and control over the flow of the commodity that are essential to better prices and larger returns to growers. The Farmers National Grain Corporation is illustrative of this. This cooperative in the first year of its participation in a full crop became the largest and one of the most successful grain concerns in the United States. Its profits of two-thirds of a million dollars on that year's business were of minor importance compared with greatly enhanced prices that were received by growers due to its activity in the markets of the United States and the world.

The Board, in meeting emergencies through stabilization, has given to agriculture and the country at large a relief of immeasurable value. In the course of a year the American farmer accumulates inventories ranging in value from ten to twelve billion dollars. These inventories are liquidated over a period of twelve months or more. They cannot be turned in the short periods that apply to most manufactured articles. Stabilization activities in wheat and cotton stayed the shock of precipitate declines that otherwise would have taken place and gave the farmer time to market his crops while adjusting himself to changing economic conditions. Vast benefits from this were reflected to every other line of business in the country. The unprejudiced and the informed admit this. They know, also, that this is the first time the Government has undertaken successfully to save the farmer from the immediate price debacle that commonly has fallen upon him in such periods of economic readjustment. Price declines that were inevitable have come about gradually instead of at once. This has saved untold millions to farmers and has prevented numerous unwarranted farm failures.

From my two years' service on the Federal Farm Board I am firmly convinced of the soundness of the Agricultural Marketing Act. I am sure it will do all that was claimed for it by you and its other advocates. The affairs of the Board are in the hands of experienced men who are actuated only by thoughts of what is best for the farmer. It has been a privilege to serve with them and with those who retired before me.

Nearness to your administration has enabled me to appreciate the more your able leadership and I wish for you every success in these troublous times.

With expressions of highest personal esteem, I remain

Very truly yours,
Samuel R. McKelvie
Member, Federal Farm Board

243

White House Statement About Latin American Debts.
June 27, 1931

THE WHITE HOUSE issued the following statement:

There is absolutely no foundation for the stories circulated in the press to the effect that this Government is considering plans for or discussions concerning South American debts. These remain, as do all private debts, solely a relationship between the debtors and creditors. Our bankers have given aid during the depression to various South American countries and so far as the administration is aware those countries are making every effort fully to maintain their credit and confidence.

NOTE: During the preceding week, Chile urged an inter-American conference to provide debt relief for Latin American countries.

244

Message to President John L. Lewis of the United Mine Workers of America About a Proposed Conference of the Coal Industry.
June 30, 1931

[Released June 30, 1931.   Dated June 29, 1931]

YOUR TELEGRAM conveying the request of the Executive Council of the United Mine Workers that a conference of coal operators and miners be convened by the Government was received during my absence from Washington.

The many intricate economic problems and competitive conditions existing in a majority of the bituminous coal mining districts of our country are of general knowledge and it is realied that the difficulties of the industry have been the subject of exhaustive investigation and study by Federal and State agencies and commissions, undertaken with the object of aiding those connected with, and interested in, this basic industry.

The Administration is desirous of lending every possible assistance to any constructive program put forward by operators and miners. Accordingly, I have referred the communications received from your Council and others to the Secretaries of Commerce and of Labor, and have asked them to advise me as to the present attitude of those directly concerned in the industry as to the manner in which the Government might contribute helpfully in any movement designed to advance the wellbeing of operators and mine-workers, as well as all others interested in the bituminous coal situation.

HERBERT HOOVER

[Mr. John L. Lewis, President, United Mine Workers of America, Indianapolis, Indiana]

NOTE: On June 11, 1931, the Executive Council of the United Mine Workers, meeting in Indianapolis, had adopted an appeal urging that a national conference of coal operators and miners be convened in Washington. The Commerce and Labor Departments sent letters to 160 operators asking them whether they favored the calling of a conference. When only 38 replied in the affirmative, the United Mine Workers were informed that the calling of a conference would serve no useful purpose.

245

Message to Haarlem House in New York City.
June 30, 1931

[Released June 30, 1931.   Dated June 29, 1931]

My dear Mr. Corsi:

Among the varied services of social agencies, one of the most important is that of promoting knowledge of the duties of citizenship among those who have come to our country from other lands. Their assumption of the duties of citizenship, as well as the enjoyment of its privileges, is highly desirable. I have been interested to learn of the Americanization work done by Haarlem House during the past thirty-four years, and I wish on the occasion of the graduating exercises of your school of citizenship on July 2nd, to extend my cordial congratulations and good wishes.

Yours faithfully,
HERBERT HOOVER

[Mr. Edward Corsi, Haarlem House, Inc., 311–313 East 116th Street, New York, N.Y.]

NOTE: The message was released on the day preceding graduation exercises at Haarlem House. The graduation exercises marked the completion of a 1-year course in English and citizenship by 87 men and women.

246

Message to the Annual Meeting of the Parent-Teachers Association.
July 1931

[Released July 1931.   Dated April 29, 1931]

My dear Mrs. Bradford:

I am deeply gratified that the annual meeting of the Parent-Teachers Association will this year have for its central theme the challenge of The Children's Charter which the White House Conference on Child Health and Protection crystallized as a working program for constructive new efforts in behalf of American childhood. Your organization is ideally constituted to render most important service in furtherance of these aspirations for a better life for the children, and I deeply appreciate their cooperation.

Yours faithfully,

HERBERT HOOVER

[Mrs. Hugh Bradford, President, Parent-Teacher Association, Hot Springs, Arkansas]

NOTE: The message was published in the July–August issue of Child Welfare Magazine.

247

Message to Wiley Post and Harold Gatty on Their Round-the-World Flight.
July 2, 1931

YOUR SUCCESSFUL world girdling flight is a striking contribution to aeronautical progress. It is dramatic testimony to the efficiency and reliability of American aircraft. It demonstrates vividly how modern science is making neighbors of all the nations of the world. All America is proud of you in the hour of your extraordinary success. You have enhanced faith in the art of flying and the science of air navigation. I congratulate you most heartily on your achievement. I look forward with pleasure to seeing you at the White House next Monday.

HERBERT HOOVER

[Messrs. Wiley Post and Harold Gatty, c/o Karl Betts, New York Athletic Club, New York City]

NOTE: Messrs. Post and Gatty flew a single-engine monoplane, the *Winnie Mae,* from New York across the Atlantic Ocean, Europe, Siberia, Alaska, and Canada in 8 days, 15 hours, and 51 minutes.

248

White House Statement on Federal
and State Expenditures for Road Programs.
July 3, 1931

IN RESPONSE to the President's request, the Federal Bureau of
Roads has completed a canvass of the whole roads program of the
country, with a view to determining the volume of construction during the current calendar year in its relation to employment.

This inquiry reveals that Federal aid for 1931 is $259,897,000, as com-
pared with $105,648,000 for 1930, an increased Federal program of
$154,249,000. It shows as well that expenditures during the year 1931 for
Federal aid, State and local roads combined, will be $1,616 million, as
compared with an expenditure of $1,601 million for the calendar year
1930, an increase of $15 million.

Some States have increased their expenditures in 1931 over 1930,
while others have made decreases. The most notable instances of increases are:

Louisiana	$34,450,000
Wisconsin	19,800,000
Illinois	10,250,000
New York	8,000,000
Texas	7,500,000
Minnesota	7,700,000
Kentucky	6,600,000
Michigan	6,500,000
Oregon	6,000,000.

The total of all increases, as shown in the accompanying table, is
$167,072,469.

Several States, however, have materially decreased their road programs. The outstanding instances are:

Pennsylvania	$29,800,000
Florida	21,150,000

Tennessee 17,900,000
California .... 13,900,000.

The total of all State and local decreases for 1931 as compared with 1930, was $152,129,361.

NOTE: The tables accompanying the statement are not printed here but are available for examination at the Herbert Hoover Presidential Library.

249

Message on the Unveiling of a Statue of Woodrow Wilson in Poznan, Poland.
July 4, 1931

DESPITE THE DISTANCES of space and the differences of speech which separate Poland and the United States, there are circumstances which make it natural for me to express an especial interest in this ceremony. It has been my own good fortune to visit Poland. It has been my good fortune to meet the illustrious citizen of Poland to whose inspiration this gathering is due. It has been my good fortune to know President Wilson, to whom it was given to play a part in the history of Poland. In so doing he cannot have been forgetful of another stormy moment of the world's affairs, when Kosciuszko, Pulaski, and other Polish volunteers, making their way across seas so much wider and more untraveled than they are now, fought in the ragged regiments of Washington. The intervening century and a half have renewed and multiplied past all count these old relations between the people of our two countries. It is therefore peculiarly touching to us that a ceremony such as this should take place in Poland, on the anniversary which stands first in our calendar. In the name of the people of the United States, as in my own, I wish to give voice to our profound appreciation of so notable a mark of remembrance, sympathy, and friendliness.

NOTE: The message was read by United States Ambassador to Poland, John N. Willys, during the unveiling ceremonies, which were broadcast in the United

States over the National Broadcasting Company networks. The statue, sculpted by Gutzon Borglum, was the gift of Ignace Paderewski, first premier of Poland.

250

Message of Sympathy on the Death of Representative George Scott Graham of Pennsylvania.
July 5, 1931

[Released July 5, 1931.   Dated July 4, 1931]

I LEARN with profound regret of the death of your husband. He was a notable figure in his chosen profession. Over a long period of years he was an outstanding member of the national House of Representatives, rendering valuable services to his State and country. Mrs. Hoover and I join in extending you our deep sympathy.

HERBERT HOOVER

[Mrs. George Scott Graham, Islip, New York]

NOTE: Representative Graham served in the Congress from 1913 until his death on July 4, 1931.

251

The President's News Conference of
July 6, 1931

THE MORATORIUM

THE PRESIDENT. I am glad to announce that the American proposal for 1 year's postponement of all intergovernmental debts and reparations has now been accepted in principle by all of the important creditor governments. The terms of acceptance by the French Government are, of course, subject to the approval of the other interested powers, for whom the American Government naturally cannot speak. Without going into technical terms, while certain payments are made by Germany for reparations account, the substance of the President's proposal is retained as the sums so paid are immediately reloaned to Germany.

The technical difficulties arising from many complicated international agreements, which involve the aggregate payment between governments of over $800 million per annum are now in the course of solution by the good will and earnest cooperation of governmental leaders everywhere.

The American part of the plan is, of course, subject to the approval by Congress, but I have received the individual assurances of support from a very large majority of the Members of both Senate and House, irrespective of political affiliations.

The acceptance of this proposal has meant sacrifices by the American people and by the former Allied Governments, who are with all others suffering from worldwide depression and deficits in governmental budgets. The economic load most seriously oppressing the peoples of Germany and Central Europe will be immensely lightened.

While the plan is particularly aimed to economic relief, yet economic relief means the swinging of men's minds from fear to confidence, the swinging of nations from the apprehension of disorder and governmental collapse to hope and confidence of the future. It means tangible aid to unemployment and agriculture.

The almost unanimous support in the United States is again profound evidence of the sincere humanity of the American people. And in this year, devoted to economic upbuilding, the world has need of solemn thought on the causes which have contributed to the depression. I need not repeat that one of these causes is the burdens imposed and the fears aroused by competitive armament. Contemplation of the past few weeks should bring a realization that we must find relief from these fundamental burdens which today amount to several times the amount of intergovernmental debts.

Q. Mr. President, does that mean that the official connection of the United States with your proposal is ended excepting the sanction of Congress? Is it over with so far as we are concerned?

THE PRESIDENT. I will talk to you on that a moment for background. The French proposal we will get over the wire in a few minutes from Paris. We have had the text by telephone but are not quite sure enough of its details to be certain about it. We know its import. The French naturally raise questions which solely concern the European participants in reparations. They are not matters of agreement with the American Government. That requires that the various participants in reparations must get together and come to a conclusion on the French proposals. I do not anticipate any great difficulty in that, as a matter of fact. But so far as we are concerned, in case they come to an agreement or they accept the French basis of anything of that kind, we have no great further official relationship to it. We simply pass it over to the State Department.

Q. Is this to be taken as a proclamation of the proposal, Mr. President? Does this mean it becomes effective as of July 1?

THE PRESIDENT. It is effective July 1.

Q. Mr. President, would you continue your narrative of this background?

THE PRESIDENT. On what other points?

Q. I thought perhaps you had something more to say in explaining it. When will these experts come together?

THE PRESIDENT. It may be that the heads of governments may need to get together. There will have to be some discussion between them. I don't want to anticipate the announcement. It means beginning 1 year after the deferred year, and in 10 annual installments.

Q. July 1, 1933, instead of 1934?

THE PRESIDENT. Yes, and go for 10 years.

Q. Mr. President, is American ratification contemplated in a special session of Congress or at the regular session in December?

THE PRESIDENT. We can do it in December. There is no actual payment due the United States until December (?),[1] with one small exception.

Q. Mr. President, could you indicate how the matters of payments in kind were finally settled?

THE PRESIDENT. It is referred to the committee of experts to work it out within the spirit of the President's proposal. It is a very technical business you will find if you get into it.

---

[1] The question mark appeared in the transcript. Foreign debt payments were due on December 15.

339

Q. Mr. President, are the payments in kind for which contracts have already been made by any process of exclusion to be reloaned to Germany?

THE PRESIDENT. That is not settled. What we said was a committee of experts to get together and work out the modification of the payment in kind plan in such a fashion as to make it conform to this proposal.

Q. You said the text of this note would be available—sent by cable or State Department?

THE PRESIDENT. By cable.

Q. Would it be exact to say that your proposal is already in effect?

THE PRESIDENT. I think it is morally in effect.

Q. As of the first of July?

THE PRESIDENT. As of the first of July. Probably what makes it effective is that nobody would put in money.

Q. What constitutes effectiveness?

THE PRESIDENT. So far as we are concerned, of course, as already stated, when those powers settle on arrangements—when they become final—that would be submitted to Congress, and then it becomes effective. As a matter of fact, the moral effect is that I doubt anybody is going to pay anything the first of July anyway.

Q. The French will make an announcement, Mr. President, won't they?

THE PRESIDENT. Either they or Mr. Mellon—I don't know which.

Q. I mean on behalf of the French Government?

THE PRESIDENT. I could not tell you.

Q. Is there to be a joint statement?

THE PRESIDENT. An understanding in the form of a written memorandum.

NOTE: President Hoover's one hundred and ninety-eighth news conference was held in the White House at 5 p.m. on Monday, July 6, 1931.

On the same day, the White House issued a text of the President's statement on the moratorium on intergovernmental debts and reparations (see Item 252).

The Department of State released a text of the agreement reached between American and French negotiators in Paris, France. The released text of the agreement follows:

After exchange of views the French Government states that it is in agreement with the United States on the essential principle of President Hoover's proposal and on the following propositions which may be expressed thus.

1. The payment of intergovernmental debts is postponed from July 1st, 1931 to June 30th, 1932.

2. However, the Reich will pay the amount of the unconditional annuity. The French Government agrees insofar as it is concerned, that the payments thus made by the Reich shall be placed by the B.I.S. [Bank for International Settlements] in guaranteed bonds of the German railways.

3. All suspended payments shall be subject to interest in accordance with the conditions suggested by the American Government payable in ten annual installments beginning with July 1st, 1933.

4. The same conditions shall apply to the bonds to be issued by the German railroads.

On the three points which it is recognized do not directly concern the American Government, the French Government makes the following observations:

A. A common action by the principal central banks acting through the medium of the B.I.S. shall be organized to assist the countries of Europe which would be particularly affected by the postponement of the payment as proposed.

B. A preliminary understanding should take place between France and the B.I.S. in order that France shall not supply the guarantee fund provided for in the Young Plan in the event of a moratorium except by monthly payments in accordance with the acknowledged rights of the creditor states after the actual transfer of payments by Germany.

C. The question of deliveries in kind and the various modifications which will become necessary as a result of the application of the American proposal and the present agreement shall be studied by a committee of experts named by the interested powers which shall reconcile the material necessities with the spirit of President Hoover's proposal.

France reserves the right to request of the German Government indispensable assurances concerning the utilization for exclusively economic purposes of the sums freed to the Reich budget.

252

Statement on the Moratorium on Intergovernmental Debts and Reparations.
July 6, 1931

THE PRESIDENT said:

"I am glad to announce that the American proposal for 1 year's postponement of all intergovernmental debts and reparations has now been accepted in principle by all of the important creditor governments. The terms of acceptance by the French Government are, of course, subject to the approval of the other interested powers, for whom the American Government naturally cannot speak. Without going into technical terms, while certain payments are made by Germany for reparations account, the substance of the President's proposal is retained as the sums so paid are immediately reloaned to Germany.

"The technical difficulties arising from many complicated international agreements, which involve the aggregate payment between governments of over $800 million per annum are now in the course of solution by the good will and earnest cooperation of governmental leaders everywhere.

"The American part of the plan is, of course, subject to the approval by Congress, but I have received the individual assurances of support from a very large majority of the Members of both Senate and House, irrespective of political affiliations.

"The acceptance of this proposal has meant sacrifices by the American people and by the former Allied Governments, who are with all others suffering from worldwide depression and deficits in governmental budgets. The economic load most seriously oppressing the peoples of Germany and Central Europe will be immensely lightened.

"While the plan is particularly aimed to economic relief, yet economic relief means the swinging of men's mind from fear to confidence, the swinging of nations from the apprehension of disorder and governmental collapse to hope and confidence of the future. It means tangible aid to unemployment and agriculture.

342

"The almost unanimous support in the United States is again profound evidence of the sincere humanity of the American people. And in this year, devoted to economic upbuilding, the world has need of solemn thought on the causes which have contributed to the depression. I need not repeat that one of these causes is the burdens imposed and the fears aroused by competitive armament. Contemplation of the past few weeks should bring a realization that we must find relief from these fundamental burdens which today amount to several times the amount of intergovernmental debts."

253

Remarks at a Ceremony Honoring Aviators Wiley Post and Harold Gatty. *July 6, 1931*

I AM HAPPY personally to congratulate you on your achievement of flying around the world in the remarkable time of less than 9 days. The first flight around the world was made only 7 years ago, when officers of the United States Army spent 15 days and 6 hours in the air, but, because of many delays and mishaps, required 175 days for the entire journey.

Your accomplishment is striking testimony of the advancement which has been made during the last few years by American pilots and American engineers. I congratulate you on your courage, determination, technical ability, and skill.

NOTE: The President spoke in ceremonies held on the White House lawn. Messrs. Post and Gatty were the honored guests at a White House luncheon on the same day.

As printed above, this item follows the text set forth in a contemporary news account.

254

Message to the Convention of the National Retail Grocers Association.
July 6, 1931

[Released July 6, 1931.   Dated June 30, 1931]

My dear Mr. Janssen:

I am interested to learn of the thirty-fourth annual convention of the National Association of Retail Grocers in Milwaukee, July 6th to 9th, and that representative members of the food and grocery industries of various European countries will also be present. Their presence is another indication of the interdependence of the various countries in the world's business. Exchange of experience and discussion of your common problems should contribute to broad and sound policies which will be reflected in the service of these industries to the consuming public.

I shall appreciate it if you will extend my cordial congratulations and good wishes to the delegates from our own country, and abroad.

Yours faithfully,

HERBERT HOOVER

[Mr. C. H. Janssen, 2388 University Avenue, St. Paul, Minnesota]

NOTE: The message was read at the 34th annual convention of the association, which met in Milwaukee, Wis. Among the 14,000 delegates to the convention were 13 grocers from European countries.

255

Message to President Paul von Hindenburg of Germany on the Moratorium on Intergovernmental Debts and Reparations.
July 9, 1931

I HAVE RECEIVED with great appreciation your communication of July 7. It is my sincere hope and expectation that this proposal which has been presented to and accepted by the nations of the world will revive confidence and promote prosperity among all peoples.

HERBERT HOOVER

[His Excellency Field Marshal Paul von Beneckendorff und von Hindenburg, President of the Reich, Berlin, Germany]

NOTE: The President's message was in response to a message from President Hindenburg, a translation of which follows:

Since the Paris negotiations have now arrived at a conclusion and the one-year moratorium proposed by you has begun, I desire to express the thanks of the German people to you and to the American people. My most sincere wish is that owing to your initiative the whole world may be led into a new era of peaceful and confident cooperation.

VON HINDENBURG
President of the Reich

[To His Excellency the President of the United States of America, the White House, Washington, D.C.]

256

The President's News Conference of *July 10, 1931*

SPECULATION IN COMMODITY MARKETS

THE PRESIDENT. It has come to my knowledge that certain persons are selling short in our commodity markets, particularly in wheat. These transactions have been continuous over the past month. I do not refer to the ordinary hedging transactions, which are a sound part of our marketing system. I do not refer to the legitimate grain trade. I refer to a limited number of speculators, and I am not expressing any views upon the economics of short selling in normal times.

But in these times this activity has a public interest. It has but one purpose and that is to depress prices. It tends to destroy returning public confidence. The intent is to take a profit from the losses of other people. Even though the effect may be temporary, it deprives many farmers of their rightful income.

If these gentlemen have that sense of patriotism, which outruns immediate profit, and a desire to see the country recover, they will close up these transactions and desist from their manipulations. The confidence imposed upon me by law as a public official does not permit me to expose their names to the public.

NOTE: President Hoover's one hundred and ninety-ninth news conference was held in the White House at 4 p.m. on Friday, July 10, 1931.

On the same day, the White House issued a text of the President's statement on speculation in the commodity markets (see Item 257).

257

Statement on Speculation in the Commodity Markets.
July 10, 1931

THE PRESIDENT said:

It has come to my knowledge that certain persons are selling short in our commodity markets, particularly in wheat. These transactions have been continuous over the past month. I do not refer to the ordinary hedging transactions, which are a sound part of our marketing system. I do not refer to the legitimate grain trade. I refer to a limited number of speculators. I am not expressing any views upon economics of short selling in normal times.

But in these times this activity has a public interest. It has but one purpose and that is to depress prices. It tends to destroy returning public confidence. The intent is to take a profit from the losses of other people. Even though the effect may be temporary it deprives many farmers of their rightful income.

If these gentlemen have that sense of patriotism, which outruns immediate profit, and a desire to see the country recover, they will close up these transactions and desist from their manipulations. The confidence imposed upon me by law as a public official does not permit me to expose their names to the public.

258

White House Statement on the
United States Tariff Commission Report.
July 13, 1931

THE WHITE HOUSE has received a great many requests for information regarding the work down by the United States Tariff Commission under the flexible clause of the Tariff Act. The attached statement deals with the activities of the reorganized Commission during the 9 months to July 1, 1931, that it has been in office.

Investigations involving 229 different articles have been authorized. Work on 110 has been fully completed, while investigations of 119 are still under consideration. Of this latter number, public hearings have been held on 33 articles. Inquiries into 51 of the remaining number of articles have advanced to the point of public hearings or are otherwise nearing completion, leaving only 35 articles awaiting preliminary action.

Of the reports submitted to the President, two, dealing with four articles, have been returned to the Commission for further study. The others have been approved. No changes in duties were made in 50 percent of the reports. A little over half of the other reports involved reductions; the balance provided for increases.

The cases brought before the Commission are being handled expeditiously. The tables presented herewith reveal that the Commission is disposing of the cases at a rate of one per week. The tables show that some 200 items relating to the strictly flexible provisions of the tariff have either been dealt with, are in process of hearings, or are in the form of applications now before the Commission.

The Tariff Act of 1930 contained 3,221 dutiable items. Of this total 2,171 were unchanged from the 1922 tariff; 890 were increased; and 235 were decreased.

Aside from the work of the Tariff Commission in respect to the flexible clause upon requests by Congress for special surveys relating to imports, the Commission has completed 4 reports dealing with 10 subjects. In addition, a fifth survey of leaf tobacco has been completed by the Commission. This survey was made by the Commission on its own initiative.

The following statement by the Tariff Commission gives in detail the statistics of its work since it was reorganized:

ACTIVITIES OF NEW TARIFF COMMISSION TO JULY 31, 1931

The Tariff Act of 1930 was passed on June 17, 1930.

The previous Tariff Commission was given ninety days pending the appointment of the new Commission for the completion of all records, etc. under the Act of 1922.

Five of the present Commissioners were given recess appointments on September 17, and have, therefore, been directly responsible for work under the Tariff Act of 1930 for a period of nine months. No decisions were made on matters of policy pertaining to applications or investigations until the sixth member of the Commission qualified, which was in October, 1930. This period was devoted to the revision of the rules of practice and procedure and mapping out the work required of the Commission.

The names of the members given recess appointments were submitted to the Senate in December, and confirmation was agreed to by the Senate in January, thus it is five months since the present Tariff Commissioners were confirmed by the Senate; six months since their names were submitted to the Senate; and nine months since the first of them were appointed.

Investigations instituted:

While the present Commission has been in office approximately nine months, or thirty-six weeks, 75 investigations and surveys have been formally instituted under the Tariff Act of 1930. Of these, 36 have already been entirely disposed of, or an average of one per week from the time of appointment of the new Commission. Of these 36 investigations, 5 were surveys which have been published (see table 1); 9 were rescinded, withdrawn or dismissed by Senate Resolution after sufficient work had been done to demonstrate that this was the proper action (see table 2);

and 22 were completed as reports and submitted to the President (see table 3). Public hearings have already been held on 10 additional investigations, and work on these is nearing completion (see table 4).

Work on 29 other surveys and investigations is also proceeding as rapidly as possible consistent with the careful study and analysis which the Commission gives each topic (see table 5). In most of these cases costs of production have been secured in the United States, and cost work is now progressing in foreign countries. Public hearings will probably be held on all of these within the next ninety days.

With reference to 46 additional applications which have been filed with the Commission, sufficient work has been done on 24 to demonstrate that complete cost investigations were not justified. Twenty of them have been denied by the Commission and dismissed without prejudice (see table 6); four have been withdrawn by the applicants (see table 6). This leaves 22 applications for investigation pending, and work is proceeding on the preliminary studies with reference to these (see table 7).

The Commission has, therefore, carried the work forward on 121 projects including applications, investigations, and surveys; has disposed of 36 of these, or an average of one per week; has dismissed 24 additional applications; work has progressed on 39 additional investigations, and preliminary study is well advanced on the 22 applications pending.

NOTE: The seven detailed tables referred to in the statement were not printed but are available for examination at the Herbert Hoover Presidential Library. A general summary with a recapitulation of the tables follow:

ACTIVITIES OF TARIFF COMMISSION, JUNE 18, 1930, TO JUNE 25, 1931

GENERAL SUMMARY

INVESTIGATIONS

Total investigations and surveys formally instituted.................... 75
    Investigations and surveys entirely disposed of............... 36
    Investigations and surveys in progress...................... 39

APPLICATIONS PENDING OR DISMISSED

Applications dismissed................................... 24
Applications pending.................................... 22

Total Projects... 121
Total Articles or Article—groups involved................... 220

RECAPITULATION OF TABLES HEREWITH

Table No.	Brief description	Number of articles or article—groups involved	Basis for action
1	5 surveys and special reports completed.	12	General powers.
2	9 investigations dismissed....	21	Flexible tariff.
3	22 investigations completed and reported to the President.	46	Flexible tariff.
4	10 investigations advanced beyond public hearings and nearing completion.	33	9 under flexible tariff; 1 under general powers.
5	29 investigations advancing to public hearing or other closing phases.	51	25 under flexible tariff; 4 under general powers.
Total	75 formal surveys and investigations.	163	
6	24 applications dismissed following preliminary surveys.	31	Flexible tariff.
7	22 applications pending, undergoing preliminary survey.	35	Flexible tariff.
Grand total	121 projects................	229	

350

259

The President's News Conference of
July 14, 1931

GERMAN FINANCIAL CRISIS

THE PRESIDENT. I have had requests from a considerable number of correspondents for discussions with me as to the background on this debt and German situation. I think it is rather more fair that if I am going to have a discussion I should have it with the whole of the press. If I am going to discuss this thing as I see it at the moment, it must be on the consideration that it is purely background material; that there is to be no quotation or ascribing to the White House, or anything of that kind. If you want the facts as I see them on that basis, I am willing to assist, but it is purely background to assist the correspondents themselves. I am able to give you these facts because they necessarily flow through this office. I want it clear it is for your advice so you can have a better understanding of what is going on. Otherwise I cannot deal with matters like these.

Now, the reparations postponement has in our view taken the most dangerous strain off the whole situation. It obviously placed $400 million of money available to the German Government, and relieved the strain on foreign exchange to the extent of $400 million, and therefore is necessarily a very considerable contribution towards the reconstitution of German finance and industry. That settlement cured the possibilities of international dissension over the situation which, of course, were looming very large, and cleared the atmosphere of that difficulty. What is more, and of equal importance, it greatly relieved the political strains in Germany so that the government goes on with orderly processes instead of disturbances.

Now, the present situation has resolved itself solely into a banking situation, in which there are elements of popular panic. The measures that have been taken by the German Government yesterday and today[1]

---

[1] On July 13 and 14, 1931, the German Government closed all stock exchanges and all banks except the Reichsbank. The holiday ended on July 15, but reopening was accompanied by stringent restrictions on withdrawals and foreign exchange transactions.

are very strong and courageous measures, and should go a long ways to get that sort of mob psychology laid and to regularize that position.

In the matter of this banking crisis there are three fairly distinct elements. There was the usual case in Germany, as there has been in all parts of the world, of overextension of some banks. They, under the strain of depression, would have been in difficulties anyway, but this situation necessarily brings them to the surface. The bank that failed yesterday [2]—the larger bank—had about the same capital and surplus as the United States bank in New York which failed without creating a ripple in the financial fabric of the United States. In other words, the effect of that failure, coming at this time, had a much greater effect on popular minds than it merited and rather more emphasis in this country than the size of it warranted.

The rather deeper than superficialities of isolated instances of weak banking was the situation of German finance in general. Germany does her foreign trade on somewhat more extended terms than any other country in the world. She gives longer terms in the sale of goods, and in the handling of that they have developed the custom or practice of issuing acceptances against these foreign trade bills and selling those acceptances to banks all over the world—in foreign currency, dollars or sterling or whatever the case may be. The foreign bills are payable to Germany in the currency of the country which received the goods. No doubt they have a considerable amount of these bills pledged. They are secured on foreign trade operations and therefore are self-liquidating bills, but they are usually for longer periods than the periods of their acceptance. They issue these for instance, carrying a 12 months credit to some foreign buyer of goods, by say 3 months acceptance, and then renew.

As the result of the situation that existed before the 20th of June, when I made the proposal for a holiday, the people in Germany had started a flight of the mark as it is called. That is an inheritance from 8 years ago when the value of the mark disappeared, and the natural tendency of the people when they see any disturbance coming on, as evidenced

---

[2] Darmstaedter und Nationalbank (Danat Bank), third largest bank in Germany.

by the visit of the German Minister to London,[3] for instance, is to immediately endeavor to cover their marks in foreign currency. That created
an instant strain on the exchange market, but worse than that, it created
a feeling amongst the holders of these acceptances that the situation in
Germany was disturbing, and a good many of those holders presented
them on their expiration for payment, and they were not prepared to
take renewed acceptances.

So you have two strains there—the first one over the flight of capital—
the flight of the mark by the threats of disturbances inside Germany, to
secure foreign exchange in a panic that the mark might depreciate, and
then its reaction abroad. And that, of course, multiplied the exchange
difficulties, and as you know, resulted in a large drainage of gold reserves and exchange from Germany.

The announcement of June 20 brought that state of feeling to an end,
and it remained sound for 4 or 5 days. The movement of exchange was
normal, but the delays in coming to a conclusion again recreated fear
in Germany, and then the fall of the mark started over again with its
repercussions abroad again. So that those strains finally developed into
a more or less popular panic, which began on Monday.

Now, the German Government has taken very strong measures to
curtail the internal flight of the mark and to stop the panic by giving
more time to have it over and by guarantees of bank deposits, and a
whole long list of activities, which we all hope are going to bring that
internal panic to an end.

Now, that is sort of an isolated question. That is a matter the Germans
have got to solve for themselves. Foreign banking discussions with foreign bankers are continuing. Naturally, the foreign banks await the
result of these measures in Germany, and so far as our bankers are concerned, they naturally await the consideration of some sort of definite
plan, in which the European banks, being on the ground, necessarily
have to take the lead and our people assist. There have been no pledges
taken in that direction, but everybody is of the mind to help. Those discussions are still going on, so that except for possible minor contradic-

---

[3] German Chancellor Heinrich Brüning and Minister of Foreign Affairs Julius Curtius visited
Great Britain from July 5 to 10, 1931.

tions in public opinion between France and Germany, the situation is
one of just a purely internal and domestic question of banking crisis
inside Germany, which is not based on the fact that the German banks
are not sound or that the Government cannot get through it but to a
panic feeling among the people. And, as I have said, that feeling is internal. It cannot be cured by any amount of action on our part. The
general tendency in all of these situations is to rather overexaggerate
them. They find their solution in rotation, and I am very much in hopes
that the activities of the German Government are going to solve the
domestic problem they are confronted with. Their government is in
no difficulty. Their budget is amply balanced by action taken. So that
they have one particular problem, and the problem is one then of foreign
exchange and local panic conditions, with a sound financial background
behind it.

Time always helps in these things, and there is no occasion for any
exaggerated anxiety about it. Of course, it is a matter that concerns us
all very greatly. We want to see a solution for it. It retards the world
generally and creates necessarily weakened or insecure commodities and
securities, and all that sort of thing, but my own impression is that time
solves these things, and cooperation if it can be developed helps out.
That is the situation as I see it. I hope it will be of help to you.

NOTE: President Hoover's two hundredth news conference was held in the White
House at 12 noon on Tuesday, July 14, 1931.

260

White House Statement on the Appointment
of Members to the Muscle Shoals Commission.
July 14, 1931

THE PRESIDENT suggested in his message to Congress on Muscle
Shoals that the States of Alabama and Tennessee, being primarily concerned, should appoint representatives, together with representatives
from agriculture and the War Department, to determine a method for
handling the Muscle Shoals plants.

The legislatures of Alabama and Tennessee have authorized representation, and the members have been appointed by the Governors.

The President today appointed Edward A. O'Neal of Alabama, president of the American Farm Bureau Federation, to represent agriculture. To represent the War Department he appointed Col. Harley B. Ferguson, Corps of Engineers, and Col. Joseph I. McMullen of the Judge Advocate General's department.

The members appointed by the States are:

MERCER REYNOLDS of Chattanooga, Tenn.

VANCE J. ALEXANDER of Nashville, Tenn.

W. A. CALDWELL of Jackson, Tenn.

And

W. F. McFARLAND of Florence, Ala.

I. N. DUNCAN of Auburn, Ala.

S. F. HOBBS of Selma, Ala.

261

Message to President Paul Doumer of France on Bastille Day.
July 14, 1931

ON THIS national holiday of the French Republic it is a great pleasure to extend to Your Excellency and to your fellow countrymen sincere congratulations both in my own name and in the name of the people of the United States.

HERBERT HOOVER

[His Excellency Paul Doumer, President of the French Republic, Paris, France]

68-611 O - 76 - 26

262

Address to the Convention of the International Christian Endeavor Societies.
July 16, 1931

FROM EVERY State in the United States, from every province of the Dominion of Canada, from Mexico, and from a score of countries beyond the seas you have assembled in San Francisco to celebrate the golden anniversary of the International Christian Endeavor Societies—an organization devoted to golden deeds and ideals.

The 50th anniversary of the International Christian Endeavor Societies is a notable moment in your history. It is significant not only to you, but to the whole Nation by reason of your past services and your potentialities for even greater usefulness in the future.

From an humble beginning in Portland, Maine, in 1881, the Christian Endeavor movement has become a world force for the promotion of spiritual advancement among our people. The 4 million members in more than 80,000 local units in 126 nations, dominions, states, and island groups present an impressive force in spiritual well-being of the world.

Despite differences of language, tradition, and custom, the youth of the world have found in the organization a common ground for spiritual training and service to their church, community, and country. It represents the most enduring monument to the idealism, insight, and organizing genius of its founder, the late Dr. Francis E. Clark.

The best index to its purposes and values are the principles it stands for. Its loyalties and ideals make for good citizenship, for character, and religious faith. It recognizes that national independence and international understanding are not incompatible. It stands for international good will and world peace. It is a mighty force for sobriety, righteousness, and respect for law, patriotism, and spiritual development in every nation.

It is an appreciated privilege, in behalf of the Nation, to greet the delegates from our own land and other lands to the convention of the World's Christian Endeavor Union at the 50th milepost of this dynamic movement. I congratulate you on the achievements of a half century of practical idealism. You have before you even higher privileges and opportunities to serve with the vigor, courage, and idealism of youth in the solution of myriads of problems of the future. Above all yours is a mission of exemplifying the standards of individual conduct which are the basis of national character. A better world is the mission of youth and it is your mission.

NOTE: The President spoke from the Cabinet Room of the White House. His address was carried by land wire to the San Francisco auditorium where the convention met, and was also broadcast over the National Broadcasting Company and the Columbia Broadcasting System radio networks.

263

Statement on the London Conference of Ministers.
July 16, 1931

THE PRESIDENT said:

"As has already been announced, Secretary Stimson will attend the Conference in London which has been called by the British Government for Monday to consider the present emergency problems in Central Europe. I have asked Secretary Mellon, if consistent with his plans, also to attend in order that we may have the benefit of his advice as well.

"It is our understanding that the Conference is limited entirely to questions of the present emergency."

264

Message to Senator Arthur Capper About the Domestic Impact of the European Economic Crisis.
July 18, 1931

YOU ARE entirely correct in your conclusion that a considerable part of the price difficulties of Kansas wheat farmers is due to the present paralysis of the export market arising from the economic crisis in Central Europe which naturally affects not only them but all countries importing our wheat. The major problem in this connection has been solved by the aid given to Germany in postponement of reparations and to other governments in postponement of debts and I am confident that we will bring about a solution to the remaining difficulties. I know of no greater immediate service to the Kansas farmer and to unemployment generally than the reestablishment of normal economic life in that quarter.

HERBERT HOOVER

[Honorable Arthur Capper, Topeka, Kansas]

265

Message to President Enrique Olaya on Colombia's Independence Day.
July 20, 1931

ON THIS memorable anniversary of the independence of the Republic of Colombia, it gives me great pleasure to express to Your Excellency in the name of the Government and people of the United States most cordial wishes for the continued welfare of your great country. To the warm greetings of my fellow countrymen, I add my own sincere wishes for your personal happiness.

HERBERT HOOVER

[His Excellency Doctor Enrique Olaya Herrera, President of the Republic of Colombia, Bogotá]

266

Statement on the London Conference of Ministers.
July 23, 1931

THE PRESIDENT said:

"The London Conference has laid sound foundations for the establishment of stability in Germany.

"The major problem is one affecting primarily the banking and credit conditions and can best be solved by the voluntary cooperation of the bankers of the world rather than by governments with their conflicting interests. Such a basis of cooperation is assured.

"The program supplements the suspension of intergovernmental debts already in effect. The combined effect should enable the German people with their resources, industry, and courage, to overcome the temporary difficulties and restore their credit.

"The program contributes to expedite recovery from worldwide depression through the overcoming of the most important elements in the crisis affecting Central Europe.

"The world is indebted to Premiers MacDonald, Laval, and Brüning, to Messrs. Stimson, Mellon, Grandi, Francqui, and other governmental representatives in this Conference. The Conference has demonstrated a fine spirit of conciliation and consideration amongst nations that will have lasting benefits in establishment of stability."

NOTE: The President referred to British Prime Minister J. Ramsay MacDonald, French Prime Minister Pierre Laval, German Chancellor Heinrich Brüning, Secretary of State Henry L. Stimson, Secretary of the Treasury Andrew W. Mellon, Italian Foreign Minister Dino Grandi, and Emile Francqui, Belgian Minister of State and Regent of the National Bank of Belgium.

The London Conference produced the standstill agreement which provided that the governments represented would recommend concerted action by their financial institutions to maintain German credits already extended. In addition, a committee of bankers was to inquire into the future needs of Germany.

267

White House Statement on the American Proposal to the London Conference of Ministers.
July 23, 1931

THE MATTER is a tempest in the teapot. The facts are these: On Friday (July 17), while still in Paris, Secretary Stimson received a cablegram from Washington setting forth a concrete proposal by the United States for consideration of the London Conference. Mr. Stimson immediately discussed the essentials of this proposal with the representatives of France and Germany. Then garbled accounts of these discussions of the American proposal appeared in the European newspapers and to some extent in the American press on Monday (July 20). Then press cables went from Washington to London on Monday that there was a new proposal. Mr. Stimson naturally denied there was a new proposal for he had received no instructions since Friday.

The American proposal transmitted Friday was issued here on Tuesday (July 21) to correct inaccurate accounts of the discussions that were based on the proposal that Mr. Stimson got on Friday.

NOTE: The statement was issued in response to stories of a rift between American leaders in Washington and those in London.

As printed above, this item follows the text set forth in a contemporary news account.

268

Messages Congratulating the Secretary of State and the Secretary of the Treasury on Their Roles in the London Conference of Ministers.
July 23, 1931

SECRETARY OF STATE HENRY L. STIMSON

I WISH to convey to you my sincere congratulations. My appreciation is the deeper from knowing the complexity of the difficulties which confronted you over the past ten days and the able manner they have been surmounted. I hope you may now secure a real vacation.

HERBERT HOOVER

SECRETARY OF THE TREASURY ANDREW W. MELLON

I WISH again to congratulate you upon a most notable public service. I trust you may now secure a real vacation.

HERBERT HOOVER

NOTE: As printed above, this item follows the text set forth in a contemporary news account.

269

Memorandum to Federal Departments and Agencies
on Expenditures for Fiscal Year 1932.
July 24, 1931

[Released July 24, 1931.　Dated July 19, 1931]

To all Departments of the Government and independent establishments:

The July 1 estimates of expenditures for the fiscal year 1932 furnished by the departments and establishments to the Bureau of the Budget indicate that in spite of all efforts for economy the expenditures as now contemplated by the departments and establishments will be in excess of those estimated as of June 1 and also in excess of those actually made during the fiscal year 1931.

In view of the fact that our receipts are falling off materially from the amount estimated at the time of the preparation of the Budget for 1932 and of the consequent large deficit indicated for the current fiscal year, I wish again to bring to your attention the seriousness of our financial situation and desire that you assure yourself that all those in your establishment are impressed with the urgent need for economies and postponements in view of this emergency. The situation is a serious one and demands that we all make the most earnest efforts to eliminate or postpone all such activities as may be so treated without serious detriment to the public welfare.

You have been requested to furnish to the Bureau of the Budget, for my information, not later than August 17, a statement of appropriations available for expenditure during the current and subsequent fiscal years with an indication of the amounts expected to be obligated therefrom and the contemplated ultimate savings.

Pending the compilation and analysis of this statement I wish to suggest that you refrain from actually obligating money available for expenditure during the current fiscal year except in those cases where such postponement or elimination will clearly be to the detriment of the public welfare.

Yours faithfully,

HERBERT HOOVER

270

White House Statement on the Retirement
of Henry P. Fletcher as Chairman
of the United States Tariff Commission.
July 28, 1931

THE WHITE HOUSE announced today that Mr. Henry P. Fletcher, who had intended to retire as Chairman of the United States Tariff Commission on September 16 next, would remain at the head of the Commission until November 15 next, at the request of President Hoover. The Commission expects that practically all pending investigations and surveys (with the exception of the vegetable and possibly one or two other investigations) will have been completed by that time.

The President believes that the Commission, under Mr. Fletcher's chairmanship, has proven that it can and will make all proper and necessary adjustments in the tariff rates and that Mr. Fletcher and the members of the Commission have performed a valuable public service in putting the Commission on an efficient operating basis, where it is commanding the confidence of the public in the absolutely fair and impartial administration of its important duties.

The President appreciates the willingness of Mr. Fletcher to remain for another 2 months, thus giving the Commission the benefit of his fine abilities.

271

White House Statement on the Maintenance of Wage Levels.
July 28, 1931

NO MEMBER of the administration has expressed the view or holds the view that the policy of the administration in advocating maintenance of wages should be changed. It has not been changed.

NOTE: The statement followed the publication on July 27, 1931, of a letter by Secretary of Commerce Robert P. Lamont to Representative Francis Condon. In the letter the Secretary declared that interference in individual cases of wage reductions was not the duty of the Government.

As printed above, this item follows the text set forth in a contemporary news account.

272

Message to the National Association of Teachers in Colored Schools.
July 28, 1931

My dear Mr. Lucas:

The National Association of Teachers in Colored Schools, which convenes in Washington this evening for its annual meeting, comprises a group of men and women whose services to their race and to our country are invaluable. To thousands of children and youth they bring not only opportunities for general education, but promotion of health, worthy home environments, vocational guidance and character training, all of which make for useful, self-reliant and law abiding lives. The schools and colleges in which they teach can render a service of great value in helping to translate into actual practice the standards and principles set forth in the Children's Charter adopted by the White House Conference on Child Health and Protection. Education is not only the foundation of personal efficiency but is the solvent of many of the problems which confront us as a nation. The work of these teachers represents a social service and practical patriotism of high order. I shall be obliged if you will extend my greetings and congratulations to the delegates and my good wishes for a convention which will lend strength and inspiration to them in their important work.

Yours faithfully,

HERBERT HOOVER

[Mr. M. Grant Lucas, President, National Association of Teachers in Colored Schools, 1738 Fifteenth Street, N.W., Washington, D.C.]

NOTE: The message was read at the opening session of the association's annual convention in Washington, D.C.

273

Message to King Prajadhipok of Siam
on His Departure From the United States.
July 29, 1931

[Released July 29, 1931.   Dated July 28, 1931]

AT THE MOMENT of Your Majesties' departure from the United States, I wish to express to Your Majesty and to Queen Rambai Barni my pleasure and that of Mrs. Hoover that Your Majesties chose to visit this country and that you gave us the pleasure of your visit to Washington. I wish you a most enjoyable and safe journey homeward and long years of usefulness as ruler of your happy and prosperous country. Mrs. Hoover joins me in thanking Your Majesties for the kind message which has just been received from you. I am certain that the American people will rejoice with me in learning that you have enjoyed your residence here and that your health has been benefited.

HERBERT HOOVER

[His Majesty The King of Siam, On Board Siamese Royal Train, Care of Station Master, Delaware and Hudson Railway, Rouses Point, New York]

NOTE: The President's message was in response to a telegram from King Prajadhipok on his departure for Canada.

During his visit to the United States, the King and his party resided at Mrs. Whitelaw Reid's home, Ophir Hall, in White Plains, N.Y.

King Prajadhipok's telegram, dated July 28, 1931, follows:

As I leave Ophir Hall on the termination of my stay in the United States of America I desire to express to you, Mr. President, my hearty appreciation of the welcome accorded to me not only at your hands and those of the officials of your government, but at the hands of the citizens of this friendly country; appreciation of the unvarying good will and of the interest evinced in the objects of my visit, and of the numerous courtesies extended to me and to my party during the three months of our residence here. In thanking you sincerely and the American people for these tokens of amity it is a pleasure to assure you that I take with me besides many pleasant memories a gratifying impression of the enhancement of the previously happy relations between our two countries and in addition a personal evidence of the skill of American physicians.

I would request you, Mr. President, to accept my warm regards and hopes for the welfare of your country and in conclusion the Queen joins me in taking leave of and in kind wishes to Mrs. Hoover.

PRAJADHIPOK

274

Message of Sympathy on the Death
of William R. McLean.
July 30, 1931

I HAVE LEARNED with deep regret of the death of your father who contributed so much to modern journalism. Please accept my heartfelt sympathy.

HERBERT HOOVER

[Mr. Robert McLean, Philadelphia Bulletin, Philadelphia, Pa.]

NOTE: Mr. McLean was the president and publisher of the Philadelphia Evening Bulletin.

275

Statement About Agricultural Relief for Drought and Grasshopper Infestations in Western Farmlands. *July 31, 1931*

THE PRESIDENT said:

"I have directed officials of the Department of Agriculture to undertake, in cooperation with local and State authorities, such organization as may be necessary to meet the situation created by local drought and grasshopper destruction in the Northwestern and Central States. The Department is engaged in a resurvey in the light of the changes in the last 2 weeks. The area affected embraces certain counties in Montana, North and South Dakota, and local sections of Iowa, Nebraska, and Minnesota.

"While suffering within the areas affected is acute, the extent of the drought and damage is comparatively minor to that which we confronted and surmounted last year. The Federal Government has already extended assistance in some portions of those localities and the Red Cross is actively engaged in relief work. Secretary Hyde is in touch with the situation. National and local resources are available and the problem will be taken care of."

NOTE: Secretary to the President Theodore G. Joslin issued the statement to the press at 4 p.m. on Friday, July 31, 1931. The President had already left for Rapidan Camp, Va.

276

Message on the Dedication of Perry's Victory Memorial. *July 31, 1931*

[Released July 31, 1931.   Dated July 29, 1931]

THE DEDICATION of the Perry's Victory Memorial to commemorate the victory of Commodore Oliver Hazard Perry and his men in the battle of Lake Erie, and an enduring peace between English-speaking peoples, is an event of more than national interest and significance. This memorial to the valour of Commodore Perry's men, and indeed, to the heroism of the combatants on both sides, also commemorates a pioneer step in the maintenance of peace through disarmament. The Rush-Bagot Treaty which followed this war provided for the permanent limitation of armaments maintained by the two nations on the Great Lakes. It stands not only as a symbol of victory at arms, but marks the establishment for the first time in history of the principle of disarmament in the policy of nations as a preventive of war. It is particularly appropriate that a tablet reproducing the Rush-Bagot agreement should be unveiled at the dedication. It comes at a time when the nations of the world are seeking solution of their common problems through cooperation and disarmament. It is my happy privilege on behalf of our nation to congratulate the Commission.

Herbert Hoover

[Mr. Webster P. Huntington, President, The Perry's Victory Memorial Commission, Put-in-Bay, Ohio]

NOTE: The message was read at dedication ceremonies at Put-in-Bay, Ohio. The memorial was built at a site overlooking the spot where Commodore Perry defeated the British in 1813.

277

The President's News Conference of *August 4, 1931*

OKLAHOMA DISTRICT ATTORNEY

THE PRESIDENT. I haven't any great wealth of news. News is not subject to manufacture. There was a District Attorney in the Western District of Oklahoma, Mr. Herbert K. Hyde, appointed this morning.

PUBLIC BUILDING PROJECTS

I have two reports which I think are of public interest. One of them is from the Treasury Department as to the progress in the public building program. As you know from previous reports, they have a total of 758 projects which have been specifically authorized at a cost of about $453 million, and, as you know, each one of those projects has to pass through a long and painful experience of advancements from one stage to another—from the determination of the site and the local conflicts that arise about it, the acquirement of the site and the local difficulties that must arise from it apparently, and the final and ultimate contract for the building. So that the Treasury reports these different stages of advancement of the projects. I will give you a shorthand note on this.

Up to date on the program they have completed 57 buildings, amounting to something over $25 million. Between May 15 and July 15—May 15 being the date of the last report—42 additional contracts have been let, bringing up the total buildings under contract to 192, with an estimated cost of $135 million. The next stage of delay is that all sites that have been acquired, plans have been completed, and are in process of being offered for bid. Forty-seven additional projects advanced to this stage since May 15, making the total now of 61 in that category, at an estimated cost of about $44 million.

Then the next category—the sites that have been acquired and the plans in course of preparation. There are 192 projects in that stage, at an estimated cost of about $181 million. And then there are the various categories of sites, negotiations, bids that have been advertised for, and so on.

The important thing about it is that the preliminaries have been gotten through in a very large majority on the sites, and the rest of the program moves with a great deal of expedition. There should be probably $300 million under contract by fall.

UNITED STATES EMPLOYMENT SERVICE

The other report is one from the Department of Labor on the development of the reorganized labor service which was authorized by Congress at the last session. It shows a very large measure of accomplishments, the details of which you can see in the report.

Otherwise than that I haven't anything of any particular interest this morning.

Q. Will the Labor report be given out?

THE PRESIDENT. Yes, in 10 or 15 minutes.

NOTE: President Hoover's two hundred and first news conference was held in the White House at 12 noon on Tuesday, August 4, 1931.

On the same day, the White House issued a text of a White House statement on public building projects (see Item 278).

A text of the Labor Department report on the United States Employment Service, dated August 3, 1931, follows:

To the President:

I have the honor to report upon the progress of the newly reorganized Employment Service in this Department as follows:

Mr. John R. Alpine, of New York, was appointed as Special Assistant to the Secretary of Labor on March 13th to direct expansion and reorganization of the Service and intensification of its efforts to relieve the situation growing out of the business depression, under the larger provisions of the last Congress.

The actual work of expansion and reorganization, at which time the very important task of selecting Industrial Superintendents of Building Trades; Mining and Quarrying; Manufacturing and Metal Trades; Transportation; Clothing and Needle Trades; Office and Mercantile, and Marine Seamen and Longshoremen, and State Directors and Assistants thereto, which were to create the personnel of this important work, was instituted on March 18, 1931. This in itself was a task of no mean proportions, but on April 20th the question of personnel had been completed with but few exceptions. On that date a meeting of those men and women who had been appointed to administer to the affairs of this reorganized United States Employment Service was held in Washington at the Department of Labor. Full instructions were given to them by Mr. Alpine, myself and other officials of the Department of Labor, and for three days the ramifications of our task of expansion was fully gone into, and the appointees given the benefit of a most extensive experience and research by the officers of the Department referred to.

In a comparatively brief period of time the new Employment Service was actually working, and from the date that its wheels were started in operation it has been gaining momentum hourly, until at this time it has demonstrated its worth in a most remarkable degree.

The concentration of effort took full shape on May 15, 1931. Our records, therefore, showing the progress of this work of reorganization and expansion should properly date as of May 15, 1931, although because of reasons comparative we will make reference data beginning April 1, 1931.

On April 1, 1931, there were 200 cooperating offices and 36 Junior Placement Offices, representing totally 236 cooperative offices.

On April 1, 1931, there were 23 Veterans' Employment Offices, and 17 Farm-Labor offices. There are now under the new plan of reorganization 56 additional Federal Employment Offices under the supervision of the various State Directors.

The number of cooperative offices as of April 1 remains unchanged, and represents 236 offices where cooperation on the part of the United States Employment Service is gratifyingly in evidence.

Totals:

Federal and cooperative offices on April 1, 1931   279
Federal and cooperative offices on July 31, 1931   332

With reference to cooperative offices, it is pleasant to record that our efforts and results in this direction are eminently satisfactory.

We have recently instituted an intensive campaign calling upon every citizen of our Country to assist in the relief of the unemployment conditions obtaining among the Veterans of our land. To this end we are working in close cooperation with the American Legion, The Veterans Administration, the Disabled American Veterans of the World War and the Veterans of Foreign Wars. While our enlarged plans in this direction are of comparative recent origin, we are making marked progress because of the splendid system of cooperation in operation between the United States Employment Service and the Veterans' Organizations referred to. We are doing everything possible to be of practical service to those men whose services were so invaluable to our Country and to all the world. This is a most important matter, and it is receiving the attention commensurate with its importance.

Total employment placements from April 1 to July 31, 1931........ 638,689

These figures are incomplete, due to the fact that full data has not been received for the month of July, but they are sufficiently accurate to demonstrate the splendid work that this enlarged United States Employment Service is doing. It is but a beginning, and as the expansion increases, so also will results increase. With the splendid season of cooperation existing with State, City and Civic Free Employment Services, and with the equally splendid cooperation existing between the various Veterans' Organziations, we confidently anticipate increasingly fine results as a consequence of our efforts in all States of the Union and in the District of Columbia.

The number of jobs that have been provided for the unemployed would undoubtedly be considered formidable under any conditions, but when the economic depression through which we are passing is taken into consideration, a little reflection will illustrate not only the importance of this task, but the splendid results that have been attained.

Obviously it is impossible to find jobs where jobs fail to exist, but the United States Employment Service, by combing the highways and byways, has succeeded in finding jobs for 281,769 unemployed from April 1st to July 31st, 1931, with complete returns not yet available, and if there are other jobs to be had, this Service proposes to locate them. We are paving the way, on solid foundation, for real Employment Service that could not be obtained by any other means.

Total placements made by all Federal and cooperative employment
offices combined.. 638,689

Despite the prevalent unfavorable economic conditions we feel that our efforts will have an appreciable effect upon the unemployment situation during the approaching winter.

Yours faithfully,
W. N. DOAK

68-611 O - 76 - 27

278

White House Statement on Public Building Projects.
August 4, 1931

THE TREASURY DEPARTMENT has furnished the following review of progress during the past 60 days of that portion of the public
building program administered by the Treasury Department. A total
of 758 projects have been specifically authorized at a cost of about $453
million. The progress of these projects is marked by stages beginning
with determination of sites, acquirement of land, design of buildings,
specifications, bids, letting of contracts, and completion.

1. *Completed buildings.* From May 15 to July 15, 6 additional projects
have been completed, bringing the total of completed buildings up to
57, at a total cost of $25,326,876.

2. *Contracted buildings.* From May 15 to July 15, contracts have been
let for 42 additional projects, bringing the total buildings now under
contract but not completed, to 192, estimated to cost $135,637,366.

3. *Sites acquired and plans completed and in process of contract.*
Forty-seven additional projects have been advanced to this stage between
May 15 and July 15, making a total now in this category of 61, of an
estimated cost of $44,249,800.

4. *Sites acquired and plans underway.* From May 15 to July 15, the
number of projects now in this category have been increased by 49, making the total 192, of an estimated cost of $181,353,023.

5. *Sites acquired or in negotiation from May 15th to July 15th.* Thirty-
four projects have been advanced to this category, there now being 100
in this stage of an estimated cost of $32,301,841.

6. *Sites advertised and bids opened.* There are now 156 projects in this
stage at an estimated ultimate total cost of $34,871,800.

It has been found that owing to local conflicts over sites, the impedi-
ments in acquiring title, condemnation proceedings, etc., the stages five
and six have proved the most fertile of delays.

THE FOLLOWING IS A REVIEW OF THE ADVANCEMENT OF THE FEDERAL BUILDING
PROGRAM SINCE THE LAST REPORT OF THE PRESIDENT ON MAY 15

	May 15		July 15	
	Number of buildings	Amount	Number of buildings	Amount
(1) Buildings completed....................	51	$23, 516, 876	57	$25, 326, 876
(2) Contracts let..........................	150	120, 213, 900	192	135, 637, 366
(3) Sites acquired, plans completed and in process of being contracted...........	56	20, 097, 000	61	44, 249, 800
(4) Sites acquired, plans partially completed..	190	192, 173, 723	192	181, 353, 023
(5) Sites acquired or in negotiation........	115	50, 622, 941	100	32, 301, 841
(6) Sites advertised, bids opened...........	196	46, 494, 800	156	34, 871, 800

279

Message to President Mustapha Kemal of Turkey
on the Nonstop Flight From New York to Istanbul
by American Aviators Boardman and Polando.
August 4, 1931

[Released August 4, 1931.   Dated August 3, 1931]

I WISH TO express my sincere appreciation of the courtesies which you
have shown the American fliers Boardman and Polando following their
successful flight from New York to Istanbul.

HERBERT HOOVER

[His Excellency Gazi Mustapha Kemal, President of the Turkish Republic, Yalova,
Turkey]

NOTE: Russell W. Boardman and John Polando set a long distance record by flying a Bellanca monoplane, the *Cape Cod,* nonstop from New York to Istanbul in 49 hours and 20 minutes. On August 5, 1931, they were honored at ceremonies in Istanbul.

280

Message Congratulating Colonel and Mrs. Edward M. House on Their Golden Wedding Anniversary.
August 4, 1931

MRS. HOOVER and I should like to join with your legion of friends in extending heartiest congratulations to you and Mrs. House on your golden wedding anniversary. We wish for you a plentitude of health and happiness.

HERBERT HOOVER

[Colonel Edward M. House, Manchester, Mass.]

281

Message of Sympathy on the Death of Walter Platt Cooke.
August 5, 1931

I HAVE LEARNED with sorrow of the death of your husband, Walter Platt Cooke. His devotion to his community and country led him into distinguished service in the United States, and his insight into world affairs enabled him to contribute greatly to the solution of the international financial problems growing out of the World War. The value of his services was recognized in the positions of responsibility which he filled in the fields of finance, law and education and by honors accorded him by the governments of France, Belgium and Italy. I wish to extend to you and your son and daughter my deepest sympathy in your bereavement.

HERBERT HOOVER

[Mrs. Walter Platt Cooke, 155 Summer Street, Buffalo, New York]

NOTE: Mr. Cooke, an internationally known lawyer, had been a member of the Reparations Commission.

282

Message to President Daniel Salamanca on the Anniversary of the Founding of the Bolivian Republic.
August 6, 1931

ON BEHALF of the Government and people of the United States of America and in my own name I ask Your Excellency to accept hearty congratulations on this great national anniversary of Bolivia.

HERBERT HOOVER

[His Excellency Daniel Salamanca, The President of Bolivia, La Paz, Bolivia]

283

The President's News Conference of
August 7, 1931

FEDERAL FARM BOARD APPOINTMENT

THE PRESIDENT. I have to announce the appointment of Mr. Frank Evans, of Salt Lake, to membership on the Farm Board. For many years he has been the attorney for farm cooperatives both in the West and in the East. He is endorsed by Mr. [Charles C.] Teague and many of the other cooperative leaders, and he takes Mr. Teague's place as the western representative on the Board.

ORGANIZATION FOR UNEMPLOYMENT RELIEF

During the last 3 weeks, as some of you may surmise, I have been engaged with other members of the administration in a study of the problems of unemployment and relief likely to confront us next winter and the organization necessary to meet that possible situation. While the improvement in a good many directions seems promising, the problem, whatever it may be, will be met. With the organized cooperation of the local and State and Federal authorities and the large number of relief and charitable organizations in the country, the problem was successfully overcome last winter, and we shall adapt the organization methods in such a manner as may be necessary to meet the next winter.

The first of the facts to be determined is the volume of the load of distress which will need to be provided for. The various bureaus of the Government are engaged in an exhaustive study of last winter's experience of all organizations in the country as to the average number in distress and their location. And a further examination is being made as to the probable increased or decreased load in different localities next winter. Those reports are not yet complete and won't be for some little time. The second requirement is to appraise the action now in progress, the agencies which are available for the winter, their resources, and the methods which have proved successful in last winter's experience, and the organization necessary to coordinate and cooperate with the various agencies. I have been in communication with a number of the Governors and with other public authorities. A number of States and municipalities have already begun to lay the foundation for action necessary to meet their problem over the winter.

I have canvassed the situation in conference with business and financial and labor leaders as to different methods of assistance in which interstate industries can be brought into greater aid.

I have had a number of conferences with the leaders of the important relief and business organizations throughout the country with view to consolidation and coordination of their efforts to support the national and local government.

We now have underway a reexamination to determine the actual number of employees probable on Federal public works. This will show a very material increase over last winter—the exact numbers we do not as yet know. And further we are canvassing the municipal and State programs, and are also canvassing the industrial programs.

The completion of these conferences and inquiries will probably require another month. At that time all the facts should be clear, both as to the load to be met and the progress and strength of the organization in different regions and the character and method of national organization necessary to coordinate and successfully cope with the problem.

That is all I have got today.

UNEMPLOYMENT STATISTICS

Q. Mr. President, how about the number of unemployed? Can you give your figure—what you are working on?

THE PRESIDENT. I am not approaching it at this time from a theoretical number. We have found on investigation that it is not merely bewildering but misleading. The problem is the load to be carried rather than any theoretical numbers. I might tell you that the 6 million of last January on investigation proves to have many flaws in it, and there is no method that I see for accurate determination. We are, however, on solid foundations when we examine the actual load of last winter and when we estimate what the probabilities will be based on the increase or decrease of employment in given localities, or factors of that kind. We get down to the ground at this time and cease talking about gross figures.

NOTE: President Hoover's two hundred and second news conference was held in the White House at 4 p.m. on Friday, August 7, 1931.

On the same day, the White House issued a text of the President's statement on the organization for unemployment relief (see Item 284).

284

Statement on the Organization for Unemployment Relief. *August 7, 1931*

THE PRESIDENT said:

"During the past 3 weeks I have been engaged, together with members of the administration, in a study of the problems of unemployment and relief likely to confront us over the coming winter and the organization necessary to meet the situation. While improvement in the situation in many directions seems promising, the problem, whatever it may be, will be met. With the organized cooperation of local and State and Federal authorities, and the large number of relief and charitable organizations, the problem was successfully handled last winter. We shall adapt organization methods in such manner as may be necessary for the coming winter.

"The first of the facts to be determined is the probable volume of the load of distress which will need to be provided for. The various bureaus of the Government are engaged in an exhaustive study of last winter's experience of all organizations in the average number of persons in distress and their location. Further examination is being made of the probable load during next winter. The economic changes during the year will materially improve certain areas and others may be worse. These reports are not yet complete.

"The second requirement is to appraise the action now in progress, the agencies which are available for the winter, the methods which have proved successful, and the organization needed to cooperate with these agencies. I have been in communication with several Governors and with other public authorities. Already many States and municipalities have begun to lay the foundation for action necessary to meet their problems.

"I have been canvassing the situation in conference with business, financial, and labor leaders as to the different methods in interstate industries which may be of aid.

"I have had a number of conferences with leaders of relief and business organizations throughout the country with view to consolidation and coordination of their efforts to support the national, State, and local action.

"We have now underway a reexamination to determine the actual number to be employed through the steadily increasing volume of Federal public works. We are canvassing State and municipal and industrial construction to ascertain what may be expected in that direction.

"The completion of these conferences and inquiries will require another month. By that time all the facts should be clear both as to the load to be met, the progress and strength of organization in different regions, and the character and method of national organization necessary to coordinate and support them."

285

Letter to the Acting Secretary of the Navy on the Selection Board for Medical Officers.
August 7, 1931

[Released August 7, 1931. Dated July 17, 1931]

My dear Mr. Secretary:

I am in receipt of your letter of even date informing me of the action of the Navy Department in convening a new board for the selection of medical officers.

I wish it to be known and recorded by the new board that the President has no interest in this matter other than to see that the best men should receive promotions.

Yours faithfully,

HERBERT HOOVER

[The Honorable, The Acting Secretary of the Navy, Washington, D.C.]

NOTE: Ernest Lee Jahncke was Acting Secretary of the Navy.

286

Radio Address to the World's Conference of the Young Men's Christian Association. *August 8, 1931*

IT IS A PLEASURE to extend in behalf of the United States most cordial greetings to the delegates from 50 nations attending the World's Conference of the Young Men's Christian Association, meeting in Cleveland tonight. Your gathering is significant, because, in the long history of your association covering more than three-quarters of a century, it is the first ever to be held on the North American Continent. I would have enjoyed welcoming you in person but the demands of public service make it impossible for me to do so. Happily the radio permits me to participate from a distance in your deliberations.

You have come from every country of Europe, from all the States of our country, from Canada, Asia, and Africa, from our sister republics in Latin America, stretching from Mexico and Cuba on the north to Chile and Argentina on the south, and from Australia, New Zealand, and other parts of the island world. You have drawn from all nations upon reservoirs of good will, enthusiasm, and devotion to spiritual ideals.

Common possession of a great spiritual ideal and a great sense of service have brought you together from all corners of the world. You have foregathered to formulate your plans that you may, with renewed vigor, foster among the youth of all lands the development of a vital faith in spiritual life, the kindling of a more passionate sense of social obligations, and the cementing of international fellowship for service to God and mankind.

You approach the problems of youth with sympathy and with confidence assured of the ultimate contributions with which they will refresh the common life of the world. You are right in the abiding confidence that the solution of all social, economic, governmental, and international problems must be guided by an idealism which finds its firm foundations in religious faith. Your interest in the activities of your association has given you an insight into public affairs and a grasp of world conditions. It has developed a leadership from within your membership that is beneficial to all nations. One of those leaders, your friend and mine, is Dr. John R. Mott. I have no need to recite to you the multitude of services he has given to the whole world by a life of complete devotion to an ideal.

The accomplishments of your associations over these many years have quickened the hopes of mankind. You have become a potent world force. No thoughtful person can overlook the profound truth that the ideas and ideals of Christ which you uphold not only have dominated the course of civilization since His time but are the foundations of our economic and social life today. Because of human weakness, the Golden Rule may have its daily violations, but this great principle, aimed at the common good, penetrates and profoundly modifies all the forces in the modern world in which we live.

Yours is an organization devoted to safeguarding the moral and spiritual heritage of youth and to guiding it in the paths of right and joy of service. In its consummation you carry forward vast constructive programs of recreation, community service, observance and obedience to law, character building, and, above all, spiritual development.

Your work has a profound unifying influence. It blends all races in its program. It welcomes to its fellowship young men of all faiths. It holds a strategic position to promote the common good not only within each nation but in international cooperation and good will. The fulfillment of these obligations is at once a challenge and an opportunity for youth itself. Recent weeks have given impressive proof of the hunger of the human spirit for a greater sense of security and a willingness to respond to a common effort to attain this goal. The desire is overpowering. It shall be realized.

In drawing attention to the nationwide and worldwide problems and service of the Y.M.C.A., however, we should not lose sight of the primary object of the organization which is to serve individual men. In all the 10,000 centers where such organizations exist, hundreds of thousands of youth can testify to what the human relationship of the Y.M.C.A. has meant to them in their individual lives. Spiritual safeguards and social influences go hand in hand with the provision of physical necessities for wholesome living. They are part of the vast programs of education which must be carried on beyond the formal schooling of our people. They are powerful forces in the warfare against downward tendencies in public morals and conduct.

Your organization is a great militant body enlisted in the fundamental advancement of human progress. The problems before the world were never greater than today. No small degree of responsibility rests upon you for their proper solution. I and my countrymen have confidence in you and the contribution you will make to the future.

NOTE: The President spoke at 8 p.m. from Rapidan Camp in Virginia, to the conference meeting in Cleveland, Ohio. His address was carried by the National Broadcasting Company and Columbia Broadcasting System radio networks.

The President referred to Dr. John R. Mott, chairman of the conference.

287

Message to the Conference of Smaller Industries.
August 10, 1931

[Released August 10, 1931.   Dated July 31, 1931]

My dear Mr. Young:

I am interested to learn that a Conference of Smaller Industries has been called at Silver Bay, New York, to promote charting of industrial courses in the light of an exchange of thought and experience by the representatives of the moderate sized units in our industrial structure. Such stock-taking of the factors of management, planning, labor, safety, costs, production and distribution, should make for sound practices and stabilization in the smaller industries and likewise have a substantial effect on industry generally. When it is realized that the smaller industries employ more than half of the nation's industrial labor the significance of your conference is clear. Business stability will be built not only on the foundations of the individual efficiency of industrial units, large and small, but upon their united efforts in analyzing their common problems and their cooperation in a sound program. I shall appreciate it if you will express to the participants in your conference my interest in their problems and my earnest hopes that your meeting will be a successful one.

Yours faithfully,
HERBERT HOOVER

[Mr. Arthur H. Young, Chairman, The Industrial Institute, Silver Bay, Lake George, N.Y.]

NOTE: The message was read at the opening session of the conference, sponsored by the Industrial Institute to consider the problems of small manufacturers. The conference was attended by approximately 200 businessmen.

288

Message to the Convention of the Army and Navy Legion of Valor.
August 10, 1931

[Released August 10, 1931.   Dated August 3, 1931]

My dear Major Cooper:

On the occasion of the Memorial Service of the Army and Navy Legion of Valor of the United States of America, I wish to extend on behalf of the nation cordial congratulations and good wishes, and to express sympathetic interest in the objectives of the organization. To cherish the memories of the valiant, to stimulate patriotism in the minds of youth and to inculcate respect for the flag, are aims which strike a responsive chord in the heart of all good citizens. I trust that your ceremonies on August 9th may contribute to the greater realization of your sound ideals.

Yours faithfully,
HERBERT HOOVER

[Major Edwin H. Cooper, D.S.C., Chief of Staff, Army and Navy Legion of Valor, 11 Glastonbury Oval, Waban, Mass.]

NOTE: The message was read at the 41st annual convention of the organization, held in Faneuil Hall in Boston, Mass.

289

Message to President Paul von Hindenburg
on the Anniversary of the Founding
of the German Republic.
August 11, 1931

I EXTEND my hearty congratulations to Your Excellency and your
fellow countrymen on this anniversary of the German Republic.

HERBERT HOOVER

[His Excellency Field Marshal Paul von Beneckendorff und von Hindenburg,
President of the Reich, Berlin, Germany]

290

White House Statement on Unemployment Relief Efforts
of the Association of Community Chests and Councils.
August 12, 1931

MR. ALLEN T. BURNS, the Executive Director of the Association of
Community Chests and Councils, has advised the President that their
organizations in 227 cities which have so far been heard from report
their complete confidence that they, in cooperation with municipalities and other local agencies, will be able wholly to undertake the
unemployment relief situation during the forthcoming winter. The
plans in these cities are going forward actively, and more cities are being
heard from daily.

291

Message on the 25th Anniversary of the National Recreation Association.
August 13, 1931

To The Boys and Girls of America:

Two and a half million of you are playing today in the playgrounds of nearly a thousand cities. Your elders rejoice with you in your fun and freckles, your sports and games and all that goes into making you happy and healthy boys and girls. Your zest in life is a precious possession and your laughter makes a joyous chorus throughout the land. Thousands of devoted men and women under the leadership of the National Recreation Association have labored for a quarter of a century to provide the playgrounds which you enjoy. We rejoice with you and with them in this boon to the boyhood and girlhood of our country.

Yours faithfully,

HERBERT HOOVER

292

Message to Frank Knox, Publisher of the Chicago Daily News.
August 13, 1931

[Released August 13, 1931.   Dated August 12, 1931]

I AM PLEASED indeed to learn that you have become the publisher of the Chicago Daily News. Your thirty years of experience as an active journalist give promise that you will maintain and enhance the high traditions of the Daily News, one of America's outstanding newspapers. I congratulate the Daily News on securing your services and wish for you personally every success in your new undertaking.

HERBERT HOOVER

[Frank Knox, Chicago Daily News, Chicago, Illinois]

NOTE: The message was in response to a telegram, dated August 11, 1931, from Frank Knox. It was published in the August 13 issue of the Chicago Daily News.

293

Message to the Annual Convention of Building and Loan Associations.
August 13, 1931

[Released August 13, 1931.   Dated August 4, 1931]

My dear Mr. Myers:

The Centennial Convention of the United States Building and Loan League and the International Congress of Building Societies and Building and Loan Associations in Philadelphia, August 11th to 14th, is an occasion of unusual historical and business significance. It marks a century of cooperative finance and individual self-help for home ownership initiated in this country in the village of Frankford, Pennsylvania in 1831. Helping to finance the building of over eight million American Homes in the intervening century is an achievement of financial importance, but of even more significant social implications.

Home owning is more than the provision of domiciles; it goes to the roots of family life, public morals and standards of living. The men who have shaped the Building and Loan plan have been pioneers in moulding a most important economic characteristic of New World civilization. The national administration has recognized the importance of home ownership by calling a conference on Home Building and Home Ownership this autumn, further to promote this phase of our community life in the light of a careful study of current conditions. The interest and cooperation of members of the Building and Loan Associations in this enterprise is cordially invited.

The savings accumulated by some twelve millions of investors in membership in Building and Loan associations in this country have acted as a stabilizing force and have illustrated the self reliance of our citizenry.

I am interested to note that other nations are joining with the American Association in the celebration of the Centennial. I should like to extend both to the delegates from our own land and those from other countries, my warmest congratulations on the substantial achievements of the Building and Loan movement, and my deep interest in your deliberations and continuing usefulness.

Yours faithfully,

HERBERT HOOVER

[Mr. R. Holtby Myers, Pres., The U.S. Building & Loan League, 740 S. Spring St., Los Angeles, Calif.]

NOTE: The message was read at the 39th annual convention of the building and loan associations, meeting in Philadelphia, Pa.

294

Letter Requesting Walter S. Gifford To Be Director of the President's Organization on Unemployment Relief. *August 19, 1931*

[Released August 19, 1931.   Dated August 17, 1931]

Dear Mr. Gifford:

It is clear that, irrespective of the improvement in employment, many localities in the United States will be faced during the coming winter with a heavy relief load due to unemployment.

In order that every preparation may be made to meet in an effective way such needs as may arise, I am asking you to set up and direct such organization as may be desirable, with headquarters in Washington to cooperate with the public authorities and reinforce the national, state and local agencies which will have responsibility for the relief activities arising out of unemployment in various parts of the nation this winter.

I am asking you to do this because of my long acquaintance with work you have done in similar fields and it is my desire that you should use your own judgment as to the type of organization you set up and its methods of work. This care of misfortune is our first duty to the nation.

The whole force of the Administration is at your disposal. Based upon my experience of some years in such problems I am sure we shall compass this task.

Yours faithfully,
HERBERT HOOVER

[Mr. Walter S. Gifford, American Telephone & Telegraph Company, New York City]

295

Statement on the Appointment of Walter S. Gifford as Director of the President's Organization on Unemployment Relief.
August 19, 1931

THE PRESIDENT said:

"I have appointed Walter S. Gifford to set up and direct such organization as may be desirable, with headquarters in Washington, to cooperate with the public authorities and to mobilize the national, State, and local agencies of every kind which will have charge of the activities arising out of unemployment in various parts of the Nation this winter. A survey of need and probable extent of the load during the next winter by various Federal agencies is now in progress.

"The work directed so splendidly by Col. Arthur Woods during the past year will be continued under the direction of Mr. Fred C. Croxton as part of the new organization, including its work on employment problems. Colonel Woods volunteered a year ago on the understanding that he must return to his other responsibilities this autumn. He will continue to give assistance to the new organization.

"Mr. Gifford is president of the American Telephone and Telegraph Company, president of the Charity Organization Society of New York, and during the war was Director of the United States Council of National Defense. I am appointing a nationwide advisory committee to assist Mr. Gifford.

388

"The task of proper assistance to the deserving is one which will again appeal to the generosity and humanity of our whole people. It is a task which our Nation will perform, for in no people is there developed a higher sense of local responsibility and of responsibility of every man to his neighbor."

NOTE: For Mr. Woods' appointment as Chairman of the President's Emergency Committee for Employment, see 1930 volume, Items 334 and 347.

296

Message of Sympathy to President Chiang Chung-cheng of China About the Flood in the Yangtze Valley. *August 19, 1931*

[Released August 19, 1931.   Dated August 18, 1931]

REPORTS OF the disastrous flood conditions in the Yangtze Valley are causing friendly concern in the United States and in my own name and in the name of the people of this country I wish to express to you and to the Chinese nation our sincere sympathy.

HERBERT HOOVER

[His Excellency Chiang Chung-cheng, The President of the National Government of the Republic of China, Nanking, China]

NOTE: In July and August 1931, China's Yangtze Valley experienced floods which destroyed a number of cities and villages, leaving millions homeless and drowning an estimated 250,000 persons.

Chiang Chung-cheng was Chiang Kai-shek.

297

The President's News Conference of
August 21, 1931

SALE OF WHEAT TO CHINA

THE PRESIDENT. I have some questions this time, so we have some inspiration. The first one is on the question of whether there is any limit on the amount of wheat which the Farm Board is willing to dispose of to China for relief purposes.[1] The amount of 15 million bushels was suggested from China, but the Farm Board is willing to accommodate the Chinese Government with any amount of wheat; 15 million is not the limit.

MAJOR GENERAL BUTLER

I have another question as to the application of Major General Smedley Butler for retirement from the Marine Corps.[2] I assume that if General Butler wishes to retire the Government will approve. The general is a very gallant officer, and I have no doubt that if the country gets into trouble again we can get him back into service.

THE PRESIDENT'S ORGANIZATION ON UNEMPLOYMENT RELIEF

I have some questions on the relief organization. I have received a very splendid response to the invitations to become members of the Advisory Committee to the Unemployment Relief Organization, as it is called. Acceptances have been received from 52 out of the 60. Two in addition have declined because of illness, and six more are out on holidays, and we have not been able to reach them yet. So that apparently the response will be complete. Some typical telegrams from those gentlemen you can see through Mr. Joslin.[3]

---

[1] The Federal Farm Board announced on August 20, 1931, that it was ready to negotiate the sale of 15 million bushels of wheat for China. The wheat was to be used for relief of refugees from the Yangtze River flood.

[2] In January 1931, Maj. Gen. Smedley D. Butler had accused Italian Prime Minister Benito Mussolini of running down a child with his automobile. The resulting controversy led to demands for a court martial of General Butler, which were later dropped. General Butler was reprimanded and on August 20, requested permission to resign from the Marine Corps.

[3] Theodore G. Joslin, Secretary to the President.

We are having a large number of communications from public officials and various organizations, especially those active over the last winter. There is a very large amount of reorganization and planning now in progress in preparation for the fall and winter. There is a very evident widespread resolution to meet the situation again. I cannot speak too highly of the actual results obtained by the multitude of committees and the organization of Federal authorities and others over last winter. They had a very large load to carry.

Whether this will be larger or less than the load of last winter cannot yet be determined, but there is a test—and a very positive test—by which the success of matters of relief can be fairly accurately determined, and that is the state of public health. I have had a great many years of experience in dealing with problems of distress and relief, as some of you know, and we have always tested efficaciously in every effort of that kind by the reflex in public health. I, therefore, made an inquiry of Surgeon General [Hugh S.] Cumming, Chief of the Public Health Service, as to what had been the state of public health over this last winter. I will give you that correspondence. In brief, it shows that the general mortality, the infant mortality, and, so far as statistics go, they are fairly accurate, the sickness in the country was less in the winter of 1931 than in the winters of full employment of 1928 and 1929. The public health has apparently never been better than it has been over the past 6 months. In arriving at those results you will see that General Cumming has taken compensation for the shift in contagious diseases and so forth, but generally, the point I wish to make is that it is a most remarkable showing for the effort which the country made last winter and one for which all those organizations are entitled to a very great deal of credit indeed.

PUBLIC WORKS EMPLOYMENT

I have one other question as to the progress of Federal employment in construction work. I have had the figures taken out anew and reduced it to a single sentence. The people directly and indirectly employed by the Federal Government in construction and maintenance work at the opening of this depression was 180,000. They touched 730,000 at the first day of August. That number will probably increase some with the increased employment in Federal road building, and it will probably decrease on the road building side with winter, but the construction contracts for public buildings will be in greater activity, and the Supervising Architect's office anticipates that by January they will be employing somewhere from 80,000 to 100,000 more than they are actually employing now.

And that is all that I have on my docket.

NOTE: President Hoover's two hundred and third news conference was held in the White House at 4 p.m. on Friday, August 21, 1931.

On August 20, 1931, the White House issued a list of persons invited to serve on the Advisory Committee to the President's Organization on Unemployment Relief. Excerpts from some of these acceptance telegrams were issued by the White House on August 21.

For the correspondence from Surgeon General Hugh S. Cumming on public health, see Item 298.

298

Letter to Surgeon General Hugh S. Cumming on the Effect of the Depression on Health Conditions. *August 21, 1931*

[Released August 21, 1931.   Dated August 13, 1931]

My dear General Cumming:

In order to assemble the entire picture of the unemployment relief problem I should like to know what the Public Health results show as to the success or failure of the organization during the past winter in relieving distress.

Therefore I would be greatly obliged if you would furnish me with such data as you have on the comparative state of the public health during the period of maximum burden of distress and relief—that is, in the early months of 1931—as compared with, say, similar months in 1928, a period of full employment. You will, of course, need to consider the effect of the irregular factors introduced by epidemics. I mention this as long experience has taught me that if there is any lowering of vitality in any section of the population, it might result in certain types of epidemics.

Generally, the final test of success or failure in efforts to meet physical distress is in the relative volume of sickness or death, and I would be glad to know what this test, applied to the last winter, shows.

Yours faithfully,

HERBERT HOOVER

[Surgeon General Hugh S. Cumming, Public Health Service, Washington, D.C.]

NOTE: Surgeon General Cumming's reply, dated August 18, 1931, follows:

My dear Mr. President:

In response to your request that you be furnished with such data as may be available on the comparative state of the public health during the period of maximum burden of distress and relief, that is, in the early months of 1931, as compared with similar months in 1928, a period of full employment, I have analyzed the existing material on this subject and submit the following for your information:

The most accurate and complete data available on health conditions in the United States are the statistics of mortality. Provisional reports of deaths in certain States are received monthly by the Public Health Service from the respective State health departments at as early a date as the data can be assembled. A compilation of available reports from 13 States (over 43,000,000 population) during the first five months of 1931 shows that the death rate was 12.0 per 1,000 as compared with 13.7 for the same period in 1928 (Table A). Rather large variations in the general death rate from year to year are more frequently due to the prevalence of influenza than to any other single cause. The times of occurrence of influenza epidemics seem to be practically beyond control, and are reflected especially in high death rates from influenza and pneumonia. Since a moderate epidemic occurred late in 1928 and early in 1929, a comparison of mortality from causes other than influenza and pneumonia has been made. The death rate with these two causes excluded was less in 1931 than in any of the three preceding years. (Table A)

It is of interest to note that records from entirely different sources indicate a similar trend. The Division of Vital Statistics of the Bureau of the Census collects statistics of deaths from industrial insurance companies having an aggregate of more than 70,000,000 policies in force. For the first six months of 1931 the death rate among those policyholders was 10.5 per 1,000; in 1928, the rate was 10.6 per 1,000 for the six months. (Table B) The death rates among about 18,000,000 industrial policyholders of the Metropolitan Life Insurance Company were 9.5 for 1931 and 9.9 for 1928 (Table C). When influenza and pneumonia are eliminated, the corresponding rates were 8.2 and 8.4.

Still another source confirms the reports above indicated. A group of large cities reporting currently to the Vital Statistics Division of the Bureau of the Census shows that the rate for the first half of 1931 (13.1 per 1,000) is less than in any of the three preceding years (13.9 for 1928). (Table D.)

Infant mortality is a rather sensitive index of health conditions. It is computed as the number of deaths under one year of age per 1,000 live births. Such rates in a group of seven States, the only ones for which data are available for each of the past four years, show that the rate (71.4) in the first five months of 1931 was less than for 1928, 75.6. (Table E.)

In a group of 13 States, with a population of over 43,000,000, the death rate from tuberculosis has continued to decline, the rate for the first five months of 1931 being only 63.4 per 100,000 against 77.5 for 1928. (Table F.)

For several years the Public Health Service has received reports of illnesses occurring among a group of wage-earner members of sick benefit associations. Sickness rates for the first half of 1931 are 104.2 per 1,000 and for 1928, 117.9, or 71.2 and 82.8, respectively, if influenza and pneumonia are omitted. (Table G.)

The reports of cases of certain communicable diseases made to the Public Health Service by State health officers for the first six months of the year 1931 may also be compared with reports for the same period of 1928. Reported diphtheria incidence during the first six months of 1931 was 26,000. For the same period of 1928, 46,000 cases were reported. For the six month period, 24,000 cases of smallpox were reported in 1931 and 29,000 cases in 1928. 4,500 cases of typhoid fever were reported for the first six months of 1931, as compared with 5,900 cases for 1928. Diphtheria, smallpox and typhoid fever are diseases which can be controlled, and the reports indicate that progress is being made, even though that progress is not as rapid as it might be.

Reports of cases of pellagra for the first six months are available from only seven of the States in which pellagra is prevalent: Virginia, South Carolina, Alabama, Mississippi, Arkansas, Louisiana and Oklahoma. In these States the number of reported cases for the first half of 1931 was 14,333; 1930, 12,203; 1929, 14,612 and 1928, 11,952.

The tables referred to in this letter are attached.

The data from these various sources indicate that 1931 has started out as a comparatively healthy year. The recent economic situation seems to have had no general adverse effect on health and mortality rates. In view of the agitation in general with respect to the effect of economic conditions on health, public health workers have been surprised at the excellent health conditions that are found upon studying the available facts.

Respectfully,

H. S. CUMMING,
Surgeon General

[The President, The White House]
Enclosures.

TABLE A—MORTALITY IN 13 STATES* DURING THE FIRST 5 MONTHS OF 1931 WITH COMPARATIVE DATA FOR THE SAME PERIOD IN THE THREE PRECEDING YEARS

First 5 months of	Death rate per 1,000 population (annual basis)	
	All causes	All causes except influenza and pneumonia
1931..............	12.0	10.2
1930..............	12.0	10.5
1929..............	13.5	10.9
1928..............	13.7	11.6

*The States were Alabama, Connecticut, District of Columbia, Indiana, Kansas, Minnesota, New Jersey, North Carolina, New York, Pennsylvania, Tennessee, Wisconsin and Iowa.

TABLE B—MORTALITY AMONG POLICY-HOLDERS OF INDUSTRIAL INSURANCE COMPANIES FOR THE FIRST 6 MONTHS OF 1931, WITH COMPARATIVE DATA FOR THE SAME PERIOD IN THE THREE PRECEDING YEARS. (POPULATION ABOUT 71,000,000 IN 1928 AND ABOUT 75,000,000 IN 1931)

First half	Death rates per 1,000 policy-holders (annual basis)
1931....................	10.5
1930....................	10.2
1929....................	11.4
1928....................	10.6

TABLE C—MORTALITY AMONG INDUSTRIAL POLICY-HOLDERS OF THE METROPOLITAN LIFE INSURANCE COMPANY FOR THE FIRST 6 MONTHS OF 1931 WITH COMPARATIVE DATA FOR THE SAME PERIOD IN THE THREE PRECEDING YEARS. (POPULATION ABOUT 18,000,000)

| First half | Death rates per 1,000 policy-holders (annual basis) | |
	All causes	All causes exclusive of influenza and pneumonia
1931................	9.5	8.2
1930................	9.4	8.2
1929................	10.5	8.5
1928................	9.9	8.4

(Includes Canada, but since the population of that country is only about one-fifteenth of that of the United States, the effect on the rates must be unappreciable.)

TABLE D—MORTALITY IN ABOUT 65 LARGE CITIES OF THE UNITED STATES DURING THE FIRST HALF OF 1931 WITH COMPARATIVE DATA FOR THE SAME PERIOD IN THE THREE PRECEDING YEARS

First half	Death rate per 1,000 population
1931.....................	13.1
1930.....................	13.4
1929.....................	14.4
1928.....................	13.9

Data are from the Weekly Health Index of the U.S. Bureau of the Census.

TABLE E—INFANT MORTALITY IN 7 STATES* DURING THE FIRST 5 MONTHS OF 1931
WITH COMPARATIVE DATA FOR THE SAME PERIOD IN THE THREE PRECEDING YEARS

First 5 months of	Deaths under 1 year per 1,000 live births
1931	71. 4
1930	70. 9
1929	80. 7
1928	75. 6

*The States were Alabama, Connecticut, Indiana, Kansas, Pennsylvania, New York and Wisconsin.

TABLE F—MORTALITY FROM TUBERCULOSIS (ALL FORMS) IN 13 STATES* DURING
THE FIRST 5 MONTHS OF 1931 WITH COMPARATIVE DATA FOR THE SAME PERIOD
IN THE THREE PRECEDING YEARS

First 5 months of	Tuberculosis death rate per 100,000 population (annual basis)
1931	63. 4
1930	71. 0
1929	76. 1
1928	77. 5

*The States were Alabama, Connecticut, District of Columbia, Indiana, Kansas, Minnesota, New Jersey, North Carolina, New York, Pennsylvania, Tennessee, Wisconsin, and Iowa. Total population in 1931—43,593,000.

TABLE G—FREQUENCY OF DISABILITY LASTING 8 CALENDAR DAYS OR LONGER IN THE FIRST HALF OF 1931 COMPARED WITH THE SAME PERIOD IN THE THREE PRECEDING YEARS

(Male Sickness Experience is of 16 Industrial Establishments which Reported Their Cases to the U.S. Public Health Service during all Four Years)

First half	Average number of males covered in the record	Annual number of 8-day and longer disabilities per 1,000 men, on account of—	
		Sickness*	Sickness* exclusive of influenza and pneumonia
1931............	108, 669	104. 2	71. 2
1930............	116, 750	103. 2	79. 3
1929............	112, 929	136. 7	80. 3
1928............	107, 227	117. 9	82. 8

*Accidents, either of industrial or of non-industrial origin, are not included.

299

The President's News Conference of *August 25, 1931*

CONSERVATION OF WATERFOWL

THE PRESIDENT. I have some questions on which I can give you a little information. The first is with regard to shortening the season for duck-shooting. I have signed a proclamation [Proc. 1965] shortening the season as recommended by the Department of Agriculture. This action is backed by 43 conservation associations and State game commissions. It is opposed by three such organizations and also by three large ammunition manufacturers. However, the proclamation has gone forth.

PRESIDENT'S ORGANIZATION ON UNEMPLOYMENT RELIEF

I have a question about additional members asked to join Mr. [Walter F.] Gifford's advisory committee. There are five more so far: Mr. James F. Bell of Minneapolis, Conrad Mann of Kansas City, P. G. Spillsbury of Phoenix, Arizona, Owen D. Young of New York, and S. P. Bush of Columbus, Ohio.

BRITISH FINANCIAL CRISIS

There are some other matters on which I can give you some information for your own use, not for quotation, but merely acceding to demands on some questions as to facts in order that you may be correctly informed.

The first is with regard to the statement that this Government has been in communication with the British in respect to the financial crisis.[1] There is not a word of truth in that statement. It is not a matter in which the American Government could properly make any communication to the British Government and I have had no such communication either by telephone or otherwise.

Next is the story that arises from a British newspaper that the Federal Reserve banks have made stipulations bearing on the change in the British ministry policies. The New York Federal Reserve Bank some time ago granted credit to the Bank of England. That credit has not been exhausted and they have received no further requests for credits from England and have had no communication of such nature.

SECRETARY OF THE TREASURY

I am asked to give Mr. Mellon's impressions of Europe. You will have to get those from Mr. Mellon.

---

[1] Gold withdrawals from Great Britain had created a financial crisis and, on August 25, 1931, led to the creation of a new National Government pledged to economy measures. The President denied the report of the London Daily Herald charging that the Federal Reserve Board and President Hoover had dictated a change in British policy and helped to bring about the fall of the Labour Cabinet.

Transportation of Wheat to China

I have a large number of questions about the transfer of Farm Board products by sea. This is solely a question for the Farm Board which makes its own arrangements. I think most commercial people will realize that when goods are sold on which the other fellow pays the freight, he also determines the shipping. The Farm Board is not paying the freight in this instance but I understand they have been trying to help out American shipping.

And that comprises the budget this morning.

NOTE: President Hoover's two hundred and fourth news conference was held in the White House at 12 noon on Tuesday, August 25, 1931.

300

Message to President Gabriel Terra on Uruguay's Independence Day.
August 25, 1931

ON BEHALF of the citizens of the United States, and in my own name, I send you cordial greetings on this anniversary of the independence of Uruguay.

HERBERT HOOVER

[His Excellency Dr. Gabriel Terra, President of the Oriental Republic of Uruguay, Montevideo]

301

Letter to the Acting Attorney General on the District of Columbia Police Force.
August 27, 1931

My dear Mr. Attorney General:

I am glad to approve, in the special circumstances of the Federal Government's relation to the District of Columbia, that the Department of

Justice should accede to the request of the District Commissioners for aid in investigation of recent charges against certain members of the Washington police.

However, we must not overlook the fact that Washington has an able and devoted police force. The vast majority of its honest men should be protected by determining if there are unworthy men in their midst. It is always possible that occasional individuals may have overstepped the law and humanity in treatment of criminals and those charged with crime, and if so, they should be severely punished. But even in such charges the police should not be prejudged on the allegations of criminals themselves or those accused of crime. There is too much tendency on the part of some people to forget the devoted work of the police, to forget the safety of society and the victims of criminals out of sympathy with criminals themselves.

Yours faithfully,

HERBERT HOOVER

[The Honorable The Acting Attorney General, Washington, D.C.]

NOTE: Thomas Day Thacher was the Acting Attorney General.

302

The President's News Conference of *September 1, 1931*

FISCAL POLICY

THE PRESIDENT. I have no questions, and I have no incidental news. I thought I might talk to you for a moment on the background in relation to future fiscal policies of the Government—solely for your information and in the hope that it might be helpful to you.

I can say at once that no serious consideration has yet been given to the policies which will be inaugurated at the time Congress meets as to taxation. For very serious reasons it is impossible to come to any conclusions on a subject of that character now, but there are a great many factors that will enter into whatever determination we will arrive at, whether to proceed without additional taxation or to impose such taxation. We do not yet know what the tendency of our income may be. Any degree of economic recovery would entirely change the whole aspect of Government receipts.

There are one or two features of our Federal income that begin to stand out with a great deal of vividness—the most important being that the corporation tax and the income tax are, both of them, profit taxes. They are dependent on the volume of governmental income, upon the progress of business and industry and, therefore, they are subject to tremendous variableness on the progress of the country as a whole. At the time those taxes were devised no doubt the amount which they might vary was little understood. The corporation tax, obviously, is a tax on profits, and as profits have diminished very greatly, that tax, of course, is very much less fertile than it used to be in good times.

The income tax is in a very large proportion a tax on earned incomes of business profits. A large amount of tax exempt securities in the country have been issued, and the Federal, State, municipal, and other tax exempt securities have furnished a refuge for unearned income, as it is called, and the result is that our Federal taxation system is fairly unreliable in its yield as between good times and bad. So that the amount of income which we would have to predicate for both this fiscal year and the next fiscal year is purely a question of the economic outlook, and we are not able to formulate at the present moment any judgment on that question. So that for that reason alone we would not be coming at the present time to any conclusions.

Furthermore, the tendency of expenditures during the present fiscal year and the next fiscal year cannot now be determined. The question, of course, is always open as to whether there will be added expenditure during this fiscal year as the result of congressional action, and also a question as to how far we can safely impose economies in the governmental expenditure during the present and next fiscal year. We are making every effort to hold down the expenditures of the Government in the present fiscal year, but we have, of course, the tremendous burden of Federal aid to the unemployment situation. You will recollect that the various programs of the Federal Government in aid to unemployment have resulted in an increase of our construction and maintenance expenditure from somewhere about $250 million, as you already know, of normal amount, to somewhere about $700 million to $750 million. In other words, we are carrying a burden of somewhere about $500 million in our Federal budget which is the product of the depression and the contribution of the Federal Government to that situation.

As I have told you before, the total number of men employed directly and indirectly on Federal construction and maintenance work in January 1930, was about 180,000, whereas it is now about 760,000. That is an indication of the increased budgetary burden which we are now carrying. That undoubtedly continues through this fiscal year. What would be the necessary conclusion about that for the next fiscal year we cannot begin to arrive at at the present time. Obviously, if there was a turn in the economic tide we would be able to diminish that burden on the Government and make very large economies in the subsequent fiscal year, but even that cannot be determined just now.

Aside from any further burden which Congress may think necessary to impose on the budget for this fiscal year, some things have arisen which are likely to increase our expenditures, particularly the loans on the bonus certificates. If those loans continue at their present rate we shall probably need to appropriate anything between $200 million and $300 million for further loans during this fiscal year. That will be a direct burden on the budget. You will recollect that there had already been distributed about $300 million prior to the passage of the act and since the passage of the act about $800 million to $850 million has been distributed, which almost exhausted the provision made by Congress in the last session for the service. We will be able to get through, until Congress opens, with the amounts which we still have available, but a continuation of that demand is likely to necessitate very considerable appropriations. And as to what that will result in it is too early to determine. It may be that all of the veterans who are going to take advantage of the provision have now done so, and that we will not be faced with that burden.

I might mention incidentally that the two long-term loans which have been recently made, the one of June for $800 million and the one of now for $800 million—one of those, the June one, just covers the deficit of last

403

year—does not quite cover it. The one made now might be said to cover the payments on bonus certificates. So that you cannot derive any conclusion as to Government policies by the fact that we are issuing loans for purposes of covering moneys which we have already expended. There is no anticipatory gospel in that.

You will recollect that in the last fiscal year we had a deficit of something over $900 million, of which something over $400 million was due to statutory retirement of the debt, and the actual increase in the debt was somewhere approximately $500 million. We, therefore, absorbed that amount of fat out of the previous excess redemption of the debt. It does not necessarily imply that we can go on living indefinitely on our fat until it is exhausted. How far the Government should go in that direction will depend on the economic outlook. If the economic situation improves, obviously the Government could live a while on its fat, but it could not go on indefinitely. And the economic outlook, I might say parenthetically, is very much dominated by the European situation. Our whole economy during the last 6 months has been practically continued by the difficulties in Europe; that Europe has not been able to purchase our agricultural commodities in any very considerable degree. It has gone through two very severe financial crises, in it two of the greatest governments in the world, something almost unparalleled in history, and the reaction in the United States has been greatly to retard our recovery. If, by the arrangements which have been set up in those governments, they have reached stability it ought to release forces in the United States which would give a good deal of encouragement here. That is another reason why another 2 or 3 months study of this situation is necessary before we can come to any fiscal conclusions.

The present situation is a little better in some particulars. In that I don't want to minimize the problem which we have to carry over the next winter. The change is largely in seasonal and governmental activities. The statistics of the Department of Labor cover the manufacturing industries and one or two service industries, together with quarrying and mining, but they do not cover such things as public works and things of that character only where they indirectly reflect into manufactures. So that if you start with the supposed 6 million unemployed last winter, we have a good many seasonal factors which at least give temporary strength to this situation. There are, as I have said, somewhere about 300 million to 380 million more people employed directly or indirectly by the Federal Government than there were last January. There are somewhere near a million, as nearly as we can compute, from the State and local expenditure on roads by the State and local authorities outside of the Federal, more than there were last winter. And there are some 750 million people employed on wages in agriculture, purely seasonal, and there are a number of other seasonal industries which have taken up a good deal of the slack of last January. And there are some industries which have shown a substantial improvement. Both the shoe and textile industries show very great improvement over last winter. Altogether it amounts to the strengthening of the situation temporarily from an employment point of view—temporarily perhaps—more than has been accredited. That, however, does not solve our problem over the winter, but I mention it to you as one of the things giving some strength and some encouragement from some of our other difficulties.

In any event, the primary problem and the only problem in governmental fiscal questions is the maintenance of the social obligations of the Government to a population that are in difficulties; that no government of a substantial character and of any humane aspect will see its people starve or go hungry or go cold, and every agency of a government, whether local, State, or Federal, must be implemented to that end. So that we have to consider that problem, and we have another problem which bears indirectly on that same one, and that is that we must maintain the complete stability and confidence in our Federal Government. That is the root of all confidence and stability in our country, and upon that maintenance bears the recovery of the country and the maintenance of employment and of all the other necessary humane considerations that come out of good government. So that we are all endeavoring to approach this problem solely from the point of view of these many factors, for their adequate determination and the best judgment we can bring to bear. And it is entirely too early to come to any conclusions on it at the present time.

I don't know that that is of any great importance to you, but you might as well know what I have in my own mind about it, and if it is useful to you I would be glad to handle some of the other problems in the same way. I am not in a position to make any statement to the press because the problems are all too implicated. It is very difficult to convey all of the problems of the situation into a discussion of this character because they are enormously involved.

Q. Mr. President, may this be used in the third category?

THE PRESIDENT. No, this is for your own information. I do not think you can present such an involved question properly from such a discussion as this. It is just for your own information.

NOTE: President Hoover's two hundred and fifth news conference was held in the White House at 12 noon on Tuesday, September 1, 1931.

On August 6, 1931, the White House issued a statement on the status of loans on adjusted service certificates for the period ending July 31, 1931.

303

The President's News Conference of
September 4, 1931

FAMINE RELIEF FOR CHINA

THE PRESIDENT. The Chinese Government has accepted the proposal of the Farm Board for the purchase of wheat and flour, to be used exclusively for famine relief purposes. And the Chinese Government has undertaken the transportation, and they have undertaken that an equal opportunity shall be given to American flagships in the bidding for charters. The amount settled is about 15 million bushels, and I understand the Farm Board is willing to expand that amount if the Chinese Government wishes and if it is needed for famine purposes.

FEDERAL FARM LOAN BOARD

Mr. Floyd Harrison has resigned as a member of the Federal Farm Loan Board to accept a position on the staff of the Federal Reserve

Board—not a member of the Federal Reserve Board but on the staff. And I have appointed Mr. James B. Madison, of Charleston, West Virginia, to membership on the Federal Farm Loan Board. Mr. Madison has been for some years the head of the Virginia Joint Stock Land Bank at Charleston, West Virginia.

STATE RELIEF EFFORTS

I have a telegram from the Governor of Delaware, in which he states that the citizens of Delaware can be counted upon to provide whatever financial help is required for those in need during the coming winter. That adds Delaware to California, Michigan, Connecticut, Illinois, and New York as States undertaking their own burden. Other Governors are making surveys, reorganizing their committees. No doubt we will have word from them later on.

PRESIDENT'S ORGANIZATION ON UNEMPLOYMENT RELIEF

I will give you out here a list of some further additions to Mr. [Walter S.] Gifford's organization by way of 14 State representatives and 6 members of the advisory committee at large.

PUBLIC BUILDINGS CONTRACTS

I have handed out today a summary of the public buildings contracts for the month of August and up to date, but as there was some complaint about the amount of statistics you are called upon to handle by telegram we have marked it for Monday morning, so you can mail it out if you want. It shows as a matter of fact more contracts let for the month of August than in any whole year in the history of the United States up to 1927.

WHEAT PRODUCTION

And I have some questions bearing on economic matters. One or two in particular which I was asked to discuss in background for you. I am perfectly willing to tell you what I know but only for your own information. I haven't any public pronouncements to make about them at all.

One of them is in regard to wheat. I am not going to make any recommendations or suggestions, but there are some phases of the wheat problem that are not well appreciated, I think. The difficulties in which the wheat farmers are—or the wheat production—are not wholly or even in fact in any major extent a problem of the depression. It is a problem the seat of which goes back much farther. Some of you will know that due to the advancement of work by the agricultural authorities various varieties of wheat have been developed and methods of cultivation developed that took in an immense semiarid area of land not formerly cultivated for wheat production, resulting in a very large expansion of the wheat area in this country, particularly in western Kansas and Texas and Oklahoma and sections of Colorado, western Nebraska and so on. Parallel with that development in agricultural science has been the revolution in mechanical developments for handling wheat. The development of the tractor plow and the combine and other mechanical devices has come parallel with this application of wheat growing in these areas.

This has been going on steadily for 10 years. The result has not alone affected the United States, but it has extended the wheat area enormously in the Argentine, in Australia, in Russia, and in Canada, and it has made possible the production of wheat at very low cost in those areas throughout the world. One effect of it has been a constantly accumulating surplus of wheat year by year since 1925. Every year has been a surplus of wheat of larger and larger dimensions in the areas with cheaper production as against the older areas of wheat production at higher costs.

The difficulties in the situation lie very largely, as I have said, outside the area of the depression. As a matter of fact, depressions rather increase the consumption of wheat. Wheat is the cheapest food in the world, and there is a very distinct tendency for the consumption of wheat to increase during a depression. So it is not a question of underconsumption we are dealing with but in fact a revolution in the production of wheat as important as the revolution in transportation when steam was applied to draw cars.

I don't know whether there is anything in that that helps you. But it has certain phases that separates that from other agriculural problems.

COTTON PRODUCTION

The cotton problem is to a small extent of that type but not in any major sense. There has been, of course, an expansion of cotton areas in Texas particularly. The boll weevil is more under control. There has been expansion in Egyptian production, but of course cotton has not been accumulating over a period of 6 or 7 years as stocks have been in wheat. And cotton would be all right with normal consumption. Cotton consumption obviously greatly decreases with a depression, and the cotton problem is a good deal a depression problem as distinguished from the other difficulties.

GOLD ACCUMULATIONS

There was one other subject, and that is the gold accumulation in the United States. As you know, we have the largest gold supply we have ever had. I don't know what the proportion is there—half the world's gold, I guess. But that gold is not accumulated to any large degree as the result of trade balances.

There is another phenomenon which is operating in that which causes a great deal of anxiety, and that is the flight of capital from practically the whole world to the United States in refuge. A very moderate estimate of the amount in capital in refuge here would be, I should think, anywhere near 2 billions. In one country alone where a survey has been made, it has 790 millions, and it is not one of the largest in the world either. It is money sent here by individuals and banks for deposit in the United States. So that we are dealing with foreign exchange again that is very puzzling.

We are also dealing with a gold question that is abnormal in the whole history of the world. I don't think that experience has ever been met with before, and we are not to be accused of hoarding this gold. I don't know of anything on the part of American citizens or the American Government or anything that Americans have done that has resulted in these accumulations. It is fundamentally due to the lack of confidence of people in their own governments and their own circumstances in their home countries. Its solution lies in the rehabilitation of confidence abroad and on the return of that capital to their own countries and its use in those countries. The difficulty that we are having over foreign exchange and the situation in various countries in a financial way is due to the migration of capital by individuals into the United States and therefore the denuding of their own countries of that capital and the multiplying of our difficulties.

I do not offer you any solution. I just offer you the explanation of what has happened. I might mention that that solution, however, as I have said, is the restoration of confidence abroad. I don't know that this accumulation of gold does the United States the slightest harm, and, therefore, we are not particularly suffering under it, but when people complain that we are hoarding it they ought to realize that it is not our doing. It is the hoarder who is sending it within our borders and putting it in our banks because he feels they are safer than any other banks in the world.

Q. Mr. President, what is the gold supply in this country now?

THE PRESIDENT. I think it was announced this morning—something over 5 billion. I don't recollect the figure.

And that is all I have got on this occasion.

NOTE: President Hoover's two hundred and sixth news conference was held in the White House at 4 p.m. on Friday, September 4, 1931.

On the same day, the White House issued a text of the President's statement on famine relief for China (see Item 304), and a text of the telegram from Governor C. D. Buck of Delaware. During this period, similar letters and telegrams endorsing the President's position on unemployment relief were issued by the White House. For release dates, see Appendix A. See also Item 329.

Lists of additional members of the Advisory Committee of the President's Organization on Unemployment Relief were issued by the White House on September 4 and 17, 1931.

304

Statement on Famine Relief for China.
September 4, 1931

THE PRESIDENT said:

"The Chinese Government has accepted the proposal of the Farm Board for the purchase of wheat and flour, to be used exclusively for famine relief purposes, on terms of payment over a period of years.

"The Chinese Government undertakes the transportation, and it has given assurances that it will give equal opportunity to American flagships in the charters made for this purpose.

"The amount at present settled is about 15 million bushels."

NOTE: The Government of the Republic of China agreed to purchase, at market prices, 450,000 tons of wheat, and to make payments from 1934 to 1936 with 4 percent interest.

305

Letter Accepting the Resignation of Floyd R. Harrison as a Member of the Federal Farm Loan Board.
September 4, 1931

Dear Mr. Harrison:

I have your letter of September 2nd, tendering your resignation as a member of the Federal Farm Loan Board, which I accept, as you request, effective at the close of September 15, 1931. I take this action with very sincere regret and cannot let the occasion pass without expressing my appreciation of your long and notable public service, first in the Department of Agriculture and later as a member of the Board of Directors of the War Finance Corporation, and a member of the Federal Farm Loan Board. In positions of large responsibility you have displayed fine capacity for efficient administration and it is my pleasure to say that the ability, energy and devotion to the public interest which you have manifested in the discharge of every duty are worthy of the highest commendation. As you leave the Farm Loan Board, you carry with you my best wishes for success in the new work which you are about to undertake in the Federal Reserve System.

Yours faithfully,

HERBERT HOOVER

[Honorable Floyd R. Harrison, Federal Farm Loan Bureau, Washington, D.C.]

NOTE: Mr. Harrison's letter, dated September 2, 1931, and released with the President's letter, follows:

Dear Mr. President:

I hereby tender my resignation as a member of the Federal Farm Loan Board.

I have greatly appreciated the honor of serving as a member of the Board during the past four years and it is with much regret that I sever my connection with the Farm Loan System. As you know, however, an opportunity has come to me for service in another field and I feel that I should avail myself of it. I hope, in the circumstances, that you will find it convenient to accept my resignation effective at the close of September 15, 1931.

With all good wishes, I am

Sincerely yours,

FLOYD R. HARRISON

[The President, The White House]

306

Message to the National Air Races.
September 4, 1931

[Released September 4, 1931. Dated September 3, 1931]

Dear Mr. Greve:

I have noticed with interest the day-by-day accounts of the National Air Race event now being held in Cleveland, and for which the City of Cleveland has made such elaborate preparation. It is indeed gratifying to observe that the American people are so greatly interested in the progress of aeronautics. I trust that this interest, not only in the present accomplishments of air-craft and air transportation but in the future possibilities as well, will serve to sustain in increasing measure our airmen, our manufacturers, and all others who are putting forth their best efforts to keep America first in the air.

Yours faithfully,

HERBERT HOOVER

[Mr. W. L. Greve, President, National Air Races, Cleveland, Ohio]

NOTE: The President's message was read over the broadcasting system at Cleveland Airport, site of the National Air Races of 1931.

307

Statement on Public Building Projects.
September 7, 1931

THE PRESIDENT said:

"That portion of the Federal program of aid to unemployment comprised in the great expansion of public buildings under the Treasury Department shows the following progress since the report of July 15. There are a total of 750 projects which have so far been specifically authorized, and 164 firms of architects are engaged in plans and supervision. The attached tables show the progress of individual projects which may be summarized:

"First: A total of 115 buildings have been completed at a total cost of $39,869,569. Three buildings have been completed during the past month.

"Second: There were 229 buildings in construction at the first of September by contract, at an estimated cost of $181,393,100. There having been 37 contracts let during the last month, of a total value in excess of $25,000,000.

"Third: There are 65 projects in which the sites have been arranged, drawings are completed, for which construction contracts have been invited, of a total estimated cost of $19,319,600.

"Fourth: There are 202 projects in which sites have been selected and on which plans are now under way of a total estimated cost of $178,766,523.

"Fifth: At the first of this month there were 199 projects in which the sites have been determined upon and are in process of being acquired. The estimated cost of the buildings thereon being $49,545,400.

"It is estimated that the number of men now directly and indirectly employed on this program is 39,000. It is estimated that the number that will be directly and indirectly employed on January 1st is 100,000.

"Tables showing the progress of the different projects in the different categories are attached thereto."

NOTE: The White House issued the statement following the President's news conference of September 4, 1931, but embargoed its release until Monday, September 7, 1931. Detailed tables and lists issued with the statement are not printed but are available for examination at the Herbert Hoover Presidential Library.

308

Message on Rosh Hashanah.
September 7, 1931

[Released September 7, 1931. Dated July 14, 1931]

ROSH HASHANAH, the Jewish New Year, affords an appropriate occasion to recall the contributions of an ancient people to the contemporary world. Jewish deeds and idealism are written indelibly on the scroll of time. Down through the centuries to our own time there has flowed a continuing stream of enrichment of the spiritual and cultural life of the world. In business, the arts, the professions, philanthropy, citizenship and, above all, in the evolution of the spiritual life of mankind, the race has contributed elements of strength, beauty and tolerance which are the common heritage of all men. On the occasion of the happy festival now being celebrated I wish to extend my heartiest congratulations and most cordial good wishes.

HERBERT HOOVER

309

Message to Ceremonies Honoring Julius Rosenwald.
September 8, 1931

[Released September 8, 1931.   Dated September 4, 1931]

My dear Mr. Sargent:

The Merit Awards sponsored by the Rotary Club of Chicago for distinguished public service by residents of that community, are not only appropriate recognition of usefulness but are an incentive to citizens to contribute to the common good through unselfish personal service. I regret that I was unable on account of the pressure of the public business, to accept your kind invitation to attend the presentation of the first of these awards on September 8th. I shall appreciate it if you will express my cordial good wishes to those gathered for the occasion and my hearty congratulations to Mr. Julius Rosenwald, the recipient of the premier award.

Yours faithfully,
HERBERT HOOVER

[Mr. Fred W. Sargent, Rotary Club of Chicago, Hotel Sherman, Chicago, Ill.]

NOTE: The message was read at a luncheon honoring Julius Rosenwald with the first of three annual merit awards. Due to ill health Mr. Rosenwald was unable to attend the luncheon, but a scroll summarizing his achievements was accepted by his son Lessing J. Rosenwald.

310

Radio Address on the 50th Anniversary of the First Red Cross Chapter House.
September 9, 1931

THE LAW provides that the Chief Executive of the Nation shall also be the President of the American National Red Cross. This fact adds to the sense of personal pleasure in the privilege which I have today of greeting by the radio those who have assembled at Dansville, New York, to commemorate the 50th anniversary of the founding of Clara Barton Chapter Number One, the first Red Cross chapter in America. This chapter has the distinction of being organized by Clara Barton herself in 1881. It is a great distinction which your chapter enjoys both for the association with Miss Barton and as the beginners of one of the most beneficent institutions of our history.

The beginnings of human enterprises derive their significance from the service which time proves their ability to perform for humanity. The Nation joins in your celebration because of the success of the great humanitarian agency which sprang from the mind of Clara Barton and the spirit of your community. The establishment of the pioneer chapter in the village of Dansville was the forerunner of 3,500 chapters now in existence throughout the United States, enrolling at times of national need as many as 20 million members. In its lifetime the Red Cross has raised and expended nearly a billion of money in the relief of human distress. The national organization has become our Nation's assurance of adequate, prompt, and efficient handling of any catastrophe within our borders. It is the flowering of the spiritual impulse to serve the common need. It represents both the common impulse of sympathetic help and the mechanism for its practical expression. It stands as a monument to individual and local initiative. It proves the ability of a democracy to create from the people themselves the agencies for their service.

More than a century has passed since Clara Barton was born. And it may be well said that the institution was not only founded by a noble woman but it has been carried on very largely by the womanhood of our country. The 50 years which have passed since that pioneer beginning have written a chapter in the worldwide relief of human suffering which is a fitting memorial to Miss Barton and a proud tradition to her countrymen.

Women's interest in the prevention of suffering and in ministrations of mercy to those in sickness, peril, and need, is the foundation of the Red Cross organization which has been fittingly described as "The Greatest Mother of Them All." To Miss Barton, Miss Mabel Boardman, and the many thousands of other devoted women, in all localities of this broad

416

land, the cause of prompt, effective, and sympathetic alleviation of suffering and distress owes its debt of gratitude and remembrance. To the men who give their service—of whom there is no greater example than Judge Payne—I also pay tribute.

It is my privilege, on behalf of the Nation, to acknowledge the debt, both to the pioneer founders of the organization and to their successors who are carrying on today.

NOTE: The President spoke at 1 p.m. from his office in the White House to the assembly in Dansville, N.Y. The Columbia Broadcasting System and the National Broadcasting Company radio networks carried the address.

Mabel T. Boardman was Secretary and John Barton Payne was Chairman of the American National Red Cross.

A reading copy of this item with holograph changes by the President is available for examination at the Herbert Hoover Presidential Library.

311

The President's News Conference of *September 11, 1931*

UNEMPLOYMENT AND RELIEF

THE PRESIDENT. I haven't any news today. I have a subject I would like to talk to you about in purely a personal way. I don't think there is any news in it, but a matter in which I think you could be very helpful. You all realize that the public mind is disturbed and some of that disturbance relates to possible over-exaggeration of the unemployment situation and what is likely to happen during the winter. A good deal of that is due to the confusion of ideas. I am not talking for publication at all.

The problem of relief to take care of the destitute, prevent hunger and cold, is a very different problem from that involved in general employment. With our experience last winter when we had on census enumeration about 6 million unemployed, so that there were somewhere between 2 million and 4 million people who had to be looked after—they fell into two categories. First were the unfortunate and the sick and others who had to have actual allowances. And then there was the larger category

417

who were helped out with made work or work directly developed to take care of the unemployed from day to day. Had those measures developed all over the country, and in fact, in probably 2,000 cities and towns succeeded in the task, in the face of the fact that there were 6 million unemployed.

It requires a little economic analysis to show why the actual burden of relief as distinguished from the unemployment problem is essentially a different question. Now, that 6 million unemployed theoretically represents 30 million people by way of their families, and one hears a good deal of discussion going on in the country as to the 30 million destitute who were unemployed at the time of the enumeration. All of our economists for many years have agreed that there are always 1½ million people unemployed in the shift of occupation amongst the 49 million of people who are gainfully employed. We have to allow only something like 2 weeks interregnum in the normal turnover of industry and business. Just at the time that census was taken there was a very large measure of seasonal unemployment; that is the maximum point. During the last summer we have seen a decrease in unemployment due to seasonal character. Normally 200,000 people are working on the roads and 750,000 on farm labor. And the increase in railroad employees hauling crops, and in the lake trades, and a lot of other things, all of which indicate the degree of seasonal unemployment at the time that census was taken. And then you have overriding all that the fact that there are 17 breadwinners in every 10 families. So that just by deduction we would have arrived at a problem of somewhere from 3 to 5 million people that would probably have been in need, and the deduction made last winter and the actual experience of the winter corroborated it. So that the problem we face next winter is not the problem of 30 million people again but the problem of that number who will be destitute and the number may be larger than it was last winter. In some localities, like New England States, it will apparently be less. We certainly will not have the care of some 3 million people that had to be fed during the drought. Certainly we will have a serious problem, and it will require a great deal of resolution and courage and generosity to solve it, but the envisaging of the

418

problem in the light of large numbers is very seriously disturbing the public minds, undermining confidence, and creating a great deal of fear, and one result of that is the tightening of people's belts who have resources and decreasing the purchasing in the country, and thereby increasing unemployment again. So that on that I may suggest that when you have an opportunity or it comes to you to interpret the facts as a matter of objective action in a contribution to the settling of the public mind, I would hope that you would make these distinctions.

As I say, we have a serious problem for the winter, but surely the 120 million people in the United States can take care of it. There is no question of doubt that nobody will starve or go hungry in the United States. There was nothing of the kind except perhaps an isolated case during the last winter. That can be easily demonstrated by the extraordinary results in public health, which could only come about by the unusual solicitude for the underdog. That we have proof that such was the case is that with the burden of last winter it was amply taken care of and it will be next winter. There is no question of public alarm over that if we can give public support to the various agencies in action. But certainly the public mind has been a good deal disturbed the last 2 weeks by the exaggeration of the problem and the misunderstanding of its fundamentals. So that I just make that suggestion to you in the work you do that it is in national interest that we should keep the public mind properly advised and keep the people steady in the boat. We have enough problems without these exaggerating ones on our shoulders.

NOTE: President Hoover's two hundred and seventh news conference was held in the White House at 4 p.m. on Friday, September 11, 1931.

68-611 O - 76 - 30

312

Message to Boston Newspapers on the Opening of Their New Plant.
September 11, 1931

[Released September 11, 1931. Dated September 9, 1931]

My dear Mr. Choate:

On the occasion of the opening of the new plant of The Boston Herald and The Boston Traveler, I send you cordial congratulations and all good wishes for the continued prosperity and public service of these papers.

Yours faithfully,

HERBERT HOOVER

[Mr. Robert B. Choate, Managing Editor, The Boston Herald and The Boston Traveler, Boston, Massachusetts]

NOTE: The message was read at exercises opening the new plant of the Boston Herald and the Boston Traveler. During the ceremony the President touched a key in the telegraph room of the White House which started the presses.

313

The President's News Conference of
September 15, 1931

WHITE HOUSE CONFERENCE ON HOME BUILDING AND HOME OWNERSHIP

THE PRESIDENT. A year ago, after a conference with some 20 associations interested in the subject, I undertook to call a general conference on questions of homebuilding and homeownership.[1] Growing out of that meeting some 15 to 20 different committees were appointed for investigation of the fact, and those committees are now ready to develop their work still further. They represent the substantial people of the country in every branch of that problem, and a major conference will

---

[1] See 1930 volume, Items 250 and 302.

take place on the 5th of December.[2] I am giving you here an extended statement in respect to the whole of it which you will have a chance to read without my going over it.

APPOINTMENTS

I have a few questions here of background character.

"Has the President appointed Mr. [Walter W.] Head, a banker of Omaha, on the Farm Board?" The answer is in the negative.

"Is the President prepared to announce the appointment of anyone to the vacancies on the Tariff Commission?" I am not able to do so at the present time.

TRADE

"Has the President any plan for the expansion of foreign purchase of American cotton?" There is no definite plan on my part. There was a plan some time ago—and this is background—to the bankers that they should arrange a credit basis system for export of cotton to Europe. They have taken it up and they are in negotiation both between themselves and the other side. I haven't any further information that I can report about it. That has not yet been concluded. That is all I can enlighten you on that subject.

I understand that I am supposed to go on the radio tomorrow night for something important—and I haven't myself yet heard of it.

NOTE: President Hoover's two hundred and eighth news conference was held in the White House at 12 noon on Tuesday, September 15, 1931.

On the same day, the White House issued a text of the President's statement on the White House Conference on Home Building and Home Ownership (see Item 314).

At the conclusion of the news conference, the President referred to rumors to the effect that he intended to call a conference on world trade. For White House denial of these rumors, see Item 315.

---

[2] The Conference was held December 2–5, 1931.

314

Statement Announcing the White House Conference on Home Building and Home Ownership. *September 15, 1931*

THE PRESIDENT said:

"I wish to announce that the President's Conference on Home Building and Home Ownership for which preparations have been in progress for something over a year will be held in Washington, Wednesday, December 2 to Saturday, December 5, inclusive. About 400 persons have assisted in the preparatory work and 1,000 representative citizens from the 48 States, associated with building and housing activities, are expected to participate in the Conference. The Conference has been organized under the chairmanship of Secretary Lamont, of the Department of Commerce. Dr. John M. Gries is the Executive Secretary.

"I decided a year ago after a conference with interested leaders in various parts of the country to undertake the organization of an adequate investigation and study, on a nationwide scale, of the problems presented in homeownership and homebuilding, with the hope of developing the facts and a better understanding of the questions involved and inspiring better organization and the removal of influences which seriously limit the spread of homeownership, both town and country.

"A Planning Committee, comprising representatives of some 20 voluntary associations, was created to make the study and set up a national conference for consideration of the data and recommendations of expert committees. The plan is somewhat similar to that of the White House Conference on Child Health and Protection, held in Washington in November 1930. Funds have been provided privately to cover research and other activities of the committees of the housing conference.

"Among the associations represented in the Planning Committee were the following:

American Civic Association
American Farm Bureau Federation
American Federation of Labor

American Home Economics Association
American Institute of Architects
Associated General Contractors
Association of Life Insurance Presidents
Better Homes in America
Chamber of Commerce of the United States
General Federation of Women's Clubs
National Association of Builders' Exchanges
National Association of Real Estate Boards
National Congress of Parents and Teachers
National Farmers Union
National Grange
National Housing Association
Russell Sage Foundation
Savings Bank Division of the American Bankers Association
United States League of Building and Loan Associations
Women's National Farm and Garden Association

"The Conference in December will be the first of its kind on this scale in the United States. It will deal with the whole question of home construction and ownership, and of the home environment. It will embrace finance, design, equipment, city planning, household management, and many other aspects.

"Twenty-five committees headed by men and women of authority and experience in various phases of the question, have been engaged for months in gathering and analyzing available information and in making additional studies and inquiries. Their work is being correlated so that, on the basis of the facts, a collective judgment may be formulated upon the best contemporary experience of leaders who have special knowledge of the subjects. It, obviously, is not our purpose to set up the Federal Government in the building of homes. But the Conference will, I believe, afford a basis for the development of a sound policy and inspire better voluntary organization to cope with the problem.

"Adequate housing goes to the very roots of well-being of the family, and the family is the social unit of the Nation. The question involves important aspects of health, morals, education, and efficiency. Nothing

423

contributes more to social stability and the happiness of our people than the surroundings of their homes. Although we have a larger proportion of adequate housing than any other country, we have not yet reached our ideal of homes for all our people. It should be possible in our country for any person of sound character and industrious habits to provide himself with adequate and suitable housing and preferably to own his own home.

"This principle, I believe, to be sound and controlling at all times. It is unnecessary to point out the beneficial effect which a well-considered nationwide program directed to the extension of homebuilding and homeownership in the immediate future would have upon our current unemployment and economic situation. The forthcoming Conference, however, was initiated to deal with the question under a long-range plan. It will be doubly fortunate if it should result not only in a sounder permanent policy, but in some degree of relief of current unemployment and in stimulation of the industries upon which building depends.

"The question touches many phases of both public and private activity. One of the important questions is finance. The present depression has given emphasis to the fact that the credit system in homebuilding is not as satisfactorily organized as other branches of credit. Commerce, industry, and to a large extent farm mortgages, all have more effective financial reservoirs. In order to enable the purchase of homes on what amounts to the installment plan, it is necessary to place first and, often enough, second mortgages. The building and loan associations have performed a great service in this field, but they cannot without assistance carry the burden. First mortgages, carried so largely by the savings banks and insurance companies, have been affected by competition with bonds and other forms of investment. Second mortgages are also necessary to many people. In the period of expansion preceding the current depression rates for second mortgages, including commissions, discounts, and other charges, rose in many cities to the equivalent of 20 or 25 percent per annum. This not only stifled homeownership, but led to the loss of many homes through foreclosure. The present depression has been marked by unemployment in the trades involved.

"Since a principal object of home construction and homeownership is to provide the best possible environment for the growing child, it is obvious that the work of the women's committees on homemaking and related subjects is a most vital phase of the Conference.

"Special attention is being devoted to the problems of farm and village housing.

"A committee of representative civic leaders of the Negro race are devoting attention to the problems of Negro housing.

"Twenty-five committees have been charged each with the study of a special field within the general problem covered by the Conference. Six correlating committees deal with questions of aim and method common to the 25 committees. These correlating committees concern themselves with standards and objectives, legislation and administration, education and service, organization programs, local and national and technological developments.

"The scope of the Conference and the quality of leadership upon which it has drawn is indicated by the list of the committees and their chairmen, which is as follows:

1. Types of Dwellings: John Ihlder, executive director, Pittsburgh Housing Association, Pittsburgh, Pa.
2. Fundamental Equipment: Prof. Collins P. Bliss, dean of the College of Engineering, New York University, New York, N.Y.
3. Kitchens and Other Work Centers: Miss Abby L. Marlatt, professor of home economics, director of courses in home economics, University of Wisconsin, Madison, Wis.
4. Utilities for Houses: Morris Knowles, author of "Industrial Housing," Morris Knowles, Inc., Pittsburgh, Pa.
5. Subdivision Layout: Harland Bartholomew, president, National Conference on City Planning, St. Louis, Mo.
6. Business and Housing: Harry A. Wheeler, former president of the Chamber of Commerce of the United States, Chicago, Ill.
7. Industrial Decentralization and Housing: Stuart W. Cramer, president-treasurer, Cramerton Mills (provides homes for employees), Cramerton, N.C.

8. Blighted Areas and Slums: Abram Garfield, architect, member of the (National) Commission of Fine Arts, Cleveland, Ohio.

9. Reconditioning, Remodeling and Modernizing: Frederick M. Feiker, Director, Bureau of Foreign & Domestic Commerce (formerly managing director, Associated Business Papers, Inc.), Washington, D.C.

10. Construction: A. P. Greensfelder, president, Associated General Contractors of America, St. Louis, Mo.

11. Design: William Stanley Parker, president, Architect's Small House Service Bureau, Boston, Mass.

12. City Planning and Zoning: Frederic A. Delano, president, American Civic Association; chairman, Regional Plan of New York and Its Environs, Washington, D.C.

13. Finance: Frederick H. Ecker, president, Metropolitan Life Insurance Co., New York, N.Y.

14. Taxation: Dr. T. S. Adams, professor, political economy, Yale University, and Economic Advisor, U.S. Treasury Department since 1917, New Haven, Conn.

15. Home Ownership and Leasing: Ernest T. Trigg, president, John Lucas Paint Company (former chairman of Committee of Civic Development Department, Chamber of Commerce of the United States), Philadelphia, Pa.

16. Home Furnishing and Decoration: Miss Ruth Lyle Sparks, Miss Sparks, Inc. (president, Interior Decorators Club of New York), New York, N.Y.

17. Landscape Planning and Planting: Mrs. Junius S. Morgan, Princeton, N.J.

18. Household Management: Miss Effie Raitt, professor and head of department of home economics, University of Washington, Seattle, Wash.

19. Housing and the Community: Dr. Joseph Hersey Pratt, past president of the American Climatological and Clinical Association, and of the American Society for Clinical Investigation, Boston, Mass.

20. Farm and Village Housing: Provost A. R. Mann, Cornell University (formerly dean of N.Y. State Colleges of Agriculture and Economics), Ithaca, N.Y.

21. Negro Housing: Miss Nannie H. Burroughs, president, National Training School for Women and Girls, Washington, D.C.

22. Home Information Centers: Miss Pearl Chase, chairman, Plans and Planting Branch of Community Arts Association, Santa Barbara, Calif.

23. Homemaking: Miss Martha Van Rensselaer, director, N.Y. State College of Home Economics, Cornell University, Ithaca, N.Y.

24. Large Scale Operations: Alfred K. Stern, Julius Rosenwald Fund, Chicago, Ill.

25. Relationship of Income and the Home: Prof. Niles Carpenter, head of department of sociology, University of Buffalo, Buffalo, N.Y.

CORRELATION COMMITTEES

A. Standards and Objectives: Lawrence Veiller, secretary-director, National Housing Association, New York, N.Y.

B. Research: Prof. James Ford, department of sociology, Harvard University; executive director Better Homes in America, 1653 Pennsylvania Ave., N.W., Washington, D.C.

C. Legislation and Administration: Bernard J. Newman, managing director, Philadelphia Housing Association, Philadelphia, Pa.

D. Education and Service: Dr. Albert Shaw, editor, American Review of Reviews, New York, N.Y.

E. Organization Programs, Local and National: Miss Harlean James, executive secretary, American Civic Association, Inc., Washington, D.C.

F. Technological Developments: Dr. George K. Burgess, Director, National Bureau of Standards, Washington, D.C.

315

White House Statement About
an International Conference on World Trade.
September 15, 1931

CABLE DISPATCHES set forth that the London Daily Herald has announced that President Hoover is considering a proposal to call a world conference to deal with world trade. The announcement is erroneous. The facts are these: The Herald telephoned the White House yesterday asking that the President comment on its editorial advocating such a conference. I said that there was no comment to be made here. The Herald asked if the editorial would be considered. I replied that if the American press carried the editorial it would be read. That was the extent of the telephone conversation.

316

Message on the 80th Anniversary
of the New York Times.
September 17, 1931

My dear Mr. Ochs:
    The most obvious thing in democracy is that it cannot function except when accompanied by a free and constructive press. Our Government is and must be responsive to the will of the people expressed through considered public opinion. That expression is more guided and revealed through the press than any other agency, but it implies great responsibility on the press that the news shall be accurately presented without bias or color that the public may have an opportunity of formulating its views on the actual facts and that its expressed opinion shall be based upon considered and constructive editorial suggestions. Any newspaper, great or small, that accurately disseminates information aids in the promotion of good Government and in the sound development of the Nation. All these are truisms of self Government but vitally

important. The New York Times has always been a conspicuous example of accurate reporting by impartial and far-flung news gathering facilities. The space it devotes to National and International affairs is a great and constructive contribution. The conscientiousness of its editorial expression is notable whether we agree with it or not. I wish to congratulate it on the observance of its eightieth anniversary.

Yours faithfully,

HERBERT HOOVER

[Mr. Adolph Ochs, The New York Times, New York City]

NOTE: The message was printed in the September 18, 1931, issue of the New York Times.

317

Statement on the Death
of David Starr Jordan.
September 19, 1931

DR. JORDAN'S loss will be felt by the many thousands of students who came to him over fifty years of active leadership in education. Few men in his calling had won so universal affection and devotion. He was a great educator and was a scholarly contributor to science, to the advancement of education and to thought upon public questions.

HERBERT HOOVER

NOTE: David Starr Jordan was the first president of Stanford University and an internationally known educator, scientist, and peace advocate.

318

Address to the American Legion
at Detroit, Michigan.
September 21, 1931

My fellow countrymen of the American Legion:

I wish to thank you for the heartening cordiality of your reception. It is a pleasure to accept the invitation of your commander to attend your convention. I am led to do so at a time of most pressing public duties, because I wish to lay frankly and simply before you important facts which I am sure you will wish to have, and I wish to point to an opportunity of service which you can give not alone to your members but to the country at large.

I need not recount to you that the world is passing through a great depression fraught with gruelling daily emergencies alike to individual men and to governments. This depression today flows largely from Europe through the fundamental dislocations of economic and political forces which arose from the World War in which your service brought bloodshed to an end and gave hope of reconstruction to the world. Our economic strength is such that we would have recovered long since but for these forces from abroad. Recovery of the world now rests and awaits in no small degree upon our country, the United States of America. Some individuals amongst us may have lost their nerve and faith but the real American people are digging themselves out of this depression with industry and courage. We have the self-containment, the resources, the manhood, and the intelligence, and by united action we will lead the world in recovery.

The American Legion, born of world emergency, wields a great influence throughout our country because it speaks for a generation which has proven its citizenship by offering its all to its country. You of the Legion have a peculiarly sacred stake in the future of the country which you fought to preserve. You have proven your devotion in camp and in battle. You have built up your organization to serve in peace as in war.

You are aware that during the past year our national expenditures have exceeded our income. Today the national government is faced with another large deficit in its budget. There is a decrease in the annual yield of income taxes alone from $2,400 million that we received in the years of prosperity to only $1,200 million today. Simultaneously, we are carrying a high and necessary extra burden of public works in aid to the unemployed, of aids to agriculture, and of increased benefits and services to veterans. In these circumstances I am directing the most drastic economy in every non-vital branch of Government, yet the essential services must be maintained. These obviously, include the adequate and generous provision for our disabled veterans and the continuation of our present programs of work for the unemployed and our aids to agriculture. Whatever the arguments made, I do not wish you to be misled by those who say that we need only to tax the rich to secure the funds which we need. We must face the absolute fact that the rich can be taxed to the point of diminishing returns, and still the deficit in our ordinary and necessary expenditures would not be covered upon a basis even of the utmost economy. Make no mistake. In these circumstances it is those who work in the fields, at the bench and at the desk who will be forced to carry an added burden for every added cent to our expenditures.

Whatever the deficit may be and in whatever manner it may ultimately be met, every additional expenditure placed upon our Government in this emergency magnifies itself out of all proportion into intolerable pressures, whether it is by taxation or by loans. Either loans or taxes beyond the very minimum necessities of government will drain the resources of industry and commerce and in turn will increase unemployment. Such action can easily defeat our hopes, our plans, and our best efforts for the recovery of our country and so indefinitely delay the return of prosperity and employment. We can carry our present expenditures without jeopardy to national stability. We cannot carry more without grave national risks.

The imperative moment has come in our history when increase in Government expenditures must be avoided, whether it be ill-considered, hasty, or uninformed legislation of any kind, or whether it be for new services meritorious in themselves. Any alternative will strike down the earnest efforts of the citizenry of our Nation to start us back upon the economic paths to which we must return if we and our children are to have the destiny which everyone has the right to hope and the heart to give.

During the past week your national commander and the members of the Legion's unemployment committee came to me and offered to the Nation the combined strength of your million men and your 10,000 posts to help in relief over this forthcoming winter. I here accept that offer with the thanks of the Nation in the fine spirit in which it is submitted. But there is today an even greater service to our country. And that is the determined opposition by you, as a great body of influential men, to any additional demands upon the Nation until we have won this war against world depression. I am not speaking alone of veterans' legislation which may be but a minor part, and that may be urged before this convention, but I am speaking equally of demands for every other project proposed in the country which would require increased Federal expenditure. It is an attitude and an action in the whole field of Government expenditures that is before us today. The very first stone in the foundations of stability and of recovery, both at home and in the world, is the stability of the Government of the United States. It is my purpose to maintain that stability, and I invite you to enlist in that fight. The country's need of this service is second only to war. I invite you to study the relation of their governmental finance to the daily welfare and security of every man, woman, and child in the history of Europe during these past 6 months alone. It is for us to observe these lessons and to be helpful but our first duty is to the people of the United States. Nothing will give a greater glow of confidence to our country today than your enlistment and the vigorous support which you are capable of bringing to this effort to prevent additional burdens on the Government from whatever quarter they may come.

You would not have the President of the United States plead with any citizen or any group of citizens for any course of action. I make no plea to you. But you would have your President point out the path of service in this Nation. And I am doing that now. My mind goes back to the days of the war when you and I served in our appointed tasks. At the end of those years of heart sickness over the misery of it all, when the peace came, you and I knew that the wounds of the world were unhealed and that there would be further emergencies still before our country and the world when self-denial and courageous service must be given. Your organization was born at that time and dedicated to that service by the very preamble of your magnificent constitution. No man can doubt the character and idealism of men who have gone into the trenches in defense of their country. I have that faith. This is an emergency and these are the times for service to which we must put full heart and purpose to help and not retard the return of the happy days we know are ahead of your country and of mine.

With the guidance of the Almighty God, with the same faith, courage, and self-sacrifice with which you, backed by the Nation, won victory 14 years ago, so shall we win victory today.

NOTE: The President spoke to the opening session of the 13th annual convention of the American Legion, assembled in Olympia Arena, Detroit, Mich.

The above text is a transcript taken from a sound recording of the address. An advance text of the address was issued on the same day.

319

White House Statement on Federal Expenditures for Public Works and Drought Relief.
September 21, 1931

THE FOLLOWING table shows distribution of Federal construction, maintenance, and drought relief expenditures for the calendar year 1930–1931, and the estimated expenditures for the first half of 1932. It also shows the distribution of those expenditures by States. The expenditures on all these items for the calendar years are:

    1930, $452,301,000.
    1931, $787,587,000.
    1st half 1932, $373,593,000.

The prospective expenditures for the first half of 1932 are divided into the following headings:

Public buildings and lands	$126, 980, 000
Construction other than buildings and construction work by Engineer Corps	95, 737, 000
Works under direction of Engineer Corps	40, 000, 000
Repairs and maintenance	37, 283, 000
Roads	73, 593, 000
Total	373, 593, 000

This rate of expenditure for the first half of 1932 in aid of unemployment, if continued over the whole year would mean a continued rate of expenditure of $746,186,000 for the calendar year.

The total expenditure of the Federal Government in aid to unemployment since the depression began (omitting drought relief) will by the end of the present fiscal year aggregate over $1,550 million.

NOTE: The table referred to is not printed but is available for examination at the Herbert Hoover Presidential Library.

320

The President's News Conference of
September 22, 1931

GREAT BRITAIN'S DEPARTURE FROM THE GOLD STANDARD

THE PRESIDENT. I have been asked by two of your members to discuss something of the British demonetization or departure from the gold standard. I can only do that by way of background. I cannot make a public statement in the matter.

I think you will understand that this situation has been pending for a good many months. There has been a large amount of British investment in the United States, and that amount, estimated by the Department of Commerce, aggregates something over $1,500 million.

That is not flight of capital but steadily increasing expenditures here which naturally affects the exchanges. It has taken place not only in the past few months but for some years back. That, of course, has affected the problem of exchange. There has been some piling up of immediate cash in our banks from that quarter.

The course resolved upon by the British Government creates some temporary dislocations in the international world, but they are due more to the confusion arising out of readjustment of quotations and values than in their effect on the values of either securities or commodities.

The first effect of the decrease in the gold value of the pound is a rise in prices of commodities in Great Britain, at least in all international commodities where the price is made by international action, such as in wheat and other raw materials. There is involved a large amount of transaction based on the readjustment of those prices. A certain amount of confusion comes out of that, and the effect on our commodity markets has been a decrease in prices. There has been a rise in price in England in consequence and our prices are practically unchanged yesterday and today.

The fact that the pound is taken off its fixed value of $4.86 is not the abandonment of the gold standard even for the pound; as international commerce revolves in these days all transactions will be measured in some gold value, whether in dollars, francs, gulden, or any other of the fixed gold currencies. No transaction can take place unless it has some basis of measurement of that character. It really means that the fixed gold standard has been abandoned and a variable standard adopted which may change momentarily. But in any event all values in international commerce are bound to revolve on gold values or some measuring stick in gold. It is more or less a case of abandoning a fixed standard and adopting a variable one so far as international commerce is concerned.

The effect in England will undoubtedly be to increase exports, which amounts to price reduction compared with the standard of measurement in gold, and it should act as a stimulant and thus should increase employment and increase the demand again for raw materials. Obviously, it amounts to a reduction in standards of living temporarily in

435

those commodities which are imported, of course raw materials, but wages and rank will lag behind. Production costs will be lower, and consequently, exports will be stimulated.

The tendency also may be to decrease imports to some extent especially for highly competitive goods. On the export side, the effect is not going to be very material on the United States because there are comparatively small volume of British and American goods which are highly competitive in neutral markets. A study made some time ago of the Argentine showed that there were only about 10 percent of the exports of the United States to the Argentine and correspondingly 10 percent of the British exports to the Argentine that were competitive. We are exporting goods which we can peculiarly produce to the best advantage, and it might mean competition in respect to that small fraction over toward the neutral market. But it would not be any appreciable volume.

There might be some decrease in imports into Great Britain, especially in luxuries, but our trade with Great Britain consists largely of raw materials and manufactured goods. If there is stimulation of British exports our exports would be more likely to increase than decrease. I mention that only to indicate that the effect of it is not as far-reaching as some people may think.

On the financial side there are no consequential balances of American banks in England. They will always have sufficient of their own capital. So there are no losses there of any consequence at all. All together the action, no doubt necessary on the British side, is not, we feel, going to have any great effect in the United States. The probabilities are that it will considerably improve the situation in England, and we will benefit in the long run. In any event, when there is a question pending over the world's economic life, the actual realization of it is much less severe on us than is the constant possibility of it such as has been the case for the past 3 or 4 months. All together if we are going to have an important economic shift it is better to have it over than to have it hanging about.

You will realize also that this is not the first time that the pound has been off the gold basis. I do not know of any nation in the world which manages to maintain through its national life the gold value of its currency. There was a long period in the United States after the Civil War when we certainly could not maintain it. The pound was off the gold basis from some point in the war to 3, 4, or 5 years afterwards, but gradually the economic situation readjusts itself. These things are temporary and go back again to their original position.

And that is all I have today.

NOTE: President Hoover's two hundred and ninth news conference was held in the White House at 12 noon on Tuesday, September 22, 1931.

On September 20, 1931, the British Government had announced its abandonment of the gold standard, and the next day the Parliament passed legislation halting the exchange of the pound sterling for gold.

321

Message to the Parents' Magazine.
September 23, 1931

[Released September 23, 1931. Dated July 31, 1931]

My dear Mr. Hecht:

Often the best way to help children is to help their parents. The Parents' Magazine does this by making available to parents the rich and significant store of information which child health authorities, educators, psychologists and others are developing on methods of rearing children. The recent White House Conference on Child Health and Protection recognized that anything which better fits our fathers and mothers for the paramount profession of parenthood helps to realize the rights and standards of health and protection embodied in the Children's Charter. On the occasion of the fifth anniversary of your useful magazine I extend to you my cordial congratulations and good wishes.

Yours faithfully,

HERBERT HOOVER

[Mr. George J. Hecht, President, The Parents' Magazine, 255 Fourth Ave., New York City]

NOTE: The message was made public in conjunction with the magazine's fifth anniversary celebration.

322

Message to Dedication Ceremonies for the Institute of Paper Chemistry at Lawrence College.
September 23, 1931

[Released September 23, 1931.   Dated September 18, 1931]

My dear Mr. Mahler:

I regretted that the pressure of the public business prevented my accepting your gracious invitation to address the dedication of the new building of the Institute of Paper Chemistry at Lawrence College. The organization of the Institute has been widely recognized as a progressive and pioneer step. It helps to ground the industry in sound scientific knowledge and to assure trained technicians to bring the benefits of continuing research to the business. This not only makes for sound development within the industry, but enables it more intelligently and adequately to serve the public demand. I congratulate those responsible for bringing the enterprise to the stage signalized by the dedication of the building to serve as a center of your constructive activities.

Yours faithfully,

HERBERT HOOVER

[Mr. Ernst Mahler, President, The Institute of Paper Chemistry, Appleton, Wisconsin]

NOTE: The message was read at the dedication ceremonies.

323

Message on National Radio Week.
September 24, 1931

[Released September 24, 1931.   Dated September 16, 1931]

My dear Mr. Aitken:

Within a decade radio has become a major factor in our system of communication. Its results have been as far-reaching as its rise has been dramatic. As a medium for the universal dissemination of ideas it is an important factor in the formation of sound public opinion and the promotion of good citizenship. It is, in fact, an art and utility of indispensable value in our national life.

National Radio Week sponsored by the National Federation of Radio Associations and associated organizations has grown to be an event of importance, both to the industry and to the public. I shall appreciate it if you will extend my heartiest greetings to all those participating in the observance.

Yours faithfully,

HERBERT HOOVER

[Mr. James Aitken, President, National Federation of Radio Associations, 32 West Randolph St., Chicago, Ill.]

NOTE: The message was made public at the Radio World's Fair held in Madison Square Garden, New York City.

324

The President's News Conference of
September 25, 1931

FEDERAL EXPENDITURES

THE PRESIDENT. The American Legion has set an example to other voluntary bodies in the country in its determination to make no demands on the next Congress.[1] A large part of the pressures for increased expenditure by the Federal Government arises, as you know, from the action of voluntary associations, group or sectional interest, or business, or the thousand other activities in the country. This Office is already in receipt of many resolutions of such bodies recommending expenditure for new undertakings by the next Congress. I have no doubt the Members of Congress are receiving some pressure, also.

Everybody in Washington is familiar with the process by which these bodies, often with meritorious projects, pass resolutions and instruct their representatives in Washington to become active during the session both in respect to the administration and the Congress. You are also aware of their activities in assembling support at home and carrying on constant drives for such increased expenditures. This is a time when the other organizations of the country should realize that this is not an occasion for the increase but rather for the decrease of Federal expenditure.

I have before me a review by the Bureau of the Budget of 271 pieces of legislation introduced by the 71st Congress—from which all duplications as to subject have been eliminated—upon which the executive branches of the Government were asked to pass opinion. They fall in two categories: first, those where the total proposed expenditure is expressed, like construction projects, et cetera; and second, those which would create an annual recurring expenditure. Those in the first category upon which adverse report was made, amounted to $4,900 million and those in the second category to $1,200 million annually. Taking a 10-year period the latter category would amount to some $12 billion.

Now, the only pertinent interest in that table is that it discloses fairly well the character and origin of pressures for increased governmental expenditure, and unless there is a pretty general recognition of the situation we will be faced with the same pressures at the next session of Congress. It is important that there should be a great effort on the part of such organizations to discourage every form of increased Federal ex-

---

[1] On September 24, 1931, the American Legion adopted an antibonus resolution calling upon its members to refrain from placing unnecessary financial burdens on the Government.

penditure and to themselves withhold projects, even though meritorious, until sometime when the country is in better condition.

COUNCIL OF NATIONAL DEFENSE

For some background and perhaps amusement, I was interested in a proposal to revive the Council of National Defense as a service in the present situation. I have no notion that we will arrive at any such situation but it seemed to have been overlooked that the Council of National Defense, to read the text of the act, "shall be nominated by the President, et cetera, and shall comprise the Secretary of War, Secretary of the Navy, Secretary of the Interior, Secretary of Agriculture, Secretary of Commerce and Secretary of Labor." Those gentlemen are all present and in constant service today. Further than that it provides for an advisory committee of seven men to be chosen from industry, the duties of the group are as follows:

"It shall be the duty of the Council of National Defense to supervise and direct investigations and make recommendations to the President and the heads of executive departments as to the location of railroads with reference to the frontier of the United States so as to render possible expeditious concentration of troops and supplies to points of defense; the coordination of military, industrial, and commercial purposes in the location of extensive highways and branch lines of railroad; the utilization of waterways; the mobilization of military and naval resources of defense; the increase of domestic production of articles and materials essential to the support of armies and of the people during the interruption of foreign commerce; the development of seagoing transportation; data as to amounts, location, method and means of production, and availability of military supplies; the giving of information to producers and manufacturers as to the class of supplies needed by the military and other services of the Government, the requirements relating thereto, and the creation of relations which will render possible in time of need the immediate concentration and utilization of the resources of the Nation."

The bill goes on to further define the duties, one of which is the creation of a board of ordnance and fortification, relates to alien enemies, espionage, arsenals, armories, arms and war materiel generally; willful destruction of war materiel and especially interference with homing pigeons owned by the United States; the manufacture, distribution, storage, use and possession, and such allied subjects.

As a matter of fact, in the creation of Mr. Gifford's commission I think we have set up an effective body of the character which will compass the situation. I mention this because there is a general impression that we need more advisory bodies. We certainly get enough advice and little enough action in these days.

NOTE: President Hoover's two hundred and tenth news conference was held in the White House at 4 p.m. on Friday, September 25, 1931.

On the same day, the White House issued a text of the President's statement on Federal expenditures (see Item 325).

Walter S. Gifford was Chairman of the President's Organization on Unemployment Relief.

325

Statement on Federal Expenditures.
September 25, 1931

THE PRESIDENT said:

"The American Legion has set an example to other voluntary bodies in the country in its determination to make no requests of the next Congress. A very large part of the pressures for increase in expenditures of the Federal Government arises from the action of voluntary associations, whether they be group interests, sectional interests, business, or a thousand other activities in the country. This Office is already the recipient of many resolutions recommending expenditures and undertakings by the Government at the next session. I have no doubt that Members of Congress are receiving them also.

"Everyone in Washington is familiar with the process by which such bodies, often with meritorious projects, instruct their representatives in Washington to promote these activities to the administration and Congress. We are all familiar with the energies they show both in direct

442

pressures upon Congress and the administration and the propaganda which they carry on in the country to induce citizens to exert their individual influence in the massing up of pressures. This is a time when they should emulate the American Legion in standing with what is the wish of the administration and the great majority of Congressmen and Senators—that is, not to increase but to decrease the expenditures of the Federal Government.

"I have before me a review from the Bureau of the Budget of 271 bills introduced into the last Congress asking for increased Federal expenditures which were referred to the executive agencies for report. These fall into two categories: those in which the total obligation is expressed in the bill; and those which would result in a continued annual obligation. After eliminating all duplicates the bills which were reported adversely by the administration during the 71st Congress amounted to $4,900 million of the first category and an annual expenditure in the second category of $1,200 million. Taking only a 10-year period, this latter category would amount to an expenditure of some $12 billion, or a total of nearly $17 billion.

"The main interest in this table is the fact that it discloses how largely these bills arise from pressures of group and sectional interests. Unless there is a general recognition that this is no time for such activities these same pressures will again arise. It is important that there should be a great effort on the part of organizations of our country to express their disapproval of such expenditures now even though the projects may be most meritorious. They should be withheld until the country is in better condition."

NOTE: On September 4, 1931, the American Legion adopted an antibonus resolution calling upon its members to refrain from placing unnecessary financial burdens on the Government.

326

Message to the Regional Conference of the New Jersey Chapters of the American National Red Cross.
September 25, 1931

[Released September 25, 1931.   Dated September 22, 1931]

My dear Mr. Eisner:

Please present my greetings to those assembled for the annual Regional Conference of the American Red Cross at Fort Monmouth. I trust that the deliberations of the representatives of the New Jersey Chapters may be fruitful in effective plans to meet the current demands upon the organization.

Yours faithfully,

HERBERT HOOVER

[Mr. Monroe Eisner, 107B Monmouth Street, Red Bank, New Jersey]

NOTE: The message was read at the annual regional conference.

327

The President's News Conference of
September 29, 1931

BACKGROUND INFORMATION

THE PRESIDENT. I have one or two subjects on which I can talk to you from the point of view of background. I think we need a reunderstanding of what background consists of—it is the desire on my part to help the correspondents with the facts about various things on which I do not desire to be quoted. There seems to be a little departure from that idea. If the correspondents do not think it worthwhile it is not a matter with which I am greatly concerned.

Navy Department Appropriations

We have had some discussion about Navy appropriations, and as I say, I am talking for background. I have had each of the departments here and have asked them to reconsider their proposed appropriations for the forthcoming year in order that we may, so far as is physically possible, meet the financial situation with which we are confronted. The Navy budget was $401 million as proposed for the fiscal year 1933, compared with $360 million for 1932—an increase of about $41 million. In the budget of 1932, construction activities involved about $50 million and the Navy is reconsidering whether or not, with some extension of construction programs, possibly bringing it up to $65 million. It would not be possible to make economies in other directions so as to bring the total appropriation for the year down to $340 million, to maintain the present rate of construction activities with some slight increase, and at the same time orient the Navy in a fashion that we would certainly not exceed the appropriation for the current year, but reduce it.

Similar suggestions have been made to other departments of the Government and I would like to add one thing to that discussion. The problem of reducing Government expenditures is a difficult one and affects great numbers of people. This makes it doubly difficult for the President and Cabinet officers to handle the problems if departmental people are going to start backfire in the press against the administration in efforts of this character. I regret that the Navy Department has considered it in the interest of their activities that they carry this fight into the press. If they wish to, I welcome it and will go to the American people on the question of whether the departments have the right to dictate to the American people what they shall expend. That is a matter that lies in the recommendation of the administration to Congress and, in finality, the action by Congress.

German Chancellor Heinrich Brüning

Another small background question is the statement about Mr. Brüning's possible visit to the United States. We have heard nothing of it.

TAXATION

Another question is on the tax question. I told you some weeks ago that we would continue to explore the question of our expenditures and the course to be pursued to the time Congress meets, and there has been no departure from that policy either by the Executive or by the Treasury. There is nothing I can add to that.

WORLD SERIES

Finally, and this is not background, I propose to attend the baseball game in Philadelphia next Monday and will welcome all the press support on that occasion that you feel you can give.

SECRETARY OF THE NAVY

Q. Mr. President, would it be permissible to ask if there has been any rift at all between you and Secretary Adams?

THE PRESIDENT. That is not at all a nice question to ask, but there is nothing of the kind and has been no thought of such a thing. Secretary Adams is devoting himself to carrying out his job and there has never been any question of his loyalty.

Q. I asked it only because there have been rumors to that effect.

THE PRESIDENT. I am glad you asked the question because it is only fair to Secretary Adams that such rumors should be cleared up. There is absolutely no truth to it. Such things do not happen in sound government.

NOTE: President Hoover's two hundred and eleventh news conference was held in the White House at 12 noon on Tuesday, September 29, 1931.

328

Radio Remarks on the Opening of the Waldorf-Astoria Hotel.
September 30, 1931

OUR HOTELS have become community institutions. They are the center points of civic hospitality. They are the meeting place of a thousand community and national activities. They have come to be conducted in far larger vision than mere profit earning. If we considered them solely from an economic point of view we would find them among the nine leaders of American industry.

The opening of the new Waldorf-Astoria is an event in the development of hotels even in New York City. It carries on a great tradition in national hospitality. It was 137 years ago that the first so-called great hotel was opened in New York—the old City Hotel—which was then heralded as an immense establishment and comprised 73 rooms. It was visited from all parts of the country as one of the fine exhibits of our national growth. A long line of constantly improving hotels from that day to this has marked the measure of the Nation's growth in power, in comfort, and in artistry.

The erection of this great structure at this time has been a contribution to the maintenance of employment and is an exhibition of courage and confidence to the whole Nation. This occasion is really but the moving day of an old institution with all its traditions of hospitality and service into a new and better structure. I have faith that in another 50 years the growth of America in wealth, science, and art will necessitate the institution's moving again to an even finer and more magnificent place and equipment.

I wish to congratulate the management on the consummation of its plan for the magnificent new home perpetuating the Waldorf-Astoria.

NOTE: The President spoke at 6:05 p.m. from the Cabinet Room in the White House to an assembly in the new Waldorf-Astoria in New York City. The National Broadcasting Company radio network carried the President's remarks.

329

Statement on Unemployment Relief Efforts in the State of Missouri.
October 1, 1931

THE PRESIDENT said:

"I am glad to announce that the Governor of Missouri has informed me that the State of Missouri is completing its organization to care for its unemployed. I have received the following telegram from the Governor:

'Jefferson City, Missouri, September 30, 1931

The President

The White House

In your efforts to mobilize the strength of the nation to the end that no one go hungry or suffer needless privation this winter, you may be interested to know that the State of Missouri and the communities and cities of our state are organizing to do their share toward that same goal. I share your feeling that this problem should be met by private effort and that great good would result could each community take care of its own citizens. Nothing solidifies and strengthens a people like joint action to meet a common disaster. Those cities whose citizens band together and give unselfishly of their time, their energies and their money in order that their neighbors may not suffer in this time of distress will come out of this trial stronger and greater. You doubtless will receive the details of what we are doing from the Missouri members of your relief committee. I would like you to know however from me that our leaders of all parties of all creeds and of all walks of life are forgetting many of their differences and cooperating in a vigorous effort to enable Missouri and Missouri communities to take care of their own citizens this winter.

Henry S. Caulfield
Governor of Missouri.'

"The following States in addition to Missouri have indicated their ability to undertake their own problem: Rhode Island, Indiana, Michigan, Connecticut, Illinois, New York, California, West Virginia, and Delaware."

NOTE: During this period, the White House issued the texts of similar letters and telegrams from other States and localities endorsing the President's position on unemployment relief. For release dates, see Appendix A.

330

Message of Sympathy on the Death of Edward Alfred Simmons.
October 3, 1931

[Released October 3, 1931.   Dated October 2, 1931]

My dear Mrs. Simmons:

I was greatly shocked to learn of the death of Colonel Simmons who had long been my friend. He had a distinguished career of public service and his passing is indeed a great loss.

I am in hopes you will have the strength to bear up under this burden.

Yours faithfully,

HERBERT HOOVER

[Mrs. Edward A. Simmons, 1625 Ditmas Avenue, Brooklyn, N.Y.]

NOTE: Mr. Simmons, president of the Simmons-Boardman Publishing Company, died on September 30, 1931.

331

Message to Boris III, King of the Bulgarians, on His Birthday.
October 3, 1931

ON THIS auspicious anniversary I send to Your Majesty sincere felicitations and best wishes for Your Majesty's continued happiness and well-being.

HERBERT HOOVER

[His Majesty Boris III, King of the Bulgarians, Sofia]

332

Message to the Federation for the Support of the Jewish Philanthropic Societies.
October 4, 1931

[Released October 4, 1931. Dated October 2, 1931]

My dear Mr. Block:

My attention has been called to the work which the Federation for the Support of Jewish Philanthropic Societies of New York City is about to start or the ninety-one institutions which it supports, and so I send to you and to all the men and women who are assisting you in this drive for funds, my very best wishes for a successful campaign.

In these days when every agency in the country is doing so nobly toward those who are in need, because of lack of employment or other reasons, we must not forget the private philanthropic societies which are the foundation of charity work, and without whom thousands of sufferers and orphans and aged persons would have little, if any attention.

Leaving Christ Episcopal Church in Alexandria, Va.
with granddaughter Peggy Ann

With Secretary of War Patrick J. Hurley aboard U.S.S. *Arizona*

With members of his party and Navy officers aboard U.S.S. *Arizona* en route to Porto Rico and the Virgin Islands

U.S. Navy

U.S. Navy

With Porto Rican Governor Theodore Roosevelt in San Juan

President and Mrs. Hoover attending services at New Friends Meeting House

International Newsreel

With Wiley Post
and Harold Gatty

With James G. Ray,
following his landing
an autogiro on the
White House lawn

Mary Pickford
presenting a
ticket to a
benefit for the
unemployed
sponsored
by the movie
industry

Placing a wreath
on the tomb of
Warren G. Harding
during
the Harding
memorial
dedication

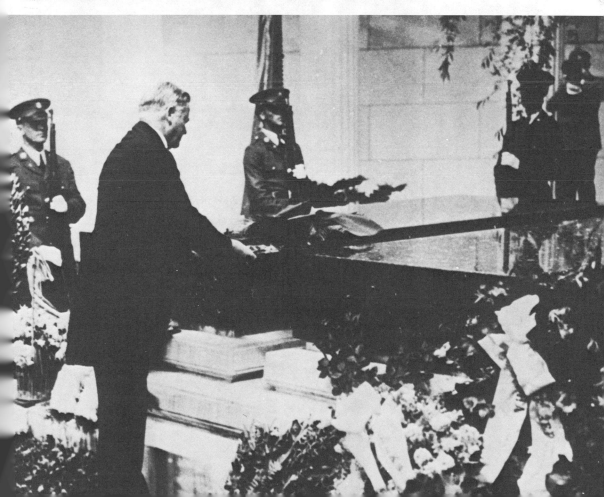

Inspection tour of the U.S.S. *Constitution*

President and Mrs. Hoover with
French Prime Minister Pierre Laval and daughter Josette

With Dr. R. A. Millikan, Dr. Vernon L. Kellogg,
and Governor John G. Pollard upon arrival at Cape Henry, Va.,
for celebration commemorating the 324th anniversary
of the landing of the first English colonists in America

Armistice Day address at the dedication of
the District of Columbia War Memorial

And so I commend you all for this eminent work of charity and as it deserves success, I feel quite certain you will accomplish it.

Yours faithfully,

HERBERT HOOVER

[Mr. Paul Block, 247 Park Avenue, New York City]

NOTE: The message was read at a fundraising dinner held in the Commodore Hotel in New York City.

333

Statement on Financial and Economic Problems.
October 4, 1931

OWING to the prolonged business depression, the succession of events abroad, the failure of banks in constantly increasing numbers, and the destruction of confidence and increasing fear throughout the country, a situation exists which calls for concerted action on the part of our leading bankers and strong banks to avert a possible threat to our entire credit structure.

You know the picture better than I do, but it may be worth while to review it briefly.

1. Since January 1st, 1,215 banks, involving $967,000,000 deposits, have closed their doors. Of this number, 698 have suspended since June , involving $792,000,000 deposits. These failures follow 1,345 bank failures in 1930, involving $864,000,000 deposits. Thus, in the course of nineteen months, no less than $1,831,000,000 have been tied up through bank suspensions; and if to this be added some $800,000,000 of cash withdrawals for boarding purposes, it is perfectly apparent that these events have resulted in pressure which must of necessity not only have affected prices, and restricted business activity to a very severe extent, but which also has severely impaired the confidence of the public and bankers as well. But what we are concerned with tonight is the threat to the banking structure.

2. The obvious method followed by a bank threatened with pressure from its depositors is to meet its obligations either by recourse to its

Federal Reserve Bank or its city correspondent, by the sale of securities, or by the disposition of other liquid assets. There is no need of emphasizing the effect which the sale of securities has on the security markets, both in the case of banks seeking to make themselves liquid, and in the case of banks that have been closed and that are being liquidated either by the Comptroller or the State banking authorities. In any event, the process has been going on and is going on in this country until every bank is seeking to increase its liquidity and to the extent that the strong banks are succeeding in doing so, to that extent they are making less liquid their weaker brethren. This process is well illustrated by the fact that the Clearing House banks in New York, I am informed, are on the average 60% liquid, whereas nothing like this degree of liquidity is true of banks in most other sections of the country. Such a process obviously cannot be continued indefinitely.

Prior to the establishment of the Federal Reserve Bank system, it would probably have been met in large measure through the relationship between the banks in the principal centers and their out of town correspondents, but, with the establishment of the Federal Reserve System, there grew up a tendency to feel that it was to the Federal Reserve System rather than to the banks in central reserve cities that all banks should look. This supposition in times like these is faulty in two respects, first, the number of State Banks that are members of the Federal Reserve System is comparatively small in number, and, second, the amount of eligible paper held by banks which may be perfectly solvent but which are, nevertheless, threatened, may be totally inadequate to meet immediate emergencies. One way to meet this handicap would be to extend the eligibility provisions of the Federal Reserve Act, but that obviously would require time. This, therefore, must be considered in the light of a future possibility rather than as a program available to meet our immediate needs. If, however, in carrying out the obligation of the strong banks in the principal financial centers to the banks throughout the country, we could set up one or more central organizations which would furnish rediscount facilities to banks throughout the country on the basis of sound assets not legally eligible for rediscount at the Federal Reserve Bank, we would not only restore liquidity to solvent institutions, but, what is even more important, we would at once tend to restore confidence now sadly lacking among all classes of bank depositors in all sections of the country. There would be no danger to the banks in the principal financial centers not only because of their existing liquidity but because of their ability to get exceptionally large accommodations from the Federal Reserve Banks which are in an unusually strong position.

3. I have, therefore, asked you to come here to make the definite suggestion to you that you proceed to the creation of such an organization, and make available to it such resources as will insure its adequate functioning. I am not concerned with the precise form which it should take, whether you should create a central organization or local organizations acting through the various Clearing Houses, but I do say that I consider some such program essential in the public interest, and that the carrying out of such a program does not admit of delay. I am confident that the Secretary of the Treasury and the leaders of the Federal Reserve System will cooperate with you in every way in the working out of such a program. If present tendencies are allowed to continue unchecked, there is no telling where the movement will stop.

4. The problem created by the vast sums tied up in closed banks is also one that should also be dealt with, not only in the interests of millions of depositors, who in times like these are faced with unusual hardships because of the tie-up of their savings, but because in the general interest it is essential to arrest this process of deflation and to restore public confidence in our banks. I would, therefore, suggest that another organization be set up that would as promptly as possible make available to depositors some reasonable percentage of the amounts due them on the basis of assets selected in accordance with sound business judgment.

NOTE: The statement was read to a group of New York bankers who were meeting with the President in the home of Secretary of the Treasury Andrew W. Mellon.

334

Letter to George L. Harrison, Federal Reserve Board of New York, on Financial and Economic Problems.
October 5, 1931

Dear Mr. Harrison:

The request which I laid before the leading New York bankers last night for cooperation in unity of national action to assure credit security can, in the light of our discussion, be simplified to the following concrete measures:

1. They are to take the lead in immediate formulation of a national institution with a capital of $500,000,000. The function of this institution to be:

(a) The rediscount of bank assets not now eligible in the Federal Reserve System in order to assure the stability of banks throughout the country from attack by unreasoning depositors. That is to prevent bank failures.

(b) Loans against the assets of closed banks to enable them to pay some early dividend to depositors and thus revive many business activities and relieve many families from destitution.

2. It is proposed that the capital be underwritten by the banks of the United States as a national effort, possibly with the support of the industrials. New York being the financial center of the nation must of necessity assume both the initiative and the major burden. The effort should be participated in by the country at large by appropriate organization.

3. As I said last night, we are in a degenerating vicious cycle. Economic events of Europe have demoralized our farm produce and security prices. This has given rise to an unsettlement of public mind. There have been in some localities foolish alarm over the stability of our credit structure and considerable withdrawals of currency. In consequence bankers in many other parts of the country in fear of the possibility of such unreasoning demands of depositors have deemed it neces-

sary to place their assets in such liquid form as to enable them to meet drains and runs. To do this they sell securities and restrict credit. The sale of securities demoralizes their price and jeopardizes other banks. The restriction on credit has grown greatly in the past few weeks. There are a multitude of complaints that farmers cannot secure loans for their livestock feeding or to carry their commodities until the markets improve. There are a multitude of complaints of business men that they cannot secure the usual credit to carry their operations on a normal basis and must discharge labor. There are complaints of manufacturers who use agricultural and other raw materials that they cannot secure credits beyond day to day needs with which to lay in their customary seasonal supplies. The effect of this is to thrust on the back of the farmer the load of carrying of the nation's stocks. The whole cumulative effect is today to decrease prices of commodities and securities and to spread the relations of the debtor and creditor.

4. The only real way to brake this cycle is to restore confidence in the people at large. To do this requires major unified action that will give confidence to the country. It is this that I have asked of the New York bankers.

5. I stated that if the New York banks will undertake to comply with this request, I will seek to secure assurance from the leaders of appropriate committees in Congress of both political parties to support my recommendation at the next session for

(a) The extension of rediscount eligibility in the Federal Reserve System.

(b) If necessity requires to recreate the War Finance Corporation with available funds sufficient for any emergency in our credit system.

(c) To strengthen the Federal Farm Loan Bank System.

Yours faithfully,
HERBERT HOOVER

[Hon. George Harrison, Federal Reserve Bank, New York City]

NOTE: George L. Harrison's response, dated October 7, 1931, follows:

Dear Mr. President:

I want very much to thank you for your letter of October 5, which was delivered to me by messenger late that afternoon. The summary which it contained of the request you made to the New York bankers who were present at the meeting in Washington Sunday night was most helpful.

Now that your proposal has been placed before the public in the morning papers, it occurs to me that you might be interested in some short review of the situation as it now stands as we see it.

Immediately after our return from Washington on Monday morning a committee of New York bankers was appointed to consider your proposal. They authorized me late Monday afternoon to tell Mr. Mills (a) that they were prepared to support your suggestion to the bankers of the United States to form a corporation of $500,000,000 for the purpose of making funds available to banks requiring accommodation upon the basis of sound banking assets not now legally eligible for rediscount at the Federal Reserve Banks; (b) that, as requested by you, they would assume the leadership in the formation of such a corporation; and (c) that the twenty four members of the New York Clearing House Association would no doubt agree by the next day to contribute their share by pledging $150,000,000, which is approximately two percent of their net demand and time deposits. This they have since done, as I informed you late yesterday afternoon. You may be interested to know that there has been quite general and enthusiastic support throughout New York to your proposal, not merely as to the formation of the $500,000,000 corporation but also as to the enlargement of the rediscount facilities of the Reserve System; the revival of some such institution as the War Finance Corporation; the strengthening of the Federal Farm Loan System, and your statement regarding a possible reconsideration of inter-governmental debts in the light of present conditions. Their agreement with your program cannot better be illustrated than by the prompt response they have made in the pledge of subscriptions to the new corporation.

You may remember that in your letter you indicated that the corporation should be organized not merely for the purpose of advancing funds to going banks on ineligible assets in order to prevent bank failures, but also to make loans against assets of closed banks. As I explained to Mr. Mills on Monday, the New York bankers' committee felt, and I agreed with them, that it would have been unwise if not impossible to have the proposed corporation undertake the task of making loans against the assets of closed banks as distinguished from the rediscounting of ineligible but sound assets in going institutions. The technical difficulties with respect to disposing of the assets of closed banks as well as the amounts involved made it seem impossible to include in the proposed new $500,000,000 corporation any provision designed to tackle this part of the program. I understood from Mr. Mills that this modification of the proposal, as outlined in your letter to me, was agreeable to you and that, to the extent that this aspect of the problem must be taken care of, it would have to be done independently of the proposed corporation.

We have also made progress in drafting a plan by which the proposed corporation may be quickly organized to function effectively. The proper and expeditious administration of a national institution of such scope may be difficult to insure, but I believe that with the cooperation of the various clearing houses as well as other voluntary associations of banks throughout the country it will be possible promptly and safely to make the funds of the corporation available in the different communities where they may be needed. Obviously, it would be impossible for one central group to determine the needs or to pass upon the merits of the applications of banks in remote sections of the country. This will probably have to be done through some sort of local association of banks which will pass upon the need for accommodation, the merits of assets to be rediscounted, and then jointly and severally guarantee the loan made by the corporation. This, you will remember, was the procedure followed in the flood pool and is somewhat similar to the procedure set up under the emergency Aldrich-Vreeland law.

I feel that your proposal to the bankers on Sunday night was a most constructive and important step in the present emergency. It will do much to provide liquidity for those banks which may need it, and there are perhaps many of them. Unfortunately, however, there are a great many banking institutions in the United States where the difficulty is not one of liquidity but of solvency, solvency which has been prejudiced by the continued depreciation in the value of the bank's assets. In this district, where I happen to be more familiar with the situation than in other sections of the country, the principal cause of bank failures has not been a lack of liquidity but rather insolvency caused by need for a drastic writeoff in bond portfolios. In other districts, I understand, many banks are threatened with insolvency because of losses in real estate loans as well as bonds.

So, while the proposed corporation will do much promptly to provide liquidity for certain solvent institutions needing cash, thus avoiding the forced sale of their assets at substantially depreciated values, it will not unfortunately be able to aid materially in improving the banking situation in those districts where the principal difficulty is the threat of insolvency through depreciation of bond or real estate values. The country banks in this district, and I believe it to be the case also in the Boston and Philadelphia districts and perhaps to a lesser extent elsewhere, have their resources very largely employed in bonds. Indeed, outside of half a dozen of our larger cities, nearly fifty percent of the assets of the banks in this district are in bonds. The proposed corporation will be helpful in this situation to the extent that it relieves some of the selling pressure upon the bond market. But if the bond market is not substantially bettered very promptly the country banking situation in this district, and possibly in other districts as well, will still remain a critical problem.

I mention this now only that I might frankly emphasize what appears to be the unavoidable limitations of the proposed $500,000,000 corporation, and the real need for such other prompt action as will tend to enhance the value of assets in banks which are now threatened with insolvency on account of the drastic cut in bond and real estate values.

I have for some weeks surveyed the possibility of a bond pool. Apparently such a pool is not considered practicable or wise even if possible. I am told that it would only be a palliative which might only worsen the situation ultimately unless there is some fundamental improvement in the earning powers of the obligors of the bonds. This is especially true of the railroads. If the Interstate Commerce Commission fails to grant a rate increase it will no doubt, sentimentally at least, have a most reactionary influence upon the railroad bond market and thus largely nullify the immediately favorable response to your announcement this morning. This would no doubt be true, even though there is a growing belief in many circles that a rate increase would probably have relatively little effect upon railroad earnings at the present time. The important objective it seems to me, therefore, is to start some favorable or constructive steps before any unfavorable announcement possibly comes from the Interstate Commerce Commission.

In view of what appears to be the imperative necessity of no further reaction but rather a prompt betterment of the bond market, which is now largely influenced by the railroad bond situation, I cannot avoid the conviction that something must be done and must be done promptly. Whether this should be a rate, increase, wage reductions, or some form of banking support may raise differences of opinion. Even if you cannot take the initiative for the various reasons which you have pointed out, might it not be possible for you to talk with some of the more influential railroad presidents with a view to ascertaining more or less definitely what they think should be done. If you ask them to reach some sort of an agreement among themselves as to what they want and to formulate a program, then there might be some concerted effort on the part of the Administration and the banking community to cooperate in carrying out a program. As I see it, we are now in a deadlock on the railroad situation, and through it in the bond market, unless the railroads themselves promptly take stock and formulate their own program for submission to the necessary parties, whether governmental or financial.

The problem of those banks which have suffered large losses on mortgage loans is perhaps even more difficult of solution than that of those with large losses in their bonds. The suggestion you made on several occasions last week with reference to a possible mortgage rediscount system, if feasible, might ultimately prove of real relief in that regard. But even if the real estate problem is not capable of immediate solution, there is no reason on that account alone to delay whatever constructive steps might be taken with respect to bond values, an improvement of which would also indirectly affect the value of other bank assets.

I hope you will please forgive my bothering you with such a lengthy letter, but I feel that you have already taken such an important and helpfully constructive step looking towards the correction of a very substantial part of the problem, that I would not be frank with you if I did not point out the very real need for fundamental improvement in the condition of a great many banks now threatened with insolvency and failure because of capital impairment through the severe depreciation of their assets—whether based on bonds or real estate.

Faithfully yours,

GEORGE L. HARRISON

[Hon. Herbert Hoover, The White House, Washington, D.C.]

335

Statement on the Death
of Senator Dwight W. Morrow.
October 5, 1931

THE COUNTRY has suffered a great loss in the death of Senator Dwight Morrow. His character as a neighbor and a friend; his public spirit as a private citizen; his services during the war; his accomplishments as Ambassador to Mexico; his unique contribution to the success of the London Naval Conference—are the record of that sort of an American who makes our country great.

NOTE: Mr. Morrow served as Ambassador to Mexico from 1927 to 1930 and as Senator of New Jersey from 1930 until this death.

336

Message to the Central New York Conference of the Methodist Episcopal Church.
October 5, 1931

My dear Mr. Hebblethwaite:

Thank you for your telegram of October 1st, conveying the resolution adopted by the Central New York Conference of the Methodist Episcopal Church at its recent meeting. I appreciate your wiring.

Yours faithfully,

HERBERT HOOVER

[Mr. R. C. Hebblethwaite, Secretary, Central New York Conference, Methodist Episcopal Church, Oneida, New York]

NOTE: In his message, the President referred to a resolution which had commended him for his stand on law enforcement and urged that the 18th amendment not be repealed.

337

White House Statement Announcing a Conference With Certain Members of Congress on Economic Problems.
October 5, 1931

A CONFERENCE has been called of the Members of some of the Senate and House committees who are available for the general purpose of securing unity of action in dealing with the many economic problems thrust upon us by the events in Europe. There being no conclusive action determined upon, there is nothing to give out at the present time. I have consulted and am continuing to consult with every group that can be helpful.

NOTE: The President called the conference to discuss plans for a new credit association and related measures.

338

Message of Sympathy on the Death
of Senator Dwight W. Morrow.
October 6, 1931

I DEEPLY appreciate your wire advising me of the death of your
brother. His passing is a shock to me and a loss to the world. Mrs. Hoover
and I wish to express our heartfelt sympathy to you and yours.

HERBERT HOOVER

[Jay J. Morrow, Englewood, N.J.]

339

Message to Certain Members of Congress
About a Conference on Economic Problems.
October 6, 1931

[Released October 6, 1931.   Dated October 3, 1931]

I AM ASKING leaders in certain committees who may be in reach to
meet with me at the White House at nine o'clock Tuesday evening next
upon an urgent national matter. I am anxious that you should come. In
order to avoid harmful speculation I should deeply appreciate it if no
information of the call should be given out. I will be glad to place a plane
at your disposal if you desire.

HERBERT HOOVER

NOTE: On the same day, the White House issued a list of 26 Members of the Congress to whom the telegram was sent.

340

Message to the Annual Convention of the National Council of Catholic Women. *October 6, 1931*

[Released October 6, 1931.   Dated October 5, 1931]

My dear Miss Hawks:

I shall be greatly obliged to you if you will present my cordial greetings to the delegates to the annual convention of the National Council of Catholic Women in session here. The National Capital delights to welcome the representatives of a nation-wide organization whose activities mean so much to the cause of good citizenship, the preservation of family life, the care of the unfortunate and the enrichment of the spiritual life and ideals of our people. I trust that your meeting may advance the sound objectives for which your organization so nobly stands.

Yours faithfully,

HERBERT HOOVER

[Miss Mary G. Hawks, President, National Council of Catholic Women, Hotel Mayflower, Washington, D.C.]

NOTE: The message was read to the annual convention in Washington, D.C.

341

The President's News Conference of *October 6, 1931*

CONFERENCE ON ECONOMIC PROBLEMS

THE PRESIDENT. As I stated yesterday, I have asked for a conference this evening with leaders of the two Houses and Members of some of the committees who may be available around Washington. And the purpose of that conference is to advance a program of national unity in setting up of constructive forces in place of destructive forces now working in this depression. I feel that it is not proper in advance of this conference to make any announcement.

Now, I would like to talk with you a little confidentially—perhaps even more confidentially than background—on a difficulty that confronts the President of the United States. I think you will agree with me that this is a position of very unusual responsibility, a position of unusual difficulty, a position of many discordant forces, a position in which it is difficult enough to secure the unity of action which the Nation absolutely demands at the present time. In the endeavor to bring various groups into coordinated action, it is necessary that I shall have conferences with those groups. I have had many such conferences, and I continue to have them—at this office, and by telephone, or any place else that is convenient for such purposes. I shall continue to do so. It is your natural business, and I admire you for it, to endeavor to find out anything you can find out. That is the proper function of newspaper correspondents. I have no feeling on that subject.

I think you will realize as citizens, however, that the disclosure of discussions, programs, and ideas that are put forward, when they are in their formative stage and when they must be hammered out on the anvil of debate with many groups, may lead to oppositions which are wholly unnecessary and increase the difficulties of the times. I am asking you to suppress nothing. I ask you to go and find out everything you can. But I think you will bear with me if I don't discuss these matters with you. Nothing would be more pleasant to me than to be able to tell you in detail everything that has taken place in the last 3 weeks, to tell you of the difficulties that have been plunged upon us by the situation in Europe, the endeavors we are making to meet them, but it would not be fair to the American people that I should start crosscurrents that are bound to rise from partial programs. So that I hope you will bear with me, and I have to bear with you.

Q. Mr. President, cannot you, after tonight's conference, give us some rather definite statement. It is coming out piecemeal if you don't. You are going to have people there—a great many groups—they will tell things and in fact be all mixed up. The condition of the financial men of the country is such now that all these rumors will have a very bad effect.

THE PRESIDENT. I would like to make an arrangement, but I don't think it is possible. I don't think that I ought even to suggest it to you, because there are persons who think I am endeavoring to suppress the news. Tonight's conference will have certain results. I cannot anticipate what they may be. I have got to have time to formulate those results in a proper public statement. When you have finished a conference at 12 o'clock at night it is not the time to sit down and endeavor to prepare a statement on those difficult subjects we have to meet. I propose to make a statement tomorrow. I don't want you to announce now or any other time I am going to do so. I am wondering whether or not I could make an arrangement with you that you will forebear any of this incidental comment that may come out of this conference. It is impossible to have a group of men who don't, some of them, wish to convey impressions, and as you say, it mixes the situation very badly and makes it very difficult for me. I don't put that up to you otherwise than as a thought of mine: that it would be helpful in this very difficult situation if you were prepared to just leave this generally alone and forebear any attempt to pry into what may take place tonight and allow me until tomorrow, that I may have at least a few hours to formulate the conference into a program.

Q. Of course, Mr. President, I don't have a morning paper. But no individual newspaper can do that. You cannot effect an agreement among newspapermen on that.

THE PRESIDENT. That is why I started off with the premise that such a thing was impossible. I am giving you my feeling and what I think would be in the interest of the American people. I leave it to you and ask for no promises. I don't even put it up as a matter you should abide by. You are absolutely free to do whatever you please.

Q. Mr. President, harking back to your words as to the purpose of the conference—is it largely with respect to the domestic situation or international as well?

THE PRESIDENT. Largely domestic. It has bearings and roots from abroad.

464

So that is all I am able to say to you at the present time.

NOTE: President Hoover's two hundred and twelfth news conference was held in the White House at 12 noon on Tuesday, October 6, 1931.

On the same day, the White House issued a text of the President's statement about the conference on economic problems with certain Members of Congress (see Item 342).

342

Statement About the Conference on Economic Problems With Certain Members of Congress.
October 6, 1931

THE PRESIDENT said:

"The purpose of my conference with Members of Congress tonight is to advance a national unity in the setting up of constructive forces in place of destructive forces now working in the depression. I feel that it is not proper in advance of this conference to make any announcement."

343

Statement on Financial and Economic Problems.
October 7, 1931

[Released October 7, 1931. Dated October 6, 1931]

THE PRESIDENT said:

"The prolongation of the depression by the succession of events in Europe, affecting as they have both commodity and security prices, has produced in some localities in the United States an apprehension wholly unjustified in view of the thousandfold resources we have for meeting any demand. Foolish alarm in these sections has been accompanied by wholly unjustifiable withdrawal of currency from the banks. Such action results in limiting the ability of the banks in these localities to extend credit to businessmen and farmers for the normal conduct of business, but beyond this, to be prepared to meet the possibility of unreasoning demands of depositors, the banks are compelled to place their assets in liquid form by sales of securities and restriction of credits so as to enable them to meet unnecessary and unjustified drains. This affects the conduct of banking further afield. It is unnecessary to specify the unfortunate consequences of such a situation in the districts affected both in its further effect on national prices of agricultural products, upon securities, and upon the normal conduct of business and employment of labor. It is a deflationary factor and a definite impediment to agricultural and business recovery.

"There is no justification for any such situation in view of the strength of our banking system and the strong position of our Federal Reserve System. Our difficulty is a diffusion of resources and the primary need is to mobilize them in such a way as to restore, in a number of localities, the confidence of the banker in his ability to continue normal business and to dispel any conceivable doubt in the mind of those who do business with him.

"In order to deal with this wholly abnormal situation and to bring about an early restoration of confidence, unity of action on the part of our bankers and cooperative action on the part of the Government is essential. Therefore, I propose the following definite program of action, to which I ask our citizens to give their full cooperation:

1. To mobilize the banking resources of the country to meet these conditions, I request the bankers of the Nation to form a national institution of at least $500 million. The purpose of this institution to be the rediscount of banking assets not now eligible for rediscount at the Federal Reserve banks in order to assure our banks, being sound, that they may attain liquidity in case of necessity, and thereby enable them to continue their business without the restriction of credits or the sacrifice of their assets. I have submitted my proposal to the leading bankers of New York. I have been advised by them that it will receive their support, and that at my request they will assume the leadership in the formation of such an organization. The members of the New York City Clearing House Association have unanimously agreed to contribute their share by pledging $150 million, which is 2 percent of their net demand and time

466

deposits. I have been assured from other large centers, as far as I have been able to reach, of their support also. I consider that it is in the national interest including the interest of all individual banks and depositors that all the banks of the country should support this movement to their full responsibility. It is a movement of national assurance and of unity of action in an American way to assist business, employment, and agriculture.

2. On September 8, I requested the Governors of the Federal Reserve banks to endeavor to secure the cooperation of the bankers of their territory to make some advances on the security of the assets of closed banks or to take over some of these assets in order that the receivers of those banks may pay some dividends to their depositors in advance of what would otherwise be the case pending liquidation. Such a measure will contribute to free many business activities and to relieve many families from hardship over the forthcoming winter, and in a measure reverse the process of deflation involved in the tying up of deposits. Several of the districts have already made considerable progress to this end, and I request that it should be taken up vigorously as a community responsibility.

3. In order that the above program of unification and solidarity of action may be carried out and that all parts of the country be enlisted, I request the Governors of the Federal Reserve banks in each district to secure the appointment of working committees of bankers for each Reserve district to cooperate with the New York group and in carrying out the other activities which I have mentioned.

4. I shall propose to the Congress that the eligibility provisions of the Federal Reserve Act should be broadened in order to give greater liquidity to the assets of the banks, and thus a greater assurance to the bankers in the granting of credits by enabling them to obtain legitimate accommodation on sound security in times of stress. Such measures are already under consideration by the Senate Committee on Currency and Banking.

5. Furthermore, if necessity requires, I will recommend the creation of a finance corporation similar in character and purpose to the War Finance Corporation, with available funds sufficient for any legitimate call in support of credit.

467

6. I shall recommend to Congress the subscription of further capital stock by the Government to the Federal land banks (as was done at their founding) to strengthen their resources, so that on the one hand the farmer may be assured of such accommodation as he may require and on the other hand their credit may be of such high character that they may obtain their funds at low rates of interest.

7. I have submitted the above mentioned proposals which require legislation to the Members of Congress whose attendance I was able to secure on short notice at this evening's meeting—being largely the Members of committees particularly concerned—and they approve of them in principle.

8. Premier Laval of France is visiting the United States. It is my purpose to discuss with him the question of such further arrangements as are imperative during the period of the depression in respect of intergovernmental debts. The policy of the American Government in this matter is well known and was set out by me in a public statement on June 20 in announcing the American proposal for a year's postponement of debt payments. Our problem in this respect is one of such adjustment during the period of depression as will at the same time aid our own and world recovery. This being a subject first of negotiation with foreign governments was not submitted for determination at this evening's conference.

9. The times call for unity of action on the part of our people. We have met with great difficulties not of our own making. It requires determination to overcome these difficulties and above all to restore and maintain confidence. Our people owe it not only to themselves and in their own interest but they can by such an example of stability and purpose give hope and confidence in our own country and to the rest of the world."

NOTE: The White House issued the statement at 12:40 a.m. on October 7, 1931, following the President's conference with certain Members of Congress on economic problems, which was held on the evening of October 6.

344

The President's News Conference of
October 7, 1931

HOME FINANCING

THE PRESIDENT. This conference this afternoon has little or no relation to the current problem. It is just by way of background that I can tell you about it. I have no public statement to make. The committees of the Housing Conference, which is going to meet in December, have been working on various problems in connection with finance of home-ownership, looking to the long view rather than the short. They wanted to have a discussion with me as to the views they have developed before final conclusions, and they are working along the line of some sort of organization of building and loan societies and in cooperation with such societies to make them more liquid and stronger. But it is not a question of the emergency at all. It is one of those series of ideas in process of development that have not reached any finality. It is not part of the economic plan.

Q. It has been suggested that you might create some sort of central agency to liquidate mortgages.

THE PRESIDENT. The real estate people have been suggesting a central mortgage rediscount bank as a permanent institution but that committee is not in agreement and have not completed their arguments. Another suggestion is that a central rediscount institution should be created by the building and loan associations in order to expand and assure their position, but this is typical of the questions brought up. There is nothing conclusive about any of them. They have a number of investigations going on endeavoring to determine facts bearing on these various problems. A number of agencies like the mutual insurance companies and the building and loans are not entirely in accord with the ideas of the real estate people, although they have ideas leading in the same direction. But there is no finality to their plans.

This meeting today was a progress meeting and there will be no final results until the meeting in December. They are working toward having an effective program for that meeting. The major object is to build up some better form, more reliable and substantial form of finance for homeownership. That is the purpose of the committee and the point toward which they are driving. At the present moment they are investigating half a dozen different ideas. There is that problem of frozen mortgages. A proposal made this morning will undertake to assist that situation, as part of the object of the general plan now in progress to take care of the situation.

NOTE: President Hoover's two hundred and thirteenth news conference was held in the White House at 5:45 p.m. on Wednesday, October 7, 1931.

Prior to the news conference, the President and Secretary of Commerce Robert P. Lamont met with members of the Finance Committee of the White House Conference on Home Building and Home Ownership, representing insurance, mortgage, building and loan, and construction interests (see Appendix E, October 7, 1931).

345

Message of Sympathy on the Death
of Daniel Chester French.
October 7, 1931

I DEEPLY REGRET to learn of the death of your husband, Daniel Chester French. He was recognized not only in this country but throughout the world as an artist of preeminent skill and power. He wrought in marble imperishable incidents and personages of American history. His statute of Abraham Lincoln in the Lincoln Memorial in the National Capital will be a National shrine forever. I extend to you and your daughter heartfelt sympathy in your sorrow.

HERBERT HOOVER

[Mrs. Daniel Chester French, Stockbridge, Mass.]

NOTE: Daniel Chester French was a noted sculptor and creator of numerous monuments and memorials. Among his most notable works were statues of Abraham Lincoln, the Minute Man, and Ralph Waldo Emerson.

346

Message to the Annual Convention
of the Atlantic Deeper Waterways Association.
October 7, 1931

[Released October 7, 1931.   Dated October 3, 1931]

My dear Mr. Moore:

Transportation facilities adequate for current requirements are an essential element of national progress. The annual convention of the Atlantic Deeper Waterways Association in Boston deals with an essential aspect of the national problem, and your deliberations are important both to commerce and to national defense. The association is to be commended for its efforts in stimulating waterway construction as a measure of unemployment relief. I trust that your deliberations may be fruitful in the formulation and execution of helpful policies, and shall appreciate it if you will present my cordial greetings and good wishes to the delegates.

Yours faithfully,

HERBERT HOOVER

[Mr. J. Hampton Moore, President, Atlantic Deeper Waterways Association, 1405 Widener Building, Philadelphia, Pa.]

NOTE: The message was read to the association's 24th annual convention in Boston, Mass.

347

Address to the Fourth Pan American Commercial Conference.
October 8, 1931

Gentlemen of the Conference:

I am most happy to extend to you the warmest possible welcome on behalf of the Government and people of the United States. We are grateful to you for coming to Washington at this time to discuss the commerical problems of common interest to the nations of America. You are meeting during a period of widespread economic depression, but this fact emphasizes rather than diminishes the necessity for the nations of this continent to take counsel with one another.

We recognize that the prosperity of each and every nation contributes to the prosperity of all. It is important that at conferences such as this the experience of each and every nation should be placed at the disposal of all in order that we may profit by our successes as well as learn the lessons of our failures.

There is one lesson from this depression to which I wish to refer, and I can present it no more forcibly than by repeating a statement which I made to this conference just 4 years ago, when we were in the heyday of foreign loans. I stated, in respect to such loans, that they are helpful in world development, "provided always one essential principle dominates the character of these transactions. That is, that no nation as a government should borrow or no government lend and nations should discourage their citizens from borrowing or lending unless this money is to be devoted to productive enterprise.

"Out of the wealth and the higher standards of living created from enterprise itself must come the ability to repay the capital to the borrowing country. Any other course of action creates obligations impossible of repayment except by a direct subtraction from the standards of living of the borrowing country and the impoverishment of its people.

"In fact, if this principle could be adopted between nations of the world—that is, if nations would do away with the lending of money for the balancing of budgets for purposes of military equipment or war purposes, or even that type of public works which does not bring some direct or indirect productive return—a great number of blessings would follow to the entire world.

"There could be no question as to the ability to repay; with this increasing security capital would become steadily cheaper, the dangers to national and individual independence in attempts of the lender to collect his defaulted debts would be avoided; there would be definite increase in the standard of living and the comfort and prosperity of the borrower.

472

"There could be no greater step taken in the prevention of war itself. This is perhaps a little further toward the millennium than our practical world has reached, and I do not propose that these are matters that can be regulated by law or treaty. They are matters that can be regulated solely by the commercial and financial sentiment of each of our countries; and if this body may be able to develop the firm conviction, develop the understanding that the financial transactions between nations must be built upon the primary foundation that money transferred is for reproductive purposes, it will have contributed to the future of the Western Hemisphere in a degree seldom open to a conference of this character."

I repeat this today, because had it been followed during these past 5 years our problems throughout the world would be far different, our difficulties infinitely less.

I have learned with particular interest and gratification that by far the greater number of those in attendance at this conference are not governmental delegates, but representatives of the commercial and financial establishments of the several American Republics. Particularly do we in the United States hold to the theory that commercial enterprise, except as rare emergency action, is essentially a private undertaking, and that the sole function of government is to bring about a condition of affairs favorable to the beneficial development of private enterprise. It is the failure to comprehend this conception of the relation between the function of government and the function of private enterprise that sometimes leads the thoughtless to assume the existence of an international indifference which does not in fact exist.

The larger significance of your meeting is attested by the fact that at stated intervals the accredited representatives of the governments and of the commercial organizations of this continent come together with a view to interchange of experience and fostering that mutual confidence without which the development of international commerce is impossible. Your work possesses a significance far beyond the concrete problems with which you will have to deal.

Permit me in closing to combine with my welcome the confident expectation that your deliberations will redound to the benefit of all the nations of this continent.

NOTE: The President spoke at approximately 11 a.m. to an audience of some 600 delegates assembled in the Pan American Building in Washington, D.C. His address was broadcast nationally and through an international radio hookup to Latin America.

348

Letter Accepting the Resignation
of Benjamin M. Day as Commissioner of Immigration
at the Port of New York.
October 8, 1931

[Released October 8, 1931.   Dated September 22, 1931]

My dear Captain Day:

I have been holding up your letter of resignation as I was in hopes it might be withdrawn. I learn from Mr. Hilles, however, that you wish to have it accepted so I cannot do other than comply with your wish.

I take this occasion to express my appreciation for the devoted public service you have given during the past years.

Yours faithfully,

HERBERT HOOVER

[Captain Benjamin M. Day, Commissioner of Immigration, Ellis Island, N.Y.]

NOTE: Charles D. Hilles was Republican national committeeman of New York.

On the same day, the White House issued an announcement of the appointment of Edward Corsi to be Commissioner of Immigration at the Port of New York and biographical data on Mr. Corsi.

Mr. Day's letter of resignation, dated September 2, 1931, and released with the President's letter, follows:

Mr. President:

I desire to be relieved of my duties as Commissioner of Immigration in the New York District, and accordingly tender to you herewith my resignation.

I will always be appreciative of the privilege of having served during your administration.

Respectfully yours,
BENJAMIN M. DAY

[The President, The White House, Washington, D.C.]

349

Message to the National Convention
of the Morris Plan Bankers Association.
October 8, 1931

[Released October 8, 1931. Dated September 29, 1931]

My dear Mr. Ball:

On the occasion of the National Convention of the Morris Plan Bankers Association in Columbus, will you kindly express my cordial greetings and my interest in their deliberations. I am impressed with the record of the Morris Plan Banks, which in a little more than two decades have loaned more than one and one-half billion dollars to more than seven million people. This record is the best evidence of the service which they render to borrowers requiring that type of credit service. The sound principles on which the system is conducted are indicated by the maintenance of the factor of safety of both principal and interest even during a time of stress upon the country's credit facilities. These banks not only render a most practical service, but promote thrift and thereby eventually increase the patronage of banks generally. I extend my good wishes for a successful convention.

Yours faithfully,
HERBERT HOOVER

[Mr. J. Rodney Ball, President, Morris Plan Bankers Association, 431 Statler Building, Boston, Mass.]

NOTE: The message was read to the annual convention in Columbus, Ohio.

350

The President's News Conference of
October 9, 1931

PRESS RELATIONS

THE PRESIDENT. I have nothing today but background. I want to express my appreciation to the representatives of the press for the way you have handled the pretty difficult situation during the last 4 or 5 days. You contributed very materially to producing that unity of action which is essential in the presence of national difficulties of this character. I know it has been difficult for you and difficult for me in relation to the press as well. And it is always difficult to bring about a unity of view amongst discordant elements. We had plenty of difficulty in bringing unity of action amongst financial institutions by which they must make some sacrifice to the national good, some special effort. And I think we had a very remarkable occasion last Tuesday evening, when 40 public men of divergent political parties were willing to arise entirely above politics, and with a discordant note of only one or two out of the whole group, within 3 hours were able to reach that unity of action as to what amounts to a very major legislative program.

CREDIT RESOURCES

In that connection, and still as a matter of background, I am wondering if we could get clear possibly to the public what we are really trying to do. When one is dealing with complex questions a man understands by instinct perhaps more than by experience. Some instances that have come up in the vast correspondence that comes in here rather indicate what the service is that we are trying to perform. There are some sections of the country where farmers are unable to obtain credit for production purposes with even unencumbered farms, and they are unable to obtain credit to carry their commodities over, and in that way they are forced into the market. There are localities where the flour millers and the spinners are only able to secure credit from day to day for their raw material instead of buying seasonally as is the normal practice in the trade, which thrusts the burden of carrying commodities back on the farmer and limits his market. Likewise in these localities where there are difficulties the manufacturers are not able to obtain their usual credit and are compelled to reduce their labor, which contributes to unemployment.

Now, these situations arise because of the lack of the ability of the bankers to serve their communities and their lack of ability is largely due to unreasoning withdrawals of deposits. Fortunately, those areas are very limited, but the whole purpose of the plan is to mass the pool credit in sufficient volume to take care of those areas. There are some things about the banking situation that are not generally understood—that the banks of the country have probably 3½ billions, or over 3 billions at least, of eligible paper which they can turn into the Federal Reserve System at any time they like, but those are not the banks under consideration but the stronger banks out of the stress areas. So that the purpose of this mobilization of credit is not alone to take care of—I will put it the other way. The banks in stress areas of course are using their eligible paper with the Federal Reserve and the purpose of this credit pool is to make advances against noneligible paper, that is, other assets, so as not alone to give them resources to meet any unreasoning demands but perhaps of more importance altogether, to give them the courage to go on with their normal business with the feeling that they can always reach out in case they are subject to pressure. None of those measures are measures of inflation. They are measures of stemming the tide of deflation. So that all that I mean that for is perhaps some of you may want to endeavor to get this down to the understanding of the people on the street who do not ordinarily grasp the meaning of credit flow when it emanates from large institutions.

The Moratorium

There is one other background question, and that is this moratorium. I can advise you that there has been no suggestion of any general extension or postponement of moratorium. I would suggest that you reread my statement on the 20th of June, which was referred to in the statement we gave out on Tuesday morning. In that statement there appears a very definite statement that the basis of settlement of our debts was the capacity to pay under normal conditions. And it is consistent with our own policies and principles that we take into consideration abnormal situations which exist. I stated there I was sure the American people had no desire to attempt to extract any sum of money beyond the capacity of any debtor to pay, and that in the view of the administration, supported at that time as on this occasion generally, that we had to recognize the situation that exists. That complete year's postponement was an emergency measure to take care of an emergency situation for the normal development of readjustments that affect the economic situation. I have the same thought now, that it is not customary amongst decent individuals or amongst nations to require a debtor to make payment of any kind beyond the capacity of the individual or nation to pay, but that does not imply for one moment that individuals and nations should not pay their full obligations within their capacity. In fact, that is the very foundation of both morals and economic life. It is not a subject I care to make any public statements about, or to give out anything out on authority from here. But I thought you might be glad to know that that is the basis on which we are acting. We are not doing anything revolutionary at the moment.

And that is all that I have got on my mind today.

NOTE: President Hoover's two hundred and fourteenth news conference was held in the White House at 4 p.m. on Friday, October 9, 1931.

351

Remarks to a Delegation of the Women's International League for Peace and Freedom. *October 10, 1931*

"I APPRECIATE deeply your coming to me. You realize as well as I the favorable attitude of the President on the limitation of world armaments. I am grateful for your effort to mobilize public opinion. No head of a government can go beyond the support that can be gained from public opinion in a world where democracy rules. There is no statesman at the head of any government in the world today that has not expressed himself as desirous of attaining these ends.

"I am glad to receive your petitions and will act as their custodian until you wish to use them elsewhere."

NOTE: The President spoke at 12:45 p.m. to a delegation of the United States Section of the league in the East Room at the White House. Prior to speaking, the President received a universal disarmament petition bearing some 150,000 signatures.

352

Message on National Pharmacy Week.
October 10, 1931

[Released October 10, 1931.   Dated September 25, 1931]

My dear Mr. Mayes:

The observance of National Pharmacy Week, October 11th to 17th, is an appropriate time to recognize the service which pharmacy renders to the public health. Research in scientific laboratories constantly adds to the armamentorium of our health forces. The drug stores of the land are the channels through which these new resources for treatment of the sick and the prevention of disease are brought promptly within reach of the people. Pharmacists are the indispensable allies of the physicians. The importance of high standards of product and professional practice in pharmacy may well be more generally recognized, and Pharmacy Week is a commendable educational effort to that end.

Yours faithfully,
HERBERT HOOVER

[Mr. Herbert R. Mayes, Editor, American Druggist, 57th Street at Eighth Avenue, New York City]

NOTE: The message was made public in conjunction with the beginning of National Pharmacy Week.

353

Message to President Chiang Chung-cheng on China's Independence Day.
October 10, 1931

I EXTEND to you and your fellow countrymen my sincere felicitations on this anniversary of the Republic of China.

HERBERT HOOVER

[His Excellency Chiang Chung-cheng, President of the National Government of the Republic of China, Nanking, China]

NOTE: Chiang Chung-cheng was Chiang Kai-shek.

354

Statement on Columbus Day.
October 12, 1931

THE ACCOMPLISHMENTS of Christopher Columbus can never lose their color and significance. Recurrence of the anniversary of his discovery of America recalls afresh the triumph of his great adventure and its import to the whole world. In him action matched imagination and courage conquered all obstacles. His pioneering spirit symbolizes the tradition of the nation built in the New World which he discovered. On the anniversary of his landing we not only pay tribute to his genius, but may draw inspiration from the vast influence of the New World upon civilization itself.

NOTE: The statement was read at the 35th charitable festival of the Italian Benevolent Society, held in the Central Opera House in New York City.

355

Radio Remarks to the Annual Convention of the International Association of Chiefs of Police. *October 12, 1931*

IT IS MY PRIVILEGE on behalf of the Government to greet the delegates to the 38th annual convention of the International Association of Police Chiefs meeting at St. Petersburg. I wish to add a cordial welcome to those delegates and guests who have come from beyond our shores.

In the United States a major responsibility rests upon the shoulders of our Chiefs of Police. Ours is a form of government where the task and responsibility of maintenance of organized society through its never-ending battle against crime rests upon each local community. The Chiefs of Police occupy a position of high command in that service. In not a few of our communities the police have been subject to criticism. That criticism arises from the exception and not the rule in police conduct. Moreover, there is a sentimentalism in some people which makes popular heroes out of criminals which needs replacement by a sentimentalism that makes a popular hero of the policeman for the courage and devotion he shows in protection of our citizens. Instead of the glorification of cowardly gangsters we need the glorification of policemen who do their duty and who give their lives in public protection.

The police perform an unending task, not alone in the mothering of the children on our streets and in the good humored dissolution of traffic jams, but in this incessant war against criminals. If the police had the vigilant, universal backing of public opinion in their communities, if they had the implacable support of the prosecuting authorities and the courts, if our criminal laws in their endeavor to protect the innocent did not furnish loopholes through which irresponsible, yet clever, criminal lawyers daily find devices of escape for the guilty, I am convinced that our police would stamp out the excessive crime and remove the worldwide disrepute which has disgraced some of our great cities.

The police by instinct are the enemies of gang activities, robberies, holdups, and ruthless murder. But so long as criminals can proceed with the smug assurance that they can defeat the law there is a constant discouragement to the police. I wonder at times that they maintain the vigilance and courage they do against the odds with which they have to contend.

I extend to you my cordial good wishes for a helpful convention. I know there will emerge from collective counsel at your meeting an increased skill and resourcefulness and deeper devotion in advancement of public welfare. I look forward confidently to the day when the moral forces of every community will rally to your support in the fight against crime everywhere.

NOTE: The President spoke at 12:45 p.m. from the Cabinet Room in the White House via radio to the association's 38th annual convention in St. Petersburg, Fla. The National Broadcasting Company and the Columbia Broadcasting System radio networks carried the remarks.

A reading copy of this item with holograph changes by the President is available for examination at the Herbert Hoover Presidential Library.

356

Message to the Annual Safety Congress of the National Safety Council.
October 12, 1931

[Released October 12, 1931.   Dated September 24, 1931]

My dear Mr. Bergquist:

Although substantial progress has been made in diminishing industrial accident rates, one cannot complacently contemplate the fact that there are still 99,000 accidental deaths a year in the United States as well as a vast number of injuries. There is clearly a tremendous field still for organized efforts to promote accident prevention, especially in the home and on the highways, and to a considerable extent in industry, in spite of a decrease of one-third in industrial accidents in the past two decades. The fact that there are 33,000 motor vehicle deaths annually in the United States is a challenge to the efforts of safety organizations and the cooperation of every motor-vehicle operator. The National Safety Council renders a conspicuously important service in promoting safety measures. Please present to its members gathered for the annual Safety Congress in Chicago my congratulations on their achievements. I trust that the meeting may be conducive to still greater effort to safeguard human life and property.

Yours faithfully,
HERBERT HOOVER

[Mr. C. W. Bergquist, President, National Safety Council, Chicago, Ill.]

NOTE: The message was read to the 20th annual congress, meeting in the Hotel Stevens in Chicago, Ill.

357

Message on the Formation of the Committee of One Hundred in Dayton, Ohio. *October 14, 1931*

[Released October 14, 1931.   Dated October 13, 1931]

I CONGRATULATE Dayton upon its formation of the Committee of One Hundred and I wish to express my appreciation of your leadership in the movement. I understand the immediate purpose of this community movement on the part of Dayton is to cooperate in furtherance of the request I made last week for "national unity of action in an American way to assist business, employment and agriculture." Dayton's method of responding to this emergency is characteristically American in its quick initiative, its energy and its flexibility to local conditions and needs. The fundamental essence of your plan is community action carried out through voluntary cooperation. That is the American way.

HERBERT HOOVER

[Hon. James M. Cox, Dayton, Ohio]

68-611 O - 76 - 35

NOTE: The message was read to 100 Dayton citizens, representing commercial, industrial, and civic groups, at a meeting called by former Governor James M. Cox.

358

The President's News Conference of
October 16, 1931

GOVERNMENT EXPENDITURES

THE PRESIDENT. I have received a number of questions about naval expenditure. Apparently the press is much more interested in the Navy than they are in the other departments, where equal reduction of expenditure is under consideration.

I have received the proposals of the high officials of the Navy of their plans for reducing expenditures. They are being considered in the light of maintaining efficiency in the Navy itself. As I said, such plans are underway in every department of the Government. All of these proposals of the departments are part of the process of final working out of the budget. No conclusions have been reached as to any particular proposed reduction in expenditure of the departments as yet. Final decision will not be reached until the budget is ready for presentation to Congress itself. All of the principal officers of the Government are cooperating to bring down expenditures. As a matter of fact, the processes of the budget are somewhat different this year from normal in that we have asked the departments to take into full consideration the economic situation of the country and to propose specific methods by which they can cooperate. In times when the income of the people is reduced and when taxes and loans stifle economic recovery, there is only one fiscal policy and that is to reduce the expenditure of the Government to the last cent consonant with the obligations of the Government itself.

There are two difficulties that confront us in reducing expenditures. The first is the large proportion of Federal expenditures that are irreducible. You will recollect that the interest must be paid on the public debt; statutory reduction of the debt must be continued; the pay allowances, pensions to veterans, pensions to civil servants, and a number of other expenditures are statutory, and they comprise nearly 2 billions of expenditure that is impossible of reconsideration. So that any reductions in Government expenditures have to be applied to one-half of the budget.

The second difficulty is that the Federal Government must make its contribution to expand employment so long as this situation continues. That is a little difficult to interpret for the prospect of a budget beginning the 1st of next July. I am in hopes that a change in the situation by that time will make it possible for us to lighten up the burden of the Government in that direction.

I realize that governmental economy as a whole is strongly desired by the public, yet every variety of expenditure has its adherents. They are all naturally solicitous that their special project be continued, even in times of national difficulty, and they are somewhat impatient with reductions and deferments and delays of projects. Public opinion supports drastic economies in general, and it will need to reach out into every special project and drive. And what is more, the public must support the administration—should support the administration in discouragement of special interests who desire to expand services of the Government in these periods. The essential services of the Government must and will be maintained, but these are times, when we have a large deficit facing the country, that even meritorious projects must and will be deferred.

COTTON

I have received word today of the plans worked out by the Southern banks under the leadership in cooperation with the Federal Farm Board in a definite plan for pooling a certain proportion of the cotton crop and financing the farmer members of that pool. All of which is constructive action of the type that the country needs. That is, that the banking community and the commercial community should join together in cooperation with governmental agencies to solve problems of this character.

I understand further meetings have taken place in the South in connection with these plans, and I am in hopes that they will meet with success.

I haven't anything further today that is going on around the Government, but you may find it in the departments if you can.

NOTE: President Hoover's two hundred and fifteenth news conference was held in the White House at 12 noon on Friday, October 16, 1931.

On the same day, the White House issued a text of the President's statement on Government expenditures (see Item 359).

At a conference in New Orleans on October 12, representatives of the Federal Farm Board, the American Cotton Co-operative Association, and the banking institutions of the cotton-growing States reached an agreement to hold some 6,800,000 bales of cotton off the market until July 31, 1932. Under the terms of the agreement the banks promised to extend loans secured by cotton up to a figure of 3,500,000 bales, the Federal Farm Board to finance the holding of 2 million bales by the American Cotton Co-operative Association, and the Federal Farm Board's Cotton Stabilization Corporation to continue holding its accumulation of 1,300,000 bales. The plan was implemented in November 1931, following ratification by the State bankers' associations.

359

Statement on Government Expenditures.
October 16, 1931

THE PRESIDENT said:

"I have received the proposals of the high officials of the Navy of plans for reduction of expenditures. They are being considered in the full light of maintained efficiency of the Department. Such studies and revisions are equally in progress in every other department of the Government. The proposals of all the departments will require study and consideration. No conclusions have been reached on any particular proposed expenditure or economy. Final decision will not be reached until the final budget is presented to Congress. All of the principal officers of the Government are cooperating to bring about reductions. In times when the income of the people is reduced and when taxes or loans may stifle economic recovery there is only one course of sound fiscal policy, and that is to reduce the expenditure of the Government to the last cent consonant with the obligations of the Government.

"There are two great difficulties which confront us in programs of reduced expenditures. The first is the very large proportion of Federal expenditures that are irreducible. We must meet interest payments on the statutory redemption of the public debt; we must pay allowances and pensions to veterans and pensions to civil servants, et cetera. Thus over 2 billion of the Federal budget is in fixed obligations, and such reductions as we can bring about must need be concentrated on less than one-half of the budget.

"The second difficulty is that the Federal Government must make its contribution to expanded employment so long as the present situation continues.

"I fully realize that while governmental economy as a whole is strongly desired by the public, yet every variety of expenditure has its adherents throughout the country, all of whom are naturally solicitous that their special project should be continued even in times of national difficulty, and they are impatient of reduction or deferment or delays of their projects. Public opinion in support of drastic economies will need to reach into these directions. It must extend also to discouragement of special interests desirous of securing new expenditures for the special projects. The essential services of the Government must and will be maintained, but these are times when, with the large deficit facing the country, even meritorious projects can, must, and will be deferred."

360

Radio Address to the Nation
on Unemployment Relief.
October 18, 1931

My fellow citizens:

This broadcast tonight marks the beginning of the mobilization of the whole Nation for a great undertaking to provide security for those of our citizens and their families who, through no fault of their own, face unemployment and privation during the coming winter. Its success depends upon the sympathetic and generous action of every man and woman in our country. No one with a spark of human sympathy can contemplate unmoved the possibilites of suffering that can crush many of our unfortunate fellow Americans if we shall fail them.

The depression has been deepened by events from abroad which are beyond the control either of our citizens or our Government. Although it is but a passing incident in our national life, we must meet the consequences in unemployment which arise from it with that completeness of effort and that courage and spirit for which citizenship in this Nation always has and always must stand.

As an important part of our plans for national unity of action in this emergency I have created a great national organization under the leadership of Mr. Walter Gifford to cooperate with the Governors, the State and the local agencies, and with the many national organizations of business, of labor, and of welfare, with the churches and our fraternal and patriotic societies so that the countless streams of human helpfulness which have been the mainstay of our country in all emergencies may be directed wisely and effectively.

Over a thousand towns and cities have well-organized and experienced unemployment relief committees, community chests, or other agencies for the efficient administration of this relief. With this occasion begins the nationwide movement to aid each of these volunteer organizations in securing the funds to meet their task over the forthcoming winter.

This organized effort is our opportunity to express our sympathy, to lighten the burdens of the heavy laden, and to cast sunshine into the habitation of despair.

The amounts sought by the committee in your town or city are in part to provide work, for it is through work that we wish to give help in keeping with the dignity of American manhood and womanhood. But much of their funds are necessary to provide direct relief to those families where circumstances and ill fortune can only be met by direct assistance. Included in many community appeals are the sums necessary to the vital measures of health and character building, the maintenance of which were never more necessary than in these times.

The Federal Government is taking its part in aid to unemployment through the advancement and enlargement of public works in all parts of the Nation. Through these works, it is today providing a livelihood for nearly 700,000 families. All immigration has been stopped in order that our burdens should not be increased by unemployed immigrants from abroad. Measures have been adopted which will assure normal credits and thus stimulate employment in industry, in commerce, and in agriculture. The employers in national industries have spread work amongst their employees so that the maximum number may participate in the wages which are available. Our States, our counties, our municipalities, through the expansion of their public works and through tax-supported relief activities, are doing their full part. Yet, beyond all this, there is a margin of relief which must be provided by voluntary action. Through these agencies Americans must meet the demands of national conscience that there be no hunger or cold amongst our people.

Similar organization and generous support were provided during the past winter in localities where it was necessary. Under the leadership of Colonel Woods, we succeeded in the task of that time. We demonstrated that it could be done. But in many localities our need will be greater this winter than a year ago. While many are affected by the depression, the number who are threatened with privation is a minor percentage of our whole people.

This task is not beyond the ability of these thousands of community organizations to solve. Each local organization from its experience last winter and summer has formulated careful plans and made estimates completely to meet the need of that community. I am confident that the generosity of each community will fully support these estimates. The sum of these community efforts will meet the needs of the Nation as a whole.

To solve this problem in this way accords with the fundamental sense of responsibility, neighbor to neighbor, community to community, upon which our Nation is founded.

The possible misery of helpless people gives me more concern than any other trouble that this depression has brought upon us. It is with these convictions in mind that I have the responsibility of opening this nationwide appeal to citizens in each community that they provide the funds with which, community by community, this task shall be met.

The maintenance of a spirit of mutual self-help through voluntary giving, through the responsibility of local government, is of infinite importance to the future of America. Everyone who aids to the full extent of his ability is giving support to the very foundations of our democracy. Everyone who from a sympathetic heart gives to these services is giving hope and courage to some deserving family. Everyone who aids in this service will have lighted a beacon of help on the stormy coast of human adversity.

The success and the character of nations are to be judged by the ideals and the spirit of its people. Time and again the American people have demonstrated a spiritual quality, a capacity for unity of action, of generosity, a certainty of results in time of emergency that have made them great in the annals of the history of all nations. This is the time and this is the occasion when we must arouse that idealism, that spirit, that determination, that unity of action, from which there can be no failure in this primary obligation of every man to his neighbor and of a nation to its citizens, that none who deserve shall suffer.

I would that I possessed the art of words to fix the real issue with which the troubled world is faced in the mind and heart of every American man and woman. Our country and the world are today involved in more than a financial crisis. We are faced with the primary question of human relations, which reaches to the very depths of organized society and to the very depths of human conscience. This civilization and this great complex, which we call American life, is builded and can alone survive upon the translation into individual action of that fundamental philosophy announced by the Savior 19 centuries ago. Part of our national suffering today is from failure to observe these primary yet inexorable laws of human relationship. Modern society cannot survive with the defense of Cain, "Am I my brother's keeper?"

No governmental action, no economic doctrine, no economic plan or project can replace that God-imposed responsibility of the individual man and woman to their neighbors. That is a vital part of the very soul of a people. If we shall gain in this spirit from this painful time, we shall have created a greater and more glorious America. The trial of it is here now. It is a trial of the heart and the conscience, of individual men and women.

In a little over a month we shall celebrate our time-honored festival of Thanksgiving. I appeal to the American people to make November 26 next the outstanding Thanksgiving Day in the history of the United States; that we may say on that day that America has again demonstrated her ideals; that we have each of us contributed our full part; that we in each of our communities have given full assurance against hunger and cold amongst our people; that upon this Thanksgiving Day we have removed the fear of the forthcoming winter from the hearts of all who are suffering and in distress—that we are our brother's keeper.

I am on my way to participate in the commemoration of the victory of Yorktown. It is a name which brings a glow of pride to every American. It recalls the final victory of our people after years of sacrifice and privation. This Nation passed through Valley Forge and came to Yorktown.

NOTE: The President spoke at 6:21 p.m. from the Commandant's residence at Fort Monroe, Va. The National Broadcasting Company and the Columbia Broadcasting System radio networks carried the address to the Nation.

The address inaugurated a 6-week campaign to raise local relief funds. Cooperating in the drive were some 1,000 local committees or community chests plus the advertising media, the film industry, and an array of public speakers.

The above text is a transcript taken from a sound recording of the address. An advance text of the address was issued on the same day.

361

Message of Sympathy on the Death of Thomas Alva Edison.
October 18, 1931

MR. EDISON was as great in his brave fight for life as he was in the achievements which have made the whole world his debtor. I mourn his passing not only as one of the greatest men our nation has produced but as a personal friend. On behalf of the nation I express the profound sympathy of all our people and Mrs. Hoover and I personally extend our deepest sympathy to you and your son and daughter in your irreparable loss.

HERBERT HOOVER

[Mrs. Thomas A. Edison, Llewellyn Park, West Orange, N.J.]

NOTE: Thomas Alva Edison was a noted scientist and inventor.

362

Statement on the Death of Thomas Alva Edison. *October 18, 1931*

THE PRESIDENT said:

"It is given to few men of any age, nation, or calling to become the benefactor of all humanity. That distinction came abundantly to Thomas Alva Edison whose death in his 85th year has ended a life of courage and outstanding achievement. His lifelong search for truth, fructifying in more than a thousand inventions, made him the greatest inventor our Nation has produced, and revolutionized civilization itself. He multiplied light and dissolved darkness; he added to whole wealth of nations. He was great not only in his scientific creative instinct and insight but did more than any other American to place invention on an organized basis of the utilization of raw materials of pure science and discovery. He was a rare genius. He has been a precious asset to the whole world.

"Every American owes a personal debt to him. It is not only a debt for great benefactions which he has brought to every American, but also a debt for the honor he brought to our country. By his own genius and effort he rose from a newsboy and telegrapher to the position of leadership amongst men. His life has been a constant stimulant to confidence that our institutions hold open the door of opportunity to those who would enter. He possessed a modesty, a kindliness, a staunchness of character rare among men. His death leaves thousands bereft of a friend, the Nation bereft of one of its notable citizens, and the world bereft of

492

one of its greatest benefactors. I mourn his passing as a personal friend over a quarter of a century."

363

Message on the 19th Anniversary of the German Evangelical Church of Brooklyn, New York. *October 18, 1931*

[Released October 18, 1931.   Dated October 16, 1931]

My dear Mr. Peters:

Please present to the members of the German Evangelical Church of Brooklyn, my hearty congratulations on the ninetieth anniversary of the establishment of the church. I wish it all success in continuing its contribution to the spiritual advancement of the community.

Yours faithfully,

HERBERT HOOVER

[Rev. Herbert H. Peters, Pastor, German Evangelical Church, 61 Schermerhorn Street, Brooklyn, N.Y.]

NOTE: The message was read at ceremonies commemorating the church's anniversary.

364

Address on the 150th Anniversary of the Surrender of General Cornwallis at Yorktown, Virginia. *October 19, 1931*

Our guests and my fellow countrymen:

No person here present, no schoolchild of the millions listening in on this occasion, needs reminder of the significance of the Battle of Yorktown. If we judge it by the standard of battles in which the contrary result would have essentially varied the whole course of history, then it becomes one of the very few decisive battles in the history of the world.

Six years of war for independence had sorely exhausted the resources, depleted the forces, and sapped the support of that group of men whose genius gave freedom to our country. With the inroads the mother country had made in subjection of the northern colonies, it is extremely doubtful if the struggle for independence could have succeeded had Washington lost at Yorktown. Certainly with the victory at Yorktown, our independence was won.

In military history, Yorktown is distinguished as one of the great battles in which land and sea forces coordinated. The naval cooperation was furnished by France, herself also at war with Great Britain. For that cooperation we have held during these 150 years a grateful remembrance. That sentiment, continuing down through our history, finally flowered in the cooperation which the American people gave to France in their defense against an overwhelming enemy. The presence of Marshal Pétain and General Pershing here today symbolizes this second comradeship in arms, so magnificently begun by De Grasse, Lafayette, and Rochambeau.

We assemble here to celebrate a victory for our own independence, but not essentially a victory over the British. The long span of history will interpret the American War for Independence and this battle more in the light of a struggle amongst English-speaking people for the establishment in government of an extension of a common philosophy of human rights begun at Runnymede. The principles and ideas for which America contended had many adherents and much sympathy in England at that time. The victory of the Americans gave impulse to the new order throughout the world; and while the sovereignties of America and England definitely diverged at Yorktown, yet the march of the ideals for which the Americans fought also went forward and triumphed in England itself.

The common acceptance of many of these principles has aligned the English-speaking people side by side for a century of peace, concord, sympathy, and devotion to a liberty defined and assured under a reign of law. The triumph of these new ideas in America strengthened the impulses for liberty in France.

"It is not to be doubted," wrote Lafayette, in sending the keys of the Bastille to Washington, "that the principles of America opened the Bastille."

Our purpose today is to pay homage to a glorious event in our national history. Among many benedictions offered to us by this ceremony, one is renewed acquaintance with the spirit of George Washington. The campaign which led to its final climax here established his military genius. It was the crown of victory which placed his name among the great commanders of all time.

It is not too much to say that without Washington the war for independence would not have been won.

Washington's greatness was far more than a great general; it lay in his soul and his character. Of him, in sober, critical judgment, a gifted modern historian, James Truslow Adams, has written: "In the travail of war and revolution, America had brought forth a man to be ranked with the greatest and noblest of any age in all the world. There have been no greater generals in the field and statesmen in the cabinet in our own and other nations. There has been no greater character. When we think of Washington, it is not as a military leader, nor as executive or diplomat. We think of the man who by sheer force of character held a divided and disorganized country together until victory was achieved, and who, after peace was won, still held his disunited countrymen by their love and respect and admiration for himself until a nation was welded into enduring strength and unity."

This national shrine stands for more than a glorious battle. It is a shrine which symbolizes things of the spirit. The victory of Yorktown was a victory for mankind. It was another blaze in the great trail of human freedom. Through these ideas and ideals the minds of a people were liberated, their exertions and accomplishments stimulated.

The primary national consequence of the independence we finally won here was the release of our national mind from all hampering restraints put upon us by subjection to another nation and an older civilization. Here America became free to be America. We acquired the

495

opportunity for unrestrained development of a government and culture that should be our own. It has made possible the realization of those visions of government and organized society which arose among us as a result of individuality of temperment born of the frontiers of a new continent.

If we look back over these 150 years, we see our Nation marking progress with every decade. From these communities of 3 million people scattered along the Atlantic seaboard, it has grown to more than 120 million. It has marked the full sweep of the continent to the Pacific Ocean with magnificent cities, homes, and farms, with a degree of comfort and security hitherto unknown in human history. It has grown in education and knowledge, from which invention and discovery have been accelerated, with every year bringing a harvest of new comforts and inspirations. It has unfolded a great experiment in human society, builded new and powerful institutions born of new ideas and new ideals, new visions of human relations. It has attained a wider diffusion of liberty and happiness and more of material things than humanity has ever known before. It has attained a security amongst nations by which no thought ever comes that an enemy may step within our borders.

While temporary dislocations have come to us because of the World War, we must not forget that our forefathers met similar obstacles to progress time and again, and yet the Nation has swept forward to ever-increasing strength. The unparalleled rise of America has not been the result of riches in lands, forests, or mines; it sprung from the ideas and ideals which liberated minds and stimulated the spirits of men. In those ideas and ideals are the soul of the people. No American can review this vast pageant of progress without confidence and faith, without courage, strength, and resolution for the future.

Selfishness is poison in the veins of human life. Wholehearted unselfishness makes the real beauty of holiness for men and nations. In hard times we are always tempted to think we must shut up our hearts of fellowship and human feeling, that we must look out for ourselves. But in hard times we must open our hearts and consider our neighbors and brothers. We *are* coming to our national thanksgiving festival, but we cannot fitly give thanks to the Father of us all if we close our eyes to our brother whom we see to be in need. Hearts that are grateful toward God must not be hard toward their fellow men. We are all of us His children and must now bear ourselves toward our brothers as His children should. Thus only may we look for His "Well done." And those words I want the United States now to hear.

NOTE: The President spoke at 11 a.m. to an estimated 30,000 people gathered at the surrender site. Included in the assembly were members of the Cabinet, Governors, military and diplomatic officials, and a number of distinguished guests. During the afternoon, the President, accompanied by Marshal Henri Pétain and General John J. Pershing, viewed a reenactment of the Yorktown surrender.

365

Remarks at a Luncheon of the Yorktown Sesquicentennial Commission in Yorktown, Virginia.
October 19, 1931

IT IS BOTH my duty and pleasure to express the appreciation of your many guests to both the Commission and the people of Virginia for your bounteous hospitality. The hospitality of Virginia has been the highest expression of courtesy in our country now for more than two centuries.

No one steps upon the soil of Virginia without inspiration from the part she has played in the winning of our liberties and the building of our institutions. It needs only to be remarked that from within a few score miles of this shrine have come five Presidents of the United States. And high character and deep patriotism which directed the events from which sprung these shrines have also been the inspiration of national leaders throughout our history.

We thank you not alone for fine courtesy but for the inspiration which comes from Virginia.

NOTE: During luncheon ceremonies, William and Mary College awarded the President an honorary degree.

A reading copy of this item written in the President's hand is available for examination at the Herbert Hoover Presidential Library.

366

Statement on a National Tribute to Thomas Alva Edison.
October 20, 1931

THE PRESIDENT said:

"The grief of every American in the passing of one of the great benefactors of humanity has manifested itself in the suggestion from hundreds of citizens that the Nation should join in a solemn tribute to the memory of Thomas Alva Edison.

"In response to this universal desire to pay personal respect to Mr. Edison's memory, I suggest that all individuals should extinguish their lights for one minute on Wednesday evening, October 21, at 7 o'clock Pacific time, 8 o'clock mountain time, 9 o'clock central time and 10 o'clock eastern time. It is my understanding that the broadcasting companies will undertake a brief program in respect to Mr. Edison's memory at this moment.

"The suggestion had been made that the electrical current at generating plants should be turned off at these hours, but on inquiry I find—and this is confirmed by Thomas Edison, Jr.—that this would constitute a great peril to life throughout the country because of the many services dependent upon electrical power in protection from fire, the operation of water supply, sanitation, elevators, operations in hospitals and the vast number of activities which, if halted even for an instant, would result in death somewhere in the country. It is not, therefore, advisable. This demonstration of the dependence of the country upon electrical current for its life and health is in itself a monument to Mr. Edison's genius."

NOTE: On Tuesday, October 20, 1931, Thomas Alva Edison was buried at Rosedale Cemetery in East Orange, N.J. Lou Henry Hoover attended the funeral services.

367

Message Welcoming Prime Minister Pierre Laval of France.
October 21, 1931

AS YOU NEAR the shores of the United States, I take great pleasure in extending to you a most cordial welcome in my own name and in that of my fellow country men.

HERBERT HOOVER

[His Excellency Pierre Laval, President of the Council of Ministers of France, *SS. Ile de France*]

NOTE: Prime Minister Laval and his daughter Josette arrived at New York on Thursday, October 22, 1931. The Prime Minister's entourage included economic. financial, and military experts as wel as a group of French newspaper correspondents.

368

White House Statement on Discussions With Prime Minister Laval.
October 23, 1931

BOTH the President and Premier Laval wish it made clear that the conversations upon which they are engaged are solely in respect of such policies as each of the two governments can develop to expedite recovery from the world economic depression. There is no remote basis whatever for statements as to "demands," "terms of settlement," or any other like discussions. Happily, there are no controversies to be settled between France and America. None such exist. The sole purpose of these conversations is the earnest, frank exchange of views with view to finding common ground for helpful action in the promotion of constructive progress in the world.

499

369

The President's News Conference of
October 24, 1931

PRIME MINISTER LAVAL'S VISIT

THE PRESIDENT. I am very glad to welcome the correspondents of the French press to the United States. We are glad that you may enlarge your acquaintance in our country and amongst our people.

I wanted to express the appreciation that I feel and that I know the whole country feels at the coming of the President of the Council of Ministers of France. He has done a great honor to our country, and especially so in these times of very grave responsibilities. I am confident that his visit will result in profits for the future. I need not repeat to you that the purpose of our conversations has been to find fields from which contributions can be made to the enlargement of good will and confidence both in the relations of both our countries and in the economic world.

I have sometimes said that we are suffering more from frozen confidence than we are from frozen securities. And the press of our country plays a major part in the development of good will and such confidence as the world is today in need of, in search for fields for cooperation and constructive action. And I trust that the French press may carry away with you pleasant recollections of the United States, and that you will realize the thorough good will and the friendliness of the American people.

The President of the Council and myself have been engaged in drafting up a preliminary draft—a short statement to be issued upon Mr. Laval's departure, and we are to have a further meeting at 10:30 tomorrow to consider that draft.

Further than that, I haven't anything more that I can tell you today.

NOTE: President Hoover's two hundred and sixteenth news conference was held in the White House at 3 p.m. on Saturday, October 24, 1931.

On the same day, the White House issued a text of the President's statement on the visit of Prime Minister Laval (see Item 370).

500

370

Statement on the Visit
of Prime Minister Laval.
October 24, 1931

THE PRESIDENT said:

"The President of the Council of Ministers of France has done us great honor in coming to our country, especially so in these times of grave responsibilities. I am confident that his visit will be profitable in results for the future.

"I need not repeat that the purpose of our conversations has been to find fields from which contribution can be made to enlargement of confidence in the relations between nations and in the economic world. I have on some occasions stated that the world is suffering more from frozen confidence than from frozen securities.

"The press plays a major part in the development of the good will on which such confidence must rest by its search for fields in which cooperation and constructive action can be evolved. I trust that you of the French press may carry away with you pleasant recollections of your visit and that you will realize the good will and friendliness of the American people."

371

Joint Statement With Prime Minister Laval.
October 25, 1931

THE TRADITIONAL friendship between the United States and France, the absence of all controversy between our two Governments, a record of many events in collaboration toward peace of the world, embracing among its recent phases the adoption of the Kellogg-Briand Pact, render it possible and opportune for the representatives of our Governments to explore every aspect of the many problems in which we are mutually interested.

Indeed the duty of statesmen is not to overlook any means of practical cooperation for the common good. This is particularly true at a time when the world looks for leadership in relief from a depression which reaches into countless homes in every land. Relations of mutual confidence between governments have the most important bearing upon speeding the recovery which we seek. We have engaged upon that mission with entire frankness. We have made real progress.

We canvassed the economic situation in the world, the trends in international relations bearing upon it; the problems of the forthcoming conference for limitation and reduction of armaments; the effect of the depression on payments under intergovernmental debts; the stabilization of international exchanges and other financial and economic subjects.

An informal and cordial discussion has served to outline with greater precision the nature of the problems. It has not been the purpose of either of us to engage in commitments binding our governments, but rather, through development of fact, to enable each country to act more effectively in its own field.

It is our joint purpose that the conference for limitation of armaments will not fail to take advantage of the great opportunity which presents itself and that it will be capable of meeting what is in reality its true mission, that is, the organization on a firm foundation of permanent peace.

Insofar as intergovernmental obligations are concerned we recognize that prior to the expiration of the Hoover year of postponement, some agreement regarding them may be necessary covering the period of business depression, as to the terms and conditions of which the two governments make all reservations. The initiative in this matter should be taken at an early date by the European powers principally concerned within the framework of the agreements existing prior to July 1, 1931.

Our especial emphasis has been upon the more important means through which the efforts of our governments could be exerted toward restoration of economic stability and confidence. Particularly we are convinced of the importance of monetary stability as an essential factor in the restoration of normal economic life in the world in which the maintenance of the gold standard in France and the United States will serve as a major influence.

It is our intent to continue to study methods for the maintenance of stability in international exchanges.

While in the short time at our disposal it has not been possible to formulate definite programs, we find that we view the nature of these financial and economic problems in the same light and that this understanding on our part should serve to pave the way for helpful action by our respective governments.

372

Radio Remarks to the Methodist Ecumenical Congress.
October 25, 1931

I AM very happy to speak briefly to the representatives of world Methodism assembled in Atlanta. I sincerely regret that public duties make it impossible for me to accept your invitation to address you in person.

Your conference meets at a time of universal but temporary difficulties. No country represented in your body is exempt from conditions that are trying and difficult. Unemployment walks before you as something much more real than a specter. It presents not simply an economic difficulty but an acute problem for human beings.

Crime and lawlessness undoubtedly will engage your serious attention not simply as problems of law but as problems of life. I am sure you have been sobered by the state of the world. I am equally sure you will not yield to despair or let your courage and faith fail.

Governments have their normal limitations. They must depend largely upon churches and schools to create, preserve, and increase the spiritual and moral basis essential to the life of the states themselves. They must have the cooperation of bodies like yours, of all religious faiths alike, working in their proper sphere, in the making of necessary attitudes and the creation of essential human tempers, such as a keen, quick consciousness of human needs and a high sense of human values. With

you lies a great responsibility in negation of that spiritual laissez faire—
that I am not my brother's keeper. Governments are tested at last by
their attitudes to the welfare of men and women. No thoughtful person
in a place of high trust can forget the dramatic picture, drawn by the
Great Teacher, of nations being sent away into torment because they
had neglected the sick, the naked, the hungry, and the unfortunate.
Hardly anything in modern civil life is more encouraging than the new
human feeling, the deep human interest now so widespread among
governments.

In this devotion to human life they gladly recognize the real assistance and leadership of the churches, which constantly hold before their
governments the ideals of courage and charity, sympathy, honor, gentleness, goodness, and faith. The governments know that the life of the
world cannot be saved if the soul of the world is allowed to be lost.

The age in which we live has seen marvelous material achievements,
and we cannot tell what new victories and discoveries lie just ahead of
us. But all this brings to human life a problem of its own—the problem
of keeping our physical achievements from mastering us and our material possessions from controlling us. And we must depend upon the
churches to help men and women everywhere to see that life does not
consist in the abundance of things, that along with devotion to men's
physical well-being must run the eternal purpose to keep the soul of the
world alive and regnant.

And I am sure you will let me say that the churches in every land
must never fail to help the governments to establish and maintain plain,
simple righteousness.

The kinds of evil now rampant in all lands are not alone a menace
to government. They are destructive to all that human life for which
governments and churches alike exist. All crimes are crimes against
human interest and welfare. The centuries have taught no lesson more
plainly than that righteousness exalts nations and evil breaks them
down.

May I close this brief message with a word upon a theme very close
to my heart and I believe equally close to yours? I refer to peace among

504

all men that dwell on the Earth, to a future free from the horrors, the wrongs, and the results of wars between nations. It seems strange and incredible that after all the centuries of man's experience with war we still have to discuss it and to argue against it. It seems even more strange that with all the crushing burdens resting upon every nation because of wars we still make progress against them at snail's pace. The nations groan under taxation, people in all lands suffer daily from economic depression, governments are perplexed—and yet we go on using incalculable sums in evident dread of those that may come upon us. A new mind must be made in the world on this subject; a new spirit must be created within the nations and between the nations. And I appeal to you as representatives of Methodists everywhere to unite with all other lovers of good will and followers of the Prince of Peace for the making of human brotherhood, in which the peace of God shall prevail in the lives of men.

I sincerely thank you for this privilege of speaking to you and wish you all the richest blessings of Earth and Heaven.

NOTE: The President spoke at 4:45 p.m. from the Cabinet Room in the White House to the Methodist Ecumenical Congess, meeting in Atlanta, Ga. The remarks were carried over a nationwide radio hookup.

A reading copy of this item with holograph changes by the President is available for examination at the Herbert Hoover Presidential Library.

373

White House Statement on the Polish Corridor.
October 25, 1931

A PRESS STATEMENT that the President has proposed any revision of the Polish Corridor is absolutely without foundation. The President has made no suggestions of any such character.

374

Message on the 25th Anniversary
of the Church of the Good Shepherd,
Brooklyn, New York.
October 25, 1931

[Released October 25, 1931.   Dated October 23, 1931]

PLEASE present my hearty congratulations to the members of the Church of the Good Shepherd, Brooklyn, on its twenty-fifth anniversary, and all good wishes for the continuance of its service in behalf of spiritual advancement in the community.

HERBERT HOOVER

[Rev. William F. Sunday, 7420 Ridge Blvd., Brooklyn, N.Y.]

NOTE: The message was read at the anniversary service on October 25, 1931.

375

Message of Sympathy on the Death
of Representative Fletcher Hale.
October 25, 1931

[Released October 25, 1931.   Dated October 23, 1931]

I AM SADDENED to learn of the death of your husband, Fletcher Hale, in the midst of a career which had already been of great service to his state and to the country. His character and ability made him a highly important member of the highest councils of the nation. Mrs. Hoover and I extend to you and your sons our deepest sympathy in your bereavement.

HERBERT HOOVER

[Mrs. Fletcher Hale, c/o Franklin Fort, 47 South Grove Street, East Orange, N.J.]

NOTE: Congressman Hale of New Hampshire served in the House of Representatives from 1927 to 1931.

376

Radio Remarks to the Annual Convention of the National Association of Broadcasters.
October 26, 1931

IT GIVES ME great pleasure to greet the ninth annual convention of the National Association of Broadcasters meeting this week in Detroit. As Secretary of Commerce I had the pleasure of wide acquaintance with the purposes of your association in the Annual National Radio Conferences which were called at that time for the development of the national policies in relation to radio.

The decisions reached at that early date have been of unending importance. The determination that radio channels were public property and should be controlled by the Government; the determination that we should not have governmental broadcasting supported by a tax upon the listener, but that we should give license to use of these channels under private enterprise where there would be no restraint upon programs, has secured for us far greater variety of programs and excellence of service without cost to the listener. This decision has avoided the pitfalls of political and social conflicts in the use of speech over the radio which would have been involved in Government broadcasting. It has preserved free speech to the country.

These principles are now strongly imbedded in our law and in our entire public system. The industry has constantly faced new and complex problems in developing policies and practices abreast of development and need. Your association has contributed greatly to their solution. I am confident that you recognize the responsibility which rests upon you in public interest. It is needless to mention the many-sided importance of radio in modern life. Its dissemination of entertainment, of knowledge, and of public opinion and topics of the public welfare, has become an essential element in the intellectual development of our country. It has brought most of the supposed values which were formerly available exclusively to life in the cities to every home throughout the land, for the treasures of music, of entertainment, and of information

507

have been brought to the loneliest farm and the most remote hamlet. It is an incalculable extension of happiness and contentment.

I extend to you my most cordial greetings and good wishes for your meeting, with the confidence that you will develop still further policies of sound management and public service.

NOTE: The President spoke at 12 noon from the Cabinet Room in the White House to the convention in Convention Hall in Detroit, Mich. The National Broadcasting Company carried the President's remarks.

A reading copy of this item with holograph changes by the President is available for examination at the Herbert Hoover Presidential Library.

377

Exchange of Messages With Prime Minister Laval on His Departure From the United States.
October 26, 1931

ON BEHALF of the American people I bid you bon voyage on your return to France from this memorable visit to the United States. It has afforded me much pleasure to welcome you among us and I personally appreciate the cordial contacts resulting from our conversations.

HERBERT HOOVER

[His Excellency Pierre Laval, President of the Council of Ministers of France, Waldorf Astoria Hotel, New York City]

NOTE: Prime Minister Laval's response to the President's message, dated October 27, 1931, follows:

I wish to express to you my gratitude for your kind telegram. I am returning to France greatly pleased with our cordial conversations and I feel confident that their results will be beneficial to the cause of French American relations, as well as to world reconstruction. May I ask you to convey to Mrs. Hoover my profound respects and my appreciation for her great kindness to my daughter. I beg you to accept my most sincere gratitude for your personal hospitality as well as for the welcome that I received in the United States.

Respectfully yours,
PIERRE LAVAL

[President Herbert Hoover, The White House, Washington, D.C.]

378

The President's News Conference of
October 27, 1931

PHILIPPINE INDEPENDENCE

THE PRESIDENT. On Secretary Hurley's return, at the Cabinet meeting this morning, we discussed the Philippine question at considerable length. We have explored the subject but formulated no conclusive policies in the matter. These discussions will be continued. Independence of the Philippines at sometime has been directly or indirectly promised by every President and by the Congress. In accord with those undertakings, the problem is one of time. In the interest of the Philippine people, the time element involves the necessity that independence must be assured of durability and the Government of the Philippines must be assured of stability. For instance, the economic independence of the Philippines must be attained before political independence can be successful. Independence tomorrow without assured economic stability would result in the collapse of Philippine Government revenues and the collapse of all economic life in the islands. We propose to give further consideration to the whole question during the immediate future.

NATIONAL CREDIT ASSOCIATION

I have some questions here on the matter of the National Credit Association and its progress. I haven't any public statement to make about it as yet, but for background purposes I can inform you that I had a meeting on Saturday night and Sunday morning with the Chairman and the President of the new association—that is, Mr. [George] Reynolds of Chicago is the Chairman, and Mr. [Mortimer N.] Buckner of New York, who is the President—in order to learn the progress being made. They reported that the country was organizing itself very rapidly into the necessary associations; the subscriptions were being developed, and that they had no doubt as to the completion of the entire project, so far as minimum subscription is concerned, by the end of this week. They are already interesting themselves in the banking situations in various quarters, and they find the whole country is rallying to their quotas and their interest in the association. The organization, as you perhaps know, rests fundamentally on the existing clearinghouse associations where they exist—where they are now established—and upon associations of country banks and others where there are no existing clearinghouse associations. A committee is set up in each of these new associations that will conduct the work of the Credit Association. In States where they have not had clearinghouse associations, such as the State of Iowa, for instance, they are forming the Iowa State Association, covering the entire State and all of the banks in the State. That is the case in a great number of other States that lie outside of the larger banking centers. Those associations have already been started in practically every locality, and their first function of their committees is to secure the subscriptions of the banks, and then they pass on to the problems that they have immediately before them.

Very fine progress is being made, and the project is meeting with almost universal support from the banking world. I am confident that it is already performing a considerable function in the restoration of confidence, and that it has made some direct accomplishments more specifically.

And that is all I have this morning.

NOTE: President Hoover's two hundred and seventeenth news conference was held in the White House at 12 noon on Tuesday, October 27, 1931.

On the same day, the White House issued a text of the President's statement on Philippine independence (see Item 379).

379

Statement on Philippine Independence.
October 27, 1931

THE PRESIDENT said:

"With Secretary Hurley's return, the Cabinet this morning discussed the Philippine question at considerable length. We explored the subject, but formulated no conclusive policies in the matter. These discussions will be continued. Independence of the Philippines at sometime has been directly or indirectly promised by every President and by the Congress. In accord with those undertakings, the problem is one of time. In the interest of the Philippine people, the time element involves the necessity that independence must be assured of durability and the Government of the Philippines must be assured of stability. For instance, the economic independence of the Philippines must be attained before political independence can be successful. Independence tomorrow without assured economic stability would result in the collapse of Philippine Government revenues and the collapse of all economic life in the islands. We propose to give further consideration to the whole question during the immediate future."

NOTE: Secretary of War Patrick J. Hurley visited the Philippines from August 31 to September 26, 1931.

380

Statement on Navy Day.
October 27, 1931

NAVY DAY offers a special opportunity for national consideration of our defense and an opportunity to express national appreciation to the body of men who give so high a service to the Nation.

The first necessity of our Government is the maintenance of a navy so efficient and strong that, in conjunction with our army, no enemy may ever invade our country. The commanding officers of our forces inform me that we are maintaining that strength and efficiency.

Ours is a force of defense, not offense. To maintain forces less than that strength is to destroy national safety; to maintain greater forces is not only economic injury to our people but a threat against our neighbors and would be righteous cause for ill will amongst them. Our problem is to assure the adjustment of our forces to the minimum based upon the outlook in the world; to strive for lower armament throughout the whole world; to promote good will among nations; to conduct our military activities with rigid economy; to prevent extremists on one side from undermining the public will to support our necessary forces, and to prevent extremists on the other side from waste of public funds.

We are fortunate in having a navy with long, high-spirited tradition. It possesses a personnel of officers and men who have never been excelled in our whole history. The Nation has reason for confidence in their ability.

381

Message of Sympathy on the Death
of George Washington Ochs Oakes.
October 27, 1931

I AM greatly shocked and saddened by the death of your brother, George Washington Ochs Oakes. His patriotism was reflected in all his service to the public welfare. I prized his friendship and mourn his loss as a friend and a splendid American. I extend to you my deep sympathy and shall appreciate it if you will convey to Mr. Ochs Oakes' sons an expression of my sorrow in their bereavement.

HERBERT HOOVER

[Mr. Adolph S. Ochs, New York Times, 229 West 23rd Street, New York City]

NOTE: Mr. Oakes, a director of the New York Times Company and editor of Current History Magazine, died at his home in New York City on October 26, 1931.

382

Message of Sympathy on the Death
of Charles A. Comiskey.
October 27, 1931

[Released October 27, 1931.   Dated October 26, 1931]

EVERY American interested in clean and honest sportsmanship will grieve with you in the death of your father, Charles A. Comiskey. His career coincided with the evolution of baseball into our national sport. His rugged character was reflected in the ideals and standards which he valiantly championed in his responsible connections with the sport. Please accept for yourself and your associates my deep sympathy in your loss.

HERBERT HOOVER

[Mr. Louis Comiskey, Eagle River, Wisconsin]

NOTE: Mr. Comiskey, president of the Chicago White Sox baseball team, died on October 26, 1931, in Eagle River, Wis.

383

Letter to Frank P. Walsh, Chairman of the Power Authority of the State of New York.
October 27, 1931

[Released October 27, 1931.   Dated October 15, 1931]

Dear Mr. Walsh:

I have your letter of October 14th. I think you will realize that I should not personally conduct the negotiations to which you refer inasmuch as they properly lie in the province of the Department of State, which has responsibility for the handling of our foreign affairs.

Your letter is one therefore which should properly come up for discussion with the Department of State.

Yours faithfully,
HERBERT HOOVER

[Mr. Frank P. Walsh, Chairman, The Power Authority of the State of New York, 80 Center Street, New York City]

NOTE: In April 1931, New York established a State Power Authority to undertake power development on the St. Lawrence River. To protect its interest State officials urged that it be made a party to Canadian-American treaty negotiations. Continuing requests and public protests led Secretary of State Henry L. Stimson to invite the chairman of the Power Authority to meet with him on October 28.

384

Message to President Thomas G. Masaryk
on Czechoslovakia's Independence Day.
October 28, 1931

ON BEHALF OF my fellow countrymen and in my own name I
extend to Your Excellency on this memorable anniversary most cordial felicitations and the renewed assurances of my high regard and best
wishes.

HERBERT HOOVER

[His Excellency Thomas G. Masaryk, President of Czechoslovakia, Prague,
Czechoslovakia]

385

Statement Announcing a Committee of Inquiry
Into Misstatements by the President of the Navy League.
October 29, 1931

THE PRESIDENT issued the following statement:

The Navy League states in its announcements that it has "for a quarter
of a century specialized in accurate information as to navy matters" and
"the principal activity of the League is to disseminate facts bearing on
navy matters to the press."

In order that the country may know the untruth and distortions of
fact in Chairman Gardiner's recent pronouncement, I will appoint a
committee including members of the Navy League to whom agencies
of the Government will demonstrate these untruths and distortions of
fact. Such an inquiry will absolve the members of the League who have
not participated in this statement. Upon its completion I shall expect
Mr. Gardiner to make a public correction of his misstatements and an
apology therefor.

It is desirable for the public to know the character of this indirect
campaign of misinformation to defeat the efforts of the high officials of

the Navy Department and the administration for reduction of Federal expenditure not immediately essential in order that we may avoid increased taxation of the people in these times.

NOTE: On October 28, 1931, William Howard Gardiner, president of the Navy League, released a pamphlet charging that the President's policy would reduce the United States to a third-rate naval power.

386

Message to President Mustapha Kemal on Turkey's Independence Day.
October 29, 1931

ON THIS auspicious anniversary which the people of Turkey are celebrating today I take pleasure in extending to Your Excellency in my own name and on behalf of my fellow countrymen most cordial greetings and best wishes for your health and happiness and the continued prosperity of the Turkish Republic.

HERBERT HOOVER

[His Excellency Gazi Mustapha Kemal, President of the Turkish Republic, Ankara, Turkey]

387

The President's News Conference of
October 30, 1931

UNEMPLOYMENT RELIEF IN THE DISTRICT OF COLUMBIA

THE PRESIDENT. A conference was held this afternoon with the Chairman of the District of Columbia Unemployment Committee, representatives of the District Community Chest, Mr. [Fred C.] Croxton of Mr. [Walter S.] Gifford's organization,[1] and the District Commissioners, in the matter of coordination of the activities of the District with

---

[1] The President's Organization on Unemployment Relief.

515

the Federal departments and Federal agencies in the matter of unemployment this winter. The District authorities will present a plan by which the departments and contractors working on public construction in the District can cooperate to handle unemployment problems.

DOMESTIC CREDIT CONDITIONS

I am happy to note the very great change that is evident in the credit situation which has gradually taken place since the announcement made on October 7. Following the abandonment of the gold standard in England a wave of great apprehension spread over the United States and reached dimensions which were not appreciated generally at that time. The hoarding of currency rose to a high point of $200 million a week and country bank failures rose to over 25 a day. At the same time the drain of gold due to the alarm of foreign holders of American credits had in this period risen to as high as over $200 million a week.

Evidence over the last week indicates that hoarding has not only ceased but we actually gained $24 million in return deposits to the banks. Small bank failures have almost ceased, the last report showing only 7 out of 20,000 country banks. Foreign exchanges have returned to the basis where it is not longer advantageous to ship gold and the most practical evidence of what these more or less vague things mean is the fact that there has been a recovery of 10 or 12 cents in the price of wheat and $15 to $20 increase per bale in cotton.

NAVY LEAGUE

The other question I have takes this for answer: I am awaiting the receipt of a list of members of the Navy League and as soon as that list is obtainable I shall select a committee from its membership, which committee will have the duty of establishing the untruths promulgated by the president of that body.

I thank you.

NOTE: President Hoover's two hundred and eighteenth news conference was held in the White House at 4 p.m. on Friday, October 30, 1931.

On the same day, the White House also issued texts of the President's statements on unemployment relief in the District of Columbia (see Item 388), domestic credit conditions (see Item 389), and on the committee of inquiry into misstatements by the president of the Navy League (see Item 390).

388

Statement on Unemployment Relief in the District of Columbia.
October 30, 1931

A CONFERENCE was held this afternoon with the Chairman of the District Unemployment Committee, representatives of the Community Chest, the District Commissioners, Mr. Gifford's committee, and others in the matter of coordination between the Federal departments with the District activities in relief to unemployment over the winter.

The District authorities will present a plan by which the departments and contractors working on public construction can actively cooperate to handle such unemployment problems as may arise in the District.

NOTE: Walter S. Gifford was Director of the President's Organization on Unemployment Relief.

389

Statement on Domestic Credit Conditions.
October 30, 1931

THE PRESIDENT said:

"I am happy to note the very great change which is evident in the credit situation since the announcement of financial plans on October 7.

"Following the abandonment of the gold standard in England a wave of great apprehension spread over the country. Hoarding of currency rose to the high point of $200 million a week between that time and the announcement of the credit pool and other credit measures. Country bank failures had risen to nearly 25 a day during this period. At the same time the drain of gold abroad due to the alarm of foreign holders

517

of American credits had in this period risen to as high as over $200 million a week.

"Evidence over the last week indicates that not only has hoarding ceased, but actually $24 million of hoarded money has returned to the banks. The small bank failures have almost ceased—the last report showing only 7 out of 20,000 total. Foreign exchanges are returned to a basis at which it is no longer advantageous to ship gold abroad.

"The practical effect of this recovery is shown in an increase in the price of wheat by 10 cents or 12 cents a bushel and cotton by $15 to $20 a bale."

390

Statement on the Committee of Inquiry Into Misstatements by the President of the Navy League. *October 30, 1931*

THE PRESIDENT said:

"I am waiting to secure a list of the members of the Navy League. As soon as that list is obtainable, I shall select representation from the membership on a committee which will be able to establish the untruths promulgated by the president of that body."

NOTE: William Howard Gardiner was president of the Navy League.

391

Message to the National Organization for Public Health Nursing. *November 1931*

[Released November 1931.   Dated September 3, 1931]

My dear Miss Nelson:

Public Health Nursing in the United States has become one of the most potent forces for raising the level of health and efficiency of the

518

people. It not only brings the boon of trained nursing service to even the humblest homes, but is a bulwark against neglect and suffering and a powerful influence in constructively promoting the public health. I am interested to learn of the plans of the National Organization for Public Health Nursing to increase its service by broadening its membership. Its efforts and objectives commend themselves to all citizens. I wish you the fullest measure of success in your current undertaking and your continued program for improving the health of the people.

Yours faithfully,

HERBERT HOOVER

[Miss Sophie C. Nelson, R.N., President, National Organization for Public Health Nursing, Inc., 450 Seventh Avenue, New York City]

NOTE: The message was published in the November 1931 issue of the Child Health Bulletin.

392

White House Statement on Appointments to the Committee of Inquiry Into Misstatements by the President of the Navy League.
November 2, 1931

THE PRESIDENT today appointed a committee comprised of Admiral Hugh Rodman, John Hays Hammond, Eliot Wadsworth, Under Secretary of State William R. Castle, Jr., Assistant Secretary of the Navy Ernest Lee Jahncke, to examine the accuracy of such statements of President Gardiner of the Navy League as may be readily determined from departmental records. This inquiry is solely into the assertions of fact made by President Gardiner in his statement of October 28, not into his opinions or conclusions nor into budgetary or general policies of the Navy.

NOTE: Mr. Hammond, Mr. Wadsworth, and Mr. Jahncke were members of the Navy League.

The committee's letter and report, dated November 6, 1931, were released by the

White House on November 7. A copy of the report is available for examination at the Herbert Hoover Presidential Library. A text of the committee's letter follows:

Dear Mr. President:

Your committee appointed on November 2, 1931 to examine and report on the statement of the Navy League of the United States dated October 28, 1931, submits herewith its unanimous report. The committee, pursuant to your statement of November 2, has directed its inquiry to the accuracy of statements and assertions of fact made by the President of the Navy League. It has not inquired into the budgetary or general policies of the Navy.

In order that the facts found by the committee may readily be compared with the statements contained in the Navy League's publication of October 28, 1931 the committee's findings in detail and the pertinent text of Mr. Gardiner's statement are set forth in parallel columns. These findings are submitted herewith in the attached report.

Certain of the erroneous statements and assertions appearing in the Navy League's publication are summarized below, together with the committee's findings in regard thereto.

First: That the Washington Naval Treaty established a ratio of 10–6 as between the American and Japanese fleets as a whole.

As is well known, the Washington Naval Treaty established ratios for capital ships and aircraft carriers only. All other types of combatant vessels were left entirely unrestricted, and no ratio for them was established until the London Naval Treaty went into force on January 1, 1931, to become effective December 31, 1936.

Second: That the ratios established by the London Naval Treaty are effective prior to December 31, 1936.

Under the terms of Part 3 of the London Naval Treaty the tonnage limits mentioned therein do not become effective until December 31, 1936, and there is manifestly no obligation to attain these limits or the ratios resulting therefrom prior to that time. The committee finds that the United States has at present more treaty tonnage under construction than any other nation.

Third: That the President and the British Prime Minister admittedly reached agreements during their conversations which have never officially been divulged in their entirety.

The assertion that secret agreements were "admittedly" reached during the President's conversations with the British Prime Minister is erroneous. There were no secret agreements.

The incorrectness of the assertion that there were such agreements between the United States and Great Britain which "have never officially been divulged in their

520

entirety" has been shown by the President's message to Congress of July 11, 1930. This message reads in part as follows:

> "I take this opportunity to repeat with the utmost emphasis that in these negotiations there were no secret or concealed understandings, promises or interpretations, nor any commitments whatever except as appear in the Treaty itself and in the interpretive exchange of notes recently suggested by your Committee on Foreign Relations, all of which are now in the hands of the Senate."

In the joint statement issued at the close of the Rapidan conversations, it was announced that an agreement on naval armaments could not be completed without the cooperation of other naval powers. This statement referred to the termination of competitive building between the two countries by "agreeing to parity of fleets category by category". Over two months before the conversations took place, the British Government's acceptance of this principle had been made public on July 23, 1929, by the British Prime Minister.

Furthermore, the Secretary of State on October 30, 1931, said that the assertion of the existence of such secret agreements was "entirely false and had been publicly refuted many times".

Fourth: That the administration refused to allow even an executive session of the Senate Committee on Foreign Relations to see the full record of its negotiations and possible commitments preparatory to the London Naval Conference of 1930.

This statement is without foundation. In answer to Senate Resolution 320, the President's message to Congress of July 11, 1930, contains the following: "No Senator has been refused an opportunity to see the confidential material referred to, provided only he will agree to receive and hold the same in the confidence in which it has been received and held by the Executive. A number of Senators have availed themselves of this opportunity." Furthermore, two members of the Committee, Senator Robinson and Senator Reed, were delegates to the London Naval Conference and were familiar with every phase of the negotiations from beginning to end, and their knowledge was available to all members of the committee.

Fifth: That President Hoover, in 1929, held up the building of the first five of the fifteen cruisers just ordered by Congress as a gesture preparatory to the Naval Conference, which was not commensurately copied by other prospective participants.

This assumption is manifestly incorrect. The President on July 24, 1929, announced in a public statement that he would delay the laying down of the keels of three cruisers, not five as alleged. The construction of these three American cruisers was not postponed beyond the period stipulated by Congress for laying down. The so-called Fifteen Cruiser Bill, which authorized this building included a clause stating that if the construction of any vessel authorized was not undertaken either in the fiscal year ending June 30, 1929, or in the fiscal year ending June 30, 1930, it might be undertaken in the next succeeding year. These three cruisers were laid down within the prescribed period. Two cruisers in addition to the five are now in the course of construction, making a total of seven now building, as two of the 1929 program were earlier laid down.

The President's statement postponing the building of these cruisers appeared on the same day that a declaration was made in the House of Commons by the British Prime Minister, several months before he came to the United States. The Prime Minister said that his Government had decided (1) to suspend all work on the cruisers *Surrey* and *Northumberland;* (2) to cancel the submarine tender *Maidstone;* (3) to cancel two contract submarines; and (4) to slow down dockyard work and other naval construction. This proves that there was commensurate action by Great Britain.

Sixth: That the President intended under the one year "holiday" to forego our treaty rights to carry on the construction of 87,600 tons of naval vessels, including the seven cruisers now building.

This refers to the proposed one year holiday in the starting of new construction and is based on the erroneous assumption repeatedly made in the Navy League statements and in its tables that construction now under way would be held up during this period. This projected armaments truce does not contemplate stopping work on vessels already under construction or for which contracts have been let. There is in the truce nothing to prevent the United States from attaining treaty ratios after its expiration. The proposed truce, designed to create an atmosphere of confidence which will prepare the ground for the successful conclusion of the General Disarmament Conference to be held next February and to prevent competition in armaments, does not in any way affect authorizations already made.

In concluding this summary, it is desirable in order that the situation may be clearly understood, to list the naval vessels now under construction or contracted for, with approximate figures of their estimated cost:

7 Cruisers at $17,000,000 each	$119,000,000
1 Aircraft Carrier at $19,000,000	19,000,000
3 Submarines at $4,400,000 each	13,200,000
5 Destroyers at $4,700,000 each	23,500,000
Approximate total	$174,700,000

In addition the Navy Department is also proceeding with the modernization of three battleships—*Idaho, Mississippi* and *New Mexico*—at an authorized cost of $30,000,000.

This program covers all combatant vessels authorized and appropriated for by Congress, with the exception of six destroyers which have been temporarily postponed.

The committee finds that the economy of $61,000,000 proposed in the naval budget of 1932–33 out of the $401,000,000 estimate does not affect the continuance of the above construction program nor result in the decommissioning of a single combatant unit.

Notwithstanding the implication contained throughout Mr. Gardiner's report, there is no basis for an assumption that the President intends to abandon the Washington and London Treaty ratios, nor do the armaments truce or the emergency economies contemplated at the present time interfere with the ultimate achievement in fact of these ratios in all categories.

For a fuller discussion of the statements and assertions which appear erroneous we invite your attention to the parallel columns of the report in which each paragraph of the statement of the President of the Navy League is dealt with in detail. It is there brought out for example that the inclusion of a series of tables, known by him to be obsolete at the time the statement was issued, should have been so labelled to avoid misleading the public.

The report unanimously adopted by this committee compares Mr. Gardiner's statements with publicly known and officially recorded facts. The report clearly shows that Mr. Gardiner's statement contains many inaccuracies, false assertions and erroneous conclusions, and that his assumption as to the President' attitude toward the Navy is wholly unwarranted.

> Respectfully yours,
> JOHN HAYS HAMMOND,
> *Chairman*
> HUGH RODMAN
> ELIOT WADSWORTH
> WILLIAM R. CASTLE, JR.
> ERNEST LEE JAHNCKE

393

Message to President Ricardo J. Alfaro
on Panama's Independence Day.
November 3, 1931

PLEASE ACCEPT my most cordial congratulations on this auspicious
anniversary and the assurances of the good will which this Government
and people bear for Your Excellency's country.

HERBERT HOOVER

[His Excellency Ricardo J. Alfaro, The President of Panama, Panama City]

394

Statement on Public Building Projects.
November 4, 1931

THE PRESIDENT said:

"That portion of the Federal program of aid to unemployment comprised in the great expansion of public buildings under the Treasury
Department shows the following progress since the report of September 1. There are a total of 817 projects which have so far been specifically
authorized, and 222 firms of architects are engaged in plans and supervision. The attached tables show the progress of individual projects
which may be summarized:

"*First:* A total of 131 buildings have been completed at a total cost of
$41,934,569. Sixteen buildings have been completed during the months of
September and October.

"*Second:* There were 270 buildings in construction at the 1st of
November by contract, at an estimated cost of $229,772,700. There have
been 41 contracts let during the months of September and October with
a total value in excess of $48,000,000.

"*Third:* There are 64 projects in which sites have been arranged, drawings are completed, for which construction contracts have been invited,
of a total estimated cost of $19,970,500.

"*Fourth:* There are 240 projects in which sites have been selected and on which plans are now under way of a total estimated cost of $141,947,923.

"*Fifth*: At the first of this month there were 100 projects in which the sites have been determined upon and are in process of being acquired. The estimated cost of the buildings thereon is $31,133,500.

"*Sixth:* There are 12 projects held for amended legislation or for other reasons with a total estimated cost of $3,145,000.

"It is estimated that the number of men now directly and indirectly employed on this program is 50,000. It is estimated by the Treasury Department that the number that will be directly and indirectly employed on January 1 is 100,000.

"Tables showing the progress of the different projects in the different categories are attached thereto."

NOTE: The tables issued with the statement are not printed but are available for examination at the Herbert Hoover Presidential Library.

395

White House Statement on Conferences
About Financing of Homeownership.
November 4, 1931

THE CONFERENCES of the President during the past few days with the representatives of the building and loan associations and the members of the Finance Committee of the Housing Conference relate to the consideration of better long view financing of homeownership and the present emergencies in small mortgages upon urban and farm property used for homes. No conclusions have yet been reached but in any event the projects discussed do not look to replacing the functions of the national credit pool among the banks as has been reported in some quarters.

NOTE: On November 3, 1931, the White House released a list of the members of the Finance Committee of the White House Conference on Home Building and Home Ownership who attended a meeting with the President that morning (see Appendix E, November 3).

396

Message on the Dedication
of the Red Cross Chapter House
in New York City.
November 5, 1931

I EXTEND to you and your co-workers my warmest congratulations upon the occasion of the dedication today of the new chapter house of the American Red Cross in New York City. From this fine edifice made possible by a gift from the Conrad Hubert fund I am sure that the fine record of a quarter of a century of service in New York City by your Red Cross Chapter will be carried on with increasingly great appreciation from your community.

HERBERT HOOVER

[General James G. Harbord, Chairman, New York Chapter, American Red Cross, 315 Lexington Avenue, New York City]

NOTE: The message was read at the dedication ceremonies.

397

The President's News Conference of
November 6, 1931

FEDERAL BUDGET

THE PRESIDENT. Some of the departmental budgets are not yet complete, that is, the budgets for the fiscal year beginning July. But we have proceeded far enough to enable me to state that the appropriations that will be proposed to Congress for that fiscal year will be about 350 million below the original departmental requests. Every department in the Government is cooperating, and every item has been cut, and every item postponed that can be done without injury to the fundamental purposes of the services or damaging their efficiency.

You will realize that nearly half of the expenditure of the Government is for interest, sinking fund, and veterans, and this represents a very essential degree of cooperation. And it is a real contribution of all the departments, bureau heads, and every agency of the Government in an endeavor to meet the necessities of the taxpayer and the general economic situation.

I would like also again to refer to the many sectional interests of the country which are pressing for increased expenditures for the next fiscal year. Such action only embarrasses the administration and the Congress in its endeavor to maintain governmental finance on a sound footing. There are many new plans for increased expenditures in various sections of the country that are meritorious and will need to be undertaken by the Government at sometime, but this is not the time. We will have to defer them until the country can pay for them. There is nothing that can contribute more to a return of prosperity than to maintain a sound fiscal position for the Federal Government.

CHARLES A. LINDBERGH

I have one appointment—in the shape of Mr. Charles A. Lindbergh as a member of the National Advisory Committee for Aeronautics.

FEDERAL BUDGET

Q. Mr. President, did you say 350 million below the original estimates? Is it possible to make any speculation as to how far it will be below the last appropriations?

THE PRESIDENT. No, there is a difficulty in that. The appropriations are very badly scattered through the whole year, and it is a little bit difficult to tell what the 1932 expenditures will be, yet. Part of the appropriations made last winter were for expenditure applicable to both the fiscal year 1931 and 1932, and it is impossible, even yet, to tell what it will be—at the end of the year we will be able to.

Q. Mr. President, have you a comparable figure with last year's original budget?

THE PRESIDENT. No, I haven't here. I think it is somewhere about 280 million roughly, below the appropriations of last year. That figure is not precise, and it may be 20 million greater than that.

NOTE: President Hoover's two hundred and nineteenth news conference was held in the White House at 4 p.m. on Friday, November 6, 1931.

On the same day, the White House issued a text of the President's statement on the Federal budget (see Item 398).

398

Statement on the Federal Budget.
November 6, 1931

THE PRESIDENT said:

"The departmental budgets for the fiscal year beginning next July have proceeded far enough to enable me to state that appropriations which will be proposed to the Congress will show a reduction of at least $350 million below that of original departmental requests. Every department in the Government is cooperating; every item has been cut; every item postponed that can be done without injury to the fundamental purpose of the departments and the efficiency of the services. As nearly half the expenditures of the Government are for interest, sinking fund, veterans' services and other items which are irreducible, this cut represents most earnest cooperation by all the departments of the Government in their endeavor to meet the necessities of the taxpayer and the present economic situation.

"Again I wish to refer to the many sectional interests throughout the country who are asking us to increase expenditures. Such action can only embarrass the earnest efforts of the administration and the Congress to maintain our governmental finance on a sound basis. Many new plans of different sections, meritorious in themselves, must be deferred until the country can afford to pay for them. Nothing will contribute more to the return of prosperity than to maintain the sound fiscal position of the Federal Government."

399

Message to the Annual Convention
of the Intracoastal Canal Association
of Louisiana and Texas.
November 6, 1931

[Released November 6, 1931.   Dated November 5, 1931]

PLEASE PRESENT my cordial greetings to the citizens of Louisiana
and Texas attending the annual convention of the Intracoastal Canal
Association celebrating the early completion of the waterway from
Mississippi to Corpus Christi. The ultimate extension of this waterway
to the Rio Grande and the Mexican border would bring important
benefits to the Southwest. I trust that your convention may give impetus
to the development of inland waterways and a coordinated system of
transportation.

HERBERT HOOVER

[Mr. Roy Miller, Vice President, Intracoastal Canal Association of Louisiana &
Texas, Corpus Christi, Texas]

NOTE: The message was read at the opening session of the association's 27th annual
convention, which met in Corpus Christi, Tex.

400

Letter to Justice Louis D. Brandeis
on His 75th Birthday.
November 8, 1931

[Released November 8, 1931.   Dated October 29, 1931]

My dear Mr. Justice:

Mrs. Hoover and I wish to be early in conveying to you our warmest
congratulations on your seventy-fifth birthday. It is not necessary for us
to remind you of the many satisfactions which have crowned your

529

public service and that you reflect a heart and mind which have made the nation your debtor.

Even during your service as a member of the highest Court in the land you have found time to give service to the advancement of the Jewish homeland and I have no doubt this has brought happiness and comfort to thousands.

We wish you many happy returns of the day.

Yours faithfully,

HERBERT HOOVER

[Hon. Louis D. Brandeis, Associate Justice of the Supreme Court, Florence Courts West, Washington, D.C.]

NOTE: The letter was released through the Jewish Telegraphic Agency on November 8, 1931. Justice Brandeis celebrated his 75th birthday on November 13.

401

Message to the National Hotel Exposition.
November 8, 1931

[Released November 8, 1931.   Dated November 3, 1931]

My dear Mr. McKowne:

I have been interested to learn of your plans for the sixteenth National Hotel Exposition in New York, and especially of your plans to align the industry with the constructive influences and forces working for economic recovery. It is to the lasting credit of the American business man that he is facing the future with courage and confidence. It is that spirit, plus the necessary reordering and readjusting of our economic life to current conditions, which will eventually solve the difficulties which confront us. I trust that your exposition may give impetus to improvement not only in the hotel industry, but in business generally.

Yours faithfully,

HERBERT HOOVER

[Mr. F. A. McKowne, President, Hotel Ass'n. of New York City, 221 West 57th Street, New York City]

NOTE: The message was released in conjunction with the opening of the exposition at the Grand Central Palace in New York City.

402

Message to the St. Louis Globe-Democrat
on the Opening of Its New Building.
November 8, 1931

[Released November 8, 1931.   Dated October 23, 1931]

My dear Mr. Ray:

Please accept for yourself and your associates my hearty congratulations as the St. Louis Globe-Democrat moves into its new building. I hope that the occasion may mark the beginning of an era of even greater service to the community and the country. The Globe-Democrat has an enviable and deserved reputation for enterprise and impartiality in publishing the news and for independence, fairness and insight in editorial interpretation. Such a conception of its responsibility helps to bring to our public life and the public service the strength of an informed and potent public opinion. You have my best wishes for continued prosperity and growth.

Yours faithfully,

HERBERT HOOVER

[Mr. E. Lansing Ray, President, St. Louis Globe-Democrat, St. Louis, Missouri]

NOTE: The message was made public in conjunction with the opening of the Globe-Democrat's new building in St. Louis, Mo.

68-611 O - 76 - 38

403

The President's News Conference of
November 10, 1931

GOVERNMENT EMPLOYEES AND UNEMPLOYMENT RELIEF

THE PRESIDENT. I have a question with respect to the action of the Federal Government on the recommendations of Mr. [Walter S.] Gifford's committee under Mr. Wheeler [1] as to staggering employment amongst civil servants. I asked Governor [Thomas E.] Campbell, Chairman of the Civil Service Commission, to get in contact with the various departments of the Government and to consider the nature of the contribution which Federal employees could make towards the unemployment situation. And it quickly developed that no plan of staggering could be worked out under the civil service law, aside from the fact of the difficulties in other directions that arose over the plan. On the other hand, the committee has endeavored to work out a method by which the Civil Service can make a proper contribution to the unemployment situation throughout the country, and that will be ready for submission in a day or two. I find that the employees throughout the departments are anxious to have some definite form of organization by which they can contribute to the unemployment situation.

Q. Mr. President, does that plan contemplate a shorter working week?

THE PRESIDENT. No, something in the nature of direct contribution—some sort of regular contribution of all Government employees, both here in Washington and in each locality. Nothing compulsory about it, purely voluntary.

APPOINTMENTS

I haven't anything else of any great news value. For the next 2 or 3 weeks—and for the last week—we will be mostly engaged in getting

---

[1] On October 28, 1931, the Committee on Employment Plans and Suggestions of the President's Organization on Unemployment Relief recommended a number of relief and recovery measures. One of the recommendations was a proposal that public employees share governmental work with some of those on relief. Harry A. Wheeler headed the Committee.

ready to present to Congress the necessary appointments for vacancies. Those have not yet been determined. We have two vacancies on the Tariff Commission, one on the Farm Board, and some 10 or 15 vacancies in the Judiciary, and I hope to have those ready to present immediately after Congress assembles.

ANNUAL MESSAGES TO CONGRESS

Also, I am necessarily engaged in consulting with different departments and agencies of the Government with regard to the recommendations to be made in the annual message. This year the budget message will be of as great importance as the general message. This requires a good deal more thought than usual because there are a number of emergency actions which will need to be presented to Congress to take care of the situation. So that is largely our occupation, rather than to produce sensations.

NOTE: President Hoover's two hundred and twentieth news conference was held in the White House at 12 noon on Tuesday, November 10, 1931.

404

Armistice Day Address at the Dedication of the District of Columbia War Memorial. *November 11, 1931*

GREAT SHRINES in our National Capital mark reverent remembrance of those who have given sacrifice and glory to the Nation. Marble and bronze, in their eloquence of silence and beauty, tell the deathless story of heroic deeds done for our country.

We gather here today to dedicate a new shrine to those residents of the District of Columbia who served in the World War. This temple will recall for all time their services and sacrifices.

It is particularly fitting that these services should be held on Armistice Day, when, throughout the Nation, our citizens pause to honor all those who gave their lives in the greatest conflict which has ever engulfed the world.

Thirteen years to the day and hour have passed since the guns ceased their destruction of life, and nations began their march back to peace and reconstruction. That day was a day of rejoicing in victory, a day of pride in the valor of our Army and Navy, a day of hope for peace in a better world. With each succeeding year, Armistice Day has come to be a day to pay tribute to the millions who valiantly bore arms in a worthy cause and to renew resolves that the peace for which these men sacrificed themselves shall be maintained.

However great our desire for peace, we must not assume that the peace for which these men died has become assured to the world or that the obligations which they left to us, the living, have been discharged. The minds of many races still are stirred by memories of centuries of injustice; in others there is ever present the fear of invasion and domination; many peoples are filled with hopes of liberty and independence. The boundaries of many nations are but zones of age-old contention. The growth of population and economic striving press against the borders of others. Worldwide expansion of commerce and industry, with its vast interchange of citizens, brings the daily obligation of self-respecting nations to see that their nationals abroad in pacific pursuits shall not be unjustly imperiled as to life and property. In every country men can secure public attention and even a living by stirring malignant forces of fear and hate of their neighbors. As a result of these forces the world is more heavily armed than even before the Great War.

All of these dangers present to statesmen a world where peace cannot be had by resolution and injunction alone. Peace is the product of preparedness for defense, the patient settlement of controversy, and the dynamic development of the forces of good will. It is the result of the delicate balance of that realism born of human experience and of idealism born of the highest of human aspirations for international justice.

The backwash of forces loosened by the Great War has grown until during the past 2 years the stability of many nations has been greatly shaken. This, with their fears and discouragement for the future, weakened confidence throughout the whole financial and economic world. That loss of confidence added enormously to unemployment, to the

534

distress of agriculture and business everywhere. From it all we have been passing through an emergency second only to the Great War.

But the emergency has brought a realization that the outstanding problem of statesmanship today in every country and in every part of the world is to reestablish confidence, not alone each nation in its own institutions, but among nations. And no greater contribution can be made to economic relief than day-to-day conclusive demonstration that progress is being made in relieving stress and strain which now so oppress the atmosphere of the family of nations.

Such action requires no treaties, no documents, and no commitments. It requires only that each nation realize the situation that exists; that it contribute in its own policies and within its own best interest to the building of good will and the rebuilding of confidence.

That progress is being made. It has been made by frank, sincere, and direct personal conferences on mutual problems between heads of states throughout the world. It has been made by similar action among the financial, industrial, and social institutions of the world. These discussions have developed common action and have increased good will and confidence. These consistent efforts are providing new avenues of relief and are assuredly turning the tide for a greatly suffering world.

It is by building good will and constructive effort among nations that we can best honor the memory of the men who died that the world should have peace. This monument stands for men who fought not alone for their country but to establish the principles of justice and peace. We pay tribute here to their valor. We honor them for their sacrifice. We respect their memory by renewing our obligations to the purposes and ideals for which they fought.

NOTE: The President spoke at 11 a.m. at the dedication of the memorial to the soldiers and sailors of World War I from the District of Columbia.

405

Message to the Seventh Fall Convention of the American Newspaper Publishers Association. *November 11, 1931*

[Released November 11, 1931.   Dated November 3, 1931]

My dear Mr. Chandler:

Will you please present my most cordial greetings to the American Newspaper Publishers Association at their fall meeting in Los Angeles. I deeply regret that the pressure of imperative duties prevents my accepting your kind invitation to address the meeting. I wish especially to express appreciation for the generous and immeasureably helpful cooperation of the press of the nation in promoting an understanding of unemployment relief needs in their respective communities and supporting efforts to provide for all those in want.

It is natural that the economic dislocation through which we have been passing should elicit divergent views as to causes and remedies. Recovery and stability can return only through a return of confidence, and no agency can make so great a contribution to the restoration of confidence and a return of normal activity as the newspapers. I hope that your meeting will be productive of sound policies within your own profession and industry and that the publishers of the country will align themselves with the constructive forces which are promoting recovery.

Yours faithfully,

Herbert Hoover

[Mr. Harry Chandler, President, American Newspaper Publishers Association, Los Angeles, California]

NOTE: The message was read at the opening session of the association's fall convention, which met at the Ambassador Hotel in Los Angeles, Calif.

406

Statement on the Budget for the Department of the Navy.
November 12, 1931

THE PRESIDENT said:

"The Navy budget which will be presented to Congress for the fiscal year beginning the 1st of next July has been fixed at $343 million. This is a decrease of about $17 million under the appropriations for the present fiscal year. It is a decrease of about $59 million from the $401 million originally proposed by the Navy some months ago and prior to the development of the evidence of large deficiency in the national budget.

"This budget for the next fiscal year does not decrease the personnel of the Navy below its present status by a single man. It does not decommission any fighting ships although the rotation plan will be continued. It does not propose to abandon any of the navy yards at the present time although the Navy officials are convinced that the products of some of these yards could be made more cheaply elsewhere. To close these yards would produce undue hardship to labor at the present time. The budget provides for the maintenance of the frigate *Constitution* and for the maintenance of the Navy bands. It is proposed to take care of the problem of the Philadelphia hospital in conjunction with the Veterans' Bureau.

"In the matter of appropriations for 'increase in the Navy' that is, for the expansion of combatant ships, the program is set up in such fashion that $57 million will be expended either through appropriations or from carryovers in the fiscal year beginning the 1st of next July. This is an increase of from $53 million estimated expenditure this present fiscal year and it is interesting to note the amount of actual expenditures on this item since 1926:

1926	25, 249, 796
1927	27, 430, 330
1928	36, 934, 985
1929	46, 758, 720
1930	49, 872, 209

1931	37, 944, 048
1932 (Estimated Nov. 1, 1931)................	53, 375, 000
1933 proposed............................	57, 000, 000

"The budget provides for the continued construction of every one of the treaty ships authorized by Congress except 6 destroyers. The deferment of these 6 destroyers out of 11 authorized has not only been a measure of economy but a policy of maintaining even construction in destroyer programs and maintenance of evenness of employment in the yards. The program proposed under this budget will not decrease but will slightly increase the total direct and indirect employment in the Navy in naval construction in the next fiscal year over and above that of the present year. The tonnage of combatant ships actually in construction by the United States today is nearly double that of Great Britain and in addition we are engaged in the modernization of three battleships.

"These are times when the American people have a right to rigid economy on the part of their Government. Navy officials have cooperated and have taken pride in the development of a proper program that would contribute to this economy.

"In keeping with established practice, the details of the budget will not be made public until transmitted to Congress."

407

The President's News Conference of
November 13, 1931

HOME LOAN DISCOUNT BANK SYSTEM

THE PRESIDENT. I have what I regard as rather an important statement, and I am giving it to you for release for the morning papers because I think it will require a little thought on your part. And rather than read all of it to you I thought I would sketch it and leave you to study it.

It is a proposal for the establishment of a system of home loan discount banks, and is the result of some 3 months of conferences with various groups interested in that subject from all parts of the country.

So that what I say to you is background and is, in fact, merely a condensation of the statement itself.

The proposal is for four purposes: That is, for the present emergency purpose of relieving the financial strains on the building and loan associations, savings banks and the deposit banks, and the farm loan banks that have been giving credit through small mortgage loans on small farms and homes. Its purpose is to relieve the pressures on homeowners and farmowners and to put these various types of institutions in the position to assist in the revival of construction in many parts of the country, with a resultant increase in employment. It also has the purpose of safeguarding against such experience in the future as we have been going through in the last 6 months in this particular. And it has the long-view purpose of strengthening those institutions that are promoting homeownership, particularly the building and loan associations. The immediate credit situation has, for the time being, restricted rather severely the operations of all this type of institutions in relation to small mortgages, and they have not only been unable to extend credit for new mortgages on farms and homes, but have been unable to renew mortgages and to give consideration to those in difficulty in these times. So that there has been a great deal of resultant hardship to borrowers and an unduly large amount of liquidation of real estate.

A good deal of the unemployment in the country is due to the breakdown in residential construction. We normally build a matter of 200,000 homes a year—new homes—which represents an expenditure estimated with the furnishings and everything else of a couple of billions, and it is a good deal more than one-half diminished—probably diminished by two-thirds at the present time. So that if we can revive the activities of various institutions that have to deal with these questions, we should obtain a considerable revival of employment in that quarter.

I want to point out to you that this statement is very carefully prepared and this I am giving you is just background. And I hope you will study it over.

The farm mortgage situation presents a great deal of difficulty. A large part of it is being taken care of by the insurance companies and Federal land banks, but a considerable segment has been taken care of by the smaller banks and other institutions where there is a good deal of pressure. So the plan itself is to establish 12 home loan discount banks, one in each Federal Reserve district, under the direction of a central board in Washington. The capital of these banks to be initially from 5 to 30 million, depending upon the needs in the various districts. The proposed banks are not to make initial or direct mortgages, but to loan only on obligations of loaning institutions secured by mortgage loans as collateral in such a fashion as to assure the expansion of the functions of those institutions. The building and loan associations, and savings banks, and deposits banks, and the farm loan banks, et cetera, may become members of the system on evidence as to eligibility as fixed by the board. The mortgage loans eligible for collateral shall not exceed $15,000 so as to limit it to urban and farm property used for home purposes. The maximum amount to be advanced against mortgage collateral not to exceed more than 50 percent of the unpaid balance on unamortized or short-term mortgages and not more than 60 percent on the unpaid balance of amortized long-term mortgages. On that basis, with proper appraisal of the property, these loans by the discount bank would cover from 25 to 30 percent of the appraised value of the property. Discount banks in turn to issue bonds or short-term notes to the public for investment. Those bonds or notes would thus be secured first by the notes of the borrowing institutions borrowing from the discount bank, and then the collateral, and further secured by the obligations and capital of the discount banks, so that they would have a firm security. It is suggested that they should be made acceptable for security for governmental and postal savings bank deposits.

If the aggregate initial capital of these banks should amount to $150 million, they would have on a 12 to 1 ratio any issue of securities, which by the way compares with 20 to 1 in the Federal land banks. They would have an ability to finance a matter of $1,800 million of discounts.

Now, it is proposed to find the initial capital for these discount banks in the same fashion, so far as it is applicable, as the capital was found for the Federal Reserve banks. In that case an organization committee is set up in each district. The capital stock shall be offered to the institutions participating, and that capital stock if undersubscribed shall be subscribed temporarily by the Government. It is proposed to follow that line in this case, and that institutions which might join afterwards and thus make use of the facilities, to purchase a certain amount of the stock held by the Government in the same fashion that they purchase the stock of the Federal land banks, so that in a short time, as was the case of the farm loan banks, the capital all went over to private hands. So that the Government, if at all, would only be temporarily in the business.

Now, the details I have given here are somewhat to give clarity to the central idea rather than inflexible conclusions. The whole plan is necessarily subject to the action of Congress, and a great many parts of it will no doubt have further development.

There is no element of inflation in this plan, but simply a better organization of credit facilities. This proposed setup does not in any way displace the National Credit Association, because that occupies an entirely different field of action from that which is proposed here. It is somewhat difficult to get any statistical ideas as to the volume of credit of this kind current in the country, but it is generally estimated at anything from 200 to a million (?)[1] from one quarter or another of small size mortgages. And the margin required in order to unfreeze the situation and get the various institutions active to get work restarted in these directions, and to loosen up in agricultural land credits is probably not very much—largely a question of assurance to those institutions that they would be able to secure cooperation in an emergency rather than perhaps actual capital.

In any event, the program is the result, as I have said, of many months of discussion with various groups, and it has been submitted in all parts of the country in its general outlines, and I have received a very wide measure of approval of the principal ideas which were circulated amongst various types of institutions, such as building and loan, savings banks, and others.

---

[1] The question mark appears in the transcript. Press accounts indicate that the estimate of small mortgages given by the President was $20 to $30 billion.

The necessity for institutions of this kind are not so great in the Northeastern part of the United States as in the rest of the country. In sections with larger supplies of capital, they are not so pressed in the present situation as the area outside of the Northeast.

That is all. I have marked it for release for tomorrow morning's papers.

Q. Mr. President, will you please tell us if the Members of Congress have been shown this?

THE PRESIDENT. To some extent, but not at great length.

That is all.

NOTE: President Hoover's two hundred and twenty-first news conference was held in the White House at 4 p.m. on Friday, November 13, 1931.

On the same day, the White House issued a text of the President's statement proposing the establishment of the home loan discount bank system (see Item 408), which was embargoed for release on November 14, 1931.

408

Statement Proposing the Establishment
of the Home Loan Discount Bank System.
November 14, 1931

THE PRESIDENT said:

"I shall propose to Congress the establishment of a system of home loan discount banks for four purposes:

"1. For the present emergency purpose of relieving the financial strains upon sound building and loan associations, savings banks, deposit banks and farm loan banks that have been giving credit through the medium of small mortgage loans upon urban and farm properties used for homes. Thereby to relieve pressures upon home and farm owners.

"2. To put the various types of institutions loaning on mortgage in a position to assist in the revival of home construction in many parts of the country and with its resultant increase in employment.

"3. To safeguard against the repetition of such experiences in the future.

"4. For the long-view purpose of strengthening such institutions in the promotion of homeownership particularly through the financial strength thus made available to building and loan associations.

"The immediate credit situation has for the time being in many parts of the country restricted severely the activities of building and loan associations, deposit banks including country banks, and savings departments, savings banks and farm loan companies in such a fashion that they are not only not able to extend credit through new mortgages to home and farm owners, but are only too often unable to renew mortgages or give consideration to those in difficulty with resultant great hardships to borrowers and a definite depreciation of real estate values in the areas where such pressures exist.

"A considerable part of our unemployment is due to stagnation in residential construction. It is true there has been some overbuilding in certain localities in the boom years. But even in these localities the inevitable need is obscured by the tendency of the population to huddle temporarily due to unemployment. The real need steadily accumulates with increasing population and will become evident and insistent as we come out of the depression. The high importance of residential construction as a matter of employment is indicated by the fact that more than 200,000 individual homes are erected annually in normal times, which with initial furnishing contribute more than two billions to our construction and other industries. This construction has greatly diminished. Its revival would provide for employment in the most vital way. As a people we need at all times the encouragement of homeownership, and a large part of such action is only possible through an opportunity to obtain long-term loans payable in installments. It is urgently important, therefore, that we provide some method for bringing into continuing and steady action the great facilities of such of these great national and local loaning concerns as have been under pressure and should provide against such difficulties in the future.

"The farm mortgage situation presents many difficulties to which this plan would give aid.

"I have consulted with representatives of the various groups granting credit on mortgage loans for the home and farm as well as Government officials and other economic agencies, and as a practical solution from the various needs and the various ideas advanced I propose the following general principles for the creation of an institution for such purpose:

"(a) That there be established 12 home loan discount banks (if necessary) one in each Federal Reserve District under the direction of a Federal home loan board.

"(b) The capital of these discount banks shall be initially of minimum of 5 to 30 million as may be determined by the Federal board upon the basis of the aggregate of such mortgage loans and probable needs of the particular district.

"(c) The proposed discount banks to make no initial or direct mortgages but to loan only upon the obligations of the loaning institutions secured by the mortgage loans as collateral so as to assure and expand the functioning of such institutions.

"(d) Building and loan associations, savings banks, deposit banks, farm loan banks, etc. may become members of the system after they have satisfied the conditions of qualifications and eligibility that may be fixed by the Federal board.

"(e) The mortgage loans eligible for collateral shall not exceed $15,000 each and shall be limited to urban and farm property used for home purposes.

"(f) The maximum amount to be advanced against the mortgage collateral not to exceed more than 50 percent of the unpaid balance on unamortized or short-term mortgage loans and not more than 60 percent of the unpaid balance of amortized long-term mortgages, and no advance to be made on mortgages in default. Such loans are to be made on the basis that there are sound appraisals of the property upon which such mortgages have been made. In other words, given sound appraisals, there will be advanced in the case of short-term or unamortized loans 25 percent of the appraisal and in case of amortized long-term loans, 30 percent of the appraised value of the property.

"(g) The discount banks as their needs require from time to time to issue bonds or short-term notes to investors to an amount not to exceed in the aggregate 12 times the capital of the issuing bank. The bonds of these discount banks would be thus secured by the obligations of the borrowing institutions, the mortgages deposited as collateral against

544

such obligations and the capital of the discount banks. These bonds to be acceptable for security for Government and postal deposits. The result would be a bond of high grade as to quality and security.

"(h) If the aggregate initial capital of the discount banks should in the beginning be fixed at $150 million it would be possible for the 12 banks to finance approximately something over $1,800 million of advance to the borrowing institutions which could be further expanded by increase in their capital.

"(i) It is proposed to find the initial capital stock for the discount banks in much the same way, in so far as is applicable, as the capital was found for the Federal Reserve banks—that is, that an organization committee in each district should first offer the capital to the institutions which would participate in the service of the bank. And as was provided in respect to the Federal Reserve banks, if the initial capital is not wholly thus provided, it should be subscribed by the Federal Government; and further somewhat as was provided in the case of the Federal land banks other institutions using the facilities of the discount banks should be required to purchase from time to time from the Government some proportionate amount of its holdings of stock if there be any. In this manner any government capital will gradually pass over to private ownership as was the case in the Federal land banks.

"The above details of the proposal are put forward as suggestions in order to give clarity to the central idea rather than as inflexible conclusions. The whole plan would necessarily be subject to the action of Congress and many parts of it will no doubt need development.

"There is no element of inflation in the plan but simply a better organization of credit for these purposes.

"This proposed institution does not in any way displace the National Credit Association which occupies an entirely different field of action."

NOTE: The White House issued the President's statement following the news conference on November 13, 1931, and embargoed its release until November 14.

409

Radio Remarks Endorsing Liberal Arts Colleges.
November 14, 1931

I AM GLAD to express appreciation of the service of the liberal arts college, that is the small college. I do this the more freely because of the more than 600 such institutions in our land. Most of them have little, if any, endowment or State support. In these times of trends toward larger units, the difficulties of the unsupported small college multiply, which make their successful operations less hopeful and, in many cases, a desperate struggle.

The important place which these institutions hold in our system of education renders their support of the utmost importance. Whatever be the magnificent services of the larger and highly specialized universities, the liberal arts college places an emphasis upon personal contacts of teacher and student which render them a vital part of our educational system.

A primary purpose of education is a product of high character and noble ideals, which regard moral and spiritual qualities superior to mere material things, without which any purely economic system would collapse.

Throughout our history these colleges have been and are now the seedbeds of leadership. They have contributed a large part to the presence in our land of nearly 2 million college-trained men and women. Theirs is a great honor roll of men and women in our Nation. The finest traditions of our country are rooted in their associations and their inspiration.

The disadvantage of the small college is obvious. The dramatic element in education does not play a great part in its activities. It must remain content with the character of service it renders to the individual man and woman and to the public weal. In the last analysis the chief service to higher education in our country must rest not with the few highly endowed universities but, in large degree, with the more than 600 smaller colleges for whose future welfare I am now speaking.

It is through them that each State and section must maintain ample cultural opportunities for the youth within reasonable distance from their homes and in circumstances fitted to the needs of each community and its people.

That service for the youth is a guarantee of equality of cultural opportunity and a bulwark for the spiritual life of the generation in which our children will have to live, a service which I sincerely commend.

NOTE: The President spoke at 9 a.m. from the Cabinet Room in the White House. His remarks were part of a radio program in which educational leaders appealed for public support of small liberal arts colleges. The program, sponsored by the Liberal Arts College Association, was carried over the National Broadcasting Company radio network.

A reading copy of this item with holograph changes by the President is available for examination at the Herbert Hoover Presidential Library.

410

Message on the 100th Anniversary of the Chillicothe News-Advertiser. *November 16, 1931*

[Released November 16, 1931.   Dated September 28, 1931]

My dear Mr. Hunter:

On the occasion of the one hundredth anniversary of the founding of The Chillicothe News-Advertiser, I wish to extend my hearty congratulations and all good wishes for the continuance of its service to the community. Newspapers have an unparalleled opportunity to exercise leadership in creating sound public opinion on the vital problems which confront the Nation today.

Yours faithfully,

HERBERT HOOVER

[Mr. J. K. Hunter, President and Manager, The Chillicothe News-Advertiser, Chillicothe, Ohio]

NOTE: The message was published in the November 16, 1931, edition of the Chillicothe News-Advertiser.

411

The President's News Conference of *November 17, 1931*

United States Tariff Commission

THE PRESIDENT. I have this morning Mr. [Henry P.] Fletcher's resignation as Chairman of the Tariff Commission. You have already been advised of this, but he attaches to his letter a complete report of the work of the Commission to date showing that by November 30 the docket will be clear of all applications and all Senate references, and we will have it mimeographed and given to you today.

Q. Mr. President, when does he officially leave?

THE PRESIDENT. The end of this month.

Italian Minister of Foreign Affairs

As you know Mr. Grandi has arrived. He is a national guest and I have some conversations with him beginning at 4 this afternoon, in conjunction with Secretary of State Stimson.

Home Loan Discount Banks

The only other item here is the continuous flood of telegrams concerning the mortgage discount bank which are coming from every town and village in the United States. That, of course, is not of so much interest to you for publication, but it is an interesting phenomenon that it has received such extraordinary universal support.

Other than that I have nothing this morning.

Italian Minister of Foreign Affairs

Q. Will you have conversations with Mr. Grandi tomorrow?

THE PRESIDENT. I don't know yet.

NOTE: President Hoover's two hundred and twenty-second news conference was held in the White House at 12 noon on Tuesday, November 17, 1931.

Italian Minister of Foreign Affairs Dino Grandi arrived in the United States on November 16, 1931.

On the same day, the White House issued the texts of representative letters and telegrams of endorsements of the Federal home loan discount bank system.

412

Letter Accepting the Resignation of Henry P. Fletcher as Chairman of the United States Tariff Commission. *November 17, 1931*

My dear Chairman Fletcher:

I have your letter of November 17th tendering your resignation as Chairman of the United States Tariff Commission, to be effective November 30th.

In accepting it I wish to express the keen appreciation I have for the great public service you have rendered. Under your Chairmanship the work of the Commission has made great progress in consummation of the hopes which were placed in its reorganization and increased authority. That a large number of cases have been considered and disposed of and the heavy docket for the year almost completed, all bespeak the devotion and effectiveness of the Commission's work.

Yours faithfully,

HERBERT HOOVER

[Hon. Henry P. Fletcher, U.S. Tariff Commission, Washington, D.C.]

NOTE: Mr. Fletcher served as Chairman of the United States Tariff Commission from September 1930 until his resignation. His letter of resignation and a memorandum on the work of the Commission, both dated September 17, 1931, and released with the President's letter, follow:

Dear Mr. President:

I hereby tender my resignation as Chairman and Member of the United States Tariff Commission effective November 30 next.

I enclose a memorandum summarizing the work accomplished since the Commission was reorganized fourteen months ago. This memorandum shows that with one or two exceptions all the investigations requested by Senate or House Resolutions have been completed. The petroleum, copper, and vegetable oil investigations are in final form and will be submitted, as requested by the Resolutions, to the Congress when it assembles next month. The most important investigation now pending is that relating to raw and refined sugar which was recently ordered and which in the nature of the case may be protracted as growing as well as refining costs both at home and abroad are involved. Work on this and all other pending applications and investigations is proceeding as rapidly as circumstances permit.

The recent depreciation in exchange in a number of countries exporting to the United States has rendered our cost data, secured before these countries departed from the gold standard, inapplicable in view of the present instability of exchange values and negative reports were sometimes unavoidable in cases where the exchange factor entered. The facts gained in our investigations, however, are all assembled and can be utilized in case further investigation may become necessary.

The Commission has been completely reorganized and is, I believe, thoroughly equipped to perform its important functions.

It is a pleasure to express my appreciation of the loyal and efficient cooperation and support I have received from my colleagues on the Commission and from every member of its staff.

Faithfully yours,

HENRY P. FLETCHER

[The President, The White House]

Enclosure.

MEMORANDUM

WORK OF THE UNITED STATES TARIFF COMMISSION

Since the Tariff Commission was reorganized, its work may be briefly summarized as follows:

By November 30, the effective date of the Chairman's resignation:

—39 separate rate investigations, covering a very large number of items, and different rates of duty, will have been completed and reported upon under Section 336 of the Tariff Act.

—11 important surveys (not involving rate changes) will also have been completed.

—Of the 9 investigations discontinued, 8 were dismissed by Senate Resolutions.

—5 applications were withdrawn by proponents.

—28 applications were dismissed by the Commission after careful preliminary investigation.

—Thus 92 cases will have been disposed of.

550

There remains on the Commission calendar 10 rate investigations and 1 survey, all in response to Senate Resolutions, and 8 rate investigations of other origin, making a total of 19 investigations and surveys in progress.

Twenty-one applications for investigations are on file, some of which may be granted and some denied, depending upon the facts developed by preliminary investigation by the Commission.

Thus the Commission has 40 investigations, surveys, and applications on its books compared with 92 disposed of since reorganization.

The Commission is, of course, engaged in other routine work assigned to it including the American Valuation study called for under Section 340 of the Tariff Act of 1930, investigations under Section 337, Surveys, etc.

The first seven of the following surveys have been completed and the reports published, while the last four are practically completed and reports are being prepared for submission to the Congress next month:

Commodity	Investigation No.	Resolution or Application No.
Crude petroleum production cost	Survey	Tariff Act of 1930.
Sugar differential	..do	Committee on Ways and Means.
Anthracite coal industry of Soviet Russia	..do	Do.
Fish and other marine products	..do	S. Res. 314.
Cigar-wrapper tobacco	..do	
United States-Philippine tariff and trade relations	..do	
Census of dyes and of other synthetic organic chemicals	..do	
Petroleum, crude and refined products thereof	..do	II. Res. 391.
Copper	..do	S. Res. 434.
Vegetable oils	..do	S. Res. 323.
Creosote oil	..do	S. Res. 470.

The following rate investigations (Sec. 336) have been completed.

Commodity	Investi-gation No.	Resolution or Application No.
Pigskin leather	16	S. Res. 313.
Woven wire fencing and netting	4	S. Res. 295.
Ultramarine blue	8	S. Res. 309.
Wood flour	12	S. Res. 313.
Wool floor coverings, nspf.	18	S. Res. 313.
Straw hats	21	S. Res. 313.
Maple sugar and maple sirup	23	S. Res. 313.
Fourdrinier wires and cylinder wires	22	S. Res. 313.
Wool felt hats	17	S. Res. 313.
Tomatoes, prepared or preserved	28	S. Res. 324.
Smokers' articles	14	S. Res. 313; application 21.
Cherries, sulphured or in brine	27	S. Res. 324; application 30.
Edible gelatin	38	Application 47.
Pig iron	10	S. Res. 309.
Bentwood furniture	36	Application 5.
Hides and skins	24	S. Res. 313.
Cheese	26	S. Res. 324; application 59.
Bells	3	S. Res. 295.
Organs	13	S. Res. 313; application 18.
Dried eggs	42	S. Res. 389; application 29.
Hemp cords	56	Application 8.
Olive oil	25	S. Res. 324.

Hearings have been held and reports are being prepared for submission to the President before November 30 in the following investigations:

Commodity	Investi- gation No.	Resolution or Application No.
Tomatoes in their natural state......	45	S. Res. 414; application 7.
Peppers in their natural state........	46	S. Res. 414; application 6.
Peas, green or unripe...............	47	S. Res. 414.
Beans, snap or string, green or unripe..	58	Application 82.
Lima beans......................	50	Application 32.
Eggplant in its natural state........	48	Application 31.
Cucumbers in their natural state.....	49	Application 31.
Okra...........................	51	Application 33.
Pineapples......................	41	S. Res. 397; applications 34 and 44.
Pens...........................	39	S. Res. 360 and 438.
Window glass....................	20	S. Res. 313.
Crin vegetal, spanish moss, flax tow..	54	S. Res. 468.
Cement.........................	5	S. Res. 295.
Lumber and timber................	19	S. Res. 313 and 321; applications 38 and 5.
Gauge glass tubes.................	57	Application 79.
Crude feldspar.	63	Application 90.
Boots and shoes..................	1	S. Res. 313 and 295.
Blown glass tableware.............	35	S. Res. 330; application 28.
Furniture of wood.................	2	S. Res. 295; application 2.

Another list of more than 30 applications have been carefully investigated by the Commission and applications either denied or dismissed without prejudice, or withdrawn by those who made the original applications. The following items appear on this list:

Denied and dismissed	Application No.	Withdrawn	Application No.
Hats, bonnets, hoods, manufactured by machine.	49	Bamboo handle toothbrushes.	11
Wool, waste, shoddy, rags, etc..	4	Crude barytes Ore...	45
Hemp yarn................	8	Artificial flowers....	70
Men's and boys' woolen clothing.	19	Parachlormetacresol.	16
Incandescent lamps............	22	Live cattle........	108
Tulip bulbs..................	24		
Cut flowers..................	39, 57		
Rough tanned walrus leather....	50		
Paintings, pastels, drawings, etc.	77		
Collodion emulsion............	64		
Cylinder watch parts, Swiss.....	48		
Grapefruit...................	35		
Pipes and smokers' articles of clay.	52		
Sugar cane in its natural state....	85		
Soybeans....................	46		
Men's silk and opera hats.......	41, 42, 61		
Hot rolled diameter tubing......	37		
Cork insulation..............	83		
Woven fabrics of flax, etc.......	73		
Jute paddings and interlinings....	74		
Calf and kip shoe leather........	81		
Antifriction steel balls..........	89		
Springrings..................	91		
Yarn guiding apron (Sec. 337)...	36		
Lumber and timber (Sec. 337)....	109		
Ground pumice stone...........	102–10–15–16		
Ground chicory..............	111		
Raw lime juice................	93		

The following is a list of investigations undertaken mostly in response to Senate Resolutions, which were rescinded and dismissed, before public hearings were held, largely in response to withdrawal of Senate Resolutions:

Commodity	Investigation No.	Resolution or Application No.
Shoe lacings	7	S. Res. 308.
Laces	11	S. Res. 311.
Reptile leather	15	S. Res. 313.
Sugar candy and confectionery	29	S. Res. 324.
Matches	32	S. Res. 325.
Cigarette paper	33	S. Res. 325.
Refined sugar	34	S. Res. 309 and 325.
Cocoa and chocolate	40	S. Res. 380.
Soups	37	Application 1.

The following investigations called for by Senate Resolutions are under way at the present time, and in most cases the investigations are nearing completion. The investigations in progress are as follows:

Commodity	Investigation No.	Resolution or Application No.
Umbrellas	9	S. Res. 312, 309.
Infants' wear of wool	31	S. Res. 325.
Agricultural hand tools	6	S. Res. 295.
Laminated products	30	S. Res. 324.
Velvets and velveteens	52	S. Res. 440.
Casein	43	S. Res. 390; application 40.
Nonedible gelatin and glue	53	S. Res. 458.
Dried beans	44	S. Res. 411.
Lead	Survey	S. Res. 441.

Some of these, the Commission has been informed, will be dismissed by the Senate.

Other investigations in progress, based upon applications, include:

Commodity	Investigation No.	Application No.
Alsimin................................	55	43.
Candied fruit........................	61	62.
Flaxseed and linseed oil.............	62	17.
Sponges..............................	64	92.
Mackerel, fresh, salted, etc..........	65 ⎱	94, 95, 98, 99, 100, 101,
Sugar and molasses..................	66 ⎰	103, 107.
Cherries, sulphured or in brine.......	59	Request of President.
Tomatoes, prepared or preserved......	60	Do.

There remains on the calendar the following applications for investigation under the provisions of section 336 of the Tariff Act of 1930. These applications are receiving the usual preliminary study at the present time:

APPLICATIONS PENDING

Commodity	Application No.
Lemons...	80
Dried or fresh mushrooms, prepared or tinned.............	60, 96
Barley malt..	53
Pulpboard in rolls for use in manufacture of wallboard.....	10
Filaments and yarns of rayon, etc.......................	69
Linen huck towels.....................................	51
Gloves of leather......................................	58
Towels and napkins of flax, hemp, ramie.................	75
Crepe and tissue paper hats, etc........................	88
Whole eggs, etc., frozen, prepared, preserved, etc.........	86, 87
Fluorspar...	97
Chocolate, sweetened, in bars, etc......................	104

Commodity	Application No.
Canvas rubber-soled footwear, waterproof.................	105
Rubber insulated wires and cables........................	106
Wooden and aluminum folding rules......................	112
Crude sperm oil...	113
Ribbon fly catchers......................................	114
Long staple cotton....................................	117, 119, 120, 121
Upholsterers' nails, thumb tacks, chair glides.............	118
Bicycle chains..	122
Antimony oxide; antimony regulus or metal...............	123

413

Memorandum About Unemployment Relief.
November 17, 1931

[Released November 17, 1931.   Dated November 16, 1931]

To the officers and employees of the departments and independent establishments and of the Government of the District of Columbia:

I have been glad to learn of the earnest desire of Government employees to have an opportunity to join in relieving distress growing out of unemployment. The officers and employees of Federal and District establishments were most generous in their response last year to the appeal of the local relief agencies, and I am confident that current needs will find equally hearty support.

To this end I commend to your favorable consideration, the plan of organization now formulated, by which every officer and employee will have the opportunity to satisfy his own charitable impulse to contribute wholeheartedly to unemployment and dependency relief. It is understood that an integral part of the plan includes provision for creating work as far as possible to give to unemployed persons, and that direct relief will be accorded only in necessitous cases.

I believe we will be brought closer together in this unified effort to relieve the distress of our fellow citizens, and will learn lessons of future fruitfulness in meeting the social problems of our community.

Yours faithfully,
HERBERT HOOVER

NOTE: The plan, as made public by the United States Civil Service Commission, called for all Federal employees to contribute 3 days' pay to relief organizations.

414

Message to the World Affairs Institute.
November 17, 1931

[Released November 17, 1931.   Dated November 9, 1931]

My dear Mrs. Adams:

I deeply regret that pressure of the public business prevented my accepting your kind invitation to address the World Affairs Institute sponsored by the Westchester County Federation of Women's Clubs and allied groups. An encouraging sign of our times is the trend toward greater citizen interest in national and international problems. I am confident that your meetings will contribute to an informed and enlightened public opinion helpful not only to the Westchester community, but to the Nation. I shall appreciate it if you will extend my most cordial greetings to the participants in your Institute and my best wishes for an occasion fruitful in promoting international understanding and concord.

Yours faithfully,
HERBERT HOOVER

[Mrs. Lucy G. Adams, Chairman, Westchester County World Affairs Institute, 170 Elm St., New Rochelle, N.Y.]

NOTE: The message was read to the institute's evening session, meeting in White Plains, N.Y.

415

Message on the Opening
of the Whitney Museum of American Art.
November 17, 1931

[Released November 17, 1931.   Dated November 10, 1931]

My dear Mrs. Whitney:

I profoundly regret that the pressure of imperative public duties prevents my accepting your kind invitation to speak at the opening of the Whitney Museum of American Art. It is an enterprise which makes a strong appeal to my own interest and I am sure that this permanent, pioneer museum devoted exclusively to American paintings and sculpture will appeal to the country as a benefaction of nation-wide interest. It is a promising step toward placing American art in the position of importance and dignity which its excellence and individuality merit. It should quicken our national sense of beauty and increase America's pride in her own culture. Please accept for yourself my heartiest congratulations on the consummation of your plans and the appreciation which I know every American must feel for so notable a contribution to the nation.

Yours faithfully,
HERBERT HOOVER

[Mrs. Harry Payne Whitney, Whitney Museum of American Art, 10 West Eighth Street, New York City]

NOTE: The message was read at ceremonies opening the Whitney Museum of American Art in New York City.

416

Statement on the Report
of the Muscle Shoals Commission.
November 19, 1931

THE PRESIDENT said:

"I am issuing today the unanimous report of the Commission on Muscle Shoals. This Commission was appointed to recommend methods for the disposal of Muscle Shoals and consists of three members each appointed by the legislatures and Governors of the States of Alabama and Tennessee, together with one member from the Engineer Corps, one from the Judge Advocate General's office and one from the agricultural organizations.

"The Commission has made a 4-months' intensive study of the subject, has had many public hearings at which all interested parties have been encouraged to send representatives. It is a representative body and its conclusions speak for themselves. At an appropriate time I shall transmit the report to the Congress."

NOTE: On the same day, the White House issued a text of the Muscle Shoals Commission report, dated November 14, 1931, which follows:

To the President of the United States and to the Governors of the States of Tennessee and Alabama:

The Muscle Shoals Commission has the honor of submitting this report of its findings and conclusions:

ORIGIN OF COMMISSION

Acting upon the suggestion contained in the message from the President of the United States to the Senate dated March 3, 1931, returning without approval Senate Joint Resolution No. 49, the Legislature of the State of Tennessee by Senate Joint Resolution No. 38, approved March 23, 1931, appointed three commissioners as representatives of the State of Tennessee to consult with any commission created by the State of Alabama and such other commission as the President might designate in connection with the consideration of the problem of utilizing the United States plants at Muscle Shoals, Alabama, for the purpose of quantity production of fertilizers and the development of the resources and industries of the Tennessee Valley.

By House Joint Resolution No. 331, approved June 30, 1931, the Legislature of the State of Alabama authorized the Governor to appoint three commissioners to represent the State of Alabama to consult with the commissioners appointed by the State of Tennessee and any similar commission which might be appointed by the President, for the consideration of the problem.

Pursuant to the authority granted in H. J. Res. No. 331, the Governor of the State of Alabama appointed three commissioners.

In conformity with the foregoing, the President appointed a commission of three members to meet with the commissioners appointed by the States of Alabama and Tennessee, and on July 14, 1931, announced the Muscle Shoals Commission.

MEMBERSHIP OF COMMISSION

The membership of the Muscle Shoals Commission is as follows:

Representing National Farm Organizations

    EDWARD A. O'NEAL, Chicago, Illinois, President, American Farm Bureau Federation

Representing the State of Tennessee

    MERCER REYNOLDS, Chattanooga, Tennessee

    J. F. PORTER, Columbia, Tennessee

    R. L. MOORE, Jellico, Tennessee

Representing the State of Alabama

    W. F. McFARLAND, Florence, Alabama

    WILL HOWARD SMITH, Prattville, Alabama

    S. F. HOBBS, Selma, Alabama—Chairman

Representing the War Department

    COLONEL HARLEY B. FERGUSON, Corps of Engineers, United States Army

    COLONEL JOS. I. McMULLEN, J.A.G.D., United States Army

By vote of the Commission at its first meeting on August 3, 1931, Honorable S. F. Hobbs of Selma, Alabama, was elected Chairman of the Commission.

SCOPE OF INQUIRY BY COMMISSION

The general scope of the inquiry by the Commission is outlined in Section 124 of the National Defense Act and the Acts of the legislatures of the states of Alabama and Tennessee enacted pursuant to the suggestion of the President, in his message to the Senate dated March 3, 1931, which returned without approval Senate Joint Resolution No. 49. The purpose of the Commission has been to inquire into the problem of applying the benefits available at the United States Plants at Muscle Shoals, Alabama, to agriculture and to consider the development of the resources of the Tennessee Valley in the interest of agriculture and industry.

INVESTIGATIONS MADE

From the outset the Commission recognized the fact that any successful plan for the operation of the properties must be based upon sound economic principles. With that thought in mind, the Commission assembled and considered all available practical data relative to the engineering and industrial possibilities of the plants. Much authentic and valuable information was gleaned from the reports of prior investigators, of which there have been many. Since there has been a very marked advance in the fertilizer, chemical, and power industries during the past ten years, it was necessary to make careful surveys of these industries to determine the present existing situation. Additional surveys were made to obtain specific engineering data pertinent to the situation. Various technical experts in the industries concerned were consulted. Since it is proposed that agriculture is to be the beneficiary of any plan, the advice of representatives of farm organizations and agronomists was sought. For the purpose of obtaining the views of individual farmers and small groups of farmers, public hearings were held in various cities of the states of Alabama and Tennessee. These meetings were well attended and much basic information was obtained.

Through the press and the mail, the general public and all industrial organizations which might be interested were solicited to submit bids and proposals for the operation or disposition of the properties. Eight bids and proposals were obtained from this source and while they evidenced careful thought and serious intention, none was sufficiently satisfactory to warrant the endorsement of the Commission.

CONCLUSIONS

From the mass of information obtained from various sources and from a careful consideration of the views of representatives of various enterprises including farm organizations, fertilizer and chemical industries and those dealing with raw materials incident to fertilizer and chemical fields and from exhaustive studies by experts, the Commission unanimously arrived at the following conclusions:

1. It is economically feasible and desirable to use and operate the Muscle Shoals properties for the following purposes:
    (a) Primarily for quantity production of types of commercial fertilizer and/or fertilizer ingredients of greater concentration, than those which are now generally sold to the farmer.
    (b) Cooperative scientific research and experimentation for the betterment of agriculture.
    (c) Manufacture of chemicals.
2. It is the definite conclusion of the Commission that the foregoing public benefits can best be obtained by private operation under lease contracts through competitive negotiations.

562

The Commission unanimously adopted the following recommendations:

3. The enactment of the necessary enabling legislation by Congress empowering the President or such agency as he may elect to negotiate and to conclude a lease contract for the United States properties at Muscle Shoals, Alabama, and to supervise operations thereunder, for and on behalf of the United States.

4. In addition to usual and necessary covenants, the lease contract covering the properties should contain provisions giving effect to the following terms:

(a) Such power as may be necessary, and such lands, buildings, fixtures and other equipment belonging to the nitrate plants as may be serviceable, will be used for making fertilizer and/or fertilizer ingredients in form suitable for quantity production, or for home mixing, or for direct application to the soil.

(b) Fertilizer and fertilizer ingredients in form suitable for home mixing or for direct application to the soil, so produced, will be sold to farmers or their authorized purchasing agents under conditions providing for equitable distribution and reasonable profit limitations.

(c) All power necessary for the production of a required initial minimum amount of fertilizer or fertilizer ingredients, and for the production of increasing amounts from time to time in response to reasonable market demands, and for the manufacture of chemicals, should be guaranteed and allocated for such purposes.

(d) The lessee shall pay a fair and reasonable rental on mutually agreeable terms.

(e) Up river development, including Cove Creek Dam, and equalization dam below Wilson Dam, to increase the rental in fair proportion to the benefits derived therefrom.

(f) Term of lease shall be 50 years, with Boulder Dam clause on re-negotiation as to rental.

5. In behalf of the development of the Tennessee Valley, there should be authority to sell or use surplus Muscle Shoals property and to sell or dispose of, on an equitable basis, surplus power at the switchboard; states, counties, municipalities and chemical operations to have preference; the remainder of such surplus power shall be subject to recall on reasonable notice for the purposes above named.

6. Power rentals accruing to the United States and proceeds from lease or sale of surplus property should be expended, not exceeding 25% for research and investigation, under the direction of a Board to be named from organized agriculture, and not exceeding 75% for the creation of a revolving fund for the operation and financing of the purchase and storage of fertilizer and fertilizer material, and the development of better methods of manufacture and distribution

of fertilizer by a farmers cooperative, representing national farm organizations. Any surplus of funds not needed for such operations will be applied to the Wilson Dam share of the amortization of the cost of Cove Creek Dam.

7. Preference as a lessee should be accorded a corporation exclusively owned and controlled by organizations of farmers, operated without profit.

8. Cove Creek Dam should be constructed by the Government. This is justified and recommended for the benefits to accrue to navigation, flood control and incidental power development, there, and at points downstream. It would greatly enhance the value of Wilson Dam and greatly encourage the building of other high dams on the Tennessee River. The construction of Cove Creek Dam should be begun immediately after the disposition, by lease or otherwise, of the Muscle Shoals project has been authorized.

9. The right of recapture of the dams involved in this report, at the termination of the lease or amortization period of fifty years, by the States of Tennessee and Alabama preferably, should be recognized, under the terms of existing laws.

10. In the opinion of the Commission, based upon careful study and survey, if such enabling legislation is enacted by Congress, such a contract will be readily negotiable, at a fair and reasonable rental, and the benefits to agriculture to be derived therefrom would be immeasurable.

The publication of all of the information which was made available and considered by the Commission in arriving at its conclusions would be very voluminous. It is believed, however, that the public might be interested in a part of that record information. Accordingly, the Commission proposes to publish a booklet setting forth certain documentary and other evidence pertinent to the solution of the problem. Some parts of this evidence received the endorsement of the Commission and other parts did not.

Most respectfully submitted,
S.F. Hobbs, *Chairman*
Edward A. O'Neal
Harley B. Ferguson
Jos. I. McMullen
Mercer Reynolds
J.F. Porter
R.L. Moore
W.F. McFarland
Wm. Howard Smith

417

Letter on the Presentation
of the American Hebrew Medal
to Archbishop Edward J. Hanna.
November 19, 1931

[Released November 19, 1931.   Dated November 16, 1931]

My dear Rabbi Landman:

I have learned with pleasure that the American Hebrew Medal for the Promotion of Better Understanding between Christian and Jew will be presented this year to Archbishop Edward J. Hanna of San Francisco. This distinguished Prelate has done much to promote that comity, resulting from better understanding, which forwards the objective this award has in view. I wish to congratulate, through you, the committee making the award and its worthy recipient.

Yours faithfully,
HERBERT HOOVER

[Rabbi Isaac Landman, 71 West 47th Street, New York City]

NOTE: The message was released in conjunction with the presentation ceremonies, which were held in the Hotel Pennsylvania in New York City.

418

Message to the New England Council.
November 19, 1931

[Released November 19, 1931.   Dated November 11, 1931]

Dear Mr. Knight:

I have been advised that the New England Council is about to hold its annual conference. I wish to avail myself of this opportunity to express to you and through you to the members of the Council my deep appreciation of the work of your organization has done and is doing.

The Council has taken upon itself the duties and the responsibilities that it alone can best discharge. It has labored earnestly and effectively for the good of the six states it serves. Furnishing a model of farsighted and intelligent cooperation, it has courageously shown the way to the entire country.

The people of New England have true cause for gratitude for the splendid efforts of the Council in behalf of the unemployed. There has been no finer cooperation with the agencies concerned with unemployment than that accorded by the Council.

The work done by the Council is most gratifying. I have every confidence the Council will continue its unstinted efforts.

Yours faithfully,

HERBERT HOOVER

[Mr. Harry C. Knight, President, New England Council, Statler Building, Boston, Massachusetts]

NOTE: The message was read to the opening session of the annual conference of the council, meeting in Boston, Mass.

419

Message to the Americanization Committee of the Newspaper Post of the Veterans of Foreign Wars. *November 21, 1931*

[Released November 21, 1931. Dated November 18, 1931]

Dear Colonel Grove:

I wish to emphasize the significance of the Americanization program under the auspices of the Newspaper Post of the Veterans of Foreign Wars of the United States. The purpose of this meeting, I am advised, is to explain to newly naturalized citizens the value of the heritage they are acquiring in becoming citizens of the United States.

There is no more sacred obligation among citizens of the United States today than to be awake to the duties of citizenship. Good citizenship connotes love of country and reverence for its laws; recognition of civic duties and defense of country in time of emergency; proper respect for the rights and property of others; and consideration for the feelings of our fellowmen. Such a spirit of good citizenship, of patriotism and unselfishness was exemplified by the membership of your organization in the conflicts in which our country was involved. It is equally important that these responsibilities be recognized in time of peace, and no less than in time of war should all citizens be worthy examples in the duties of citizenship to those newly assuming those duties.

Yours faithfully,

HERBERT HOOVER

[Colonel Walter E. Grove, Commander, The Americanization Committee of the Newspaper Post, No. 1955, Veterans of Foreign Wars of the United States, 216 West 50th Street, New York City]

NOTE: The letter was read at Naturalization Day ceremonies in City Hall Plaza in New York City.

420

The President's News Conference of *November 24, 1931*

UNITED STATES TARIFF COMMISSION

THE PRESIDENT. I have to announce that Mr. Robert Lincoln O'Brien of Boston has been appointed Chairman of the Tariff Commission. Mr. [Theodore G.] Joslin will give you a note about his background and history. As you know, for many years he was the editor of the Boston Herald.

BRITISH TARIFF POLICY

Just for background, there are one or two points on the recent British action with regard to tariffs. One of the difficulties which confronted the English people for the last 2 years has been the growing adverse trade balance and the drain which it placed on their exchange and gold situation. And the purpose of their action is to correct that situation by a decrease in the volume of imports.

The American goods affected amount to 1.6 percent only of the total exports of the United States to Great Britain. Its effect is very much larger in its proportions to other countries than ourselves. The fact of the case is that our American foreign trade is much less competitive than is generally thought, and that is a fair indication of the ratio of competitive goods in our exports. In diminishing the amount of competitive goods to England in competition with their own industry, the list, as I have said, works out at less than 1.6 percent of our total exports to Great Britain.

There is no disposition in the United States to take any action whatever about it. It is entirely within the domestic authority of Great Britain. It is not our concern. We have a concern for the strengthening of the British financial situation. The prosperity of Great Britain adds to the prosperity of the whole world. Just as we insist upon conducting our own domestic policies, so we have no right to criticize anyone else for any domestic arrangements which they may set up in their own protection and interest.

Q. Mr. President, does your information tell you what countries are more seriously affected by the British proposals than our own?

THE PRESIDENT. No, I haven't got the data here.

The British going off the gold standard obviously lowers the production costs in Great Britain, and might presumably increase exports of the British to the United States. That event happened on the 21st of September, as I recollect, and there has been no evidence of any increased imports into this country yet of any character. The British have been able to compete with our people in the matter of coal trade in some foreign points more severely, but otherwise than that we see no effect of it at all on our foreign trade. And again it comes back to the fact that a large part of the British exports to the United States are not competitive with our goods either. If production costs in England should turn out to be so much lowered in competitive goods as to cause dumping in the United States, the Tariff Commission can deal with those questions within its authorities, but I do not anticipate that anything of the kind is going to happen.

Otherwise than that I haven't any news today.

NOTE: President Hoover's two hundred and twenty-third news conference was held in the White House at 12 noon on Tuesday, November 24, 1931.

On the same day, the White House issued biographical data on Robert Lincoln O'Brien.

On November 20, 1931, Great Britain adopted an emergency tariff act authorizing its Board of Trade to impose emergency duties of up to 110 percent on importation that it held to be abnormal. The initial order under the law levied duties amounting to 50 percent ad valorem on a long list of articles.

421

Message to the Governor of Rhode Island on State Unemployment Relief Efforts.
November 25, 1931

I WISH to congratulate the people of Rhode Island and you personally on the sturdy manner in which the state has undertaken and provided for its burdens.

HERBERT HOOVER

[Hon. Norman S. Case, Governor of Rhode Island, Providence, R.I.]

NOTE: The message was in response to a letter from Governor Case, informing the President on the status of State and local unemployment relief efforts. For release dates of similar letters and telegrams issued by the White House, see Appendix A.

The text of Governor Case's letter follows:

I know that you will be interested to learn that the three community chest drives in Rhode Island which closed yesterday, exceeded their quota in each instance. Notwithstanding the fact that the Providence community chest quota was approximately eighty thousand dollars in excess of last year, over eight hundred and fifteen thousand dollars was raised, representing a twenty-five thousand dollar oversubscription. Cranston's chest went five thousand dollars over the top, and for the first time the Pawtucket and Blackstone Valley chest raised its quota and exceeded it by fifteen thousand dollars. The showing by employees in each case was remarkable, as for instance, wage earners in Providence contributed over one hundred thousand dollars to this fine humanitarian cause, this on a one per cent payroll basis. Also that the Rhode Island General Assembly in a one day session, for which the legislatures received no pay, adopted the Governor's plan appropriating one million five hundred thousand dollars for unemployment relief to such cities and towns as will require assistance in order to care for their responsibilities in this matter this money to be loaned out of the States unincumbered surplus at an interest rate of three per cent annually on notes, each town to be limited in its borrowings to one-tenth of one per cent of its total assessed valuation.

These facts confirm my telegram to you of recent date, in which I stated that Rhode Island will provide for its own.

Norman S. Case
Governor of Rhode Island

[The President, Washington, D.C.]

422

Message on the Special Statewide Observance of Thanksgiving Day in Arkansas. *November 26, 1931*

[Released November 26, 1931.   Dated November 19, 1931]

I WAS ADVISED today of the special plan for statewide observance of Thanksgiving Day in Arkansas.

The remarkable recovery of Arkansas from the effects of the drought during 1930, which had followed floods in 1927, is evidence of the courage and energy of the people and of the blessings of Almighty Providence.

Reports show that Arkansas has been fortunate indeed. Weather conditions have been most favorable. Its harvest is the largest and most varied in years. Larders that were empty last year are now filled almost to overflowing. The people have enjoyed immunity from disease and pestilence.

It is not difficult for one to understand why its people, remembering that the first Thanksgiving centered about a harvest following a period of hardship and near famine, have come to realize its true significance.

Please will you convey my appreciation for this exemplification of the spirit of our people to the Chairman of the Statewide Committee having charge of the Thanksgiving observance as well as to the ministers, churches and other organizations.

Herbert Hoover

[Harvey Couch, Pine Bluff, Arkansas]

NOTE: Mr. Couch read the message during a Thanksgiving Day radio broadcast sponsored by the State advisory committee on relief.

423

Message of Sympathy on the Death of Alfred A. Taylor. *November 26, 1931*

[Released November 26, 1931. Dated November 25, 1931]

MRS. HOOVER and I are greatly saddened to learn of the death of your husband, Alfred A. Taylor. In his public career as Governor of the State and member of Congress he served the public welfare with ability and devoted diligence, and his character was reflected in a high sense of duty in all his relationships. Please accept for yourself and members of your family our deepest sympathy in your loss.

HERBERT HOOVER

[Mrs. Jennie Anderson Taylor, Milligan College, Tennessee]

NOTE: Mr. Taylor, former Governor of Tennessee, died in Johnson City, Tenn., on November 25, 1931.

424

Message to the National Tuberculosis Association on the Christmas Seal Campaign. *November 30, 1931*

[Released November 30, 1931. Dated November 23, 1931]

I COMMEND to all our people the annual sale of Christmas Seals conducted by the National Tuberculosis Association and its affiliated State and local associations. These seals sold during the holiday season provide the funds which make possible the organized campaign for the prevention of tuberculosis. These efforts are showing encouraging results in a diminishing death rate. The proceeds of the seal sale make possible one of the most valuable of all services to mankind in helping to check and destroy a disease which endangers millions of homes and weakens millions of citizens, especially the children and youth of the nation. It is especially important at this time to protect the health and physical stamina of our people.

Herbert Hoover

NOTE: The message was made public in conjunction with the launching of the 25th annual Christmas Seal campaign.

425

Address to the White House Conference on Home Building and Home Ownership.
December 2, 1931

YOU HAVE COME from every State in the Union to consider a matter of basic national interest. Your purpose is to consider it in its long view rather than its emergency aspects. Next to food and clothing the housing of a nation is its most vital social and economic problem. This Conference has been called especially to consider one great segment of that problem—that is, in what manner can we facilitate the ownership of homes and how can we protect the owners of homes?

The Conference also has before it some phases of that other great segment of housing; that is, the standards of tenement and apartment dwellings. While at this time we give primary emphasis to homeownership in city, town, and farm, we are all of us concerned in the improvement of city housing. I hope we may at some future time subject the question of city housing to more definitely organized national intelligence through which we shall further establish standards which will give impetus to public understanding and public action to this, the question of blighted areas and slums in many of our great cities. I am confident that the sentiment 'for homeownership is so embedded in the

American heart that millions of people who dwell in tenements, apartments, and rented rows of solid brick have the aspiration for wider opportunity in ownership of their own homes. To possess one's own home is the hope and ambition of almost every individual in our country, whether he lives in hotel, apartment, or tenement.

While the purpose of this Conference is to study and advise upon the very practical questions of home design, of materials, of building regulations, of zoning, of taxes, of transportation, of financing, of parks and playgrounds, and other topics, yet behind it all every one of you here is impelled by the high ideal and aspiration that each family may pass their days in the home which they own; that they may nurture it as theirs; that it may be their castle in all that exquisite sentiment which it surrounds with the sweetness of family life. This aspiration penetrates the heart of our national well-being. It makes for happier married life, it makes for better children, it makes for confidence and security, it makes for courage to meet the battle of life, it makes for better citizenship. There can be no fear for a democracy or self-government or for liberty or freedom from homeowners no matter how humble they may be.

There is a wide distinction between homes and mere housing. Those immortal ballads, Home, Sweet Home; My Old Kentucky Home; and the Little Gray Home in the West, were not written about tenements or apartments. They are the expressions of racial longing which find outlet in the living poetry and songs of our people. They were written about an individual abode, alive with the tender associations of childhood, the family life at the fireside, the free out of doors, the independence, the security, and the pride in possession of the family's own home—the very seat of its being.

That our people should live in their own homes is a sentiment deep in the heart of our race and of American life. We know that as yet is not universally possible to all. We know that many of our people must at all times live under other conditions. But they never sing songs about a pile of rent receipts. To own one's own home is a physical expression of individualism, of enterprise, of independence, and of the freedom of spirit. We do not in our imagination attach to a transitory place that expression about a man's home being his castle, no matter what its constitutional rights may be.

But to return to our practical problems. Over 30 committees embracing the collective skill and experience of our country have been voluntarily engaged for the past year in collecting the best of national experience from every part of our country, in collating it into definite recommendations for your consideration. Like the solution of all practical problems, the facts first must be discovered; they must be assembled in their true perspective; and the conclusions to be drawn from them must be the inexorable march of logic. This Conference has not been called primarily on legislative questions. Its major purpose is to stimulate individual action. It seeks a better planned use of our Nation's energies and resources, especially those that are rooted in neighborliness and mutual help, and those that find expression in our great national voluntary organizations, in our schools and colleges, and in our research laboratories. The Conference represents a place in our mastery of the forces that modern science and modern technology place at our disposal. It is not to set up government in the building of homes but to stimulate individual endeavor and make community conditions propitious. The basis of its action is to collate the whole of our experience to date, to establish standards, to advance thought to a new plane from which we may secure a revitalized start upon national progress in the building and owning of homes.

About a year ago we held in Washington such a conference as this in relation to the health and protection of children.[1] That conference established new standards and a new and higher plane of understanding and action. It presented a set of standards and conclusions, and those conclusions, I am informed, have now been printed in literally millions of copies—through the associations which were interested, through State authorities, and municipal authorities. They have penetrated the thought and permeated the practice of the Nation. Many conferences have been called by the Governors of many States, by the mayors of many cities, to consider and apply their conclusions. Their actions have already

[1] See 1930 volume, Items 140 and 142.

wielded a powerful influence in the administrative functions of government from the Federal Government down to the smallest community. They have been made the basis of legislative action. They have lifted the sense of public and individual responsibility in the Nation. And it is a result of this kind which we are confidently expecting from this Conference.

I notice that some—not the members of these committees—have contended that the development of city and urban life necessarily has driven us to less and less possible ownership of homes. I do not agree with that. The very development of transportation, the advantages of distribution of industry today make the ownership of homes far more feasible and desirable than ever before. But it involves vast problems of city and industrial management which we should have the courage to face. It involves also a great problem of finance. The newly married pair setting out upon the stream of life seldom come to their new state with sufficient resources to purchase or enter upon that great adventure of life of building a home.

It has long been my opinion that we have fairly creditably solved every other segment of our credit structure more effectively than we have solved this one. In normal times the Federal Reserve System has given mobility to financing of commercial transactions. The agricultural banks and the insurance companies have given mobility to farm credit. The public exchanges have given mobility to the financing of industrial credit through stocks and bonds. Through various discount companies we have established mobility for the sale of automobiles and radio sets and fur coats on the installment plan, where 20 or 25 percent cash payments are gratefully accepted.

We have in normal times, through the savings banks, insurance companies, the building and loan associations, and others, provided abundant and mobile finance for 50 percent of the cost of a home through the first mortgage. But the definite problem is not presented by those who can find 50 percent of the cost of a home. Our chief problem in finances relates to those who have an earnest desire for a home, who have a job and therefore possess sound character credit, but whose initial resources run to only 20 or 25 percent. These people would willingly work

575

and apply all their rent and all their savings to gain for themselves this independence and security and social well-being. Such people are a good risk. They are the very basis of stability to the Nation. To find a way to meet their need is one of the problems that you have to consider; that is, how we can make a home available for installment purchase on terms that dignify the name credit and not upon terms and risks comparable to the credit extended by a pawnbroker. Our building and loan and many other associations have made an effort to find a solution for this group, but it is as yet largely unorganized and the question substantially unsolved.

I recently made a public proposal for the creation of a system of home loan discount banks. That proposal is familiar to you, and I will not traverse its details at the present time. It was brought forward partially to meet the situation presented by the present emergency, to alleviate the hardships that exist amongst homeowners today, and to revitalize the building of homes as a factor of economic recovery, but in its long-distance view it was put forward in the confidence that through the creation of an institution of this character we could gradually work out the problem of systematically promoted homeownership on such terms of sound finance as people who have the homeowning aspiration deserve in our country.

And there are many other problems involved in your investigations which bear equal importance to the problem of home financing. The surroundings in which such homes are to be built; the very method of their building; transportation and other facilities which must be provided for them; and the protection that must be given to them from the encroachment of commerce and industry. All of these and many other subjects you will compass. You should be in a position when you complete your work to advise our country of new standards and new ideals for our country.

I wish to express our gratitude, in which I know you will all join, to the hundreds of committee members who have labored so devotedly and capably in preparation for your Conference. I assure you of my appreciation for your coming and my confidence of the high results that will flow from your deliberations.

576

NOTE: The President spoke at 9:30 p.m. to some 3,000 delegates assembled in Constitution Hall. The National Broadcasting Company and the Columbia Broadcasting System radio networks carried the address.

The Conference continued through December 5, 1931, and produced a continuing program. The 31 committee reports and other materials were published in an 11-volume Conference series.

A reading copy of this item with holograph changes by the President is available for examination at the Herbert Hoover Presidential Library.

426

White House Statement on Reports
of the United States Tariff Commission.
December 2, 1931

THE PRESIDENT announced today that he had approved each of the reports on 17 investigations recently completed and submitted to him by the Tariff Commission. This is the largest group of reports submitted at any one time since the passage of the Tariff Act. Eight of them are on mining and industrial products and nine are on agricultural products.

Increases were made in the rates of duty on McKay sewed shoes and on fresh green peas. Decreases were specified on window glass, turned shoes, crude feldspar, green peppers, and eggplant. No change was made on cement, ground feldspar, lumber, crin vegetal, flax upholstery tow, Spanish moss, pens, gauge glass tubes, and shoes other than turned or the McKay sewed types, the last three because of the currency situation in England, the chief competing country. No change was specified in the rates of fresh tomatoes and green snap beans because of the Mexican currency situation, and on cucumbers, lima beans, okra, and pineapples no revision was proposed because of the abnormality of the cost periods or the difference in the seasons during which the domestic and foreign products are produced and marketed.

The report on window glass contained a reservation by one Commissioner. In the case of cement one Commissioner attached a short dissenting statement.

The new rates proclaimed by the President will be effective January 1, 1932.

Canada, the United Kingdom, Belgium, Czechoslovakia, Switzerland, Mexico, and Cuba, were the principal foreign countries concerned in the trade in these imports.

Senate resolutions were responsible for 10 of the investigations and applications from private sources led to 7 investigations.

The accompanying tables summarize the details.

NOTE: The tables accompanying the statement are not printed but are available for examination at the Herbert Hoover Presidential Library.

On the same day, the White House issued the report of the United States Tariff Commission on tariff changes approved by the President.

427

Message to the American Bible Society on Universal Bible Sunday.
December 4, 1931

[Released December 4, 1931.   Dated November 25, 1931]

My dear Mr. Brown:

I am interested to know that December 6th is to be observed as Universal Bible Sunday. Our institutions and common life are grounded in spiritual ideals. I hope that the observation of Bible Sunday will quicken the spiritual impulses of our people and contribute to the spiritual advancement which underlies our stability, service and progress as a nation and as individuals.

Yours faithfully,

HERBERT HOOVER

[Mr. George W. Brown, General Secretary, American Bible Society, Bible House, Astor Place, New York City]

NOTE: The message was released in conjunction with a campaign to make December 6 of each year Universal Bible Sunday.

428

Message on the Award
of the Montclair Yale Bowl
to Eugene Meyer.
December 5, 1931

[Released December 5, 1931.   Dated November 30, 1931]

My dear Mr. Roberts:

I am happy to be informed that the Yale Club of Montclair will award
its Yale Bowl this year to Honorable Eugene Meyer, Governor of the
Federal Reserve Board. Mr. Meyer's service to the country during the
war and as Federal Farm Loan Commissioner, member of the Federal
Farm Loan Board and of the Federal Reserve Board, have made the
nation his debtor. His financial acumen and insight have been invaluable in dealing with problems of the first magnitude in the field of
international as well as national credit organization and stability. The
award represents discrimination and judgment on the part of the givers
as well as recognizing the merit of the receiver of this honor.

Yours faithfully,

HERBERT HOOVER

[Mr. Nicholas Roberts, 565 Fifth Avenue, New York City]

NOTE: The message was read at the annual gathering of the Yale Club of Montclair, N.J.

429

Message to the Lord's Day Alliance.
December 6, 1931

[Released December 6, 1931.   Dated December 3, 1931]

My dear Dr. Bowlby:

I am interested to learn that the Lord's Day Alliance of the United
States will celebrate its forty-third anniversary on December 6th–7th.

579

Its vigilant work in promoting reverent respect for the Sabbath Day is a potent factor in preserving the sacredness of that Day against secularization.

Yours faithfully,
HERBERT HOOVER

[Rev. H. L. Bowlby, D.D., General Secretary, Lord's Day Alliance of the United States, 156 Fifth Avenue, New York City]

NOTE: The message was read at services commemorating the organization's 43d anniversary.

430

Annual Message to the Congress on the State of the Union.
December 8, 1931

To the Senate and House of Representatives:

It is my duty under the Constitution to transmit to the Congress information on the state of the Union and to recommend for its consideration necessary and expedient measures.

The chief influence affecting the state of the Union during the past year has been the continued world-wide economic disturbance. Our national concern has been to meet the emergencies it has created for us and to lay the foundations for recovery.

If we lift our vision beyond these immediate emergencies we find fundamental national gains even amid depression. In meeting the problems of this difficult period, we have witnessed a remarkable development of the sense of cooperation in the community. For the first time in the history of our major economic depressions there has been a notable absence of public disorders and industrial conflict. Above all there is an enlargement of social and spiritual responsibility among the people. The strains and stresses upon business have resulted in closer application, in saner policies, and in better methods. Public improvements have been carried out on a larger scale than even in normal times. The country is richer in physical property, in newly discovered resources, and in productive capacity than ever before. There has been constant gain in knowledge and education; there has been continuous advance in science and invention; there has been distinct gain in public health. Business depressions have been recurrent in the life of our country and are but transitory. The Nation has emerged from each of them with increased strength and virility because of the enlightenment they have brought, the readjustments and the larger understanding of the realities and obligations of life and work which come from them.

NATIONAL DEFENSE

Both our Army and Navy have been maintained in a high state of efficiency. The ability and devotion of both officers and men sustain the highest traditions of the service. Reductions and postponements in expenditure of these departments to meet the present emergency are being made without reducing existing personnel or impairing the morale of either establishment.

The agreement between the leading naval powers for limitation of naval armaments and establishment of their relative strength and thus elimination of competitive building also implies for ourselves the gradual expansion of the deficient categories in our Navy to the parities provided in those treaties. However, none of the other nations, parties to these agreements, is to-day maintaining the full rate of construction which the treaty size of fleets would imply.

Although these agreements secured the maximum reduction of fleets which it was at that time possible to attain, I am hopeful that the naval powers, party to these agreements, will realize that establishment of relative strength in itself offers opportunity for further reduction without injury to any of them. This would be the more possible if pending negotiations are successful between France and Italy. If the world is to regain its standards of life, it must further decrease both naval and other arms. The subject will come before the General Disarmament Conference which meets in Geneva on February 2 next.

FOREIGN AFFAIRS

We are at peace with the world. We have cooperated with other nations to preserve peace. The rights of our citizens abroad have been protected.

The economic depression has continued and deepened in every part of the world during the past year. In many countries political instability, excessive armaments, debts, governmental expenditures, and taxes have resulted in revolutions, in unbalanced budgets and monetary collapse and financial panics, in dumping of goods upon world markets, and in diminished consumption of commodities.

Within two years there have been revolutions or acute social disorders in 19 countries, embracing more than half the population of the world. Ten countries have been unable to meet their external obligations. In 14 countries, embracing a quarter of the world's population, former monetary standards have been temporarily abandoned. In a number of countries there have been acute financial panics or compulsory restraints upon banking. These disturbances have many roots in the dislocations from the World War. Every one of them has reacted upon us. They have sharply affected the markets and prices of our agricultural and industrial products. They have increased unemployment and greatly embarrassed our financial and credit system.

As our difficulties during the past year have plainly originated in large degree from these sources, any effort to bring about our own recuperation has dictated the necessity of cooperation by us with other nations in reasonable effort to restore world confidence and economic stability.

Cooperation of our Federal reserve system and our banks with the central banks in foreign countries has contributed to localize and ameliorate a number of serious financial crises or moderate the pressures upon us and thus avert disasters which would have affected us.

The economic crisis in Germany and Central Europe last June rose to the dimensions of a general panic from which it was apparent that without assistance these nations must collapse. Apprehensions of such collapse had demoralized our agricultural and security markets and so threatened other nations as to impose further dangers upon us. But of

582

highest importance was the necessity of cooperation on our part to relieve the people of Germany from imminent disasters and to maintain their important relations to progress and stability in the world. Upon the initiative of this Government a year's postponement of reparations and other intergovernmental debts was brought about. Upon our further initiative an agreement was made by Germany's private creditors providing for an extension of such credits until the German people can develop more permanent and definite forms of relief.

We have continued our policy of withdrawing our marines from Haiti and Nicaragua.

The difficulties between China and Japan have given us great concern, not alone for the maintenance of the spirit of the Kellogg-Briand Pact, but for the maintenance of the treaties to which we are a party assuring the territorial integrity of China. It is our purpose to assist in finding solutions sustaining the full spirit of those treaties.

I shall deal at greater length with our foreign relations in a later message.

THE DOMESTIC SITUATION

Many undertakings have been organized and forwarded during the past year to meet the new and changing emergencies which have constantly confronted us.

Broadly the community has cooperated to meet the needs of honest distress, and to take such emergency measures as would sustain confidence in our financial system and would cushion the violence of liquidation in industry and commerce, thus giving time for orderly readjustment of costs, inventories, and credits without panic and widespread bankruptcy. These measures have served those purposes and will promote recovery.

In these measures we have striven to mobilize and stimulate private initiative and local and community responsibility. There has been the least possible Government entry into the economic field, and that only in temporary and emergency form. Our citizens and our local governments have given a magnificent display of unity and action, initiative and patriotism in solving a multitude of difficulties and in cooperating with the Federal Government.

For a proper understanding of my recommendations to the Congress it is desirable very briefly to review such activities during the past year.

The emergencies of unemployment have been met by action in many directions. The appropriations for the continued speeding up of the great Federal construction program have provided direct and indirect aid to employment upon a large scale. By organized unity of action, the States and municipalities have also maintained large programs of public improvement. Many industries have been prevailed upon to anticipate and intensify construction. Industrial concerns and other employers have been organized to spread available work amongst all their employees, instead of discharging a portion of them. A large majority have maintained wages at as high levels as the safe conduct of their business would permit. This course has saved us from industrial conflict and disorder which have characterized all previous depressions. Immigration has been curtailed by administrative action. Upon the basis of normal immigration the decrease amounts to about 300,000 individuals who otherwise would have been added to our unemployment. The expansion of Federal employment agencies under appropriations by the Congress has proved most effective. Through the President's organization for unemployment relief, public and private agencies were successfully mobilized last winter to provide employment and other measures against distress. Similar organization gives assurance against suffering during the coming winter. Committees of leading citizens are now active at practically every point of unemployment. In the large majority they have been assured the funds necessary which, together with local government aids, will meet the situation. A few exceptional localities will be further organized. The evidence of the Public Health Service shows an actual decrease of sickness and infant and general mortality below normal years. No greater proof could be adduced that our people have been protected from hunger and cold and that the sense of social responsibility in the Nation has responded to the need of the unfortunate.

To meet the emergencies in agriculture the loans authorized by Congress for rehabilitation in the drought areas have enabled farmers to produce abundant crops in those districts. The Red Cross undertook and magnificently administered relief for over 2,500,000 drought sufferers last winter. It has undertaken this year to administer relief to 100,000 sufferers in the new drought area of certain Northwest States. The action of the Federal Farm Board in granting credits to farm cooperatives saved many of them from bankruptcy and increased their purpose and strength. By enabling farm cooperatives to cushion the fall in prices of farm products in 1930 and 1931 the Board secured higher prices to the farmer than would have been obtained otherwise, although the benefits of this action were partially defeated by continued world overproduction. Incident to this action the failure of a large number of farmers and of country banks was averted which could quite possibly have spread into a major disaster. The banks in the South have cooperated with the Farm Board in creation of a pool for the better marketing of accumulated cotton. Growers have been materially assisted by this action. Constant effort has been made to reduce overproduction in relief of agriculture and to promote the foreign buying of agricultural products by sustaining economic stability abroad.

To meet our domestic emergencies in credit and banking arising from the reaction to acute crisis abroad the National Credit Association was set up by the banks with resources of $500,000,000 to support sound banks against the frightened withdrawals and hoarding. It is giving aid to reopen solvent banks which have been closed. Federal officials have brought about many beneficial unions of banks and have employed other means which have prevented many bank closings. As a result of these measures the hoarding withdrawals which had risen to over $250,000,000 per week after the British crisis have substantially ceased.

FURTHER MEASURES

The major economic forces and weaknesses at home and abroad have now been exposed and can be appraised, and the time is ripe for forward action to expedite our recovery.

Although some of the causes of our depression are due to speculation, inflation of securities and real estate, unsound foreign investments, and mismanagement of financial institutions, yet our self-contained national economy, with its matchless strength and resources, would have enabled us to recover long since but for the continued dislocations, shocks, and setbacks from abroad.

Whatever the causes may be, the vast liquidation and readjustments which have taken place have left us with a large degree of credit paralysis, which together with the situation in our railways and the conditions abroad, are now the outstanding obstacles to recuperation. If we can put our financial resources to work and can ameliorate the financial situation in the railways, I am confident we can make a large measure of recovery independent of the rest of the world. A strong America is the highest contribution to world stability.

One phase of the credit situation is indicated in the banks. During the past year banks, representing 3 per cent of our total deposits have been closed. A large part of these failures have been caused by withdrawals for hoarding, as distinguished from the failures early in the depression where weakness due to mismanagement was the larger cause of failure. Despite their closing, many of them will pay in full. Although such withdrawals have practically ceased, yet $1,100,000,000 of currency was previously withdrawn which has still to return to circulation. This represents a large reduction of the ability of our banks to extend credit which would otherwise fertilize industry and agriculture. Furthermore, many of our bankers, in order to prepare themselves to meet possible withdrawals, have felt compelled to call in loans, to refuse new credits, and to realize upon securities, which in turn has demoralized the markets. The paralysis has been further augmented by the steady increase in recent years of the proportion of bank assets invested in long-term securities, such as mortgages and bonds. These securities tend to lose their liquidity in depression or temporarily to fall in value so that the ability of the banks to meet the shock of sudden withdrawal is greatly lessened and the restriction of all kinds of credit is thereby increased. The continuing credit paralysis has operated to accentuate the deflation and liquidation of commodities, real estate, and securities below any reasonable basis of values.

All of this tends to stifle business, especially the smaller units, and finally expresses itself in further depression of prices and values, in restriction on new enterprise, and in increased unemployment.

The situation largely arises from an unjustified lack of confidence. We have enormous volumes of idle money in the banks and in hoarding. We do not require more money or working capital—we need to put what we have to work.

The fundamental difficulties which have brought about financial strains in foreign countries do not exist in the United States. No external drain on our resources can threaten our position, because the balance of international payments is in our favor; we owe less to foreign countries than they owe to us; our industries are efficiently organized; our currency and bank deposits are protected by the greatest gold reserve in history.

Our first step toward recovery is to reestablish confidence and thus restore the flow of credit which is the very basis of our economic life. We must put some steel beams in the foundations of our credit structure. It is our duty to apply the full strength of our Government not only to the immediate phases, but to provide security against shocks and the repetition of the weaknesses which have been proven.

The recommendations which I here lay before the Congress are designed to meet these needs by strengthening financial, industrial, and agricultural life through the medium of our existing institutions, and thus to avoid the entry of the Government into competition with private business.

FEDERAL GOVERNMENT FINANCE

The first requirement of confidence and of economic recovery is financial stability of the United States Government. I shall deal with fiscal questions at greater length in the Budget message. But I must at this time call attention to the magnitude of the deficits which have developed and the resulting necessity for determined and courageous policies. These deficits arise in the main from the heavy decrease in tax receipts due to the depression and to the increase in expenditure on construction in aid to unemployment, aids to agriculture, and upon services to veterans.

During the fiscal year ending June 30 last we incurred a deficit of about $903,000,000, which included the statutory reduction of the debt and represented an increase of the national debt by $616,000,000. Of this, however, $153,000,000 is offset by increased cash balances.

In comparison with the fiscal year 1928 there is indicated a fall in Federal receipts for the present fiscal year amounting to $1,683,000,000, of which $1,034,000,000 is in individual and corporate income taxes alone. During this fiscal year there will be an increased expenditure, as compared to 1928, on veterans of $255,000,000, and an increased expenditure on construction work which may reach $520,000,000. Despite large economies in other directions, we have an indicated deficit, including the statutory retirement of the debt, of $2,123,000,000, and an indicated net debt increase of about $1,711,000,000.

The Budget for the fiscal year beginning July 1 next, after allowing for some increase of taxes under the present laws and after allowing for drastic reduction in expenditures, still indicates a deficit of $1,417,000,000. After offsetting the statutory debt retirements this would indicate an increase in the national debt for the fiscal year 1933 of about $921,000,000.

Several conclusions are inevitable. We must have insistent and determined reduction in Government expenses. We must face a temporary increase in taxes. Such increase should not cover the whole of these deficits or it will retard recovery. We must partially finance the deficit by borrowing. It is my view that the amount of taxation should be fixed so as to balance the Budget for 1933 except for the statutory debt retirement. Such Government receipts would assure the balance of the following year's budget including debt retirement. It is my further view that the additional taxation should be imposed solely as an emergency measure terminating definitely two years from July 1 next. Such a basis will give confidence in the determination of the Government to stabilize its finance and will assure taxpayers of its temporary character. Even with increased taxation, the Government will reach the utmost safe limit of its borrowing capacity by the expenditures for which we are already obligated and the recommendations here proposed. To go further than these limits in either expenditures, taxes, or borrowing will destroy confidence, denude commerce and industry of its resources, jeopardize the financial system, and actually extend unemployment and demoralize agriculture rather than relieve it.

Federal Land Banks

I recommend that the Congress authorize the subscription by the Treasury of further capital to the Federal land banks to be retired as provided in the original act, or when funds are available, and that repayments of such capital be treated as a fund available for further subscriptions in the same manner. It is urgent that the banks be supported so as to stabilize the market values of their bonds and thus secure capital for the farmers at low rates, that they may continue their services to agriculture and that they may meet the present situation with consideration to the farmers.

Deposits in Closed Banks

A method should be devised to make available quickly to depositors some portion of their deposits in closed banks as the assets of such banks may warrant. Such provision would go far to relieve distress in a multitude of families, would stabilize values in many communities, and would liberate working capital to thousands of concerns. I recommend that measures be enacted promptly to accomplish these results and I suggest that the Congress should consider the development of such a plan through the Federal Reserve Banks.

Home-Loan Discount Banks

I recommend the establishment of a system of home-loan discount banks as the necessary companion in our financial structure of the Federal Reserve Banks and our Federal Land Banks. Such action will relieve present distressing pressures against home and farm property owners. It will relieve pressures upon and give added strength to building and loan associations, savings banks, and deposit banks, engaged in extending such credits. Such action would further decentralize our credit structure. It would revive residential construction and employment. It would enable such loaning institutions more effectually to promote home ownership. I discussed this plan at some length in a statement made public November 14, last. This plan has been warmly indorsed by the recent National Conference upon Home Ownership and Housing, whose members were designated by the governors of the States and the groups interested.

RECONSTRUCTION FINANCE CORPORATION

In order that the public may be absolutely assured and that the Government may be in position to meet any public necessity, I recommend that an emergency Reconstruction Corporation of the nature of the former War Finance Corporation should be established. It may not be necessary to use such an instrumentality very extensively. The very existence of such a bulwark will strengthen confidence. The Treasury should be authorized to subscribe a reasonable capital to it, and it should be given authority to issue its own debentures. It should be placed in liquidation at the end of two years. Its purpose is that by strengthening the weak spots to thus liberate the full strength of the Nation's resources. It should be in position to facilitate exports by American agencies; make advances to agricultural credit agencies where necessary to protect and aid the agricultural industry; to make temporary advances upon proper securities to established industries, railways, and financial institutions which can not otherwise secure credit, and where such advances will protect the credit structure and stimulate employment. Its functions would not overlap those of the National Credit Corporation.

FEDERAL RESERVE ELIGIBILITY

On October 6th I issued a statement that I should recommend to the Congress an extension during emergencies of the eligibility provisions in the Federal reserve act. This statement was approved by a representative gathering of the Members of both Houses of the Congress, including members of the appropriate committees. It was approved by the officials of the Treasury Department, and I understand such an extension has been approved by a majority of the governors of the Federal reserve banks. Nothing should be done which would lower the safeguards of the system.

The establishment of the mortgage-discount banks herein referred to will also contribute to further reserve strength in the banks without inflation.

BANKING LAWS

Our people have a right to a banking system in which their deposits shall be safeguarded and the flow of credit less subject to storms. The need of a sounder system is plainly shown by the extent of bank failures. I recommend the prompt improvement of the banking laws. Changed financial conditions and commercial practices must be met. The Congress should investigate the need for separation between different kinds of banking; an enlargement of branch banking under proper restrictions; and the methods by which enlarged membership in the Federal reserve system may be brought about.

POSTAL SAVINGS BANKS

The Postal Savings deposits have increased from about $200,000,000 to about $550,000,000 during the past year. This experience has raised important practical questions in relation to deposits and investments which should receive the attention of the Congress.

RAILWAYS

The railways present one of our immediate and pressing problems. They are and must remain the backbone of our transportation system. Their prosperity is interrelated with the prosperity of all industries. Their fundamental service in transportation, the volume of their employment, their buying power for supplies from other industries, the enormous investment in their securities, particularly their bonds, by insurance companies, savings banks, benevolent and other trusts, all reflect their partnership in the whole economic fabric. Through these institutions the railway bonds are in a large sense the investment of every family. The well-maintained and successful operation and the stability of railway finances are of primary importance to economic recovery. They should have more effective opportunity to reduce operating costs by proper consolidation. As their rates must be regulated in public interest, so also approximate regulation should be applied to competing services by some authority. The methods of their regulation should be revised. The Interstate Commerce Commission has made important and far-reaching recommendations upon the whole subject, which I commend to the early consideration of the Congress.

ANTITRUST LAWS

In my message of a year ago I commented on the necessity of congressional inquiry into the economic action of the antitrust laws. There is wide conviction that some change should be made especially in the procedure under these laws. I do not favor their repeal. Such action would open wide the door to price fixing, monopoly, and destruction of healthy competition. Particular attention should be given to the industries founded upon natural resources, especially where destructive competition produces great wastes of these resources and brings great hardships upon operators, employees, and the public. In recent years there has been continued demoralization in the bituminous coal, oil, and lumber industries. I again commend the matter to the consideration of the Congress.

UNEMPLOYMENT

As an aid to unemployment the Federal Government is engaged in the greatest program of public-building, harbor, flood-control, highway, waterway, aviation, merchant and naval ship construction in all history. Our expenditures on these works during this calendar year will reach about $780,000,000 compared with $260,000,000 in 1928. Through this increased construction, through the maintenance of a full complement of Federal employees, and through services to veterans it is estimated that the Federal taxpayer is now directly contributing to the livelihood of 10,000,000 of our citizens.

We must avoid burdens upon the Government which will create more unemployment in private industry than can be gained by further expansion of employment by the Federal Government. We can now stimulate employment and agriculture more effectually and speedily through the voluntary measures in progress, through the thawing out of credit, through the building up of stability abroad, through the home loan discount banks, through an emergency finance corporation and the rehabilitation of the railways and other such directions.

I am opposed to any direct or indirect Government dole. The breakdown and increased unemployment in Europe is due in part to such practices. Our people are providing against distress from unemployment in true American fashion by a magnificent response to public appeal and by action of the local governments.

General Legislation

There are many other subjects requiring legislative action at this session of the Congress. I may list the following among them:

Veterans' Services

The law enacted last March authorizing loans of 50 per cent upon adjusted-service certificates has, together with the loans made under previous laws, resulted in payments of about $1,260,000,000. Appropriations have been exhausted. The Administrator of Veterans' Affairs advises that a further appropriation of $200,000,000 is required at once to meet the obligations made necessary by existing legislation.

There will be demands for further veterans' legislation; there are inequalities in our system of veterans' relief; it is our national duty to meet our obligations to those who have served the Nation. But our present expenditure upon these services now exceeds $1,000,000,000 per annum. I am opposed to any extension of these expenditures until the country has recovered from the present situation.

Electrical-Power Regulation

I have recommended in previous messages the effective regulation of interstate electrical power as the essential function of the reorganized Federal Power Commission. I renew the recommendation. It is urgently needed in public protection.

MUSCLE SHOALS

At my suggestion, the Governors and Legislatures of Alabama and Tennessee selected three members each for service on a committee to which I appointed a representative of the farm organizations and two representatives of the War Department for the purpose of recommending a plan for the disposal of these properties which would be in the interest of the people of those States and the agricultural industry throughout the country. I shall transmit the recommendations to the Congress.

REORGANIZATION OF FEDERAL DEPARTMENTS

I have referred in previous messages to the profound need of further reorganization and consolidation of Federal administrative functions to eliminate overlap and waste, and to enable coordination and definition of Government policies now wholly impossible in scattered and conflicting agencies which deal with parts of the same major function. I shall lay before the Congress further recommendations upon this subject, particularly in relation to the Department of the Interior. There are two directions of such reorganization, however, which have an important bearing upon the emergency problems with which we are confronted.

SHIPPING BOARD

At present the Shipping Board exercises large administrative functions independent of the Executive. These administrative functions should be transferred to the Department of Commerce, in keeping with that single responsibility which has been the basis of our governmental structure since its foundation. There should be created in that department a position of Assistant Secretary for Merchant Marine, under whom this work and the several bureaus having to do with merchant marine may be grouped.

The Shipping Board should be made a regulatory body acting also in advisory capacity on loans and policies, in keeping with its original conception. Its regulatory powers should be amended to include regulation of coastwise shipping so as to assure stability and better service. It is also worthy of consideration that the regulation of rates and services upon the inland waterways should be assigned to such a reorganized board.

REORGANIZATION OF PUBLIC WORKS ADMINISTRATION

I recommend that all building and construction activities of the Government now carried on by many departments be consolidated into an independent establishment under the President to be known as the "Public Works Administration" directed by a Public Works Administrator. This agency should undertake all construction work in service to the different departments of the Government (except naval and military work). The services of the Corps of Army Engineers should be delegated in rotation for military duty to this administration in continuation of their supervision of river and harbor work. Great economies, sounder policies, more effective coordination to employment, and expedition in all construction work would result from this consolidation.

LAW ENFORCEMENT

I shall present some recommendations in a special message looking to the strengthening of criminal-law enforcement and improvement in judicial procedure connected therewith.

INLAND WATERWAY AND HARBOR IMPROVEMENT

These improvements are now proceeding upon an unprecedented scale. Some indication of the volume of work in progress is conveyed by the fact that during the current year over 380,000,000 cubic yards of material have been moved—an amount equal to the entire removal in the construction of the Panama Canal. The Mississippi waterway system, connecting Chicago, Kansas City, Pittsburgh, and New Orleans, will be in full operation during 1933. Substantial progress is being made upon the projects of the upper Missouri, upper Mississippi, etc.

Negotiations are now in progress with Canada for the construction of the St. Lawrence Waterway.

68-611 O - 76 - 42

THE TARIFF

Wages and standards of living abroad have been materially lowered during the past year. The temporary abandonment of the gold standard by certain countries has also reduced their production costs compared to ours. Fortunately any increases in the tariff which may be necessary to protect agriculture and industry from these lowered foreign costs, or decreases in items which may prove to be excessive, may be undertaken at any time by the Tariff Commission under authority which it possesses by virtue of the tariff act of 1930. The commission during the past year has reviewed the rates upon over 254 items subject to tariff. As a result of vigorous and industrious action, it is up to date in the consideration of pending references and is prepared to give prompt attention to any further applications. This procedure presents an orderly method for correcting inequalities. I am opposed to any general congressional revision of the tariff. Such action would disturb industry, business, and agriculture. It would prolong the depression.

IMMIGRATION AND DEPORTATION

I recommend that immigration restriction now in force under administrative action be placed upon a more definite basis by law. The deportation laws should be strengthened. Aliens lawfully in the country should be protected by the issuance of a certificate of residence.

PUBLIC HEALTH

I again call attention to my previous recommendations upon this subject, particularly in its relation to children. The moral results are of the utmost importance.

CONCLUSION

It is inevitable that in these times much of the legislation proposed to the Congress and many of the recommendations of the Executive must be designed to meet emergencies. In reaching solutions we must not jeopardize those principles which we have found to be the basis of the growth of the Nation. The Federal Government must not encroach upon nor permit local communities to abandon that precious possession of local initiative and responsibility. Again, just as the largest measure of responsibility in the government of the Nation rests upon local self-government, so does the largest measure of social responsibility in our country rest upon the individual. If the individual surrenders his own initiative and responsibilities, he is surrendering his own freedom and his own liberty. It is the duty of the National Government to insist that both the local governments and the individual shall assume and bear these responsibilities as a fundamental of preserving the very basis of our freedom.

Many vital changes and movements of vast proportions are taking place in the economic world. The effect of these changes upon the future can not be seen clearly as yet. Of this, however, we are sure: Our system, based upon the ideals of individual initiative and of equality of opportunity, is not an artificial thing. Rather it is the outgrowth of the experience of America, and expresses the faith and spirit of our people. It has carried us in a century and a half to leadership of the economic world. If our economic system does not match our highest expectations at all times, it does not require revolutionary action to bring it into accord with any necessity that experience may prove. It has successfully adjusted itself to changing conditions in the past. It will do so again. The mobility of our institutions, the richness of our resources, and the abilities of our people enable us to meet them unafraid. It is a distressful time for many of our people, but they have shown qualities as high in fortitude, courage, and resourcefulness as ever in our history. With that spirit, I have faith that out of it will come a sounder life, a truer standard of values, a greater recognition of the results of honest effort, and a healthier atmosphere in which to rear our children. Ours must be a country of such stability and security as can not fail to carry forward and enlarge among all the people that abundant life of material and spiritual opportunity which it has represented among all nations since its beginning.

HERBERT HOOVER

The White House,
    December 8, 1931.

431

Message to the United Campaign Appeal of Philadelphia.
December 8, 1931

[Released December 8, 1931.   Dated December 7, 1931]

My dear Mr. Curtis:

I have received your telegram and do feel gratification that the United Campaign Appeal of Philadelphia has been oversubscribed. I wish most heartily to congratulate you and your colleagues and the people of Philadelphia on the fine spirit shown.

Yours faithfully,

HERBERT HOOVER

[Mr. Cyrus H. K. Curtis, Chairman, Welfare Federation, Philadelphia, Pa.]

NOTE: The message was in response to a message from Mr. Curtis, dated December 7, 1931, and released with the President's message, as follows:

The President:

You perhaps will feel gratification that the United Campaign of Philadelphia which was undertaken for unemployment relief and the maintenance of our Welfare Federation during the coming year recorded at its final meeting today total subscriptions of $10,000,000 against its goal of $9,000,000.

CYRUS H. K. CURTIS,
Chairman

432

Annual Budget Message to the Congress,
Fiscal Year 1933.
December 9, 1931

To the Congress of the United States:

I have the honor to transmit herewith the Budget of the United States for the fiscal year ending June 30, 1933. The receipts and expenditures shown in detail in the Budget are summarized in the following statement:

SUMMARY OF RECEIPTS AND EXPENDITURES (EXCLUSIVE OF POSTAL REVENUES AND POSTAL EXPENDITURES PAID FROM POSTAL REVENUES)

	1933	1932	1931
General fund receipts...........	$2,473,515,772.00	$2,204,257,200.00	$3,103,336,105.16
Special fund receipts.............	103,014,430.00	34,621,600.00	86,303,975.14
Total, general and special fund receipts...........	2,576,530,202.00	2,238,878,800.00	3,189,640,080.30
General fund expenditures........	3,889,223,050.00	4,284,411,800.00	3,987,148,133.52
Special fund expenditures........	107,449,400.00	77,428,000.00	104,515,774.89
Total, general and special fund expenditures.......	3,996,672,450.00	4,361,839,800.00	4,091,663,908.41
Excess of general and special fund expenditures over general and special fund receipts...........	1,420,142,248.00	2,122,961,000.00	902,023,828.11
Excess of trust fund receipts over trust fund expenditures........	3,192,800.00	277,315.00	....
Excess of trust fund expenditures over trust fund receipts........	....	....	693,016.96
Total, excess of expenditures..................	1,416,949,448.00	2,122,683,685.00	902,716,845.07

From this statement it will be seen that, in spite of an estimated increase of over $337,000,000 in receipts for next year and an estimated reduction in expenditures of more than $365,000,000, a large excess of expenditures is still indicated for the fiscal year 1933 under present laws. This condition requires that I make, in accordance with section 202 of the Budget and Accounting Act, recommendations to Congress for new taxes, loans, or other appropriate action to meet the estimated deficiency. My recommendations appear later in this message.

1932

For the fiscal year ending June 30, 1932, the receipts, originally estimated at $3,956,000,000, are now expected to fail of realization because of the severity of the depression and will fall below the estimates by $1,717,-000,000. The principal elements entering into this decline in revenues are income-tax receipts, $1,140,000,000; customs receipts, $202,000,000; miscellaneous internal-revenue receipts, $132,000,000, and postponement of payments of principal and interest on the foreign debt, $247,000,000.

Expenditures are expected to increase over the original estimates by $437,000,000. This is the net difference between many items of increase and decrease. The principal increases, in part due to subsequent legislation, include added benefits to veterans, $135,000,000; speeding up of public works to aid unemployment, $160,000,000; Federal Farm Board revolving loan fund, $80,000,000; interest on the public debt, $24,000,000; postal deficit, $81,000,000; and settlements under the war claims act, $37,000,000. There are many other individual items of increase over the expenditures estimated a year ago which would materially swell the total of increases. Rigid reduction of expenses elsewhere supplemented by decreases in public-debt expenditures on account of the moratorium and smaller tax refunds than were originally estimated serve to offset the total increases. These changes in receipts and expenditures indicate a deficit of $2,123,000,000 which includes statutory debt retirement or a probable net debt increase of $1,711,000,000.

1931

For the fiscal year ending June 30, 1931, the actual receipts fell short of those estimated a year ago by $516,000,000. The principal elements in this falling off were internal revenue and customs receipts which, together, account for $506,000,000. The actual expenditures exceeded those estimated for the year by $207,000,000, and may be attributed to the special legislation calling for emergency drought relief and increased public works to relieve unemployment, coupled with the advance payment of $112,000,000 to the adjusted-service certificate fund, offset in part by reductions and economies in other directions. The net result was a deficit of $902,000,000, which included $440,000,000 for statutory debt retirement, or a net increase in the debt of $462,000,000, plus additional cash in the Treasury of $153,000,000, or a total debt increase of $615,000,000.

TAXES

We are now face to face with a situation where for a time the current revenues of the Government under our existing laws have fallen below the amounts required to meet the absolutely necessary expenses. This brings the question directly before us of the course that shall be pursued. As already stated the deficit for the fiscal year 1931 is $902,000,000 and the estimated deficits for 1932, $2,123,000,000, and 1933, $1,417,000,000, or a total of $4,442,000,000, which, after deducting statutory debt redemptions and increased cash in the Treasury, show for these three fiscal years a total probable net increase in the national debt of $3,247,000,000. Rightly or wrongly our tax system is very largely based upon business profits and in consequence is subject to great variables.

We can not maintain public confidence nor stability of the Federal Government without undertaking some temporary tax increases. It is obviously impossible to impose a degree of taxation which will balance the Budget for the current fiscal year. We should endeavor by increase of taxes and rigid curtailment of expenditures to balance the Budget for the next fiscal year except to the extent of the amount required for statutory debt retirements. We should assure its balance, including statutory debt retirements, for the fiscal year following.

I recommend that Congress provide for an increase in taxation for a definite limited period and upon the general plan of taxation which existed under the revenue act of 1924 with such changes as may be appropriate in the light of altered conditions. The Secretary of the Treasury has prepared recommendations along these lines which he will present at the proper time. It is proposed that this increase shall be definitely terminated in two years from next July. This plan, it is estimated, will realize $920,000,000 next year and thus meet the above conditions of balancing the Budget for the fiscal year 1933 except for the statutory debt retirement. It would balance the Budget including debt retirement in the fiscal year beginning July 1, 1933. It would provide about $390,000,000 for the current year, leaving us with the necessity of borrowing an amount which will represent a net increase in the public debt by about $1,320,000,000.

The plan of approximately reenacting the revenue act of 1924 has the great advantage that the Government is equipped by experience with similar legislation for its systematic and economical collection. The public has paid such taxes in the past and has found them not intolerable and has found that they do not prevent increased prosperity. By providing a definite date for termination of the temporary increase it will allow taxpayers to look forward to definite relief.

I further recommend that Congress inquire into the economic effect of the provisions of the present law relating to capital gains and losses.

APPROPRIATIONS

The estimates of appropriations recommended in this Budget for the fiscal year 1933, to carry out the financial program recommended above, are summarized in the following statement showing increases or decreases as compared with actual appropriations for the current fiscal year.

	Estimates, 1933	Increases	Decreases
Legislative establishment:			
Senate...................	$3,241,564.00	....	$7,728.00
House of Representatives........	8,177,374.00	....	6,238.00
Architect of the Capitol........	4,257,415.00	....	5,401,007.00
Botanic Garden..............	231,022.00	$57,140.00	....
Library of Congress..........	2,489,777.00	....	72,305.00
Government Printing Office......	3,274,000.00	....	20,000.00
Miscellaneous..............	185,050.00	....	3,000.00
Total, legislative establishment.................	21,856,202.00	57,140.00	5,510,278.00
Executive office..............	429,380.00	....	43,000.00
Independent establishments:			
American Battle Monuments Commission.................	400,000.00	95,750.00	....
Arlington Memorial Bridge Commission.................	1,000,000.00	....	....
Board of Mediation..........	169,865.00	....	18,320.00
Board of Tax Appeals.........	635,000.00	....	18,640.00
Bureau of Efficiency..........	199,940.00	....	330.00
Civil Service Commission.......	1,542,720.00	....	115,622.00
Commission of Fine Arts........	9,775.00	....	....

	Estimates, 1933	Increases	Decreases
Independent establishments—Continued			
Employees' Compensation Commission	4, 986, 926.00	255, 946.00	. . . .
Federal Board for Vocational Education	10, 285, 405.00	199, 425.00	. . . .
Federal Farm Board	1, 880, 000.00	. . . .	100, 020, 000.00
Federal Oil Conservation Board	17, 500.00	. . . .	2, 500.00
Federal Power Commission	362, 020.00	43, 550.00	. . . .
Federal Radio Commission	431, 360.00	. . . .	34, 020.00
Federal Reserve Board	1, 692, 800.00	83, 600.00	. . . .
Federal Trade Commission	1, 266, 500.00	. . . .	495, 266.00
General Accounting Office	4, 290, 820.00	. . . .	6, 800.00
George Rogers Clark Sesquicentennial Commission	500, 000.00	. . . .	300, 000.00
George Washington Bicentennial Commission	452, 230.00	114, 035.00	. . . .
Interstate Commerce Commission	9, 661, 410.00	. . . .	2, 251, 063.00
Mount Rushmore National Memorial Commission	25, 000.00	25, 000.00	. . . .
National Advisory Committee for Aeronautics	1, 012, 310.00	. . . .	38, 760.00
National Capital Park and Planning Commission	. . . .	. . . .	4, 000, 000.00
Personnel Classification Board	195, 116.00	. . . .	23, 734.00
Puerto Rican Hurricane Relief Commission	. . . .	. . . .	1, 000, 000.00
Protecting interests of the United States in oil leases and oil lands	. . . .	. . . .	60, 000.00
Public Buildings and Public Parks of the National Capital	4, 701, 575.00	. . . .	1, 092, 042.00
Public Buildings Commission	125, 000.00	. . . .	. . . .
Smithsonian Institution	1, 250, 964.00	44, 540.00	. . . .
Supreme Court Building Commission	2, 000, 000.00	. . . .	1, 750, 000.00
Tariff Commission	1, 150, 500.00	. . . .	89, 500.00
United States Geographic Board	11, 678.00	1, 000.00	. . . .
U.S. Shipping Board and Merchant Fleet Corporation	423, 270.00	. . . .	36, 982, 730.00
Veterans' Administration	1, 072, 064, 527.00	124, 624, 649.00	. . . .
Total, Executive Office and independent establishments	1, 123, 182, 591.00	125, 487, 495.00	148, 342, 327.00
Department of Agriculture	197, 454, 976.00	. . . .	49, 828, 154.00
Department of Commerce	44, 719, 304.00	. . . .	9, 615, 926.00
Department of the Interior	70, 627, 152.33	. . . .	14, 667, 954.40

	Estimates, 1933	Increases	Decreases
Department of Justice..............	53, 900, 364. 00	2, 671, 163. 00	....
Department of Labor..............	14, 488, 397. 00	....	505, 803. 00
Navy Department.................	343, 000, 000. 00	....	17, 101, 593. 00
Post Office Department:			
Postal Service payable from post-			
al revenues..................	658, 724, 487. 00	12, 240, 710. 00	....
Postal deficiency payable from			
Treasury....................	155, 000, 000. 00	....	40, 000, 000. 00
State Department.................	16, 714, 071. 89	....	1, 792, 234. 45
Treasury Department..............	293, 735, 857. 00	24, 798, 440. 00	....
War Department, including Panama			
Canal.........................	423, 940, 302. 00	....	36, 138, 348. 00
District of Columbia..............	47, 331, 919. 00	....	1, 640, 719. 00
Total, ordinary, including Pos-			
tal Service.................	3, 464, 675, 623. 22	165, 254, 948. 00	325, 143, 336. 85
Reduction in principal of the public			
debt:			
Sinking fund..................	426, 489, 600. 00	14, 718, 300. 00	....
Other redemptions of the debt...	70, 313, 878. 00	70, 138, 878. 00	....
Principal of the public debt..........	496, 803, 478. 00	84, 857, 178. 00	....
Interest on the public debt...........	640, 000, 000. 00	35, 000, 000. 00	....
Total, including Post Office			
Department and Postal Serv-			
ice........................	4, 601, 479, 101. 22	285, 112, 126. 00	325, 143, 336. 85
Deduct Postal Service payable from			
postal revenues....................	658, 724, 487. 00	12, 240, 710. 00	....
Total, payable from the Treas-			
ury.......................	3, 942, 754, 614. 22	272, 871, 416. 00	325, 143, 336. 85
Annual appropriations..............	2, 657, 011, 886. 22	....	156, 807, 584. 85
Permanent appropriations............	1, 285, 742, 728. 00	104, 535, 664. 00	....
Total.......................	3, 942, 754, 614. 22	104, 535, 664. 00	156, 807, 584. 85

The bare comparison between appropriations proposed for the next fiscal year and those made for the current fiscal year, as shown in the above statement, fails to present a true picture of Government operations to the extent that in neither year do these appropriations represent the full amount available for expenditure, due largely to continuing appropriations from previous years. It is necessary to consider total expenditures in order to arrive at a true comparison between the two years. That comparison is given in the opening paragraph of this message and shows that the expenditures for 1933 are estimated at $365,000,000 less than those for the current fiscal year.

In framing this Budget, I have proceeded on the basis that the estimates for 1933 should ask for only the minimum amounts which are absolutely essential for the operation of the Government under existing law, after making due allowance for continuing appropriations. The appropriation estimates for 1933 reflect a drastic curtailment of the expenses of Federal activities in all directions where a consideration of the public welfare would permit it. Even with such reductions in the estimates of appropriations, the anticipated receipts under existing law, as stated above will be $1,417,000,000 short of the amount needed to meet Federal expenditures, including statutory debt retirement.

In viewing our financial requirements for 1933 the fact should not be overlooked that of the total of $3,942,000,000 of the estimates of appropriations payable from the Treasury contained in this Budget, $1,285,000,000 is represented by permanent definite and indefinite appropriations which by law are automatically made each year without further action by the Congress. Taking into consideration that in addition to this sum of $1,285,000,000 of permanent definite and indefinite appropriations there are other expenditures of the nature of fixed charges amounting to approximately $1,000,000,000 for which annual estimates of appropriations must be submitted, there is in reality an area of only about $1,700,000,000 of the total of $3,942,000,000 presented in this Budget which is available for consideration in seeking means to curtail our expenditures.

SHIPPING BOARD

The estimates for the Shipping Board for 1933 show a decrease from the appropriations for 1932 of $36,972,000. This is due mainly to the fact that no further appropriation is needed at this time for the construction loan fund for which $35,000,000 was appropriated in 1932, it being contemplated that the unexpended balance of that appropriation, together with repayments of loans and sales receipts transferred to the fund, will be sufficient to meet expenditures from the fund during 1933. For the shipping fund for which $1,970,000 was appropriated in 1932, no estimate for a further appropriation is being presented, as it is expected that the operating loss for 1933, which is estimated at about $5,250,000, can be met by utilizing cash balances and reserves.

VETERANS' ADMINISTRATION

There is requested in this Budget a total of slightly more than $1,072,000,000 for the Veterans' Administration, compared with a total appropriation for 1932 of approximately $947,000,000. About $21,000,000 of each of these amounts pertains to the civil service retirement and disability fund and is not properly chargeable to the annual cost of caring for our veterans, which thus becomes $926,000,000 for 1932 and $1,051,000,000 for 1933. Comparison of these amounts indicates on its face a net increase of $125,000,000 for 1933. However, it is now known that additional appropriations will be required for the fiscal year 1932 to the approximate amount of $260,000,000 of which $200,000,000 is to meet obligations due to the increase in the loan value of adjusted-service certificates and $60,000,000 to meet the requirements for military and naval compensation, Army and Navy pensions, and aid to State and Territorial homes for disabled veterans.

Taking these supplemental requirements for 1932 into consideration, the above indicated net increase of $125,000,000 becomes a net decrease of approximately $135,000,000. This net decrease, however, is due largely to the adjusted-service certificate fund requirements, which are $162,-000,000 less for 1933. If the adjusted-service certificate fund be excluded from both 1932 and 1933, the estimates for 1933 represent an ultimate net increase over 1932 of $27,000,000. This amount is the net difference between several items of increase and decrease. The principal item of increase is found in military and naval compensation, which is up $42,000,000. Resulting from the increase in hospital and domiciliary facilities, the cost of administration, medical, hospital, and domiciliary services shows an increase of $4,460,000, and there is a further increase of $1,527,000 in the item for hospital and domiciliary facilities. Offsetting these increases is a decrease of $9,000,000 in Army and Navy pensions, $4,500,000 in military and naval insurance, and $7,762,000 in the Government life-insurance fund.

AGRICULTURE

The estimates for the Department of Agriculture for 1933 carry approximately $49,800,000 less than the appropriations for 1932. This decrease is accounted for in part by the fact that the 1932 appropriations contained $22,000,000 for seed loans and agricultural relief for which no estimate is required for 1933. There is a further reduction of $20,000,-000 in the 1933 estimates from the 1932 appropriations for Federal-aid roads and forest roads and trails, as the regular programs for these works under existing authorizations were advanced to that extent in 1931 and 1932 by the funds made available in the emergency construction appropriations. The balance of the decrease is reflected in a reduction of $1,750,000 in the estimate for the acquisition of additional forest lands and $4,800,000 for other activities of the department.

TREASURY DEPARTMENT

The estimates for practically all of the organization units in the Treasury Department for the fiscal year 1933 are less than the appropriations for 1932, the notable exception being an increase of $57,400,000 in the items for the construction of new Federal buildings authorized and now in some stage of development and for the operation and maintenance of completed buildings. The principal items of decrease are $26,000,000 for refunding internal-revenue taxes illegally collected, funds now available for this purpose being considered sufficient for the fiscal year 1933, $3,200,000 for the Coast Guard, due principally to the completion of its programs for the construction of buildings and vessels; $934,000 for customs administration, as a result of falling receipts; and $512,000 for the Public Health Service, due principally to nonrecurring expenditures for equipping new hospitals and quarantine stations.

The prospective operations under permanent indefinite appropriation items in the fiscal year 1933 will be largely in excess of the current year. To provide for interest on our enlarged public debt, $35,000,000 additional will be required. Public-debt retirements required to be made from ordinary receipts will require $85,000,000 additional for the purposes of the cumulative sinking fund, receipts from foreign governments to be applied to debt retirements, and retirements from franchise-tax receipts from Federal reserve banks.

BUILDINGS

The Federal public building program authorized by the act of May 25, 1926, as amended, is being advanced in a marked degree in furtherance of the movement for the relief of the unemployed. The total authorizations now amount to $620,000,000 in addition to the amounts authorized for certain old projects specifically brought into the program by the original act and amounting to upwards of $9,000,000. Of the total amount authorized $190,000,000 is for land and buildings in the District of Columbia. Moreover, at places where abandoned sites and buildings are sold the proceeds are to be applied against the cost of the new project. The estimated sale value of sites and buildings to be so replaced amounts to approximately $69,000,000 and about $6,700,000 has been realized from such sales up to the present time.

In accordance with the provisions of the legislation above referred to specific authorizations have been made for 817 projects at limits of cost aggregating $466,800,000. Under authority of these authorizations obligations have been incurred, up to June 30, 1931, amounting to $175,-560,000, of which $73,633,000 were incurred in the fiscal year 1931. It is expected that obligations to be incurred in the fiscal year 1932 will amount to $155,000,000, and if this is brought about there will be a balance of over $136,000,000 available for obligation in the fiscal year 1933. It is apparent, therefore, that specific authorizations for individual projects already made are sufficient to carry the construction program through the fiscal year 1933.

To finance the projects which have been specifically authorized, on the basis of providing for maturing obligations, appropriations aggregating $207,030,000 have been made. The total expenditures thereunder to the close of the fiscal year 1931 amounted to $117,890,000, leaving an unexpended balance of $89,140,000, and it is estimated that $140,000,000 additional will be required to meet payments which will become due up to the close of the fiscal year 1933. To provide the additional funds which will be necessary to meet payments to the close of the fiscal year 1932 a supplemental estimate for $20,000,000 will be transmitted to Congress for consideration in connection with the first deficiency bill, and $120,000,000 is included in this Budget for payments to be made in the fiscal year 1933.

In addition to the building program referred to above, additional appropriations aggregating $28,680,000 have been made for the purchase of land in the District of Columbia. The expenditures thereunder to the close of the fiscal year 1931 amounted to $22,569,000, leaving an unexpended balance of $6,111,000 available for subsequent purchases. Additional appropriations under this authorization are not required at this time.

The War Department is also carrying forward a building program for the housing of military personnel, for hospitals, utilities, and administration activities, and for technical buildings for the Air Corps made necessary by the need for replacing World War temporary construction and to provide generally for the increase in the pre-war strength of the Regular Army, including the expansion of the Air Corps. There has already been appropriated $89,311,000 which, with the contract authorization of not to exceed $3,000,000 contained in the War Department appropriation act for 1932, practically exhausts the authorizations so far granted by law for continuing the program. The estimates for 1933 carry $2,250,000 to meet obligations under the contract authorization of $3,000,000. For the Panama Canal the estimates for 1933 provide $700,000 for new buildings and structures.

For the Veterans' Administration this Budget provides $12,877,000 for additional hospital and domiciliary facilities. Of this amount $10,877,000 is covered by the authorization of $20,877,000 provided by the act approved March 4, 1931, leaving $5,000,000 yet to be appropriated thereunder, and $2,000,000 is for completing the authorizations contained in the acts approved June 21, 1930, and July 3, 1930, for the erection of two national soldiers' homes, one in the South and one in the Northwest.

For the Navy Department, estimates aggregating $4,337,000 are included in the Budget to provide for hospitals, barracks, shop buildings, hangars, storehouses, etc.

For the Interior Department, a total of $1,815,200 is provided for new buildings, of which $642,510 is for the Indian Service, $312,700 for the National Park Service, and $860,000 for Howard University.

The estimates for the District of Columbia provide $3,818,500 for various buildings, including $1,600,000 for continuing the construction of the municipal center, $1,491,000 for school buildings, $490,000 for hospitals, and $237,500 for other purposes.

The estimates for the Department of Justice provide $962,000 for construction at the various penitentiaries and the industrial reformatory; for completion of the United States Southwestern Reformatory at El Reno, Okla., and the United States Hospital for Defective Delinquents at Springfield, Mo., $1,850,000 and $1,250,000, respectively; for Federal jails, $100,000; and for the National Training School for Boys, Washington, D.C., $124,000; a total of $4,286,000.

For the Department of State, $450,000 is provided to continue the acquisition of sites and buildings and the initial furnishing of buildings for the use of diplomatic and consular establishments and other agencies of the United States in foreign countries.

The total amount provided in this Budget for the procurement of sites and the construction of buildings is, therefore, $150,534,000—a very large increase over normal activities in this direction.

NATIONAL DEFENSE

The estimates for national defense under the War and Navy Departments for 1933 aggregate $644,650,000 as compared with the appropriations for 1932 for this purpose totaling $695,691,000, a decrease of $51,041,000. These amounts exclude all items of a nonmilitary nature.

The net decrease for the War Department amounts to $33,952,000.

This is due mainly to the fact that owing to lowered commodity costs there will be carried forward into 1933 large stocks of subsistence, clothing, and other supplies, and to a decrease in the present estimates from the appropriations for 1932 of funds to carry forward the Army building program. The postponement of other projects where practicable without serious detriment to the maintenance, operation, and training of the Army has also been a material factor in effecting reductions in the estimates for 1933.

Provision is made in these estimates for average active strengths of 12,000 commissioned officers, 924 warrant officers, and 118,750 enlisted men of the Regular Army, and 6,500 enlisted men of the Philippine Scouts; for an actual average strength of 185,000 officers and men of the National Guard; for the training of 20,722 members of the Organized Reserves for varying periods; for the enrollment and instruction of 127,565 students in Reserve Officers' Training Corps units in schools and colleges and the training of 7,200 of this number in 42 camps; and for 30 days' attendance at citizens' military training camps of 37,500 trainees. With one or two very minor exceptions these strengths are the same as those provided for 1932.

For the Navy Department the items contained in the estimates for purposes of national defense for 1933 amount to $342,606,000. The comparable amount appropriated for 1932 is $359,694,000. This indicates a decrease under 1932 of $17,088,000. This decrease includes $15,000,000 for ordinary maintenance and operating expenses of the fleet and the shore establishment, $8,000,000 for shore projects, and $7,150,000 for construction of new ships. It provides an increase of $15,000,000 for modernization of battleships. The items for ordinary maintenance and operation of the fleet and shore establishments provide for maintaining during 1933 an average of 79,700 enlisted men of the Navy, the same as provided for 1932, and an average of 15,343 enlisted men of the Marine Corps as against 17,500 men provided for 1932. Under these estimates no fighting vessels will be decommissioned and no navy yards or training stations will be closed. Other decreases in requirements are due in part to the continuation of the so-called "rotation plan" for the employment of vessels, recently adopted by the Navy Department, which lends

611

itself to both economy and efficiency in fleet operations, and in part to reduced costs of supplies and materials.

The estimates of $31,400,000 for the construction of new vessels, compared with the appropriation of $38,550,000 for 1932, indicates a decrease of $7,150,000. This, however, is a facial decrease only. When the cash balances to be carried forward from prior years, and the amount to be made available by transfer from the naval supply account fund, are taken into consideration, the total that will be available for ship construction in 1933 is estimated at $57,000,000. The availability for 1933 exceeds in amount the expenditures for ship construction in any one of the last 10 years. The expenditures in 1923 were $46,682,000; 1924, $41,697,000; 1925, $34,022,000; 1926, $25,250,000; 1927, $27,430,000; 1928, $36,935,000; 1929, $46,760,000; 1930, $49,872,000; 1931, $37,944,000; and for 1932 are estimated at $53,000,000. The amount available for 1933 will provide for normal progress in construction of every vessel now authorized by law and permitted under treaty restrictions except six destroyers the laying down of which has been postponed and, in addition, for beginning construction of one more 8-inch-gun cruiser in January, 1933, which is the earliest date permitted under the terms of the London treaty.

RIVERS AND HARBORS AND FLOOD CONTROL

The estimate for the annual appropriation for the maintenance and improvement of existing river and harbor works contained in this Budget is in the same amount as was appropriated for 1932, namely, $60,000,000. The emergency appropriations made last December for public works with a view to increasing employment contained $22,500,000 for rivers and harbors, which is in addition to the annual appropriations of $55,000,000 for 1931 and $60,000,000 for 1932. Viewed alone this advance in the program would indicate that some reduction from $60,000,000 would be justified in the estimate for 1933. This, however, is not the case, as the Government has given tentative assurances as to early dates of fulfillment which will require the full amount of the appropriation requested for 1933.

For flood control the 1933 estimates of annual appropriations are $3,000,000 less than the appropriations for 1932, this difference being the amount of the emergency appropriation made last December.

The total of the estimates contained in this Budget for rivers and harbors (including maintenance and operation of Dam No. 2, Muscle Shoals) and flood control is $104,182,000, of which $70,142,000 is for rivers and harbors and $34,040,000 for flood control. The total of $104,-182,000 includes $10,537,000 to meet the requirements under authorizations of law covering permanent specific and indefinite appropriations, advances and contributions, for rivers and harbors and flood control work.

RETIREMENT FUNDS

Pending a revaluation of the civil service retirement and disability fund, the estimate contained in this Budget for the financing of the Government's liability to the fund calls for the same amount as was appropriated for 1932, $20,850,000. For the Foreign Service retirement and disability fund, however, the estimate contained in this Budget is $416,000, as against an estimate and appropriation of $215,000 for 1932. This increase is based upon an actuarial valuation recently made by the Bureau of Efficiency and clearly indicates that the Government's liability to the fund was substantially increased by the act approved February 23, 1931. That act, however, continues without change the provision contained in the act of May 24, 1924, that the aggregate appropriations to meet the Government's liability under the retirement fund should at no time exceed the aggregate total of the contributions of the Foreign Service officers theretofore made, and accumulated interest thereon. While the estimate of $416,000 for 1933 may be made without exceeding the limitation contained in this provision, the restrictions thereof will preclude appropriations for 1934 in excess of about $322,000, and for subsequent fiscal years in excess of about $178,000 based on the present pay roll of the Foreign Service officers. Federal contributions of these amounts will be totally inadequate to maintain the solvency of the retirement fund.

The continuation in the act of February 23, 1931, of this restrictive provision indicates clearly that it was not the intention of Congress in the enactment of that law to confer additional retirement benefits upon Foreign Service officers which would prevent the solvency of the retirement fund being maintained by Federal contributions equal to, but not exceeding in the aggregate, the total of the contributions of the Foreign Service officers and accumulated interest on such contributions. The recent actuarial valuation, however, shows conclusively that some further legislative action will be necessary if we are to maintain the solvency of the Foreign Service retirement and disability fund. The Secretary of State is aware of this situation and will make appropriate recommendation to the Congress during the present session.

UNEXPENDED BALANCES

Last year in submitting the Budget for 1932 I called attention to the fact that in the preparation of the estimates of appropriations I had refrained from recommending that the requirements for 1932 be met in part by a reappropriation or extension of the availability of unexpended balances of appropriations for the then current or prior fiscal years. In making appropriations for the fiscal year 1932 Congress concurred in this change in policy, and I am therefore submitting the estimates of appropriations for 1933 on the same basis. I mention this because efforts for such economy as would be consistent with the public welfare have resulted in unexpended balances, both actual for last year and estimated for this year, which would have made it possible substantially to reduce the amount of direct appropriations requested in many of the estimates contained in this Budget had the old practice been continued. This reduction would have totaled about $70,000,000.

CONCLUSION

We have recently closed one fiscal year and are now advanced into another year where the depression in business has resulted, on the one hand, in a heavy falling off in receipts and, on the other hand, in large

Federal expenditures to provide work to assist in the relief of unemployment.

The welfare of the country demands that the financial integrity of the Federal Government be maintained. This is a necessary factor in the rebuilding of a sound national prosperity. This Budget, with its recommended reductions in appropriations and increases in revenues, presents a definite program to this end involving three steps—first, a material reduction in the anticipated deficit for the current fiscal year; second, a relation between receipts and expenditures for the fiscal year 1933 which will avoid a further increase in the public debt during that year; and third, a balanced Budget for 1934.

To carry out this program it is important to emphasize the fact that we are now in a period where Federal finances will not permit of the assumption of any obligations which will enlarge the expenditures to be met from the ordinary receipts of the Government.

I am confident that the Congress realizes this situation and will give it full consideration in passing upon matters which may contemplate any such additions to our spending program. To those individuals or groups who normally would importune the Congress to enact measures in which they are interested, I wish to say that the most patriotic duty which they can perform at this time is to themselves refrain and to discourage others from seeking any increase in the drain upon public finances.

HERBERT HOOVER

DECEMBER 7, 1931.

NOTE: On December 14, 1931, the White House issued a summary of the Budget on a functional basis, with an account of expenditures on construction work in aid to unemployment.

433

Message to the Congress
on United States Foreign Relations.
December 10, 1931

To the Senate and House of Representatives:

In my message of the 8th instant I stated that I should address the Congress at greater length upon our foreign affairs.

WORLD WAR DEBT POSTPONEMENT

With the support of a large majority of the individual Members of the Senate and House, I informed the governments concerned last June that—

"The American Government proposes the postponement during one year of all payments on intergovernmental debts, reparations, and relief debts, both principal and interest, of course not including obligations of governments held by private parties. Subject to confirmation by Congress, the American Government will postpone all payments upon the debts of foreign governments to the American Government payable during the fiscal year beginning July 1 next, conditional on a like postponement for one year of all payments on intergovernmental debts owing the important creditor powers."

In making this proposal, I also publicly stated:

"The purpose of this action is to give the forthcoming year to the economic recovery of the world and to help free the recuperative forces already in motion in the United States from retarding influences from abroad.

"The world-wide depression has affected the countries of Europe more severely than our own. Some of these countries are feeling to a serious extent the drain of this depression on national economy. The fabric of intergovernmental debts, supportable in normal times, weighs heavily in the midst of this depression.

"From a variety of causes arising out of the depression, such as the fall in the price of foreign commodities and the lack of confidence in

616

economic and political stability abroad, there is an abnormal movement of gold into the United States which is lowering the credit stability of many foreign countries. These and the other difficulties abroad diminish buying power for our exports and in a measure are the cause of our continued unemployment and continued lower prices to our farmers.

"Wise and timely action should contribute to relieve the pressure of these adverse forces in foreign countries and should assist in the re-establishment of confidence, thus forwarding political peace and economic stability in the world.

"Authority of the President to deal with this problem is limited, as this action must be supported by the Congress. It has been assured the cordial support of leading members of both parties in the Senate and the House. The essence of this proposition is to give time to permit debtor governments to recover their national prosperity. I am suggesting to the American people that they be wise creditors in their own interest and be good neighbors.

"I wish to take this occasion also to frankly state my views upon our relations to German reparations and the debts owed to us by the allied Governments of Europe. Our Government has not been a party to, or exerted any voice in determination of, reparation obligations. We purposely did not participate in either general reparations or the division of colonies or property. The repayment of debts due to us from the Allies for the advance for war and reconstruction were settled upon a basis not contingent upon German reparations or related thereto. Therefore, reparations is necessarily wholly a European problem with which we have no relation.

"I do not approve in any remote sense of the cancellation of the debts to us. World confidence would not be enhanced by such action. None of our debtor nations have ever suggested it. But as the basis of the settlement of these debts was the capacity under normal conditions of the debtor to pay, we should be consistent with our own policies and principles if we take into account the abnormal situation now existing in the world. I am sure the American people have no desire to attempt to extract any sum beyond the capacity of any debtor to pay, and it is our view that broad vision requires that our Government should recognize the situation as it exists.

"This course of action is entirely consistent with the policy which we have hitherto pursued. We are not involved in the discussion of strictly European problems, of which the payment of German reparations is one. It represents our willingness to make a contribution to the early restoration of world prosperity in which our own people have so deep an interest.

"I wish further to add that while this action has no bearing on the conference for limitation of land armaments to be held next February, inasmuch as the burden of competitive armaments has contributed to bring about this depression, we trust that by this evidence of our desire to assist we shall have contributed to the good will which is so necessary in the solution of this major question."

All the important creditor governments accepted this proposal. The necessary agreements among them have been executed, and creditor governments have foregone the receipt of payments due them since July 1, 1931.

The effect of this agreement was instantaneous in reversing the drift toward general economic panic and has served to give time to the peoples of those countries to readjust their economic life. The action taken was necessary. I am confident it commends itself to the judgment of the American people.

Payments due to the United States Government from many countries, both on account of principal and interest, fall due on December 15th. It is highly desirable that a law should be enacted before that date authorizing the Secretary of the Treasury, with the approval of the President, to postpone all payments due us on account of debts owed by foreign governments to the United States Government during the year ending June 30, 1932, and to provide for their payment over a 10-year period, beginning July 1, 1933.

As we approach the new year it is clear that a number of the governments indebted to us will be unable to meet further payments to us in full pending recovery in their economic life. It is useless to blind ourselves to an obvious fact. Therefore it will be necessary in some cases to make still further temporary adjustments.

The Congress has shared with the Executive in the past the consideration of questions arising from these debts. I am sure that it will commend itself to the Congress, that the legislative branch of the Government should continue to share this responsibility. In order that we should be in position to deal with the situation, I recommend the re-creation of the World War Foreign Debt Commission, with authority to examine such problems as may arise in connection with these debts during the present economic emergency, and to report to the Congress its conclusions and recommendations.

DISARMAMENT

The United States has accepted an invitation to take part in the World Disarmament Conference which convenes on February 2 at Geneva. The efforts of this conference will be in line with the endeavors in which the American Government has taken a leading part beginning with The Hague Conference in 1899. Up to the present time the record of achievement has been almost entirely in the field of naval disarmament. It is to be hoped that further progress can be made in reduction of naval arms and that limitation and reduction so urgently needed can be extended to land arms.

The burden of taxes to support armament is greater to-day than before the Great War, and the economic instability of the world is definitely due in part to this cause and the fears which these huge armaments at all times create. No discouragements should be permitted to turn the world from sane and reasonable limitation of arms.

With a view to establishing an atmosphere of confidence for the opening of this World Disarmament Conference, more than forty Governments, including all the principal military and naval powers, have joined in accepting the principle of one-year armaments truce. This truce, which is the outgrowth of a proposal advanced last September by the Foreign Minister of Italy, is designed to prevent the expansion of armaments program during the coming months in the hope of removing the threat of a sudden revival of competition in arms before and during the conference. These steps were fully approved by our War and Navy Departments.

MANCHURIA

We have been deeply concerned over the situation in Manchuria. As parties to the Kellogg-Briand Pact and to the Nine Power Treaty, we have a responsibility in maintaining the integrity of China and a direct interest with other nations in maintaining peace here.

When this controversy originated in September the League of Nations was in session and China appealed to the Council of that body which at once undertook measures of conciliation between China and Japan. Both China and Japan have participated in these proceedings before the Council ever since. Under the Kellogg-Briand Pact all of the signatories, including China and Japan, have covenanted to seek none but pacific means in the settlement of their disputes. Thus the ultimate purpose of proceedings under this section of the Kellogg-Briand Pact and of conciliation proceedings by the League Covenant coincide. It seemed, therefore, both wise and appropriate rather to aid and advise with the League and thus have unity of world effort to maintain peace than to take independent action. In all negotiations, however, the Department of State has maintained complete freedom of judgment and action as to participation in any measures which the League might finally be determined upon.

Immediately after the outbreak of the trouble this Government advised both Japan and China of its serious interest. Subsequently it communicated its views to both governments regarding their obligations under the Kellogg-Briand Pact. In this action we were joined by other nations signatory of the pact. This Government has consistently and repeatedly by diplomatic representations indicated its unremitting solicitude that these treaty obligations be respected. In the recurring efforts of the nations to bring about a peaceful settlement this Government has realized that the exercise of the utmost patience was desirable, and it is believed that public opinion in this country has appreciated the wisdom of this restraint.

At present a resolution is pending before the meeting at Paris, with hopes of passage, under which Japan and China will agree to take no initiative which might lead to renewed conflict; in which Japan has reiterated its intention to withdraw the Japanese troops to the railway zone as soon as lives and property of Japanese nationals in Manchuria can be adequately protected; and under which both nations agree to a neutral commission to meet on the ground, to which commission all matters in dispute can be referred for investigation and report.

St. Lawrence Waterway

Conversations were begun between the Secretary of State and the Canadian minister at Washington on November 14 looking to the framing of a treaty for the development of the St. Lawrence seaway. The negotiations are continuing. I am hopeful that an agreement may result within a reasonable time enabling us to begin work on this great project, which will be of much importance economically to Canada and to the United States.

Visits of M. Laval and Signor Grandi

The President of the Council of Ministers of France, M. Laval, visited Washington in October in order to discuss problems of outstanding world interest, in the solution of which it was felt that the two countries could be of assistance. The informal and cordial conversations served to bring into relief the respective positions of the two Nations.

The visit in November of the Royal Italian Minister for Foreign Affairs also afforded an opportunity for a cordial exchange of views respecting the many world problems in which this Government and the Goverment of Italy are interested.

It was not the purpose of these meetings to engage in any commitments or to conclude agreements. However, the visits of M. Laval and Signor Grandi, together with the various meetings of statesmen in Europe and the visit of the Secretary of State to European countries, have brought about valuable understanding of the nature of the problems confronting different governments which should aid in their solution.

NICARAGUA

In compliance with the agreement made in May, 1927, the Nicaraguan Government requested supervision by an electoral commission from the United States of the congressional elections held in 1930. This year a member of the commissions of 1928 and 1930 was sent to Nicaragua as an observer during the election of municipal authorities in order that, on the basis of his observations, it might be possible to arrange the many necessary details of the supervision of the 1932 presidential election in Nicaragua.

Armed forces of the United States maintained in Nicaragua have been reduced to the minimum deemed necessary to the training of the Nicaraguan Constabulary and the rendering of appropriate support for such instruction. It is proposed to withdraw completely American armed forces from Nicaragua after their presidential election in 1932.

Nicaragua suffered a terrible disaster in the destruction of Managua, the capital, by earthquake and fire in March last. With their usual generosity the American people, through the Red Cross, went wholeheartedly to the assistance of the stricken country. United States marines and engineers of the War Department, who were in the country making a survey of the proposed canal route, joined in rendering service. The American Legation building was destroyed with all its contents, but the minister and his staff continued to carry on their official duties and worked ceaselessly in the face of unusual hardships. The Nicaraguan Government has expressed its deep gratitude for the aid rendered.

HAITI

Substantial progress has been made in carrying out the program for the withdrawal of our activities in Haiti recommended by the Commission which, with the support of the Congress, made an investigation of Haitian affairs in 1930, and by its good offices laid the foundation for the present popularly elected Government of that Republic.

After protracted negotiations an accord was reached with the Haitian Government on August 5 providing for the return to Haitian control of important Government services heretofore carried on under American supervision by virtue of general obligations arising through the provisions of our treaty with Haiti. In accordance with this agreement the Haitian Government on October 1 assumed definitely the administration and control of the Department of Public Works, the Sanitary Service, and the Technical Service of Agriculture, which includes the industrial educational system. All American personnel was withdrawn from these services. To minimize the possibility of epidemics, and in order that the health of the American troops and officials still stationed in Haiti might be adequately protected, the accord provided that an American scientific mission, consisting of three American naval officers and six hospital corpsmen, should be charged with the control of sanitation in the cities of Port au Prince and Cape Haitien.

The accord makes appropriate provision for the continuance of adequate financial control and assistance on the part of our Government. The liberty of action, both of the Government of the United States and the Government of Haiti with respect to questions of financial administration, is, of course, limited. In this connection it must be borne in mind that investors have supplied capital desired by Haiti and that securities have been issued to them on the faith and credit of the provisions of that treaty and the American financial control which it provided during the life of the bonds.

BOLIVIA AND PARAGUAY

In 1929 the Government of the United States together with the Governments of Cuba, Colombia, Mexico, and Uruguay, formed the Commission on Inquiry and Conciliation, Bolivia-Paraguay, which had the good fortune of being able to terminate an international incident which for a time threatened to cause war between the countries involved. The five neutral governments then offered their good offices to Bolivia and Paraguay, with a view to furthering a settlement of their difficulties. This offer was accepted in principle. I am happy to state that representatives of both countries are now meeting in Washington, with the hope of concluding a pact of nonaggression between them.

ARBITRATION OF THE BOUNDARY DISPUTE
BETWEEN GUATEMALA AND HONDURAS

It has been the privilege of this Government to lend its good offices on several occasions in the past to the settlement of boundary disputes between the American republics. One of the most recent occasions upon which the disinterested services of this Government were requested was in connection with the settlement of the dispute which for almost a century has been outstanding between the Republics of Guatemala and Honduras with respect to their common boundary. Conferences extending over a period of some months were held in 1930 in the Department of State, and eventually on July 16, 1930, a treaty was signed submitting the question to arbitration, and there was also signed a supplementary convention providing for the delimitation of the boundary after the Arbitral Tribunal hands down its award. Ratifications were exchanged on October 15, 1931. The Tribunal, which will meet in Washington, will be presided over by the Chief Justice of the United States, who has set December 15, 1931, as the date for the first meeting.

MEXICO

The period for hearings before the General and Special Claims Commissions between this country and Mexico expired in August, 1931. Pursuant to a resolution of the Senate under date of February 28, 1931, and under instructions from the Department of State, the American Ambassador at Mexico City is carrying on negotiations with the Mexican Government looking to the renewal of the activities of the commissions, in order that the claims of American citizens still pending may be heard and adjudicated.

The Governments of the United States and Mexico have approved in principle certain engineering plans submitted by the International Boundary Commission, United States and Mexico, for the rectification of the Rio Grande in the vicinity of El Paso, Tex., to prevent periodical floods in that region. Negotiations are being carried on between the two Governments in an effort to reach an agreement by which this important international project may be undertaken.

TREATIES AND CONVENTIONS BEFORE THE SENATE

There have been transmitted to the Senate, from time to time, treaties and conventions which have failed during recent sessions to obtain that body's consideration or final decision. Inasmuch as these treaties affect numerous phases of private and public endeavor, I earnestly commend their early conclusion to the attention of the Congress.

In the past session of the Congress I transmitted to the Senate protocols providing for adherence by the United States to the Permanent Court of International Justice. Upon that occasion I expressed my views fully not only of the wisdom of such action, but that the safeguards against European entanglements stipulated for by the Senate had been in effect secured and the interests of the United States protected. I need not repeat that for over twelve years every President and every Secretary of State has urged this action as a material contribution to the pacific settlement of controversies among nations and a further assurance against war.

By consideration of legislation during its last session, the Congress informed itself thoroughly regarding the merits of the Copyright Convention signed at Berlin on November 13, 1908. I hope that necessary legislation will be enacted during this Congress which will make it possible for further consideration to be given to the Copyright Convention.

The Sockeye Salmon Fisheries Treaty, entered into with Canada to afford protection to the industry, which was signed on May 26, 1930, merits the attention of the Senate during the present session.

The United States sent a delegation to the Conference on Safety of Life at Sea, which was held in London in 1929. The convention, which was signed by the more important maritime nations of the world on May 31, 1929, has unified the standards of safety in accordance with modern developments of engineering science and in compliance with the governments' obligation to their citizens to reduce the perils of travel to a minimum by requiring high efficiency in seamanship.

The Convention for the Supervision of the International Trade in Arms and Ammunition and in Implements of War, signed at Geneva, June 17, 1925, represents another of the steps taken in the general field

625

of restriction of armament. It has been ratified unconditionally by some nations, conditionally by others. With the added impetus which ratification by the United States would lend to such a move, it is quite possible that the fourteen ratifications necessary by treaty stipulation would be received to bring the convention into force.

Among the other treaties and conventions which remain before the Senate for its consideration and of no less importance in their respective fields are a treaty regarding consular agents of American States (Sixth International Conference of American States, Havana, 1928); a treaty relating to Maritime Neutrality with American States (Sixth International Conference of American States, Havana, 1928); the General Treaty of Inter-American Arbitration, signed at Washington January 5, 1929; the convention relating to prisoners of war, signed at Geneva on July 27, 1929; a convention signed on the same date for the amelioration of the condition of wounded and sick of armies in the field (the Red Cross Convention); and the convention for the unification of certain rules relating to bills of lading for the carriage of goods by sea, signed at Brussels on behalf of the United States on June 23, 1925.

NEW TREATIES AND CONVENTIONS

Since my message to the Seventy-second Congress and by virtue of the power vested in the office of the Chief Executive, I have continued to commission representatives of this Government to negotiate treaties with the representatives of other countries which affect the amicable, political, commercial, and juridical relations of this country, as well as treaties dealing with humanitarian matters.

Important treaties and conventions which have been signed recently by representatives of this Government are as follows:

1. Treaty of arbitration and conciliation with Switzerland, signed February 16, 1931.

2. Treaty modifying the conciliation convention with Italy (Bryan Peace Treaty), signed September 23, 1931.

3. Extradition treaty with Greece, signed May 6, 1931.

4. Protocol relating to military obligations in certain cases of double nationality, multilateral, signed December 31, 1930.

5. Treaty of friendship, commerce, and consular rights with Poland, signed June 15, 1931.

6. Treaty with reference to establishment and sojourn with Turkey, signed October 28, 1931.

These treaties and conventions will be transmitted to the Senate in due course, with a view to obtaining its advice and consent to ratification.

HERBERT HOOVER

The White House,
   December 10, 1931.

434

Message to the Congress Transmitting Documents Relating to United States Participation in the International Exposition at Seville, Spain.
December 10, 1931

To the Congress of the United States:

I am forwarding, for the consideration of the Congress, a report from the Secretary of State transmitting the following documents in connection with the participation of this Government in an exposition which was held a Seville, Spain, the preparation and work in connection with such participation having extended from 1927 to 1931:

I. Report of the Commissioner General of the United States of America to the International Exposition at Seville, Spain.

II. Photographs to accompany the report of the commissioner general.

III. Departmental reports to accompany the report of the commissioner general.

IV. Financial statement of appropriations and expenditures for the International Exposition at Seville, Spain, 1927–1931.

V. Pamphlets distributed by the United States commission to accompany the report of the commissioner general.

HERBERT HOOVER

The White House,
   December 10, 1931.

627

435

Remarks on Presenting the Herbert Schiff Memorial Trophy.
December 10, 1931

Lieutenant Commander Whitehead:

As the United States Naval Reserve Aviation Base at Floyd Bennett Field in Brooklyn, New York, has been awarded the Herbert Schiff Memorial Trophy for the fiscal year ending June 30, 1931, I take pleasure in turning over to you, as the Commanding Officer of that Base, this splendid memorial trophy. The record of your base, with 3,441 hours of flying time, without accident to personnel or material, is an accomplishment well worthy of commendation. Please accept for the officers and men under your command my heartiest congratulations.

NOTE: The President presented the trophy to Lt. Comdr. Richard P. Whitehead at 12:30 p.m. Secretary of the Navy Adams, Adm. William A. Moffett, and William Schiff, donor of the trophy, also attended. The award was made annually to the naval squadron flying the greatest number of hours without accident.

436

The President's News Conference of
December 11, 1931

ECONOMIC RECOVERY PROGRAM

THE PRESIDENT. In the recommendations that I have laid before Congress and in the organizations created in the last few months there is a very definite rounded program for turning the tide of deflation and starting the country on the road to recovery. That program has been formulated after consultation with men in public life, leaders of labor, of agriculture, of industry, and of commerce. A considerable part of it depends on voluntary action. That is already in motion. A part of it requires legislation. The legislation part of it is entirely nonpartisan. I am interested in the principles involved more than in the details, and I do appeal for unity of action for its early consummation.

Now, the major steps that we have to take are domestic. The action needed is in the home field, and it is urgent. The reestablishment of stability abroad is helpful to us, and I am confident that that is in progress, but we must depend upon ourselves. And if we do devote ourselves to our urgent domestic questions we can make a very large recovery independent and irrespective of any foreign influences. In order that the country may get the program thoroughly in mind, I want to review to you the major parts of it. And I may tell you that you will get a shorthand note of this.

One: Provision for distress amongst the unemployed by voluntary organization and the united action of local communities in cooperation with the Unemployment Relief Organization, whose appeal for organization and funds has met with a response that has been unparalleled since the war. Almost every locality in the country has reported now that it can take care of its own. But in order to assure that there will be no failure to meet problems as they arise, the organization will be continued over the winter.

The second point: Our employers have organized and will continue to give part-time work instead of discharging a portion of their employees. That plan is now literally assisting millions of people who otherwise would have no resources. And the Government will continue the very large Federal construction program over the winter. That program now is running at the rate of over $60 million a month.

Third: We are proposing to strengthen the Federal land bank system in the interest of the farmer.

Fourth: We are proposing assistance to homeowners, both agricultural and urban, who are in difficulties, in securing renewals of mortgages by strengthening the country banks, the savings banks, and building and loan associations through a system of home loan discount banks. I am confident that in restoring these institutions to their normal functioning we will see a revival in employment in new construction.

Fifth: Development of a plan to assure the early distribution to depositors in closed banks and thus relieve distress amongst millions of smaller depositors and smaller businesses.

Sixth point is: The enlargement under full safeguards of the discount facilities of the Federal Reserve banks in the interest of more adequate credits.

Seventh: The creation for the period of the emergency of a Reconstruction Finance Corporation to furnish the necessary credit otherwise unobtainable under existing circumstances, and so give full confidence to agriculture and industry and labor against any further paralyzing influences or shocks, but especially by the reopening of credit channels to assure the maintenance of normal working of the commercial fabric.

Eighth: This program has a proposal to assist all the railways by protection from unregulated competition, and to the weaker ones by the formation of a credit pool, as authorized by the Interstate Commerce Commission, and by other measures, thus affording security to the bonds held by our insurance companies, our savings banks, and other benevolent trusts, so as to protect the interest of every family and promote the recuperation of railway employment.

Ninth: Revision of the banking laws so as better to safeguard depositors.

Tenth: Safeguarding and support of banks through the National Credit Association, which has already given great confidence to bankers and extended their ability to make loans to commerce and industry.

Eleventh: Maintenance of the public finance on a sound basis by drastic economy; by resolute opposition to the enlargement of Federal expenditure until after recovery; and by temporary increase in taxation, so distributed that the burden may be borne in proportion to the ability to pay amongst all groups and in such a fashion as not to retard recovery.

Twelfth: The maintenance of our American system of individual initiative and individual and community responsibility in all these various problems.

The broad purpose of all this program is to restore the old job instead of creating a new made job; to help the worker at the desk as well as the worker at the bench, and to restore their buying power for the farmers' products to assist him. In fact, the program is to turn the processes of liquidation and deflation and to start the country forward.

The program affects favorably every man, woman, and child. It does not affect especially any one group or class. One of its purposes, of course, is to start the flow of credit now impeded by fear and uncertainty, to the detriment of every manufacturer, businessman, and farmer. In fact, to reestablish the normal functioning is what we need at this hour.

GREAT BRITAIN: TRADE, TARIFFS, AND WAR DEBTS

There is one other subject on which I can talk to you for a minute as background. This is not for quotation. It has an indirect bearing on the question of the foreign debt. Our total exports last year were about $3,800 million. Of this $678 million went to the United Kingdom and about $322 million—making it up to about a billion—went to other parts of the British Empire outside of Canada; that is, those parts peculiarly dependent on the United Kingdom. About $660 million went to Canada, which is also placed in that same complex. So that nearly one-half of the whole exports of the United States went to the British Empire.

Now, the British have lately passed two tariff bills. The first of these affected only $11,800,000 of American products. The second one, which was passed a few days ago, affected a larger volume of products and yet only affected $350,000, or practically no American products. In other words, out of all this vast volume of trade, that is direct trade to Great Britain, of $678 million, only $12,100,000 has been affected by their tariff provisions.

I will not give you the figures as to how it affects other countries, but they are very different from the relation to the United States. Now, the income of the British people is in sterling. They are off the gold basis. The payments that they have to make to us are in dollars. So that if you take the normal payment on British debt to us and convert it into the burden at the present exchange, you will find that that debt payment has increased 50 percent by virtue of their going off the gold standard.

I might mention one other fact in connection with it. There has been some discussion about these actions being undertaken to assist American bankers, and this I can tell you, that the British have more money in American banks than they owe to American banks—in fact, it is about the same—not very much either way. So that the American banker is not interested in what we do in this matter so far as his personal interest is concerned.

I give you these figures in juxtaposition because there is such a thing as national interest, and it is well worthwhile for the American people to consider where their financial interest lies in their relations to international economic problems.

As I say, that is entirely for background for you. It is not for quotation or authority, but I think that you ought to understand that we are not proceeding here without some regard for our own interests when we say that there are some of the people who owe us money on this debt who obviously will not be able to pay until they have made further recovery, and there are some people to whom it is a profit in consideration.

Thank you.

NOTE: President Hoover's two hundred twenty-fourth news conference was held in the White House at 4 p.m. on Friday, December 11, 1931.

On the same day, the White House released a text of the President's statement on the economic recovery program (see Item 437).

On November 30, 1931, the White House issued the text of a letter, dated November 28, from Walter S. Gifford, Chairman of the President's Organization on Unemployment Relief, on the progress made in the relief of unemployment.

437

Statement on the Economic Recovery Program.
December 11, 1931

THE PRESIDENT said:

"In my recommendations to Congress and in the organizations created during the past few months, there is a definite program for turning the tide of deflation and starting the country upon the road to recovery. This program has been formulated after consultation with leaders of every branch of American public life, of labor, of agriculture, of commerce, and of industry. A considerable part of it depends on voluntary organization in the country. This is already in action. A part of it requires legislation. It is a nonpartisan program. I am interested in its principles rather than its details. I appeal for unity of action for its consummation.

"The major steps that we must take are domestic. The action needed is in the home field, and it is urgent. While reestablishment of stability abroad is helpful to us and to the world, and I am confident that it is in progress, yet we must depend upon ourselves. If we devote ourselves to these urgent domestic questions we can make a very large measure of recovery irrespective of foreign influences.

"That the country may get this program thoroughly in mind, I review its major parts:

"1. Provision for distress among the unemployed by voluntary organization and united action of local authorities in cooperation with the President's Unemployment Relief Organization, whose appeal for organization and funds has met with a response unparalleled since the war. Almost every locality in the country has reported that it will take care of its own. In order to assure that there will be no failure to meet problems as they arise, the organization will continue through the winter.

"2. Our employers are organized and will continue to give part-time work instead of discharging a portion of their employees. This plan is affording help to several million people who otherwise would have no resources. The Government will continue to aid unemployment over the winter through the large program of Federal construction now in progress. This program represents an expenditure at the rate of over $60 million a month.

"3. The strengthening of the Federal land bank system in the interest of the farmer.

"4. Assistance to homeowners, both agricultural and urban, who are in difficulties in securing renewals of mortgages by strengthening the country banks, savings banks, and building and loan associations through the creation of a system of home loan discount banks. By restoring these institutions to normal functioning, we will see a revival in employment in new construction.

"5. Development of a plan to assure early distribution to depositors in closed banks, and thus relieve distress amongst millions of smaller depositors and smaller businesses.

"6. The enlargement under full safeguards of the discount facilities of the Federal Reserve banks in the interest of a more adequate credit system.

"7. The creation for the period of the emergency of a reconstruction finance corporation to furnish necessary credit otherwise unobtainable under existing circumstances, and so give confidence to agriculture, to industry and to labor against further paralyzing influences and shocks, but more especially by the reopening of credit channels which will assure the maintenance and normal working of the commercial fabric.

"8. Assistance to all railroads by protection from unregulated competition, and to the weaker ones by the formation of a credit pool, as authorized by the Interstate Commerce Commission, and by other measures, thus affording security to the bonds held by our insurance companies, our savings banks, and other benevolent trusts, thereby protecting the interest of every family and promoting the recuperation of the railways.

"9. The revision of our banking laws so as better to safeguard the depositors.

"10. The safeguarding and support of banks through the National Credit Association, which has already given great confidence to bankers and extended their ability to make loans to commerce and industry.

"11. The maintenance of the public finance on a sound basis:

(a) By drastic economy.

(b) Resolute opposition to the enlargement of Federal expenditure until recovery.

(c) A temporary increase in taxation, so distributed that the burden may be borne in proportion to ability to pay amongst all groups and in such a fashion as not to retard recovery.

"12. The maintenance of the American system of individual initiative and individual and community responsibility.

"The broad purpose of this program is to restore the old job instead of create a made job, to help the worker at the desk as well as the bench, to restore their buying power for the farmers' products—in fact, turn the processes of liquidation and deflation and start the country forward all along the line.

"This program will affect favorably every man, woman and child— not a special class or any group. One of its purposes is to start the flow of credit now impeded by fear and uncertainty, to the detriment of every manufacturer, business man and farmer. To reestablish normal functioning is the need of the hour."

438

Message on the Completion of
the Regional Plan of New York and Its Environs.
December 11, 1931

[Released December 11, 1931.   Dated December 9, 1931]

My dear Mr. Delano:

It was my privilege nearly ten years ago to attend the initial meeting in the interest of the Regional Plan of New York and its Environs. I am now particularly interested to know that the final volume embodying the research and study of a decade has been completed for presentation to the citizens of the New York region. This marks an important stage in your enterprise. From the vision of a new conception of city building you proceeded to painstaking fact-finding and to the formulation of a plan. You now approach the stage of realizing the plan in practice. Its realization will be facilitated by the sound foundation which has been laid. The work of the organization, so generously made possible by the Russell Sage Foundation, is a contribution to sound, farsighted municipal planning of preeminent importance in this country, if not in the world.

Yours faithfully,

HERBERT HOOVER

[Mr. Frederic A. Delano, Chairman, Regional Plan of New York and its Environs, 407 Hibbs Building, Washington, D.C.]

NOTE: The message was read at a dinner celebrating the completion of the plan, which was held in the Hotel Roosevelt in New York City.

439

Address to the Gridiron Club.
December 12, 1931

Members of the Gridiron Club and guests:

I know that I represent all of the guests in expressing our gratitude to the Gridiron Club for their hospitality and entertainment. We have had a highly educational evening. We guests fully realize that this is the semiannual occasion when the representatives of the press make their contribution to lofty ideals, to unity and solidarity of national action in the presence of national danger by rubbing the salt of wit, the vinegar of hyperbole, and the iodine of satire into the raw wounds of politics. That is all natural and appropriate, for just as the village gossip satisfies the soul of both Main Street and Wall Street, also the gossip and the humor of politics and public life are always more interesting and surely more relaxing than striving to serve one's fellow men, especially after dinner.

For nearly 20 years I have attended Gridiron dinners. On each occasion I have listened to the solemn announcement that "ladies are always present and reporters never present." During all of these years I have wondered about that statement. I do not challenge its honest intent, but every one of you will read in the Sunday newspapers a full account of these proceedings, except, I hasten to add, the partially extemporaneous efforts of Mr. Blythe [1] and myself. If you are conversant with the news-

---

[1] Samuel G. Blythe was president of the Gridiron Club in 1907.

paper world, you will know that this account of the proceedings is always released by the Gridiron Club itself a week in advance. It is not a leak, it is a flood. The procedure no doubt enables the Gridiron members conscientiously to obey their sacred rule, because the murder has already been committed. Another explanation may be that secrecy is limited to addresses by guests, because either the Gridiron Club has no confidence in the humor of its guests, wishes to protect the public from it, or considers it must be censored.

In any event the news release of a week ago describing what has taken place here tonight, contained description of a skit on White House censorship. That is a thorny subject, as old as the Government and involving the theory that the principal job of Presidents is to make news for both morning and afternoon editions each day, and particularly that it shall have a mixed flavor of human-interest story and a dog fight that will please the village gossips. A revered President, long since dead, once told me that there was no solution to this relation of the White House to the press; that there never would be a President who could satisfy the press until he was 20 years dead.

Let me say from some experience that the conduct of public business, both domestic and foreign, nine times out of ten is a matter of delicate negotiation, of long and patient endeavor to bring about the meeting of many minds. One critical essential in all such negotiations is to avoid the rock of announced positions and the inflammation of public controversy by which measures affecting men and nations may be wrecked before a common understanding may be reached through the long and tedious process of give and take. But naturally the correspondents under pressure to discover every step of such processes and to envisage every difference of opinion in those terms of combat, to satisfy the village gossips would require to have minute-by-minute access to the most confidential conversation—for both morning and evening editions—and to have mimeographed copies of all foreign dispatches. Not always having these facilities given to them they must satisfy the managing editor somehow at least by a column damning the Government for secrecy, with forebodings and a dark conspiracy against public interest with Wall Street, or Downing Street, or some other dark alley. Yet if all of these facilities were offered minute-by-minute the press would be entirely upset because such facilities are of no importance unless given as individual scoop to the exclusion of every other newspaper.

As a matter of fact things are not that bad. On the contrary, the access of the press to the President and other officials here in Washington is without parallel in any nation. Moreover, the vast majority of the correspondents possess an amazing ability to follow the intricate movements of this most gigantic of all organizations on Earth. Considering the time at their disposal, they report them intelligently, objectively, with astounding accuracy and penetration. They possess a sense of honesty, public responsibility, a deep patriotism, and the high importance of a scoop.

The press suffers from many other impositions. I recently received an explanation of some of them from my friend, Dr. [William A.] White, who heads St. Elizabeths Hospital for the insane in the District of Columbia. You are aware that Dr. White is a leader of the modern school of psychotherapy. This is an important and growing branch of the physician's science. The discoveries made in it have been most helpful in accounting for human behavior. Our language and our ideas have been enriched by its discoveries. A new nomenclature has grown up from it.

Dr. White informs me that there is a very definite pathological type which is known as the "exhibitionists" and that they peculiarly congregate in our National Capital.

I will not go into the doctor's definition of an exhibitionist; suffice it to say they comprise those who have an abnormal desire to preen into public. One well-defined form is represented by those who visit the White House to say a hurried few words to the President and on leaving hand out a long statement to the reporters at the door on subjects that have never been or little discussed with the President, but with the firm confidence that the implication of their visit will put them on page one, column one. There are other varieties of exhibitionists and dwellers in that twilight of near sanity, illuminated only with brainstorms, who collect around this neighborhood; but as I make it a practice never to say anything that cannot be forgiven, I shall not pursue the subject.

You have heard something tonight about cooperation between the political parties. The country needs cooperation. But do not forget that ours is a government built upon political parties. There is no method by which the American people can express their public will except through party organization. The day that we begin coalition government you may know that our democracy has broken down. Constructive opposition is an essential to the very functioning of our democracy, and no less certainly destructive opposition at this stage of the world's history is the road to the abyss. Political leaders can cooperate and maintain their identity. And political parties, having been elected to power whether in the executive or in the Congress, have a definite and positive responsibility to the people and an expectation from them of patriotic action which overrides all partisanship. No party can stand among the American people which will not accept its full responsibilities.

The Republican administration has the responsibility and duty of providing a program in a time of great national emergency. That program has been provided. It is not partisan. It favors no group except those in need. It calls for sacrifice evenly, each according to his means. It will provide such further recommendations as the times may require. I am as confident of the actual cooperation of our Democratic colleagues in national service as I am confident of their patriotism, but I do not doubt that they will contribute to the anvil of debate.

I need not remind you that these are difficult times. Never in peacetime has the Executive and the Congress been confronted with greater responsibilities. They are times which require broad sympathies and great sacrifices. They are times which require stern and resolute action of Government and it requires equally stern and resolute action by citizens.

The whole situation requires unity of action in our Nation. It demands cooperation. It demands courageous action by governments and by men. It demands that men rise above party and political advantage.

NOTE: The President spoke at a dinner meeting held in the Willard Hotel in Washington, D.C.

The Gridiron Club, an organization of Washington newsmen, met semiannually for a dinner and satirical review of current political events. Remarks at the dinners were off-the-record, but President Hoover's were later published.

440

Message to the Congress Transmitting the Report of the Muscle Shoals Commission. *December 17, 1931*

To the Congress of the United States:

In my message to the Senate on March 3d last returning without my approval Senate Joint Resolution No. 49, I suggested that as the solution of the Muscle Shoals problem was a matter of major interest to the States of Tennessee and Alabama these States should set up a commission of their own representatives to cooperate with a like commission appointed by me to consider the disposition of the Muscle Shoals project.

On March 20, 1931, the Legislature of the State of Tennessee passed the accompanying resolution which was approved by the Governor on March 23, 1931. Under this resolution Mr. Mercer Reynolds, Mr. Vance J. Alexander and Mr. W. A. Caldwell were appointed members of the commission. As Mr. Alexander and Mr. Caldwell were unable to serve, the Governor subsequently appointed Mr. J. F. Porter and Mr. R. L. Moore to fill the vacancies. On June 30, 1931, the Assembly of Alabama passed the accompanying resolution, which was approved by the Governor on June 30, 1931, and under it Mr. S. F. Hobbs, Mr. Will Howard Smith, and Mr. W. F. McFarland were appointed members of the commission. On July 14, 1931, I appointed Colonel Harley B. Ferguson, Corps of Engineers, United States Army, Colonel Joseph I. McMullen, office of the Judge Advocate General, United States Army, and Mr. Edward A. O'Neal, President of the American Farm Bureau Federation, as members of the commission.

Hearings were held and after long consideration of the subject, the commission rendered to me a unanimous report which I now transmit for the consideration of the Congress. In addition the commission has prepared a brochure showing the evidence on which its recommendations are based. This I also transmit for the information of the Congress.

HERBERT HOOVER

The White House,
    December 17, 1931.

NOTE: The message and accompanying papers are printed as Senate Document 21 (72d Cong., 1st sess.).

441

Message to King Alexander I of Yugoslavia Offering Birthday Greetings.
December 17, 1931

IT GIVES ME much pleasure on this Your Majesty's birthday to extend to you and the people of Yugoslavia cordial felicitations on behalf of my fellow countrymen and in my own name and to wish for Your Majesty a long and prosperous reign.

HERBERT HOOVER

[His Majesty Alexander I, King of Yugoslavia, Belgrade, Yugoslavia]

442

Statement on Financial Assistance to Railroads.
December 18, 1931

THE PRESIDENT said:

"In consequence of the fall in prices of railway bonds, I have a number of telegrams from different parts of the country and inquiries from the press as to the status of the various agencies which are proposed to assist those railways which are not earning their fixed charges across the trough of the depression without further consequential defaults on bonds or receiverships. These inquiries are natural, because the standing of railway bonds is a fundamental matter to thousands of publicly-owned institutions. As shown by the Interstate Commerce Commission, excluding those roads already in receivership, the number of railways earning less than fixed charges is only about 16 percent or 17 percent of the whole. This, however, includes some roads that are parts of larger systems able to look after them. It will be remembered that the carriers have now organized the Railway Credit Corporation on the plan provided between them and the Interstate Commerce Commission for assisting railways with deficient earnings from the special income authorized by the Commission. This income is estimated at something over $100 million. The Railway Credit Corporation has been approved by the Railway Executives and the Commission, and is now in course of confirmation by the Boards of the different railway companies. Proposals are in progress by which financial assistance can be provided by the Railway Credit Corporation in anticipation of the collection of the increased rates assigned for this purpose.

"Beyond this, the Reconstruction Finance Corporation which I have proposed to the Congress, aside from its purposes to aid agricultural credit associations and the export of agricultural commodities and other stiffening of the credit situation, will under those recommendations be able to give emergency aid in this situation also if it should be necessary. I, of course, regard the enactment of the authority to create this corporation as a most urgent matter.

"It is my understanding that progress is being made on the proposal from the Conference of Railway Brotherhoods at Chicago that they should appoint a committee with power to act with the Railway Executives on wage questions, subject to confirmation of their locals, and that the Railway Executives are likewise appointing a committee with power to act on their behalf.

"Altogether this problem is receiving most serious attention."

NOTE: The above is taken from the mimeographed handout for the President's news conference of December 18, 1931. No transcript of the news conference has survived. Press accounts indicate that in the news conference the President amplified his prepared statement by saying that "the railroad bonds amount to $9 billion and are held by public institutions of all kinds with direct relationship to the people at large."

443

Message of Sympathy on the Death of Herbert Knox Smith.
December 18, 1931

I DEEPLY REGRET to learn of the death of your husband, Herbert Knox Smith, whose career was one of such distinguished public service. Mrs. Hoover and I extend our deepest sympathy to you in your bereavement.

HERBERT HOOVER

[Mrs. Gertrude D. Smith, "Westward," Farmington, Connecticut]

NOTE: Mr. Smith, head of the Bureau of Corporations from 1907 to 1912, died at his home in Farmington, Conn., on December 17, 1931.

444

Christmas Message to Disabled Veterans.
December 20, 1931

To All Disabled Veterans:

It is my privilege to convey to you at this holiday season the nation's tribute of remembrance and gratitude for your service in defense of our country.

Your sacrifices and sufferings have called forth the solicitude of the nation expressed in the services which have been established to minister to your needs.

In extending to you a greeting of good cheer at Christmas I express my earnest personal wish and that of all our people that the New Year may bring to you abundant blessings of contentment, health, hope and restoration. I send you renewed assurance of the nation's gratitude and devotion to your needs.

HERBERT HOOVER

NOTE: The message was sent to various veterans' organizations and hospitals throughout the country.

68-611 O - 76 - 45

445

Message to the Congress Requesting Appropriations for the American Delegation to the General Disarmament Conference at Geneva. *December 21, 1931*

To the Congress of the United States:

In my message on foreign affairs which was communicated to the Congress on the 10th day of this month, I spoke of the invitation which this Government has accepted to participate in the General Disarmament Conference which is to meet at Geneva on February 2, 1932. I spoke also in that message of the interest of this Government in supporting the efforts of this conference in accordance with the traditional policy of the American Nation to meet with the other nations of the world and to offer its cooperation in any endeavor which has in view the reduction of the huge burdens which result from unnecessarily heavy and costly armaments.

I am transmitting herewith and I commend to the favorable consideration of the Congress a report on the subject from the Secretary of State in which he requests that authorization be made for an appropriation to defray the expenses of sending an American delegation to Geneva for the purpose of representing the United States at the conference.

HERBERT HOOVER

The White House,
    December 21, 1931.

NOTE: The message and accompanying papers are printed as Senate Document 26 (72d Cong., 1st sess.).

446

The President's News Conference of
December 22, 1931

ECONOMIC RECOVERY PROGRAM

THE PRESIDENT. In the many conferences that I have had with the leaders of the House and Senate they all assure me that Congress will devote itself to the expeditious passage of the emergency economic program which I proposed for the amelioration of the agricultural, employment, and credit situations. I had urged that the proposed congressional holiday should be shortened, but the leaders inform me that they do not believe it is possible to maintain a quorum before January 4. They do assure me, however, that the measures which are uncompleted before the holidays will receive immediate attention after reconvening and that I may be assured that the Reconstruction Finance Corporation will be the first to receive consideration, and that there is amply sufficient cohesion in Congress to assure its very rapid passage.

HOLIDAYS FOR GOVERNMENT EMPLOYEES

I have received requests from Federal employees of the District that they should be given two periods of holidays so as to cover the Saturday following Christmas and from New Year's Day to January 4. While I see little objection to the day following Christmas in order that Federal employees may have an opportunity to join their families out of town, I do not feel that we should extend the holidays at New Year's. We cannot suspend functioning of the Federal Government in these times.

U.S. DELEGATION TO THE GENERAL DISARMAMENT CONFERENCE

General [Charles G.] Dawes will head the disarmament delegation. Mr. [Henry P.] Fletcher finds that he will not be able to accept membership on the Commission, I am sorry to say. The whole question of disarmament is and has been of profound interest to the women of the United States. They have shown great interest in it for many years, and I have determined to appoint a leading woman as a member of the delegation. I am now in discussion with a lady of qualities and prominence as to her acceptance of that mission.

That is, I think, all that I have on this occasion.

NOTE: President Hoover's two hundred and twenty-fifth news conference was held in the White House at 12 noon on Tuesday, December 22, 1931.

On the same day, the White House issued texts of the President's statements on the economic recovery program (see Item 447), the holidays for Government employees (see Item 448), and the United States delegation to the General Disarmament Conference (see Item 449).

447

Statement on the Economic Recovery Program.
December 22, 1931

THE PRESIDENT said:

"Leaders of both Houses have assured me that Congress will devote itself to the economic emergency program which I have proposed for the amelioration of agricultural, unemployment, and credit situations. I had urged that the proposed congressional holidays should be shortened but leaders have informed me that they do not believe it possible to secure a quorum before January 4. They assure me, however, that the measures which are uncompleted before the holidays will receive immediate attention after reconvening, and I am assured that the Reconstruction Finance Corporation will be the first to receive consideration and that it has sufficient support to be passed by the Congress."

448

Statement on Holidays for Government Employees.
December 22, 1931

THE PRESIDENT said:

"I have received requests from Federal employees in the District that they should be given two periods of holidays so as to cover the Saturday following Christmas Day, and from New Year's Day until January 4. While I see little objection to the day following Christmas in order that Federal employees may have the opportunity of joining their families out of town, I do not feel that we should extend the holiday at New Year's. We cannot suspend the functioning of the Federal Government at such a time."

NOTE: On the same day, the President signed Executive Order 5764, closing Government offices on December 26.

449

Statement on the United States Delegation to the General Disarmament Conference.
December 22, 1931

THE PRESIDENT said:

"General Dawes will head the American Delegation to the Geneva Conference. Mr. [Henry P.] Fletcher, I am sorry to say, finds that he will not be able to accept membership on the Commission. The whole question of disarmament is and has been of profound interest to the women of the United States. They have shown great interest in it for many years. I have determined to appoint a prominent woman as a member of the delegation. I am now conferring with a lady of high fitness for the position as to her acceptance of that important mission.

NOTE: Charles G. Dawes was U.S. Ambassador to Great Britain.

The General Disarmament Conference was scheduled to meet in Geneva, Switzerland in February 1932.

450

Statement on Signing the Foreign Debt Moratorium Resolution.
December 23, 1931

THE PRESIDENT said:

"I have signed the act authorizing the foreign debt postponement for one year. I am gratified at the support it received in the Congress as indicated by the approval—including those absent yet who expressed their views—of 79 Senators as against 15 opposed, and the approval of 317 Members of the House of Representatives as against 100 opposed. It is further gratifying that both political parties strongly supported this proposal.

"The suggestion of our Government for the year's postponement of intergovernmental debts among all principal nations of which ours is only a part, averted a catastrophe, the effects of which would have reached to the United States and would have caused the American people a loss of many times the amount involved. No part of the debt owing to us has been cancelled or reduced; the postponed amounts are repayable over a period of about 10 years with interest at 4 percent.

"In saving the collapse of Germany by the year's postponement the American people have done something greater than the dollars and cents gained from the maintenance of our agricultural markets, the prevention of panic and unlimited losses. They have contributed to maintain courage and hope in the German nation, to give opportunity for the other European countries to work out their problems."

NOTE: As enacted, House Joint Resolution 147 is Public Resolution No. 5 (47 Stat. 3).

451

Christmas Greeting to the Nation.
December 24, 1931

Mr. Vice President, the people of Washington and of our whole country-wide:

This is the season and this is the occasion when the whole Nation unites in good cheer and good wishes. We dedicate it particularly to our children, and we give devotion to the faith from which it is inspired.

It gives me great pleasure to join in this ceremony of the lighting of this tree, which is indeed symbolic of that in every household in our country. I ardently wish to every home a Merry Christmas and a Happy New Year.

NOTE: The President spoke at 5 p.m. during ceremonies in which he lighted the national community Christmas tree in Sherman Square, Washington, D.C. The National Broadcasting Company radio network carried the remarks.

As printed above, this item follows the text set forth in a contemporary news account.

452

Message to the Nation's Christmas Tree Association. *December 25, 1931*

[Released December 25, 1931. Dated December 3, 1931]

To the Nation's Christmas Tree Association:

Your annual Christmas service held at the foot of a living tree antedating the birth of Christ, is a dramatic and inspiring event of national interest. It symbolizes and vivifies our greatest Christian festival with its eternal message of unselfishness, joy and peace.

HERBERT HOOVER

NOTE: The message was read at the annual ceremony around the General Grant tree in Grant National Park, Calif. The tree, believed to be the world's oldest living thing, had been designated in 1925 as the Nation's Christmas tree.

453

The President's News Conference of *December 29, 1931*

GENERAL DISARMAMENT CONFERENCE

THE PRESIDENT. I have appointed Mr. Norman Davis, who was formerly the Under Secretary of State, as a member of the delegation to the Disarmament Conference. There may be one or two more members.

ECONOMY IN GOVERNMENT

The question of economy in government is prominently before the country—economy in Federal expenditure especially. The most constructive direction for economy in Federal expenditure beyond the rigid reduction of appropriations and the resolute opposition to any new legislation, lies in the consolidation of Government bureaus and the general reorganization of the Federal Government. I have delivered various public addresses and messages to Congress on this—the addresses over the last 10 years and the messages to Congress over the last 2 years—repeatedly. And one of those recommendations in particular has been carried out in the Veterans' Bureau where we consolidated all the veterans' activities. General Hines [1] reports to me that the administrative savings in consequence run somewhere from 10 to 15 million a year.

And outstanding amongst those reorganizations is the creation of an administrator of public works to cover all construction activities of the Government as a service agency to all the other departments. There are very large economies to be made there by a thorough reorganization of all construction activities. We have, I should think, 10 different agencies of the Government engaged in construction at the present time; each one of them with its separate organization spread over the entire country; every one of them with a separate organization in Washington, with duplication of engineers and architects and activities, and competition in the purchase of supplies; no one of which can be properly eliminated unless we can bring all those activities under one head.

We could accomplish very great savings if we could consolidate all the merchant marine activities and all the services to the merchant marine into the Department of Commerce. I have referred a great number of times in messages, particularly in the last message, as to the necessity of consolidating into the Department of Commerce the merchant marine.

We could make economies if we could consolidate the conservation activities of the Government in the same manner, as well as the public health activities which are scattered through several different depart-

---

[1] Frank T. Hines, Administrator of Veterans' Affairs, Veterans' Administration.

ments; the educational activities that I think are in eight different departments of the Government. There are a great number of activities of the same general major purpose that now lie in all sorts of commissions and departments and scattered hither and yon all through the Government.

However, the consolidation does not alone lie in the elimination of overlaps but it lies also in having single-headed direction under which policies can be formulated and where they will be much more under public inspection, and especially, as a remedy to a sort of self-growth of bureaus, the placing of these things into groups under a single head will prevent much additional future expenditure.

This subject is a very old one, but now that economy is absolutely the first necessity of the Government, it is an appropriate time for Congress to take the matter up. In fact, such an action would constitute a major accomplishment at the present session of Congress.

And that is all I have got today.

Q. Mr. President, do you plan a message on this?

THE PRESIDENT. I have stated all this in three different messages. Mr. Joslin can give you an extract from those messages—each one of them. I also in the last message referred to the fact that I would send up some more information on the subject later in the session, so that I shall send up still a further message but not for a month or two until we have dealt with the emergency measures and the economy program.

Otherwise I haven't anything today.

Q. Mr. President, you speak of public works first. Do I assume that will be the first one in the message? You emphasized that in your talk just now.

THE PRESIDENT. I would put it parallel with the merchant marine reorganization. Both of them are very important, and both of them offer unusual opportunities for economies.

Q. Mr. President, you speak of that consolidation under an administrator——

THE PRESIDENT. Setting up an agency similar to the Veterans' Bureau.

Q. Without representation in the Cabinet?

THE PRESIDENT. The Veterans' Administration was a new type of organization in the Government. As public construction relates to every department of the Government, I think it would be better to set up a similar type of organization to that which we have in the Veterans' Bureau rather than put it in one of the departments.

Q. That would take the Supervising Architects from the Treasury [1] and Public Roads from Agriculture [2] and Rivers and Harbors——

THE PRESIDENT. Yes, Rivers and Harbors from the Army.[3] In my message to Congress I suggested that the Engineers continue to administer Rivers and Harbors as in the past. The Department of the Interior covers a very large measure of construction in the reclamation service [4] and the Boulder Dam. Lighthouse service [5] have construction activities. The Department of Justice builds prisons. The War Department builds buildings of one kind or another. I do not propose to put the actual military construction in such an activity, of course. The construction of navy yards and other things of that kind are necessary and military matters would have to remain in those two departments.

Q. Mr. President, do I understand that Rivers and Harbors is to remain in the War Department?

THE PRESIDENT. No, to transfer to this new agency, but to transfer the Army Engineers for service—not to take them out of the Army but to delegate them to the administration of that service as before.

Q. And on the merchant marine——

THE PRESIDENT. The proposal was that the Shipping Board should return to its function as an advisory and regulatory body and remove all of its administrative functions to the Department of Commerce. There are a number of shipping lines which could be economized on and various other things that could be done if properly consolidated. There are various other merchant marine activities in the Government.

Q. Mr. President, has there been any estimate of the possible saving on this?

---

[1] Office of Supervising Architect, Department of the Treasury.

[2] Bureau of Public Roads, Department of Agriculture.

[3] Board of Engineers for Rivers and Harbors, Office of Chief of Engineers, Department of War.

[4] Bureau of Reclamation, Department of the Interior.

[5] Bureau of Lighthouses, Department of Commerce.

THE PRESIDENT. There has been no attempt to estimate them. We thought the savings of the veterans' activities was an indication. It is difficult to tell until you get them together cheek and jowl where we could get at the overlap.

NOTE: President Hoover's two hundred and twenty-sixth news conference was held in the White House at 12 noon on Tuesday, December 29, 1931.

On the same day, the White House issued a text of the President's statement on economy in Government (see Item 454).

For the excerpts of the messages distributed by Theodore G. Joslin, Secretary to the President, see 1929 volume, Item 295, page 431 and this volume, Item 430, pages 594 and 595.

454

Statement on Economy in Government.
December 29, 1931

THE PRESIDENT said:

"The most constructive direction for economy in Federal expenditure beyond a rigid reduction of appropriations and the resolute opposition to new appropriations lies in the consolidation of Government bureaus and general reorganization of the Federal Government. I have recommended this reorganization in public addresses, reports and messages to Congress throughout the past 10 years.

"I particularly emphasized this necessity as the basis of constructive economy in my message to the second session of the 71st Congress. I again referred to it in the message to the third session of that Congress, and in my message to the present Congress I again traversed the subject. Some of my recommendations have been carried out, the most notable one being the consolidation of all veterans' activities into the Veterans' Administration. As a result, General [Frank T.] Hines reports that we are saving somewhere from 10 to 15 millions a year in this service alone.

"Outstanding amongst these reorganizations would be consolidation of all construction activities of the Government under an administrator of public works to serve all the departments. Other cases are the consolidation of all merchant marine activities into the Department of Commerce; the consolidation of the conservation activities of the Government; of the public health services, of educational activities and numerous other groups on the same major purpose under single-headed responsibility. Such action would result in the elimination of many expensive agencies and overlap resulting in very great economies. These economies would run into many millions.

"In addition to the actual economy by concentrated administration and elimination of overlap, further great economies would be brought about through the curtailment of the self-expanding capacity of scattered bureaus which could be much better controlled if they were grouped together. It would enable policies in connection with different Government activities to be better developed and better directed.

"The subject is an old one and now that economy absolutely must be the first order in government it is an appropriate time for Congress to take up the question and bring it to conclusion. Such action would comprise a major accomplishment of the present session of Congress."

455

New Year's Message
to Foreign Service Officers.
December 31, 1931

To Diplomatic and Consular Officers:

I send cordial greetings at the advent of the New Year to our diplomatic and consular officers abroad with all good wishes for the satisfactions which your service merits. The government draws upon the personnel of its Foreign Service throughout the world for much in the way of information, negotiation, and tactful relationships. The New Year will bring many problems, but if we at home and you abroad maintain our industry, courage, and confidence in the principles and institutions which this country exemplifies, we can do much to promote economic recovery and international friendship. A sound and stable United States is a contribution to the well-being of the world.

HERBERT HOOVER

456

Message of Sympathy on the Death of Richard V. Oulahan. *December 31, 1931*

[Released December 31, 1931.   Dated December 30, 1931]

Dear Mrs. Oulahan:

I have learned with profound regret of the death of your husband. Richard V. Oulahan was an outstanding journalist, a good friend and a wise counsellor. Few writers of our day have done more to disseminate truth regarding national affairs, always for the advancement of our country. He was highly deserving of the designation voluntarily given to him by his fellow journalists, "dean" of the corps of Washintgon correspondents. His passing is a personal loss to me. Mrs. Hoover joins with me in expressing heartfelt sympathy to you and yours.

Yours faithfully,
HERBERT HOOVER

[Mrs. Richard V. Oulahan, 1518 31st Street, Washington, D.C.]

NOTE: Mr. Oulahan, chief Washington correspondent for the New York Times, died on December 30, 1931.

Supplement I

The President's Diary of Developments
of the Moratorium
May 6–July 22, 1931

NOTE: Although this item is identified as a diary account of the President's involvement in negotiating the moratorium on foreign debts, the format of intermittent entries and the inclusion of supplementary materials suggests that it would more correctly be described as a journal. It should be noted also that the entries extend beyond the date of the announcement of the moratorium (June 20, 1931).

The text printed below follows the final, typed format found in the President's files. It includes holograph additions which are shown in brackets.

May 6

Ambassador Sackett just arrived from Germany; states situation is gradually developing towards a critical climax. While he does not feel that there is any immediate danger, he is convinced that unless the tide turns in the economic world that by fall the German situation must collapse. The political disturbances are so extreme, the misery of the people is so great, unemployment has been increasing steadily; that the pressure of reparations is so great that he does not believe the present form of Government will stand in Germany, and that we must face the possibilities of a debacle or revolution unless something can be done. He is most earnest that we take up the question to see whether there is any suggestion or contribution that we should make.

I told him that we, of course, were vitally interested, but it was difficult to see what could be done as we were not a party to reparations; that I felt that one of the fundamental difficulties of all Europe was the increasing armament, which had now reached the stage where the total expenditure of the civilized nations was nearly $5,000,000,000 per

657

annum; that this sum amounted to many times the whole debt weight of the world, but that this did not so much directly concern Germany. I asked him if he thought a suspension of reparations under the Young plan would do any good—he thought it would help.

I undertook to make a study of this situation and to discuss the matter with him when he returned at the end of the month.

I discussed with Ambassador Sackett the speech which I had made on disarmament before the International Chamber of Commerce; that I had the feeling that we were approaching the time when some definite action would need to be taken, but that it did seem to me that we must get over both to the American people and abroad at least one of the malevolent forces that was producing and keeping up this depression.

May 7

I requested Dr. Klein, the Assistant Secretary of Commerce, to furnish me with various memoranda showing the relation of war debts of the different countries; the intergovernmental debts; the military expenditures; the movement of imports and exports into and out of European countries in relation to the United States and between themselves.

I also requested the State Department to give me what information they had on the interrelation of in and out payments of intergovernmental debts of the various countries, particularly Great Britain, France, and Belgium.

Requested Mr. Silas Strawn to draw out the German delegates to the International Chamber of Commerce as to their view of the situation in Germany, upon which he reported that they took the gloomiest view.

May 8

Invited the Belgian delegates to dinner at the White House, and discussed with them at some length the situation both in Belgium, which they stated was not bad, and in Germany, which they stated was very bad, both socially and economically.

May 11

Discussed with Secretary of State the statements made by Sackett and suggested to him that we might give thought to the fact that both the American debt settlements and German reparations were predicated upon capacity to pay in normal times; that of course there was no relationship between reparations and the debts due the American government, as the American debt had been settled irrespective of any income of the Allied Governments from reparations, but that it began to look possible that the depression had reached such depths as to make the whole fabric of intergovernmental debt beyond the capacity to pay under depression conditions.

May 13

[Obscure] press [despatch] carries news of the failure of Creditanstalt, which in my recollection was the most important banking institution in the old Austrian Empire. That confirms Sackett's view of the dangers in that quarter.

May 14

I informed Stimson that we might get some light on the situation from the conferences at Geneva assembled by the various Allied Powers to consider methods of ending depression.

May 15

Dispatch from Minister Roosevelt at Budapest, outlining the excitement created in Hungary through the collapse · of the Austrian Creditanstalt, and the great dangers which were arising, with fear in

659

Hungary that a total collapse was imminent in Austria, which was undermining the Hungarian situation; although he says it would be some weeks before the full effect of the situation is felt.

May 19

Again took up with the Secretary of State the question of intergovernmental debts. Read to him a paragraph to be included in a speech which I propose to make at Indianapolis early in June, indicating that our debt had been settled on the basis of capacity to pay in normal times; that the American people would not wish to extort more than the capacity of these nations to pay ny [by] virtue of the world-wide depression, which, of course, was unexpected at the time the settlements were made, and opposing cancellation or permanent revision. He approved of the idea of laying the groundwork for possible future action.

(*Subsequently struck this out of speech.*)

May 20–22

Conversations with Chairman Meyer of the Federal Reserve Board as to the international situation and the effect upon the United States of further European degeneration. He informed me that there were very large amounts of German foreign trade bills held all over the world, of which considerable amounts were held in the United States; that these bills are self-liquidating by the countries to whom the goods had been sold, and were therefore safe. He pointed out the very wide distribution of German Government and local bonds in the United States, and that the French Government had deposits in various American banks of probably six or eight hundred millions of dollars, the movement of all of which might be affected by difficulties in Central Europe. He felt that our system could handle the shock; that the Federal Reserve could at any moment expand the credit facilities by the purchase of more governments, etc.

Supplement I

May 21

Stimson agrees that press reports indicate that conferences going on at Geneva for the purpose of ending the world depression have come to an end with no constructive suggestion.

May 26–29

Number of dispatches from Minister Stockton at Vienna on the acute crises which had taken place in Austria as the result of the failure of the Creditanstalt and the jeopardy of the Austrian National Bank; reciting at length the acute economic situation and the great danger of total collapse in Austria and its effect upon surrounding states.

May 28

Press reports indicate Austrian Government today guaranteed all bank deposits in an endeavor to prevent financial collapse.

Stockton advises that the situation has become almost impossible of recovery.

May 30

Press carries the report of that the Central Banks have agreed to stand behind the Central Bank of Austria by furnishing a large credit.

German Chancellor announces that they will pay a visit to Chequers for discussion of their situation.

June 1

Stockton reports on situation in Austria that there is now hope crisis is passed.

June 2

Ambassador Sackett came to Washington for discussion with Secretary of State and myself on the German situation. He is sailing at once for Germany.

I explained to him that I felt that we would need to assist in the crisis, and that he could assure the German Ministry that we would endeavor to be helpful. I told him of my view that the whole reparations and debt complex could well be [temporarily] reviewed in the light of capacity to pay under depression conditions, and that he might advise upon his arrival the reaction from the German Government.

Stockton advises the Austrian crisis developed much worse. He remarks that if capitalistic system weathers the storm, its obligations may be met.

June 2–4

Ambassador Dawes [and Ambassador Gibson] my guests at White House. I asked his views upon my idea of a review of all intergovernmental debts to determine capacity to pay under depression conditions, this not to disturb agreements under normal conditions—limiting the reduced basis to two years. We discussed situation in all European countries at great length. [They] agreed with my idea. He considered there was ample time to do so provided the date of reductions was first fixed, say, July 1st.

June 3

Stockton reports that situation has improved and it looks like condition may be carried on for some time further.

German Government announces a drastic tax increase and reduction of expenditures.

Press dispatches carry statement from Germany that the Germans will seek moratorium on reparations.

June 5

I asked Secretaries Stimson, Mellon and Undersecretary Mills to attend at the White House. I explained to them that I felt the European situation had been degenerating much faster during the past month due to the failure of the Creditanstalt; that we were endangered by a general financial collapse in that quarter; that while the Germans as yet had made no move I felt that their situation was weakening and that the political forces in motion might result in revolution and overthrow if any financial crisis should develop; that it seemed to me the drift of gold to the United States was paralyzing central banking institutions the world over. I stated that the idea which I had discussed with Stimson during the past two weeks of a re-examination of capacity to pay under depression conditions would not work fast enough. I had a definite proposal to lay before them. That was that we should postpone all collections on allied debts for one year in consideration of all the allies making similar postponements of reparations and all claims during the same period. I further explained that the world needed some strong action which would change the mental point of view and that I felt perhaps such an action might serve this purpose of general reestablishment of courage and confidence. I read them a rough memo I had prepared.

Mr. Stimson favored it. Mr. Mellon stated his unqualified disapproval. Mr. Mills stated that there was no executive authority except so far as payments on principal were concerned amounting to less than $80,000,000 out of the $250,000,000, that it would be impossible to secure without a special session of Congress because it would break down the debt structure, and that he entirely disapproved.

I reiterated my position but stated that I thought it desirable to make further inquiries and suggested that Mr. Mills go to New York to examine the financial situation both there and abroad and that as Mr. Mellon was leaving next day for Europe, that he should make independent inquiries there and that Mr. Stimson should also make renewed inquiries through agencies of the State Department and that I would get in contact with the Department of Commerce. I stated that I feared we were in the presence of a great crisis.

(*Proposed statement*)

The most constructive thing that can be done in the whole world economic situation today is that payments on the intergovernmental obligations arising out of war, which may become due between July 1, 1931, and July 1, 1932, be deferred for payment until the third year from now, upon such basis of distribution as may subsequently be agreed upon, thus giving the whole world one year to restore its domestic economy and removing the fears and apprehensions of moratoriums and defaults from the world, and giving a year's breathing spell in which to rearrange internal economy and recover from depression.

Our debt settlement agreements provide partially for such a postponement, but any action of this kind to be of any value must apply in full to all German, Austrian, Hungarian and Bulgarian reparations payments, and must likewise apply in full to all debts from former allies due to Great Britain or to France and any other and all such intergovernmental obligations.

I know of nothing that would contribute more to restore employment and the demand for goods over the whole world. During this proposed year of recovery we shall be holding the conference on reduction of land armaments. Action by that conference could lift an economic burden upon people of the world which would several times outweigh these international payments.

New York bankers have apparently got wind of my discussions with different people on the question of reviewing of capacity to pay. Lamont of Morgan & Company rang up to say that he thought it was desirable that we should use the government influence to see that the Germans did not give notice of a deferment of the reparations during their visit at Chequers, as that would precipitate matters. He said that it had been suggested from Washington that we might give notice to the Allied Governments that we would have no objection to their deferring the payments on principal of the debt. I informed him that I had considered this, but that it was of no purpose, as the total amounts they could defer were under $80,000,000 a year, and this would furnish no basis for discussions for amelioration of the German situation. I asked him if he had discussed the situation with Senator Morrow. He said not. He stated that his firm had no money in Germany but that other institutions probably had. I did not communicate to him any feature of my plan for a year's deferment.

June 6

Brüning issued a statement in London, indicating that Germany must have assistance.

I telegraphed and telephoned Senator Morrow that I would be glad if he would discuss German situation with New York bankers and endeavor to find how serious they regarded the condition of the Reichbank and the Austrian Banks. I told him confidentially not to be passed on what I had in mind. He undertook to make inquiries on Monday (8th).

I telegraphed and telephoned Senator Morrow that I would be glad if he would investigate the opinion of German situation by New York bankers and endeavor to find how serious they regarded the condition of the Reichbank and the Austrian banks, and to feel out if they were prepared to assist Reichbank.

June 8

German Ministry in London discussing their situation. I suggested to Mr. Stimson that he call up Mr. MacDonald and ask him on the telephone the character of their presentation and his own impressions. Mr. MacDonald's view was that the situation was becoming critical, but

665

Mr. MacDonald stated that the Germans had assured him that while they would ultimately need to seek relief on reparations, that the position would not become acute before September; that they had no notion of taking any action prior to that date. He did not think that the matter was at present imminent; and stated that he had discouraged any attempt at a European conference over intergovernmental debts.

June 9

Had Senator Morrow and Secretary Mills to dinner to discuss situation. They agreed that we should take action at some point. Morrow agreed with me that New York bankers were panicky over the situation in Germany and Austria and that we must allow it to develop a little before we could present my plan to political leaders on both sides and to the Governments of Europe with any hope of success. That the rapidly developing situation in Germany would bring the world to a realization that something real must be done. He or Mills suggested sending Harrison of the Federal Reserve Bank of New York to Europe to report upon the situation as he was levelheaded. I agreed and Harrison agreed to go.

June 12–13

Mr. Stimson held conference with Owen D. Young, Ogden Mills, and Mr. Gilbert, the former Director General of the Reparations Committee in Germany, as to their views on the situation. They urged that immediate action be taken without even waiting for consultation with political leaders.

June 13–14

Saturday and Sunday at the Rapidan Secretary Stimson and Mr. Mills telephoned me at great length upon the situation which had rapidly developed as the result of the German Minister's visit to London. That the statements made by them had precipitated runs on Central European banks and that a crisis had developed much more rapidly than had been anticipated. The project which had been discussed of sending Harrison to Europe to make further inquiries into the position was useless as Harrison had to remain in New York to take care of possible crisis there. They had repeated sessions with Owen Young and others, and they considered the time had come when we must act. They forwarded to me the draft of a statement they proposed I should issue, covering my suggestion of the one-year debt holiday.

I informed them that the position had reoriented itself by the action of the German Ministers, and that instead of being able to predicate action on the general movements for world recovery we were faced with a bankers' panic and action by the Germans which greatly embarrassed all preliminary negotiation; that I could not act without approval of the leaders of both political parties with any hope of securing cooperation by Congress; that I must have time in which to develop this, and that I could not possibly undertake the necessary negotiations with political parties to prepare the way for action until I returned from the West, although I would institute such discussions along the road; that to do this without such authority would instantly become a political issue and that we would be able to carry no conviction to the world of our ability to carry the issue in Congress; that our second plight would be infinitely worse than the first.

I therefore declined their repeated telephone urgings to take action and stated that I preferred to keep in touch with the situation during my trip with view to taking action on my return and that if the situation became so distressing as to require it I would have the leaders of both parties meet me in Washington on my return.

June 14

Telephoned Eugene Meyer at Mt. Kisco, and asked him to get into contact with Mr. Baruch and explain to him our problem. Later Baruch called me and I further explained it to him, asked him to give it consideration and to make inquiries as to necessary and feasibility of plan. Both Meyer and Baruch agreed that action was not desirable until situation developed more pressure, lest we fail to get support at home and abroad.

With view to possibly alleviating the situation, Mr. Castle gave a hint that we might review the debt situation in the light of the depression.

Mr. Mellon reported [from Europe] that his inquiry showed the situation was absolutely critical.

June 15

Redrafted possible statement proposing year's holiday in all interallied debts on the train.

June 16

Consulted Ambassador Dawes, Senator Watson, and Senator Fess, who approved of the project.

June 18

Told Stimson that in view of Sackett's telegrams as to the urgency of the situation and the possible outbreaks of widespread disorder at any moment we ought to have a clear cut statement signed by the highest German authority of the need for action.

Upon my return to Washington I had a conference with Secretaries Stimson and Mills. Mr. Mellon had cabled that the situation was urgent and strongly recommended that I should take immediate action on the lines I had proposed on the 5th instant entirely reversing the previous views. Mr. Mills presented the views of the Treasury Department, entirely the reverse from those expressed in our conference on the 5th.

I at once began to feel out Members of the Senate and House with whom I could get in contact. Made appointment with Senators Walsh and Glass for the following morning.

June 18–20

Interviewed Senators Glass, Walsh, Ashurst, and other Democratic leaders.

June 18

Called Baruch who felt we were in the right line; said he had already taken it up in principle with Democratic leaders generally most helpful. Discussed situation again on 19th. Baruch systematically canvassing Democratic Senators.

June 19

I consider it desirable to issue a short statement on the question of German relief.

(two statements follow:)

Together with Under Secretary Mills, I interviewed Senator Walsh of Montana, Senators Swanson, Glass, King and Harris, setting out the European situation and suggesting one year's postponement of inter-governmental debts, conditional upon approval of the Congress. They expressed strong support of the proposal.

Mr. Mills placed the proposal before Senator Harrison, Representatives Crisp, Collier, and Byrns (by telephone) and they approved.

I personally interviewed Senators Bingham and Reed and by telephone placed the situation before Senators Borah, Morrow, Watson, Couzens and Vandenberg. All except Senator Couzens fully approved and he stated he would raise no opposition. I had previously spoken to Senator Fess, who approved.

I have also by telephone, placed the matter before Congressman Hawley, and personally interviewed Representative Tilson, Ramseyer, and Bacharach. Mr. Mills placed the matter before Representatives Chindblom, Mapes, Estep, Michener, Wood and Snell—all of whom cordially supported the proposal.

Both Mr. Owen D. Young and Ambassadors Dawes and Gibson strongly support it.

The President said:

"Since my return from the Central West yesterday I have conferred with those leaders of both political parties who are present in Washington with respect to certain steps which we might take to assist in economic recovery both here and abroad.

"These conversations have been particularly directed to strengthening the situation in Germany. No definite plans or conclusions have yet been arrived at but the response which I have met from the leaders of both parties is most gratifying.

"Any statement of any plan or method is wholly speculative and is not warranted by the facts."

June 20

Having succeeded to a large degree with the leaders of the House and Senate, although failing to secure positive support of Senator Robinson and Congressman Garner, we considered we would be safe in going to the world with the proposal. We had expected Senator Robinson in Washington on Sunday and to employ the time up to Sunday evening with Members of the House and Senate. We learned, however, that the program had leaked to the press and that garbled accounts which might cause great conflict in Europe were going to publication. We also found that Senator Robinson had not come to Washington and in the presence of Stimson and Mills I telephoned him and secured his approval of my making the statement which he would not oppose although he would not give his support or allow the use of his name in that connection. He did agree that he would not make any opposition to the proposal. Both Mr. Mills and I discussed the matter with Garner by telephone but could not secure support from him altho he agreed he would make no statement pro or con prior to the meeting of Congress. We then determined to issue the proposal the terms of which I wrote myself.

June 21

Statement of the American proposal appears in the press.

June 24–25

Long arguments Stimson and Mills who want to accept most of the French proposals. I have insisted that we simply could not go to the American people with any proposal that did not apply equally everywhere and I would not do so.

July 3

Drafted with Castle, Morrow, and Mills, a memo for the French, setting out the basis for an agreement, including my idea of a technical commission to settle all reparations in kind and technical questions "in the spirit" of my original proposal. I did not like the dispatch very much as it was too lawyerlike, too technical, and befuddled people's minds on the big issues.

July 4

Published our dispatch anyway. Mellon stated on the phone that the French objected to it and were preparing a note.

Later Mellon telegraphed paragraph of French note on reparations in kind. Mellon stated that the French note contained many jokers. He was very discouraged. French very ugly.

Left for Rapidan at 11 o'clock. Castle and Mills to cable our thoughts on day's transactions to Mellon.

July 5

At Rapidan received by telephone part text of French note in reply to ours of July 4. At once ordered car and came to Washington, bringing Senator Reed, who was a guest. Arrived at 3:30 and called Mills and Castle. I outlined a change in strategy:

1. To put up a simple formula to French in a formal dispatch as a proposed joint statement that would be impossible for them to refuse before the world, especially the settlement of their attempt to nibble off reparations in kind by referring it to commission to settle "in the spirit" of President's proposal.

2. To advise the press of the nature of our note generally—in advance of French receiving it, so that they could not blanket it by more Paris propaganda.

3. Dissect and expose the French note of July 4th to Mellon and be prepared to publish a devastating analysis of it, showing that the French had raised eight new questions after two weeks, all impossible of acceptance.

4. Advise Mellon we did not care what view the French took of our formula; that we only wanted yes or no; that we proposed to finally test their honesty and to force their hands. Mills vehemently opposed and drafted a long technical agreement to be offered to them. Reed and Castle agreed with my strategy. Mills very vehement that I was bringing the world to ruin.

July 6

I dictated a press statement for Castle to issue, forecasting the note. Issued at 10 o'clock. 10:30 talked with Mr. Mellon by phone three times. First he described the consternation and anger of French ministers over my cabled formula, said he had gotten them partly pacified. Implored us not to publish the note itself. We agreed not to, but told him a general summary had gone out. Told him to try to induce the French to make a note of "reservations" upon our formula. If they put up anything like their note of July 4th we would publish the two documents and then would state that Europe must pull itself together and settle its own differences before anything could be done; that MacDonald had agreed to at once announce an immediate conference of all heads of states and force the French into line. Drafted statement which I would issue.

Second telephone from Mellon. He asked amplification of instructions.

Third call Mellon said French had caved in and had written a paraphrase of my formula in order to save their face, which he submitted. We at once agreed to it.

At 4:30 o'clock I issued a statement announcing completion in principle.

Had Sackett called and told to have Germany make complimentary remarks in such form as to make amenities to other governments. Also had Castle hint that British would insist on further years in repayment period.

July 12

(Proposed statement from Mills—phoned from Rapidan.)

The position of the Federal Government in the present phase of the German situation is clear. Through the President's plan the German crisis in international obligations has been relieved and over 400,000,000 made available for devotion to the rehabilitation of industry and commerce during the next year instead of payment upon reparations. The strain has been greatly reduced thereby. That is the only direction in which the American Government has either opportunity or authority to intervene.

The situation has now resolved itself into an internal banking crisis in Germany and is one which can only be resolved by the banking world.

The Federal Government has neither funds which it can loan for such purposes, nor has it any authority to determine the policies of the banking world. It is naturally anxious for a solution as assisting the German people and in the interest of the whole problem of world recovery.

(Proposed statement from Harrison.)

I have seen Mr. Mills' statement. I am sure the Federal Reserve Banks and our bankers generally are anxious for a solution of the German Banking crisis. But any plan of solution must naturally originate by a definite program from the German Banks in cooperation with the Banks of Europe. I am sure our Banks would give most earnest consideration to such a plan.

(Proposed statement from Castle.)

The intergovernmental relief of Germany has been solved by the President's action and the whole situation greatly aided and clarified. The German position is now solely a banking crisis and is solvable only by their banks. The heads of the principal European National Banks including the Bank of England, are meeting tomorrow morning in Basle together with the Bank of International Settlements. They will no doubt consider the crisis. Obviously any plan for banking solution must originate from these bankers and it is my understanding that our bankers are prepared to consider assistance in any effective plan of relief that will be evolved by them.

July 17

I sent for Mills and explained that the conference going on in Paris was heading us into an utterly impossible situation of political entanglements and at the same time would utterly wreck the situation in Germany. I told him I had thought out a plan which I believed might solve the situation which I outlined to him. I then dictated an analysis of the whole situation which was telegraphed to Messrs. Stimson and Mellon.

July 18

(Telegram from Stimson read over phone by Castle to President at Rapidan Camp.)

Yesterday afternoon I saw the German Ambassador and talked with him frankly on conciliatory measures that could be taken. I warned him that the Germans could not expect further financial assistance from America except on commercial basis. The conversation was long and satisfactory. I told him frankly that from my observation of the French I thought the Germans had no reason to anticipate unfair treatment. In the evening I had a similar talk with Flandin who will be a delegate at London, in which I stressed the importance from the world economic standpoint that there should be no arbiter in the French-German negotiations. I pointed out how the market had risen on the news of the coming meeting, as well as the fact that the adverse loan market might be greatly ameliorated before the London conference was over. I assured him on the strength of MacDonald presiding over the meeting that the French would have fair treatment in London. He responded so warmly that today I saw Laval and had a talk with him informing him of my interview with the German Ambassador. He responded satisfactorily and assured me there would be no arbiter if he could prevent it and promised to have satisfactory press reports. The English press report that troubled the President has been entirely relieved and Henderson and I will attend the meeting Sunday morning after which Laval is giving a luncheon and I then take the 4 o'clock train for London. The only adverse incident has been the foolish and dangerous cable sent by Lamont about which I spoke to the President. At a time when Laval has been struggling with his own bank trying to rise out of the extreme depression the last few days such a blow was peculiarly unfortunate and has delayed the improvement to which we are all striving.

(Transatlantic call started here.)

———————

Mr. Stimson apparently did not react to the plan still insisting that we had to work along with the French. I insisted that there was no genuinity to the French proposal, that they were the road to a political morass and the demoralization of Germany. On discussion with Mills and Castle I resolved to place the matter in a formal note which could be presented at the London conference and asked Mills and Castle to formulate such a note on the basis of the telegraphic plan of yesterday.

July 19

At the Rapidan I received the draft from Castle and Mills which followed closely my original telegram to Stimson and approved its being dispatched with some alterations. Inasmuch as our people were still under the spell of the French and disposed to be critical I drafted and sent an extension telegram of criticism of the French situation indicating my belief that there was no genuinity in it.

(Phoned to Castle at 11 a.m., incomplete)

In respect to our telegram today it seems to us that the following considerations are likely to arise in the conference:

1. It will be insisted that while our proposal is only the first step, it is inadequate to the present needs. Upon this the banking world has no satisfactory or convincing information. The Germans naturally feel they should have more credits but it will be impossible to satisfy the banking world on this point without some further information.

2. The Germans should realize that as a result of the German crisis the whole financial world has been placed in extreme difficulty and that the provision of further credits is a greater financial difficulty today than it would have been three months ago; that the first thing necessary is to restore confidence even though Germany should remain short of working capital for a certain period of time. They should also realize that all countries are short of capital at this time and that each country has now to seek safeguards for its own financial situation.

3. When the President put forward his proposal on the 20th of June, the external run upon Germany practically ceased but with the delays of the French in acceptance, unrest was recreated both in Germany and

abroad. As a result Germany has been called upon to meet from various quarters the payment of a great deal of these short term credits. The result of these demands has been to undermine the President's proposal. Our information is that the American banks have stood up to a very large percentage and some of them have responded for even further assistance. On the other hand it is said that the French have decreased their holdings of German short term obligations by over $200,000,000. It is stated that the banks of Switzerland, Holland, Denmark, Italy have done likewise. This action by those groups is in itself largely responsible for the present situation and a moral obligation rests upon them to restore these credits and take their part in the world burden. This can be done in one of two ways—either that each country as a whole should restore its situation to what it was on the 20th of June, or alternatively that we take, say the British or American position of today, and insist that every nation restore its credits up to the same proportion which the British and Americans now extend as against those of June 20th. In other words if our bankers have decreased credits by 20% then these other nations should restore their situation to 80% of that existing on the 20th of June.

4. We cannot say that our bankers would not be prepared to make some further short term advances but they have the right to know that other nations have restored their proportional situations and that they will take their proportion of whatever the new load may be.

5. At some point in the negotiations you might suggest that if the other nations are prepared to put up renewed credits, that up to a sum of $120,000,000 the American government will undertake to finance raw materials in wheat and cotton in the same terms that other nations will extend credits to Germany. In other words instead of furnishing banking credits our governmental agencies will extend credits to Germany with which to purchase from these agencies raw materials. Such a service is exactly equal to banking credits.

6. As to the French Government's assertion that they are the only government willing to meet this crisis you can put forward the following effective statement:

1. That the Americans today are carrying more than half the whole

load of German short term credits; that the French are carrying less than 3%; that the French have, even since the Presidents statement, reduced these credits and further embarrassed the situation; that they would come with clean hands into the conference if they restore these credits to the situation in the same proportion as the Americans who, at the request of the President, have held open their short term credits; that the American Government is prepared to assist further credit to the government either through further extension of banking credits or in any event through furnishing of supplies as above mentioned.

7. On the information we have received indirectly from the Reichbank officials we believe that the immediate situation can be taken care of by the holding open of present lines of credit. It certainly can be taken care of if other nations will restore credit to the same proportion as the Americans now hold to that which existed on the 20th of June. We are fearful, however, that if the standard of the provision of some sum of new money to Germany shall be erected by this conference as an implied condition upon which the conference is a success or failure, the whole world will stagger until such time as this loan is consummated. On the other hand if the immediate step is taken to keep open present lines of credit the world will feel that the situation has been stabilized and it will begin to recover confidence and out of this confidence will grow the possibility of further action.

July 20

Talked with Stimson and he was entirely changed. The French press had attacked him bitterly. I pointed out, however, that the French had been leaking the conversations which he had with them and the Germans on the basis of my plan and that this created a difficult situation here. I suggested that we should make a statement. He strongly advised against it. Later in the day we called again and urged that some statement could be issued but he replied that he did not wish any statement issued until after he had presented the plan at the conference the following morning, said that it would be all right for us to publish whatever we saw fit coincident with his presentation.

July 21

We published the text of the note sent on Sunday founded on the telegram of the previous Friday, Mr. Castle giving some explanation to the press. For some reason Stimson denied that there was any such plan or that he had presented anything to the conference although reports of the conference show that he did raise an essential to the plan although he did not present it as provided in the note.

July 22

Publication of the plan clarified the air and brought the conference in London down to realities. Stimson, however, has thrown a cloud over the whole business by an interview with the press in which he accredited MacDonald with having initiated the plan.

Supplement II
Excerpts From an Interview
With the President

NOTE: The following statements were made by President Hoover during an interview with correspondent Frazier Hunt on November 25, 1930. Mr. Hunt's article on the interview appeared in the February 1931 issue of Cosmopolitan. This was the first interview in which the President permitted his exact words to be quoted.

INCOME AND EXPENDITURES

"We spend more in this country, but we earn more," the President went on. "You know, contrary to the old maxim, it isn't so much what we spend that counts—it's what we earn. I am more interested in increasing people's incomes than in worrying over their expenditures. Before we are a spending nation we are an earning nation. . . .

"I remember hearing an argument three or four years ago between an old retired middle-western farmer and his son. The father was criticizing his son for spending so much money. He explained how hard he and the young man's mother had worked and how little they had spent—as against the all-year hired hand and the trips and the two motor cars of the present day. But the son changed his father's tune when he proved that today the farm was earning five times more gross than during his father's day—and so he had a right to better things and to spend five times as much on them."

STANDARDIZATION

"You know there is a certain type of individual who chides this country about our so-called 'standardization,'" the President went on. "Well, I don't mind how much we standardize or what we standardize so long as everybody gets it and uses it. The purpose of standardizing is to make things cost less and to make them accessible to everybody. Take bathtubs. I wouldn't care if every bathtub was exactly the same, if all people had them and would use them. And the same way with the radio; it isn't the type or style that's important—it's their universal use and what comes out of them that's all-important. Standardized tools, radios, automobiles, typewriters, lead pencils, do no harm to the human mind; in fact, they add variety to life and joy to millions who would not otherwise know them. It's all right to standardize so long as we standardize UP and not DOWN."

DEPRESSION

"But we are really cheerful humans and consequently optimistic people and so it is a passing thing and before long we will wake up and find the depression and the fear passed and prosperity again with us."

SCIENCE AND INVENTION

"We are facing a changing world of science and invention. No twelve months go by but that there is some great advancement, some discovery, some development, in the field of practical science. It is all so swift and changing that we cannot begin to follow it. Take the one matter of rays, all but unknown a generation ago. Today the harnessing of certain of these strange elements makes possible our radios and a score of other inventions.

"Fifteen years ago there were less than a hundred industrial research laboratories, operated at a total cost of perhaps a million dollars a year. Now there are more than a thousand of these laboratories where pure science becomes the handmaid of invention. One great organization alone is spending $5,000,000 annually for experimental purposes and research.

"So it is that before our very eyes a new world of science and industry is being built and constantly rebuilt. It is a changing world with new and changing problems. What, for instance, will our grandchildren do with the added leisure that efficient machinery, and its consequent shorter hours of labor, will give them? Will this future generation have the discipline and education and the spiritual upbringing and the

682

fine moral background to withstand the new temptations of the high-speed city life that will be theirs?"

NEW GENERATION OF CHILDREN

"Only children of a New Generation—a New American—can stand against this future world. First of all, their health must be looked after—this civilization would decay in a generation of physical weaklings; then comes their play environment, their schooling, their discipline, their morals. These are but a few items in this endless and many-sided task of seeing that a New Generation is ready for the New World.

"One of the biggest of all problems is to drive in this idea of the necessity of properly born, trained, educated and healthy moral children to the voters and officials of America. This Child Health Conference was a start—but only that. We must keep it alive and burning. This Conference was the aftermath of years of investigation and experience of the best and most devoted of Americans. It evolved a 'Charter for Children' of nineteen points that needs be in every household and every government office. We must follow this National Conference with a series of state conferences, then group, and finally individual town and city conferences, and the 'Charter for Children' must be drawn into the activities of government and of social institutions.

"Think what this New Generation built upon that constitution will mean to the single problem of the young criminal. The present rate of criminal increase is disheartening beyond measure. Today, there are more than 100,000 criminals in our Federal and state prisons—and there are that many more criminals at large who should be behind the bars. . . . This New Generation of children, healthy, trained and mentally inspired, would go a long way towards solving all this. Most of our native criminal class are products of city slums. If the character and quality and health of these children were watched and nurtured, a criminal type of child would not develop. It would be difficult to overestimate what the single item of adequate playground facilities would mean in the bringing-up of normal city children.

"Proper food is another all-important part in planning the New Generation, for, according to the Conference, one hundred percent of all deficient children are simply the product of bad feeding. And while this goes back to the home, health education must largely originate in the school—and for the time being, in proper and periodic examination.

"We must see that their roots have proper soil to put their precious tendrils into. City children must not be denied grass and flowers, fields and streams—all the imaginative surroundings that are a part of nature.

"And of tremendous importance, too, are the million and a half especially gifted children scattered by the winds of chance among our 45,000,000 children. They have 'gifts' that must be nurtured. They come from all classes and kinds; they are the 'sports' of nature. They must be used to the limits of their special talents in the building-up of this great new national life. One of the major problems is to find leadership capable of coping with its increased complexity."

"Ten years will see the start of this new generation. We can move swiftly after that. . . . But I repeat, we must keep pounding and repeating the whole idea until it becomes as much of an accepted part of our national life and thought as, say, our national defense is. Why, today we think little of spending $700,000,000 annually on our two great arms of defense—and yet it is with difficulty that we vote a twentieth part of that sum towards national health and national education. Somehow, it is hard to 'sell' an intangible thing like protection of children, yet we 'buy' a $17,000,000 cruiser without raising an eyebrow."

Appendix A—Additional White House Releases

NOTE: This appendix lists those releases not printed as items in this volume. A complete listing of Proclamations and Executive orders for 1931 appears in Appendix B and are printed in full in "Proclamations and Executive Orders, Herbert Hoover, 1929–1933."

Date	Subject
January	
5	List of endorsers for D. Lawrence Groner to be an Associate Justice of the Court of Appeals of the District of Columbia
5	List of endorsers for William Hitz to be an Associate Justice of the Court of Appeals of the District of Columbia
6	List of endorsers for Harry A. Hollzer to be United States District Judge of the Southern District of California
8	List of endorsers for William H. Sawtille, Tucson, Ariz.
18	List of leading citizens accepting President's invitation to become members of a committee to sponsor the Red Cross drought relief campaign
22	Advance text of radio address on the American National Red Cross drought relief campaign
23	Nomination sent to the Senate for Benedict Crowell to be a brigadier general in the Army Reserve Corps
28	List of endorsers for Thomas M. Kennedy to be United States District Judge for the Southern District of Texas
28	List of endorsers for Walter H. Evans to be United States Judge of the Customs Court
29	List of endorsers and biographical data for Albert M. Sames to be United States District Judge for the District of Arizona

Appendix A

Appendix A

687

Appendix A

Appendix A

689

Appendix A

Appendix A

68-611 O - 76 - 48

Appendix A

Appendix B—Messages to the Congress

NOTE: This appendix lists those messages not printed as items in this volume. Presidential reports to the Congress are not included and are listed separately in Appendix D.

71st Congress, 3d Session

693

Appendix B

Appendix B

Appendix B

Appendix B

72d Congress, 1st Session

699

Appendix B

Appendix C—Presidential Proclamations and Executive Orders

[The texts of these documents are printed in "Proclamations and Executive Orders, Herbert Hoover, 1929–1933."]

PROCLAMATIONS

No.	Date	Subject
	1931	
1930	Jan. 5	Bryce Canyon National Park, Utah, lands added
1931	Jan. 16	Hiawatha National Forest, Mich., lands added
1932	Jan. 27	Ottawa National Forest, Mich., establishment
1933	Feb. 5	Maple sugar and maple sirup, decrease in rate of duty
1934	Feb. 5	Woven-wire fencing and netting, increase in rate of duty
1935	Feb. 5	Pigskin leather, decrease in rate of duty
1936	Feb. 5	Wood flour, decrease in rate of duty
1937	Feb. 5	Hats, bonnets, and hoods, decrease in rate of duty
1938	Feb. 12	Marquette National Forest, Mich., name changed and consolidation of lands
1939	Mar. 2	Brazil, exportation of arms and ammunitions, prohibition revoked
1940	Mar. 16	Fourdrinier wires, cylinder wires, and woven-wire cloth, increase in rate of duty
1941	Mar. 16	Wool-felt hats and bodies therefor, decrease in rates of duty

No.	Date	Subject
	1931	
1942	Mar. 16	Edible gelatin, decrease in rates of duty
1943	Mar. 17	Migratory game bird regulations, amendment
1944	Mar. 30	George Washington Birthplace National Monument, Va., lands added
1945	Apr. 1	Canyon De Chelly National Monument, Ariz., establishment
1946	Apr. 7	Nezperce and Bitterroot National Forests, Idaho, boundaries modified
1947	Apr. 7	Child Health Day
1948	Apr. 13	Pinnacles National Monument, Calif., lands added
1949	Apr. 16	Emergency Board, Louisiana and Arkansas Railway Co., labor dispute
1950	Apr. 24	Katmai National Monument, Alaska, lands added
1951	May 1	Harney National Forest, S. Dak., lands added
1952	May 4	Byrce Canyon National Park, Utah, lands added
1953	June 19	Immigration quotas
1954	June 24	Bells, increase in rate of duty
1955	June 24	Hemp cordage, increase in rate of duty
1956	June 24	Dried whole eggs, dried egg yolk, and dried egg albumen, increase in rate of duty
1957	June 24	Pipe organs, decrease in rate of duty
1958	June 24	Bentwood furniture, decrease in rate of duty
1959	June 24	Olive oil, decrease in rate of duty

Appendix C

Appendix C

EXECUTIVE ORDERS

Appendix C

No.	Date	Subject
	1931	
5533	Jan. 16	Oregon, Federal Power Commission, authorization to issue a project license to the Odell Lake Co. for construction on Reservoir Site Reserve No. 16
5534	Jan. 21	Montana and Nevada, land withdrawal for Public Water Reserve No. 137
5535	Jan. 21	Montana, restoration of lands withdrawn for Power Site Reserve No. 510
5536	Jan. 21	Montana, restoration of lands withdrawn for Power Site Reserve No. 397
5537	Jan. 21	California, restoration of lands withdrawn for Potash Reserve No. 2, California No. 1
5538	Jan. 23	Colorado, land withdrawal for resurvey
5539	Jan. 23	Ponca Indian Reservation, Okla., extension of trust period on allotments
5540	Jan. 26	Charles Sheldon Wildlife Refuge, Nev., establishment
5541	Jan. 27	Oregon, restoration of lands withdrawn for power site reserves
5542	Jan. 27	California, land withdrawal for resurvey
5543	Jan. 30	Idaho, restoration of lands withdrawn for Power Site Reserve No. 283
5544	Jan. 30	Civil Service Rules, Schedule A, Subdivision III, amendment
5545	Jan. 30	Civil Service Rules, Schedule B, Subdivision I, Paragraph 7, revocation
5546	Jan. 31	Cheyenne River Indian Reservation, S. Dak., extension of trust period on allotments

No.	Date	Subject
	1931	
5547	Jan. 31	New Mexico, land withdrawal for resurvey
5548	Jan. 31	New Mexico, land withdrawal for resurvey
5549	Feb. 5	Instructions to Diplomatic Officers, amendment
5550	Feb. 6	California, land withdrawal for classification and in aid of the administration and control of the Government-owned oil and gas deposits in Kettleman Hills Field
5551	Feb. 7	New Mexico, land withdrawal for resurvey
5552	Feb. 9	Utah, revocation of lands withdrawn containing oil shale to permit the issuance of trust patents to Ma-chook-a-rats (Chester) and Jimmie Colorow, Uncompahgre Ute Indians
5553	Feb. 9	Mrs. Nixon S. Plummer, exemption from civil service rules on appointment
5554	Feb. 9	Helen R. Witt, exemption from civil service rules on appointment
5555	Feb. 11	New Mexico, land withdrawal for resurvey
5556	Feb. 11	Prairie Band of Potawatomi Indians, Kans., extension of trust period on allotments
5557	Feb. 13	Pine Ridge Indian Reservation, S. Dak., extension of trust period on allotments
5558	Feb. 16	New Mexico, land withdrawal for resurvey
5559	Feb. 16	Colorado, land withdrawal pending legislation to make such land grants to the Colorado School of Mines
5560	Feb. 16	Civil Service Rules, Schedule A, amendment
5561	Feb. 18	Hawaii, restoration of lands withdrawn for a United States agricultural station

No.	Date	Subject
	1931	
5562	Feb. 20	Mississippi, land withdrawal for lighthouse purposes
5563	Feb. 23	Margaret Kane, exemption from civil service rules on appointment
5564	Feb. 25	Oregon, restoration of lands withdrawn for Power Site Reserves No. 145 and 566
5565	Feb. 25	Foreign Service, regulations governing appointments
5566	Feb. 27	Virgin Islands, government transferred from the jurisdiction of the Navy Department to the Interior Department
5567	Feb. 28	Montana, restoration of lands withdrawn for Power Site Reserve No. 512
5568	Mar. 3	Chugach National Forest, Alaska, exclusion of lands from, and such lands opened to entry
5569	Mar. 3	Florida, revocation of lands withdrawn for survey and such lands opened to entry
5570	Mar. 3	Civil Service Rule IX, Section 1, amendment
5571	Mar. 5	Arizona, land withdrawal for resurvey
5572	Mar. 7	Idaho, authorization to approve L. E. Strout's application for right-of-way for an irrigation project across lands withdrawn for classification
5573	Mar. 7	Utah, land withdrawal for classification and possible inclusion in a national monument
5574	Mar. 11	Chugach National Forest, Alaska, exclusion of lands from, and such lands opened to entry
5575	Mar. 12	Fond du Lac Band of Chippewa Indians, Minn., extension of trust period on allotments

707

Appendix C

No.	Date	Subject
	1931	
5576	Mar. 13	New Mexico, revocation of lands withdrawn for resurvey and such lands opened to entry
5577	Mar. 13	Oakland, Calif., customs port of entry abolished
5578	Mar. 13	Port of San Francisco, Calif., designation changed to the port of San Francisco-Oakland and extension of port limits
5579	Mar. 16	Crescent Lake Wildlife Refuge, Nebr., establishment
5580	Mar. 16	Agua Caliente Band of Mission Indians, Calif., extension of trust period on allotments
5581	Mar. 17	California, land withdrawal for classification and pending legislation
5582	Mar. 18	Alaska, land withdrawal for the investigation, examination, and classification of coal lands
5583	Mar. 30	Rates of rental and subsistence allowances for officers of the various services
5584	Mar. 30	Civil Service Rules, Schedule A, Section VIII, Paragraph 5(d), amendment
5585	Mar. 30	California, land withdrawal for resurvey
5586	Mar. 30	North Dakota, land withdrawal for classification and possible inclusion in a wildlife refuge
5587	Mar. 30	Colorado, revocation of lands withdrawn for resurvey and such lands opened to entry
5588	Mar. 31	Civil Service Rules, Schedule A, amendment
5589	Apr. 1	Idaho, land withdrawal for townsite purposes
5590	Apr. 1	Montana, restoration of lands withdrawn for Petroleum Reserve No. 40, Montana No. 1

708

Appendix C

Appendix C

710

No.	Date 1931	Subject
5620	May 13	Dorothy I. Sinnott, exemption from civil service rules on appointment
5621	May 13	Consular Regulations, amendment
5622	May 15	Philippine Islands, Federal employees, inclusion in the classified service
5623	May 15	California, land withdrawal for resurvey
5624	May 15	Foreign Service quarters, regulations for the occupation and maintenance
5625	May 18	Interior Department, Field Service, Saturday working hours
5626	May 18	Kickapoo Indians, Kans., extension of trust period on allotments
5627	May 20	Federal employees residing in Arlington, Va., permission to participate in local government
5628	May 20	Amy Cowing, exemption from civil service rules on appointment
5629	May 21	Montana, land withdrawal for Public Water Reserve No. 141
5630	May 25	Washington, lands transferred from the jurisdiction of the Navy Department to the Interior Department and reservation of part of the lands for lighthouse purposes
5631	May 26	California, land withdrawal for municipal water supply purposes
5632	May 27	North Dakota, revocation of lands withdrawn for classification and such lands opened to entry
5633	May 28	California, land withdrawal for resurvey
5634	June 1	Washington, transfer of lands from Mount Baker National Forest to Snoqualmie National Forest

No.	Date	Subject
	1931	
5635	June 2	Arthur B. Landt, exemption from civil service rules on appointment
5636	June 3	Civil Service Rules, Schedule B, amendment
5637	June 4	Hawaii, restoration of portion of Keaahala Military Reservation
5638	June 8	Radio frequencies, assignment to Government radio stations
5638A	June 8	Radio frequencies, assignment to Government radio stations
5639	June 8	Wyoming, coal land withdrawal, Wyoming No. 1, modification to permit the withdrawal of lands for an aviation field
5640	June 8	California, land withdrawal for resurvey
5641	June 8	Alaska, restoration of lands from Salmon Hatchery Reservation
5642	June 8	Foreign Service, regulations for administering
5643	June 8	Foreign Service, representation and post allowances, regulations governing
5644	June 8	Foreign Service, designation of "unhealthful" posts
5645	June 8	Alien Property Custodian, delegation of further powers under the Trading with the Enemy Act
5646	June 9	Idaho, transfer of lands from Selway National Forest to Bitterroot National Forest
5647	June 9	Income tax returns, inspection
5648	June 11	Foreign Service, regulations governing accounts and returns
5649	June 12	Helen Terrill Mays, exemption from civil service rules on appointment

No.	Date	Subject
	1931	
5650	June 18	Oregon, land withdrawal for Public Water Reserve No. 142
5651	June 18	Minnesota, revocation of lands withdrawn for classification and such lands opened to entry
5652	June 18	Colorado, land withdrawal for resurvey
5653	June 20	Colorado, restoration of lands withdrawn for Power Site Reserve No. 81
5654	June 20	Montana, land withdrawal for an addition to Duck Creek Ranger Station for the administration of Helena National Forest
5655	June 22	Arizona, restoration of lands withdrawn for Public Water Reserve No. 72
5656	June 22	Wyoming, land withdrawal for resurvey
5657	June 24	Civil Service Rules, Schedule A, Subdivision II, Paragraph 2, amendment
5658	June 24	Executive orders and proclamations, regulations governing form, style, and safeguarding of the text
5659	June 25	Florence R. Hopkins, exemption from civil service rules on appointment
5660	June 26	Nevada, lands, transfer of jurisdiction from the Navy Department to the Interior Department
5661	July 1	Consular Regulations, amendment
5662	July 1	Civil Service Rules, Schedule A, Subdivision IX, amendment
5663	July 1	Horace Paul Bestor, designation as a Farm Loan Commissioner
5664	July 2	Nevada, land withdrawal for use as a naval ammunition depot

713

Appendix C

No.	Date	Subject
	1931	
5665	July 2	A. D. Forsythe, exemption from civil service rules on appointment
5666	July 3	Commerce Department, persons holding local offices, permission to receive an appointment in the Commerce Department
5667	July 6	Oregon, land withdrawal for resurvey
5668	July 6	Wyoming, land withdrawal for target range
5669	July 14	Montana and Utah, restoration of lands withdrawn for Public Water Reserve No. 49, Montana No. 4 and Public Water Reserve No. 1, Utah No. 1
5670	July 22	Oregon, transfer of lands from the War Department to Suislaw National Forest
5671	July 29	Wisconsin, Minnesota, North Dakota, Montana, Wyoming, Idaho, Washington, and Oregon, land withdrawal pending legislation
5672	Aug. 3	Colorado and Wyoming, land withdrawal for Public Water Reserve No. 143
5673	Aug. 4	Tongass National Forest, Alaska, exclusion of lands from, and such lands opened to entry
5674	Aug. 7	California, revocation of lands withdrawn for resurvey and such lands opened to entry
5675	Aug. 7	Utah, revocation of lands withdrawn for resurvey and such lands opened to entry
5676	Aug. 7	Washington, Reservoir Site Reserve No. 1, modification, Federal Power Commission, authorization to issue a project license
5677	Aug. 10	New Mexico, revocation of lands withdrawn for resurvey and such lands opened to entry

714

No.	Date	Subject
	1931	
5678	Aug. 10	Utah, revocation of lands withdrawn for resurvey and such lands opened to entry
5679	Aug. 10	Wyoming, revocation of lands withdrawn for resurvey and such lands opened to entry
5680	Aug. 10	Civil Service Rule II, Schedule A, Subdivision VIII, Section 3, amendment
5681	Aug. 12	California, land withdrawal for resurvey
5682	Aug. 12	New Mexico, land withdrawal for resurvey
5683	Aug. 12	Oregon, land withdrawal for lookout station
5684	Aug. 12	Utah, land withdrawal for classification
5685	Aug. 12	New Mexico, revocation of lands withdrawn for resurvey and such lands opened to entry
5686	Aug. 12	California, Reservoir Site Reserve No. 17, modification, Federal Power Commission, authorization to issue a project license
5687	Aug. 18	Wyoming, land withdrawal for resurvey
5688	Aug. 18	Colorado, revocation of lands withdrawn for resurvey and such lands opened to entry
5689	Aug. 18	Arizona, authorization for Western Gas Co. to run a natural gas pipeline within the United States-Mexico international boundary strip
5690	Aug. 20	Philippine Islands, land withdrawals in the provinces of Zambales and Luzon for chromite deposits
5691	Aug. 21	Civil Service Rules, Schedule A, Subdivision XVIII, amendment

No.	Date	Subject
	1931	
5692	Aug. 24	Hawaii, Aiea Military Reservation, amendment of land description
5693	Aug. 24	Hawaii, Punchbowl Hill Military Reservation, correction of land description
5694	Aug. 25	Oregon, land withdrawal pending legislation
5695	Aug. 27	Marie V. Abernethy, exemption from civil service rules on appointment
5696	Aug. 27	Civil Service Rules, Schedule B, Subdivision IV, amendment
5697	Aug. 28	Caroline J. Skilton, exemption from civil service rules on appointment
5698	Aug. 31	Colorado, revocation of lands withdrawn for resurvey and such lands opened to entry
5699	Aug. 31	Oregon, revocation of lands withdrawn for resurvey and such lands opened to entry
5700	Aug. 31	Public Health Service officers, permission to hold territorial, local, and State offices and territorial, local, and State health officer and employees permission to hold office in the Public Health Service upon approval or necessity
5701	Aug. 31	John W. Harrison, exemption from civil service rules on appointment
5702	Sept. 1	Oregon, land withdrawal for a sea lion refuge
5703	Sept. 1	Wyoming, restoration of lands withdrawn for Power Site Reserve No. 137
5704	Sept. 2	Panama Canal Zone, delimiting of judicial districts
5705	Sept. 3	Adolph G. Wolf, designation as Acting Judge of the District Court of the United States for Porto Rico

716

No.	Date	Subject
	1931	
5706	Sept. 4	Mary J. A. Hangliter, Margaret B. Hillyard, Catherine Lehmkuhl, and Frances N. Kane, exemption from civil service rules on appointments
5707	Sept. 4	Foreign Service quarters, regulations governing occupation and maintenance
5708	Sept. 8	Uintah Railway Co., authorization for a right-of-way across certain withdrawn lands in Utah
5709	Sept. 11	California, land withdrawal for resurvey
5710	Sept. 14	Naval airspace and defensive sea areas, reservation for national defense and other governmental purposes
5711	Sept. 14	Montana, land withdrawal for classification and pending legislation
5712	Sept. 14	Arizona, land withdrawal pending legislation
5713	Sept. 14	Wyoming, coal land withdrawal, Wyoming No. 1, modification to permit the withdrawal and use of lands for the maintenance of air navigation facilities
5714	Sept. 15	California, land withdrawal for Soldiers Mountain and Sugar Loaf lookout sites for the administration of Shasta National Forest
5715	Sept. 16	Hawaii, restoration of portion of Barracks Lot Military Reservation
5716	Sept. 16	National Commission on Law Observance and Enforcement, records transferred to the Justice Department
5717	Sept. 17	California, Federal Power Commission, authorization to issue a license for a project on Public Water Reserve No. 116
5718	Sept. 17	California, revocation of lands withdrawn for classification

Appendix C

718

No.	Date	Subject
	1931	
5734	Oct. 17	Warm Springs Indian Reservation, Oreg., extension of trust period on allotments
5735	Oct. 20	New Mexico, revocation of lands withdrawn for resurvey and such lands opened to entry
5736	Oct. 20	Philippine Islands, land withdrawal for military purposes
5737	Oct. 22	Consular Regulations, amendment
5738	Oct. 29	Louise A. Gallivan, exemption from civil service rules on appointment
5739	Oct. 30	Idaho, restoration of lands withdrawn for Power Site Reserve No. 117
5740	Oct. 31	St. Marks Migratory Bird Refuge, Fla., establishment
5741	Nov. 2	Wyoming, revocation of lands withdrawn for resurvey and such lands opened to entry
5742	Nov. 3	William C. White, exemption from civil service rules on appointment
5743	Nov. 7	Arkansas, revocation of lands withdrawn for classification and such lands opened to entry
5744	Nov. 7	Colorado, restoration of lands withdrawn for Power Site Reserve No. 2
5745	Nov. 7	Wyoming, restoration of lands withdrawn for Power Site Reserves No. 5 and 30
5746	Nov. 10	Yakima Indian Reservation, Wash., extension of trust period on allotments
5747	Nov. 11	Big Lake Bird Reservation, Ark., exclusion of lands from, and an addition of other lands

No.	Date *1931*	Subject
5748	Nov. 12	Savannah River Bird Refuge, S.C., abolished and the Savannah River Wildlife Refuge, Ga., S.C., established
5749	Nov. 20	Colorado, revocation of lands withdrawn for resurvey and such lands restored to the Rio Grande National Forest
5750	Nov. 23	California, revocation of lands withdrawn for lighthouse purposes
5751	Dec. 3	Colorado, land withdrawal for classification
5752	Dec. 3	New Mexico, transfer of lands from Datil National Forest to Cibola National Forest and the name of Manzano National Forest changed to Cibola National Forest
5753	Dec. 7	Civil Service Rule VII, Section 2, amendment
5754	Dec. 7	Alaska, land withdrawal for Public Water Reserve No. 144
5755	Dec. 10	Mississippi, land withdrawal for classification and possible inclusion in a national forest
5756	Dec. 16	Montana, transfer of lands from Lewis and Clark National Forest to Helena National Forest
5757	Dec. 16	Montana, transfer of lands from Madison National Forest to Deerlodge National Forest and from Deerlodge National Forest to Beaverhead National Forest
5758	Dec. 16	Montana, transfer of lands from Lolo National Forest to Cabinet National Forest
5759	Dec. 16	Montana, transfer of lands from Madison, Missoula, and Helena National Forests to Deerlodge National Forest and exclusion of certain lands from Deerlodge National Forest
5760	Dec. 16	Montana, transfer of lands from Madison National Forest to Gallatin National Forest

720

No.	Date	Subject
	1931	
5761	Dec. 16	Montana, transfer of lands from Bitterroot and Missoula National Forests to Lolo National Forest
5762	Dec. 18	Florence F. Burton, exemption from civil service rules on appointment
5763	Dec. 22	Christmas, 1931
5764	Dec. 22	Civil Service Rule V, Section 4, amendment
5765	Dec. 24	New Mexico, transfer of lands from Datil National Forest to Gila National Forest
5766	Dec. 30	Yetta B. Floyd, exemption from civil service rules on appointment
5767	Dec. 30	Hallie D. Stotler, exemption from civil service rules on appointment
5768	Dec. 30	Indian reservations, extension of trust period on allotments
5769	Dec. 30	Idaho, restoration of lands withdrawn for Phosphate Reserve No. 9, Idaho No. 2
5770	Dec. 30	Port Everglades, Fla., designation as a customs port of entry

Appendix D—Presidential Reports to the 71st and 72d Congresses During 1931

Subject	Published	Sent to the Congress
United States Civil Service Commission		
47th annual	....	Jan. 5
48th annual	....	Dec. 10
Yellowstone National Park Boundary Commission, final	H. Doc. 710	Jan. 5
American Samoan Commission	S. Doc. 249	Jan. 9
National Commission on Law Observance and Enforcement	H. Doc. 722	Jan. 20
	H. Doc. 166	Dec. 10
Alien Property Custodian, annual	H. Doc. 543	Feb. 6
Director General of Railroads, annual	H. Doc. 789	Feb. 27
War Policies Commission	H. Doc. 163	Dec. 10
Alaska Railroad	....	Dec. 10
Arlington Memorial Amphitheater, commission on erection of memorials and entombment of bodies	....	Dec. 10
Bureau of Efficiency	....	Dec. 10
Committee on Conservation and Administration of the Public Domain	....	Dec. 10
Council of National Defense, 15th annual	....	Dec. 10

723

68-611 O - 76 - 50

Appendix D

Appendix E—The President's Calendar

NOTE: This appendix is a compendium of the President's appointments and activities selected from the Executive Office calendar and the records maintained by the Chief Usher of the White House. It is intended both as a record of business appointments and an indication of the many ceremonial demands placed upon the time of the Chief Executive.

This listing follows the sequential order of the President's day. It does not include Mrs. Hoover's engagements, such social activities as automobile tours of the area, or visits to the White House by members of the family. Titles and first names have been supplied when not included in the original calendar.

Researchers interested in detailed information regarding the specific hour of meetings and in additional activities should write to the Herbert Hoover Presidential Library, West Branch, Iowa 52358.

1931

January 1

Arthur de Maro and Charles P. Ruby

New Year's public reception

Lunch—Col. Campbell B. Hodges, Capt. Russell Train, and Capt. Frank B. Goettge

Walter E. Hope, Assistant Secretary of the Treasury

Dinner—Judge and Mrs. Irvine Luther Lenroot

January 2

Breakfast—Senator James E. Watson, Senate majority leader

Cabinet

Representative Frederick R. Lehlbach

Lunch—Mr. and Mrs. Myron C. Taylor

Washington Correspondents

Raymond Benjamin, assistant chairman of the Republican National Committee

Dinner—Dr. and Mrs. Augustus Taber Murray and Mrs. Charles D. Walcott

January 3

Breakfast—Mark Sullivan, journalist

Representative James G. Strong, Kansas

Percy Long, San Francisco, Calif.

Representative Robert G. Simmons, Nebraska

J. Butler Wright, United States Minister to Uruguay

Albert C. Dent, New York, Chemical National Bank

1931

Lenna L. Yost, Republican National Committee, and Mrs. Alexander

Arthur Woods, Chairman of the President's Emergency Committee for Employment

Dinner—Representative and Mrs. Arthur M. Free and Mr. and Mrs. Ashmun N. Brown

January 4

Lunch—Senator and Mrs. Frederic C. Walcott and sons, Alexander and William

Walter E. Hope, Assistant Secretary of the Treasury

January 5

Breakfast—Representative John Q. Tilson and Walter H. Newton

J. Clawson Roop, Director of the Budget

Senator Joseph E. Ransdell

Mrs. Harvey W. Wiley and National Woman's Party delegation

Representative Franklin W. Fort

Dinner—Mr. and Mrs. Wilfred W. Fry

January 6

Cabinet

Washington Correspondents

Henry J. Allen, former Senator of Kansas

Representative Albert H. Vestal

Dinner—Representative and Mrs. Wallace H. White, Jr.

National Automobile Show in New York, telephoned greetings

January 7

Breakfast—Dr. Joel T. Boone

Senator Samuel M. Shortridge and Victor R. McLucas

Senators Porter H. Dale and Frank C. Partridge

Adolph C. Miller, Federal Reserve Board of Governors

Representative Andrew J. Montague, Virginia

Military Order of the World War, delegation

Lawrence W. Wallace, executive secretary of the American Engineering Council

Ralph B. Williamson, Federal Power Commission

Lunch—Frank J. Loesch, National Commission on Law Observance and Enforcement

Frank B. Kellogg, former Secretary of State

Raymond Benjamin, assistant chairman of the Republican National Committee

Dinner—Mr. and Mrs. Howard E. Coffin

January 8

Breakfast—Mr. and Mrs. Howard E. Coffin

Representative John Q. Tilson and Emanuel Strauss

Senators Hiram Bingham and Guy D. Goff

Representative George P. Darrow

Arthur Woods, Chairman of the President's Emergency Committee for Employment

Cleveland A. Newton, general counsel of the Mississippi Valley Association

Ethan T. Colton, Y.M.C.A.

Charles S. Dewey

Chester H. Gray and Edward A. O'Neal, American Farm Bureau Federation

Charles E. Mitchell, United States Minister to Liberia

Secretary of Commerce Robert P. Lamont

Representative Robert Blackburn

Thornton Green

J. Clawson Roop, Director of the Budget

Representative Allen T. Treadway

Dinner—Diplomatic Corps

January 9

Breakfast—Mark Sullivan, journalist

Cabinet

William E. Fowler, chairman of the Los Angeles Republican Committee

Representative Robert G. Simmons

Lawrence W. Wallace, executive secretary of the American Engineering Council, and Ralph E. Flanders, vice president of the American Society of Mechanical Engineers

Panamanian Minister, Ricardo J. Alfaro, on departure

John Lord O'Brian, Assistant to the Attorney General

Lunch—John Barton Payne, Chairman of the American National Red Cross

Washington Correspondents

Dinner—Senator and Mrs. Dwight W. Morrow

January 10

Breakfast—Bernard M. Baruch

Col. M. S. Guggenheim, Army Reserve Corps

Representative Lindley H. Hadley, Washington

Representative Albert F. Carter, California

Representative S. Wallace Dempsey, New York

Representative Menalcus Lankford and delegation of Virginia lawyers

Senator Ellison D. Smith

John Barton Payne, Chairman of the American National Red Cross

Secretary of Agriculture Arthur M. Hyde

Attorney General William D. Mitchell

Mr. and Mrs. Carl Hanna

January 11

Breakfast—Mr. and Mrs. Carl Hanna

Raymond Benjamin, assistant chairman of the Republican National Committee

Lunch—Mr. and Mrs. Carl Hanna

Secretary of War Patrick J. Hurley, Secretary of Agriculture Arthur M. Hyde, Secretary of the Interior Ray Lyman Wilbur, Postmaster General Walter F. Brown, Under Secretary of State Joseph P. Cotton, and Assistant Secretary of the Treasury Walter E. Hope

1931

January 12

Breakfast—Mark Sullivan, journalist
Inspected Arlington Memorial Bridge
Representative Edgar Howard, Nebraska
Representative S. Wallace Dempsey, New York
Arthur S. Draper, New York Herald Tribune
J. A. Aasgard, Bishop of the Norwegian Lutheran Church of America
A. Johnston, George W. Laughlin, and W. J. Burk, representatives of the Brotherhood of Locomotive Engineers
William M. Calder, White House Conference on Home Building and Home Ownership
National Grange, executive committee
Warren Olney, Jr., San Francisco, Calif.
Glenn B. Skipper and Clara C. Grace, Florida Republican national committee members
Secretary of Agriculture Arthur M. Hyde
Louis J. Taber, master of the National Grange, and delegation
Dinner—Representative and Mrs. John Q. Tilson

January 13

Senator James E. Watson, Representative Fred S. Purnell, Paul Bausman, and Harry Fenton
Sydney Anderson, General Mills, Inc.
Cabinet
Washington Correspondents

Edward F. Colladay
Joseph C. Swan and delegation from Alabama
Lunch—Henry J. Allen and Frank E. Gannett
James P. Goodrich, former Governor of Indiana
Newbold Noyes, Washington Evening Star
J. Clawson Roop, Director of the Budget
Ernest Lee Jahncke, Assistant Secretary of the Navy
George H. Lorimer, Curtis Publishing Co.
Representative Franklin W. Fort
Dinner—with Secretary of State and Mrs. Henry L. Stimson at their residence

January 14

Breakfast—Mark Sullivan, journalist
William H. Hill
James F. Burke, general counsel of the Republican National Committee
Secretary of War Patrick J. Hurley
Ernest Lee Jahncke, Assistant Secretary of the Navy
Senator Arthur R. Robinson, Indiana
Joseph C. Swan
W. Kingsland Macy, New York Republican national committeeman
Representative Ruth Hanna McCormick, Illinois
Representative Sol Bloom

Senator Simeon D. Fess and delegation from the George Washington Bicentennial Commission

Representative Melvin J. Maas, Minnesota

George W. Rightmire, president of Ohio State University, and executive committee of the Association of Land Grant Colleges and Universities

Maurice Cahill, department commander of the American Legion for Iowa

Paul B. McKee, president of Electric Company of Brazil

Duquesne University basketball team

Lunch—Frank T. Hines, Administrator of Veteran's Affairs, and Ralph T. O'Neill

Henry J. Haskell, editor of the Kansas City Star

Arch W. Shaw, Chairman of the President's Committee on Recent Social Trends

Dinner—James F. Burke, general counsel of the Republican National Committee, and Warren C. Fairbanks, president of the Indianapolis News Publishing Co.

January 15

Breakfast—Warren C. Fairbanks, president of the Indianapolis News Publishing Co.

Senator Otis F. Glenn and Charles F. Drake

Ogden L. Mills, Under Secretary of the Treasury

Senator Arthur Capper, Representative-elect Harold McGugin, and Alfred Langdon, chairman of the Independent Oil Producers of Kansas

Robert Maisel, New York

Mrs. Nathaniel Thayer, Massachusetts Republican national committeewoman

Samuel Hill and Frank Terrace

Belle Sherwin, president of the National League of Women Voters

Belgium Chargé d'Affaires, Vicount de Lantsheere, to present Dr. Jules Duesberg of the University of Liege

Thomas E. Campbell, President of the Civil Service Commission

Samuel Crowther, author

J. Clawson Roop, Director of the Budget

Secretary of Labor William N. Doak

James R. Garfield, Chairman of the Committee on the Conservation and Administration of the Public Domain

Senators Frederic C. Walcott and Simeon D. Fess

Edgar Rickard

Reception—Members of the Senate

January 16

Breakfast—Dr. Joel T. Boone

Cabinet

Paul C. Wolman, commander in chief of the Veterans of Foreign Wars

Frank T. Hines, Administrator of Veterans' Affairs, and governors of the National Soldiers' Homes

Wallace Townsend, Arkansas Republican national committeeman

729

Lincoln Ellsworth, presented with special gold medal awarded by the Congress

John Barton Payne, Chairman of the American National Red Cross, Secretary of Commerce Robert P. Lamont, Under Secretary of the Treasury Ogden L. Mills, and Assistant Secretary of the Treasury Walter E. Hope

Lunch—Lincoln Ellsworth

Richard Lloyd Jones, editor of the Tulsa Tribune

Mrs. Fitzsimmons

H. V. Kaltenborn, Brooklyn, N.Y.

Secretary of the Interior Ray Lyman Wilbur

January 17

Breakfast—Mark Sullivan, journalist

Louis K. Liggett, president of the United Drug Company

Senator David A. Reed

Representative Edmund F. Cooke, New York

Representative W. W. Chalmers

Representative Albert F. Carter and Joseph R. Knowland, president and publisher of the Oakland (Calif.) Tribune

C. E. Grunsky, San Francisco, Calif.

Caroline McCormick Slade, vice president of the New York League of Women Voters

Senator Frederick Steiwer

George deB. Keim and officers of the General Society of Colonial Wars

Representative Archie D. Sanders of New York and Mr. Knapp

Ernest Lee Jahncke, Assistant Secretary of the Navy

L. W. Boe, president of St. Olaf's College

Jefferson S. Coage, Recorder of Deeds for the District of Columbia

Lunch—William Z. Ripley and Marie M. Meloney

C. Bascom Slemp

Eugene Meyer, Governor of the Federal Reserve Board

Representative John Q. Tilson

Raymond Benjamin, assistant chairman of the Republican National Committee

Dinner—Senator and Mrs. George H. Moses, Senator Samuel M. Shortridge, Representative and Mrs. Lindley H. Hadley, Representative and Mrs. William E. Evans, Capt. and Mrs. John F. Lucey, and Aida de Acosta Breckinridge

January 18

Breakfast—Dr. Joel T. Boone

Raymond Benjamin, assistant chairman of the Republican National Committee

George Akerson and Lawrence Richey

Lunch—Senator and Mrs. David A. Reed and Mrs. Shepston

Secretary of War Patrick J. Hurley, Secretary of the Interior Ray Lyman Wilbur, Secretary of Agriculture Arthur M. Hyde, Under Secretary of the Treasury Ogden L. Mills, Assistant Secretary of the Treasury Walter E. Hope, and Secretary to the President Walter H. Newton

Mark Sullivan, journalist

Dinner—Mr. and Mrs. Frank B. Kellogg, Senator and Mrs. Arthur H. Vandenberg, Mr. and Mrs. Henry P. Fletcher, and Mr. and Mrs. Howard Sutherland

January 19

George W. Wickersham, Chairman of the National Commission on Law Observance and Enforcement

Arlington Memorial Bridge Commission

Senator Hamilton F. Kean, New Jersey

Silas H. Strawn, president of the Chamber of Commerce of the United States

Senator Carl Hayden, Arizona

James R. Garfield, Chairman of the Committee on Conservation and Administration of the Public Domain

Senator Arthur R. Gould

Lunch—Secretary of State Henry L. Stimson

Dinner—Charles D. Hilles

January 20

Breakfast—Walter E. Hope and Walter H. Newton

Senator Frederick Hale

Cabinet

Joseph S. Frelinghuysen, president of the Harding Memorial Association, and Secretary of the Treasury Andrew W. Mellon

Herbert D. Brown, Chief of the Bureau of Efficiency

Herbert Longworth

Dinner—Mr. and Mrs. John Walter Drake and daughters, Rosalie, Barbara, and Elizabeth Drake

Congressional Club reception, attendance at

January 21

Senator Reed Smoot

William M. Chadbourne, New York

Emily K. Kneubuhl, executive secretary of the National Federation of Business and Professional Women's Clubs

Federal Life Insurance Company, delegation of agents

James E. Jewel, of Fort Morgan, Colo., and Samuel R. Van Sant, of Minnesota, former commanders in chief of the Grand Army of the Republic

Lunch—Nathan W. MacChesney

Representative Carl R. Chindblom and Mrs. Frank Schaedler

Representative Allen T. Treadway and Horace A. Moses

Representative David Hopkins

Theodore C. Wallen, New York Herald Tribune

Representative Willis C. Hawley

Ira E. Bennett, editor of the Washington Post

1931

Speaker of the House Nicholas Long-
worth, Under Secretary of the Treas-
ury Ogden L. Mills, Secretary to the
President Walter H. Newton, and
Representatives Carl E. Mapes, Addi-
son T. Smith, Leonidas C. Dyer, Ber-
trand H. Snell, Allen T. Treadway,
Isaac Bacharach, Robert G. Simmons,
Earl C. Michener, Scott Leavitt, Wil-
lis C. Hawley, Homer Hoch, George
P. Darrow, William P. Holaday, John
Q. Tilson, Frederick R. Lehlbach, and
Lindley H. Hadley

January 22

Breakfast—Mark Sullivan and Mark L.
Requa
Inspected Arlington Memorial Bridge
Representative Frank M. Ramey
Mrs. M. D. Cameron, Nebraska Repub-
lican national committeewoman
Senator John Thomas, Idaho
George W. Malone, Commission on
the Conservation and Administra-
tion of the Public Domain
Otto T. Mallery, National Recreation
Association
Frank T. Hines, Administrator of Vet-
erans' Affairs
Ogden L. Mills, Under Secretary of the
Treasury
Representative Frederick M. Davenport
Representative Carl R. Chindblom
J. Clawson Roop, Director of the
Budget

Representative John Q. Tilson, House
majority leader
Dinner—Supreme Court

January 23

Cabinet
Richard Dix and Estelle Taylor, screen
stars, and Floyd Gibbons, journalist
Remington Rand representatives
Lunch—William M. Butler, former
Senator of Massachusetts
Washington Correspondents
Henry P. Fletcher, Chairman of the
United States Tariff Commission

January 24

Senator Charles S. Deneen and Carl
L. Birdsall
Representative Louis C. Cramton
Representative Sol Bloom
Representative J. Banks Kurtz, Penn-
sylvania
Elihu Root
John R. Alpine, American Federation of
Labor
Frank B. Noyes, Associated Press
Lenna L. Yost, Republican National
Committee
Lunch—Mrs. William Howard Taft
and Mr. and Mrs. Robert A. Taft
Hugh Lincoln Cooper, New York
John G. Brown, Indiana
Clara B. Burdette
Representative Franklin W. Fort

1931

Dinner—Mr. and Mrs. Mark Sullivan, Dr. and Mrs. Vernon L. Kellogg, Assistant Secretary of State and Mrs. William R. Castle, Jr., Alfred Castle, Mr. and Mrs. Ernest I. Lewis, Capt. and Mrs. Russell Train, Mr. and Mrs. Mark L. Requa, Maj. and Mrs. Earl C. Long, Representative Franklin W. Fort, Barbara Fort, and Mildred Hall

January 25

Mark L. Requa

January 26

Breakfast—Charles S. McCain, president of Chase National Bank, and Winthrop W. Aldrich, president of Equitable Trust Co. of New York

Senator Simeon D. Fess and Marshall Sheppey of Toledo, Ohio

Senator Tasker L. Oddie

Senator Arthur H. Vandenberg, Governor and Mrs. Wilber M. Brucker, State Attorney General and Mrs. Paul W. Voorhees, and State Senator James G. Frey, all of Michigan

Charles C. Paulding and Alfred Erskine Marling, Union League Club, New York

Robert L. Owen, former Senator of Oklahoma

Church Organizations on Permanent Preventives of Unemployment, conference delegation

Ralph A. Collins, New York Sun

John Lord O'Brian, Assistant to the Attorney General

Secretary of State Henry L. Stimson

Secretary of Agriculture Arthur M. Hyde

Samuel R. McKelvie, Federal Farm Board

William F. McDowell, bishop of the Methodist Episcopal Church, Washington, D.C.

January 27

Breakfast—Mark Sullivan, journalist

Cabinet

Washington Correspondents

Lunch—Henry Leigh Hunt

William S. Fitzpatrick, Prairie Oil and Gas Co., Kans.; Edwin B. Reeser, president of American Petroleum Institute; and Secretary of Commerce Robert P. Lamont

Secretary of Commerce Robert P. Lamont

Edward B. Clements, Missouri Republican national committeeman

Capt. John F. Lucey

Joseph R. Nutt, Republican National Committee

Senator Frederic C. Walcott

Dinner—with Secretary of the Treasury and Mrs. Andrew W. Mellon

January 28

Breakfast—Gwen Martin

Senator Otis F. Glenn, Illinois

C. L. Marshall, Johnson City, Tenn.

Eugene P. Booze, Mound Bayou, Miss.

Post Wheeler, United States Minister to Paraguay

Fred B. Smith

733

Theodore G. Joslin, Boston Evening
Transcript
Will H. Hays
Dinner—George Barr Baker

January 29

Senators Robert D. Carey and John B.
Kendrick and Representative Vincent
Carter
Senator William E. Brock, Tennessee
Malcolm Muir, president of McGraw-
Hill Co.
Representative B. Carroll Reece and
Mr. and Mrs. Charles McElwain
Cora W. Baker and Mrs. Franklin W.
Withoft, American Battle Monu-
ments Commission
Lunch—Crate D. Bowen, Miami, Fla.,
and Walter H. Newton, Secretary to
the President
Henry P. Fletcher, Chairman of the
United States Tariff Commission
Secretary of Commerce Robert P. La-
mont
J. Clawson Roop, Director of the
Budget
Reception—House of Representatives

January 30

Representative L. J. Dickinson, Iowa
Cabinet
William O. Thompson, president
emeritus of Ohio State University
E. W. Sawyer, Interior Department, to
present maps
C. Bascom Slemp and officials of the
Washington Gas Light Company

Wilma Hoyal, president of the Ameri-
can Legion Auxiliary, and delegation
from the Women's Patriotic Confer-
ence on National Defense
Lunch—Mr. and Mrs. Walter Teller
and Mendel Silverberg
Herbert D. Brown, Chief of the Bureau
of Efficiency
Canadian Chargé d'Affaires, Hume
Wrong, to present Prime Minister
Richard B. Bennett of Canada
Washington Correspondents
Dinner—Prime Minister Richard B.
Bennett, Chargé d'Affaires Hume
Wrong, Secretary of State Henry L.
Stimson, Assistant Secretary of State
William R. Castle, Jr., Hanford Mac-
Nider, Maj. Herridge, and Henry M.
Robinson

January 31

Breakfast—Mark Sullivan, journalist
Pressed electric button starting flow of
natural gas from Pennsylvania and
West Virginia to the District of
Columbia
Hanford MacNider, United States
Minister to Canada
Postmaster General Walter F. Brown
Ernest Lee Jahncke, Assistant Secretary
of the Navy
Secretary of State Henry M. Stimson
Representative Arthur M. Free, Cali-
fornia
Representative William R. Coyle, Penn-
sylvania
Arthur Woods, Chairman of the Presi-
dent's Emergency Committee for
Employment

Honduran Minister, Ernesto Argueto, on departure

Representative Herbert J. Drane of Florida and B. C. Skinner

Edgar Jadwin, former Chief of Engineers of the Army

Lunch—Wallace B. Donham, dean of the Graduate School of Business Administration at Harvard University

Secretary of State Henry L. Stimson and Class of 1888 of Yale University

Mrs. Ogden Reid

February 1

Lunch—Governor and Mrs. John G. Winant of New Hampshire

Senator Reed Smoot

Senator Samuel M. Shortridge

Dinner—Mr. and Mrs. Jay Cooke

February 2

Breakfast—Senator David A. Reed, Under Secretary of the Treasury Ogden L. Mills, and Mr. and Mrs. Jay Cooke

Secretary of the Navy Charles F. Adams

Representative Edith Nourse Rogers

Representative Addison T. Smith and delegation of Western Members of the House

Alfred K. Nippert, Cincinnati, Ohio

Representative Wallace H. White, Jr., Maine

Howard Osterhault, New York City attorney

Senator Frederic C. Walcott

February 3

Breakfast—Senator James E. Watson, Senate majority leader

Cabinet

Washington Correspondents

C. Bascom Slemp and Anne Madison

Gen. Peyton C. Marsh, former Chief of Staff of the Army

Rome C. Stephenson, president of the American Bankers Association

Secretary of State Henry L. Stimson

Secretary of the Treasury Andrew W. Mellon

Secretary of War Patrick J. Hurley

Secretary of the Navy Charles F. Adams

Secretary of Labor William N. Doak

Secretary of Commerce Robert P. Lamont

Harvey C. Couch

Dinner—with Secretary of War and Mrs. Patrick J. Hurley at their residence

February 4

Breakfast—Senators James E. Watson and Charles L. McNary, and Walter H. Newton

Representative William Williamson, South Dakota

Representative Robert G. Simmons, Nebraska

Amon G. Carter, newspaper publisher, Fort Worth, Tex.

Senator Otis F. Glenn and Clarence F. Buick, former Illinois State Senator

Representative Charles L. Underhill and Massachusetts Institute of Technology boxing team

Samuel S. Koenig

Dr. Leonard B. Smith and committee from the Methodist Protestant Church

Representative Menalcus Lankford and delegation of Virginia Members of the House

Lunch—Kent Cooper, president of the Associated Press of Germany

Dinner—former Senator Henry J. Allen and Henrietta Allen

Representatives John Q. Tilson, William R. Wood, and Louis C. Cramton, and Walter H. Newton, Secretary to the President

February 5

Senators Dwight W. Morrow and Hamilton F. Kean, and committee of Ocean City, N. J. officials

Representative J. Will Taylor, Tennessee

P. T. Myhand, Mercer, Calif.

Henry S. Pritchett, president emeritus of Carnegie Foundation for Advancement of Teaching

Fred H. Bixby, Long Beach, Calif.

Lunch—James F. Burke, Earle S. Kinsley, and Daniel Pomeroy, Republican National Committee

Henry P. Fletcher, Chairman of the United States Tariff Commission

James R. Garfield, Chairman of the Committee on the Conservation and Administration of the Public Domain

J. Clawson Roop, Director of the Budget

Washington Correspondents

Dinner—Speaker's dinner

February 6

Breakfast—Mark Sullivan, journalist

Harvey C. Couch

Cabinet

Marie M. Meloney, New York Herald Tribune

Representative Franklin W. Fort

Representative Joe J. Manlove

William Loeb, Jr., vice president of the American Smelting and Refining Co.

Dinner—Dr. and Mrs. Stanley M. Rinehart

February 7

Breakfast—Mark Sullivan, journalist

Ogden L. Mills, Under Secretary of the Treasury

Representative Franklin W. Fort

David Lawrence, editor of the U.S. Daily

Senator Simeon D. Fess and Harry S. Kissell, president of the National Association of Real Estate Boards

Senator Federick H. Gillett

Bainbridge Colby, former Secretary of State

Representative Edith Nourse Rogers

736

1931

George M. Powell, Jacksonville, Fla.

Curtis M. Johnson, Minnesota

Gutzon Borglum, sculptor and painter

David B. Robertson, Brotherhood of Locomotive Firemen and Enginemen

Lunch—Edward G. Lowry, journalist

February 8

French Strother, Administrative Assistant to the President

Walter E. Hope, Assistant Secretary of the Treasury

Representative John Q. Tilson, House majority leader

February 9

Representative Franklin W. Fort

Ogden L. Mills, Under Secretary of the Treasury

Senator Joseph E. Ransdell

Representative Ruth Bryan Owen

Carlton K. Matson, editor of Buffalo Times

Representative Godfrey Goodwin

Representative Joseph C. Shaffer, Virginia

J. Clawson Roop, Director of the Budget

Representative Ruth Pratt

Senator Frederick Hale

Henry M. Robinson, Los Angeles banker

Raymond Benjamin, assistant chairman of the Republican National Committee

February 10

Cabinet

Washington Correspondents

Walter E. Hope, Assistant Secretary of the Treasury

Representative Homer Hoch and Alfred Langdon

Dinner—with Attorney General and Mrs. William D. Mitchell at their residence

February 11

Senator Robert D. Carey, Wyoming

Representative Olger B. Burtness, North Dakota

Representative Richard J. Welch, California

Arthur Woods, Chairman of the President's Emergency Committee for Employment, and John Barton Payne, Chairman of the American National Red Cross

Edward A. Simmons, New York

Herbert Fleishhacker, San Francisco banker

Lafayette B. Gleason, New York

British Ambassador, Sir Ronald Lindsay, to present Capt. Malcolm Campbell

J. Matt Chilton, Republican National Committee

Thomas E. Green, American National Red Cross

J. Horace McFarland

John C. Chaney, former Representative of Indiana

Group of Internal Revenue Collectors in Charge

737

National Association of Marine Engineers, convention delegation

Lunch—Frank T. Hines and Walter H. Newton

Senator William H. King and Representatives Scott Leavitt and Don B. Colton

James R. Garfield, Chairman of the Committee on the Conservation and Administration of the Public Domain

Charles S. Smith, Associated Press

Harry A. Garfield, president of Williams College

Secretary of the Treasury Andrew W. Mellon and Senator David A. Reed

Senators Reed Smoot, David A. Reed, Dwight W. Morrow, James E. Watson, and Charles L. McNary

Dinner—Mrs. Horatio A. Small, Mr. and Mrs. Louis B. Mayer, and Mr. and Mrs. W. Kingsland Macy

Reception—Army and Navy

February 12

Breakfast—Mrs. Horatio A. Small, and Mr. and Mrs. Louis B. Mayer, and Mr. and Mrs. W. Kingsland Macy

Senators James E. Watson and Guy D. Goff

Senator George H. Moses

Senator Lawrence C. Phipps, Colorado

Kenneth Mackintosh, National Commission on Law Observance and Enforcement

James E. Freeman, Episcopal Bishop of Washington Diocese, and Harry Roberts Carson, Bishop of Haiti

Representative Philip D. Swing, California

Secretary of Commerce Robert P. Lamont and George A. Sloane, president of the Cotton Textile Institute, Inc.

Representative William E. Evans, California

William T. Ellis, Swarthmore, Pa.

C. B. Denman, Federal Farm Board

Herbert D. Brown, Bureau of Efficiency, and a committee from Virgin Islands

Representative Richard B. Wigglesworth

Canadian Chargé d'Affaires, Hume Wrong, to present Hugh Guthrie, Minister of Justice of Canada

Mark L. Requa

J. Clawson Roop, Director of the Budget

Representative Willis C. Hawley

Dinner—Thomas T. C. Gregory

Lincoln Day Address from the White House

February 13

Breakfast—Senator Frederic C. Walcott and Mark Sullivan

Senator Duncan U. Fletcher, Florida

Cabinet

Leon C. Faulkner, president of the American Prison Association, and its directors

Ralph J. Totten, United States Minister to South Africa

738

Robert Linton, California

Lt. Col. Joseph I. McMullen and John Hays Hammond

Henry M. Robinson, Los Angeles banker

Raymond Benjamin, assistant chairman of the Republican National Committee

Julius Barnes, chairman of the board of the Chamber of Commerce of the United States

February 14

Breakfast—Representative John Q. Tilson and Moses Strauss

Representative Franklin W. Fort

Secretary of War Patrick J. Hurley

Louis B. Mayer, president of Metro-Goldwyn-Mayer Co., Inc.

James C. Stone, Federal Farm Board

Harry Lapidus, Omaha, Nebr.

Senators Dwight W. Morrow and Hamilton F. Kean

Albert C. Mattei

February 15

George Akerson, former Secretary to the President

February 16

Breakfast—Mark Sullivan, journalist

J. Clawson Roop, Director of the Budget

Senator Arthur R. Robinson, Indiana

Representative Frederick W. Dallinger, Massachusetts, and Marion Angeline Howlett

National Credit Men's Association, delegation

Walter E. Garrison and California Water Conservation Committee

William C. Deming, former President of the Civil Service Commission

Mrs. Lowell Fletcher Hobart, Daughters of the American Revolution

Representative Donald F. Snow

Columbia Regional Conference of Credit Bureau Executives, delegates

Haitian Minister, Dantes Bellegarde, to present letters of credence

Secretary of Labor William N. Doak

Orville Bullington, Wichita Falls, Tex.

Reception—for officials of the Departments of the Treasury, Post Office, Interior, Agriculture, Commerce, and Labor

February 17

Breakfast—Mark Sullivan and Assistant Secretary of the Treasury Walter E. Hope

Senator George H. Moses

Cabinet

Washington Correspondents

William Blease, vice president of the Oakland Motor Co.

Representative Samuel A. Kendall

E. S. Clark

Lunch—Henry M. Robinson, Los Angeles banker

Senator Reed Smoot

Representative David Hopkins, Missouri

Ralph Snyder, president of the Kansas Farm Bureau

739

Senator David A. Reed

Frank T. Hines, Administrator of Veterans' Affairs, Ogden L. Mills, Under Secretary of the Treasury, and Walter E. Hope, Assistant Secretary of the Treasury

Dinner—Assistant Secretary of the Treasury Walter E. Hope

February 18

Breakfast—Senator James E. Watson, Senate majority leader

Charles D. Hilles

Representative Ruth Pratt, New York

Secretary of Agriculture Arthur M. Hyde

Michael Gallagher

Henry P. Fletcher, Chairman of the United States Tariff Commission

William S. Bennett, general counsel for the Edward Hines Lumber Co.

Representative Andrew J. Montague, Virginia

Mr. and Mrs. Fred W. Kiesel and daughter of Sacramento, Calif.

Nathan Clayton

Lunch—David W. Mulvane, Republican National Committee, and Judge Steward

Anne O'Hare McCormick

Attorney General William D. Mitchell

George W. Wickersham

February 19

Vermont delegation in Congress

Senator Charles W. Waterman

Walter E. Garrison, director of the California Public Works

John H. Walker, Springfield, Ill.

Luncheon—Dr. and Mrs. William Palmer Lucas and Mr. and Mrs. Fred W. Kiesel and daughter

Henry P. Fletcher, Chairman of the United States Tariff Commission

J. Clawson Roop, Director of the Budget

Raymond Benjamin, assistant chairman of the Republican National Committee

Representative Franklin W. Fort and Raymond Benjamin

February 20

Representative Daniel A. Reed, Pennsylvania

Henry J. Allen, former Senator of Kansas

Cabinet

Senator Simeon D. Fess and president of the Union League of New York

Representative Edith Nourse Rogers

James M. Hazlett, chairman of Republican Citizens Committee

Lunch—Frank T. Hines, Administrator of Veterans' Affairs

Lt. Col. Joseph I. McMullen

Washington Correspondents

Representative Ruth Pratt, New York

February 21

Representative John Q. Tilson and John A. Campbell, New York Life Insurance Co.

Senator Lawrence C. Phipps

Representative Charles A. Eaton, New Jersey

Representative U. S. Stone, Oklahoma

Attorney General William D. Mitchell and Assistant Attorney General Charles P. Sisson

Frank J. Loesch

Marie M. Meloney, New York Herald Tribune

Postmaster General Walter F. Brown

Secretary of Commerce Robert P. Lamont

Edward Klauber, assistant to the president of the Columbia Broadcasting System

Herbert D. Brown, Bureau of Efficiency and Paul M. Pearson, Governor of the Virgin Islands

Representative Edmund F. Cooke and Americanization group

Lunch—Secretary of State Henry L. Stimson

Alice M. Dickson and Lillian M. Gilbreth

Judge Irvine Luther Lenroot

Dinner—White House Correspondents Association, New Willard Hotel

February 22

Raymond Benjamin, assistant chairman of the Republican National Committee

Lunch—French Strother, Administrative Assistant to the President

February 23

Breakfast—Mark Sullivan, journalist

Representative Harold Knutson, Minnesota

Senator John Thomas, Idaho

Secretary of Agriculture Arthur M. Hyde

Representative Wallace H. White, Jr., Maine

DeMolay boys from New Jersey

J. Clawson Roop, Director of the Budget

Henry M. Robinson, Los Angeles banker

Lunch—Mrs. James W. Corrigan, Mrs. Armstrong Taylor, Mrs. Kermit Roosevelt, Hazel Corbin, and Mabel Choate

William Hard, journalist

Dinner—Senator Frederic C. Walcott and former Senator Henry J. Allen

February 24

Breakfast—Ogden Reed and Geoffrey Parsons

Representative Edward B. Almon

Senator Arthur Capper and Representative Homer Hoch

Cabinet

Paul S. Wowrer, European correspondent of the Chicago Daily News

Washington Correspondents

Lynn High School football team

Representative Franklin W. Fort, New Jersey

Harvey C. Couch

Frank T. Hines, Administrator of Veterans' Affairs

Senator Joseph E. Ransdell

Senator William E. Borah

February 25

Breakfast—Mark Sullivan, journalist

Senator Frederick H. Gillett

741

Senator Charles S. Deneen

Senator William E. Brock

Representatives Miles C. Allgood and Lister Hill

Representative Charles Finley, Kentucky

Samuel Edgar Nicholson

W. M. Wiley, California

George B. Dolliver, president of the National Editorial Association

German Ambassador, Friedrich von Prittwitz, to present Herman Schmitz

Louis L. Babcock and delegation from Erie County, N. Y.

Grand Masters of Masons in the United States

Senator Arthur R. Gould

Representative J. Russell Leech, Pennsylvania

Representative William L. Nelson and group

H. Paul Bestor, Farm Loan Commissioner, and W. W. Martin

Mrs. U. S. Guyer

Lunch—Allan Fox and Alida M. Henriques

February 26

Andrew Furuseth, president of the International Seamen's Union of America

Representative Edmund F. Cooke, New York

Representative J. A. Garber, Virginia

Representative Effiegene Wingo and delegation from Arkansas

Representative Edward B. Almon and congressional delegation from the South

Representative Elva R. Kendall, Kentucky

Willis J. Abbott, Christian Science Monitor

Chester H. Gray, American Farm Bureau Federation

Italian Ambassador, Nobile Giacomo de Martino, to present a group of students of the Institute of Physical Education in Rome, Italy

Representatives of Presbyterian-Dutch-German Reformed Churches

J. Clawson Roop, Director of the Budget

Attorney General William D. Mitchell

Secretary of Commerce Robert P. Lamont

Secretary of War Patrick J. Hurley

Edwin C. Dinwiddie and committee from the National Temperance Bureau

February 27

Breakfast—Senators James E. Watson, Frederick Hale, Henry W. Keyes, and Lawrence C. Phipps; Representatives William R. Wood, Burton L. French, Guy U. Hardy, and John Taber; and Walter H. Newton

Representative Franklin W. Fort to present his successor Representative-elect Peter A. Cavicchia, New Jersey

Cabinet

Judge and Mrs. Albert H. Watson

742

Lawrence H. Rupp, Grand Exalted Ruler of the Elks

Pressed electric key in the White House telegraph room starting the new presses of the Portland (Maine) Evening News

Ray Clapper, United Press Associations Washington Correspondents

Dinner—Mr. and Mrs. Eugene Meyer

February 28

Breakfast—Mark Sullivan, journalist

Senator Frederick Hale and Maine congressional delegation

Senator J. Thomas Heflin, Alabama

Senator John Thomas and Representatives Addison T. Smith and Burton L. French, Idaho

Representative B. Carroll Reece, Tennessee

Representative Maurice H. Thatcher and Kentucky congressional delegation

William F. Schilling, Federal Farm Board

Representative Ruth Pratt, Charles D. Hilles, and W. Kingsland Macy

Henry J. Allen, former Senator of Kansas, to present group of independent oil producers, headed by Orville Bullington of Wichita Falls, Tex.

Greek Minister, Charalambos Simopoulos, to present Monsignor Athenagoras, Archbishop of the Greek Orthodox Church in the United States

C. Bascom Slemp

Mabel Walker Willebrandt and a committee on aeronautical law of the American Bar Association

Representative Ruth Bryan Owen and a group of Florida citizens

Henry M. Robinson, Los Angeles banker

March 1

Breakfast—Henry M. Robinson, Los Angeles banker

Secretary of War Patrick J. Hurley

Lunch—Representative John Q. Tilson, House majority leader

Secretary of War Patrick J. Hurley and Gen. Lytle Brown

Senator Frederic C. Walcott

Dinner—Senator and Mrs. Charles L. McNary, Representative William R. Wood, and Representative and Mrs. Clyde Kelly

March 2

Thomas E. Wilson, Frederic S. Snyder, and William W. Woods, from the Institute of American Meat Packers

Representative Franklin W. Fort

James Owen, Colorado

Clarence M. Young, Assistant Secretary of Commerce, and Robert Buck

Edward V. Babcock, Pittsburgh, Pa.

Mr. and Mrs. Charles Klem, New York

Ogden L. Mills, Under Secretary of the Treasury

Speaker of the House Nicholas Longworth

Secretary of War Patrick J. Hurley

March 3

Frank T. Hines, Administrator of Veterans' Affairs
Cabinet
Senator John Thomas, Idaho, and E. R. Whitla
Dinner—Mr. and Mrs. Roy Verum, Assistant Secretary of the Treasury and Mrs. Walter E. Hope, and Mr. and Mrs. Walter A. Strong

March 4

Breakfast—Mark Sullivan, journalist
To the Capitol to sign bills and joint resolutions before close of session
Photographed with Cabinet, leaders of Congress, and Government officials following adjournment of Congress
Dinner—Senator Simeon D. Fess, Representative and Mrs. William E. Evans, Representative-elect and Mrs. Charles F. Curry, and Gertrude Bowman

March 5

Breakfast—Mark Sullivan, journalist
Representative William R. Wood, Indiana
B. Carroll Reece, former Representative of Tennessee
Senator Clarence C. Dill
Representative Thomas J. B. Robinson, Iowa
Charles O'Connor, former Representative of Oklahoma
Frederick D. MacKay and S. Parkes Cadman

Albert Foster Dawson, former Representative of Iowa
W. W. Chalmers, former Representative of Ohio
Representative Charles L. Gifford
Charles L. Lawrence and a delegation from the board of governors of the Aeronautical Chamber of Commerce of America, Inc.
Senator Peter Norbeck
Isadore Dockweiler and Grace Strohmer, Los Angeles, Calif.
Charles S. Wilson, Federal Farm Board, and Mr. Gracie
Lunch—Senators Daniel O. Hastings and Frederic C. Walcott
Alexander Legge, Chairman of the Federal Farm Board
J. Clawson Roop, Director of the Budget
Secretary of War Patrick J. Hurley
Attorney General William D. Mitchell
Secretary of the Interior Ray Lyman Wilbur
Raymond Benjamin, assistant chairman of the Republican National Committee

March 6

Breakfast—Senator James E. Watson, Senate majority leader
Senator Robert D. Carey, Wyoming
Cabinet
Senator Roscoe C. Patterson and former Representative Edgar C. Ellis
Senator Jesse H. Metcalf
Representative Louis Ludlow, Mrs. A. P. Flynn of Logansport, Ind., Mrs. Cortland C. Gillen, and Mrs. S. R. Rariden of Greencastle, Ind.

Senator Walter F. George and Martha Berry

Senator Samuel M. Shortridge

Grange group from western New York

Lunch—Mrs. Charles D. Walcott, Mrs. Charles Lea, and Anthony Czarnecki

James C. Stone, Vice Chairman of the Federal Farm Board

Secretary of Commerce Robert P. Lamont and William Wallace Atterbury, president of Pennsylvania Railroad

Washington Correspondents

Julius Barnes, chairman of the board of the Chamber of Commerce of the United States

March 7

Breakfast—Mark Sullivan, journalist

Representative Willis C. Hawley

Arthur Woods, Chairman of the President's Emergency Committee for Employment

Richard N. Elliott, former Representative of Indiana

Senator Otis F. Glenn, Illinois

James R. Garfield, Chairman of the Committee on the Conservation and Administration of the Public Domain

C. B. Denman, Federal Farm Board

Charles H. Burke, Commissioner of the United States to the International Exposition of Colonial and Overseas Countries

Leo S. Rowe, Director General of the Pan American Union

Clarence W. Greene, president of Parsons College, Fairfield, Iowa

William Gude to present flowers from the National Florists Association

Departed for Asheville, N.C., to visit Herbert Hoover, Jr.—accompanied by Mrs. Hoover, Lawrence Richey, Dr. Joel T. Boone, and Miss Fisher

March 8

In Asheville, N.C.

March 9

Returned from Asheville, N.C.

Secretary of Labor William N. Doak

Secretary of Agriculture Arthur M. Hyde

Representative Edith Nourse Rogers

Mr. Tuthill

Frank T. Hines, Administrator of Veterans' Affairs

James F. Burke, general counsel to the Republican National Committee

March 10

Senator Samuel M. Shortridge

Senator Simeon D. Fess

Cabinet

Jay G. Hayden and the executive committee of the Gridiron Club

Representative John W. Summers, Washington

Charles McK. Saltzman, Chairman of the Federal Radio Commission

Ashmun N. Brown, Providence (R.I.) Journal

Theodore G. Joslin, Boston Evening Transcript

Stephen B. Davis

Dinner—James F. Burke and Will Irwin

March 11

Breakfast—Will Irwin
Representatives Carl E. Mapes, Earl C. Michener, and Joseph L. Hooper
Mrs. Bina West Miller
Matthew Woll, American Federation of Labor
Representative Hamilton Fish, Jr.
Oscar K. Davis, executive secretary of the National Foreign Trade Council
Charles F. Abbott, executive director of the American Institute of Steel Construction
William Curtis Bok, treasurer of the American Foundation
D. Lawrence Groner, Judge of the District of Columbia Court of Appeals
Joseph H. Milans, grand commander, and committee from the Knights Templar of the District of Columbia
C. G. Mathis and a committee from the Monroe Centennial Memorial Commission
Thomas Gibson, Denver, Colo.
Lunch—Secretary of State Henry L. Stimson
Secretary of Labor William N. Doak
R. S. Pickens, Associated Press
C. Bascom Slemp

March 12

Breakfast—Walter H. Newton and Robert H. Lucas
Senator Arthur R. Robinson, Indiana

J. Matt Chilton, Republican National Committee
Representative Burton L. French, Idaho
Mrs. Henry W. Keyes
Senator David A. Reed
Merryle S. Rukeyser, journalist
John F. O'Ryan and delegation from the National World Court Committee
John J. Leary, Jr., New York, journalist
Mrs. Edward A. Harriman, chairman of the League of Republican Women
Representative James C. McLaughlin, Michigan
Senator David A. Reed
Washington Correspondents
Henry P. Fletcher, Chairman of the United States Tariff Commission
J. Clawson Roop, Director of the Budget
Eugene Meyer, Governor of the Federal Reserve Board
Albert W. Atwood, writer for the Saturday Evening Post
William D. L. Starbuck, Federal Radio Commission

March 13

Breakfast—Mark Sullivan, journalist
Senator Otis F. Glenn
Cabinet
Frank T. Hines, Administrator of Veterans' Affairs
Edward D. Stair, Detroit Free Press, and George deB. Keim, secretary of the Republican National Committee

Mrs. John F. Sippel and Julia K. Jaffray, Federation of Women's Clubs

James C. Stone and Samuel R. McKelvie, Federal Farm Board

Senator Tasker L. Oddie

Julius Klein, Assistant Secretary of Commerce

Harold A. LaFount, Federal Radio Commission

Dinner—Representative and Mrs. Adam M. Wyant and Representative and Mrs. Maurice H. Thatcher

March 14

Senator Joseph T. Robinson, Arkansas

Representative Kent E. Keller, Illinois

William T. Rawleigh, Freeport, Ill., manufacturer

Secretary of Agriculture Arthur M. Hyde

Charles C. Teague, Federal Farm Board

Representative Charles A. Eaton, New Jersey

Secretary of Labor William N. Doak

Dinner—Mr. and Mrs. Mark Sullivan

March 15

Breakfast—Dr. Joel T. Boone

Raymond Benjamin, assistant chairman of the Republican National Committee

Lunch—Secretary of Agriculture Arthur M. Hyde, and Earl C. Smith

George Akerson, former Secretary to the President

March 16

Henry P. Fletcher, Chairman of the United States Tariff Commission

John Thomas Taylor, American Legion

Raymond B. Stevens, adviser on foreign affairs to the King of Siam

John A. L. Waddell, New York

Frank B. Noyes, president of the Associated Press

Brazilian Ambassador, S. Gurgél do Amaral

Grand Council Order of DeMolay

Bishop of England High School basketball team, Charleston, S.C.

Lunch—Frank T. Hines and John H. Cowles

Ogden L. Mills, Under Secretary of the Treasury

Mr. Leary

Secretary of Agriculture Arthur M. Hyde

Raymond Benjamin, assistant chairman of the Republican National Committee

Secretary of Commerce Robert P. Lamont

Charles J. Hepburn

Dinner—Secretary of Commerce and Mrs. Robert P. Lamont

March 17

Breakfast—Mark Sullivan, journalist

Senator Frederick Steiwer

Eugene Meyer, Governor of the Federal Reserve Board

Cabinet

Washington Correspondents

Georgia Wentz

Senator Peter Norbeck and Paul E. Bellamy, Rapid City, S. Dak.

George M. James, Federal Reserve Board

Lunch—Mr. and Mrs. Thomas E. Campbell and Col. and Mrs. C. E. Thompson

Thomas E. Campbell, President of the Civil Service Commission, and Margaret Flynn

Albert W. Atwood, writer for the Saturday Evening Post

C. Bascom Slemp

Arthur Woods, Chairman of the President's Emergency Committee for Employment

March 18

Senator Reed Smoot

Senator Thomas D. Schall, Minnesota

George W. Angerstein, Chicago, Ill.

Lunch—Senator William E. Borah

Departed for Porto Rico and Virgin Islands

March 19–March 28

Porto Rican and Virgin Islands tour

March 29

Returned from Porto Rico and Virgin Islands

Theodore G. Joslin and Walter H. Newton, Secretaries to the President

March 30

Breakfast—Dr. Joel T. Boone

Secretary of Agriculture Arthur M. Hyde

J. Clawson Roop, Director of the Budget

Lunch—Secretary of State Henry L. Stimson

Vice President Charles Curtis

Secretary of State Henry L. Stimson and Assistant Secretary of State James G. Rogers

Secretary of Labor William N. Doak

Senator Simeon D. Fess

Dinner—Henry J. Allen, former Senator of Kansas

March 31

Breakfast—Senator James E. Watson, Senate majority leader

Cabinet

Washington Correspondents

Justices James M. Proctor and Alfred A. Wheat of the Supreme Court of the District of Columbia

Guilford (S.C.) College choir

Lunch—Frank B. Kellogg, former Secretary of State

Raymond Benjamin, assistant chairman of the Republican National Committee

Dinner—Frederick H. Ecker, president of the Metropolitan Life Insurance Co.

April 1

Breakfast—Walter E. Hope, former Assistant Secretary of the Treasury, and Frederick H. Ecker, president of the Metropolitan Life Insurance Co.

Henry P. Fletcher, Chairman of the United States Tariff Commission

Senator Peter Norbeck

John M. Robsion, former Senator of Kentucky

Ernest O. Thompson, mayor of Amarillo, Tex.

Joseph E. Ransdell, former Senator of Louisiana

John Barton Payne, Chairman of the American National Red Cross

Elmer T. Peterson, editor of Better Homes and Gardens magazine

John W. Hutchinson, New York

Representative James S. Parker, New York

Mrs. Philip Moore, St. Louis, Mo.

Representative Oscar B. Lovette and Hugh McCall Tate, Interstate Commerce Commission

Laurits S. Swenson, United States Minister to the Netherlands

Representative Louis Ludlow and group from Indiana

Lunch—Secretary of Commerce Robert P. Lamont

Secretary of the Navy Charles F. Adams

Julius Barnes, chairman of the board of the Chamber of Commerce of the United States

Mr. and Mrs. J. C. Penney

April 2

Senator Otis F. Glenn

Representative Scott Leavitt, Montana

Representative William R. Wood, Indiana

William M. Calder, former Senator of New York

Edgar J. Goodrich, Board of Tax Appeals

George C. Dyer, Assistant United States Attorney at St. Louis

Mrs. Frederick T. Connor and daughter of Evanston, Ill.

Lunch—James C. Stone, Chairman of the Federal Farm Board, and George S. Milnor

Belgian Ambassador, Paul May, to present letters of credence

Wilson M. Compton, National Lumber Manufacturers' Association

J. Clawson Roop, Director of the Budget

Dinner—Mr. and Mrs. Russell Doubleday and Representative and Mrs. John Q. Tilson and children

April 3

Breakfast—Mr. and Mrs. Russell Doubleday and Representative and Mrs. John Q. Tilson

Cabinet

James G. Brown, Indianapolis, Ind.

Henry P. Fletcher, Chairman of the United States Tariff Commission

Representative Ruth Bryan Owen and Howard R. Driggs and Oregon Trail Memorial Association delegation

Lunch—Mr. and Mrs. William J. Maier and family

A. R. Johnson, Ohio

Representative William R. Coyle and Fred B. Gernerd, former Representative of Pennsylvania

Washington Correspondents

Dinner—Mrs. Sidney Mitchell

April 4

Breakfast—Mark Sullivan, journalist

Senator L. J. Dickinson, Iowa

Senator Warren R. Austin, Vermont

Mrs. John Hays Hammond and Harris Hammond

Secretary of Commerce Robert P. Lamont and George A. Martin, president of the Railroad Cooperative Building and Loan Association

Canadian Chargé d'Affaires, Hume Wrong, to present Raoul Dandurand

Elizabeth E. Stout

Lunch—Senator and Mrs. Warren R. Austin

Dinner—Mr. and Mrs. Timothy Hopkins

April 5

Breakfast—Mr. and Mrs. Timothy Hopkins

Knights Templar Easter Service at Arlington Cemetery

Lunch—Dr. and Mrs. Augustus Taber Murray, Mrs. Francis Murray, and Mr. and Mrs. Timothy Hopkins

Dinner—Secretary of Commerce and Mrs. Robert P. Lamont, Mr. and Mrs. Eugene Meyer, Miss Meyer, Mrs. Vernon L. Kellogg, Jean Kellogg, Miss Bradbury, Miss Cavey, Mr. and Mrs. Clarence M. Woolley, and Myron C. Taylor

April 6

Breakfast—Charles K. Field, Mr. and Mrs. Clarence M. Woolley, and Myron C. Taylor

William E. Lamb, former Solicitor of the Department of Commerce

Rev. and Mrs. William A. Sunday

Stanley C. Wilson, Governor of Vermont, and delegation

Civic service clubs, executives

Paul E. Haworth, House Committee on War Claims

Postmaster General Walter F. Brown

Lunch—Mr. and Mrs. Frank P. Stockbridge, Janet Stockbridge, Clara B. Burdette, Emma G. Wheeler, Charles K. Field, Harold Titcomb, Royden Peacock, Lt. Willis, John Titcomb, and Judge and Mrs. James F. Burke

Dinner—Jeremiah Milbank and James F. Burke, Republican National Committee

April 7

Breakfast—Judge and Mrs. James F. Burke

British Ambassador, Sir Ronald Lindsay, to present Montagu Norman, Governor of the Bank of England

Cabinet

Washington Correspondents

Ralph T. O'Neill, national commander of the American Legion

Representative Clay Stone Briggs

Rabbi Bookhaven and 5 Eagle Scouts

Lunch—Judge and Mrs. James F. Burke

Henry P. Fletcher, Chairman of the United States Tariff Commission

Raymond Benjamin, assistant chairman of the Republican National Committee

Dinner—Judge and Mrs. James F. Burke

April 8

Breakfast—Edgar Rickard

Lawrence C. Phipps, former Senator of Colorado

Secretary of War Patrick J. Hurley

Walter Lyman Brown, New York

Frank H. Hitchcock, former Postmaster General

Clarke Griffith and Eddy Eynon, Washington Baseball Club

Hungarian Minister, Count Laszlo Szechenyi, to present Count Bela Hadik and Lt. Col. S. A. Beldy

Cicero Murray, chairman of the Oil States Advisory Committee

George Easter, Jacksonville, Fla.; Thorlief Knudtzen, Oak Park, Ill.; and Wilfred Schurink, Mobile, Ala., winners of the National Committee on Wood Utilization contest

Lunch—Mr. and Mrs. Stanley Washburn, Mr. and Mrs. William B. Poland, and Edgar Rickard

Frederick William Wile, journalist

John Barton Payne, Chairman of the American National Red Cross

Robert H. Lucas, executive director of the Republican National Committee

Dinner—Senator and Mrs. L. J. Dickinson, Mr. and Mrs. George Rublee, Mr. and Mrs. French Strother, and Edgar Rickard

April 9

Senator Claude A. Swanson

Lt. Col. Joseph I. McMullen

Adolph Lewisohn

Charles S. Barrett, former president of the National Farmers' Union

Group of Brooklyn, N.Y., schoolteachers

Lunch—George W. Wickersham

Secretary of Commerce Robert P. Lamont and Russell Cornell Leffingwell

Secretary of War Patrick J. Hurley and Secretary of the Interior Ray Lyman Wilbur

G. Gould Lincoln, Washington Star

J. Clawson Roop, Director of the Budget

Julius Klein, Assistant Secretary of Commerce

Dinner—former Senator Henry J. Allen and Mr. and Mrs. Edward B. Robinette

751

April 10

Breakfast—Wesley C. Mitchell, Chairman of the Research Committee on Social Trends, and Mr. and Mrs. Edward B. Robinette

Cabinet

Senator David A. Reed and Thomas S. Baker, president of Carnegie Institute of Technology

George Otis Smith, Chairman of the Federal Power Commission

Harvey C. Couch

Senator Duncan U. Fletcher; C. H. Reeder, mayor of Miami; and A. H. Heermance, secretary-treasurer of the Greater Miami Airport Association

Lucy Peabody, president of the Woman's National Law Enforcement Commission

William R. Castle, Jr., Under Secretary of State

George W. Pepper, former Senator of Pennsylvania

Henry J. Allen, former Senator of Kansas

Arthur Woods, Chairman of the President's Emergency Committee for Employment

Hanford MacNider, United States Minister to Canada, to present Robert J. Manion, Canadian Minister of Railways and Canals

Representative John Q. Tilson, House majority leader

Dinner—Senator and Mrs. David A. Reed and Mrs. Walter C. Wycoff

Departed for Cincinnati, Ohio

April 11

Attended Nicholas Longworth's funeral in Cincinnati, Ohio

April 12

Returned from Cincinnati, Ohio

Lunch—Mr. and Mrs. Hanford MacNider

Dinner—Under Secretary of the Treasury and Mrs. Ogden L. Mills, John Fell, and Dorothy Fell

April 13

Breakfast—Dr. Joel T. Boone

National Recreation Association board of directors, 25th annual meeting, in Cabinet Room

American National Red Cross, address at Continental Memorial Hall

Secretary of Commerce Robert P. Lamont and Matthew E. Sloan, president of the New York Edison Company

Austin T. Levy, Burrillville, R. I.

Eugene Meyer, Governor of the Federal Reserve Board

William Randolph Hearst, Jr.

National Woman's Democratic Law Enforcement League, delegation

Lewis A. Sexton and members of the National Hospital Day Committee of the American Hospital Association

Lunch—N. A. Fletcher and Robert S. Regar

Panamanian Minister, Harmodio Arias, to present letters of credence

Henry P. Fletcher, Chairman of the United States Tariff Commission

Lt. Col. Joseph I. McMullen

John Hays Hammond

Raymond Benjamin, assistant chairman of the Republican National Committee

April 14

Albert W. Jefferis, former Representative of Nebraska

Cabinet

Governing Board of the Pan American Union, radio address to special session

Ben Casanus and a committee on unemployment relief for the city of New Orleans, La.

Lunch—Secretary of the Navy Charles F. Adams, Rev. and Mrs. Fletcher Homan, Mrs. Louis A. Frothingham, and Leverett Saltonstall

Opening baseball game between Philadelphia and Washington

Radio address from the Lincoln study in the White House on the 50th anniversary of Tuskegee Institute

Julius Barnes, chairman of the board of the Chamber of Commerce of the United States

Dinner—with Secretary of the Navy and Mrs. Charles F. Adams at their residence

April 15

Breakfast—Mr. and Mrs. Herter, Mrs. P. Fuller, and George Fuller

Arch W. Shaw, Chairman of the President's Committee on Recent Social Trends

Frank B. Noyes, president of the Associated Press

Representative Jesse P. Wolcott, Michigan

Edward Smith, Minneapolis, Minn.

Mrs. Harry E. Thomas, Wisconsin Republican national committeewoman

Mrs. Henry R. Rea, Central Committee of the American National Red Cross

Douglas Malloch, author

Army Chaplains, convention delegates

Representative Robert G. Simmons, Nebraska

Mr. and Mrs. Duffield, Mason City, Iowa

Women's Organization for National Prohibition Reform, members

Lunch—Arch W. Shaw and Mrs. Harry E. Thomas

Senator Charles L. McNary

G. Gould Lincoln, Washington Star

Secretary of State Henry L. Stimson

Japanese Ambassador, Katsuji Debuchi, to present Prince Takamatsu and his Princess Consort

Roy A. Roberts, Kansas City Star

Dinner—Prince Takamatsu and his Princess Consort

April 16

Senator Wesley L. Jones, Washington

Senator Wallace H. White, Jr., Maine

Secretary of Agriculture Arthur M. Hyde

B. Carroll Reece, former Representative of Tennessee

753

1931

Marie M. Meloney, New York Herald Tribune

Charles A. Freeman, editor of the Olean Herald

Isaac R. Pennypacker and committee from the Valley Forge Park Commission

John Hays Hammond, mining engineer, and William E. Hall, president of the Boys' Club Federation of America

William R. Castle, Jr., Under Secretary of State, and Professor O. K. Allen of Oxford University, England

Carl Byer

National Society of Dames of the Loyal Legion, members

Society Daughters of Founders and Patriots of America, officers and delegates

Lunch—Marie M. Meloney, New York Herald Tribune

J. Clawson Roop, Director of the Budget

Henry Ford, automobile manufacturer

American Society of Editors, members

April 17

Breakfast—Mark Sullivan, journalist

Cabinet

Representative Menalcus Lankford and Luther B. Way, Judge of the Federal District Court for the Eastern District of Virginia

Clara Estabrook, Presque Isle, Maine

Mr. and Mrs. Watson Stokes, New York

Lunch—Mrs. Giles Whiting and Mrs. Swain

Senators Phillips Lee Goldsborough and Daniel O. Hastings

Mrs. George Horace Lorimer

Washington Correspondents

Dinner—With Chief Justice and Mrs. Charles Evans Hughes at their residence

April 18

Breakfast—Solicitor General Thomas D. Thacher, Assistant Secretary of the Treasury Ferry K. Heath, Mr. and Mrs. Walter H. Newton, Lawrence Richey, Dr. and Mrs. Joel T. Boone, Mark Sullivan, and Assistant Secretary of the Navy Ernest Lee Jahncke

To Rapidan Camp, Va.—the above breakfast guests and Justice and Mrs. Harlan Fiske Stone, Secretary of Agriculture and Mrs. Arthur M. Hyde, and Mrs. Thomas D. Thacher

April 19

Returned from Rapidan Camp, Va.

April 20

Breakfast—Secretary of Agriculture Arthur M. Hyde, James C. Stone of the Federal Farm Board, and Alexander Legge

Alexander F. Osborn and A. H. Schoellropf of the Buffalo Unemployment Committee

Horace C. Gardner, Chicago, Ill.

William E. Humphrey, Federal Trade Commission

William M. Ritter

Thomas S. Wright and committee of the National Funeral Directors Association

John Dyneley Prince, United States Minister to Yugoslavia

Mr. and Mrs. John W. Craddock, New Orleans, La.

Secretary of Labor William N. Doak

Lunch—Thomas E. Campbell, President of the Civil Service Commission

National Conference of Business Paper Editors, delegation

Dinner—Mr. and Mrs. Frank E. Gannett

April 21

Breakfast—Mr. and Mrs. Frank E. Gannett and Viscountess Harcourt

J. Clawson Roop, Director of the Budget

Cabinet

Washington Correspondents

Irish Free State Minister, Michael Mac-White, to present George Russell

Pan American Conference of Directors of Public Health, delegates

Planted tree on north White House grounds in connection with the George Washington Bicentennial Celebration

Dinner—With Secretary of the Interior and Mrs. Ray Lyman Wilbur at their residence

April 22

T. V. O'Connor, Chairman of the United States Shipping Board

C. Bascom Slemp

Spanish Ambassador, Alejandro Padilla y Bell

Secretary of Labor William N. Doak and State superintendents of the Federal Employment Service

Harold F. Pitcairn of Philadelphia, presented with the Collier Trophy by the President

Federal Council of Churches of Christ of America, delegation

Representative Samuel S. Arentz and daughter to present commemorative coin on behalf of Las Vegas Chamber of Commerce

World Conference on Work for the Blind, delegates

Lunch—Helen Keller, Mrs. Macy, Miss Thompson, Dr. and Mrs. Glenn Frank, and Dr. and Mrs. William J. Hutchins

Arthur Woods, Chairman of the President's Emergency Committee for Employment

Reception—Daughters of the American Revolution

Dinner—Mr. and Mrs. Samuel Crowther

April 23

Breakfast—Mr. and Mrs. Samuel Crowther

Mrs. William Cumming Story

Thomas E. Campbell, President of the Civil Service Commission

755

Carl Jones

James G. McDonald, chairman of the board of the Foreign Policy Association, Inc.

Swedish Minister, Wollmar F. Bostrom, to present Ivar Tengbom

Hazel Viola Markinson presented "Buddy Poppy" to the President

Reginald D. Johnson of Los Angeles, presented gold medal by the President, for winning architectural competition of the Better Homes in America

Society of the Children of the American Revolution, delegation

Lunch—to the Better Homes luncheon at the Girl Scouts' little house

A. D. Noyes, New York Times

April 24

Breakfast—Mark Sullivan, journalist

Senator Charles L. McNary

Cabinet

Senator L. J. Dickinson, Iowa

Mrs. Ben Wylie, State president of the Georgia Daughters of the American Revolution, and Mrs. G. H. Norris

Mordecai W. Johnson, president of Howard University, and committee from the Columbian Educational Association of the District of Columbia

Negro Housing Committee of the White House Conference on Home Building and Home Ownership

Brazilian Ambassador, Rinaldo de Lima e Silva, to present letters of credence

Lt. Col. Julian L. Schley, Deputy Governor of Panama Canal Zone

Washington Correspondents

April 25

Breakfast—Mark Sullivan, journalist

Secretary of Commerce Robert P. Lamont

Departed for Cape Henry, Va. on board the *Sequoia,* accompanied by Mrs. Hoover, Robert A. Millikan, Dr. and Mrs. Vernon L. Kellogg, Capt. Russell Train, Col. Campbell B. Hodges, Dr. Joel T. Boone, and Lawrence Richey

April 26

At Cape Henry, Va., memorial ceremonies commemorating 324th anniversary of the landing of the first English colonists in America

April 27

Returned from Cape Henry, Va.

Senator George H. Moses and Albert H. Hislop

Lenna L. Yost, Republican National Committee

Frederick L. Devereux, New York

Arthur Woods, Chairman of the President's Emergency Committee for Employment

Washington, D.C. high school cadets, colonels

Rev. and Mrs. David McInnis

Lunch—Senator James E. Watson

James T. Williams, Jr., editor of Universal Service

Reception—National Society of the United States Daughters of 1812

Dinner—Gridiron Club, accompanied by Theodore G. Joslin

April 28

Breakfast—Mark Sullivan, journalist, and George Barr Baker

Cabinet

Horace Stillwell, Florida

Professor and Mrs. M. J. Thue, Chicago, Ill.

Woodmen of the World, convention delegates

Lunch—Mr. and Mrs. John A. Swanson and George Baldwin

Dinner—With Secretary of Agriculture and Mrs. Arthur M. Hyde at their residence

April 29

Breakfast—Mr. and Mrs. George B. Longan

Received the King and Queen of Siam

Returned the call of the King and Queen of Siam

Dr. Jordan, University of Virginia

Representative Allen T. Treadway

State Dinner—King and Queen of Siam

April 30

Representative Edith Nourse Rogers

S. Wallace Dempsey, former Representative of New York

George Otis Smith, Chairman of the Federal Power Commission

Robert Barry and Harry H. Atkinson, United States Attorney for Nevada

Representative Bertrand H. Snell and Lake Placid Olympic Games committee

Gilbert T. Hodges and committee of the Advertising Federation of America

Compton brothers—Karl, Arthur, and Wilson

Building Trades Department of the American Federation of Labor, executive council

Sylvia Diedech, winner of the Chicago Times radio spelling bee

Clara Estabrook, Presque Isle, Maine

Lunch—Dr. and Mrs. Karl T. Compton, Dr. and Mrs. Arthur H. Compton, and Mr. and Mrs. Wilson M. Compton

Senator Felix Hebert

Mr. Scott of Iowa

Samuel Perkins, Tacoma, Wash.

Called on the King and Queen of Siam to say goodbye

Dinner—George Harrison

May 1

Breakfast—George Harrison

Royal O. Kloeber, Acting Director of the Budget

Pressed electric button opening doors to the new Empire State Building in New York City

Cabinet

Lunch—Secretary of Labor William N. Doak and William Green, president of the American Federation of Labor

Washington Correspondents

Raymond Benjamin, assistant chairman of the Republican National Committee

Dinner—A. E. Kinnelly and George Ewing

May 2

Secretary of Commerce Robert P. Lamont

Franklin W. Fort, former Representative of New Jersey

Attended wedding of Secretary Lamont's daughter

Secretary of the Interior Ray Lyman Wilbur

May 3

Breakfast—Silas H. Strawn, president of the Chamber of Commerce of the United States

Lunch—Under Secretary of State and Mrs. William R. Castle, Jr. and George Ewing

Dinner—Mr. and Mrs. Leland W. Cutter

Dan Lawrence

May 4

Breakfast—Mark Sullivan, journalist

International Chamber of Commerce, address in Constitution Hall

Merle Thorpe, editor of the Nation's Business

Belgian Ambassador, Paul May, to present Professor and Mrs. Maurice Philippson

Mrs. Paul Fitzsimmons, Rhode Island Republican national committeewoman

Frank I. McCoy, former Chief Justice of the Supreme Court of the District of Columbia

William J. MacCracken, Jr., secretary of the American Bar Association

Gary, W. Va., high school band

Phil Cook

Lunch—Daniel Willard, railroad president

Robert H. Lucas, executive director of the Republican National Committee

Dinner—The Little Cabinet, i.e., Under Secretaries of the various departments

May 5

Fred C. Croxton, President's Emergency Committee for Employment

Cabinet

Washington Correspondents

Attorney General William D. Mitchell, Richard Bancroft, and H. R. Johnston

Roy D. Chapin and directors of the National Automobile Chamber of Commerce

Mrs. Lightfoot

Mrs. W. G. Knight and party from Milo, Maine

Herbert S. Huston

John Moorman, Indiana

Lunch—Mr. and Mrs. Edward A. Dickson, James Grant, and Howard Heinz

William Hard

Reception—Colonial Dames of America

Raymond Benjamin, assistant chairman of the Republican National Committee

Dinner—With Secretary of Commerce and Mrs. Robert P. Lamont

May 6

Breakfast—Mark Sullivan, journalist

Frederic M. Sackett, United States Ambassador to Germany

William S. Culbertson, United States Ambassador to Chile

Francis B. Loomis

Louie W. Strum and Scott M. Loftin, Florida

Henry S. Dennison, Massachusetts

Thomas B. Morgan, United Press representative in Rome, Italy

David W. Mulvane

Arthur A. Henning and Mr. and Mrs. John McCutcheon and son

Anna Martin and sister, Greenville, Ohio

Robert B. Armstrong, Los Angeles Times

Lunch—Lewis E. Pierson of New York and Howard Heinz of Pittsburgh, Pa.

Senator Simeon D. Fess

Julius Barnes, chairman of the board of the Chamber of Commerce of the United States

Dinner—Mr. and Mrs. Hamlin Garland, Mr. and Mrs. William Hard, and David W. Mulvane

May 7

Breakfast—Mark Sullivan, journalist

Senator Charles L. McNary

Edward L. Ryerson, Chicago, Ill.

Lawrence W. Wallace, executive secretary of the American Engineering Council, and committee from the building industry

Herschel C. Walker, Philadelphia, Pa.

William M. Chadbourne, New York

Judson Hannigan, president of the Republican Club, Massachusetts

John F. Sinclair, financial editor of the North American Newspaper Alliance

Mrs. A. F. Hassan and delegates to the American Women's Legion convention

Lunch—Charles H. Sherrill

Julius Barnes, chairman of the board of the Chamber of Commerce of the United States

Walter F. Dillingham

Senator Phillips Lee Goldsborough and Morris A. Soper

Charles P. Sisson, Assistant Attorney General

Reception—International Chamber of Commerce delegates

Dinner—Mr. and Mrs. John A. Hartford

May 8

Breakfast—Mark Sullivan, journalist, and Mr. and Mrs. John A. Hartford

Royal O. Kloeber, Acting Director of the Budget

Cabinet

Albert F. Dawson, former Representative of Iowa

Ernest Lee Jahncke, Assistant Secretary of the Navy, and John N. Jackson, chairman of the Republican State Central Committee of Louisiana

British Chargé d'Affaires, Ronald Ian Campbell, to present Edwin Thompson, Lord Mayor of Liverpool, England; Gen. Edward Higgins, commander in chief of the Salvation Army; Right Hon. Ampthill, Right Hon. Lord Wraxall of the British Privy Council; C. R. S. Nicholl, and Bainbridge Colby

Lunch—P. A. Rowley, president of Manhattan Co. of New York

Arthur Brisbane, editor of the Chicago Herald and Examiner

Frederick D. Young, Illinois

Washington Correspondents

Reception—American Law Institute delegates

Silas H. Strawn and Julius Barnes, Chamber of Commerce of the United States

Dinner—Belgian Ambassador Paul May, Mr. Theunis, M & Mme Philippson, Ambassador and Mrs. Frederic M. Sackett, Mr. and Mrs. Silas H. Strawn, Edgar Rickard, Mrs. Marble, and Sue Dyer

May 9

Breakfast—Secretary of War Patrick J. Hurley, Representative William R. Wood, Gen. Douglas MacArthur, Lawrence Richey, Dr. Joel T. Boone, and Edgar Rickard

Rapidan Camp, Va.—The above breakfast guests and Maj. Gen. George V. Moseley, General and Mrs. Lytle Brown, Quartermaster General and Mrs. J. L. DeWitt, Mr. and Mrs. Earle S. Kinsley, and Mr. and Mrs. Theodore G. Joslin

May 10

Returned from Rapidan Camp, Va.

LeRoy T. Vernon, Chicago Daily News

Dinner—Mr. and Mrs. Earle S. Kinsley and Edgar Rickard

May 11

Breakfast—Mr. and Mrs. Earle S. Kinsley

Charles Kerr

Senator Duncan U. Fletcher, Representative Ruth Bryan Owen, and delegation from Florida

John R. Mott, president of the World's Alliance of the Young Men's Christian Association

Charles S. Dewey, financial adviser

William Fox, former head of Fox Film Corporation

Mrs. Roland Craw, Oxford, Ind.

Albert W. Atwood, writer for the Saturday Evening Post

Secretary of War Patrick J. Hurley and Manuel Quezon, president of the Philippine Senate

May 12

Breakfast—Mark Sullivan, journalist

Cabinet

Washington Correspondents

Representative Thomas H. Cullen, New York

Lunch—Dr. and Mrs. Vernon L. Kellogg, Carl Hoffman, Mrs. H. E. Manville, Mr. and Mrs. Howard Fisher, and J. Parke Channing

Dinner—General and Mrs. Edward Martin

May 13

Breakfast—General and Mrs. Edward Martin

Mrs. Nathaniel Thayer, Massachusetts Republican national committeewoman

F. Richard Schaaf, president of the First National Bank, Gary, Ind.

David Lynn, Architect of the Capitol, and Harvey W. Corbett, architect of New York

Francis P. Gaines, president of Washington and Lee University

Senator Phillips Lee Goldsborough and William C. Chesnut

Robert B. Armstrong and Mayor and Mrs. John C. Porter of Los Angeles, Calif.

Frederick Ring

Lunch—Albert Shaw

Pressed electric button in White House starting the presses for the publication of the golden anniversary edition of the Chicago Examiner

Dinner—Governor Percival Baxter of Maine

May 14

Breakfast—Mark Sullivan, journalist

Wilson M. Compton, National Lumber Manufacturers' Association

Representative Burton L. French, Idaho

Paul Shoup, president of the Southern Pacific Railroad Company

Frank J. Loesch

Paul Wooten, New Orleans Times-Picayune, and Paul Aldrich

Disabled American War Veterans, committee

Chilean Ambassador, Carlos G. Davila, to present Comdr. Arturo B. Merino, Capt. Dario Mergica, and Lt. Felipe Latorre

Ora S. Spillman, former attorney general of Nebraska

Methodist Protestant Church convention delegates

Mrs. R. A. Wolff, New Kensington, Pa., and group of children

Lunch—Walter W. Head, president of the Morris Plan Corporation of America

May 15

Cabinet

Lamont Rowlands

British Ambassador, Sir Ronald Lindsay, to present Dr. J. C. Carlisle

International Association of Torch Clubs, convention delegates

Senator David A. Reed

Representative Frank Murphy, Ohio

Washington Correspondents

Dinner—Secretary of War and Mrs. Patrick J. Hurley, and Mr. and Mrs. Edward H. Butler

May 16

Breakfast—Senator Daniel O. Hastings, Lawrence Richey, and Dr. Joel T. Boone

Rapidan Camp, Va.—Secretary of the Interior and Mrs. Ray Lyman Wilbur, Assistant Secretary of the Interior Joseph M. Dixon, Assistant Secretary of the Interior and Mrs. John H. Edwards, Senator Daniel O. Hastings, Mr. and Mrs. Horace M. Albright, Mr. and Mrs. Charles J. Rhoads, Mr. and Mrs. Charles C. Moore, Mr. and Mrs. W. C. Mendenhall, Mr. and Mrs. William J. Cooper, Mr. and Mrs. Elwood Mead, Mr. and Mrs. Edward H. Butler, Mr. and Mrs. Theodore G. Joslin, Lawrence Richey, and Dr. Joel T. Boone

May 17

Returned from Rapidan Camp, Va.
Dinner—Hugh Gibson, United States Ambassador to Belgium

May 18

Maj. Edwin H. Cooper, Waban, Mass., Army and Navy Legion of Valor

Arthur Coleman, associate editor of Holland's magazine

Fred C. Croxton, member of the President's Emergency Committee for Employment

Representative George F. Brumm, Pennsylvania

Henry J. Allen, former Senator of Kansas

George W. Wickersham

Dinner—Representative John Q. Tilson, William H. Crocker, and Hugh Gibson

May 19

Cabinet
Wayland W. Magee, Federal Reserve Board

May 20

Breakfast—Mark Sullivan, journalist

Harry F. Guggenheim, United States Ambassador to Cuba

Francis V. Keesling, San Francisco lawyer

Union of South Africa Minister, Eric Hendrick Louw, to present group of citizens from South Africa

Representative Harold Knutson, Minnesota

R. Hansen

Two sons of Edgar Gleason, managing editor of the San Francisco Bulletin

Father Bergs of Pittsburgh, Pa.

National Association of Mutual Savings Banks, convention delegates

Mr. and Mrs. Eugene Steinaker, Janesville, Wis.

John Barton Payne, Chairman of the American National Red Cross, to present Max Huber, Switzerland, president of the International Red Cross

Lunch—Jasper N. Tincher, former Representative of Kansas

Colombian Minister, Fabio Lozano Torrijos, to present letters of credence

Dinner—Mr. and Mrs. Charles C. Teague and Mr. and Mrs. Milton Teague

May 21

Breakfast—Bernard M. Baruch

B. Carroll Reece, former Representative of Tennessee

Richard V. Oulahan, New York Times

Senator James J. Davis, Pennsylvania

H. Paul Bestor, Farm Loan Commissioner

Stephen Duggan, director of the Institute of International Education

Whiting Williams, author

A. S. Brown, Jr., Boston, Mass.

Edward A. O'Neal, president of the American Farm Bureau Federation

Representative Ruth Bryan Owen

Representative William E. Hull, Illinois, and Maj. Gen. T. Q. Ashburn, Inland Waterways Corporation

Dinner—American National Red Cross, at Willard Hotel, address

May 22

Breakfast—Mark Sullivan, journalist

Herbert Bayard Swope, journalist

Cabinet

J. Leonard Replogle, New York manufacturer

John W. O'Leary, president of the Chicago Association of Commerce

Mr. and Mrs. Gould C. Dietz, Omaha, Nebr.

National oratorical contest finalists

Lunch—Mr. and Mrs. John D. Rockefeller, Jr.

Lt. Col. Joseph I. McMullen

Harry E. Barnard, Director of the White House Conference on Child Health and Protection

Washington Correspondents

Dinner—Ambassador Hugh Gibson

National Advisory Council on Radio in Education, radio introduction of Dr. Robert A. Millikan

May 23

Breakfast—Postmaster General Walter F. Brown, Assistant Postmasters General Warren I. Glover, John W. Philp, and Arch Coleman, Lawrence Richey, and Dr. Joel T. Boone

Rapidan Camp, Va.—Postmaster General and Mrs. Walter F. Brown, Assistant Postmasters General Warren I. Glover and John W. Philp, Assistant Postmaster General and Mrs. Arch Coleman, Assistant Postmaster General and Mrs. Frederic A. Tilton, Governor and Mrs. Theodore Roosevelt, Major General and Mrs. John A. Lejeune and Miss Lejeune, Professor and Mrs. William Starr Myers, Mr. and Mrs. Edsel Ford, Lawrence Richey, Theodore G. Joslin, and Dr. Joel T. Boone

Radio address in connection with the dedication of the War Memorial Hall at Cornell University, Ithaca, N.Y.

May 24

At Rapidan Camp, Va.

May 25

Returned from Rapidan Camp, Va.

Harvey C. Couch

Representative William I. Sirovich, New York

Fred B. Smith, chairman of the World Alliance for International Friendship

Representative Harold Knutson, Minnesota

Samuel H. Thompson, Federal Farm Board, and Mrs. Sewall

National Retail Dry Goods Association, convention delegates

Lunch—Edgar Rickard

Ernest I. Lewis, Interstate Commerce Commission

Dinner—Edgar Rickard

Raymond Benjamin, assistant chairman of the Republican National Committee

May 26

Breakfast—Mark Sullivan, journalist

Cabinet

White House Correspondents Association, committee

Lunch—Calvin W. Rice, Dexter S. Kimball, Conrad N. Lauer, and John V. W. Reynders

Dedication of the Titanic Memorial in Potomac Park

Silas H. Strawn and Julius Barnes, Chamber of Commerce of the United States

Dinner—Mrs. Alvin T. Hert

May 27

Breakfast—Senator Simeon D. Fess

Fred C. Croxton, President's Emergency Committee for Employment, and Rufus Jones, Mrs. Lewis, and Mr. Leeds

Representative William R. Wood, Indiana

Harry L. Bowlby, Lord's Day Alliance of the United States

British Ambassador, Sir Ronald Lindsay, to present Sir John Reith, director general of the British Broadcasting Corporation

Charles S. Barrett and R. G. Elbert

National spelling bee, finalists

Charlotte Davis, South Carolina

International tennis, exhibition game on White House lawn between American and Argentine teams

Lunch—John S. Fisher, former Governor of Pennsylvania

May 28

Breakfast—Mark Sullivan, journalist

Henry P. Fletcher, Chairman of the United States Tariff Commission

Lt. Col. Joseph I. McMullen

George H. Carnahan, president of Intercontinental Rubber Co.

H. S. Hicks, Mark Graves, and Henry Long, representatives of State Tax Commissions of Illinois, New York, and Massachusetts

George H. Bailey

Danish Minister, Otto Wadsted, and members of the Danish Brotherhood

Representative Harold Knutson, Minnesota

George W. Wickersham

Secretary of the Treasury Andrew W. Mellon

Senator William E. Borah

May 29

Senator Hiram Bingham

Cabinet

C. Frank Reavis, former Representative of Nebraska

Departed for Philadelphia

Dinner at the Union League Club in Philadelphia, remarks

May 30

Departed Philadelphia for Valley Forge

Memorial Day address, parade ground, Valley Forge Park

Returned to Washington, D.C.

Theodore G. Joslin, Secretary to the President

Dinner—Mr. and Mrs. Mark Sullivan, Dr. and Mrs. Vernon L. Kellogg, and Capt. and Mrs. Russell Train

June 1

Breakfast—Walter E. Hope, former Assistant Secretary of the Treasury

Fred C. Croxton, President's Emergency Committee for Employment

Anson C. Goodyear, New York manufacturer

Senator Otis F. Glenn

Chester H. Gray, Charles E. Hearst, C. R. White, and W. R. Ogg, Special Committee of the American Farm Bureau Federation

Theodore M. Schenck and mother, Brooklyn, N.Y.

Rotary International, group of officials

Lunch—Paul B. Williams, editor of the Utica Daily Press

Christian Gauss, dean of Princeton University

Department of Agriculture executives

Senator Otis F. Glenn

Dinner—Frank Knox, publisher of the Chicago Daily News

June 2

Breakfast—Frank Knox, publisher of the Chicago Daily News

Cabinet

Washington Correspondents

Lunch—Harley L. Clarke, president of Fox Film Corporation, Chicago

Frederic M. Sackett, United States Ambassador to Germany

June 3

Breakfast—Mark Sullivan, journalist, and Ambassador Charles G. Dawes

Senator James Couzens

R. W. Dunlap, Assistant Secretary of Agriculture, and father, Nelson J. Dunlap

Senator Pat Harrison and delegation from Mississippi and Georgia

765

Polish Minister Tytus Filipowicz, to present Peter Lot-Galusinski, assistant editor of Krakow Kurier

Reformed Church convention delegation

Boys Club Federation, officials

New York State George Washington Bicentennial Commission, members

Elizabeth Child

Mr. and Mrs. Oscar Berg

C. W. Warburton, Director of Extension Work, Department of Agriculture, and group of 4–H Club prize winners

Hooverville High School graduating class

Lunch—Ambassador Charles G. Dawes

June 4

William M. Chadbourne, New York

William S. Bennett, Edward Hines Lumber Co.

Representative Hamilton Fish, Jr.

Marie M. Meloney, New York Herald Tribune

Matilda Lindsay, National Women's Trade Union League of America

Representatives Riley J. Wilson and John H. Overton, Louisiana

Belgian Ambassador, Paul May, to present Professor Rehenir Gregoire, University of Brussels

British Ambassador, Sir Ronald Lindsay, to present Arthur Salter

James C. Stone, Chairman of the Federal Farm Board

J. Clawson Roop, Director of the Budget

June 5

Breakfast—Mr. and Mrs. Will H. Hays

Cabinet

Archbishop Aglipay, of the Independent Church of the Philippine Islands

James R. Garfield, Chairman of the Committee on the Conservation and Administration of the Public Domain

Lenna L. Yost, Republican National Committee

Washington Correspondents

Rapidan Camp, Va.—Ambassador Hugh Gibson, Assistant Secretary of the Navy Ernest Lee Jahncke, Adm. William V. Pratt, Theodore G. Joslin, and Dr. Joel T. Boone

June 6

At Rapidan Camp, Va.—Joining group already there were: Secretary of the Navy and Mrs. Charles F. Adams, Assistant Secretary of the Navy David S. Ingalls, Mrs. William V. Pratt, Maj. Gen. and Mrs. Benjamin H. Fuller, Rear Adm. and Mrs. Ridley McLean, Rear Adm. and Mrs. A. L. Parsons, Capt. and Mrs. Russell Train, Mr. and Mrs. Robert G. Simmons, Allan Hoover, Hugh Cumming, Richard Trent, and J. Clawson Roop

June 7

At Rapidan Camp, Va.

June 8

Returned from Rapidan Camp, Va.

Secretary of State Henry L. Stimson

British Ambassador, Sir Ronald Lindsay, to present J. F. Darling

Representative Louis Ludlow, Indiana

National safety competition in mining and quarrying, representatives of winning companies

Dinner—Charles D. Hilles

June 9

Breakfast—Mark Sullivan, journalist

Cabinet

Thomas McClintock, Denver, Colo.

Lunch—Louis Wiley, New York Times business manager

Eugene Meyer, Governor of the Federal Reserve Board

Dinner—Under Secretary of the Treasury and Mrs. Ogden L. Mills, Senator Dwight W. Morrow, and Mr. and Mrs. George H. Lorimer

June 10

Breakfast—Mr. and Mrs. George H. Lorimer

Ogden L. Mills, Under Secretary of the Treasury

Herbert D. Brown, Chief of the Bureau of Efficiency

Representative George P. Darrow, Pennsylvania

Osro Cobb, Little Rock, Ark.

Senator Simeon D. Fess

Representative Leonidas C. Dyer, Missouri

Martin H. Kennedy

John B. Chaffee

Jefferson Myers, United States Shipping Board

Lunch—Victor F. Ridder

Lawn party for veterans

Senator James J. Davis

Dinner—Secretary of War Patrick J. Hurley

June 11

Chinese Minister, Chao Chu Wu, to say goodbye

Edward N. Hurley, former Chairman of the Emergency Fleet Corporation

German Chargé d'Affaires, Rudolph Leitner, to present Emil Ludwig

Danish Minister, Otto Wadsted, to present Peter Freuchen

Dean and Mrs. Allen G. Flowers, Baylor University Law School

Walter Scott Pratt III and group of children from the Rhinehart School for the Deaf and Dumb of Montgomery County, Md.

Ben T. Epps, Jr.

Representative Arthur P. Lamneck and a group from the Reserve Officers Training Corps

Flagg Council of the United Commercial Travelers of America, convention delegates

Lunch—Willis H. Booth

J. Clawson Roop, Director of the Budget

Dinner—George Barr Baker, Gertrude B. Lane, and former Governor James P. Goodrich

June 12

Breakfast—former Governor James P. Goodrich and Gertrude B. Lane

John Barton Payne, Chairman of the American National Red Cross

Cabinet

Representative Addison T. Smith, Idaho

Samuel R. McKelvie, Federal Farm Board

Senator J. Hamilton Lewis

Lunch—Elbert L. Carpenter

John Foster Dulles

Young Republicans

Rapidan Camp, Va.—Mark Sullivan, Garet Garrett, Lawrence Richey, and Dr. Joel T. Boone

June 13

At Rapidan Camp, Va.—Additional guests: Mrs. Mark Sullivan and children, Mr. and Mrs. William Hard, Mr. and Mrs. Ashmun N. Brown, Janet Large, Mr. and Mrs. R. D. Mohun, Peggy Rickard, George Hoyt, and Maj. and Mrs. Earl C. Long

June 14

Left Rapidan Camp, Va. for Indianapolis, Ind.

June 15

Indiana Editorial Association dinner— address at Indianapolis

June 16

Dedication of Harding Memorial at Marion, Ohio, address

Grand Army of the Republic parade at Columbus, Ohio, remarks

June 17

Dedication of the remodeled Lincoln Tomb, Springfield, Ill., address

June 18

Returned from trip to Indiana, Ohio, and Illinois

Dinner—Representative and Mrs. John Q. Tilson

Eugene Meyer, Governor of the Federal Reserve Board

June 19

Breakfast—Senator David A. Reed and Representative and Mrs. John Q. Tilson

Senator Thomas J. Walsh

Senator Hiram Bingham

Senator Carter Glass

Cabinet

Mary Berry Hocker, founder of the Daughters of the American Constitution

Martha McClure, Iowa Republican national committeewoman

Lenna L. Yost and Mrs. Barnett E. Marks, Republican National Committee

Lewis Wood and South Carolina Press Association

Ogden L. Mills, Under Secretary of the Treasury; Julius Klein, Assistant Secretary of Commerce; and Representative Isaac Bacharach

Washington Correspondents

J. Clawson Roop, Director of the Budget

Boy Scouts from Pennsylvania, Maryland, Delaware, and Virginia

Dinner—Charles K. Field

Ogden L. Mills, Under Secretary of the Treasury

June 20

Breakfast—Mark Sullivan, journalist

Senator Henry F. Ashurst

Senator David I. Walsh

Senator Duncan U. Fletcher

Senator James F. Byrnes

Secretary of Commerce Robert P. Lamont

Ogden L. Mills, Under Secretary of the Treasury

Lunch—Arthur Brisbane, editor of the Chicago Herald and Examiner

Secretary of State Henry L. Stimson

Dinner—Charles K. Field

Rapidan Camp, Va.—Under Secretary of the Treasury Ogden L. Mills, Senator Reed Smoot, Charles K. Field, Mark Sullivan, George L. Harrison, Dr. and Mrs. Vernon L. Kellogg, Mr. and Mrs. Theodore G. Joslin and sons, Dr. and Mrs. Joel T. Boone, Lawrence Richey, and Walter Newton

June 21

At Rapidan Camp, Va.

June 22

Returned from Rapidan Camp, Va.

Secretary of State Henry L. Stimson

John Hammill, former Governor of Iowa

Mrs. R. D. Matthews and son

Argentine Ambassador, Manuel E. Malbran, who is leaving to become Argentine Ambassador to England

Mrs. Mark Sullivan

Ferry K. Heath, Assistant Secretary of the Treasury, and Maxine Weaver, Michigan Cherry Queen

Lunch—Walter H. Newton and Frederick E. Murphy

Henry P. Fletcher, Chairman of the United States Tariff Commission

Ogden L. Mills, Under Secretary of the Treasury

Raymond Benjamin, assistant chairman of the Republican National Committee

June 23

Senator Reed Smoot

Cabinet

C. C. Young, former Governor of California, and daughter

Senator Pat Harrison

National 4-H Club convention delegates

Lunch—Winthrop W. Aldrich

Canadian Minister, William Duncan Herridge, to present letters of credence

Frank T. Hines, Administrator of Veterans' Affairs

Secretary of War Patrick J. Hurley

Eugene Meyer and Adolph C. Miller, Federal Reserve Board of Governors

June 24

Breakfast—Mark Sullivan, journalist

Representative William R. Wood

Howard E. Coffin and Charles S. Barrett

Ralph Budd, president of the Great Northern Railroad

Representative J. Will Taylor, Tennessee

Joseph S. Cullinan, Houston, Tex.

W. J. McCabe, Duluth, Minn.

Francis A. Adams, New York

John E. Edgerton, president of the National Association of Manufacturers, and H. L. Derby, president of Kalbfleisch Corporation

Secretary of State Henry L. Stimson and Acting Secretary of the Treasury Ogden L. Mills

Francis B. Loomis, San Francisco, Calif.

Neca Jones, Oberton, Nev., representing 4-H Clubs of Nevada

Lunch—Franklin W. Fort, former Representative of New Jersey

E. T. Clark

Earle S. Kinsley, Vermont Republican national committeeman

June 25

Breakfast—James F. Burke and Joseph R. Nutt, Republican National Committee

Secretary of State Henry L. Stimson and Acting Secretary of the Treasury Ogden L. Mills

Senator Pat Harrison

Daniel A. Poling, president of the World's Christian Endeavor Union

Samuel McClintock Hamill, American Child Health Association

Representative August H. Andresen, Minnesota

Representative Albert Johnson, Washington

Mrs. J. C. Griswold, Texas Republican national committeewoman

Chilean Ambassador, Carlos G. Davila, to present Senator Rafael Lewis Barahona of Chile

J. Clawson Roop, Director of the Budget

Dinner—Attorney General and Mrs. William D. Mitchell and Secretary of Commerce Robert P. Lamont

June 26

Theodore Roosevelt, Governor of Porto Rico

James C. Stone, Chairman of the Federal Farm Board

Secretary of State Henry L. Stimson and Acting Secretary of the Treasury Ogden L. Mills

Cabinet

1931

Nathan Adams, Dallas, Tex., and S. A. Grieberson, director of the American Petroleum Institute

Silas H. Strawn and Julius Barnes, Chamber of Commerce of the United States

Lunch—Secretary of State Henry L. Stimson

Dominican Republic Minister, Roberto Despradel, to present letters of credence

Dinner—William R. Castle, Jr., Under Secretary of State

June 27

Breakfast—Mark Sullivan, journalist

Rapidan Camp, Va.—George W. Wickersham, Mr. and Mrs. Bruce Barton, Mr. and Mrs. Newbold Noyes, Mr. and Mrs. Edgar Rickard, Dr. and Mrs. Vernon L. Kellogg, Lawrence Richey, and Dr. Joel T. Boone

June 28

At Rapidan Camp, Va.

June 29

Returned from Rapidan Camp, Va.

William R. Castle, Jr., Under Secretary of State

Senator Reed Smoot

Senator Millard E. Tydings

Fred C. Croxton, member of the President's Emergency Committee for Employment

Marie M. Meloney, New York Herald Tribune

Martha McClure, Iowa Republican national committeewoman

Curtis D. Wilbur, former Secretary of the Navy

Secretary of Labor William N. Doak

Kappa Delta Sorority, delegates

Phi Delta Fraternity, delegates

Lunch—Under Secretary of State William R. Castle, Jr., Under Secretary of the Treasury Ogden L. Mills, and Senator Dwight W. Morrow

James S. Stone, Chairman of the Federal Farm Board, and George S. Milnor, president of the Chicago Grain Stabilization Corporation

Dinner—Alanson B. Houghton, former Ambassador to Great Britain

June 30

William R. Castle, Jr., Under Secretary of State, and Ogden L. Mills, Under Secretary of the Treasury

Cabinet

Spanish Ambassador, Salvador de Madariaga, to present letters of credence

Ogden L. Mills, Under Secretary of the Treasury

Charles D. Hilles

William R. Castle, Jr., Under Secretary of State, and Ogden L. Mills, Under Secretary of the Treasury

July 1

Breakfast—Mark Sullivan, journalist, and Senator Dwight W. Morrow

771

William R. Castle, Jr., Under Secretary
of State
Kenneth Mackintosh
Ralph Metcalf, Tacoma, Wash.
Mary J. Elenbaum, Cavalier, N. Dak.
William Walt, Dalmatia, Pa.
Delta Sigma Fraternity, delegates
Lunch—Edwin C. Jameson
Dinner—Judge and Mrs. Warren
Olney, Jr., and Senator Dwight W.
Morrow
Capt. and Mrs. Russell Train

July 2

Breakfast—Senator Dwight W. Morrow
William R. Castle, Jr., Under Secretary
of State, and Ogden L. Mills, Under
Secretary of the Treasury
Senator Hiram Bingham
Mrs. J. C. Griswold, Texas Republican
national committeewoman
William R. Castle, Jr., Under Secretary
of State; Ogden L. Mills, Under Sec-
retary of the Treasury; Eugene
Meyer, Governor of the Federal Re-
serve Board; and Secretary of Com-
merce Robert P. Lamont
Lunch—Alonzo E. Taylor, Under Sec-
retary of State William R. Castle, Jr.,
and Under Secretary of the Treasury
Ogden L. Mills
J. Clawson Roop, Director of the
Budget
William R. Castle, Jr., Under Secretary
of State, and Ogden L. Mills, Under
Secretary of the Treasury

Dinner—Senator Dwight W. Morrow
and William L. Ward

July 3

Breakfast—Mark Sullivan, journalist
William R. Castle, Jr., Under Secretary
of State; Ogden L. Mills, Under Sec-
retary of the Treasury; and Eugene
Meyer
Cabinet
Washington Correspondents
Dinner—Under Secretary of State Wil-
liam R. Castle, Jr., Under Secretary
of the Treasury Ogden L. Mills,
George L. Harrison, Mark Sullivan,
and Lawrence Richey

July 4

Breakfast—Dr. Joel T. Boone
Rapidan Camp, Va.—Attorney Gener-
al and Mrs. William D. Mitchell,
Senator and Mrs. David Reed, Mr.
and Mrs. Lewis L. Strauss, Mr. and
Mrs. Mark Sullivan and Narcissus
Sullivan, Mr. and Mrs. George Cole
Scott and George Scott, Evelyn W.
Allen, Lawrence Richey, Dr. Joel T.
Boone, and Mr. and Mrs. Frank Kent

July 5

Returned from Rapidan Camp, Va.
William R. Castle, Jr., Under Secretary
of State; Ogden L. Mills, Under Secretary of the Treasury; and Edward
S. Beck

Dinner—Mr. and Mrs. Lewis L. Strauss
and Lawrence Richey
Mark Sullivan, journalist

July 6

Breakfast—Mark Sullivan, journalist
William R. Castle, Jr., Under Secretary
of State
Lt. Col. Joseph I. McMullen
William R. Castle, Jr., Under Secretary
of State, and Ogden L. Mills, Under
Secretary of the Treasury
Mr. and Mrs. Hugh R. Pomeroy, Los
Angeles, Calif.
Jacob A. O. Preus, former Governor of
Minnesota
William R. Castle, Jr., Under Secretary
of State, and Ogden L. Mills, Under
Secretary of the Treasury
Wiley Post and Harold Gatty, around-
the-world fliers
Modern Woodmen of America, group
Lunch—Wiley Post and Harold Gatty
William R. Castle, Jr., Under Secretary
of State, Ogden L. Mills, Under Sec-
retary of the Treasury, and Senator
David A. Reed
Dinner—Secretary of War Patrick J.
Hurley and Mrs. Sidney Cloman

July 7

William R. Castle, Jr., Under Secretary
of State
Cabinet
Washington Correspondents

Ogden L. Mills, Under Secretary of the
Treasury
Mr. White of Arkansas
Mr. Peterbaugh
William R. Castle, Jr., Under Secretary
of State; Hanford MacNider, United
States Minister to Canada; and Wil-
liam D. Herridge, Canadian Minis-
ter
James H. McGraw, Jr., and Malcolm
Muir
Representative C. Murray Turpin and
group of bankers
Argentine Ambassador, Felipe A. Espil,
to present letters of credence
Attended baseball game between Phil-
adelphia and Washington
Dinner—Vice President Charles Cur-
tis, Mrs. Edward E. Gann, Secretary
of the Navy Charles F. Adams, Sur-
geon General and Mrs. Hugh S.
Cumming, and Mr. and Mrs. George
A. Hastings

July 8

Breakfast—Mark Sullivan, journalist
John Barton Payne, Chairman of the
American National Red Cross
Ogden L. Mills, Under Secretary of the
Treasury
William R. Castle, Jr., Under Secretary
of State
Secretary of Commerce Robert P. La-
mont
Henry P. Fletcher, Chairman of the
United States Tariff Commission, and
Walter H. Newton

773

Irving Fisher, Yale University economist

Secretary of War Patrick J. Hurley

British Ambassador, Sir Ronald Lindsay, to present Maynard Keynes

Mr. and Mrs. Thompson and Miss Mitchell

Boys and girls participating in tests relating to sound films in public school instruction

Winners of model airplane contest

French Ambassador Paul Claudel and Under Secretary of State William R. Castle, Jr.

John Spargo

Eugene Meyer, Governor of the Federal Reserve Board

Carl Williams and Stanley F. Reed, Federal Farm Board

James L. Wright, Buffalo Evening News

Dinner—Secretary of Labor William N. Doak and Senator Arthur Capper

Mr. and Mrs. Walter H. Newton

July 9

Breakfast—George Cole Scott, Jr., and Dr. Joel T. Boone

Henry J. Allen, former Senator of Kansas

Charles F. Scott

Henry Rushton Fairclough, Stanford University, Calif.

James T. Williams, Jr., Hearst Publications

Representative J. Will Taylor, Tennessee

Secretary of War Patrick J. Hurley and Maj. Gen. Robert U. Patterson, Surgeon General of the Army

Edward N. Hurley, former chairman of the Emergency Fleet Corporation

National Convention of Baptist Young People's Union, delegates

Lunch—Michael Gallagher and George Fulmer Getz

Frank T. Hines, Administrator of Veterans' Affairs

J. Clawson Roop, Director of the Budget

Richard V. Oulahan, New York Times

Dinner—Henry J. Allen and Henry Rushton Fairclough

July 10

Breakfast—Mark Sullivan, journalist

Michael Gallagher

Martin Egan, J. P. Morgan & Co.

Cabinet

J. W. T. Duvel, Agriculture Department

Representative Charles A. Eaton, New Jersey

Representative Harry P. Beam, Illinois

Dr. and Mrs. Joseph Martin Dawson, Waco, Tex.

Charles Drew and party

Anthony Czarnecki, Chicago, Ill.

Henry J. Allen, former Senator of Kansas

Washington Correspondents

Rapidan Camp, Va.—Secretary of Commerce and Mrs. Robert P. Lamont, Lawrence Richey, and Dr. Joel T. Boone

Appendix E

1931

July 11

At Rapidan Camp, Va.—other weekend guests: Vice President Charles Curtis, Mr. and Mrs. Edward T. Gann, Under Secretary of State and Mrs. William R. Castle, Jr., Assistant Attorney General and Mrs. Seth W. Richardson, Assistant Secretary of Commerce Julius Klein, Allan Fox, Mr. and Mrs. Thomas Healy, and Mr. and Mrs. Robert H. Angell

July 12

At Rapidan Camp, Va.

July 13

Returned from Rapidan Camp, Va.

William R. Castle, Jr., Under Secretary of State, and Ogden L. Mills, Under Secretary of the Treasury

Lunch—George W. Truett and Walter H. Newton

Secretary of War Patrick J. Hurley and Gen. Douglas MacArthur

William R. Castle, Jr., Under Secretary of State

Dinner—Ernest I. Lewis, Interstate Commerce Commission

July 14

Breakfast—Mark Sullivan, journalist

Senator Royal S. Copeland

Frank H. Hitchcock, Tucson, Ariz.

William R. Castle, Jr., Under Secretary of State, and Ogden L. Mills, Under Secretary of the Treasury

Cabinet

Washington Correspondents

Representative William E. Evans, California

Mrs. Gilgan and Mrs. Warren, Idaho

Mr. Robinson, Mitchell, S. Dak.

Mr. and Mrs. Joe Werner and Mr. and Mrs. E. K. Spencer

Secretary of Commerce Robert P. Lamont

Lt. Col. Joseph I. McMullen

Eugene Meyer, Governor of the Federal Reserve Board

Ogden L. Mills, Under Secretary of the Treasury, and J. Clawson Roop, Director of the Budget

Carl William, Federal Farm Board

William R. Castle, Jr., Under Secretary of State

Dinner—Adolph C. Miller, Federal Reserve Board

William Hard

July 15

Breakfast—Mark Sullivan, journalist

Secretary of Commerce Robert P. Lamont

William R. Castle, Jr., Under Secretary of State, and Ogden L. Mills, Under Secretary of the Treasury

Secretary of Labor William N. Doak

John R. Alpine, Employment Service, Department of Labor

Rev. and Mrs. G. A. Papperman

Michael Gallagher

William R. Castle, Jr., Under Secretary of State

William R. Castle, Jr., Under Secretary of State, and Harvey H. Bundy, Assistant Secretary of State

Dinner—Secretary of Commerce and Mrs. Robert P. Lamont, and T. W. Lamont

July 16

William R. Castle, Jr., Under Secretary of State, and Ogden L. Mills, Under Secretary of the Treasury

Shepherd Morgan, New York

Senator James E. Watson and William F. McDowell, bishop of the Methodist Episcopal Church of Washington, D.C.

Arthur R. Thompson and W. J. Howey, St. Petersburg, Fla.

Lunch—Under Secretary of State William R. Castle, Jr., and Under Secretary of the Treasury Ogden L. Mills

International Christian Endeavor Union, 50th anniversary meeting in San Francisco, Calif., radio address

Frank T. Hines, Administrator of Veterans' Affairs

Herbert Bodman, president of the New York Produce Exchange and Walter S. Case, Pomeroy and Co. of New York

William R. Castle, Jr., Under Secretary of State, and Ogden L. Mills, Under Secretary of the Treasury

J. Clawson Roop, Director of the Budget

Dinner—Myron C. Taylor, U.S. Steel Corporation

July 17

Breakfast—Mark Sullivan, journalist

William R. Castle, Jr., Under Secretary of State, and Ogden L. Mills, Under Secretary of the Treasury

Henry P. Fletcher, Chairman of the United States Tariff Commission

Cabinet

Lunch—Ogden L. Mills, Under Secretary of the Treasury

James R. Garfield, Chairman of the Commission on the Conservation and Administration of the Public Domain

Dinner—C. Bascom Slemp

July 18

Eugene Meyer, Governor of the Federal Reserve Board

Ogden I. Mills, Under Secretary of the Treasury

Roy Vernon

W. G. Skelly, Tulsa, Okla., president of the Skelly Oil Co.

William R. Castle, Jr., Under Secretary of State, and Ogden L. Mills, Under Secretary of the Treasury

Lunch—Eugene Meyer and Mr. and Mrs. Henry P. Fletcher

Rapidan Camp, Va.—Mr. and Mrs. Eugene Meyer, Mr. and Mrs. Henry P. Fletcher, Mr. and Mrs. Jeremiah Milbank, Senator and Mrs. Otis F. Glenn, Theodore C. Wallen, Theodore G. Joslin, and Dr. Joel T. Boone

July 19

At Rapidan Camp, Va.

July 20

Returned from Rapidan Camp, Va.

William R. Castle, Jr., Under Secretary of State

Senator Dwight W. Morrow, Ambassador to Great Britain Charles G. Dawes, and Under Secretary of State William R. Castle, Jr.

E. T. Clark, vice president of Drugs, Inc.

John R. Mott, president of the World's Alliance of the Y.M.C.A.

Ogden L. Mills, Under Secretary of the Treasury

Citizen's Military Training Corps from Fort Washington, Md. and Fort Myer, Va.

Lunch—Ogden L. Mills, Under Secretary of the Treasury

Ogden L. Mills, Under Secretary of the Treasury

Senator James E. Watson, Senate majority leader

Dinner—Senator Dwight W. Morrow, Ambassador Charles G. Dawes, and Under Secretary of State William R. Castle, Jr.

Charles F. Scott

Samuel H. Thompson, Federal Farm Board

July 21

Breakfast—Mark Sullivan, journalist

William N. Reynolds, Winston-Salem, N.C.

Senator Dwight W. Morrow, Ambassador to Great Britain Charles G. Dawes, Under Secretary of State William R. Castle, Jr., and Under Secretary of the Treasury Ogden L. Mills

Cabinet

A. A. Moody

Representative Samuel A. Kendall

Senator Dwight W. Morrow, Ambassador Charles G. Dawes, and Under Secretary of the Treasury Ogden L. Mills

William R. Castle, Jr., Under Secretary of State, and Eugene Meyer, Governor of the Federal Reserve Board

July 22

Roy A. Roberts, Kansas City, Mo.

Ogden L. Mills, Under Secretary of the Treasury

Secretary of War Patrick J. Hurley

Senator Dwight W. Morrow and Under Secretary of the Treasury Ogden L. Mills

David E. Kaufman, United States Minister to Siam

Curtis N. Terry, Louisville, Ky.

Representative John W. Boehne, Jr., Indiana

R. S. Pickens

Secretary of Commerce Robert P. Lamont

Senator Dwight W. Morrow and Under Secretary of the Treasury Ogden L. Mills

Eugene Meyer, Governor of the Federal Reserve Board

William R. Castle, Jr., Under Secretary of State

July 23

Breakfast—Mark Sullivan, journalist

William R. Castle, Jr., Under Secretary of State, and Ogden L. Mills, Under Secretary of the Treasury

Ernest Lee Jahncke, Assistant Secretary of the Navy

Frederic William Wile, broadcast journalist

Representative Edgar Howard, Nebraska

William M. Chadbourne, New York

Representative Frederick M. Davenport, New York

Mr. and Mrs. George B. Nichols, Buffalo, N.Y.

Representative Allen T. Treadway, Massachusetts

National Aeronautic Association, convention delegates

Indiana schoolteachers, group

South Carolina schoolteachers, group

Lunch—Representatives Allen T. Treadway and Frederick M. Davenport

Julius Klein, Assistant Secretary of Commerce

Secretary of War Patrick J. Hurley

William R. Castle, Jr., Under Secretary of State

Ernest Lee Jahncke, Assistant Secretary of the Navy

July 24

Breakfast—Mark Sullivan, journalist

Roy A. Roberts, Kansas City, Mo.

Representative Sol Bloom, New York

George G. Allen, New York

Senator James E. Watson, Senate majority leader

Cabinet

Ernest Lee Jahncke, Assistant Secretary of the Navy

Dorothy Thompson

Dr. Blake, California

Lunch—Senator Arthur H. Vandenburg, Mark Sullivan, Theodore G. Joslin, and Dr. Joel T. Boone

Rapidan Camp, Va.—Senator Arthur H. Vandenberg, Mark Sullivan, Mr. and Mrs. Byron Price, former Senator and Mrs. David Baird, Jr., Henry M. Robinson, Mr. and Mrs. Theodore G. Joslin, and Dr. Joel T. Boone

July 25–27

At Rapidan Camp, Va.

July 28

Returned from Rapidan Camp. Va.

Cabinet

Laurence M. Benedict, Los Angeles Times

Eugene Meyer, Governor of the Federal Reserve Board, and Ogden L. Mills, Under Secretary of the Treasury

Representative Archie D. Sanders, New York

National intelligence contest, prize winners

Senator George H. Moses

William R. Castle, Jr., Under Secretary of State, and Ogden L. Mills, Under Secretary of the Treasury

1931

Fred C. Croxton, President's Emergency Committee for Employment

Dinner—Raymond Robins

July 29

Breakfast—Edgar Rickard

Secretary of War Patrick J. Hurley

John Barton Payne, Chairman of the American National Red Cross

Representative Royal C. Johnson, South Dakota

Representative Frederick R. Lehlbach

Henry B. Rust, Pittsburgh, Pa.

Samuel W. McNabb, United States District Attorney for Southern District of California

Representative Sol Bloom and George M. Cohan, song writer

Edgar S. Vaught, Oklahoma City, Okla.

Mrs. Lamar Jeffers and friends

Miss Lineberger and Miss Thayer

Edgar W. McCormack

Lunch—Edgar Rickard

Honduran Minister, Celeo Davila, to present letters of credence

Julius Klein, Assistant Secretary of Commerce

William R. Castle, Jr., Under Secretary of State, and Ogden L. Mills, Under Secretary of the Treasury

Edwin B. Kimball

Secretary of Labor William N. Doak

Dinner—Secretary of the Navy Charles F. Adams, Adm. and Mrs. David F. Sellers, Mr. and Mrs. Wallace M. Alexander, and Edgar Rickard

July 30

Breakfast—Edgar Rickard

Secretary of War Patrick J. Hurley and Manuel Quezon, president of the Philippine Senate

George A. Allen, New York

James G. McDonald, chairman of the board of the Foreign Policy Association, Inc.

Senator Porter H. Dale and Representative Ernest W. Gilson

Thomas C. Angerstein, Chicago, Ill.

Beatrice Creamery Co., plant managers

President of the Great Western Sugar Co.

Lunch—Edgar Rickard

Secretary of War Patrick J. Hurley

Ogden L. Mills, Under Secretary of the Treasury

William R. Castle, Jr., Under Secretary of State

Raymond Benjamin, assistant chairman of the Republican National Committee

July 31

Representative James S. Parker, New York

Cabinet

William S. Moscrip, Lake Elmo, Minn.

Mr. Gustafson

W. R. Linch and family, Lincoln, Nebr.

Richard V. Oulahan, New York Times

Lunch—Representative James S. Parker, New York

Rapidan Camp, Va.—Representative James S. Parker, Lawrence Richey, and Dr. Joel T. Boone

779

Appendix E

1931

August 1

Rapidan Camp, Va.—Other guests: Secretary of Labor and Mrs. William N. Doak, Representative and Mrs. Arthur M. Free, Mr. and Mrs. Will Irwin, Mr. and Mrs. Ellis A. Yost, Thomas E. Campbell, Jay G. Hayden

August 2

At Rapidan Camp, Va.

August 3

Returned from Rapidan Camp, Va.
William R. Castle, Jr., Under Secretary of State
Lunch—Will Irwin
Ferry K. Heath, Assistant Secretary of the Treasury
Dinner—Frederick H. Payne, Assistant Secretary of War

August 4

Breakfast—Mark Sullivan, journalist
Joseph R. Nutt, treasurer of the Republican National Committee
Cabinet
Washington Correspondents
Swiss Chargé d'Affaires, Etienne Lardy, to present Alfred Plinckiger
Argentine Ambassador, Felipe A. Espil, to present Lt. Col. Francisco Lajous and officers of the Argentine Training Ship *Presidente Sarmiento*
John Hammill, former Governor of Iowa
George deB. Keim, secretary of the Republican National Committee

Lunch—George W. Hill, president of the American Tobacco Co.
Joseph R. Nutt, treasurer of the Republican National Committee
Henry M. Robinson, Los Angeles banker
Fred C. Croxton, Rufus Jones, Lucy B. Lewis, Clarence E. Pickett, and Henry T. Brown
Dinner—Henry M. Robinson, Los Angeles banker

August 5

Breakfast—Mark Sullivan, journalist
Felix Cordova Davila, Resident Commissioner from Porto Rico
Frederick H. Payne, Assistant Secretary of War, and Theodore Swann of Birmingham
Secretary of Labor William N. Doak and C. L. Richardson
Representative Emanuel Celler, New York
Representative Arthur M. Free
Counselor of the Brazilian Embassy, Paulo Coelho de Almeida, to present Austregesilo de Athayde
Edward McE. Lewis and Tell W. Nicolet, American Legion
Order of the Sons of Italy, delegation
Lunch—Victor Heintz, former Representative of Ohio
William M. Steuart, Director of the Census
Lt. Col. Joseph I. McMullen
Fred C. Croxton, Allen J. Burns, Henry Sharke, Linton B. Smith, and William J. Ellis

780

Dinner—Under Secretary of the Treasury Ogden L. Mills, Governor of the Federal Reserve Board Eugene Meyer, and Walter Stewart

August 6

Breakfast—Walter S. Gifford, president of the American Telephone and Telegraph Co.

Representative George P. Darrow, Pennsylvania

C. W. Warburton, Department of Agriculture

William F. Schilling, Federal Farm Board

Representatives J. Will Taylor and Oscar B. Lovette, Tennessee

Representative Edith Nourse Rogers

William R. Castle, Jr., Under Secretary of State

C. E. Driver, Chicago, Ill.

Counsellor of the British Embassy, D. G. Osbourne, to present A. J. Cummings

Boy Scout Troop of Clearfield, Pa.

John B. Hollister, Cincinnati, and Cooper Pogue, chairman of the Ohio Republican Campaign Committee

Secretary of Labor William N. Doak and Robert McBirnie, mayor of Boone, Iowa

Lunch—Mr. and Mrs. Harvey C. Couch and family

Ogden L. Mills, Under Secretary of the Treasury, and H. Paul Bestor, Federal Farm Loan Bureau

Silas H. Strawn and Julius Barnes, Chamber of Commerce of the United States

J. Clawson Roop, Director of the Budget

Ernest Lee Jahncke, Assistant Secretary of the Navy

Raymond Benjamin, assistant chairman of the Republican National Committee

Dinner—William M. Butler, former Senator of Massachusetts

August 7

Franklin W. Fort, former Representative of New Jersey

Cabinet

Uruguayan Minister, Jacobo Varela

Boy Scouts, delegation from Alexandria, Va.

Mr. and Mrs. Robert Littler, California

Lunch—Frank Crowell

William R. Castle, Jr., Under Secretary of State

Washington Correspondents

Rapidan Camp, Va.—Henry M. Robinson, Mark Sullivan, Senator and Mrs. Felix Hebert, Mr. and Mrs. Edward T. Clark, Mr. and Mrs. Charles S. Groves, Mr. and Mrs. Paul Wooten, Mr. and Mrs. Lamont Rowlands, and Dr. Joel T. Boone

August 8

At Rapidan Camp, Va.

Radio address to World's Conference of Young Men's Christian Associations, meeting in Cleveland, Ohio

781

August 9

At Rapidan Camp, Va.

August 10

Returned from Rapidan Camp, Va.

Lt. Col. Joseph I. McMullen

Frederick H. Payne, Acting Secretary of War

William R. Castle, Jr., Under Secretary of State

Frank Shutts, Miami, Fla.

Senator Simeon D. Fess, Ohio

Lunch—Senator Simeon D. Fess

Roy Roberts, managing editor of the Kansas City Star

William M. Steuart, Director of the Census

Frank T. Hines, Administrator of Veterans' Affairs

Col. Campbell B. Hodges, Military Aide to the President

Secretary of Labor William N. Doak and Thomas Leary

Ogden L. Mills, Under Secretary of the Treasury, and George L. Harrison

August 11

Carl Williams, Federal Farm Board

Cabinet

Alvin Moody, Texas

William P. MacCracken, Jr., secretary of the American Bar Association

Seth W. Richardson, Assistant Attorney General

Young Men's Christian Association, delegates from the World's Conference

William D. B. Ainey

Lunch—Leslie Reed, Richmond, Va.

Abraham C. Ratchesky, United States Minister to Czechoslovakia

Fred C. Croxton, Chairman of the President's Emergency Committee for Employment

August 12

Breakfast—Walter S. Gifford, president of the American Telephone and Telegraph Co.

Mr. Hill, Binghamton, N.Y.

Roy Vernon

Lamont Rowlands

E. E. Hunt, Secretary of the President's Committee on Recent Economic Changes

Lenna L. Yost, Republican National Committee

Mr. and Mrs. Victor Sandel, St. Cloud, Minn.

Allen T. Burns, executive director of the Association of Community Chests and Councils

William R. Castle, Jr., Under Secretary of State

Alan C. Collins, editor of World's Work

Ray Clapper, United Press Associations

Eugene Meyer, Governor of the Federal Reserve Board

Dinner—Ferry K. Heath, Assistant Secretary of the Treasury

August 13

Fred C. Croxton, Chairman of the President's Emergency Committee for Employment

David Hinshaw

Alfred P. Thom, general counsel of the Association of Railway Executives

Walter F. Dexter, president of Whittier College

Palmer E. Pierce, Philip P. Campbell, and committee representing the National Foreign Trade Council

Richard H. Waldo, McClure Newspaper Syndicate

Robert H. Angell, Virginia

John B. Chapple, managing editor of the Ashland (Wis.) Daily News

Roy St. Lewis, Assistant Attorney General

William R. Castle, Jr., Under Secretary of State

Robert S. Pickens

William F. Ogburn, President's Research Committee on Social Trends

Hugh S. Cumming, Surgeon General of the Public Health Service

August 14

Joseph M. Dixon, Assistant Secretary of the Interior

Cabinet

Senator L. J. Dickinson

John H. Sherburne and Paul Howland

David Hinshaw and Walter L. Hopkins

German Chargé d'Affaires, Rudolf Leitner, to present Bishop Ernst Stoltenhoff

Egyptian Minister, Sesostris Sidarous Pasha, to present letters of credence

Maurice Leon, New York

Dinner—Ira E. Bennett, editor of the Washington Post

August 15

Breakfast—Mr. and Mrs. Charles D. Hilles and Mr. and Mrs. Wilbur Forrest

Rapidan Camp, Va.—Mr. and Mrs. Wilbur Forrest, Frederick H. Payne, Gen. Douglas MacArthur, Mr. and Mrs. Charles D. Hilles, Theodore G. Joslin, and Dr. Joel T. Boone

August 16

At Rapidan Camp, Va.—arriving with Mrs. Hoover were Surgeon General and Mrs. Hugh S. Cumming

August 17

Returned from Rapidan Camp, Va.

Fred C. Croxton, Chairman of the President's Emergency Committee for Employment

Lunch—Henry M. Robinson, Los Angeles banker

Representative Frank H. Foss, Massachusetts

Frank T. Hines, Administrator of Veterans' Affairs

William R. Castle, Jr., Under Secretary of State

Mr. Butcher

Raymond Benjamin, assistant chairman of the Republican National Committee

Mark Sullivan, journalist

August 18

Breakfast—Mark Sullivan, journalist
Representative Sol Bloom
Fred C. Croxton, President's Emergency Committee for Employment, and Mr. Barrett
Adolph C. Miller, Federal Reserve Board of Governors
Cabinet
Representative Allen T. Treadway
Paul S. Clapp, managing director of the National Electric Light Association
Arthur R. Gould, former Senator of Maine
George E. McKinnis, Oklahoma
Anton Koerber
Hugh S. Cumming, Surgeon General of the Public Health Service
Arthur A. Ballantine, Assistant Secretary of the Treasury
Secretary of Agriculture Arthur M. Hyde
Silas H. Strawn, president of the Chamber of Commerce of the United States
Dinner—Mr. and Mrs. Adolph C. Miller

August 19

Breakfast—Mark Sullivan, journalist
Mr. Hooper, Mr. Wilson, and Mr. Hoeck
Representative Albert H. Vestal, Indiana

T. C. Davis of New York and Mr. Parker
Representative Howard W. Smith, Virginia
Argentine Ambassador, Felipe A. Epsil
T. V. O'Connor, Chairman of the United States Shipping Board
Walter S. Hallanan, West Virginia Republican national committeeman
Lunch—Mrs. Arthur Livermore
Eugene Meyer, Governor of the Federal Reserve Board
William C. Redfield, former Secretary of Commerce
Capt. F. M. Williams and American Polar Expedition committee
Frank T. Hines, Administrator of Veterans' Affairs
Mr. Scott
Secretary of Agriculture Arthur M. Hyde
Silas H. Strawn, president of the Chamber of Commerce of the United States

August 20

Breakfast—Mark Sullivan, journalist
Capt. Russell Train
Fred C. Croxton, Chairman of the President's Emergency Committee for Employment
Ira E. Bennett, editor of the Washington Post
Kermit Roosevelt, vice president of the International Mercantile Marine
Thomas E. Campbell, President of the Civil Service Commission

1931

Bryce M. Stewart, member of the President's Emergency Committee for Employment

Edgar C. Snyder and committee on Public Relations of the District of Columbia Bicentennial Commission

William R. Castle, Jr., Under Secretary of State

William R. Castle, Jr., Under Secretary of State

Theodore Wallen, correspondent

J. Clawson Roop, Director of the Budget

Julius Barnes, chairman of the board of the Chamber of Commerce of the United States

August 21

Breakfast—Mark Sullivan, journalist

Cabinet

Lunch—Henry M. Robinson, Los Angeles banker

Maj. Gen. Lytle Brown, Chief of Engineers of the Army

National Beet Growers Association, committee

Washington Correspondents

Dinner—Senator and Mrs. James E. Watson and Henry M. Robinson

August 22

C. Bascom Slemp

Mr. Polson, Washington

Walter S. Gifford, Director of the President's Organization on Unemployment Relief

Rapidan Camp, Va.—Secretary of Agriculture Arthur M. Hyde, Senator John G. Townsend, Jr., and Miss Townsend, Representative William R. Wood, Assistant Secretary of State and Mrs. James G. Rogers, Walter S. Gifford, Mr. and Mrs. Fred C. Croxton, Mr. and Mrs. A. H. Kirchhofer, Mr. and Mrs. Charles M. Morrison, Henry M. Robinson, Mildred Hall, Theodore G. Joslin, and Dr. Joel T. Boone

August 23

At Rapidan Camp, Va.

August 24

Returned from Rapidan Camp, Va.

William R. Castle, Jr., Under Secretary of State

Mr. Scott

J. Russell Young, Washington Star

Edward A. O'Neal, president of the American Farm Bureau Federation

Harry A. Wheeler, Chicago, Ill.

German Ambassador, Friedrich von Prittwitz

Wallace Townsend, Arkansas Republican national committeeman

William R. Castle, Jr., Under Secretary of State

Dinner—Mr. and Mrs. George Horace Lorimer

August 25

Breakfast—Mr. and Mrs. George Horace Lorimer

1931

Cabinet

Washington Correspondents

John H. Edwards, Assistant Secretary of the Interior

Representative Fred A. Hartley, Jr.

Representative William R. Wood and boys and girls band of Whiting, Ind.

Eagle Scouts group from Mississippi

Lunch—Patrick H. Callahan, Louisville, Ky.

Henry Chalmers, Bureau of Foreign and Domestic Commerce

George E. Lichty, Waterloo, Iowa

Ernest Walker Sawyer

J. Russell Young, Washington Star

Secretary of the Treasury Andrew W. Mellon

Luther H. Reichelderfer, Commissioner of the District of Columbia, and William W. Bride, District Corporation Council

August 26

Breakfast—Mark Sullivan, journalist

Guy D. Goff, former Senator of West Virginia

Representative William R. Wood, Indiana

George R. Stobbs, former Representative of Massachusetts

Richard H. Waldo, McClure Newspaper Syndicate

Mrs. Worthington Scranton

Samuel S. Sandberg, United States Shipping Board

Godfrey Dewey, president of the III Olympic Winter Games Committee

Group of aviators from Czechoslovakia, Germany, Great Britain, Italy, and Poland

Senator James E. Watson and group of Boy Scouts from Indiana

Secretary of Agriculture Arthur M. Hyde

Lunch—Henry M. Robinson

J. W. Pole, Comptroller of the Currency

Ashmun N. Brown, Providence (R.I.) Journal

Col. Campbell B. Hodges, Military Aide to the President

Raymond Benjamin, assistant chairman of the Republican National Committee

Dinner—Secretary of the Treasury Andrew W. Mellon, Eugene Meyer, George W. Davison, Charles S. McCain, William C. Potter, James T. Lee, and Henry M. Robinson

August 27

Breakfast—Mark Sullivan, journalist

Representative Harold Knutson

Edward Price Bell, journalist

Samuel H. Barker, president of the Bankers Trust Co.

Joseph E. Ransdell, former Senator of Louisiana

Atlee Pomerene, former Senator of Ohio

Representative Charles R. Crisp, Georgia

H. F. Arthur Schoenfeld, United States Minister to the Dominican Republic

786

1931

John B. Sosnowski, former Representative of Michigan

Chester H. Gray, American Farm Bureau Federation, and Mr. Martindale

Dudley Moulton, director of California Department of Agriculture

American Air Mail Society, delegation

Lunch—Walter S. Gifford, Director of the President's Organization on Unemployment Relief

William R. Castle, Jr., Under Secretary of State

J. Clawson Roop, Director of the Budget

Dinner—Warren C. Fairbanks, president of the Indianapolis News Publishing Co.

August 28

Breakfast—Warren C. Fairbanks, president of the Indianapolis News Publishing Co.

Cabinet

Representative William R. Wood

Russell W. Boardman and John Polando, transatlantic aviators

Secretary of Labor William N. Doak

Rapidan Camp, Va.—John Lord O'Brian, Col. U.S. Grant, 3d, Frank Knox, Mr. and Mrs. James C. Rogers, Mr. and Mrs. Warren C. Fairbanks, Mr. and Mrs. Mark Sullivan, Mr. and Mrs. Theodore G. Joslin, Lawrence Richey, and Dr. Joel T. Boone

August 29–30

At Rapidan Camp, Va.

August 31

Returned from Rapidan Camp, Va.

J. Matt Chilton, Republican National Committee

Secretary of Labor William N. Doak

Representative Frank Crowther, New York

Lieutenant Governor of Mississippi and party

Mrs. Hendricks and sons of St. Louis, Mo.

Frank Evans, Federal Farm Board

Senator James J. Davis

Secretary of Agriculture Arthur M. Hyde

Lem C. Speers, New York Times

Dinner—William R. Castle, Jr., Under Secretary of State

September 1

Breakfast—Mark Sullivan, journalist

Senator Daniel O. Hastings

Cabinet

Washington Correspondents

Thomas J. Hamilton, editor of the Augusta (Ga.) Chronicle

Justice and Mrs. Thomas H. MacGregor, Louisiana State Court of Appeals

Hollywood, Calif., girls baseball team

Boy and girl tennis players

William Hamilton

Samuel J. Prescott

Lunch—Walter S. Gifford, Director of the President's Organization on Unemployment Relief

Muscle Shoals Commission

Theodore C. Wallen, New York Herald Tribune

1931

Dinner—James F. Bell, member of the President's Organization on Unemployment Relief

September 2

Breakfast—Mark Sullivan, journalist

Representative Cyrenus Cole, Iowa

Representative William R. Wood, Indiana

William R. Castle, Jr., Under Secretary of State

Senator Simeon D. Fess and committee representing small colleges of the country

Ralph F. Bradford, director of conservation for Illinois

N. W. Knapp, New York

Arthur K. Foran

Representative Oscar De Priest

W. R. Wilcox

Polly Moran

German Ambassador, Friedrich von Prittwitz, to present crew of the German airplane DO–X

Curtis M. Johnson, Minnesota

Senator Henrik Shipstead

Lunch—Birge Clark

Robert S. Pickens, Associated Press

Raymond Benjamin, assistant chairman of the Republican National Committee

Dinner—Secretary of the Navy and Mrs. Charles F. Adams and Mr. and Mrs. Carl Williams

September 3

Breakfast—Mark Sullivan, journalist

Senator Ellison D. Smith, South Carolina

Karl A. Bickel, United Press

Carl H. White

Frank T. Hines, Administrator of Veterans' Affairs

Missionary Board of the Federated Council of Churches, committee

Edward A. O'Neal, president of the American Farm Bureau Federation

Randall Gould, Shanghai newspaper correspondent

Representative Wilbur M. White, Ohio

C. A. Hodges and committee in charge of the President's Cup Race

Everett Watkins and Mrs. Oliver M. Loomis

Warren H. McBryde

Printing apprentices from Chicago

David Lawrence, U.S. Daily

George R. James, Federal Reserve Board

Lem C. Speers, New York Times

Maj. Gen. George S. Gibbs and Frank Page

J. Clawson Roop, Director of the Budget

Secretary of the Treasury Andrew W. Mellon

Secretary of Agriculture Arthur M. Hyde

Robert H. Lucas, executive director of the Republican National Committee

September 4

Ferry K. Heath, Assistant Secretary of the Treasury

Russell Doubleday, New York

Cabinet

Lt. Col. Joseph I. McMullen

Ernest Lee Jahncke, Assistant Secretary of the Navy

Bolivian Minister, Eduardo Dies de Medina, upon his departure

William F. McDowell, bishop of the Methodist Episcopal Church of Washington, D.C.

Thomas Littlepage

Virginia Allors and Miss Reckinger, to present peaches

Rentfro B. Creager, Republican National Committee

Washington Correspondents

Rapidan Camp, Va.—Secretary of Commerce Robert P. Lamont, Mr. and Mrs. George Benson, Mr. and Mrs. Walter Newton, and Dr. Joel T. Boone

September 5

At Rapidan Camp, Va.—Guests arriving were Henry M. Robinson and James R. Garfield

September 6–7

At Rapidan Camp, Va.

September 8

Returned from Rapidan Camp, Va.

George R. James, Federal Reserve Board, and W. L. Clayton, of Houston

Cabinet

J. Clawson Roop, Director of the Budget

Washington Correspondents

Mrs. George V. Reynolds, St. Louis, Mo.

Lunch—Henry M. Robinson, Los Angeles banker

Eugene Meyer and George R. James, Federal Reserve Board, and W. L. Clayton

Louis J. Taber, master of the National Grange

Robert S. Pickens, Associated Press

James C. Stone, Chairman of the Federal Farm Board

Dinner Secretary of State Henry L. Stimson

September 9

Breakfast—Walter E. Hope and Mark Sullivan

Eugene Meyer, Governor of the Federal Reserve Board

Secretary of State Henry L. Stimson

Representatives John W. Summers and Burton L. French

Senator Hattie W. Carraway, Arkansas

Senator Porter H. Dale and members of the House delegation from Vermont

Secretary of the Treasury Andrew W. Mellon and Under Secretary of the Treasury Ogden L. Mills

Lafayette B. Gleason, New York

Ulysses S. Stone, former Representative of Oklahoma

Gen. John J. Pershing, Col. Campbell B. Hodges, and Col. Carlos Garfias

Paul Wooten, New Orleans Times-Picayune

789

1931

Radio address on the 50th anniversary of the founding of the first Red Cross Chapter in Dansville, N.Y.

Lunch—Walter S. Gifford, Director of the President's Organization on Unemployment Relief

Nathan W. MacChesney

LeRoy T. Vernon, Chicago Daily News

Secretary of Commerce Robert P. Lamont

Dinner—Senator James E. Watson and Henry M. Robinson, Los Angeles banker

September 10

Breakfast—Henry M. Robinson and Mark Sullivan

Senator Daniel O. Hastings

Secretary of Labor William N. Doak

William M. Chadbourne, New York

Robert Maisel, New York

Representative Carl R. Chindblom, Illinois

Representative William (Ed) Hull, Illinois

Anthony Czarnecki and son of Chicago

Ernest Merrill and delegation from West Virginia

John Thomas Taylor, American Legion

Capt. Fred Kochli, Disabled Veterans of World War, to present forget-me-nots

Lunch—Mrs. Henry M. Robinson

Senator David A. Reed

Eliot Wadsworth, former Assistant Secretary of the Treasury

J. Clawson Roop, Director of the Budget

Richard V. Oulahan, New York Times

Dinner—Representative John Q. Tilson, House majority leader, and Samuel Crowther

September 11

Breakfast—Lewis L. Strauss and Samuel Crowther

Mr. Epstein

Senators James E. Watson and Henry D. Hatfield, and George deB. Keim, secretary of the Republican National Committee

Henry P. Fletcher, Chairman of the United States Tariff Commission

Cabinet

Pressed electric button starting presses of the Boston Herald in its new plant

Julius Klein, Assistant Secretary of Commerce

Ogden L. Mills, Under Secretary of the Treasury

David Lawrence, U.S. Daily

Washington Correspondents

Clarence Poe

Secretary of Commerce Robert P. Lamont

Senator Simeon D. Fess

Dinner—Under Secretary of the Treasury Ogden L. Mills and Henry M. Robinson, Los Angeles banker

September 12

Breakfast—Mark Sullivan and H. C. Ogden

Fred C. Croxton, Assistant Director of the President's Organization on Unemployment Relief

Senator Henrik Shipstead

Secretary of the Treasury Andrew W. Mellon

Rapidan Camp, Va.—Secretary of State and Mrs. Henry L. Stimson, Postmaster General and Mrs. Walter F. Brown, Assistant Secretary of the Treasury and Mrs. Arthur A. Ballantine, Henry M. Robinson, H. C. Ogden, Mr. and Mrs. Gould Lincoln, Mr. and Mrs. Robert B. Armstrong, Lawrence Richey, Dr. Joel T. Boone, and Mark Sullivan

September 13

At Rapidan Camp, Va.

September 14

Returned from Rapidan Camp, Va.

Charles G. Johnson, State treasurer of California

National defense committee of the American Legion

Lenna L. Yost, Republican National Committee

Secretary of Agriculture Arthur M. Hyde

Henry Long, tax commissioner of Massachusetts

Lunch—John K. Ottley

Richard V. Oulahan, New York Times

Fred C. Croxton, Assistant Director of the President's Organization on Unemployment Relief

Matthew Woll, American Federation of Labor

Dinner—Eugene Meyer, Herbert K. Hallett, Robert H. Treman, Howard A. Loeb, James A. House, John K. Ottley, Melvin A. Traylor, Walter W. Smith, George H. Prince, Walter S. McLucas, Henry M. Robinson, and Walter Lechtenstein

September 15

J. Clawson Roop, Director of the Budget

Cabinet

Washington Correspondents

John Thomas Taylor and American Legion officials

Capt. Russell Train

Charles S. Groves

Whiting Williams

Secretary of the Navy Charles F. Adams

James F. Burke, general counsel of the Republican National Committee

Raymond Benjamin, assistant chairman of the Republican National Committee

Mr. and Mrs. Ernest I. Lewis

September 16

Hanford MacNider, United States Minister to Canada

Thomas H. MacDonald, Bureau of Public Roads

William E. Humphrey, Federal Trade Commission

A. C. Backus, Milwaukee, Wis.

Merryle S. Rukeyser, journalist

Austrian Minister, Edgar L. C. Prochnick, to present special medal made by the National Porcelain Factory of Austria in commemoration of President Hoover's announcement of the moratorium on war debt payments

French Embassy Chargé d'Affaires, Jules Henry, to present M. Fernand Tayen

Archibald Dresser, Boston, Mass.

Lunch—Janet Mabie Clapp, Fairfax Hall, Cambridge, Mass.

Senator Phillips Lee Goldsborough, Maryland

James J. Leary, journalist

W. A. Hildebrand, Greensboro, N.C. News

Secretary of State Henry L. Stimson

Hanford MacNider, United States Minister to Canada

Dinner—Mr. and Mrs. Hanford Mac-Nider

September 17

Samuel R. McKelvie, Federal Farm Board

Representative Frank L. Bowman, West Virginia

Harry R. Guggenheim, United States Ambassador to Cuba

Representative Fletcher B. Swank, Oklahoma

Everrett S. Owens, Dallas, Tex., and Robert M. Harris, New York

Italian Ambassador, Nobile Giacomo de Martino, to present Admiral Alfredo Acton

Frank H. Hitchcock

William Costello, Minneapolis Tribune

Bolivian Minister, Luis O. Abelli, to present letters of credence

Charles G. Edwards, New York

Jay G. Hayden, president of the Gridiron Club

J. Clawson Roop, Director of the Budget

Robert S. Pickens, Associated Press

Jim West

Capt. John F. Lucey

Myron C. Taylor, U.S. Steel Corporation

September 18

Breakfast—Mark Sullivan, journalist

Cabinet

Frank T. Hines, Administrator of Veterans' Affairs

Walter S. Gifford and Owen D. Young, President's Organization on Unemployment Relief

Bruce Barton

Chilean Ambassador, Miguel Cruchaga Tocornal, to present letters of credence

Representative Edith Nourse Rogers

Jim Wright, Buffalo News

Secretary of Agriculture Arthur M. Hyde

Richard Lee Strout, Christian Science Monitor

Joseph P. Knapp, publisher

Dinner—Secretary of State Henry L. Stimson and Secretary of the Treasury Andrew W. Mellon

September 19

Breakfast—Henry M. Robinson, Los Angeles banker

Senators Thomas J. Walsh and Burton K. Wheeler

Secretary of Commerce Robert P. Lamont

Mark Sullivan, journalist

John Wesley Hill, chancellor of Lincoln Memorial University

Lunch—Senator Frederic C. Walcott, Mr. and Mrs. William Allen White, Capt. John F. Lucey, and Henry M. Robinson

Rapidan Camp, Va.—Senator Frederic C. Walcott, Mr. and Mrs. William Allen White, Governor and Mrs. Harry G. Leslie, Mr. and Mrs. Henry P. Fletcher, Mr. and Mrs. Franklin W. Fort, Mr. and Mrs. James P. Hornaday, Capt. John F. Lucey, Mr. and Mrs. George Akerson, Lawrence Richey, and Dr. Joel T. Boone

September 20

At Rapidan Camp, Va.

Departed for Martinsburg, W. Va. to board train for Detroit, Mich.

September 21

Detroit, Mich. to address convention of the American Legion

Departed for Washington, D.C.

September 22

Returned from Detroit, Mich.

Julius Klein, Assistant Secretary of Commerce

Eugene Meyer, Governor of the Federal Reserve Board

Cabinet

Washington Correspondents

Thurman P. Hill and Oil States Advisory Committee

Dan W. Turner, Governor of Iowa

Representative John D. Clarke, New York

Lunch—Henry M. Robinson, Los Angeles banker, and Governor Dan W. Turner

Senator Daniel O. Hastings

Robert A. Taft

Secretary of the Interior Ray Lyman Wilbur

Postmaster General Walter F. Brown

Robert H. Lucas, executive director of the Republican National Committee

Dinner—Secretary of Agriculture Arthur M. Hyde, Secretary of the Interior Ray Lyman Wilbur, and George T. Cameron, publisher of the San Francisco Chronicle

September 23

Breakfast—George T. Cameron, publisher of the San Francisco Chronicle

J. Clawson Roop, Director of the Budget

Representative Harold Knutson

Meier Steinbrink, New York

Mexican Ambassador, Manuel C. Tellez, to say goodbye

Charles F. Abbott, executive director of the American Institute of Steel Construction

Lenna L. Yost, Republican National Committee

Presented gold and silver cups to George Reiss and Richard Loynes, winners of first and second places in the President's Cup Race

Earl J. Davis, Detroit, Mich.

Secretary of State Henry L. Stimson

Secretary of Agriculture Arthur M. Hyde

Lunch—Walter S. Gifford, Director of the President's Organization on Unemployment Relief, and Henry M. Robinson, Los Angeles banker

Ernest Lee Jahncke, Assistant Secretary of the Navy

Arno B. Cammerer, Assistant Director of the National Park Service

Raymond Benjamin, assistant chairman of the Republican National Committee

Dinner—Henry M. Robinson, Los Angeles banker

September 24

Breakfast—Henry M. Robinson and Mark Sullivan

James L. McConaughy, president of Wesleyan University

Representatives Fletcher B. Swank of Oklahoma and Martin Dies of Texas

Secretary of Agriculture Arthur M. Hyde

Irvine Luther Lenroot, Judge of the United States Court of Customs and Patent Appeals

William S. Bennett, Edward Hines Lumber Co.

George Vits, Wisconsin

Stuart W. Cramer

Allen M. Pope and C. T. Williams

Senator Claude A. Swanson and Representative Schuyler Otis Bland, Virginia

British Chargé d'Affaires, Ronald Ian Campbell, to present Frederick C. Sainsbury, mayor of Reading, England

Representative Norton L. Lichtenwalner, Pennsylvania

Lunch—Arthur Brisbane, editor of the Chicago Herald and Examiner

Kenneth Clark

American Institute of Architects, delegation

Secretary of State Henry L. Stimson

Lt. Col. Joseph I. McMullen

J. Clawson Roop, Director of the Budget

Reception—Polish Women's Alliance of America, delegates

Dinner—Senator James E. Watson, Senate majority leader

September 25

Breakfast—Mark Sullivan, journalist

Theodore Roosevelt, Governor of Porto Rico

Senator David A. Reed, Pennsylvania

Senator Otis F. Glenn, Illinois

Cabinet

Miss Atwood

Walter S. Gifford, Director of the President's Organization on Unemployment Relief, and committee

Interstate Commerce Commission of the Federal Bar Association

Gamma Eta Gamma Fraternity, members

Secretary of State Henry L. Stimson

G. Gould Lincoln, Washington Star

Ashmun N. Brown, Providence (R.I.) Journal

Washington Correspondents

Robert S. Pickens, Associated Press

Frederick William Wile, broadcast journalist

September 26

Bruce Barton

Harry F. Burgess, Governor of Panama Canal Zone

Senator Ellison D. Smith, South Carolina

Theodore Roosevelt, Governor of Porto Rico

Gen. James A. Drain

Lunch—Governor and Mrs. Wilbur M. Brucker, Mr. and Mrs. Fred F. Shedd, Mr. and Mrs. Harry P. Wolfe, Senator and Mrs. Hiram Bingham, Governor Theodore Roosevelt

Rapidan Camp, Va.—the above lunch guests and Lawrence Richey and Dr. Joel T. Boone

September 27

At Rapidan Camp, Va.

September 28

Returned from Rapidan Camp, Va.

Representative John J. O'Connor, Louisiana

Henry L. Stevens and Ralph R. O'Neill, American Legion

Adam Blumer and party, Monroe, Wis.

Mr. Cramer, Phillip, Wis.

Kenneth C. Ray and party, Mechanicsville, Ohio

Robert McBirnie, mayor of Boone, Iowa

Lunch—Hanford MacNider, United States Minister to Canada

Secretary of the Navy Charles F. Adams

Carl Clapp Thomas, Los Angeles, Calif.

George Akerson, former Secretary to the President

Ernest I. Lewis, Interstate Commerce Commission

Dinner—Ira E. Bennett, editor of the Washington Post

September 29

Breakfast—Mark Sullivan, journalist

H. Paul Bestor, Federal Farm Loan Bureau

Secretary of State Henry L. Stimson

Eugene Meyer, Governor of the Federal Reserve Board

Cabinet

Washington Correspondents

Silas H. Strawn, president of the Chamber of Commerce of the United States

Sheldon Whitehouse, United States Minister to Guatemala

Lunch—Harry J. Brown and Harvey Hancock

Mr. Gallagher

Mark L. Requa

Dinner—Mr. and Mrs. Paul Block

September 30

Breakfast—Mark Sullivan and Mr. and Mrs. Paul Block

Capt. Russell Train

Ogden L. Mills, Under Secretary of the Treasury

Joseph R. Nutt, treasurer of the Republican National Committee

Theodore Roosevelt, Governor of Porto Rico

Secretary of State Henry L. Stimson

James H. Rand, Jr., president of Remington Rand Co. and William P. MacCracken, Jr., secretary of the American Bar Association

Senator Robert D. Carey, Wyoming

Oscar J. Larson, former Representative of Minnesota

Samuel McCune Lindsay, professor of social legislation at Columbia University

Charles Brandon Booth, commander of the Volunteers of America

Earl Ferguson, Iowa

Lenna L. Yost, Republican National Committee

Mrs. Robert G. Simmons and friends of Nebraska

Elwood Mead, Commissioner of Reclamation and Roy R. Gill of Spokane, Wash.

Lunch—Under Secretary of State and Mrs. William R. Castle, Jr., Alfred Castle, Mrs. Raymond Robins, Mrs. Scherfesse, Emily and Mary Hydeclarke

Albert W. Atwood

Eugene Meyer, Governor of the Federal Reserve Board

Joseph R. Nutt, treasurer of the Republican National Committee

Theodore C. Wallen, New York Herald Tribune

Thomas F. Healey, Philadelphia Public Ledger

Raymond Benjamin, assistant chairman of the Republican National Committee

Radio address in connection with the opening of the Waldorf-Astoria Hotel in New York

Secretary of the Treasury Andrew W. Mellon, Under Secretary of the Treasury Ogden L. Mills, Federal Reserve Board Governor Eugene Meyer, George L. Harrison, and Albert H. Wiggins

Dinner—Mark L. Requa

October 1

Breakfast—Mark L. Requa

Ogden L. Mills, Under Secretary of the Treasury

Secretary of State Henry L. Stimson

Secretary of Commerce Robert P. Lamont

Eugene Meyer, Governor of the Federal Reserve Board

Warner D. Huntington, Manufacturing Chemists' Association of the United States

William F. Schilling, Federal Farm Board

William Stern, North Dakota

Herbert S. Houston, International Chamber of Commerce

Charles Evans Hughes, Chief Justice of the Supreme Court, and senior circuit judges

Nathan Adams, Dallas, Tex.

Ferry K. Heath, Assistant Secretary of the Treasury

William B. Poland

Lunch—Nathan Adams

Franklin D'Olier and R. R. Rogers, Prudential Insurance Co.

Ogden L. Mills, Under Secretary of the Treasury

Jeremiah Milbank and Lewis L. Strauss

J. Clawson Roop, Director of the Budget

Byron Price, Associated Press

Senator Felix Hebert

October 2

Breakfast—Mark Sullivan, journalist

Cabinet

Francis Lee Stuart, Ernest P. Goodrich, and George T. Seabury, American Society of Civil Engineers

George Hatfield, United States District Attorney, San Francisco

J. Henry Hesler, San Francisco, Calif.

William Lassiter

Maj. Gen. Edward L. King

Edward A. Rasmuson, Skagway, Alaska

Lunch—Senator William E. Borah

Secretary of Labor William N. Doak and Mr. Johnson

Eugene Meyer, Governor of the Federal Reserve Board

Ogden L. Mills, Under Secretary of the Treasury

October 3

Breakfast—Mr. and Mrs. Noel Macy, Mark Sullivan, and Bernard M. Baruch

Secretary of State Henry L. Stimson

Franklin W. Fort, former Representative of New Jersey

Hanford MacNider, United States Minister to Canada

Lunch—Under Secretary of the Treasury Ogden L. Mills, Federal Reserve Board Governor Eugene Meyer, and George L. Harrison

Secretary of the Treasury Andrew W. Mellon and Under Secretary of the Treasury Ogden L. Mills

Rapidan Camp, Va.—Judge and Mrs. Irvine Luther Lenroot, Mr. and Mrs. Julius Barnes, J. Walter Drake, Mr. and Mrs. Charles J. Hepburn, W. Kingsland Macy, Mr. and Mrs. Noel Macy, Mark L. Requa, Mr. and Mrs. Mark Sullivan, Lawrence Richey, and Dr. Joel T. Boone

October 4

Returned from Rapidan Camp, Va.

Secretary of the Treasury Andrew W. Mellon, Under Secretary of the Treasury Ogden L. Mills, and Federal Reserve Board Governor Eugene Meyer

Arthur A. Ballantine, Assistant Secretary of the Treasury

Dinner—Mr. and Mrs. Charles J. Hepburn, Mr. and Mrs. Julius Barnes, Noel Macy, Mark L. Requa, W. Kingsland Macy, Mrs. J. Walter Drake, Mr. and Mrs. Mark Sullivan, and Lawrence Richey

October 5

Breakfast—Mark Sullivan, journalist
To Philadelphia to attend World Series Baseball game between Philadelphia and St. Louis
Dinner—Under Secretary of the Treasury Ogden L. Mills and George Barr Baker

October 6

Breakfast—Mark Sullivan, journalist
Eugene Meyer, Governor of the Federal Reserve Board
Henry J. Allen, former Senator of Kansas
Frank T. Hines, Administrator of Veterans' Affairs
Senator Otis F. Glenn
Cabinet
Washington Correspondents
Representative John McDuffie, Alabama
Warren E. Green, Governor of South Dakota
Dakota Wesleyan University football team
George F. Shafer, Governor of North Dakota
Lunch—Henry J. Allen, former Senator of Kansas
Eugene Meyer, Federal Reserve Board
Secretary of Labor William N. Doak

October 7

Breakfast—Mark Sullivan, journalist
Michael Gallagher
Secretary of State Henry L. Stimson
Senator Robert D. Carey
William V. Hodges, Denver, Colo.
Polish Chargé d'Affaires, Stanislaw Lepkowski, to present Gustaw Orlícz-Dreszer
Mr. and Mrs. Graham M. Dean, Iowa City, Iowa
Capt. James G. Hall
National Council of Catholic Women, delegation
William Pulliam
Ernest L. Klein, Chicago, Ill.
Mr. Roger
Lunch—Mr. and Mrs. Atholl McBean, Peter McBean, and Mark L. Requa
Secretary of Commerce Robert P. Lamont and the following members of the Finance Committee of the White House Conference on Home Building and Home Ownership: James L. Madden, Metropolitan Life Insurance Co.; William E. Best, United States Building and Loan League; Hiram S. Cody, Cody Trust Co.; Clarence Dillon, Dillon, Read and Co.; Harry A. Kahler, New York Title and Mortgage Co.; Harry S. Kissell, National Association of Real-Estate Boards; Samuel N. Reep, Home Building and Loan Associations; W. A. Starrett, Starrett Corp.; Ernest T. Trigg, John Lucas and Co.; Clarence M. Woolley, American Radiator Co.

Dinner—Clarence M. Woolley and Norman H. Davis

October 8

Breakfast—James C. Stone and Norman H. Davis
Mr. Dennis, Chicago, Ill.
Mark L. Requa
Address at the opening meeting of the fourth Pan-American Commercial Conference in the Pan-American Building
Silas H. Strawn, president of the Chamber of Commerce of the United States
Clara B. Burdette
Secretary of Labor William N. Doak and Edward Corsi
F. W. Pickard, Wilmington, Del.
H. Paul Bestor, Federal Farm Loan Board, and J. B. Madison of Charleston, W. Va.
Rufus Woods, Wenatchee, Wash.
Lunch—Theodore Roosevelt, Governor of Porto Rico
Attorney General William D. Mitchell
Mr. Grant, San Francisco
Daniel Willard
J. Clawson Roop, Director of the Budget
Secretary of the Interior Ray Lyman Wilbur
Reception—League of Republican Women
Ernest I. Lewis, Interstate Commerce Commission

October 9

Breakfast—Mark Sullivan, journalist

Ogden L. Mills, Under Secretary of the Treasury
Senator Joseph T. Robinson, Arkansas
Cabinet
Frank T. Hines, Administrator of Veterans' Affairs, and George R. Lunn, commander in chief of the Spanish American War Veterans
Counselor of the British Embassy, Francis D. G. Osborne, to present George Frank Titt, Lord Mayor of Manchester, England
George F. Shafer, Governor of North Dakota, and Warren E. Green, Governor of South Dakota
Lunch—W. Cameron Forbes, United States Ambassador to Japan
Washington Correspondents
John Matthew Gries, Executive Secretary of the White House Conference on Home Building and Home Ownership
Hugh McCall Tate, Interstate Commerce Commission
Dinner—George Barr Baker
Clyde B. Aitchison, Interstate Commerce Commission

October 10

Secretary of Commerce Robert P. Lamont
Secretary of State Henry L. Stimson
Julius Klein, Assistant Secretary of Commerce
Louis B. Mayer, president of Metro-Goldwyn-Mayer Co., Inc.
International League for Peace and Freedom, delegation of women
Lunch—Louis B. Mayer

J. Clawson Roop, Director of the Budget

Rapidan Camp, Va.—Justice and Mrs. Harlan Fiske Stone, Mr. and Mrs. Mark Sullivan, Alida M. Henriques, Mrs. Charles D. Walcott, Mr. and Mrs. William P. MacCracken, Mr. and Mrs. William Hard, Lt. and Mrs. Fred Butler, Lawrence Richey, and Dr. Joel T. Boone

October 11

At Rapidan Camp, Va.—Chief Justice and Mrs. Charles Evans Hughes

October 12

Returned from Rapidan Camp, Va.

Ogden L. Mills, Under Secretary of the Treasury

Frank W. Blair, Detroit, Mich., and former Governor Angus W. McLean

Counselor of the British Embassy, Francis D. G. Osborne, to present Alfred E. Johns

Mr. Winkle, Dallas, Tex.

Radio address—38th annual convention of the International Association of Chiefs of Police, in St. Petersburg, Fla.

Lunch—Frederick H. Payne, Assistant Secretary of War, and Gen. Douglas MacArthur

Fred C. Croxton, Assistant Director of the President's Organization on Unemployment Relief

Secretary of State Henry L. Stimson

Reception—The Supreme Court

Dinner—Edward B. Clements, Missouri Republican national committeeman

October 13

Breakfast—Mark Sullivan, journalist

Mr. Gallagher

Ogden L. Mills, Under Secretary of the Treasury

Representative Bertrand H. Snell, New York

Charles J. Hepburn

Cabinet

Robert B. Armstrong, Los Angeles Times

Mr. Acton, managing editor of the Journal of Commerce

Mr. Koenig

J. D. Brock and Col. Ruby D. Garrett, Kansas City, Kans.

Lunch—Thomas S. Gates, president of the University of Pennsylvania

Harry J. Haas, president of the American Bankers Association

Adolph C. Miller, Federal Reserve Board of Governors

Dinner—Secretary of Agriculture Arthur M. Hyde

H. Paul Bestor, Federal Farm Loan Bureau

October 14

Breakfast—Dr. Joel T. Boone

James C. Moreland, Chicago, Ill.

Henry P. Fletcher, Chairman of the United States Tariff Commission

Ferry K. Heath, Assistant Secretary of the Treasury

1931

Frederick H. Payne, Assistant Secretary of War, and Lt. Col. Joseph I. Mc-Mullen

George W. Davison, president of the Central Hanover Bank and Trust Co.

Representatives John N. Sandlin and Riley J. Wilson, Louisiana

Harvey C. Couch and L. W. Baldwin, president of the Missouri Pacific Railway Co.

Wiley Post and Harold Gatty

H. L. Derby, National Association of Manufacturers

William Butterworth, former president of the Chamber of Commerce of the United States

Perry Weidner, Los Angeles, Calif., grand master of the Knights Templar

Counselor of the British Embassy, Francis G. D. Osborne, to present Rev. C. Snyder Smith, Rev. Robert Bond, and Rev. Edwin Fitch

French Ambassador, Paul Claudel, to present M. Andrew Citroen

Henry George Foundation of America, committee

Representative Sol Bloom of New York and State chairmen of the George Washington Bicentennial Commissions

Eugene Shoecraft

Dinner—Max C. Fleischman

Eugene Meyer, Governor of the Federal Reserve Board

Secretary of State Henry L. Stimson

Secretary of Labor William N. Doak and Assistant Secretary of the Navy Ernest Lee Jahncke

Robert B. Armstrong, Los Angeles Times

Raymond Benjamin, assistant chairman of the Republican National Committee

Dinner—Senator Charles L. McNary

October 15

Breakfast—Mark Sullivan, journalist

Frederick H. Payne, Assistant Secretary of War, and Lt. Col. Joseph I. Mc-Mullen

Secretary of Commerce Robert P. Lamont

C. Bascom Slemp

Arch W. Shaw, President's Committee on Recent Economic Changes

Charles C. Selecman, president of Southern Methodist University, Dallas, Tex.

William F. McDowell, bishop of Methodist Episcopal Church of Washington, D.C., and John L. Nielson, bishop from Switzerland

Darold D. DeCoe, commander in chief of the Veterans of Foreign Wars of the United States, and Frank T. Hines, Administrator of Veterans' Affairs

Tulsa, Okla., football team

Henry W. O. Millington and delegation from the Southern Baptist Convention, Jewish-Christian Conference

LeBlanc and party

Ogden L. Mills, Under Secretary of the Treasury

Lunch—Stephen O. Metcalf, Providence, R. I.

Secretary of the Navy Charles F. Adams

Walter S. Gifford, Director of the President's Organization on Unemployment Relief

J. Clawson Roop, Director of the Budget

William R. Castle, Jr., Under Secretary of State

October 16

Breakfast—Mark Sullivan, journalist

Senator George H. Moses

Cabinet

Franklin W. Fort, former Representative of New Jersey

Counselor of the British Embassy, Francis G. D. Osborne, to present Sir Francis Goodenough of England

University of Kentucky football team

Lunch—Walter P. Chrysler and Michael Gallagher

S. F. Hobbs, chairman of the Muscle Shoals Commission

Washington Correspondents

John D. Garrett, United States Ambassador to Italy

Senator Simeon D. Fess

October 17

Breakfast—Mark Sullivan, journalist

Ogden L. Mills, Under Secretary of the Treasury

Secretary of State Henry L. Stimson

Fred E. Stewart, Oakland; H. H. Linney, San Francisco; and R. A. Vandergrift, Sacramento, Calif.

Departed for Annapolis, Md., to board U.S.S. *Arkansas* en route to Yorktown, Va.

October 18

Spent day on board U.S.S. *Arkansas*

Radio address on unemployment from Fort Monroe, Va.

October 19

Yorktown, Va.—sesquicentennial celebration of the surrender of Cornwallis, delivered an address and attended luncheon and pageant before returning to U.S.S. *Arkansas* for return to Washington, D.C.

October 20

Returned from Yorktown, Va.

Rome C. Stephenson, South Bend, Ind.

Secretary of State Henry L. Stimson

Cabinet

Governor and Mrs. Henry Stewart Caulfield of Missouri

Minnesota group presented by Walter H. Newton

Counselor of the British Embassy, Francis D. G. Osborne, to present Lord and Lady Cornwallis, Sir Philip Colville, and Sir George Menteth Boughey and Lady Boughey

James F. Burke, general counsel of the Republican National Committee

1931

Lunch—John J. McClure

Representatives James J. Connolly, Benjamin M. Golder, George A. Welsh, Harry C. Ransley, Pennsylvania

Senators Gerald P. Nye and Lynn J. Frazier and Representative James H. Sinclair

Daniel Willard, president of the Baltimore and Ohio Railroad Co.

Hugh Wilson

Secretary of State Henry L. Stimson, Under Secretary of State William R. Castle, Jr., and Under Secretary of the Treasury Ogden L. Mills

Clyde B. Aitchison, Interstate Commerce Commission, and Walter H. Newton

Edgar Rickard

October 21

Breakfast—Edgar Rickard, Henry M. Robinson, and Mark Sullivan

Senator James J. Davis

Ernest Lee Jahncke, Assistant Secretary of the Navy

Harry M. Warner, president of Warner Bros. Pictures

David H. Blair, former Commissioner of Internal Revenue

Henry H. Heimann, executive manager of the National Association of Credit Men

James G. McDonald, chairman of the board of the Foreign Policy Association, Inc.

Belgian Ambassador, Paul May, to present Emile Francqui

Ernest Gruening, editor of the Portland (Maine) Evening News

Polish Ambassador, Tytus Filipowicz

Clarence M. Young, Assistant Secretary of Commerce for Aeronautics and aviators Hugh Herndon, Jr., and Clyde Pangborn

Negro Masonic Supreme Council, officers

Lunch—Edgar Rickard and Ernest Gruening

Louis K. Liggett, president of the United Drug Co.

Ogden L. Mills, Under Secretary of the Treasury

Senator William E. Borah

October 22

Breakfast—Henry M. Robinson and Mark Sullivan

Representative William R. Wood

Senator John G. Townsend, Jr., Delaware

Frank B. Noyes, president of the Associated Press

William D. Leppitt and W. L. Petrikin, Great Western Sugar Co., Denver, Colo.

Charles Hibbard, Spokane, Wash.

Senator Wallace H. White, Jr.

Mr. and Mrs. Edgar H. Evans and daughter

International oratorical contest finalists

American Association of Personal Finance Companies, officers and convention delegates

Eugene Meyer, Governor of the Federal Reserve Board

J. Clawson Roop, Director of the Budget

Secretary of State Henry L. Stimson

French Prime Minister Pierre Laval and daughter and French Ambassador and Mrs. Paul Claudel

Dinner—Prime Minister Pierre Laval and French delegation attending the Yorktown Sesquicentennial

October 23

Breakfast—Mark Sullivan, journalist

Henry J. Allen, former Senator of Kansas

Cabinet

National Negro Technicians Association, members

Prime Minister Pierre Laval

Prime Minister Pierre Laval, Secretary of State Henry L. Stimson, Under Secretary of the Treasury Ogden L. Mills, and Mr. Bizot

Dinner—Prime Minister Pierre Laval, Secretary of State Henry L. Stimson, Under Secretary of the Treasury Ogden L. Mills, and Mr. Bizot

October 24

Breakfast—Prime Minister Pierre Laval and daughter

Secretary of State Henry L. Stimson and Under Secretary of the Treasury Ogden L. Mills

Prime Minister Pierre Laval

Correspondents accompanying Prime Minister Pierre Laval

Washington Correspondents

Dinner—Mr. and Mrs. George M. Reynolds, Chicago, Ill.

October 25

Breakfast—M. N. Buckner, Under Secretary of the Treasury Ogden L. Mills, Federal Reserve Board Governor Eugene Meyer, George L. Harrison, Henry M. Robinson, and George M. Reynolds

Conference with Prime Minister Pierre Laval, French Ambassador Paul Claudel, Secretary of State Henry L. Stimson, Under Secretary of the Treasury Ogden L. Mills, and Mr. Bizot

Lunch—Ogden L. Mills, Under Secretary of the Treasury

Radio address to the Ecumenical Congress in Atlanta, Ga.

Dinner—Secretary of the Interior and Mrs. Ray Lyman Wilbur, Mr. and Mrs. Henry M. Robinson, and Ernest I. Lewis

October 26

Breakfast—Mark Sullivan, journalist

Secretary of War Patrick J. Hurley

Louis B. Mayer, president of Metro-Goldwyn-Mayer Co., Inc.

Radio address to the National Broadcasters' Association convention

Netherlands Minister, J. H. van Royen, to present Dr. and Mrs. de Sitter

Fred J. Lingham

Henry J. Allen, former Senator of Kansas

Appendix E

1931

Theodore Roosevelt, Governor of Porto Rico

H. Paul Bestor, Federal Farm Loan Bureau

Senator Simeon D. Fess

Dinner—Secretary of War and Mrs. Patrick J. Hurley, Mr. and Mrs. Henry M. Robinson, and Governor and Mrs. Theodore Roosevelt

October 27

Breakfast—Mark Sullivan, journalist

Representative John Q. Tilson, House majority leader

Lt. Col. Joseph I. McMullen, Muscle Shoals Commission

Walter S. Gifford, Director of the President's Organization on Unemployment Relief

Cabinet

Washington Correspondents

Turkish Ambassador, Ahmet Muhtar, to present Shukri Bey

Myers Y. Cooper, Governor of Ohio

Lunch—James C. Stone and Kermit Roosevelt

William Hard, journalist

Attorney General William D. Mitchell

Byron Price, Associated Press

Secretary of War Patrick J. Hurley

H. Paul Bestor, Federal Farm Loan Bureau

Charles Evans Hughes, Jr., and Grenville Clark

Dinner—Belgian Ambassador and Mrs. Paul May, Miss May, Hugh S. Cumming, Lt. Roger, Lt. Wall, and Lt. Willis

October 28

Senator James Couzens, Michigan

Edward B. Clements, Missouri Republican national committeeman

Representative Joseph W. Martin, Jr., Massachusetts

Sewell Abbott

Joseph A. Tolbert, United States Attorney for the Southern District of South Carolina

Representative Frank L. Bowman, West Virginia

Senator Ellison D. Smith and Representative Thomas S. McMillan, South Carolina

Representative Edith Nourse Rogers, Massachusetts

British Ambassador, Sir Ronald Lindsay, to present Henry G. Wells

Charles E. Roesch, mayor of Buffalo, N.Y., and committee

Society of Automotive Engineers, delegates to annual convention

Walter S. Gifford, Director of the President's Organization on Unemployment Relief, and I. E. Lambert, vice president of the Radio Corporation of America to present film on unemployment

Lunch—A. E. Winship, editor of Journal of Education

Ogden L. Mills, Under Secretary of the Treasury

C. J. Hughes

Dinner—Dr. and Mrs. Vernon L. Kellogg

October 29

Walter E. Hope, former Assistant Secretary of the Treasury

Representative William E. Hess, Ohio

Frank T. Hines, Administrator of Veterans' Affairs

Herbert Corey, author

German Ambassador, Friedrich von Prittwitz, to present Wilhelm Cuno

James E. Freeman and ZeBarney T. Phillips

Representative Richard Yates, Illinois

Veterans' Administration, regional managers

Secretary of State Henry L. Stimson

Henry P. Fletcher, Chairman of the United States Tariff Commission

Secretary of the Treasury Andrew W. Mellon, Assistant Secretary of the Treasury Ferry K. Heath, and architects

J. Clawson Roop, Director of the Budget

David W. Mulvane, Republican National Committee

Secretary of Commerce Robert P. Lamont and Walter E. Hope

October 30

Breakfast—Mark Sullivan, journalist

Secretary of War Patrick J. Hurley

Secretary of State Henry L. Stimson

Cabinet

Ernest Lee Jahncke, Assistant Secretary of the Navy

Edward A. O'Neal, New Orleans, La.

Fred C. Croxton, Assistant Director of the President's Organization on Unemployment Relief

Thomas Walker Page, United States Tariff Commission

Washington Correspondents

Robert Taft

H. Paul Bestor, Federal Farm Loan Bureau

Eugene Meyer, Governor of the Federal Reserve Board

Raymond Benjamin, assistant chairman of the Republican National Committee

Dinner—Mr. and Mrs. Thomas E. Campbell

October 31

Breakfast—Mark Sullivan, journalist

E. W. Kemmerer, Princeton, N.J.

Secretary of War Patrick J. Hurley

Adm. Hugh R. Rodman, Ret.

Howard Sutherland, Alien Property Custodian

Secretary of the Navy Charles F. Adams

Cleveland Newton

Senator Simeon D. Fess

Lt. Col. Joseph I. McMullen

Lunch—Hubert Work and Dr. Waldemar Lindgren

November 1

Lunch—Under Secretary of State and Mrs. William R. Castle, Jr.

Dinner—Senator and Mrs. David A. Reed

1931

November 2

Breakfast—Mark Sullivan, journalist
Senator Claude A. Swanson, Virginia
Secretary of the Navy Charles F. Adams
Secretary of Commerce Robert P. Lamont, William E. Best, and committee from the United States Building and Loan League
C. E. Grunsky, president of the American Engineering Council
Representative Howard W. Smith, Mr. Allen, and Rev. Langston, to invite President to cornerstone laying for the Vestry House of Pohick Church
John Barton Payne, Chairman of the American National Red Cross
Dinner—Mr. and Mrs. Walter H. Newton, Mrs. W. B. Chamberlain, and Gardner Cowles

November 3

Finance Committee of the White House Conference on Home Building and Home Ownership, with the following present: Secretary of Commerce Robert P. Lamont; William A. Starrett, Starrett Corp.; John Matthew Gries, Executive Secretary of the Conference; Frederick H. Ecker, Chairman of the Finance Committee; William E. Best, United States Building and Loan League; Alexander M. Bing, City Housing Corp.; Hiram S. Cody, Cody Trust Co.; Clarence Dillon, Dillon, Read and Co.; William A. Johnston, Akron, Ohio; Harry A. Kahler, New York Title and Mortgage Co.; William H. Kingsley, The

Penn Mutual Life Insurance Co.; Harry S. Kissell, National Association of Real Estate Boards; James L. Madden, Metropolitan Life Insurance Co.; L. A. McLean, Southern Trust Co.; Paul P. O'Brian, American Loan and Savings Association; Samuel N. Reep, Home Building and Loan Association; Henry R. Robins, Commonwealth Title Co. of Philadelphia; H. C. Robinson, Guardian Trust Co.; and James S. Taylor, Department of Commerce, Secretary of the Finance Committee
Cabinet
Charles A. Jonas, Republican National Committee, and Jim Duncan, North Carolina Republican State chairman
Lunch—Dr. Lyle, Albert Herter, Hans Kinsler, Mr. and Mrs. Walter Lipmann, Doris Goss, and Col. Campbell B. Hodges
Salvadoran Minister, Carlos Leiva, to present letters of credence
Senator Carter Glass
Lt. Col. Joseph I. McMullen and Col. Harley B. Ferguson, War Department representatives on the Muscle Shoals Commission
Attorney General William D. Mitchell
Secretary of Commerce Robert P. Lamont and John Matthew Gries
Dinner—Ambassador and Mrs. Walter E. Edge

November 4

Breakfast—Mark Sullivan, journalist, and Ambassador Walter E. Edge

807

Secretary of the Interior Ray Lyman
Wilbur

Ferry K. Heath, Assistant Secretary of
the Treasury

Silas H. Strawn, president of the
Chamber of Commerce of the United
States, and committee from the Chi-
cago Board of Trade

Siebel C. Harris and George H. Davis,
chairman and vice chairman of the
Grain Committee on National Affairs

David S. Ingalls, Assistant Secretary of
the Navy (Air)

Rev. H. K. Robinson, chaplain of the
Quentin Roosevelt Post #4, American Legion

Albert H. Hislop, New Hampshire Republican national committeeman

Mr. and Mrs. Peter Phillips, Yonkers,
N.Y.

Mary Lesta Wakeman and group of
Washington, D.C. Girl Reserves of
the Y.W.C.A.

Ferry K. Heath, Assistant Secretary of
the Treasury, and Thomas E. Campbell, President of the Civil Service
Commission

C. E. Grunsky, president of the American Engineering Council

James L. Wright, Buffalo News

Silas H. Strawn, president of the Chamber of Commerce of the United
States

J. Clawson Roop, Director of the
Budget

November 5

Breakfast—Mark Sullivan, journalist

Secretary of War Patrick J. Hurley

Benedict Crowell, Cleveland, Ohio, former Secretary of War

Chester H. Gray, American Farm Bureau Federation

Roy T. Davis, United States Minister to
Panama

Lunch—Lawrence M. Judd, Governor
of Hawaii

J. Clawson Roop, Director of the Budget

Joseph R. Nutt, treasurer of the Republican National Committee

Jeremiah Milbank, Southern Railway
Co.

Raymond Benjamin, assistant chairman
of the Republican National Committee

Dinner—Ambassador and Mrs. John D.
Garrett, Dr. and Mrs. Vernon L. Kellogg, Mr. and Mrs. Adolph C. Miller,
and Ferry K. Heath

November 6

Breakfast—Edgar Rickard

Henry J. Allen, former Senator of Kansas

Senator Charles L. McNary

Cabinet

Senator Henrik Shipstead

Gerrish Gassaway, president of the National Association of Commercial Organization Secretaries

Representative Albert Johnson, Washington

Vernon L. Kellogg

Appendix E

1931

Lunch—Edgar Rickard

James L. Fieser, American National Red Cross

Secretary of Agriculture Arthur M. Hyde

Washington Correspondents

Clarence Streit, Geneva correspondent for the New York Times

Senator David A. Reed

Thomas E. Campbell, President of the Civil Service Commission

George Akerson, former Secretary to the President

Dinner—Mr. and Mrs. Henry M. Robinson

November 7

Secretary of State Henry L. Stimson

Senator Hiram Bingham and Jorge Bird Arias of Porto Rico

Representative Don B. Colton, Utah

O. P. Gascoigne, Chesapeake and Potomac Telephone Co.

Representative Arthur M. Free, California

George Akerson, former Secretary to the President

Otis J. Rogers

Lunch—former Representative J. Hampton Moore of Pennsylvania

J. Clawson Roop, Director of the Budget

Dinner—Secretary of the Navy and Mrs. Charles F. Adams, and Mrs. Cox

November 8

Breakfast—Charles K. Field and Henry M. Robinson

Lunch—Senator and Mrs. James J. Davis, Judge and Mrs. Edward J. Henning, and Charles K. Field

Paul Shoup, president of the Southern Pacific Railroad Co.

Dinner—Senator and Mrs. James Couzens, Governor and Mrs. Lawrence M. Judd, Mr. and Mrs. Henry M. Robinson, Mrs. James W. Good, and Mr. and Mrs. Yaw

November 9

Secretary of State Henry L. Stimson

Representative Addison T. Smith, Idaho

Charles H. Sherrill, International Committee on the Olympic Games

John L. Richards, Boston, Mass.

John M. Morehead, United States Minister to Sweden

Governor and Mrs. Lawrence M. Judd of Hawaii

Junior Order of United American Mechanics, delegation

Representative Royal C. Johnson and committee of Veterans of Foreign Wars

Mexican Ambassador, José Manuel Puig Casauranc, to present letters of credence

Edward G. Lowry, journalist

Franklin W. Fort, former Representative of New Jersey

Ernest R. Graham, Chicago, Ill.

Walter S. Gifford, Director of the President's Organization on Unemployment Relief

J. Clawson Roop, Director of the Budget

Secretary of State Henry L. Stimson

November 10

Cabinet

Washington Correspondents

Secretary of State Henry L. Stimson

Matthew E. Hanna, United States Minister to Nicaragua

Lunch—Mr. and Mrs. Zane Grey

Dr. Shaw

Frasier Hunt, Cosmopolitan magazine

Jay G. Hayden, president of the Gridiron Club

Secretary of the Treasury Andrew W. Mellon

Dinner—Eugene Meyer, George L. Harrison, Mortimer N. Buckner, and Henry M. Robinson

November 11

Breakfast—Mark Sullivan, journalist

To Arlington Cemetery to place wreath on Tomb of the Unknown Soldier

Dedication of memorial to soldiers and sailors of World War from the District of Columbia, address

John T. Adams, member of the Advisory Committee of the Inland Waterways Corporation

Murray Garcon and party

Abraham C. Ratchesky, United States Minister to Czechoslovakia

Lunch—Mr. and Mrs. Ernest R. Graham, Thad J. Johnson, and Anna Fitzhugh

To Navy Yard to inspect the *Constitution*

Archbishop James Henry O'Connell

Eugene Meyer, Governor of the Federal Reserve Board

Dinner—Mr. and Mrs. Raymond Benjamin and Barbara Benjamin

November 12

Secretary of the Navy Charles F. Adams, Adm. W. V. Pratt, Chief of Naval Operations, and J. Clawson Roop, Director of the Budget

Representative John Q. Tilson, House majority leader

Representative Burton L. French, Idaho

Representative William R. Wood, Indiana

W. M. Wood, president of the Mississippi Valley Structural Steel Co.

Robert L. Owen, former Senator of Oklahoma

William P. MacCracken, Jr., secretary of the American Bar Association

Representative Cassius C. Dowell

William R. Castle, Jr., Under Secretary of State

Lunch—Mrs. Fairbanks, George Akerson, Mrs. Frederick Butler, Miss Goss, Dare S. McMullen, Col. Campbell B. Hodges, Maj. Howard Eager, and Lt. Ring

Edward Williams Decker, banker, Minneapolis, Minn.

Henry P. Fletcher, Chairman of the United States Tariff Commission

George Akerson, former Secretary to the President

Frasier Hunt, Cosmopolitan magazine

J. Clawson Roop, Director of the Budget

Secretary of Agriculture Arthur M. Hyde

Dinner—football players

Appendix E

November 13

Handball—football dinner guests of previous evening

Breakfast—Walter E. Hope and former Stanford football players, including Paul M. Downing, Joel Y. Field, Julius B. Frankenheimer, William H. Harrelson, W. C. Hazzard, Herbert Hicks, Will Irwin, Martin H. Kennedy, and W. W. Orcutt

Charles S. Dewey, former Assistant Secretary of the Treasury

Cabinet

British Ambassador, Sir Ronald Lindsay, to present Maharajadhiraja of Burdwan

Archbishop Edward J. Hanna of San Francisco

Senator Ellison D. Smith

Charles Fickert

Representative Wilbur M. White, Ohio

Representative Samuel S. Arentz, Nevada

Byron Price, Associated Press

Will Irwin

Washington Correspondents

Frederic William Wile, broadcast journalist

LeRoy T. Vernon, Chicago Daily News

Charles Fickert and Annie G. Lyle

Dinner—Mr. and Mrs. Henry M. Robinson

Senator William E. Borah

November 14

Breakfast—Mark Sullivan, journalist

Liberal Arts Colleges Association, radio address from Cabinet Room

J. Clawson Roop, Director of the Budget

Eugene Meyer, Governor of the Federal Reserve Board

Hanford MacNider, United States Minister to Canada

November 15

Breakfast—Senator James E. Watson, Senate majority leader

Lunch—Mr. and Mrs. Walter H. Newton

November 16

Breakfast—Mark Sullivan, journalist

Secretary of State Henry L. Stimson

James P. Goodrich, former Governor of Indiana

Samuel O. Levinson

Representative Menalcus Lankford, Virginia

Jefferson Caffrey, United States Minister to Colombia

Morris Gist

Secretary of Commerce Robert P. Lamont and Dr. Mann

E. G. Pinkham, Kansas City Star

Ezra Brainerd, Jr., Chairman of the Interstate Commerce Commission

Italian Ambassador, Nobile Giacomo de Martino, to present Dino Grandi, Minister of Foreign Affairs

November 17

Breakfast—Mark Sullivan, journalist

Senator Frederic C. Walcott

Cabinet

Washington Correspondents

811

Gridiron Club, executive committee

Harry A. Garfield, president of Williams College, and Lawrence Lowell, president of Harvard University

British Ambassador, Sir Ronald Lindsay, to present Vice Admiral Vernon Haggard

Mrs. Walter S. McLucas of Kansas City, and Mrs. Loose

Representative Ruth Pratt

Secretary of War Patrick J. Hurley

Dinner—Secretary of War Patrick J. Hurley, Secretary of the Interior Ray Lyman Wilbur, and Postmaster General Walter F. Brown

November 18

Breakfast—Mark Sullivan, journalist

Secretary of State Henry L. Stimson and Italian Minister of Foreign Affairs Dino Grandi

Senator L. J. Dickinson and Mr. Adler

Louis McGrew, Pittsburgh, Pa., publisher of Labor World

Secretary of Commerce Robert P. Lamont

Lunch—Nathan W. MacChesney

Michael Gallagher

Dinner—Italian Minister of Foreign Affairs Dino Grandi

November 19

Lt. Col. Joseph I. McMullen, Muscle Shoals Commission

Louis McGrew, Pittsburgh, Pa., publisher of Labor World

Representative William R. Eaton, Colorado

William S. Bennett, vice president of the Continental Coal Co.

B. S. Moss, New York

Mrs. W. Reginald Baker, New Jersey

German Ambassador, Friedrich von Prittwitz, to present H. Jaechk, Dean of the College of Politics, Berlin, Germany

Hugh R. Wilson, United States Minister to Switzerland

Group of citizens from South Carolina and Georgia

Lunch—A. E. Ruszkiewicz, Buffalo, N.Y.

Secretary of State Henry L. Stimson

Senator Reed Smoot

Michael Gallagher

J. Clawson Roop, Director of the Budget

Italian Minister of Foreign Affairs and Signora Dino Grandi

Robert H. Lucas, executive director of the Republican National Committee

Mr. and Mrs. William Benson Storey

November 20

Breakfast—Mark Sullivan and Mr. and Mrs. William Benson Storey

Secretary of State Henry L. Stimson

Cabinet

Japanese Ambassador, Katsuji Debuchi, to present Yukio Ozaki

Arthur J. Weaver, former Governor of Nebraska, and Missouri River Navigation Association

Mr. and Mrs. Ned Wayburn, Jr., New York

Appendix E

1931

Ernest Lee Jahncke, Assistant Secretary of the Navy, and Edward A. Parsons, president of the Louisiana Historical Society

H. E. Ford

Butler University football team

Lunch—George T. Harding

William Benson Storey

Harry F. Guggenheim, United States Ambassador to Cuba

Senator David A. Reed, Pennsylvania

James R. Garfield, Chairman of the Committee on the Conservation and Administration of the Public Domain

Raymond Benjamin, assistant chairman of the Republican National Committee

November 21

Representative John Q. Tilson, House majority leader

Secretary of State Henry L. Stimson

Fred C. Croxton, Assistant Director of the President's Organization on Unemployment Relief

Group of newsboys from Brooklyn (N.Y.) Eagle

Lunch—Mark Reed

Robert Lincoln O'Brien, Boston

Walter S. Gifford, Director of the President's Organization on Unemployment Relief

John Matthew Gries, Executive Secretary of the White House Conference on Home Building and Home Ownership

Bernard M. Baruch

November 22

Lunch—Mr. and Mrs. Thomas E. Campbell and Allan Campbell

Home Building and Home Ownership Commissioners Frederick H. Ecker, Clarence Dillon, William H. Kingsley, and Harry A. Kahler

Dinner—Secretary of Commerce and Mrs. Robert P. Lamont, Representative and Mrs. Willis C. Hawley, Representative and Mrs. Richard S. Aldrich, Mr. and Mrs. Silas H. Strawn

November 23

J. Clawson Roop, Director of the Budget

Secretary of Labor William N. Doak

Senator Tasker L. Oddie, Nevada

Representative James S. Parker, New York

Secretary of Commerce Robert P. Lamont

Ecuadorian Minister, Homero Viteri Lafronte, on departure

Representative Harold Knutson and Father J. Kromolicki of Freeport, Minn.

Mr. and Mrs. Hotchner and daughter, New York

Frank P. Washburn, commissioner of agriculture of Maine to present gift from the potato growers of Maine

Lunch—Frederick Brown, New York

Secretary of War Patrick J. Hurley

James R. Garfield and Mr. Wilson

Eugene Meyer, Federal Reserve Board

November 24

Cabinet

Washington Correspondents

British Ambassador, Sir Ronald Lindsay, to present Sydney W. Pascall, of London, president of Rotary International

Brazilian Ambassador, Rinaldo de Lima e Silva, to present Miguel Lisboa, director of the International Rotary for Latin America

University of North Dakota football team

Lunch—John N. Willys, United States Ambassador to Poland

George Barr Baker

William B. McGerarty, president of the Washington Society of Alexandria, and delegation from Alexandria, Va.

Henry F. Misslewitz, United Press Associations

Senator Simeon D. Fess

Dinner—Assistant Secretary of the Treasury and Mrs. Arthur A. Ballantine and Barbara Ballantine

November 25

Breakfast—Daniel Willard, Baltimore

Secretary of State Henry L. Stimson

Frederick H. Payne, Assistant Secretary of War, and Lt. Col. Joseph I. McMullen, Muscle Shoals Commission

Bird M. Robinson and committee from the American Short Line Railroad Association

Representative Leonidas C. Dyer, Missouri

Frank T. Hines, Administrator of Veterans' Affairs and architects John Sloane and T. M. Robertson

Representative Burton L. French, Idaho

Daniel F. Steck, former Senator of Iowa

George T. Summerlin, United States Minister to Venezuela

Senator Roscoe C. Patterson, Missouri, and Mr. and Mrs. L. B. Thompson

Secretary of the Interior Ray Lyman Wilbur and officials of the Reclamation Service

Joie-Lou Berliner and H. W. Witcover, representatives of the Child Health Crusaders

Lunch—Mr. and Mrs. Arthur C. Johnson

James G. Rogers, Assistant Secretary of State, and Henry J. Allen, former Senator of Kansas

Secretary of the Interior Ray Lyman Wilbur, Secretary of Commerce Robert P. Lamont, John Matthew Gries, and Mr. Ford

J. Clawson Roop, Director of the Budget

Raymond Benjamin, assistant chairman of the Republican National Committee

November 26

Breakfast—Mark Sullivan, journalist

Lunch—Sara Louis Arnold and Mary G. Hood

Arthur A. Ballantine, Assistant Secretary of the Treasury

1931

November 27

Walter W. Stewart, New York
Secretary of State Henry L. Stimson
Cabinet
J. Clawson Roop, Director of the Budget
Col. Herbert Deakyne, Board of Engineers for Rivers and Harbors
Mr. and Mrs. Emanuel Hertz, New York
University of Detroit football team
Wooster College, Ohio, football team
Henry J. Allen, former Senator of Kansas
Ezra Brainerd, Jr., Chairman of the Interstate Commerce Commission
Mr. Reep
Secretary of Agriculture Arthur M. Hyde
Postmaster General Walter F. Brown
Secretary of Commerce Robert P. Lamont
Richard Hooker, director of the Associated Press
Secretary of War Patrick J. Hurley
Walter S. Gifford, Director of the President's Organization on Unemployment Relief
Secretary of State Henry L. Stimson
Henry J. Allen, former Senator of Kansas
Dinner—Mr. and Mrs. Edward E. Gann, Senator and Mrs. Tasker L. Oddie, and Miss Goss

November 28

Henry J. Allen, former Senator of Kansas
J. Clawson Roop, Director of the Budget

Secretary of State Henry L. Stimson
James C. White
Adolph C. Miller, Federal Reserve Board of Governors
Walter Lippmann, New York World
Representative Willis C. Hawley
Edwin Balmer, editor of Red Book, and William H. Crawford
Secretary of Agriculture Arthur M. Hyde
Postmaster General Walter F. Brown
Lunch—Walter S. Gifford and sons, Sherman and Dick
Edwin Balmer, editor of Red Book
Chester H. Gray, American Farm Bureau Federation
Secretary of War Patrick J. Hurley
Secretary of Commerce Robert P. Lamont

November 29

Breakfast—Walter E. Hope, former Assistant Secretary of the Treasury
Lunch—Walter E. Hope
Dinner—Walter E. Hope, Ambassador and Mrs. Robert Woods Bliss, and Mr. and Mrs. Charles Warren

November 30

Breakfast—Mark Sullivan, journalist
Ferry K. Heath, Assistant Secretary of the Treasury
Senator Wesley L. Jones
Senator John Thomas and Irvin E. Rockwell
Everett Colby, chairman of the executive committee of the National World Court Committee

1931

S. Wallace Dempsey, former Representative of New York

Franklin W. Fort, former Representative of New Jersey

Julius G. Lay, United States Minister to Honduras

Archibald Rice

William Monroe Trotter and committee of the National Equal Rights League

Richard E. Pennoyer, London, England

Senator Frederick Steiwer

Lunch—Franklin W. Fort, former Representative of New Jersey

Adoph C. Miller, Federal Reserve Board of Governors

Ogden L. Mills, Under Secretary of the Treasury

Secretary of Commerce Robert P. Lamont

H. D. Paulson, editor of the Fargo (N. Dak.) Forum

December 1

Senator Frederic C. Walcott

Senator Hiram Bingham

Cabinet

Representative William R. Coyle

Henry J. Allen, former Senator of Kansas

Representative Bertrand H. Snell

Secretary of State Henry L. Stimson

Secretary of Agriculture Arthur M. Hyde

John Matthew Gries, Executive Secretary of the White House Conference on Home Building and Home Ownership

December 2

Breakfast—Mark Sullivan, journalist

Postmaster General Walter F. Brown

Representative John Q. Tilson, House majority leader

Eugene Meyer, Governor of the Federal Reserve Board

Senator Samuel M. Shortridge

Representative Robert Luce, Massachusetts

Arch W. Shaw, President's Committee on Recent Economic Changes

Ruth Morgan

Senator Robert J. Bulkley, Ohio

Leroy W. Hubbard

Capital University Choir

Lunch—Richard Scott

Ogden L. Mills, Under Secretary of the Treasury

Fred W. Kiesel, president of the California National Bank, Sacramento

William R. Castle, Jr., Under Secretary of State

Attorney General William D. Mitchell

Secretary of Commerce Robert P. Lamont

White House Conference on Home Building and Home Ownership, address at Constitution Hall

December 3

Breakfast—Mark Sullivan, journalist

Vice President Charles Curtis

Representative Bertrand H. Snell, New York

Representative Daniel A. Reed, New York

Mr. Peck, North Carolina

Senator Claude A. Swanson

J. Frank Grimes, representing Independent Grocers Alliance of America

Representative Edith Nourse Rogers, Massachusetts

P. B. Gates and F. E. Carringer, Denver

Robert Woods Bliss, United States Ambassador to Argentina

Representative Charles E. Swanson and E. P. Chase, editor of the News-Telegram of Atlantic, Iowa

National Warm Air Heating Association, 19th annual convention delegates

T. E. McDowell, Stanford University

Karl A. Bickel, president of United Press

Secretary of the Interior Ray Lyman Wilbur

Representative Ruth Pratt

J. Clawson Roop, Director of the Budget

Mrs. J. N. Barger, Albany, Mo.

Dinner—Cabinet

December 4

Julius Barnes, chairman of the board of directors of the Chamber of Commerce of the United States

Cabinet

A. C. Pearson, president of the National Publishers Association

Col. Benjamin Fly, Tucson, Ariz.

Representative Sol Bloom and State Senator Desmond of New York

Ella A. Boole, president of the National Woman's Christian Temperance Union, and delegates to the regional conference

Lunch—Mrs. Willis Martin and Mary Delano

James R. Garfield, Chairman of the Committee on the Conservation and Administration of the Public Domain

Henry J. Allen, former Senator of Kansas

Senator Otis F. Glenn

New York Real Estate president and three

Secretary of State Henry L. Stimson

Reception—Members of the White House Conference on Home Building and Home Ownership

Dinner—Mr. and Mrs. Whiting Williams

December 5

Ogden L. Mills, Under Secretary of the Treasury

Secretary of Labor William N. Doak

Secretary of War Patrick J. Hurley

Senator Otis F. Glenn

Mark Sullivan, journalist

Charles S. McDonald, chairman of South Dakota Republican State Central Committee

Stuart W. Cramer, North Carolina

Harry S. Kissell and two

Eugene Meyer, Governor of the Federal Reserve Board

Senator James E. Watson, Representative Bertrand H. Snell, and Walter H. Newton

December 6

Lunch—Secretary of the Interior and Mrs. Ray Lyman Wilbur, and Martha and Rose Van Rensselar

817

Secretary of Commerce Robert P. Lamont, Ephraim F. Morgan, and John Matthew Gries

Secretary of State Henry L. Stimson

Dinner—Senator and Mrs. Daniel O. Hastings and Dr. and Mrs. Vernon L. Kellogg

December 7

Breakfast—Mark Sullivan, journalist

Representative Charles L. Underhill

Secretary of Agriculture Arthur M. Hyde

Fred C. Croxton, Assistant Director of the President's Organization on Unemployment Relief

Senator Arthur R. Robinson, Indiana

Senator James E. Watson, Senate majority leader

Representative Hamilton Fish, Jr., New York

William T. Rawleigh, Freeport, Ill.

Franklin W. Fort, former Representative of New Jersey

George Murnane

Lawrence M. Judd, Governor of Hawaii

Daniel W. O'Donoghue, associate justice of the Supreme Court of the District of Columbia

Mr. and Mrs. Thomas A. Dunn, Pittsburgh

Lunch—Mark L. Requa

John Barton Payne, Chairman of the American National Red Cross

Senator Peter Norbeck

Senator David A. Reed, Pennsylvania

House and Senate Organization Committees

Representative Henry B. Steagall

Secretary of Labor William N. Doak and John L. Lewis, president of the United Mine Workers of America

Eugene Meyer, Federal Reserve Board

Dinner—George Barr Baker

December 8

Breakfast—Mark Sullivan, journalist

Robert Lincoln O'Brien, Chairman of the United States Tariff Commission

Secretary of Commerce Robert P. Lamont

Secretary of State Henry L. Stimson

Cabinet

Reginald H. Sullivan, mayor of Indianapolis, Ind.

Henry L. Stevens, Jr., national commander of the American Legion

Group of Republican women from Pennsylvania

J. Clawson Roop, Director of the Budget

Secretary of State Henry L. Stimson

Dinner—With Vice President Charles Curtis and Mrs. Edward E. Gann at his residence

December 9

Ogden L. Mills, Under Secretary of the Treasury

Representative Fred S. Purnell, Indiana

Senator William W. Barbour, New Jersey

Representative William E. Evans, California

Lenna L. Yost, Republican National Committee, and Miss Boswell of New York

Postmaster General Walter F. Brown

Mark L. Requa and commission from Arizona to present fruit

Representative Joe Crail and Ella C. Wheeler

W. Kingsland Macy, New York Republican national committeeman

Representative Samuel A. Kendall, Pennsylvania

Representative Edith Nourse Rogers, Massachusetts

J. Matt Chilton, Republican National Committee

Representative Gale H. Stalker, New York

Lunch—Mr. and Mrs. Warren Fairbanks

William L. Chenery, editor of Colliers Weekly, and Arthur Train

J. Clawson Roop, Director of the Budget, and Ferry K. Heath, Assistant Secretary of the Treasury

Frank B. Kellogg, former Secretary of State

Russell Doubleday

John F. Chester, Associated Press

Mark L. Requa

Representative John Q. Tilson, House majority leader

December 10

Senator George H. Moses, New Hampshire

Postmaster General Walter F. Brown

Michael Gallagher

Secretary of State Henry L. Stimson

Robert Lincoln O'Brien, Chairman of the United States Tariff Commission

Senator Ellison D. Smith, South Carolina

Senator L. J. Dickinson, Iowa

Representative Philip D. Swing, California

Senator Simeon D. Fess, A. N. Ward, president of Western Maryland College, and committee representing the liberal arts college movement

Presentation of the Herbert Schiff Memorial Trophy to Lt. Comdr. Richard P. Whitehead, for the U.S.N. Reserve Aviation Base, Floyd Bennett Field, Brooklyn, N.Y.

William Rowen, president of the Board of Education of Pennsylvania

Ogden L. Mills, Under Secretary of the Treasury

Representative James W. Collier, Mississippi

Arthur J. Barton, Wilmington, N.C.

J. Clawson Roop, Director of the Budget

Mark L. Requa

Reception—Diplomatic

December 11

Ogden L. Mills, Under Secretary of the Treasury

Representative Joseph W. Byrns, Tennessee

Cabinet

Senators Duncan U. Fletcher and Park Trammell, Florida

National radio audition finalists

Osee L. Bodenhamer and John Ewing

University of Alabama football team

Lunch—Roy A. Roberts, Kansas City Star

Harvey S. Firestone, Sr.

Roy A. Roberts, Kansas City Star

Frank Knox, publisher of the Chicago Daily News, and Mr. Ellis

Arthur Brisbane, editor of the Chicago Herald and Examiner

Washington Correspondents

Dinner—Mr. and Mrs. Sidney Kent, Mr. and Mrs. George Akerson, Mr. and Mrs. Giles Whitney, and Paul Shoup

December 12

Breakfast—Dr. Joel T. Boone

Ashmun N. Brown, Providence (R.I.) Journal

Henry P. Fletcher, former Chairman of the United States Tariff Commission

Arlington Memorial Bridge Commission, meeting in Cabinet Room

Fred C. Croxton, Assistant Director of the President's Organization on Unemployment Relief

Paul Shoup, president of the Southern Pacific Railroad Co.

William Harding, former Governor of Iowa

Senator Robert J. Bulkley, Ohio, and Governor George White of Ohio

Senator Claude A. Swanson, Virginia

Chilean Ambassador, Carlos G. Davila, to present Emilio Bello Codesido

Senator Simeon D. Fess and Marshall Sheppey

Indiana Editorial Association, delegation

Senator Robert D. Carey

Dr. Ford

Charles A. Rawson, former Senator of Iowa

Conrad Mann, President's Organization on Unemployment Relief

Lunch—Senator Otis F. Glenn and Judge Wilberson

Thomas W. Lamont

Henry P. Fletcher, former Chairman of the United States Tariff Commission

James F. Burke, general counsel of the Republican National Committee

Ogden L. Mills, Under Secretary of the Treasury, and Mr. Drexel

Senator Reed Smoot

Gridiron Dinner—Willard Hotel

Frank Knox, publisher of the Chicago Daily News

December 13

Ogden L. Mills, Under Secretary of the Treasury

Lunch—Mr. and Mrs. John Blodgett, Charles D. Hilles, and Mrs. Fitzsimmons

Postmaster General Walter F. Brown and James F. Burke, general counsel of the Republican National Committee

Richard Whitney, president of the New York Stock Exchange

Secretary of State Henry L. Stimson

820

1931

December 14

Breakfast—Mark Sullivan, journalist

Representative Bertrand H. Snell, New York

Roy G. West, former Secretary of the Interior

Senator Roscoe C. Patterson, Edward B. Clements, and Mr. Adams

Eugene Meyer, Governor of the Federal Reserve Board

Senator Frederick Steiwer and L. W. Hartman, president of the Portland, Oreg., Chamber of Commerce

Representative Ruth Bryan Owen

B. Carroll Reece, former Representative of Tennessee

Edwin Balmer, editor of Red Book, and William H. Crawford

Ernest Lee Jahncke, Assistant Secretary of the Navy, and John F. Jackson

Maj. Gen. George E. Leach, Chief of the Bureau of the Militia, Department of War

Joseph R. Nutt and Walter E. Hope

Grace Semple Burlingham, Missouri

Lunch—Members of the Republican National Committee

Willis J. Abbott, editor of the Christian Science Monitor

Senator Carter Glass, Virginia

Franklin W. Fort, former Representative of New Jersey

Senator David A. Reed, Pennsylvania

Jay Cooke

Raymond Benjamin, assistant chairman of the Republican National Committee

Dinner—executive committee of the Republican National Committee

December 15

Franklin W. Fort and Edward D. Duffield, president of the Prudential Insurance Co. of America

Secretary of War Patrick J. Hurley

Ogden L. Mills, Under Secretary of the Treasury

Cabinet

Senators Porter H. Dale and Warren R. Austin and Representative John E. Weeks, Vermont

Daniel A. Poling and group from the International Society of Christian Endeavor

J. A. Harris

Daniel A. Poling, president of the International Interdenominational Christian Endeavor Society

Mr. Harding

W. G. Skelly, president of the Skelly Oil Co.

Jay Cooke

Secretary of Labor William N. Doak

Franklin W. Fort, former Representative of New Jersey

Mark L. Requa

December 16

Breakfast—Mark Sullivan, journalist

Senator Frederic C. Walcott

Representative Robert Luce, Massachusetts

821

Representative Charles L. Underhill, Massachusetts

Ogden L. Mills, Under Secretary of the Treasury

Senator Wesley L. Jones and Representative John W. Summers, Washington

Nathan L. Miller, former Governor of New York

Representative Riley J. Wilson and Harry Jacobs, Chief Army Engineer for Louisiana

Albert Bushnell Hart and Alexander Brin, Massachusetts George Washington Bicentennial Commission

German Ambassador, Friedrich von Prittwitz, to present Dr. von Schultze Gaevernitz of Germany

Norris Brown, former Senator of Nebraska

Miss Barkley, daughter of Senator Alben W. Barkley

Dr. and Mrs. A. Chalmers Wilson

Reception—Republican National Committee

Lunch—Representative Ruth Pratt and Walter S. Hallanan

Ecuadorian Minister, Gonzalo Zaldumbide, to present letters of credence

Representatives Bertrand H. Snell and John Q. Tilson

Secretary of State Henry L. Stimson

Secretary of War Patrick J. Hurley

Representative Cassius C. Dowell, Iowa

Representative Lloyd Thurston, Iowa

Secretary of Labor William N. Doak

Joseph R. Nutt, treasurer of the Republican National Committee

December 17

Breakfast—Mark Sullivan, journalist, and Philip de László, artist

Ogden L. Mills, Under Secretary of the Treasury

Representative William Williamson, South Dakota

Edward B. Clements, Missouri Republican national committeeman

Representative Scott Leavitt

Hanna Clothier Hull, Caroline McCormick Slade, and Helen Taft Manning

S. S. Way and Mrs. Paul Rewman

Fred C. Croxton, Assistant Director of the President's Organization on Unemployment Relief

J. A. Harris

Representative Leonidas C. Dyer

Representatives John T. Buckbee and Frederick W. Dallinger to present winner of typical boy and his dog contest

Frank T. Hines, Administrator of Veterans' Affairs

Secretary of State Henry L. Stimson

Lunch—Philip de László, artist

Attorney General William D. Mitchell

J. Clawson Roop, Director of the Budget

James R. Garfield, Chairman of the Committee on the Conservation and Administration of the Public Domain

Senator Thomas D. Schall, Minnesota

Senator David A. Reed, Pennsylvania

Ogden L. Mills, Under Secretary of the Treasury

Dinner—Commander and Mrs. Beauregard and Mrs. Hert

Reception—Judicial

December 18

Breakfast—Speaker of the House John Nance Garner, and Representatives Harry T. Rainey, Bertrand H. Snell, James W. Collier, Charles R. Crisp, Willis C. Hawley, Robert Luce, Henry B. Steagall, and Allen T. Treadway, Representatives Brand and Strong, Walter H. Newton, and Ogden L. Mills

Representative Charles L. Underhill, Massachusetts

Cabinet

Attorney General William D. Mitchell

Rentfro B. Creager and Orville Bullington

Carlton A. Fisher, national commander of the Marine Corps League, and committee

Lunch—Frank E. Gannett, newspaper publisher

J. Matt Chilton and Col. Seitz

David W. Mulvane, Republican National Committee

James R. Garfield, Chairman of the Committee on the Conservation and Administration of the Public Domain

Edward G. Buckland, New Haven Railroad

Walter E. Hope, former Assistant Secretary of the Treasury

Senator James Couzens, Michigan

Norman H. Davis

Senator Frederic C. Walcott, Connecticut

Daniel Willard, president of the Baltimore and Ohio Railroad Co.

Secretary of Labor William N. Doak

Fred C. Croxton, Assistant Director of the President's Organization on Unemployment Relief

Secretary of War Patrick J. Hurley and Dwight F. Davis, Governor General of the Philippine Islands

Senator Arthur R. Robinson and Representative William R. Wood, Indiana

Senator Roscoe C. Patterson, Missouri

Representative Robert L. Bacon

John M. Robsion, former Senator of Kentucky

Ogden L. Mills, Under Secretary of the Treasury

Lunch—Philip de László, artist

C. Bascom Slemp

Frank H. Hitchcock, former Postmaster General

Eugene Meyer, Governor of the Federal Reserve Board

Norman H. Davis

Raymond Benjamin, assistant chairman of the Republican National Committee

Dinner—Col. Campbell B. Hodges, Mr. and Mrs. Arthur Train, and Mrs. Horatio Small

December 19

Breakfast—Walter E. Hope, former Assistant Secretary of the Treasury

December 20

Breakfast—Mr. and Mrs. Arthur Train and Mrs. Horatio Small

823

Dinner—Representative Allen T. Treadway, Representative and Mrs. Leonidas C. Dyer, Representative and Mrs. Carl R. Chindblom, Representative Edith Nourse Rogers, and Mr. and Mrs. Walter H. Newton

December 21

Breakfast—Senators Reed Smoot, James E. Watson, David A. Reed, Pat Harrison, William H. King, Walter F. George, Peter Norbeck, Phillips Lee Goldsborough, Frederic C. Walcott, Duncan U. Fletcher, and Carter Glass; Under Secretary of the Treasury Ogden L. Mills; Federal Reserve Board Governor Eugene Meyer; and Walter H. Newton

Senators Bronson Cutting of New Mexico and J. Hamilton Lewis, Illinois

Representative Grant E. Mouser, Jr., Ohio

Secretary of War Patrick J. Hurley

Costa Rican Chargé d'Affaires, Guillermo E. Gonzáles, to present Dr. Luis Castro Urena

Planted white oak tree from Abraham Lincoln's birthplace in Hodgenville, Ky.

Secretary of State Henry L. Stimson

Secretary of Agriculture Arthur M. Hyde

Senator Robert F. Wagner

December 22

Breakfast—Mark Sullivan, journalist

Cabinet

Washington Correspondents

T. V. O'Connor, Chairman of the United States Shipping Board

Lunch—Ralph Williams

Richard E. Sloan, former Governor of Arizona

Albert W. Atwood, Saturday Evening Post

Henry J. Allen, former Senator of Kansas

December 23

Secretary of State Henry L. Stimson

Secretary of War Patrick J. Hurley, Oscar K. Davis, and Mr. Cook

Secretary of Labor William N. Doak, C. Stanley Sterling Smith, and A. Johnson

Harry J. Haas, president of the American Bankers Association

Ferry K. Heath, Assistant Secretary of the Treasury

Representative William Williamson and Jean Darling

J. Clawson Roop, Director of the Budget

Eugene Meyer, Governor of the Federal Reserve Board

Lem C. Spears. New York Times

December 24

Breakfast—Mrs. Mark Sullivan

Philip de László, artist

Lunch—Philip de László, artist

Representative Bertrand H. Snell, New York

Arthur A. Ballantine, Assistant Secretary of the Treasury

Eugene Meyer, Governor of the Federal Reserve Board

Ogden L. Mills, Under Secretary of the Treasury

Thomas E. Campbell, President of the Civil Service Commission

Ferry K. Heath, Assistant Secretary of the Treasury

Victor S. K. Houston, Delegate of Hawaii

W. M. Ritter

Pressed electric button lighting the National Community Christmas Tree in Sherman Park

December 25

Breakfast—Mrs. Vernon L. Kellogg

Philip de László, artist

Ira E. Bennett, editor of the Washington Post

Dinner—Members of the Cabinet and their families, Mr. and Mrs. Douglas Lewis, and Alan Herrington

December 26

Senator Duncan U. Fletcher, Florida

Senator Claude A. Swanson, Virginia

Byron Price Phillip

Lunch—Mr. and Mrs. Mark Sullivan and Philip de László

George Benson

Secretary of Commerce Robert P. Lamont

December 27

Breakfast—Mark Sullivan and Philip de László

Lunch—Philip de László

Senator Pat Harrison

December 28

Breakfast—Mark Sullivan, journalist

Mr. Macklin

Charles H. Burke, former Commissioner of Indian Affairs

Secretary of Labor William N. Doak

Mrs. Powell Harrison and children

University of California football team

Kingston, Pa., Boy Scout Troop 166

Oberlin College glee club

Fred C. Croxton, Assistant Director of the President's Organization on Unemployment Relief

Representative Robert Luce, Massachusetts

Julius Klein, Assistant Secretary of Commerce

Secretary of State Henry L. Stimson

Ogden L. Mills, Under Secretary of the Treasury

December 29

Breakfast—Mark Sullivan, journalist, and Philip de László

Ogden L. Mills, Under Secretary of the Treasury

Cabinet

Washington Correspondents

William Hard

Harry S. Kissell, president of the National Association of Real Estate Boards

John B. Creighton, president of the Davenport Mortgage Company of New York

Secretary of State Henry L. Stimson

Lunch—Raymond Robins

Judson C. Welliver, president of Pullman Co.

Postmaster General Walter F. Brown

December 30

Breakfast—Philip de László

Senator Wesley L. Jones

Senator Hiram Bingham and Mr. Meyer

Senator Robert D. Carey, Wyoming

Otto L. Mallery, Philadelphia

Edward F. Colladay, Newbold Noyes, and Thomas E. Campbell

Group of newsboys

Brooklyn Daily Times newsboys

New York Junior Naval Militia

Mrs. Gilbert Grosvenor and Mrs. Clyde Kelly

Lunch—Philip de László

E. E. Hunt, secretary of the President's Research Committee on Social Trends

John F. Sinclair, financial editor of the North American Newspaper Alliance

James G. Rogers, Assistant Secretary of State

J. Clawson Roop, Director of the Budget

Frederick H. Payne, Assistant Secretary of War

Dinner—Adolph S. Ochs, newspaper publisher

December 31

Breakfast—Philip de László

H. Paul Bestor, Federal Farm Loan Bureau

Senator Duncan U. Fletcher, Florida. and Mr. Thompson

Ogden L. Mills, Under Secretary of the Treasury

Senator Arthur Capper and Richard J. Hopkins

Harry F. Burgess, Governor of Panama Canal Zone

Lunch—Secretary of War Patrick J. Hurley

Eugene Meyer, Governor of the Federal Reserve Board

Capt. Adolphus Andrews

Secretary of Agriculture Arthur M. Hyde

Rodney Dutcher, National Education Association

Appendix F—Rules Governing This Publication

[Reprinted from the Federal Register, vol. 37, p. 23607, dated November 4, 1972]

TITLE I—GENERAL PROVISIONS

Chapter 1—Administrative Committee of the Federal Register

PART 10—PRESIDENTIAL PAPERS

Subpart A—Annual Volumes

Authority: 44 U.S.C. 1506; sec. 6, E.O. 10530, 19 FR 2709; 3 CFR 1954–1958 Comp. p. 189.

Subpart A—Annual Volumes

§ 10.1 *Publication required.*

The Director of the Federal Register shall publish, at the end of each calendar year, a special edition of the Federal Register called the "Public Papers of the Presidents of the United States." Unless the amount of material requires otherwise, each volume shall cover one calendar year.

§ 10.2 *Coverage of prior years.*

After consulting with the National Historical Publications Commission on the need therefor, the Administrative Committee may authorize the publication of volumes of papers of the Presidents covering specified years before 1957.

§ 10.3 *Scope and sources.*

(a) The basic text of each volume shall consist of oral statements by the President or of writings subscribed by him, and selected from—

(1) Communications to the Congress;

(2) Public addresses;

(3) Transcripts of news conferences;

(4) Public letters;

(5) Messages to heads of State;

(6) Statements released on miscellaneous subjects; and

(7) Formal executive documents promulgated in accordance with law.

(b) In general, ancillary text, notes, and tables shall be derived from official sources.

§ 10.4 *Format, indexes, and ancillaries.*

(a) Each annual volume, divided into books whenever appropriate, shall be separately published in the binding and style that the Administrative Committee considers suitable to the dignity of the Office of the President of the United States.

(b) Each volume shall be appropriately indexed and contain appropriate ancillary information respecting significant Presidential documents not printed in full text.

§ 10.5 *Distribution to Government agencies.*

(a) The Public Papers of the Presidents of the United States shall be distributed to the following, in the quantities indicated, without charge:

(1) *Members of Congress.* Each Senator and each Member of the House of Representatives is entitled to one copy of each annual volume published during his term of office, upon his written request to the Director of the Federal Register.

(2) *Supreme Court.* The Supreme Court is entitled to 12 copies of each annual volume.

(3) *Executive agencies.* The head of each executive agency is entitled to one copy of each annual volume upon application to the Director.

(b) Legislative, judicial, and executive agencies of the Federal Government may obtain copies of the annual volumes, at cost, for official use, by the timely submission of a printing and binding requisition to the Government Printing Office on Standard Form 1.

§ 10.6 *Extra copies.*

Each request for extra copies of the annual volumes must be addressed to the Superintendent of Documents, to be paid for by the agency or official making the request.

Index

[Main references are to item numbers except as otherwise indicated]

Index

[Main references are to item numbers except as otherwise indicated]

Index

[Main references are to item numbers except as otherwise indicated]

831

[Main references are to item numbers except as otherwise indicated]

Index

[Main references are to item numbers except as otherwise indicated]

[Main references are to item numbers except as otherwise indicated]

Index

[Main references are to item numbers except as otherwise indicated]

Index

Index

[Main references are to item numbers except as otherwise indicated]

Index

[Main references are to item numbers except as otherwise indicated]

Index

[Main references are to item numbers except as otherwise indicated]

68-611 O - 76 - 58

Index

[Main references are to item numbers except as otherwise indicated]

Index

[Main references are to item numbers except as otherwise indicated]

Index

[Main references are to item numbers except as otherwise indicated]

Index

[Main references are to item numbers except as otherwise indicated]

Index

Index

Index

Index

[Main references are to item numbers except as otherwise indicated]

Index

[Main references are to item numbers except as otherwise indicated]

[Main references are to item numbers except as otherwise indicated]

[Main references are to item numbers except as otherwise indicated]

Index

[Main references are to item numbers except as otherwise indicated]

Index

[Main references are to item numbers except as otherwise indicated]

Index

Index

[Main references are to item numbers except as otherwise indicated]

855

Index

Index

[Main references are to item numbers except as otherwise indicated]

Index

Index

Index

[Main references are to item numbers except as otherwise indicated]

Index

[Main references are to item numbers except as otherwise indicated]

861

Index

[Main references are to item numbers except as otherwise indicated]

Index

[Main references are to item numbers except as otherwise indicated]

Index

Index

[Main references are to item numbers except as otherwise indicated]

Index

[Main references are to item numbers except as otherwise indicated]

[Main references are to item numbers except as otherwise indicated]

Index

[Main references are to item numbers except as otherwise indicated]

U.S. GOVERNMENT PRINTING OFFICE : 1976 O—68-611